**W9-DAY-876**

# Frommer's®

# SAN FRANCISCO
## FROM $60 A DAY

### Here's what the critics say about Frommer's:

"Amazingly easy to use. Very portable, very complete."
*—Booklist*

♦

"The only mainstream guide to list specific prices. The Walter Cronkite of guidebooks—with all that implies."
*—Travel & Leisure*

♦

"Complete, concise, and filled with useful information."
*—New York Daily News*

♦

"Hotel information is close to encyclopedic."
*—Des Moines Sunday Register*

# Frommer's ®

2nd Edition

# SAN FRANCISCO FROM $60 A DAY

## The Ultimate Guide to Comfortable Low-Cost Travel

### by Matthew R. Poole

IDG Books Worldwide, Inc.
An International Data Group Company
Foster City, CA • Chicago, IL • Indianapolis, IN • New York, NY

## ABOUT THE AUTHOR

**Matthew R. Poole,** a native Californian, has managed to combine three of his stronger passions—writing, photography, and traveling—to his advantage, and as a result has authored and contributed to more than 20 travel guides to California, Las Vegas, Hawaii, and abroad. Before becoming a full-time travel writer/photographer, Matthew worked as an English tutor in Prague, ski instructor in the Swiss Alps, and scuba instructor in Maui. Addicted to a life of chronic freedom, he spends most of his time on the road doing research and avoiding commitments. He currently lives in San Francisco.

Matthew also contributes to *Frommer's San Francisco, Frommer's California, Frommer's Portable California Wine Country, Frommer's San Francisco Walking Tours,* and *Frommer's California from $60 a Day* guides.

## IDG BOOKS WORLDWIDE, INC.

An International Data Group Company
919 E. Hillsdale Blvd.
Suite 400
Foster City, CA 94404

Find us online at **www.frommers.com**

ISBN 0-02-863030-0
ISSN 1093-698X

Editor: Naomi P. Kraus
Production Editor: Christina Van Camp
Photo Editor: Richard Fox
Design by Michele Laseau
Staff Cartographers: John Decamillis, Roberta Stockwell
Page creation by John Bitter, Natalie Evans, Sean Monkhouse, and Kendra Span
Front cover photo by John M. Roberts

## SPECIAL SALES

For general information on IDG Books Worldwide's books in the U.S., please call our Consumer Customer Service department at 1-800-762-2974. For reseller information, including discounts, bulk sales, customized editions, and premium sales, please call our Reseller Customer Service department at 1-800-434-3422.

Manufactured in the United States of America

5  4  3  2  1

# Contents

# List of Maps

## ACKNOWLEDGMENTS

Matthew would like to thank Erika Lenkert, Tuhin Roy, Tom Walton, Donalyn Mason, and Dara Colwell for their advice and contributions.

## AN INVITATION TO THE READER

When I first started writing for Frommer's, I'd call my editor after each of my books was published and excitedly ask, "Any reader mail?" I was interested to learn whether folks were enjoying our books—or actually reading them for that matter. I was disappointed when I hadn't received any mail, but my editors assured me that it was a compliment; most people write only to complain, so I must be doing something right. But the fact is, I want to hear what you think. What did you love? What did you hate? What was over- or underrated? Did you find a hotel, restaurant, bar, attraction—whatever—that we should have included? Tell me your opinion, so I can share the information with your fellow travelers in upcoming editions. That way, perhaps I'll stop accosting and questioning poor, innocent visitors when I see them carrying our guides through the streets of my favorite city. C'mon, drop me a note. Write to:

*Frommer's San Francisco from $60 a Day,* 2nd Edition
IDG Travel
1633 Broadway
New York, NY 10019

## AN ADDITIONAL NOTE

Please be advised that travel information is subject to change at any time—and this is especially true of prices. We therefore suggest that you write or call ahead for confirmation when making your travel plans. The author, editors, and publisher cannot be held responsible for the experiences of readers while traveling. Your safety is important to us, however, so we encourage you to stay alert and be aware of your surroundings. Keep a close eye on cameras, purses, and wallets, all favorite targets of thieves and pickpockets.

## WHAT THE SYMBOLS MEAN

### ✪ Frommer's Favorites

Our favorite places and experiences—outstanding for quality, value, or both.

The following abbreviations are used for credit cards:

| | | | |
|---|---|---|---|
| AE | American Express | EURO | Eurocard |
| CB | Carte Blanche | JCB | Japan Credit Bank |
| DC | Diners Club | MC | MasterCard |
| DISC | Discover | V | Visa |
| ER | EnRoute | | |

## FIND FROMMER'S ONLINE

**Arthur Frommer's Budget Travel Online** (**www.frommers.com**) offers more than 6,000 pages of up-to-the-minute travel information—including the latest bargains and candid, personal articles updated daily by Arthur Frommer himself. No other Web site offers such comprehensive and timely coverage of the world of travel.

# The San Francisco Experience

**1**

**W**e know what you're thinking: How could anyone possibly enjoy a vacation in San Francisco for as little as $60 a day? After all, the average room rate alone is $123 a night—not including taxes, tipping, and taxi fare.

But if there's one thing we underpaid travel writers know better than anyone, it's how to live large and spend little. So my team of savings-savvy researchers and I have pooled our collective wisdom into what we firmly believe is the best budget guide to San Francisco. We live here, we know this city, and we know how to have a *lot* of fun here without spending mounds of cash—in fact, we do it every day. Some of our advice is obvious (skip the Ritz), even more comes from experience (go for the bargain fixed-priced menus at the hot restaurants)—and all of it is geared to making sure that you will have a fantastic stay in the city regardless of your tax bracket.

Yes, ultra-luxury $300-per-night hotel rooms and blow-your–bank account restaurants are plentiful here, but that's not where the majority of locals (including us) hang out or dine. Traveling on a budget in San Francisco means doing what most of its denizens do every day: eating at the city's many affordable restaurants, hanging out in the city's wonderful parks and neighborhoods, and taking advantage of its wide variety of free or inexpensive attractions. Granted, you won't be sleeping on satin sheets or dining on caviar, but you're definitely more likely to experience the real San Francisco than those limo'ing from their penthouse suite to five-star restaurants and back.

But the best advice we can give you about San Francisco is to just *go*. Enjoy the cool blast of salt air as you stroll across the Golden Gate. Stuff yourself with dim sum in Chinatown. Browse the Haight for incense and crystals. Walk along the beach, pierce your nose, see a play, ride on a cable car—the list is endless and always affordable. It's all happening in San Francisco, and everyone, whether rich or in the red, is invited. All you have to do is arrive with an open mind and a sense of adventure—the rest is waiting for you.

# San Francisco at a Glance

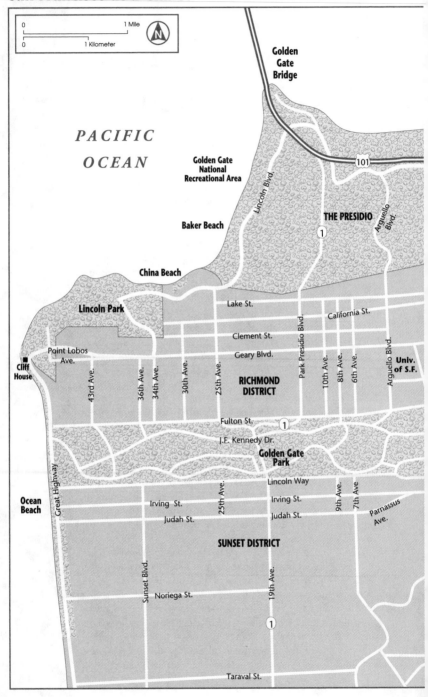

PACIFIC OCEAN

Golden Gate Bridge

Golden Gate National Recreational Area

Baker Beach

China Beach

Lincoln Blvd.

THE PRESIDIO

Arguello Blvd.

Lincoln Park

Lake St.

California St.

Clement St.

Geary Blvd.

Point Lobos Ave.

Cliff House

43rd Ave.

36th Ave.

34th Ave.

30th Ave.

25th Ave.

RICHMOND DISTRICT

Park Presidio Blvd.

10th Ave.

8th Ave.

6th Ave.

Arguello Blvd.

Univ. of S.F.

Fulton St.

J.F. Kennedy Dr.

Golden Gate Park

Lincoln Way

Ocean Beach

Great Highway

Irving St.

Judah St.

25th Ave.

Irving St.

Judah St.

9th Ave.

7th Ave.

Parnassus Ave.

SUNSET DISTRICT

Sunset Blvd.

Noriega St.

19th Ave.

Taraval St.

0          1 Mile
0          1 Kilometer
N

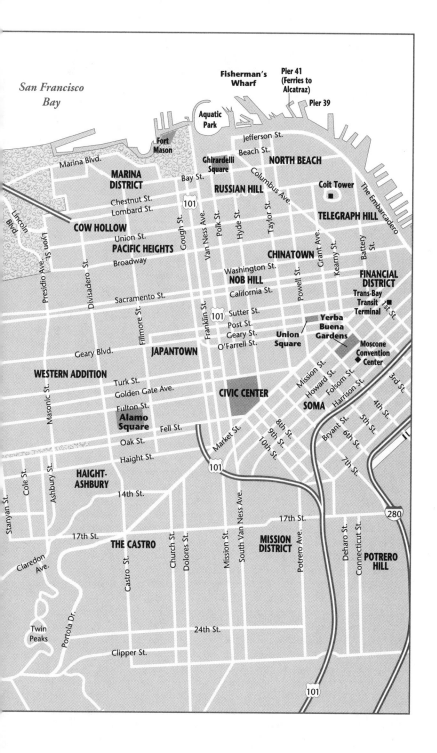

San Francisco
Bay

Fisherman's
Wharf

Pier 41
(Ferries to
Alcatraz)

Pier 39

Aquatic
Park

Jefferson St.

Fort
Mason

Beach St.

Marina Blvd.

Ghirardelli
Square

NORTH BEACH

MARINA
DISTRICT

Bay St.

Columbus Ave.

Coit Tower

Chestnut St.
Lombard St.

RUSSIAN HILL

The Embarcadero

COW HOLLOW

Union St.

TELEGRAPH HILL

PACIFIC HEIGHTS

Broadway

Gough St.

Van Ness Ave.

Polk St.

Hyde St.

Taylor St.

CHINATOWN

Grant Ave.

Kearny St.

Battery St.

Presidio Ave.

Lincoln Blvd.

Lyon St.

Divisadero St.

Fillmore St.

Sacramento St.

Washington St.

NOB HILL

California St.

Powell St.

FINANCIAL
DISTRICT

Trans-Bay
Transit
Terminal

1st St.

Franklin St.

Sutter St.
Post St.
Geary St.
O'Farrell St.

Union
Square

Yerba
Buena
Gardens

Moscone
Convention
Center

Geary Blvd.

JAPANTOWN

WESTERN ADDITION

Masonic St.

Turk St.
Golden Gate Ave.

Mission St.

Howard St.

Folsom St.

Harrison St.

3rd St.

Fulton St.

CIVIC CENTER

SOMA

Alamo
Square

Fell St.

Oak St.

Market St.

8th St.

9th St.

10th St.

Bryant St.

4th St.

5th St.

6th St.

7th St.

Haight St.

HAIGHT-
ASHBURY

Cole St.

Ashbury St.

Stanyan St.

14th St.

280

17th St.

Claredon Ave.

17th St.

THE CASTRO

Castro St.

Church St.

Dolores St.

Mission St.

South Van Ness Ave.

MISSION
DISTRICT

Potrero Ave.

Deharo St.

Connecticut St.

POTRERO
HILL

Twin
Peaks

Portola Dr.

24th St.

Clipper St.

101

101

101

101

3

# 1 Frommer's Favorite (& Mostly Free) San Francisco Experiences

- **Walking Across the Golden Gate Bridge.** Don your windbreaker and walking shoes and prepare for a wind-blasted, exhilarating walk across San Francisco's most famous landmark. It's just one of those things you have to do at least once in your life.

- **Touring Alcatraz.** Even if you loathe tourist attractions, you'll like Alcatraz. The rangers have done a fantastic job of preserving The Rock—enough to give you the heebie-jeebies just looking at it—and they give excellent guided tours. Even the boat ride across the bay is worth the price. Don't miss this one.

- **Strolling Through Chinatown.** Chinatown is a trip. We've been through it at least 100 times and it has never failed to entertain us. Skip the crummy camera and luggage stores and head straight for the outdoor markets, where a cornucopia of the bizarre, unbelievable, and just plain weird is on display. Better yet, take one of Shirley Fong Torres's Wok Wiz tours of Chinatown for the full effect.

- **Nursing a Cup of Coffee (or Three) in North Beach.** One of the most pleasurable smells of San Francisco is the aroma of roasted coffee beans wafting down Columbus Avenue. Start the day with a cup of Viennese at Caffe Trieste (a haven for true San Francisco characters), followed by a walk in and around Washington Square, lunch at Mario's Bohemian Cigar Store (à la focaccia sandwiches), book browsing at City Lights, more coffee at Caffè Greco, and dinner at L'Osteria del Forno. Finish off the day with a little flamenco dancing at La Bodega or a nightcap accompanied by Enrico Caruso on the jukebox at Tosca's.

- **Browsing the Haight.** Though flower power has wilted, the Haight is still, more or less, the Haight: a sort of resting home for aging hippies, dazed Deadheads, skate punks, and an assortment of rather pathetic young panhandlers. Think of it as visiting a people zoo as you walk down the rows of used-clothing stores and leather shops, trying hard not to stare at that girl (at least we *think* it's a girl) with the pierced eyebrows and shaved head. End the mystery tour with a plate of mussels at Cha Cha Cha, one of San Francisco's top restaurants that's a bargain to boot.

- **Getting Back to Nature at the Marin Headlands.** San Francisco's backyard of sorts, the Marin Headlands (located just across the Golden Gate Bridge to the west) offer not only the best views of the city, but also a wealth of outdoor activities. Bird watching, hiking, mountain biking, horseback riding—the list goes on—are all fair game at this glorious national park. Don't miss the Marine Mammal Center, a ward for injured or abandoned seals (cute little buggers) and sea lions.

- **Cruising the Castro.** The most populated and festive street in the city isn't just for gays and lesbians (though you'll find the best cruising in town here). There are some great shops and cafes—particularly Café Flore for lunch—but it's the people watching that makes the trip a must. And if you have the time, catch a flick at the beautiful 1930s Spanish colonial movie palace, the Castro Theatre.

- **Hanging Out in Golden Gate Park.** A day at Golden Gate Park is a day well spent. Its arboreal paths stretch from the Haight all the way to Ocean Beach, offering dozens of fun things to do along the way. Top sites are the Japanese Tea Garden and the Steinhart Aquarium. The best time to go is Sunday, when portions of the park are closed to traffic (rent skates or a bike for the full effect). Toward the end of the day, head west to the beach and watch the sunset.

- **Catching an Early-Morning Cable Car.** Skip the boring California line and take the Powell-Hyde cable car down to Fisherman's Wharf—the ride is worth the wait. When you reach the top of Nob Hill, grab the rail in one hand and hold the camera with the other, because you're about to see a view of the bay that'll make you a believer. (*Inside tip:* Don't call it a trolley.)

- **Visiting MOMA.** Ever since the MOMA opened in 1995, it has been the best place to go for a quick dose of culture. Start by touring the museum, then head straight for the gift shop (oftentimes more entertaining than the rotating exhibits). Have a light lunch at Caffè Museo, where the food is a vast improvement from most museums' mush, then finish the trip with a stroll through the Yerba Buena Gardens across from the museum.

- **Spending a Soul-Stirring Sunday Morning at Glide.** The high-spirited singers and hand-clapping worshipers at Glide turn churchgoing into a spiritual party that leaves you feeling elated, hopeful, and at one with the world. All walks of life attend the service, which focuses not on any particular religion but on what we have in common as people. It's great fun, with plenty of singing and roof-raising.

- **Walking the Coastal Trail.** Walk the forested coastal trail from the Cliff House to the Golden Gate Bridge and you'll see why San Franciscans put up with living on a fault line. Start at the parking lot just above Cliff House and head north. On a clear day you'll have incredible views of the Marin Headlands, but even on foggy days it's worth the trek to scamper over old bunkers and relish the crisp, cool air. Dress warmly.

- **Taking a Drive to Muir Woods, Stinson Beach, and Point Reyes.** If you have wheels, reserve a day for a trip across the Golden Gate. Take the Stinson Beach exit off U.S. 101, spend a few hours gawking at the monolithic redwoods at Muir Woods (this place is amazing), continue on to Stinson Beach for lunch at the Parkside Café, then head up the coast to the spectacular Point Reyes National Seashore. Rain or shine, it's a day trip you'll never forget.

## 2  Best Hotel Bets

- **Best Overall Value:** The **Marina Inn,** 3110 Octavia St. (☎ **800/274-1420**), is, without question, the best low-priced hotel in San Francisco. Rustic pinewood furnishings, full bathtubs with showers, complimentary continental breakfast, afternoon sherry, and nightly turndown service with chocolates on your pillow—all this for as little as $65 a night. Runner up: the **San Remo Hotel,** 2237 Mason St. (☎ **800/352-REMO**), whose North Beach location, friendly staff, and low prices can't be beat.

- **Best Place to Stay on a Shoestring:** It ain't heaven, but clean, quiet lodgings this close to Union Square don't come any cheaper than those at the **Temple Hotel,** 469 Pine St. (☎ **415/781-2565**), where rooms go for just $57 a night for two persons.

- **Best Splurge:** The **Petite Auberge,** 863 Bush St. (☎ **415/928-6000**), is a delightful rendering of a French country inn. The 26 rooms have attractive furnishings and lace curtains; the tiled breakfast room opens onto a small garden where guests enjoy afternoon tea and wine. If the Auberge is full, try the equally quaint **White Swan Inn,** 845 Bush St., between Taylor and Mason streets (☎ **415/775-1755**), down the street.

- **Best Castro B&B:** If you didn't make it out to the Castro in the fun-loving 1970s, a stay at the cozy **Inn on Castro,** 321 Castro St. (☎ **415/861-0321**), will give you a spin on the bygone vibe, as well as all comforts of home.

- **Best for Conventioneers:** The **Stratford Hotel,** 242 Powell St. (☎ **888/ 50-HOTEL**), may be a few blocks north of the convention center, but it's close enough. It offers all the necessities and has a perfect location for throwing your briefcase down at the end of the day and heading out to the downtown happy-hour action.
- **Best for Long-Term Stays:** If you're planning to make yourself at home, you'll find all the necessary comforts—and an affordable price tag—at **Hotel Halcyon,** 649 Jones St. (☎ **800/627-2396**).
- **Best Views:** One would think that a city surrounded on three sides by water would have a slew of ocean-view hotels, but, oddly enough, it doesn't. The **Seal Rock Inn,** 545 Point Lobos Ave. (☎ **415/752-8000**), located in the Richmond District, is the only budget hotel to offer a view of the ocean. You'll be lulled to sleep by the sound of the surf and distant foghorns.
- **Best for Families:** At **The Wharf Inn,** 2601 Mason St. (☎ **800/548-9918**), kids are within skipping distance of the world famous Fisherman's Wharf, and mom and dad don't have to sweat parking the minivan because there's plenty of free parking here.
- **Best Freebies:** With a free full breakfast, hot towel racks, voice mail, cable TV, and complimentary airport-to-hotel transport, the **Hotel David Bed & Breakfast,** 480 Geary St. (☎ **800/524-1888**), is hard to beat. However, if you're traveling by car, your best bet is the **Vagabond,** 2550 Van Ness (☎ **800/522-1555**), where the breakfast is less lavish, but the free parking (limited), free coffee and donuts, heated pool, and free local phone calls more than make up for it.
- **Best for a Romantic Rendezvous:** The hopelessly romantic **Hotel Bohème,** 444 Columbus St. (☎ **415/433-9111**), is the perfect mixture of art, style, class, and location—mere steps from the chic sidewalk cafes of North Beach. If Bette Davis were alive today, this is where she'd stay.
- **Best Moderately Priced Hotel:** The luxurious "Gramercy" rooms at the **Nob Hill Inn,** 1000 Pine St. (☎ **415/673-6080**), are among the plushest you'll find in the city for less than $100. Perks include large bathrooms with marble sinks and clawfoot tubs, antique furnishings, a comfortable full-size bed, pin-drop silence, and the distinction of staying in one of the city's most prestigious hotels.
- **Best Budget B&B:** It may not be the most centrally located place in town, but if you want a slice of old-style San Francisco, the quaint **Monte Cristo,** 600 Presidio (☎ **415/931-1875**), will do the trick. Prices start at $73 a night (including a full breakfast buffet), but the manager has been known to negotiate when his beds are empty.
- **Best Funky Hotel:** The **Phoenix Hotel,** 601 Eddy St. (☎ **800/248-9466**), wouldn't look out of place in Palm Springs. It's a favorite with the rock and movie set, including Sinead O'Connor, k.d. Lang, and the Red Hot Chili Peppers. Former flower children will prefer the 1960s-nostalgic **Red Victorian Bed, Breakfast, & Art,** 1665 Haight St. (☎ **415/864-1978**).

## 3 Best Dining Bets

- **Best Value:** Nowhere else in town will you find such heaping plates of fresh pasta at penny-pinching prices as at **Pasta Pomodoro,** 655 Union St. (☎ **415/ 399-0300**), 2027 Chestnut St. (☎ **415/474-3400**), 2304 Market St. (☎ **415/ 558-8123**), 3611 California St. (☎ **415/831-0900**); and 816 Irving St. (☎ **415/566-0900**).

- **Best Moderately Priced Restaurant:** Comfortable and casual-but-upscale **Fringale,** 570 4th St. (☎ 415/543-0573), is one of our very favorite restaurants, even compared to the pricey big boys. It offers some of the best French food in the city in a wonderful atmosphere, and at a steal of a price. Start with the mouth-watering foie gras and finish with the outstanding Basque custard torte; the middle's up for grabs.
- **Best Splurge Choice:** We say **Fringale** (see above) again! Yes, it's a "moderately priced" restaurant where you can enjoy an exquisite meal at an affordable price, but if we were really going to blow the budget, we'd still go for broke here—wine, appetizers, dessert, the works. Just remember that you'll have to make a reservation far in advance (or get really lucky and fill a cancellation) to dine here, because the word is out on this one.
- **Best Dim Sum:** Downtown and Chinatown dim-sum restaurants may be more centrally located, but that's all they have on the **Hong Kong Flower Lounge,** 5322 Geary Blvd. (☎ 415/668-8998), which serves up the best shark-fin soup, seafood dumplings, and salt-fried shrimp this side of China.
- **Best Party Scene:** Throw back a few glasses of sangría with your tapas at **Cha Cha Cha,** 1801 Haight St. (☎ 415/386-5758), and you'll start swinging with the rest of the crowd.
- **Best Pizza:** Has **Pauline's,** 260 Valencia St. (☎ 415/552-2050), perfected the pizza? Quite possibly. At least it's the best we've ever had. Pauline's only does two things—pizzas and salads—but does them both better than any other restaurant in the city.
- **Best Burritos:** We're not foolish enough to deem one burrito the king in this town. If you do nothing else while you're here, seek out at least one of the hefty and heavenly tortilla wraps we've recommended in chapter 6. (See the list of restaurants under "Mexican" in the "Restaurants by Cuisine" index in that chapter.)
- **Best Place for Picnic Supplies:** If you're anywhere near North Beach, head to San Francisco's legendary **Molinari Delicatessen,** 373 Columbus Ave. (☎ 415/421-2337), which offers a mouth-watering selection of cold salads, cheeses, and sandwiches packaged and priced to go (the Italian subs are big enough for two hearty appetites). Another good sunny-day option is a picnic lunch on Marina Green, but first stop by the **Marina Safeway,** 15 Marina Blvd. (☎ 415/563-4946), to pick up fresh-baked breads, gourmet cheeses, and other foodstuffs (including fresh cracked crab when in season).
- **Best Coffee Shop or Cafe:** With all the wonderfully unique coffee shops throughout this cafe town, there can be no one winner. We do, however, love the authentic atmosphere at **Mario's Bohemian Cigar Store,** 566 Columbus Ave. (☎ 415/362-0536), and **Caffe Trieste,** 601 Vallejo Ave. (☎ 415/392-6739). Our advice is this: If you see one you like, pull up a chair. Just do yourself one favor: Stay away from the ever-trendy Starbucks.
- **Best Happy-Hour Spread:** We've saved oodles of dinner dollars over the years by feeding our faces at the free buffet spread Monday to Friday at **MacArthur Park,** 607 Front St. (☎ 415/398-5700). Fridays are best, when flirtation's in the air and there's a stampede for the savory barbecued ribs and chicken.
- **Best Seafood:** The **Crab Cake Lounge,** 900 North Point St. (☎ 415/929-1730), located on the upper level of the glamorous McCormick and Kuleto's Seafood Restaurant, offers a huge selection of shellfish—fresh oysters on the half shell, Prince Edward mussels, Sacramento Delta crayfish, Manila clams—and light seafood dishes at very reasonable prices.

- **Best Desserts:** If for nothing else, stop by **Rumpus,** 1 Tillman Place (☎ **415/ 421-2300**), for one of the best desserts we've ever had: the pudding-like chocolate brioche cake. We've introduced it to out-of-town guests, and they've cursed us ever since because they now know that it exists and can't get it at home.
- **Funkiest Atmosphere:** San Francisco's most . . . *alternative* burger joint is **Hamburger Mary's,** 1582 Folsom St. (☎ **415/626-5767**), a popular hangout for gays, lesbians, and just about everyone else eschewing society's norms (and you don't even need leather undies to join the party).

# Planning an Affordable Trip to San Francisco

## 2

**A**s expensive as San Francisco is, there are infinite ways to enjoy the city on a pauper's pocketbook. But to get the most for your money, you'll need to do plenty of advance planning. Airfare and lodging will take the largest bites out of your travel budget, so either shop for the best bargains and secure them well in advance (especially during high season), or pay the consequences—literally.

This chapter offers lots of useful information to help you plan a great trip to San Francisco without going broke. It's devoted to insider advice, money-saving tips, and ways to stretch your budget so you keep your accommodation costs and three meals a day down to as little as $60 a day. (We assume that two adults are traveling together and that between the two of you, you have at least $120 to spend.) The cost of transportation, activities, sightseeing, and entertainment are extra, but we have plenty of insider tips to save you money on those activities as well.

## 1 Visitor Information

Visitors from outside the United States should also see chapter 3, "For Foreign Visitors," for entry requirements and other pertinent information.

**The San Francisco Convention and Visitors Bureau,** 900 Market St. (at Powell Street), Hallidie Plaza, Lower Level, San Francisco, CA 94102 (☎ **415/391-2000;** www.sfvisitor.org), is the best source for any kind of specialized information about the city. Even if you don't have a specific question, you may want to send them $3 for their 100-page magazine, *The San Francisco Book,* which includes a 3-month calendar of events, city history, shopping and dining information, and several good, clear maps, as well as an additional 50-page lodging guide. If simply need specific information faxed to you, you can call ☎ **800/220-5747;** follow the prompts and they will forward the information via fax only. The bureau only highlights members' establishments, so if they don't have what you're looking for, it doesn't mean it's nonexistent.

You can also get the latest on San Francisco at the following online addresses, which will also link you to dozens of other San Francisco Web sites:

- *Bay Guardian,* free weekly's city page: **www.sfbayguardian.com**
- Hotel accommodations, reserve online: **www.hotelres.com/**

**Travel Tip**

Strapped for cash? Call **Western Union** (☎ **800/325-6000**) for a recording listing the nearest branch to which you can have money wired, then call mom. **Money-Gram** (☎ **800/926-9400**), a fairly new service operated by American Express, can also wire emergency funds worldwide in minutes, but charges considerably less. Senders should call the above toll-free number to learn the address of the closest MoneyGram outlet. Cash, credit/charge card, or a personal check (with ID) are acceptable forms of payment. AMEX's fee for the service is $10 for the first $300, with a sliding scale for larger sums. The service includes a short Telex message and a 3-minute phone call from sender to recipient. The beneficiary must present a photo ID at the outlet where the money is received.

- *Q San Francisco,* for gays and lesbians: **www.qsanfrancisco.com/**
- *SF Gate,* the city's combined *Chronicle* and *Examiner* newspapers: **www.sfgate. com**
- Channel 7, ABC, and KGO's city guide: **www.citysearch7.com**

## MONEY

In addition to the details below, foreign visitors should see chapter 3, "For Foreign Visitors," for more information about money.

All over San Francisco, you'll find **ATMs** that are linked to a national network that most likely includes your bank at home. Withdrawing cash as you need it is really the easiest way to deal with money while you're on the road. **Cirrus** (☎ **800/424-7787;** www.mastercard.com/atm/) and **Plus** (☎ **800/843-7587;** www.visa.com/atms) are the two most popular networks. Use the 800 numbers to locate ATMs in your destination. Expect to be charged up to $3 per transaction if you're not using your own bank's ATM. *Tip:* The way around this is to ask for cash back at stores (like Safeway) that accept ATM cards and don't charge usage fees. Of course, you'll have to purchase something first.

**Traveler's checks** are something of an anachronism from the days before the ATM made cash accessible at any time. The only sound alternative to traveling with dangerously large amounts of cash, traveler's checks were as reliable as currency, unlike personal checks, but could be replaced if lost or stolen, unlike cash. These days, traveler's checks seem less necessary because most cities have 24-hour ATMs that allow travelers to withdraw small amounts of cash as needed—and thus avoid the risk of carrying a fortune around an unfamiliar environment. Many banks, however, impose a fee every time a card is used at an ATM in a different city or bank. If you're withdrawing money every day, you might be better off with traveler's checks—provided you don't mind showing identification every time you want to cash a check. They are accepted by most restaurants, hotels, and shops, and can be exchanged for cash at banks and check-issuing offices.

You can get traveler's checks at almost any bank. **American Express** offers denominations of $10, $20, $50, $100, $500, and $1,000. You'll pay a service charge ranging from 1 to 4 percent. You can also get American Express traveler's checks over the phone by calling ☎ **800/221-7282;** by using this number, Amex gold and platinum cardholders are exempt from the 1-percent fee. AAA members can obtain checks without a fee at most AAA offices. **American Express** offices are open Monday to Friday from 8:30am to 5:30pm and Saturday from 9am until 2pm. See "Fast Facts: San Francisco" in chapter 4 for office locations.

**Visa** offers traveler's checks at Citibank locations nationwide, as well as several other banks. The service charge ranges between 1½ and 2 percent; checks come in denominations of $20, $50, $100, $500, and $1,000. **MasterCard** also offers traveler's checks. Call ☎ **800/223-9920** for a location near you.

If you opt to carry traveler's checks, be sure to keep a record of their serial numbers, separately from the checks of course, so you're ensured a refund in just such an emergency.

**Credit cards** are invaluable when traveling. They are a safe way to carry money and provide a convenient record of all your expenses. Almost every place in San Francisco takes them. You can also withdraw cash advances from your credit cards at any bank (though you'll start paying hefty interest on the advance the moment you receive the cash, and you won't receive frequent-flyer miles on an airline credit card). At most banks, you don't even need to go to a teller; you can get a cash advance at the ATM if you know your PIN number. If you've forgotten your PIN number or didn't even know you had one, call the phone number on the back of your credit card and ask the bank to send it to you. It usually takes 5–7 business days, though some banks will provide the number over the phone if you tell them your mother's maiden name or pass some other security clearance. American Express cardholders can guarantee an advance against their card—in some cases up to $10,000—at an American express office. See "Fast Facts: San Francisco" in chapter 4 for office addresses.

Almost every credit card company has an emergency 800 number that you can call if your wallet or purse is stolen. They may be able to wire you a cash advance off your credit card immediately, and in many places, they can deliver an emergency credit card in a day or two. The issuing bank's 800 number is usually on the back of the credit card—though of course that doesn't help you much if the card was stolen. The toll-free information directory will provide the number if you dial ☎ **800/555-1212.** Citicorp Visa's U.S. emergency number is ☎ **800/336-8472.** American Express cardholders and traveler's check holders should call ☎ **800/221-7282** for all money emergencies. MasterCard holders should call ☎ **800/307-7309.**

Odds are that if your wallet is gone, the police won't be able to recover it for you. However, after you realize that it's gone and you cancel your credit cards, it is still worth informing them. Your credit card company or insurer may require a police report number.

# 2  45 Money-Saving Tips

While planning your trip, don't get discouraged if you've almost blown your entire vacation budget on hotels before you've even packed your bags. San Francisco is one of the most popular destinations in the world, and because of all the tourist and convention traffic, hotels can and do charge steep tariffs. But there's good news, too: Once you get here, pay for your room, and head out to explore, you'll find that many activities and attractions won't cost you a dime.

The following are some tips to help keep your traveling costs to a minimum:

## WHEN TO GO

1. Try to travel in the off-season, roughly October to April. Most room rates at the smaller hotels decrease by as much as 50% from November to February, and 10% to 15% March to May. Some hotels also offer slightly lower rates Sunday to Thursday. Case in point: A room at the Marina Inn on a summer Saturday is

| What Things Cost in San Francisco | U.S. $ | British £ |
|---|---|---|
| Taxi from airport to city center (tip included) | 36.00 | 21.60 |
| Bus fare to any destination within the city (adult) | 1.00 | 60p |
| Bus fare to any destination within the city (children and seniors) | 35¢ | 21p |
| Double room at Campton Place Hotel (expensive) | 300.00 | 180 |
| Double room at Savoy Hotel (moderate) | 140.00 | 84 |
| Double room at the Commodore International Hotel (inexpensive) | 99.00 | 60 |
| Lunch for one at Betelnut (moderate) | 20.00 | 12 |
| Lunch for one at Mario's Bohemian Cigar Store (inexpensive) | 10.00 | 6 |
| Dinner for one, without wine, at Fleur de Lys (expensive) | 70.00 | 42 |
| Dinner for one, without wine, at Fringale (moderate) | 35.00 | 21 |
| Dinner for one, without wine, at Cha Cha Cha (inexpensive) | 20.00 | 12 |
| Glass of beer | 3.00 | 1.80 |
| Coca-Cola | 2.00 | 1.20 |
| Cup of coffee | 1.30 | 80p |
| Admission to the top of Coit Tower | 3.75 | 2.25 |
| Movie ticket | 8.00 | 4.80 |
| Theater ticket | 8.00–50.00 | 4.80–30 |

$95. The same room on a weekday in February is $65. Ironically, because San Francisco's weather is so screwy, you'll have a much better chance of a sunny vacation during the winter months. Only a small percentage of hotels offer weekend/vacation packages, but it can't hurt to ask when you're snooping around for a room.

## AIRFARES

2. Surf the Internet for bargains. There are lots of sites and online services designed to find you discounted airfares, accommodations, and car rentals. See the box "Cyber Deals for Net Surfers," later in this chapter, for some Web pages worth checking out.

3. If you don't have a computer, visit a travel agent before your trip and see what can be arranged in the way of low airfares, room rates, cheap car rentals, and package deals that you don't have access to independently. Since the services of a travel agent are free, it never hurts to ask.

4. When calling the airlines directly, be sure to ask for the lowest fare, not just the coach fare. And don't forget to inquire about discounts for seniors, children, and students.

5. Read the advertisements in newspaper travel sections, which often feature special promotional fares and packages.

6. Always check the Sunday travel section for consolidators ("bucket shops") and charter flights too. Though tickets are usually heavily restricted (ask about all the details), you're likely to save a bundle—usually 20% to 35%. This can really be a great way to go if you're buying at the last minute. Consolidators you might try

include **TFI Tours International** (☎ **800/745-8000,** or 212/736-1140 in New York State); **Cheap Tickets** (☎ **800/377-1000** or 212/570-1179); and **1-800-FLY-4-LESS.** Contact the Better Business Bureau before going with an unknown or questionable company.

7. Don't take a taxi from the airport into the city. The fare from the San Francisco International Airport (SFO) to the downtown area will run $25 to $30 plus tip, so unless you're with a group who can split the fare, you're probably better off taking a bus or shuttle. Both the SFO and the Oakland International Airport, the two major airports serving the city, have convenient shuttle and bus services that will take you to a central location near your destination for far less money; many hotels also have shuttles to and from the airport.

## CAR RENTALS

8. If you plan to spend all your time in San Francisco, you probably don't need to rent a car at all. Parking's a nightmare, most hotels charge a hefty parking fee, and the city is so condensed that you can easily bus, cab, cable car, or walk it.

9. The only reason you'd really need a car is if you're planning to do any road trips to the Wine Country or other surrounding areas. If that's the case, be sure to call all the major car-rental companies (use toll-free numbers listed in "Getting Around" in chapter 4) to compare rates.

10. Don't book a rental car through an airline without doing some research first. Airlines do not offer the best deals; they merely reserve a car for you.

11. In addition to the big chains, consider renting from one of the dozens of regional rental places in San Francisco to rent from for your getaway, many of which offer lower rates. Two good ones are **A-One Rent-A-Car,** 434 O'Farrell St. (☎ **415/771-3977**), and **Bay Area Rentals,** 229 7th St. (☎ **415/621-8989**). Even after you've made your reservations, call again and check rates a few days or weeks later—you may stumble upon a lower rate.

12. Be sure to check whether your credit card or personal auto insurance policy covers you when you rent a car. If you're covered by one or the other, you'll be able to avoid the cost of collision-damage waivers (usually an additional $10 to $12 a day) that the car-rental agencies are eager to sell you.

13. Whether you're driving or not, it's a good idea to be a member of the **American Automobile Association (AAA),** which charges $40 to $60 per year (with an additional one-time joining fee) depending on where you join. Members (only those that carry their cards with them) not only receive free roadside assistance, but also have access to a wealth of free travel information (detailed maps and guidebooks). Also, many hotels and attractions in San Francisco offer discounts to AAA members—always inquire. Call ☎ **800/922-8228** or your local branch for membership information. **Amoco Motor Club** (☎ **800/334-3300**) is another recommended choice.

14. Don't bother putting expensive gas in the tank. After all, it is a rental.

## PUBLIC TRANSPORTATION

15. San Francisco's public transportation system—known as Muni—is both an easy and affordable way to get around (but certainly not the fastest or most reliable). **Muni discount passes,** called "Passports," entitle holders to unlimited rides on buses, Metro streetcars, and cable cars. A Passport costs $6 for 1 day, and $10 or $15 for 3 or 7 consecutive days. Among the places where you can purchase a Passport are the San Francisco Visitor Information Center, the Holiday Inn Civic Center, and the TIX Bay Area booth at Union Square.

## ACCOMMODATIONS

16. In addition to airfare, you'll also have better luck saving on room rates if you visit in the off-season. In winter, when hotels have a low occupancy level, they slash rates by as much as 50%; be sure to call as far in advance as possible to get these discounts.

17. The sooner you book a room, the better. The cheapest accommodations are always the first to go, so the farther in advance you commit, the better your chances of scoring a bargain.

18. Whether you make a reservation or arrive on the spot, ask for the cheapest room and about any promotions, package deals, or discounted rates for students, seniors, military personnel, or government employees—whatever applies. Also, inquire about what makes a room worth less than other options (such as shared versus private baths) and be sure that the downsides are acceptable to you.

19. When booking your hotel, find out if there's an extra charge for parking if you're going to have a car in the city. In downtown San Francisco, stashing your car can cost up to $20 per day (sometimes more) *without* in-and-out privileges. If there's a charge, be sure to ask about the availability of local street parking; hotel employees are usually more than happy to give you the lowdown on the local parking scene. Also consider staying at one of the city's few hotels offering free parking (see the box on p. 70).

20. Using toll-free numbers lets you compare hotel rates without spending a lot on long-distance phone calls; and some places, especially the chains, will give you a discount only when you use the 800 number.

21. Bargain at the front desk. A hotel makes zero dollars per night on an empty room. Hence, most hotels are willing to bargain on rates. Haggling probably won't work too well during the high season, when hotels are almost 100% booked, but if you're traveling off-season and the answer is "no," try politely speaking with a manager, with whom you might be able to negotiate a better deal. An especially advantageous time to haggle for lower rates is late afternoon or early evening on the day of your arrival, when a hotel's likelihood of filling up with full-price bookings is remote.

22. If you think "B&B" refers to "bargain and budget," think again. You're likely to pay higher prices to stay at one of these homey little spots than you are at many hotels and motels. But if your heart is set on a bed-and-breakfast, contact **Bed and Breakfast International** (☎ **800/872-4500**) and let this outfit find affordable accommodations for you. It books dozens of B&Bs ranging from $60 to $150 per night. There's a 2-night minimum.

23. If you're traveling with kids, try to book a room at a hotel where they can stay in your room for free. At first glance the rate may seem high, but when you figure in the money you'll save by booking one room instead of two and by preparing some of your own meals (many come with kitchens), the savings start to add up.

24. Even if you don't have a car, consider staying at a chain motel on the fringes of the city such as HoJo or Rodeway Inn. Rates are far lower than at downtown hotels, and it's only a $1 bus ride to anywhere in the city.

25. At budget hotels, if the first room you see is disappointing (all right, dismal), don't storm out. Ask to see other rooms; they often vary considerably, and if you're polite, the management might upgrade you to a better room for free just to keep you happy.

26. Don't make local phone calls from your hotel room if you can avoid it. Hotels often charge 75¢ for local calls, as well as inflated rates for long-distance calls. Even if you use your credit card for long-distance calls, you're often charged 50¢ to 75¢ for access. Save money by making your calls from the hotel lobby or a

nearby phone booth. If you're planning on making a lot of local calls for business or other reasons, find a hotel that offers free local calling.

27. In a fiercely competitive market, more and more hotels are offering free continental breakfast with coffee as an enticement. Find out from your hotel or travel agent if this is available at your hotel. The savings can really add up, especially if you're staying for a longer period of time. But beware: Sometimes continental breakfast means nothing but so-so coffee and processed pastries.

## DINING

28. San Francisco boasts some of the world's finest dining. If you want to try a place that's beyond your budget, consider going for lunch instead of dinner. Often the lunch menu is served until 4 or 5pm, and main courses usually cost several dollars less than the same dishes do at dinner. You probably won't be hungry for the rest of the day, and will avoid spending a fortune for dinner.

29. Keep an eye out for happy hours. Aside from cheap drink specials, many establishments provide a free snack spread that can easily replace dinner. See the box "Hog Heaven Happy Hours" in chapter 6 for details.

30. Pick up a copy of the *San Francisco Bay Guardian,* one of the city's free alternative newspapers, and look for "two-for-one" and other discount coupons for restaurants around town.

31. Fixed-price menus and early-bird dinners are big money savers. Look for restaurants that offer them. If you're traveling with children, find restaurants that offer reduced-price children's menus.

32. San Francisco is an outdoor, sporty kind of place. If weather permits, instead of dining in restaurants, consider putting together a picnic breakfast, lunch, or dinner. There's an infinite number of celestial outdoor dining spots, and hundreds of phenomenal take-out joints that will help you create a cheap feast to go; even a gourmet spread can cost less than a meal in a restaurant.

33. Sure, there's plenty of hype about California-inspired cuisine; but if you follow the locals' lead to any of the city's fantastic ethnic restaurants, you'll find that, while few of them are locally influenced, they're definitely world-class—not to mention a heck of a lot cheaper than California-style restaurants. Two taste-bud tempters: **Thep Phanom,** 400 Waller St. (☎ **415/431-2526**), for tantalizing Thai; and **Taquerias La Cumbre,** 515 Valencia St. (☎ **415/863-8205**), which cranks out hefty fresh burritos, tacos, and combination plates for less than $7.

## SIGHTSEEING

34. The **San Francisco Visitor Information Center,** on the lower level of Hallidie Plaza, 900 Market St., at Powell Street (☎ **415/391-2000**), offers money-saving coupons for restaurants, shops, and attractions in the area. To get your hands on some, call or stop by.

35. The Muni Passport fare cards (see no. 15 above) not only entitle holders to unlimited rides on buses, Metro streetcars, and cable cars, but also to admission discounts at 24 of the city's major attractions, including the M. H. De Young Memorial Museum, the Asian Art Museum, the California Academy of Sciences, and the Japanese Tea Garden (all in Golden Gate Park); the Museum of Modern Art; Coit Tower; the Exploratorium; the city zoo; and the National Mari-time Museum and Historic Ships (where you may visit the USS *Pampanito* and the SS *Jeremiah O'Brien*).

36. Most museums are open to the public free 1 day per month (sometimes 1 day a week). Call the museum of your choice to find out which day is free day or see the box "Free Culture" in chapter 7.

37. If you plan to visit all the attractions in Golden Gate Park, buy the Explorer Pass, which enables you to visit the three museums and the Japanese Tea Garden for $14. Passes are available at each individual site.

38. Check out local alternative and tourist newspapers, many of which regularly run discounts for attractions and activities in San Francisco. The *Bay Guardian* is free and is your best bet—it's widely distributed in street-corner boxes and at cafes and restaurants throughout the city. Another good one is the *San Francisco Weekly.*

39. Many attractions offer discounts to seniors, students, or military personnel. Inquire before paying full admission, and be sure to bring your ID.

40. Skip the pricey guided tours and do it yourself. Use the walking tours we've outlined in chapter 8, "City Strolls," or put together your own sightseeing itinerary based on the information included in this book (you've already paid for it so you might as well use it). But if you'd still rather have someone lead you around town, you can take one of the free neighborhood tours offered by **City Guides,** an affiliate of the San Francisco Library. Call ☎ **415/557-4266** for schedules, or pick one up at the San Francisco Visitor Information Center, on the lower level of Hallidie Plaza, 900 Market St. (at Powell St.; ☎ **415/391-2000**), or at any SF Public Library.

## SHOPPING

41. If you live out of state and make a substantial purchase while in town, it may be wise to have the store ship it to your home. You'll have to pay a shipping charge, but you won't have to pay California sales tax—or lug it along the rest of your trip.

42. San Francisco is silly with used-everything stores, and the selection is phenomenal. Two good haunts for pre-owned goods are Polk Street and Haight Street, though thrift stores abound everywhere, including ones that offer high-quality merchandise.

## NIGHTLIFE

43. Avoid clubs with high cover charges. There are plenty of bars and dance clubs with cover charges of just a couple of dollars, and some with no admission fees at all; see our recommendations in chapter 10, "San Francisco After Dark."

44. Keep your eyes peeled for bars and clubs advertising happy-hour specials, discounted covers, ladies' nights, and other money-saving theme nights.

45. If you want to see a musical or theatrical performance, contact the **TIX Bay Area** box office (☎ **415/433-7827**) to inquire about discounted or matinee shows. Also, some theaters and companies offer same-day reduced tickets, student discounts, and standing-room rates; see chapter 10 for details.

## 3 When to Go

If you're dreaming of convertibles, Frisbee on the beach, and tank-topped evenings, change your reservations and head to Los Angeles. Contrary to California's sunshine-and-bikini image, San Francisco's weather is mild and can often be downright fickle; it's nothing like that of neighboring Southern California.

## CLIMATE

Northern California weather has been extraordinary recently. In the past several years, the Bay Area has experienced two sizzling and one nonexistent summer, one winter that ended in late June (and kept Tahoe's ski lifts open until August), a series of floods, and a storm whose 80-mile-per-hour winds blew century-old trees right out of the ground. However, San Francisco's temperate, marine climate usually means relatively mild weather year-round. In summer, temperatures rarely top 70°F, and the city's chilling fog rolls in most mornings and evenings. Even when autumn's heat occasionally stretches into the 80s and 90s, you should still dress in layers, or by early evening you'll learn firsthand why sweatshirt sales are a great business at Fisherman's Wharf. In winter, the mercury seldom falls below freezing, and snow is almost unheard of, but that doesn't mean you won't be whimpering if you forgot to bring a coat. Still, compared to most of the States' varied weather conditions, San Francisco is consistently pleasant.

It's that beautifully fluffy, chilly, wet, heavy, and sweeping fog that makes the city's weather so precarious. Northern California's summer fog bank is produced by a rare combination of water, wind, and topography. It lies off the coast and is pulled in by rising air currents when the land heats up. Held back by coastal mountains along a 600-mile front, the low clouds seek out any passage they can find. And the access most readily available is the slot where the Pacific Ocean penetrates the continental wall—the Golden Gate.

## HIGH SEASON VERSUS OFF-SEASON

While summer is the most popular time to visit, it's also often characterized by foggy days, cold windy nights, crowded tourist destinations, and higher hotel and airfare rates. A good bet is to visit in spring, or better yet, autumn. Every September, right about the time San Franciscans mourn being gypped (or fogged) out of another summer, something wonderful happens: The thermostat rises, the skies clear, and the locals call in sick to work and head for the beach. It's what residents call "Indian summer." The city is also delightful during winter, when the opera and ballet seasons are in full swing, there are fewer tourists, hotel prices drop a bit, and downtown bustles with holiday cheer.

### San Francisco's Average Temperatures (°F) & Rainfall (in.)

|      | Jan | Feb | Mar | Apr | May | June | July | Aug | Sept | Oct | Nov | Dec |
|------|-----|-----|-----|-----|-----|------|------|-----|------|-----|-----|-----|
| High | 56  | 59  | 60  | 61  | 63  | 64   | 64   | 65  | 69   | 68  | 63  | 57  |
| Low  | 46  | 48  | 49  | 49  | 51  | 53   | 53   | 54  | 56   | 55  | 52  | 47  |
| Rain | 4.5 | 2.8 | 2.6 | 1.5 | 0.4 | 0.2  | 0.1  | 0.1 | 0.2  | 1.1 | 2.5 | 3.5 |

# San Francisco Calendar of Events

## January

- **San Francisco Sports and Boat Show,** Cow Palace. Draws thousands of boat enthusiasts over a 9-day period. Call **Cow Palace Box Office (☎ 415/469-6065)** for details. Mid-January.

## February

○ **Chinese New Year,** Chinatown. In 2000, the year of the dragon, public celebrations will again spill onto every street in Chinatown. Festivities begin with the "Miss Chinatown USA" pageant parade, and climax a week later with a celebratory parade of marching bands, rolling floats, barrages of fireworks, and a block-long dragon writhing in and out of the crowds; festivities go for several weeks and wrap up with a memorable parade through Chinatown. Arrive early for a good viewing spot on Grant Avenue. Make your hotel reservations early. For dates and information, call ☎ 415/982-3000.

**Travel Tip**

Even if it's sunny out, don't forget to bring a jacket. The weather can change almost instantly from sunny and warm to windy and cold. As the saying goes, "If you don't like the weather in San Francisco, wait 5 minutes."

## March

- **St. Patrick's Day Parade.** Almost everyone's honorarily Irish at this festive affair starting at 12:45pm at Market and Second streets and continuing to City Hall. But the party doesn't stop there. Head down to the Civic Center for the post-party or venture to Embarcadero's Harrington's bar after work hours and celebrate with hundreds of the Irish-for-a-day yuppies as they gallivant amid the closed-off streets and numerous pubs. Call ☎ **510/644-1164** for details. The Sunday before March 17.

## April

- **Cherry Blossom Festival,** Japantown. Meander through the arts-and-crafts and food booths aligning the blocked-off streets; watch traditional drumming, flower arranging, origami, or a parade celebrating the cherry blossom and Japanese culture. Call ☎ **415/563-2313** for information. Mid- to late April.
- ✪ **San Francisco International Film Festival,** with screening at the AMC Kabuki 8 Cinemas, at Fillmore and Post streets, and many other locations. Started 43 years ago, this is America's oldest film festival, featuring more than 200 films and videos from more than 50 countries, and awards ceremonies where renowned honorees join the festivities. Tickets are relatively inexpensive, and screenings are very accessible to the general public. Entries include new films by beginning and established directors. For a schedule or information, call ☎ **415/931-FILM.** Mid-April to early May.

## May

- **Cinco de Mayo Celebration,** Mission District. This is the day the Latino community celebrates the victory of the Mexicans over the French at Puebla in 1862. Mariachi bands, dancers, food, and a parade fill the streets of the Mission. Parade starts at 10am at 24th and Bryant streets and ends at the Civic Center. Sunday before May 5.
- ✪ **Bay to Breakers Foot Race,** Golden Gate Park. Even if you don't participate, you can't avoid this run from downtown to Ocean Beach that stops morning traffic throughout the city. Around 80,000 entrants gather—many dressed in wacky, innovative, and sometimes X-rated costumes—for the approximately 7½-mile run. If you're feeling lazy, join the throng of spectators who line the route in the form of sidewalk parties, bands, and cheerleaders of all ages to get a good dose of true San Francisco fun. The event is sponsored by the *San Francisco Examiner* (☎ **415/777-7770**). Third Sunday of May.
- ✪ **Carnival,** on Mission Street between 14th and 24th streets, and Harrison Street between 16th and 21st streets. The San Francisco Mission District's largest annual event, Carnival, is a day of festivities that culminates with a parade on Mission Street on the Sunday of the Memorial Day weekend. One of San Franciscans' favorite events, more than half a million spectators line the route, and the samba musicians and dancers continue to play on 14th Street, near Harrison, at the end of the march. Just show up, or call the **Mission Economic and Cultural Association** (☎ **415/826-1401**) for complete information.

## June

- **Union Street Art Festival,** along Union Street from Fillmore to Gough streets. With a new promotion company leading the way, the Union Street Fair is now the Union Street Art Festival, which intends to celebrate San Francisco with themes, gourmet food booths, music, and entertainment, and a juried show with more than 350 artists. No doubt the change won't deter the great-looking, young yuppie cocktailers from packing every bar and spilling out into the street. Call the Union Street Association at ☎ **415/441-7055** or the event promoters at 510/970-3217 for more information. First weekend of June.

- **Haight Street Fair.** Featuring alternative crafts, ethnic foods, rock bands, and a healthy number of hippies and young street kids whooping it up and slamming beers in front of the blaring rock 'n' roll stage. The fair usually extends along Haight between Stanyan and Ashbury streets. For details, call ☎ **415/661-8025.** In June; call for date.

- ✪ **North Beach Festival,** Grant Street in North Beach. In 1999, this party celebrated its 45th anniversary; organizers claim it's the oldest urban street fair in the country. Close to 100,000 city folk meander along Grant Avenue, between Vallejo and Union streets, to eat, drink, and browse the arts-and-crafts booths, poetry readings, swing dancing venue, and *arte di gesso* (sidewalk chalk art). But the most enjoyable part of the event is listening to music and people watching. Call ☎ **415/989-2220** for details. Usually Father's Day weekend, but call to confirm.

- **San Francisco Lesbian, Gay, Bisexual, Transgender Pride Parade & Celebration,** Market Street. A prideful event drawing up to half a million participants who celebrate all of the above–and then some. The parade's start and finish have been moved around in recent years to accommodate road construction. Regardless of its path, it ends with hundreds of food, art, and information booths and soundstages. Call ☎ **415/864-3733** for information and location. Usually the third or last weekend of June.

- ✪ **Stern Grove Midsummer Music Festival.** Pack a picnic and head out early to join thousands who come here to lie in the grass and enjoy classical, jazz, and ethnic music and dance in the Grove at 19th Avenue and Sloat Boulevard. These free concerts are held every Sunday at 2pm. Show up with a lawn chair or blanket. There are food booths if you forget snacks, but you'll be dying to leave if you don't bring warm clothes—the Sunset District can be one of the coldest parts of the city. Call ☎ **415/252-6252** for listings. Mid-June through August.

## July

- **Jazz and All That Art on Fillmore.** The first weekend in July starts off with a bang when the upscale portion of Fillmore (the section they block off is changing, so call for details) closes off traffic and fills the street with several blocks of arts and crafts, gourmet food, and live jazz. The festivities will be held on July 1 and 2 from 10am to 6pm. Call ☎ **415/346-4446** for more information.

- **Fourth of July Celebration and Fireworks.** This event can be somewhat of a joke, since more often than not, like everyone else, fog comes into the city on this day to join in the festivities. Sometimes it's almost impossible to view the million-dollar fireworks from Pier 39 on the northern waterfront. Still, it's a party and if the skies are clear, it's a damn good show.

- **San Francisco Marathon.** One of the largest marathons in the world. For entry information, contact West End Management, the event organizer, at ☎ **800/698-8699** or 415/284-9492. Usually the second weekend in July.

## August

- **Renaissance Pleasure Faire.** An expensive but enjoyable festival takes place north of San Francisco and takes you back to Renaissance times—with games, plays, and arts-and-crafts and food booths. In the past the fair was located in Black Point Forest, just east of Novato, but there's talk of a new location. The Faire opens the weekend before Labor Day, and runs six to eight weekends and on Labor Day (☎ **800/52-FAIRE** or 415/892-0937).

- ✪ **A La Carte, A La Park,** usually at Sharon Meadow, Golden Gate Park. You probably won't get to go to all the restaurants you'd like while you're visiting the city, but you can get a good sampling if you attend this annual event. Over 40 of the town's favorite restaurants, accompanied by 20 microbreweries and 20 wineries, offer tastings in the midst of San Francisco's favorite park. There's entertainment as well, and proceeds benefit the Friends of Recreation & Parks. Prices for 2000 hadn't been determined when this book went to press, but in 1999, admission was $9 adults, $7.50 seniors, and free for children under 12. Call ☎ **415/458-1988** for details. Always Labor Day weekend.

## September

- **Opera in the Park.** Each year the San Francisco Opera launches its season with a free concert featuring a selection of arias. Usually in Sharon Meadow, Golden Gate Park, on the first Sunday after Labor Day, but call ☎ **415/861-4008** to confirm the date.

- ✪ **San Francisco Blues Festival,** on the grounds of Fort Mason. The largest outdoor blues music event on the West Coast will be 28 years old in 2000 and again feature local and national musicians performing back-to-back during the 3-day extravaganza. You can charge tickets by phone through **BASS Ticketmaster** (☎ **510/762-2277**). For **schedule** information, call ☎ **415/826-6837.** Usually in late September.

- **Castro Street Fair.** Celebrates life in the city's most famous gay neighborhood. Call ☎ **415/467-3354** for information or check it out on the Web at **www.castrostreetfair.org.** Usually end of September or beginning of October.

- ✪ **Sausalito Art Festival,** Sausalito. A juried exhibit of more than 180 artists. It is accompanied by music—provided by Bay Area jazz, rock, and blues performers—and international cuisine, enhanced by wines from some 50 different Napa and Sonoma producers. Parking is impossible; take the **Blue & Gold Fleet ferry** (☎ **415/705-5555**) from Fisherman's Wharf to the festival site. For more information, call ☎ **415/332-3555.** Labor Day weekend, early September.

## October

- **Italian Heritage Parade.** The city's Italian community leads the festivities around Fisherman's Wharf celebrating Columbus's landing in America. The festival includes a parade along Columbus Avenue and sporting events, but for the most part, it's just a great excuse to hang out in North Beach and people watch. For information, call ☎ **415/434-1492.** Sunday closest to Columbus Day.

- **Reggae in the Park,** usually in Sharon Meadow in Golden Gate Park. Going into its 10th year, this event draws thousands to Golden Gate Park to dance and celebrate the soulful sounds. Big-name reggae and world-beat bands play all weekend long, and ethnic arts-and-crafts and food booths are set up along the stage's periphery. Tickets are around $15 in advance, and $17.50 on-site. Two-day passes are available at a discounted rate. Free for children under 12. Call ☎ **415/458-1988** for more details. Always the first weekend in October.

- **Exotic Erotic Halloween Ball.** The Friday or Saturday night before Halloween, thousands come dressed in costume, lingerie, and sometimes even less than that. It's a wild fantasy affair with bands, dancing, and costume contests. *Beware:* It can be somewhat cheesy. Tickets cost approximately $35 per person. For information, call ☎ **415/567-BALL** or surf over to **www.exoticeroticball.com**. For tickets, call ☎ **510/762-BASS.**
- **Halloween.** A huge night in San Francisco. A fantastical parade is organized at Market and Castro, and a mixed gay/straight crowd revels in costumes of extraordinary imagination. The past few years they've been trying to divert festivities to the Civic Center, but the action's still best in the Castro. October 31.
- **San Francisco Jazz Festival.** This festival presents eclectic programming in an array of fabulous jazz venues throughout the city. With close to 2 weeks of nightly entertainment and dozens of performers, the jazz festival is a hot ticket. Past events have featured Herbie Hancock, Dave Brubeck, the Modern Jazz Quartet, Wayne Shorter, and Bill Frisell. For information, call ☎ **800/850-SFJF** or 415/398-5655. End of October, beginning of November.

**December**
- *The Nutcracker,* War Memorial Opera House. Performed annually by the **San Francisco Ballet** (☎ **415/703-9400**). Tickets to this Tchaikovsky tradition should be purchased well in advance.

## 4  Tips for Travelers with Special Needs

### FOR TRAVELERS WITH DISABILITIES

A disability shouldn't stop anyone from traveling. There are more resources out there than ever before. *A World of Options,* a 658-page book of resources for travelers with disabilities, covers everything from biking trips to scuba outfitters. It costs $35 ($30 for members) and is available from **Mobility International USA,** P.O. Box 10767, Eugene, OR 97440 (☎ **541/343-1284,** voice and TDD; www.miusa. org). Annual membership for Mobility International is $35, which includes their quarterly newsletter, *Over the Rainbow.* In addition, **Twin Peaks Press,** P.O. Box 129, Vancouver, WA 98666 (☎ **360/694-2462**), publishes travel-related books for people with disabilities.

The Moss Rehab Hospital (☎ **215/456-9600**) has been providing friendly and helpful phone advice and referrals to travelers with disabilities for years through its **Travel Information Service** (☎ **215/456-9603**; www.mossresourcenet.org).

You can join **The Society for the Advancement of Travel for the Handicapped** (SATH), 347 Fifth Ave. Suite 610, New York, NY 10016 (☎ **212/447-7284,**

### Travel Tip

If you suffer from a chronic illness, consult your doctor before your departure. For conditions like epilepsy, diabetes, or heart problems, wear a **Medic Alert Identification Tag** (☎ **800/825-3785**; www.medicalert.org), which will immediately alert doctors to your condition and give them access to your records through Medic Alert's 24-hour hot line. Membership is $35, plus a $15 annual fee.

Pack prescription medications in your carry-on luggage. Carry written prescriptions in generic, not brand-name form, and dispense all prescription medications from their original labeled vials. Also bring along copies of your prescriptions in case you lose your pills or run out.

fax 212-725-8253; www.sath.org) for $45 annually, $30 for seniors and students, to gain access to their vast network of connections in the travel industry. They provide information sheets on travel destinations and referrals to tour operators that specialize in traveling with disabilities. Their quarterly magazine, *Open World for Disability and Mature Travel,* is full of good information and resources. A year's subscription is $13.00 ($21 outside the U.S.).

Vision-impaired travelers should contact the **American Foundation for the Blind,** 11 Penn Plaza, Suite 300, New York, NY 10001 (☎ **800/232-5463**), for information on traveling with Seeing Eye dogs.

Most of San Francisco's major museums and tourist attractions are fitted with wheelchair ramps. In addition, many hotels offer special accommodations and services for wheelchair-bound and other visitors with disabilities. These include extra-large bathrooms and ramps for the wheelchair-bound and telecommunication devices for deaf people. The San Francisco Convention and Visitors Bureau (see section 1, "Visitor Information," above) has the most up-to-date information. Travelers in wheelchairs can secure special ramped taxis by calling **Yellow Cab** (☎ **415/626-2345**), which charges regular rates for the service. Travelers with disabilities can also get a free copy of the *Muni Access Guide,* published by the San Francisco Municipal Railway, Accessible Services Program, Municipal Railway, 949 Presidio Ave., San Francisco, CA 94115 (☎ **415/923-6142**). Call this number Monday to Friday from 8am to 5pm. Many of the major car-rental companies now offer hand-controlled cars for disabled drivers. **Avis** can provide such a vehicle at any of its locations in the United States with 48-hour advance notice; **Hertz** requires between 24 and 72 hours of advance reservation at most of its locations. **Wheelchair Getaways** (☎ **800/873-4973;** www.blvd.com/wg.htm) rents specialized vans with wheelchair lifts and other features for the disabled in more than 100 cities across the United States.

Travelers with disabilities may also want to consider joining a tour that caters specifically to them. One of the best operators is **Flying Wheels Travel,** 143 West Bridge (P.O. Box 382), Owatonna, MN 55060 (☎ **800/535-6790**). They offer various escorted tours and cruises, with an emphasis on sports, as well as private tours in minivans with lifts. Other reputable specialized tour operators include **Accessible Journeys** (☎ **800/TINGLES** or 610/521-0339), for slow walkers and wheelchair travelers, and **The Guided Tour, Inc.** (☎ **215/782-1370**).

## FOR GAY & LESBIAN TRAVELERS

If you head down to the Castro—an area surrounding Castro Street near Market Street that's predominantly a gay and lesbian community—you'll understand why the city is a mecca for gay and lesbian travelers. Since the 1970s, this unique part of town has remained the colorfully festive gay neighborhood teeming with "outed" city folk who meander the streets shopping, eating, partying, or cruising. If anyone feels like an outsider in this part of town, it's heterosexuals, who, although warmly welcomed in the community, may feel uncomfortable or downright threatened if they harbor any homophobia or an aversion to being "cruised." For many San Franciscans, it's just a fun area (especially on Halloween) with some wonderful shops.

It is estimated that gays and lesbians form one-fourth to one-third of the population of San Francisco, so it's no surprise that in recent years clubs and bars catering to them have popped up all around town. Although lesbian interests are concentrated primarily in the East Bay (especially Oakland), a significant community resides in the Mission District, around 16th Street and Valencia.

Several local publications are dedicated to in-depth coverage of news, information, and listings of goings-on around town for gay men and lesbians. The *Bay Area Reporter* has the most comprehensive listings, including a weekly calendar of events, and is distributed free on Thursdays. It can be found stacked at the corner of 18th and Castro streets and at Ninth and Harrison streets, as well as in bars, bookshops, and various stores around town. It may also be available in gay and lesbian bookstores elsewhere in the country.

**GUIDES & PUBLICATIONS**    For accommodations, check with two international guides: *Odysseus* ($29) and *Inn Places* ($16). These books and others are available by mail from **Giovanni's Room,** 345 S. 12th St., Philadelphia, PA 19107 (☎ 215/923-2960; E-mail: giophilp@netaxs.com) and **A Different Light Bookstore,** 489 Castro St., San Francisco, CA 94114 (☎ 415/431-0891; www.adlbooks.com). Other locations are in New York City (☎ 212/989-4850) and Los Angeles (☎ 310/854-6601).

*Our World,* 1104 N. Nova Rd., Suite 251, Daytona Beach, FL 32117 (☎ 904/441-5367), is a magazine devoted to gay and lesbian travel worldwide. It costs $35 for 10 issues. *Out and About,* 8 W. 19th St., Suite 401, New York, NY 10011 (☎ 800/929-2268; www.outandabout.com), has been hailed for its "straight" reporting about gay travel. It profiles the best gay or gay-friendly hotels, restaurants, clubs, and other places, with coverage of destinations throughout the world. It costs $49 a year for 10 information-packed issues. *Out and About* aims for the more upscale gay or lesbian traveler and has been praised by everybody from *Travel and Leisure* to the *New York Times.* Both these publications are also available at most gay and lesbian bookstores.

**ORGANIZATIONS**    **The International Gay & Lesbian Travel Association (IGLTA),** 4331 N. Federal Hwy., Suite 304, Fort Lauderdale, FL 33308 (☎ 800/448-8550 for a voice mailbox, or 954/776-2626; www.ilgta.com), encourages gay and lesbian travel worldwide. With around 700 travel agency members, it offers quarterly newsletters, marketing mailings, and a membership directory that is updated four times a year. Travel agents who are IGLTA members will be tied into this organization's vast information resources, or you can e-mail them at IGLTA@aol.com.

**TRAVEL AGENCIES**    In California a few leading gay-friendly options for travel arrangements are **Now Voyager,** 4406 18th St., San Francisco, CA 94114 (☎ 800/255-6951 or 415/626-1169), and **Gunderson Travel Inc.,** 8543 Santa Monica Blvd., Suite 8, West Hollywood, CA 90069 (☎ 800/899-1944 or 800/872-8457 in the U.S., or 310/657-3944); e-mail them at **gundersontvl@worldnet.att.net**.

Also in California, **Skylink Women's Travel,** 1006 Mendocino Ave., Santa Rosa, CA 95401 (☎ 800/225-5759 or 707/546-9888), and **Thanks Babs!** (☎ 888/WOW-BABS;** www.skylinktravel.com), can help custom design your visit to the area.

General gay and lesbian travel agencies include **Family Abroad** (☎ 800/999-5500 or 212/459-1800; gay and lesbian); **Above and Beyond Tours** (☎ 800/397-2681;** mainly gay men); and **Yellowbrick Road** (☎ 800/642-2488; gay and lesbian).

# FOR FAMILIES

San Francisco is full of sightseeing opportunities and special activities geared toward children, and considering that much of it is free, the kids aren't likely to break your bank on this trip (unless, of course, they corner you into a visit to the famed FAO Schwarz toy store). See "Especially for Kids" and the box "Cheap Thrills: What to See & Do for Free (or Almost) in San Francisco," both in chapter 7, for information and ideas for families.

Several books on the market offer tips to help you travel with kids. Most concentrate on the U.S., but two, *Family Travel* (Lanier Publishing International) and *How to Take Great Trips with Your Kids* (The Harvard Common Press), are full of good general advice that can apply to travel anywhere. Another reliable tome with a worldwide focus, is *Adventuring with Children* (Foghorn Press).

*The Unofficial Guide to California with Kids* (Macmillan Travel) is an excellent resource covering the entire state. It rates and ranks attractions for each age group, lists dozens of family-friendly accommodations and restaurants, and suggests lots of beaches and adventures that are great for the whole clan.

*Family Travel Times* is published six times a year by TWYCH (Travel with Your Children; ☎ **888/822-4388** or 212/477-5524), and includes a weekly call-in service for subscribers. Subscriptions are $40 a year for quarterly editions. A free publication list and a sample issue are available by calling or sending a request to the above address.

**Families Welcome!,** 92 N. Main, Ashland, OR 97520 (☎ **800/326-0724** or 541/482-6121), is a travel company specializing in worry-free vacations for families.

## FOR WOMEN

Women's services are often lumped together in the lesbian category, but there are resources geared toward women without regard to sexuality. The **Bay Area Women's and Children's Center,** 318 Leavenworth St. (☎ **415/474-2400**), offers specialized services and city information to women. The **Women's Building,** 3543 18th St. (☎ **415/431-1180**), is a Mission-area space housing feminist art shows and political events and offering classes in yoga, aerobics, movement, and tai chi chuan. The **Rape Crisis Hotline** (☎ **415/647-7273**) is staffed 24 hours daily.

Several Web sites offer women advice on how to travel safely and happily. The **Executive Woman's Travel Network** (www.delta-air.com/womenexecs/) is the official woman's travel site of Delta airlines and offers women tips on staying fit while traveling, eating well, finding special airfares, and dealing with many other travel issues. **WomanTraveler** (**www.womantraveler.com/**) is an excellent guide that suggests places where women can stay and eat in various destinations. The site is authored by women and includes listings of female-owned businesses such as hotels, hostels, and so on.

## FOR SENIORS

Seniors regularly receive discounts at museums and attractions and on public transportation; such discounts, when available, are listed in this guide, under their appropriate headings. Ask for discounts everywhere—at hotels, movie theaters, museums, restaurants, and attractions. You may be surprised how often you'll be offered reduced rates.

When making airline reservations, ask about a seniors' discount, but find out if there is a cheaper promotional fare before committing yourself. Also, mention the fact that you're a senior citizen when making other travel reservations. For example, both **Amtrak** (☎ **800/USA-RAIL;** www.amtrak.com) and **Greyhound** (☎ **800/752-4841;** www.greyhound.com) offer discounts to persons over 62. And many hotels offer senior discounts; **Choice Hotels** (Clarion Hotels, Quality Inns, Comfort Inns, Sleep Inns, Econo Lodges, Friendship Inns, and Rodeway Inns), for example, give 30% off their published rates to anyone over 50, provided you book your room through their nationwide toll-free reservations numbers (that is, not directly with the hotels or through a travel agent). See Appendix B for a handy list of national toll-free numbers.

The **Senior Citizen Information Line** (☎ **415/626-1033**) offers advice, referrals, and information on city services. The **Friendship Line for the Elderly** (☎ **415/752-3778**) is a support, referral, and crisis-intervention service.

The **National Council of Senior Citizens,** 8403 Colesville Rd., Suite 1200, Silver Spring, MD 20910 (☎ **301/578-8800**), a nonprofit organization, offers a newsletter six times a year (partly devoted to travel tips) and discounts on hotel and auto rentals; annual dues are $13 per person or couple.

*The Mature Traveler,* a monthly 12-page newsletter on senior citizen travel is a valuable resource. It is available by subscription ($30 a year) from GEM Publishing Group, Box 50400, Reno, NV 89513-0400. GEM also publishes *The Book of Deals,* a collection of more than 1,000 senior discounts on airlines, lodging, tours, and attractions around the country; it's available for $9.95 by calling ☎ **800/460-6676.** Another helpful publication is *101 Tips for the Mature Traveler,* available from Grand Circle Travel, 347 Congress St., Suite 3A, Boston, MA 02210 (☎ **800/221-2610** or 617/350-7500; fax 617/346-6700).

Members of the **American Association of Retired Persons (AARP),** 601 E St. NW, Washington, DC 20049 (☎ **800/424-3410** or 202/434-2277), get discounts not only on hotels but on airfares and car rentals, too. AARP offers members a wide range of special benefits, including *Modern Maturity* magazine and a monthly newsletter.

**Mature Outlook,** P.O. Box 9390, Des Moines, IA 50306 (☎ **800/336-6330**), began as a travel organization for people over 50, though it now caters to people of all ages. Members receive discounts on hotels and receive a bimonthly magazine. Annual membership is $19.95, which entitles members to discounts and, often, free coupons for discounted merchandise from Sears.

**Golden Companions,** P.O. Box 5249, Reno, NV 89513 (☎ **702/324-2227**), helps travelers 45-plus find compatible companions through a personal voice-mail service. Contact them for more information.

**Grand Circle Travel,** 347 Congress St., Suite 3A, Boston, MA 02210 (☎ **800/221-2610** or 617/350-7500), is also one of the hundreds of travel agencies specializing in vacations for seniors Many of these packages, however, are of the tour-bus variety, with free trips thrown in for those who organize groups of 10 or more. Seniors seeking more independent travel should probably consult a regular travel agent. **SAGA International Holidays,** 222 Berkeley St., Boston, MA 02116 (☎ **800/343-0273**), offers inclusive tours and cruises for those 50 and older. SAGA also sponsors the more substantial "Road Scholar Tours" (☎ **800/621-2151**), which are fun-loving, but with an educational bent.

You may also want to peruse *The 50+ Traveler's Guidebook* (St. Martin's Press), *The Seasoned Traveler* (Country Roads Press), or *Unbelievably Good Deals and Great Adventures That You Absolutely Can't Get Unless You're Over 50* (Contemporary Books). Also check out your newsstand for the quarterly magazine *Travel 50 & Beyond.*

# 5  Getting There

## BY AIR
### THE MAJOR AIRLINES
San Francisco is serviced by dozens of carriers, including the following major domestic airlines: **American Airlines,** 433 California St. (☎ 800/433-7300);

# Cyber Deals for Net Surfers

It's possible to get some great deals on airfare, hotels, and car rentals via the Internet. Grab your mouse and surf before you take off—you could save a bundle on your trip. The Web sites highlighted below are worth checking out, especially since all services are free. Always check the lowest published fare, however, before you shop for flights online.

**Arthur Frommer's Budget Travel** (www.frommers.com)   Home of the Encyclopedia of Travel and *Arthur Frommer's Budget Travel* magazine and daily newsletter, this site offers detailed information on 200 cities and islands around the world, and up-to-the-minute ways to save dramatically on flights, hotels, car reservations, and cruises. Book an entire vacation online and research your destination before you leave. Consult the message board to set up "hospitality exchanges" in other countries, to talk with other travelers who have visited a hotel you're considering, or to direct travel questions to Arthur Frommer himself. The newsletter is updated daily to keep you abreast of the latest breaking ways to save, to publicize new hot spots and best buys, and to present veteran readers with fresh, ever-changing approaches to travel.

**Microsoft Expedia** (www.expedia.com)   The best part of this multipurpose travel site is the "Fare Tracker:" You fill out a form on the screen indicating that you're interested in cheap flights from your hometown, and, once a week, they'll e-mail you the best airfare deals on up to three destinations. The site's "Travel Agent" will steer you to bargains on hotels and car rentals, and with the help of hotel and airline seat pinpointers, you can book everything right on line. This site is even useful once you're booked. Before you depart, log on to Expedia for maps and up-to-date travel information, including weather reports and foreign exchange rates.

**Travelocity** (www.travelocity.com)   This is one of the best travel sites out there, especially for finding cheap airfare. In addition to its "Personal Fare Watcher," which notifies you via e-mail of the lowest airfares for up to five different destinations, Travelocity will track the three lowest fares for any routes on any dates in minutes. You can book a flight right then and there, and if you need a rental car or hotel, Travelocity will find you the best deal via the SABRE computer reservations system (another huge travel agent database). Click on "Last Minute Deals" for the latest travel bargains, including a link to "H.O.T. Coupons" (www.hotcoupons.com), where you can print out electronic coupons for travel in the United States and Canada.

---

**Delta Airlines,** 433 California St. and 124 Geary St. (☎ 800/221-1212); **Northwest Airlines,** 124 Geary St. and 433 California St. (☎ 800/225-2525); **Southwest Airlines,** at the airport (☎ 800/I-FLY-SWA); **TWA,** 595 Market St., Suite 2240, at the corner of Second Street (☎ 800/221-2000); **United Airlines,** 433 California St., 124 Geary, and Embarcadero One (☎ 800/241-6522); and **US Airways,** 433 California St. (☎ 800/428-4322).

Other major airlines that fly to San Francisco include: **Alaska Airlines** (☎ 800/426-0333); **America West Airlines** (☎ 800/235-9292); **Hawaiian Airlines** (☎ 800/367-5320); **Reno Air** (☎ 800/RENO-AIR; www.renoair.com); **Tower Air** (☎ 800/34-TOWER outside New York, or 718/553-8500 in New York;

**Trip.com** (www.trip.com): This site is really geared toward the business traveler, but vacationers-to-be can also use Trip.com's exceptionally powerful fare-finding engine, which will e-mail you every week with the best city-to-city airfare deals for as many as 10 routes. The site uses the Internet Travel Network, another reputable travel agent database, to book hotels and restaurants.

**E-Savers Programs**    Several major airlines offer a free e-mail service known as E-Savers, via which they'll send you their best bargain airfares on a regular basis. Here's how it works: Once a week (usually Wednesday), or whenever a sale fare comes up, subscribers receive a list of discounted flights to and from various destinations, both international and domestic. Here's the catch: These fares are usually only available if you leave the very next Saturday (or sometimes Friday night) and return on the following Monday or Tuesday. It's really a service for the spontaneously inclined and travelers looking for a quick getaway. But the fares are cheap, so it's worth taking a look. If you have a preference for certain airlines (in other words, the ones you fly most frequently), sign up with them first.

Here's a partial list of airlines and their Web sites, where you can not only get on the e-mailing lists, but also book flights directly:

- **American Airlines:** www.aa.com
- **British Airways:** www.british-airways.com
- **Canadian Airlines International:** www.cdnair.ca
- **Continental Airlines:** www.flycontiental.com
- **Northwest Airlines:** www.nwa.com
- **TWA:** www.twa.com
- **US Airways:** www.usairways.com
- **United Airlines:** www.ual.com
- **Virgin Atlantic Airways:** www.fly.virgin.com

One caveat: You'll get frequent-flier miles if you purchase one of these fares, but you can't use miles to buy the ticket.

**Smarter Living** (www.smarterliving.com)    If the thought of all that surfing and comparison shopping gives you a headache, then head right for Smarter Living. Sign up for their newsletter service, and every week you'll get a customized e-mail summarizing the discount fares available from your departure city. Smarter Living tracks more than 15 different airlines, so it's a worthwhile time saver.

www.towerair.com). **National Airlines** (☎ 888/757-JETS; www.nationalairlines.com) now offers flights to San Francisco from Chicago, New York, and Dallas through Las Vegas. The airline plans to expand to several other gateway cities in the future. All passengers may take a free stopover in Las Vegas.

If you're coming from outside the United States, refer to chapter 3, "For Foreign Visitors," which lists the major international carriers.

## FLYING FOR LESS: TIPS FOR GETTING THE BEST AIRFARES

Passengers within the same airplane cabin rarely pay the same fare for their seats. To get the lowest available fare, check your newspaper and call the airlines, asking for the lowest promotional or special fare available. Note, though, that the lowest-priced fares will often be nonrefundable, require advance purchase of 1 to 3 weeks and a certain length of stay, and carry penalties for changing dates of travel. You'll almost never see a sale during the peak summer vacation months of July and August, or during the Thanksgiving or Christmas seasons; but in periods of low-volume travel, you should pay no more than $400 for a cross-country flight.

If you can be flexible, ask if you can secure a cheaper fare by staying an extra day or by flying midweek. Many airlines won't volunteer this information. At the time of this writing, the lowest round-trip fare on one airline from New York was $324, but you had to purchase 14 days in advance, stay at least 1 Saturday night in San Francisco, and travel during certain hours. Otherwise the price was $465. From Chicago, the trip cost $360. From Los Angeles, fares ranged from $193 round-trip (21-day advance purchase) to $386 (7-day advance purchase). Of course, fares change radically depending on the time of year and whether there's a sale going on. In business class, expect to pay about $951 one way from New York and $1,335 from Chicago. First class costs about $1,500 one way from New York and $1,348 from Chicago.

Don't overlook the possibility of using a **consolidator,** or "bucket shop," when hunting for low domestic fares. By negotiating directly with the airlines, the "buckets" can sell discounted tickets, but they will also carry restrictions and penalties for changes or cancellation.

The lowest-priced bucket shops are usually local operations with low profiles and overheads. Look for their advertisements in the travel section or the classifieds of your local newspaper. Nationally advertised businesses are usually not as competitive as the smaller operations, but they have toll-free telephone numbers and are easily accessible. There are lots of fly-by-night consolidators, though, and problems can range from disputing never-received tickets to finding you have no seat booked when you get to the airport. Play it safe by going with a reputable business. Here are some suggestions: **1-800-FLY-CHEAP** (www.1800flycheap.com); **Cheap Seats** (☎ 800/451-7200; www.cheapseatstravel.com); or our favorite, **Cheap Tickets** (☎ 800/377-1000; www.cheaptickets.com). **Council Travel** (☎ 800/226-8624; www.counciltravel.com) and **STA Travel** (☎ 800/781-4040; www.sta.travel.com) cater especially to young travelers, but their bargain basement prices are available to people of all ages; **Travel Bargains** (☎ 800/AIR-FARE; www.1800airfare.com) was formerly owned by TWA, but now offers the deepest discounts on many other airlines, with a 4-day advance purchase.

Discounted fares have pared the number of **charters,** but they're still available. Most charter operators advertise and sell their seats through travel agents, thus making these local professionals your best source of information for available flights. Before deciding to take a charter flight, check the restrictions on the ticket: You may be asked to purchase a tour package, to pay in advance, to be amenable if the day of departure is changed, to pay a service charge, to fly on an airline you're not familiar with (this usually is not the case), and to pay harsh penalties if you cancel, but to be understanding if the charter doesn't fill up and is canceled up to 10 days before departure. Summer charters fill up more quickly than others and are almost sure to fly, but if you decide on a charter flight, seriously consider cancellation and baggage insurance.

**Courier flights** are primarily long-haul jobs and are usually not available on domestic flights. Companies that hire couriers use your luggage allowance for their business baggage; in return, you get a deeply discounted ticket. Flights are often offered at the last minute, and you may have to arrange a pretrip interview to make sure you're right for the job. **Now Voyager** (☎ **212/431-1616** Monday to Friday from 10am to 5:30pm and Saturday from noon to 4:30pm) flies from New York and sometimes has flights to San Francisco for as little as $199 round-trip. Now Voyager also offers noncourier discounted fares, so call the company even if you don't want to fly as a courier.

You can also join a travel club such as **Moment's Notice** (☎ **718/234-6295**) or **Sears Discount Travel Club** (☎ **800/433-9383**, or 800/255-1487 to join), which supply unsold tickets at discounted prices. You pay an annual membership fee to get the club's hotline number. Of course, you're limited to what's available, so you have to be flexible.

## THE MAJOR AIRPORTS

Two major airports serve the Bay Area: San Francisco International and Oakland International.

**San Francisco International Airport,** located 14 miles south of downtown directly on U.S. 101, is served by almost four dozen major scheduled carriers. Travel time to downtown during commuter rush hours is about 40 minutes; at other times it's about 20 to 25 minutes.

The airport offers a toll-free **hot line,** available weekdays from 7am to 5pm (PST), for information on ground transportation (☎ **800/736-2008**). During operating hours the line is answered weekdays by a real person who will provide you with a rundown of all your options for getting into the city from the airport. Each of the three main terminals also has a desk where you can get the same information.

A **taxi** from the airport to downtown will cost $28 to $32, plus tip, so unless you're with a group who can split the fare, you're probably better off taking a bus or shuttle.

**SFO Airporter** buses (☎ **415/495-8404**) depart from outside the lower-level baggage-claim area to downtown San Francisco every 15 to 30 minutes from 6:15am to midnight (picking up at hotels as early as 5am). They stop at several Union Square–area hotels, including the Grand Hyatt, San Francisco Hilton, San Francisco Marriott, Westin St. Francis, Parc Fifty-Five, Hyatt Regency, and Sheraton Palace. No reservations are needed. The cost is $10 each way, and children under 2 ride for free.

Other private shuttle companies offer door-to-door airport service, in which you share a van with a few other passengers. **SuperShuttle** (☎ **415/558-8500**) will take you anywhere in the city, charging $10 per person to a hotel; $12 to a residence or business, plus $8 for each additional person; and $40 to charter an entire van for up to seven passengers. **Yellow Airport Shuttle** (☎ **415/282-7433**) charges $10 per person. Each shuttle stops every 20 minutes or so and picks up passengers from the marked areas outside the terminals' upper level. Reservations are required for the return trip to the airport only and should be made 1 day before departure. Keep in mind that these shuttles demand they pick you up 2 hours before your domestic flight, 3 hours during holidays and for international flights.

The San Mateo County Transit system, **SamTrans** (☎ **800/660-4287** within northern California, or 650/508-6200; www.santrans.com) runs two buses between the airport and the Transbay Terminal at First and Mission streets. The 7B bus costs $2.20 and makes the trip in about 55 minutes. The 7F bus costs $3 and takes only 35 minutes, but permits only one carry-on bag. Both buses run daily. The 7B starts at 4:46am and the 7F starts at 5:30am. Both run frequently until 8pm, then hourly until about midnight.

## Car Rentals

All major car-rental agencies have locations at the airport. You don't need a car to explore San Francisco itself if you stay in a city hotel, but in case you do decide you need one, tips on car rentals can be found under "Getting Around" in chapter 4.

Located about 5 miles south of downtown Oakland, at the Hagenberger Road exit of Calif. 17 (U.S. 880), **Oakland International Airport** (☎ **510/577-4000**) is used primarily by passengers with East Bay destinations. Some San Franciscans, however, prefer this less-crowded, accessible airport when flying during busy periods.

Again, taxis from the airport to downtown San Francisco are expensive, costing approximately $45, plus tip.

**Bayporter Express** (☎ **415/467-1800**) is a shuttle service that charges $20 for the first person, $10 each additional to downtown San Francisco (it costs more to outer areas of town). **Easy Way Out** (☎ **510/430-9090**) is another option, which charges $20 per person, $10 each additional rider. Both accept advance reservations. To the right of the airport exit, there are usually shuttles that will take you to the city for around $20 per person. Keep in mind that they are independently owned and prices vary.

The cheapest way to downtown San Francisco is to take the shuttle bus from the airport to **BART** (Bay Area Rapid Transit; ☎ **510/464-6000**). The AirBART shuttle bus runs about every 15 minutes Monday to Saturday from 6am to 11:30pm and Sunday from 8:30am to 11:30pm, stopping in front of Terminals 1 and 2 near the ground transportation signs. The cost is $2 for the 10-minute ride to BART's Coliseum terminal. BART fares vary, depending on your destination; the trip to downtown San Francisco costs $2.45 and takes 20 minutes once onboard. The entire excursion should take around 45 minutes.

## BY CAR

San Francisco is easily accessed by major highways: Interstate 5, from the north, and U.S. 101, which cuts south-north through the peninsula from San Jose and across the Golden Gate Bridge to points north. If you drive from Los Angeles, you can either take the longer coastal route (437 miles and 11 hr.) or the inland route (389 miles and 8 hr.). From Mendocino, it's 156 miles and 4 hours; from Sacramento it's 88 miles and 1½ hours; and from Yosemite it's 210 miles and 4 hours.

If you are driving and aren't already a member, then it's worth joining the **American Automobile Association (AAA)** (☎ **800/922-8228**), which charges $40 to $60 per year (with an additional one-time joining fee), depending on where you join, and provides roadside and other services to motorists. **Amoco Motor Club** (☎ **800/334-3300**) is another recommended choice.

## BY TRAIN

Traveling by train takes a long time and usually costs as much as, or more than, flying, but if you have *a lot* of time on your hands and want to take a leisurely ride across America, riding the rail may be a good option.

San Francisco–bound **Amtrak** (☎ **800/872-7245** or 800/USA-RAIL) trains leave from New York and cross the country via Chicago. The journey takes about 3½ days, and seats sell quickly. At this writing, the lowest round-trip fare would cost anywhere from $314 to $570 from New York and from $256 to $464 from

Chicago. These heavily restricted tickets are good for 45 to 180 days and allow up to three stops along the way, depending on your ticket.

Round-trip tickets from Los Angeles can be purchased for as little as $92 or as much as $140. Trains actually arrive in Emeryville, just north of Oakland, and connect with regularly scheduled buses to San Francisco's Ferry Building and CalTrain station in downtown San Francisco.

**CalTrain** (☎ **800/660-4287** or 415/546-4461) operates train services between San Francisco and the towns of the peninsula. The city depot is at 700 Fourth St., at Townsend Street.

## BY BUS

Bus travel is an inexpensive and often flexible option. **Greyhound/Trailways** (☎ **800/231-2222**) operates buses to San Francisco from just about anywhere and offers several money-saving multiday passes. Round-trip fares vary, depending on your point of origin, but few, if any, ever exceed $300. The main San Francisco bus station is the **Transbay Terminal,** 425 Mission St. at First Street. For information, call ☎ **800/231-2222.**

## PACKAGE DEALS

Packages combining airfare, accommodations, and perhaps even car rentals or airport transfers are sometimes a good way to go. Though some companies offer escorted tours, others simply buy airline tickets and hotel rooms in bulk, passing on some of the discount to you (you still travel independently.) Often you'll pay much less than if you had organized the same trip by booking each component separately. To find out what tours and packages are available to you, check the ads in the travel section of your newspaper or visit your travel agent.

For information on independent fly-drive packages (no escorted tour groups, just a bulk rate on your airfare, hotel, and possibly rental car), contact **American Airlines Fly AAway Vacations** (☎ 800/321-2121), **American Express Vacations** (☎ **800/241-1700;** www.leisureweb.com), **Continental Airlines Vacations** (☎ 800/634-5555), **Delta Vacations** (☎ 800/872-7786), **TWA Getaway Vacations** (☎ 800/438-2929), **Southwest Airlines** (☎ **800/I-FLY-SWA;** www.iflysw.com), or **United Vacations** (☎ 800/328-6877). Availability varies widely based upon season and demand, but it always pays to investigate what the major air carriers are offering.

One of the biggest packagers in the Northeast, **Liberty Travel** (☎ **888/271-1584;** www.libertytravel.com) boasts a full-page ad in many Sunday papers. You won't get much in the way of service, but you will get a good deal.

For one-stop shopping on the Web, go to **www.vacationpackager.com,** a search engine that will link you to many different package-tour operators offering California vacations, often with a company profile summarizing the company's basic booking and cancellation terms.

# 3 For Foreign Visitors

The pervasiveness of American culture around the world may make you feel that you know the United States pretty well, but leaving your own country still requires an additional degree of planning. This chapter will help prepare you for the more common problems that visitors to San Francisco may encounter.

## 1 Preparing for Your Trip

### ENTRY REQUIREMENTS

Immigration laws are a hot political issue in the United States these days, and the following requirements may have changed somewhat by the time you plan your trip. Check at any U.S. embassy or consulate for current information and requirements. You can also plug into the **U.S. State Department's** Internet site at **http://state.gov**.

### DOCUMENT REGULATIONS

**VISAS**   The U.S. State Department has a **Visa Waiver Pilot Program** allowing citizens of certain countries to enter the United States without a visa for stays of up to 90 days. At press time these included Andorra, Argentina, Australia, Austria, Belgium, Brunei, Denmark, Finland, France, Germany, Iceland, Ireland, Italy, Japan, Liechtenstein, Luxembourg, Monaco, the Netherlands, New Zealand, Norway, San Marino, Slovenia, Spain, Sweden, Switzerland, and the United Kingdom. Citizens of these countries need only a valid passport and a round-trip air or cruise ticket in their possession upon arrival. If they first enter the United States, they may also visit Mexico, Canada, Bermuda, and/or the Caribbean islands and return to the United States without a visa. Further information is available from any U.S. embassy or consulate. Canadian citizens may enter the United States without visas; they need only proof of residence.

Citizens of all other countries must have (1) a valid passport that expires at least 6 months later than the scheduled end of their visit to the United States, and (2) a tourist visa, which may be obtained without charge from any U.S. consulate.

**OBTAINING A VISA**   To obtain a visa, the traveler must submit a completed application form (either in person or by mail) with a 1½-inch-square photo, and must demonstrate binding ties to a residence abroad. Usually you can obtain a visa at once or within 24 hours, but it may take longer during the summer rush from June through August. If you cannot go in person, contact the nearest U.S. embassy or consulate for directions on applying by mail. Your travel agent or airline office may also be able to provide you with visa applications and instructions. The U.S. consulate or embassy that issues your visa will determine whether you will be issued a multiple- or single-entry visa and any restrictions regarding the length of your stay.

British subjects can obtain up-to-date passport and visa information by calling the **U.S. Embassy Visa Information Line** (☎ **0891/200-290**) or the **London Passport Office** (☎ **0990/210-410** for recorded information).

**IMMIGRATION QUESTIONS**    Telephone operators will answer your inquiries regarding U.S. immigration policies or laws at the **Immigration and Naturalization Service's Customer Information Center** (☎ **800/375-5283**). Representatives are available from 9am–3pm, Monday through Friday. The INS also runs a 24-hour automated information service, for commonly asked questions, at ☎ **800/ 755-0777.** You can also call the **Immigration Office** at the San Francisco International Airport (☎ **650/876-2876**) or San Francisco's **INS Ask Immigration System** (☎ **415/705-4411**).

**PASSPORTS**    To enter the United States, you must have a valid passport. Safeguard your passport in an inconspicuous, inaccessible place like a money belt. If you lose it, visit the nearest consulate of your native country as soon as possible for a replacement. Passport applications are downloadable from the Internet sites listed below.

**Canadian residents** can pick up a passport application at one of 28 regional passport offices or most travel agencies. The passport is valid for 5 years and costs Can$60. Children under 16 may be included on a parent's passport but need their own to travel unaccompanied by the parent. Applications, which must be accompanied by two identical passport-sized photographs and proof of Canadian citizenship, are available at travel agencies throughout Canada or from the central **Passport Office, Department of Foreign Affairs and International Trade,** Ottawa, Ont. K1A 0G3 (☎ **800/567-6868;** www.dfait-maeci.gc.ca/passport). Processing takes 5 to 10 days if you apply in person, or about 3 weeks by mail.

Residents of the **United Kingdom** can pick up a passport application for a regular 10-year passport (the Visitor's Passport has been abolished), at the nearest passport office, major post office, or travel agency. You can also contact the London Passport Office at ☎ **0171/271-3000** or search its Web site at **www.open.gov.uk/ ukpass/ukpass.htm**. Passports are £21 for adults and £11 for children under 16.

**Irish** residents can apply for a 10-year passport, costing IR£45, at the Passport Office, Setanta Centre, Molesworth Street, Dublin 2 (☎ **01/671-1633;** www.irlgov.ie/iveagh/foreignaffairs/services). Those under age 18 and over 65 must apply for a IR£10 3-year passport. You can also apply at 1A South Mall, Cork (☎ **021/272-525**) or over the counter at most main post offices.

Australians should apply at the local post office or passport office or search the government Web site at **www.dfat.gov.au/passports/**. Passports for adults are A$126 and for those under 18 A$63.

**Travel Tip**

Be sure to keep a copy of all your travel papers separate from your wallet or purse, and leave a copy with someone at home should you need it faxed in an emergency.

If you are a citizen of **New Zealand,** you can pick up a passport application at any travel agency or Link Centre. For more info, contact the Passport Office, P.O. Box 805, Wellington (☎ **0800/225-050**). Passports for adults are NZ$80 and for those under 16 NZ$40.

**DRIVER'S LICENSES**   Foreign driver's licenses are recognized in San Francisco, although you may want to get an international driver's license if your home license is not written in English.

## MEDICAL REQUIREMENTS

Unless you're arriving from an area known to be suffering from an epidemic (particularly cholera or yellow fever), inoculations or vaccinations are not required for entry into the United States. If you have a disease that requires treatment with narcotics or syringe-administered medications, carry a valid signed prescription from your physician to allay any suspicions that you may be smuggling narcotics (a serious offense that carries severe penalties in the U.S.).

For HIV-positive visitors, requirements for entering the United States are somewhat vague and change frequently. According to the latest publication of *HIV and Immigrants: A Manual for AIDS Service Providers,* "Although INS doesn't require a medical exam for every one trying to come into the United States, INS officials may keep out people who they suspect are HIV positive. INS may stop people because they look sick or because they are carrying AIDS/HIV medicine."

If an HIV-positive non-citizen applying for a non-immigrant visa knows that HIV is a communicable disease of public health significance but checks "no" on the question about communicable diseases, INS may deny the visa because it thinks the applicant committed fraud. If a non-immigrant visa applicant checks "yes," or if INS suspects the person is HIV positive, it will deny the visa unless the applicant asks for a special waiver for visitors. This waiver is for people visiting the United States for a short time, to attend a conference, for instance, to visit close relatives, or to receive medical treatment. For up-to-the-minute information concerning HIV-positive travelers, contact the Center for Disease Control's **National Center for HIV** (☎ **404/332-4559;** www.hivatis.org) or the **Gay Men's Health Crisis** (☎ **212/367-1000;** www.gmhc.org). You can also contact the San Francisco Bar Association's **Immigration Project** at ☎ **415/982-1600, ext. 767.**

## CUSTOMS

Every visitor over 21 years of age may bring in, free of duty, the following: (1) 1 liter of wine or hard liquor; (2) 200 cigarettes, 100 cigars (but not from Cuba), or 3 pounds of smoking tobacco; and (3) $100 worth of gifts. These exemptions are offered to travelers who spend at least 72 hours in the United States and who have not claimed them within the preceding 6 months. It is altogether forbidden to bring into the country foodstuffs (particularly fruit, cooked meats, and canned goods) and plants (vegetables, seeds, tropical plants, and the like). Foreign tourists may bring in or take out up to $10,000 in U.S. or foreign currency with no formalities; larger sums must be declared to U.S. Customs on entering or leaving, which includes filing form CM 4790. For more specific information regarding U.S. Customs, contact your nearest U.S. embassy or consulate, or the **U.S. Customs** office (☎ **202/927-1770;** www.customs.ustreas.gov).

### WHAT YOU CAN BRING HOME

**U.K. citizens returning from a non-EC country** have a customs allowance of: 200 cigarettes; 50 cigars; 250g of smoking tobacco; 2 liters of still table wine; 1 liter of spirits or strong liqueurs (over 22% volume); 2 liters of fortified wine, sparkling wine or other liqueurs; 60cc (ml) perfume; 250cc (ml) of toilet water; and £145 worth of all other goods, including gifts and souvenirs. People under 17 cannot have the tobacco or alcohol allowance. For more information, contact HM Customs & Excise, Passenger Enquiry Point, 2nd Floor Wayfarer House, Great South West Road, Feltham, Middlesex TW14 8NP (☎ **0181/910-3744;** from outside the U.K. 44/181-910-3744), or consult their Web site at **www.open.gov.uk**.

For a clear summary of **Canadian** rules, write for the booklet *I Declare,* issued by **Revenue Canada,** 2265 St. Laurent Blvd., Ottawa K1G 4KE (☎ **613/993-0534**). Canada allows its citizens a $500 exemption, and you're allowed to bring back duty-free 200 cigarettes, 2.2 pounds of tobacco, 40 imperial ounces of liquor, and 50 cigars. In addition, you're allowed to mail gifts to Canada from abroad at the rate of Can$60 a day, provided they're unsolicited and don't contain alcohol or tobacco (write on the package "Unsolicited gift, under $60 value"). All valuables should be declared on the Y-38 form before departure from Canada, including serial numbers of valuables you already own, such as expensive foreign cameras. *Note:* The $500 exemption can only be used once a year and only after an absence of 7 days.

The duty-free allowance in **Australia** is A$400 or, for those under 18, A$200. Personal property mailed home should be marked "Australian goods returned" to avoid payment of duty. Upon returning to Australia, citizens can bring in 250 cigarettes or 250 grams of loose tobacco, and 1,125ml of alcohol. If you're returning with valuable goods you already own, such as foreign-made cameras, you should file form B263. A helpful brochure, available from Australian consulates or Customs offices, is *Know Before You Go.* For more information, contact **Australian Customs Services,** GPO Box 8, Sydney NSW 2001 (☎ **02/9213-2000**).

The duty-free allowance for **New Zealand** is NZ$700. Citizens over 17 can bring in 200 cigarettes, or 50 cigars, or 250 grams of tobacco (or a mixture of all three if their combined weight doesn't exceed 250 grams); plus 4.5 liters of wine and beer, or 1.125 liters of liquor. New Zealand currency does not carry import or export restrictions. Fill out a certificate of export, listing the valuables you are taking out of the country; that way, you can bring them back without paying duty. Most questions are answered in a free pamphlet available at New Zealand consulates and Customs offices: *New Zealand Customs Guide for Travellers, Notice no. 4.* For more information, contact New Zealand Customs, 50 Anzac Ave., P.O. Box 29, Auckland (☎ **09/359-6655**).

## INSURANCE

Although it's not required of travelers, health insurance is highly recommended. Unlike many European countries, the United States does not usually offer free or low-cost medical care to its citizens or visitors. Doctors and hospitals are expensive, and in most cases will require advance payment or proof of coverage before they render their services. Policies can cover everything from the loss or theft of your baggage and trip cancellation to the guarantee of bail in case you're arrested. Good policies will also cover the costs of an accident, repatriation, or death. Packages such as **Europ Assistance** in Europe are sold by automobile clubs and travel agencies at attractive rates. **Worldwide Assistance Services, Inc.** (☎ **800/821-2828**) is the agent for Europ Assistance in the United States.

Though lack of health insurance may prevent you from being admitted to a hospital in non-emergencies, don't worry about being left on a street corner to die: The American way is to fix you now and bill the living daylights out of you later.

**INSURANCE FOR BRITISH TRAVELERS**   Most big travel agents offer their own insurance, and will probably try to sell you their package when you book a holiday. Think before you sign. **Britain's Consumers' Association** recommends that you insist on seeing the policy and reading the fine print before buying travel insurance. **The Association of British Insurers** (☎ **0171/600-3333**) gives advice by phone and publishes the free *Holiday Insurance,* a guide to policy provisions and prices. You might also shop around for better deals: Try **Columbus Travel Insurance Ltd.** (☎ 0171/375-0011) or, for students, **Campus Travel** (☎ **0171/730-2101**).

**INSURANCE FOR CANADIAN TRAVELERS**   Canadians should check with their provincial health plan offices or call **HealthCanada** (☎ **613/957-2991**) to find out the extent of their coverage and what documentation and receipts they must take home in case they are treated in the United States.

# MONEY
## CURRENCY

The U.S. monetary system is painfully simple: The most common bills (all ugly, all green) are the $1 (colloquially, a "buck"), $5, $10, and $20 denominations. There are also $2 bills (seldom encountered), $50 bills, and $100 bills (the last two are usually not welcome as payment for small purchases). Note that a newly redesigned $100 and $50 bill were introduced in 1996, and a redesigned $20 bill in 1998. Expect to see redesigned $10 and $5 notes in the year 2000. Despite rumors to the contrary, the old-style bills are still legal tender.

There are six denominations of coins: 1¢ (1 cent, or a penny); 5¢ (5 cents, or a nickel); 10¢ (10 cents, or a dime); 25¢ (25 cents, or a quarter); 50¢ (50 cents, or a half dollar); and, prized by collectors, the rare $1 piece (the older, large silver dollar and the newer, small Susan B. Anthony coin). A new gold $1 piece will be introduced by the year 2000.

*Note:* The "foreign-exchange bureaus" so common in Europe are rare even at airports in the United States, and nonexistent outside major cities. It's best not to change foreign money (or traveler's checks denominated in a currency other than U.S. dollars) at a small-town bank, or even a branch in a big city; in fact, leave any currency other than U.S. dollars at home—it may prove a greater nuisance to you than it's worth.

## TRAVELER'S CHECKS

Though traveler's checks are widely accepted, make sure that they're denominated in U.S. dollars, as foreign-currency checks are often difficult to exchange. The three traveler's checks that are most widely recognized—and least likely to be denied—are **Visa, American Express,** and **Thomas Cook.** Be sure to record the numbers of the checks, and keep that information separately in case they get lost or stolen. Most San Francisco businesses are pretty good about taking traveler's checks, but you're better off cashing them in at a bank (in small amounts, of course) and paying in cash. *Remember:* You'll need identification, such as a driver's license or passport, to change a traveler's check.

## CREDIT CARDS & ATMS

Credit cards are the most widely used form of payment in the United States: Visa (BarclayCard in Britain), **MasterCard** (EuroCard in Europe, Access in Britain, Chargex in Canada), **American Express, Diners Club, Discover,** and **Carte Blanche.** You must have a credit or charge card to rent a car. There are, however, a handful of stores and restaurants in San Francisco that do not take credit cards, so be sure to ask in advance. Most businesses display a sticker near their entrance to let you know which cards they accept. (*Note:* Businesses often require a minimum purchase price, usually around $10, to use a credit card.)

It is strongly recommended that you bring at least one major credit card. Hotels, car-rental companies, and airlines usually require a credit card imprint as a deposit against expenses, and in an emergency a credit card can be priceless.

You'll find automated teller machines (ATMs) on just about every other block in San Francisco (particularly Wells Fargo Bank and Bank of America). Some ATMs will allow you to draw U.S. currency against your bank and credit cards. Check with your bank before leaving home, and remember that you will need your personal identification number (PIN) to do so. Most accept Visa, MasterCard, and American Express, as well as ATM cards from other U.S. banks. Expect to be charged up to $3 per transaction, however, if you're not using your own bank's ATM.

One way around these fees is to ask for cash back at grocery stores that accept ATM cards and don't charge usage fees. Of course, you'll have to purchase something first.

## SAFETY
### GENERAL SAFETY SUGGESTIONS
While most San Francisco tourist areas are generally safe, there are a few neighborhoods you should leave out of your itinerary, such as the Tenderloin and Hunter's Point areas.

Avoid deserted areas, especially at night, and don't go into any of the parks at night unless there's a concert or similar occasion that attracts crowds. Daylight assaults on tourists in San Francisco are extremely rare.

Avoid carrying valuables with you on the street, and don't display expensive cameras or electronic equipment. Hold onto your pocketbook, and place your billfold in an inside pocket. In theaters, restaurants, and other public places, keep your possessions in sight.

Remember also that hotels are open to the public, and in a large hotel, security might not be able to screen everyone entering. Always lock your room door—don't assume that once inside your hotel you are automatically safe and no longer need to be aware of your surroundings.

See "Fast Facts: San Francisco" in chapter 4, "Getting to Know San Francisco," for more city-specific safety tips.

### DRIVING SAFETY
Driving safety is important too, especially given the highly publicized carjackings of foreign tourists in Florida. Question your rental agency about personal safety and ask for a traveler's-safety-tips brochure when you pick up your car. Get written directions—or a map with the route clearly marked—from the agency showing how to get to your destination. And, if possible, arrive and depart during daylight hours.

Recently, more and more crime has involved cars and drivers. If you drive off a highway into a doubtful neighborhood, leave the area as quickly as possible. If you

---

**Travel Tip**

If the proverbial poop hits the fan, you can have someone wire money to you very quickly via Western Union. For the office nearest you, call ☎ **800/325-6000**.

have an accident, even on the highway, stay in your car with the doors locked until you assess the situation or until the police arrive. If you're bumped from behind on the street or are involved in a minor accident with no injuries and the situation appears to be suspicious, motion to the other driver to follow you. *Never* get out of your car in such situations. Go directly to the nearest police precinct, well-lit service station, or 24-hour store.

Always try to park in well-lit and well-traveled areas if possible. If you leave your rental car unlocked and empty of your valuables, you're probably safer than locking your car with valuables in plain view. Never leave any packages or valuables in sight. If someone attempts to rob you or steal your car, don't try to resist the thief/carjacker—report the incident to the police department immediately by calling ☎ **911.**

## 2 Getting to the U.S.

Traveling overseas on a budget is something of an oxymoron, but there are ways to knock down the price of a plane ticket by several hundred dollars if you take the time to shop around. For example, travelers from overseas can take advantage of the APEX (Advance Purchase Excursion) reduced fares offered by all major U.S. and European carriers. For more money-saving airline advice, see "45 Money-Saving Tips," in chapter 2, "Planning an Affordable Trip to San Francisco."

In addition to the domestic American airlines listed under "Getting There" in chapter 2, a number of international carriers also serve the Bay Area airports, including, among others: **Aer Lingus** (☎ **01/844-4747** in Dublin or 061/415-556 in Shannon; www.aerlingus.ie), **Air Canada** (☎ **800/776-3000;** www.aircanada. ca); **British Airways** (☎ **0345/222-111** in the U.K.; www.british-airways.com; with direct flights to San Francisco from London), **Canadian Airlines** (☎ **800/ 426-7000;** www.cdair.ca), **Japan Airlines** (☎ **0354/89-1111** in Tokyo; www.jal. co.jp), **Qantas** (☎ **13-12-11** in Australia; www.qantas.com.au), and **Virgin Atlantic Airways** (☎ **01293/747-747** in the U.K.; www.fly.virgin.com; direct flights to San Francisco from London). **Air New Zealand** (☎ **13-2476** in New Zealand; www.airnewzealand.co.nz) flies to Los Angeles and will book you straight through to San Francisco on a partner airline.

Major U.S. carriers, such as **Continental** (☎ **01293/776-464** in the U.K.; www.flycontinental.com), **TWA** (☎ **800/892-4141** in the U.K.; www.twa.com), **United** (☎ **020/8990-9900** in the U.K.; www.ual.com), **American** (☎ **020/ 8572-5555** in the U.K.; www.aa.com, and **Delta** (☎ **0800/414-764** in the U.K.; www.delta-air.com), also have service from Europe to the United States. **United** (☎ **02/237-8888** in Sydney, 008/230-322 in the rest of Australia) also offers flights from Sydney to San Francisco.

Visitors arriving by air, no matter what the port of entry, should cultivate patience and resignation before setting foot on U.S. soil. Getting through immigration control can take as long as 2 hours on some days, especially on summer weekends, so be sure to have this guidebook or something else to read. Add the time it takes to clear Customs, and you'll see that you should make a very generous allowance for delay in planning connections between international and domestic flights—figure on 2 to 3 hours at least.

In contrast, for the traveler arriving by car or rail from Canada, the border-crossing formalities have been streamlined to the vanishing point. And for the traveler by air from Canada, Bermuda, and some places in the Caribbean, you can sometimes go through Customs and Immigration at the point of departure, which is much quicker.

# 3  Getting Around the U.S.

**BY PLANE**   Some large airlines (for example, Northwest and Delta) offer travelers on their transatlantic or transpacific flights special discount tickets under the name **Visit USA,** allowing mostly one-way travel from one U.S. destination to another at very low prices. *These discount tickets are not on sale in the United States and must be purchased abroad in conjunction with your international ticket.* This system is the best, easiest, and fastest way to see the United States at low cost. You should obtain information well in advance from your travel agent or the office of the airline concerned, since the conditions attached to these discount tickets can be changed without advance notice.

**BY TRAIN**   International visitors can also buy a **USA Railpass,** good for 15 or 30 days of unlimited travel on Amtrak (☎ **800/USA-RAIL**). The pass is available through many foreign travel agents. Prices in 1999 for a 15-day pass are $285 off-peak, $425 peak; a 30-day pass costs $375 off-peak, $535 peak. (With a foreign passport, you can also buy passes at some Amtrak offices in the United States, including locations in San Francisco, Los Angeles, Chicago, New York, Miami, Boston, and Washington, D.C.) Reservations are generally required and should be made for each part of your trip as early as possible.

**BY BUS**   Although bus travel is often the most economical form of public transit for short hops between U.S. cities, it can also be slow and uncomfortable—certainly not an option for everyone (particularly when Amtrak, which is far more luxurious, offers similar rates). **Greyhound/Trailways** (☎ **800/231-2222**), the sole nationwide bus line, offers an **International Ameripass** that must be purchased before coming to the United States, or at the Greyhound International Office at the Port Authority Bus Terminal in New York City. The pass can be obtained from foreign travel agents and costs less than the domestic version. 1999 passes cost as follows: 7 days ($179), 15 days ($269), 30 days ($369), or 60 days ($539). Foreigners can get more info on the pass at **www.greyhound.com**, or by calling ☎ **212/971-0492** (14:00-21:00 GMT) and ☎ **402/330-8552** (all other times). In addition, special rates are available for senior citizens and students.

   Be aware that San Francisco's bus terminal is not located in the best of neighborhoods, but unless you're wandering around at 3am, it's not really dangerous.

**BY CAR**   The most cost-effective, convenient, and comfortable way to travel around the United States—especially California—is by car (although you may find a car more of a hassle than a help in the city of San Francisco itself). The Interstate highway system connects cities and towns all over the country; in addition to these high-speed, limited-access roadways, there's an extensive network of federal, state, and local highways and roads. California has no toll roads, but it does charge a toll fee at many major bridges. Some of the national car-rental companies that have offices in San Francisco include **Alamo** (☎ 800/327-9633), **Avis** (☎ 800/331-1212), **Budget** (☎ 800/527-0700), **Dollar** (☎ 800/800-4000), **Hertz** (☎ 800/654-3131), **National** (☎ 800/227-7368), and **Thrifty** (☎ 800/367-2277).

   If you plan on renting a car in the United States, you probably won't need the services of an additional automobile organization. If you're planning to buy or borrow a car, automobile-association membership is recommended. **AAA,** the **American Automobile Association** (☎ 800/222-4357) is the country's largest auto club and supplies its members with maps, insurance, and, most important, emergency road service. The cost of joining runs from $63 for singles to $87 for two members, but if you're a member of a foreign auto club with reciprocal arrangements, you can enjoy free AAA service in America. See "Getting There" in Chapter 2 for more information.

## Fast Facts: For the Foreign Traveler

**Business Hours**   See "Fast Facts: San Francisco," in chapter 4.

**Climate**   See "When to Go," in chapter 2.

**Currency & Exchange**   Foreign-exchange bureaus are rare in the United States, and most banks are not equipped to handle currency exchange. San Francisco's money-changing offices include the following: **Bank of America,** 345 Montgomery St. (☎ **415/622-2451**), open Monday to Friday from 9am to 6pm; and **Thomas Cook,** 75 Geary St. (☎ **415/362-3452**), open Monday to Friday from 9am to 5pm and on Saturday from 10am to 4pm.

**Drinking Laws**   The legal age for purchase and consumption of alcoholic beverages is 21; proof of age is required and often requested at bars, nightclubs, and restaurants, so it's always a good idea to bring ID when you go out. In San Francisco, liquor is sold in supermarkets, and grocery and liquor stores, daily from 6am to 2am. Licensed restaurants are permitted to sell alcohol during the same hours. Note that many eateries are licensed only for beer and wine.

A big no-no is having an open container of alcohol in your car or in any public area that isn't zoned for alcohol consumption. The police can, and probably will, fine you on the spot. And nothing will ruin your trip faster than getting a citation for DWI ("driving while intoxicated"); so don't even think about driving while under the influence.

**Electricity**   U.S. wall outlets give power at 110 to 115 volts, 60 cycles, compared with 220 volts, 50 cycles in most of Europe. In addition to a 100-volt transformer, small foreign appliances, such as hair dryers and shavers, will require a plug adapter (available at most hardware stores) with two flat, parallel pins.

**Embassies & Consulates**   All embassies are located in the nation's capital, Washington, D.C. In addition, several of the major English-speaking countries also have consulates in San Francisco or in Los Angeles.

The embassy of **Australia** is at 1601 Massachusetts Ave. NW, Washington, DC 20036 (☎ **202/797-3000**); a consulate-general is at 1 Bush St., Suite 700, San Francisco, CA 94104 (☎ **415/362-6160**). The embassy of **Canada** is at 501 Pennsylvania Ave. NW, Washington, DC 20001 (☎ **202/682-1740**); the nearest consulate is at 300 S. Grand Ave., 10th Floor, California Plaza, Los Angeles, CA 90071 (☎ **213/346-2700**). The embassy of the **Republic of Ireland** is at 2234 Massachusetts Ave. NW, Washington, DC 20008 (☎ **202/462-3939**); a consulate is at 44 Montgomery St., Suite 3830, San Francisco, CA 94104 (☎ **415/392-4214**). The embassy of **New Zealand** is at 37 Observatory Circle NW, Washington, DC 20008 (☎ **202/328-4800**); the nearest consulate is at 12400 Wilshire Blvd., Suite 1150, Los Angeles, CA 90025 (☎ **310/207-1605**). The embassy of the **United Kingdom** is at 3100 Massachusetts Ave. NW, Washington, DC 20008 (☎ **202/462-1340**); the nearest consulate is at 1 Sansome St., Suite 850, San Francisco, CA 94104 (☎ **415/981-3030**). The embassy of **Japan** is at 2520 Massachusetts Ave. NW, Washington, DC 20008 (☎ **202/238-6700**); the consulate-general of Japan is located at 50 Fremont St., 23rd Floor, San Francisco, CA 94105 (☎ **415/777-3533**).

If you are from another country, you can get the telephone number of your embassy by calling "Information" (directory assistance) in Washington, D.C. (☎ **202/555-1212**).

**Emergencies**    You can call the police, an ambulance, or the fire department through the single emergency telephone number ☎ **911** from any phone or pay phone (no coins needed). If that doesn't work, another useful way of reporting an emergency is to call the telephone company operator by dialing 0 (zero, not the letter O).

**Gasoline (Petrol)**    Prices vary, but expect to pay anywhere between $1.35 and $1.65 for 1 U.S. gallon (about 3.8 liters) of "regular" unleaded gasoline (petrol). Higher-octane fuels are also available at most gas stations for slightly higher prices. Taxes are already included in the printed price.

**Holidays**    On the following legal national holidays, banks, government offices, post offices, and many stores, restaurants, and museums are closed: New Year's Day (Jan 1), Martin Luther King Jr. Day (third Mon in Jan), Presidents' Day (third Mon in Feb), Memorial Day (last Mon in May), Independence Day (July 4), Labor Day (first Mon in Sept), Columbus Day (second Mon in Oct), Veterans Day (Nov 11), Thanksgiving Day (last Thurs in Nov), and Christmas Day (Dec 25). Election Day, for national elections, falls on the Tuesday following the first Monday in November. It's a legal national holiday during a presidential election, which occurs every fourth year (next in 2000).

**Mail**    If you want to receive mail, but aren't exactly sure where you'll be, have it sent to you, in your name, **℅ General Delivery (Poste Restante)** at the main post office of the city or region you're visiting (call ☎ **800/275-8777** for information on the nearest post office). In San Francisco letters can be picked up at the **Civic Center Post Office Box Unit,** P.O. Box 429991, San Francisco, CA 94142-9991 (☎ **800/275-8777**). The addressee must pick it up in person and produce proof of identity (driver's license, credit card, passport). Most post offices will hold your mail up to 1 month, and are open Monday to Saturday from 8am to 6pm.

Generally found at street intersections, mailboxes are blue and carry the inscription U.S. MAIL. If your mail is addressed to a U.S. destination, don't forget to add the five-digit zip code after the two-letter abbreviation of the state to which the mail is addressed (CA for California).

For overseas mail, **postal rates** are as follows: A first-class letter of up to one-half ounce costs 60¢ (46¢ to Canada and 40¢ to Mexico); a first-class postcard costs 50¢ (40¢ to Canada and 35¢ Mexico); and a preprinted postal aerogramme costs 50¢.

**Medical Emergencies**    To call an ambulance, dial ☎ **911** from any phone—no coins are needed. For hospitals and other emergency information, see "Fast Facts: San Francisco" in chapter 4.

**Newspapers & Magazines**    Many of San Francisco's newsstands offer a selection of foreign periodicals and newspapers, such as *The Economist, Le Monde,* and *Der Spiegel.* For information on local literature and specific newsstand locations, see "Fast Facts: San Francisco," in chapter 4.

**Post Office**    See "Mail," above.

**Radio & Television**    There are five national television networks that are broadcast over the air: ABC (Channel 7), CBS (Channel 5), NBC (Channel 4), PBS

(Channel 9), and Fox (Channel 2). Cable television includes the national networks as well as 50 or so other cable stations, including the Cable News Network (CNN), ESPN (sports channel), and MTV. Most hotels offer a dozen cable stations to choose from, as well as pay-per-view movies. You'll also find a wide choice of local radio stations, each broadcasting particular kinds of talk shows and/or music—classical, country, jazz, rock, pop, gospel—punctuated by news broadcasts and frequent commercials.

**Smoking**   Heavy smokers are in for a tough time in San Francisco. There is no smoking allowed in public buildings, sports arenas, elevators, theaters, banks, lobbies, restaurants, offices, stores, bed-and-breakfasts, most small hotels, and bars. Yes, that's right, as of January 1, 1998, you can't even smoke in a bar in California, the only exception being a bar where drinks are served solely by the owner. You will find, however, that many neighborhood bars turn the other cheek while they pass you an ashtray.

**Taxes**   In the United States, there is no value-added tax (VAT) or other direct tax at a national level. Every state, as well as every city, is allowed to levy its own local sales tax on all purchases, including hotel and restaurant checks and airline tickets. Taxes are already included in the price of certain services, such as public transportation, cab fares, phone calls, and gasoline. The amount of sales tax varies from 4% to 10%, depending on the state and city, so when you are making major purchases, such as photographic equipment, clothing, or high-fidelity components, it can be a significant part of the cost.

In addition, many cities charge a separate "bed" or room tax on accommodations, above and beyond any sales tax. None of these taxes, by the way, will be refunded to foreign tourists.

For information on sales and room taxes in San Francisco, see "Fast Facts: San Francisco" in chapter 4.

**Telephone & Fax**   Pay phones can be found almost everywhere—at street corners, in bars and restaurants, and in hotels. Outside the metropolitan area, however, public telephones are more difficult to find; stores and gas stations are your best bet.

Phones do not accept pennies and few will take anything larger than a quarter. Some public phones, especially those in airports and large hotels, accept credit cards, such as MasterCard, Visa, and American Express. Credit cards are especially handy for international calls; instructions are printed on the phone.

In San Francisco, **local calls** cost 35¢. To make local calls, dial the seven-digit local number. For domestic long-distance calls or international calls, stock up with a supply of quarters; first dial the number, then a recorded voice will instruct you when and in what quantity you should put the coins into the slot. For **domestic long-distance calls,** first dial 1 (the long-distance access code), the area code, and the seven-digit local number. For **direct overseas calls,** dial 011 first (the international access code), then the country code (Australia, 61; Republic of Ireland, 353; New Zealand, 64; United Kingdom, 44), followed by the city code, and then the local number you wish to call. To place a call to Canada or the Caribbean, just dial 1, the area code, and the local number.

Before calling from a hotel room, always ask the hotel phone operator if there are any telephone surcharges. These can sometimes be reduced by calling collect or by using a telephone charge card. Hotel charges, which can be exorbitant, may be avoided altogether by using a pay phone in the lobby.

Note that almost all calls to phone numbers in area codes 800 and 888 are toll-free, but your hotel may still charge a small fee for making the call.

For **local directory assistance** ("Information"), dial ☎ **411;** for **long-distance information** in the United States and Canada, dial 1, then the appropriate area code and **555-1212.**

For "collect" (reversed-charge) calls and for "person-to-person" calls, dial 0 (zero, not the letter O) followed by the area code and the number you want; an operator or recording will then come on the line, and you should specify that you are calling collect or person-to-person, or both. If your operator-assisted call is international, just dial 0 and wait for the operator.

Like the telephone system, **telegraph and telex** services are provided by private corporations, such as ITT, MCI, and above all, **Western Union.** You can bring your telegram to a Western Union office or dictate it over the phone (☎ **800/325-6000**). You can also telegraph money, or have it telegraphed to you, very quickly. In San Francisco, a Western Union office, located near the Civic Center, is at 61 Gough St., at Market Street (☎ **415/621-2031**). There are several other locations around town, too; call ☎ **800/325-6000** for the one nearest you.

You'll find **fax facilities** widely available. They can be found in most hotels and many other establishments. Try Mailboxes Etc. or any photocopying shop.

**Telephone Directory**   There are two kinds of telephone directories in the United States. The general directory is the so-called White Pages, in which private and business subscribers are listed in alphabetical order. The inside front cover lists the emergency number for police, fire, and ambulance, and other vital numbers (like the Coast Guard, poison-control center, crime-victims hot line, and so on). The first few pages are devoted to community-service numbers, including a guide to long-distance and international calling, complete with country codes and area codes.

The second directory, printed on yellow paper (hence its name, **Yellow Pages**), lists all local services, businesses, and industries by type of activity, with an index at the back. The listings cover not only such obvious items as automobile repairs by make of car, or drugstores (pharmacies), often by geographical location, but also restaurants by type of cuisine and geographical location, bookstores by special subject and/or language, places of worship by religious denomination, and other information that a tourist might otherwise not readily find. The Yellow Pages also include city plans or detailed maps, often showing postal zip codes and public-transportation routes.

**Time**   The United States is divided into four time zones (six, if Alaska and Hawaii are included). From east to west, these are eastern standard time (EST), central standard time (CST), mountain standard time (MST), and Pacific standard time (PST). There are also Alaska standard time (AST) and Hawaii standard time (HST). San Francisco is on Pacific standard time, which is 8 hours behind Greenwich mean time. Noon in New York City (EST) is 11am in Chicago (CST), 10am in Denver (MST), 9am in San Francisco (PST), 8am in Anchorage (AST), and 7am in Honolulu (HST).

Daylight-saving time is in effect from the first Sunday in April until 2am on the last Sunday in October, except in Arizona, Hawaii, part of Indiana, and Puerto Rico. Daylight saving time moves the clock 1 hour ahead of standard time.

**Tipping**    Service in America is some of the best in the world, and is rarely included in the price of anything. In fact, it's part of the American way of life to tip, on the principle that you must expect to pay for any service you get. Many personnel receive little direct salary and must depend on tips for their income. In fact, the U.S. federal government imposes income taxes on service personnel based on an estimate of how much they should have earned in tips relative to their employer's total receipts. In other words, they may have to pay taxes on a tip you didn't give them!

Here are some rules of thumb:

In **hotels,** tip bellhops at least $1 per piece of luggage ($2 to $3 if you have a lot of luggage) and tip the chamber staff $1 per day. Tip the doorman or concierge only if he or she has provided you with some specific service (for example, calling a cab for you or obtaining difficult-to-get theater tickets). Tip the valet parking attendant $1 every time you get your car.

In **restaurants, bars, and nightclubs,** tip service staff 15% to 20% of the check, tip bartenders 10% to 15%, tip checkroom attendants $1 per garment, and tip valet-parking attendants $1 per vehicle. Tip the doorman only if he has provided you with some specific service (such as calling a cab for you). Tipping is not expected in cafeterias and fast-food restaurants.

Tip **cab drivers** 15% of the fare.

As for **other service personnel,** tip skycaps at airports at least $1 per piece ($2 to $3 if you have a lot of luggage) and tip hairdressers and barbers 15% to 20%.

Tipping ushers at movies and theaters, and gas-station attendants, is not expected.

**Toilets**    Public toilets can be hard to find in San Francisco. There are only a handful of fancy new French stalls strategically placed on high-volume streets, and few small stores will allow you access to their facilities. You can almost always find a toilet in restaurants and bars; note, however, a growing practice in some restaurants and bars of displaying a notice that toilets are for the use of patrons only. You can ignore this sign, or better yet, avoid arguments by paying for a cup of coffee or soft drink, which will qualify you as a patron. Large hotels and fast-food restaurants are probably the best bet for good, clean facilities. Museums, department stores, shopping malls, and, in a pinch, gas stations, all have public toilets. If possible, avoid the toilets at parks and beaches, which are a real crap shoot (pun intended) when it comes to cleanliness.

# Getting to Know San Francisco

**4**

**H**alf the fun in becoming familiar with San Francisco is wandering around and haphazardly stumbling upon great shops, restaurants, and viewpoints that even locals may not know exist. But you'll find that although metropolitan, San Francisco is a small town, and you won't feel like a stranger for long. If you get disoriented, just remember that downtown is east, Golden Gate Bridge is north, and even if you do get lost, you probably won't go too far since three sides of the city are surrounded by water. The most difficult challenge you'll have, if traveling by car, is mastering the maze of one-way streets. This chapter offers useful information on how to become better acquainted with the city.

## 1 Orientation

### VISITOR INFORMATION

Once in the city, visit the **San Francisco Visitor Information Center,** on the lower level of Hallidie Plaza, 900 Market St., at Powell Street (☎ **415/391-2000;** fax 415/362-7323), for information, brochures, discount coupons, and advice on restaurants, sights, and events in the city. They can provide answers in German, Japanese, French, Italian, and Spanish, as well as English, of course. To find the office, descend the escalator at the cable-car turnaround.

Dial ☎ **415/391-2001** anytime, day or night, for a recorded message about current cultural, theater, music, sports, and other special events. This information is also available in German, French, Japanese, and Spanish.

Keep in mind that the service offers information that relates only to its member organizations, and it emphasizes tourist spots over areas with more local flavor. While there's tons of information here, it's not representative of all the city has to offer. The office is open Monday to Friday from 9am to 5:30pm, on Saturday from 9am to 3pm, and on Sunday from 10am to 2pm. It's closed on Thanksgiving Day, Christmas Day, and New Year's Day. You can get information anytime from the automated service offers information via fax if you call ☎ **800/220-5747** and follow the prompts.

Pick up a copy of the *Bay Guardian.* The city's free alternative paper lists all city happenings—their kiosks are located throughout the city and in most coffee shops.

For specialized information on Chinatown's shops and services, and on the city's Chinese community in general, contact the **Chinese Chamber of Commerce,** 730 Sacramento St., San Francisco, CA 94108 (☎ **415/982-3000**), open daily from 9am to 5pm.

The **Visitors Information Center of the Redwood Empire Association,** in The Cannery, 2801 Leavenworth, 2nd Floor, San Francisco, CA 94133 (☎ **800/ 200-8334** or 415/543-8334; www.redwoodempire.com), offers informative brochures and a very knowledgeable desk staff who are able to plan tours both in San Francisco and north of the city. Their annual 48-page *Redwood Empire Visitors' Guide* (free by mail with up to 6-week delivery, $5 if delivered by priority mail—check, cash, or money order—in the U.S.; $5.50 by mail internationally; free in person) offers information on everything from San Francisco hotels, walking tours, and museums to visit in Northern California. The office is open daily 10am to 5pm.

## CITY LAYOUT

San Francisco occupies the tip of a 32-mile-long peninsula between San Francisco Bay and the Pacific Ocean. Its land area measures about 46 square miles. Twin Peaks, in the geographic center of the city, is more than 900 feet high.

San Francisco may seem confusing at first, but it quickly becomes easy to negotiate. The city's downtown streets are arranged in a simple grid pattern, with the exception of Market Street and Columbus Avenue, which cut across the grid at right angles to each other. Hills appear to distort this pattern, however, and can be disorienting. But as you learn your way around, these same hills will become your landmarks and reference points.

**MAIN ARTERIES & STREETS**   **Market Street** is San Francisco's main thoroughfare. Most of the city's buses travel this route on their way to the Financial District from the outer neighborhoods to the west and south. The tall office buildings clustered downtown are at the northeast end of Market; 1 block beyond that lies the Embarcadero and the bay.

**The Embarcadero** curves along San Francisco Bay from south of the Bay Bridge to the northeast perimeter of the city and terminates at Fisherman's Wharf, the famous tourist-oriented pier. Aquatic Park, Fort Mason, and the Golden Gate National Recreation area are located farther on around the bay, occupying the northernmost point of the peninsula.

From the eastern perimeter of Fort Mason, **Van Ness Avenue** runs due south, back to Market Street. The area we have just described forms a rough triangle, with Market Street as its southeastern boundary, the waterfront as its northern boundary, and Van Ness Avenue as its western boundary. Within this triangle lie most of the city's main tourist sights.

**FINDING AN ADDRESS**   Since most of the city's streets are laid out in a grid pattern, finding an address is easy when you know the nearest cross street. When asking for directions, find out the nearest cross street and the neighborhood in which your destination is located, but be careful not to confuse numeric avenues with numeric streets. Numeric avenues (Third Avenue, and so on) are found in the Richmond and Sunset districts in the western part of the city. Numeric streets (Third Street, and so on) are south of Market in the east and south parts of town.

# The Neighborhoods in Brief

**Union Square**    Union Square is the commercial hub of the city. Most major hotels and department stores are crammed into the area surrounding the actual square (named for a series of violent pro-Union mass demonstrations staged here on the eve of the Civil War), and there is a plethora of upscale boutiques, restaurants, and galleries tucked between the larger buildings. A few blocks west is the **Tenderloin,** a patch of poverty and blight where you should keep your wits about you.

**Nob Hill/Russian Hill**    Bounded by Bush, Larkin, Pacific, and Stockton streets, Nob Hill is the genteel, well-heeled district of the city, still occupied by the major power brokers and the neighborhood businesses they frequent. Russian Hill extends from Pacific to Bay and from Polk to Mason. It is marked by steep streets, lush gardens, and high-rises occupied by both the moneyed and the more bohemian.

**SoMa**    In recent years, high rents have forced residents and businesses into once desolate south of Market (dubbed "SoMa"). The area is still predominantly warehouses and industrial spaces, but now many of them are brimming with life. The area is officially demarcated by the Embarcadero, Highway 101, and Market Street, with the greatest concentrations of interest around Yerba Buena Center, along Folsom and Harrison streets between Steuart and Sixth, and Brannan and Market. Along the waterfront is an array of restaurants. Farther west, around Folsom between 7th and 11th streets, is where much of the city's nightclubbing occurs.

**Financial District**    East of Union Square, this area bordered by the Embarcadero, Market, Third, Kearny, and Washington streets is the city's business district, and the stomping grounds for many major corporations. The pointy TransAmerica Pyramid, at Montgomery and Clay streets, is one of the district's most conspicuous architectural features. To its east stands the sprawling Embarcadero Center, an 8½-acre complex housing offices, shops, and restaurants. Farther east still is the World Trade Center, standing adjacent to the old Ferry Building, the city's pre-bridge transportation hub. Ferries to Sausalito and Larkspur still leave from this point.

**Chinatown**    The official entrance to Chinatown is marked by a large red-and-green gate on Grant Avenue at Bush Street. Beyond lies a 24-block labyrinth, bordered by Broadway, Bush, Kearny, and Stockton streets, filled with restaurants, markets, temples, and shops—and, of course, a substantial percentage of San Francisco's Chinese residents. Chinatown is a great place for urban exploration all along Stockton, Grant, and Portsmouth Square, and the alleys that lead off them like Ross and Waverly. This area is jam-packed, so don't even think about driving here.

**North Beach**    The Italian quarter, which stretches from Montgomery and Jackson to Bay Street, is one of the best places in the city to grab a coffee, pull up a cafe chair, and do some serious people-watching. Nightlife is equally happening; restaurants, bars, and clubs along Columbus and Grant avenues bring folks from all over the Bay Area here to fight for a parking place and romp through the festive neighborhood. Down Columbus toward the Financial District are the remains of the city's Beat-Generation landmarks, including Ferlinghetti's City Lights Bookstore

## Map Tip

For a complete map of San Francisco's neighborhoods, see "San Francisco at a Glance" on page 2.

and Vesuvio's Bar. Broadway—a short strip of sex joints—cuts through the heart of the district. **Telegraph Hill** looms over the east side of North Beach, topped by Coit Tower, one of San Francisco's best vantage points.

**Fisherman's Wharf**    North Beach runs into Fisherman's Wharf, which was once the busy heart of the city's great harbor and waterfront industries. Today, it is a tacky-but-interesting tourist area with little if any authentic waterfront life, except for recreational boating and some friendly sea lions.

**Marina District**    Created on landfill for the Pan-Pacific Exposition of 1915, the Marina boasts some of the best views of the Golden Gate, as well as plenty of grassy fields alongside the San Francisco Bay. Streets are lined with elegant Mediterranean-style homes and apartments, which are inhabited by the city's well-to-do singles and wealthy families. Here, too, are the Palace of Fine Arts, the Exploratorium, and Fort Mason Center. The main street is Chestnut between Franklin and Lyon, which is lined with shops, cafes, and boutiques. Because of its landfill foundation, the Marina was one of the city's hardest-hit districts in the 1989 quake.

**Cow Hollow**    Located west of Van Ness Avenue, between Russian Hill and the Presidio, this flat, grazable area supported 30 dairy farms in 1861. Today, Cow Hollow is largely residential and occupied by the city's Young and Yuppie. Its two primary commercial thoroughfares are Lombard Street, known for its many relatively inexpensive motels, and Union Street, a flourishing shopping sector filled with restaurants, pubs, cafes, and shops.

**Pacific Heights**    The ultra-elite, such as the Gettys and Danielle Steele—and those lucky enough to buy before the real-estate boom—reside in the mansions and homes that make up Pacific Heights. When the rich meander out of their fortresses, they wander down to Union Street, a long stretch of boutiques, restaurants, cafes, and bars.

**Japantown**    Bounded by Octavia, Fillmore, California, and Geary, Japantown shelters only about 4% of the city's Japanese population, but it's still a cultural experience to explore these few square blocks and the shops and restaurants within them.

**Civic Center**    Although millions of dollars have been expended on brick sidewalks, ornate lampposts, and elaborate street plantings, the southwestern section of Market Street remains downright dilapidated. The Civic Center, at the "bottom" of Market Street, is an exception. This large complex of buildings includes the domed and newly dapper City Hall, the Opera House, Davies Symphony Hall, and the city's main library. The landscaped plaza connecting the buildings is the staging area for San Francisco's frequent demonstrations for or against just about everything.

**Haight-Ashbury**    Part trendy, part nostalgic, part funky, the Haight, as it's most commonly known, was the soul of the psychedelic and free-loving 1960s and the center of the counterculture movement. Today, the neighborhood straddling upper Haight Street on the eastern border of Golden Gate Park is more gentrified, but the commercial area still harbors all walks of life. Leftover, aged hippies mingle with grungy, begging street kids outside Ben & Jerry's ice-cream shop (where they may still be talking about Jerry Garcia), nondescript marijuana dealers whisper "Buds" as shoppers pass, and many people walking down the street have Day-Glo hair. But you don't need to be a freak or wear tie-dye to enjoy the Haight—the food, shops, and bars cover all tastes. From Haight, walk south on Cole Street, for a more peaceful and quaint neighborhood experience.

**The Castro**   One of the liveliest streets in town, Castro is practically synonymous with San Francisco's gay community, even though technically it is only a street in the Noe Valley District. Located at the very end of Market Street, between 17th and 18th streets, Castro supports dozens of shops, restaurants, and bars catering to the gay community. Open-minded straight people are welcome, too.

**Mission District**   The Mexican and Latin American populations, along with their cuisine, traditions, and art, make the Mission District a vibrant area to visit. Because some parts of the neighborhood are poor and sprinkled with the homeless, gangs, and drug addicts, many tourists duck into Mission Dolores, cruise by a few of the 200-plus amazing murals, and head back downtown. But there's plenty more to see in the Mission District. There's a substantial community of lesbians around Valencia Street, several alternative arts organizations, and most recently the ultimate in young hipster nightlife and a full strip of fabulous affordable restaurants around 16th and Valencia. New bars, clubs, and restaurants are popping up on Mission between 18th and 24th streets and Valencia at 16th Street. Don't be afraid to visit this area, but do use caution at night.

## 2  Getting Around

### BY PUBLIC TRANSPORTATION

**The San Francisco Municipal Railway,** 949 Presidio Ave., better known as Muni (☎ 415/673-6864), operates the city's cable cars, buses, and Metro streetcars. Together, these three public transportation services crisscross the entire city, making San Francisco fully accessible to everyone. Buses and Metro streetcars cost $1 for adults, 35¢ for ages 5 to 17, and 35¢ for seniors over 65. Cable cars cost a whopping $2 for all people over 5 ($1 for seniors from 9pm to midnight and from 6 to 7am). Needless to say, they're packed primarily with tourists. Exact change is required on all vehicles except cable cars. Fares quoted here are subject to change.

For detailed route information, phone Muni or consult the bus map at the front of the Yellow Pages. If you plan on making extensive use of public transportation, you may want to invest in a comprehensive route map ($2), sold at the San Francisco Visitor Information Center (see "Visitor Information" in "Orientation," above) and in many downtown retail outlets.

Muni discount passes, called **"Passports,"** entitle holders to unlimited rides on buses, Metro streetcars, and cable cars. A Passport costs $6 for 1 day, and $10 or $15 for 3 or 7 consecutive days. As a bonus, your Passport also entitles you to admission discounts at 24 of the city's major attractions, including the M. H. De Young Memorial Museum, the Asian Art Museum, the California Academy of Sciences, and the Japanese Tea Garden (all in Golden Gate Park); the Museum of Modern Art; Coit Tower; the Exploratorium; the zoo; and the National Maritime Museum and Historic Ships (where you may visit the USS *Pampanito* and the SS *Jeremiah O'Brien*). Among the places where you can purchase a Passport are the San Francisco Visitor Information Center, the Holiday Inn Civic Center, and the TIX Bay Area booth at Union Square.

**BY CABLE CAR**   San Francisco's cable cars may not be the most practical means of transport, but these rolling historic landmarks sure are a fun ride. There are only three lines in the city, and they're all condensed in the downtown area. The most scenic, and exciting, is the **Powell-Hyde line,** which follows a zigzag route from the corner of Powell and Market streets, over both Nob Hill and Russian Hill, to a turntable at gas-lit Victorian Square in front of Aquatic Park. The **Powell-Mason**

# San Francisco Mass Transit

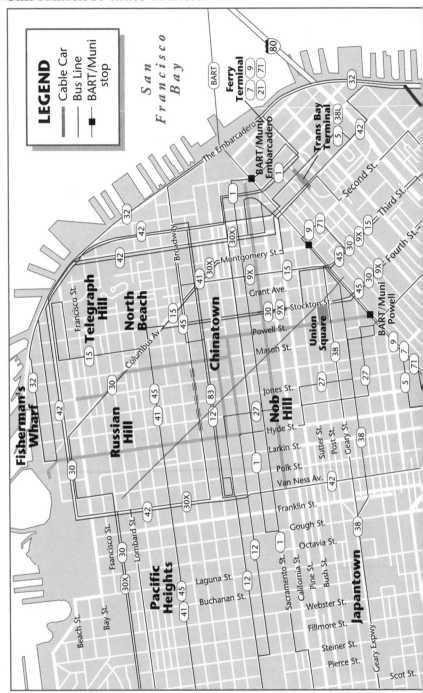

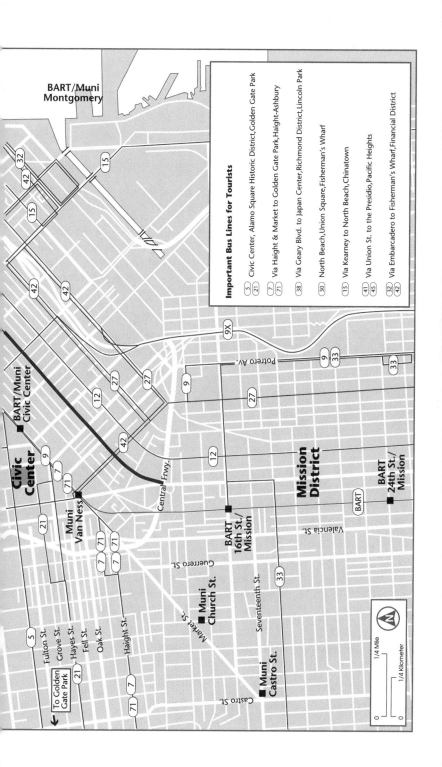

**Important Bus Lines for Tourists**

- (5) (21) Civic Center, Alamo Square Historic District, Golden Gate Park
- (7) (71) Via Haight & Market to Golden Gate Park, Haight-Ashbury
- (38) Via Geary Blvd. to Japan Center, Richmond District, Lincoln Park
- (30) North Beach, Union Square, Fisherman's Wharf
- (15) Via Kearney to North Beach, Chinatown
- (41) (45) Via Union St. to the Presidio, Pacific Heights
- (32) (42) Via Embarcadero to Fisherman's Wharf, Financial District

BART/Muni
Montgomery

Civic
Center

BART/Muni
Civic Center

Muni
Van Ness

Muni
Church St.

Muni
Castro St.

BART
16th St./
Mission

BART
24th St./
Mission

Mission
District

Central Frwy.

Potrero Av.

Valencia St.

Guerrero St.

Market St.

Castro St.

Seventeenth St.

Haight St.

Fulton St.
Grove St.
Hayes St.
Fell St.
Oak St.

To Golden
Gate Park

1/4 Mile

1/4 Kilometer

0

0

51

**line** starts at the same intersection and climbs over Nob Hill before descending to Bay Street, just 3 blocks from Fisherman's Wharf. The least scenic is the **California Street line,** which begins at the foot of Market Street and runs a straight course through Chinatown and over Nob Hill to Van Ness Avenue. All riders must exit at the last stop and wait in line for the return trip. The cable-car system operates from approximately 6:30am to 12:30am.

**BY BUS**    Buses reach almost every corner of San Francisco, and beyond—they travel over the bridges to Marin County and Oakland. Some buses are powered by overhead electric cables; others use conventional gas engines; and all are numbered and display their destinations on the front. Stops are designated by signs, curb markings, and yellow bands on adjacent utility poles, and most bus shelters exhibit Muni's transportation map and schedule. Many buses travel along Market Street or pass near Union Square and run from about 6am to midnight, after which there is infrequent all-night "Owl" service. If you can help it, for safety purposes, avoid taking buses late at night.

Popular tourist routes are traveled by bus nos. 5, 7, and 71, all of which run to Golden Gate Park; 41 and 45, which travel along Union Street; and 30, which runs between Union Square and Ghirardelli Square.

**BY METRO STREETCAR**    Five of Muni's six Metro streetcar lines, designated J, K, L, M, and N, run underground downtown and on the street in the outer neighborhoods. The sleek railcars make the same stops as BART (see below) along Market Street, including Embarcadero Station (in the Financial District), Montgomery and Powell streets (both near Union Square), and the Civic Center (near City Hall). Past the Civic Center, the routes branch off in different directions: The J line will take you to Mission Dolores; the K, L, and M lines to Castro Street; and the N line parallels Golden Gate Park. Metros run about every 15 minutes—more frequently during rush hours. Service is offered Monday to Friday from 5am to 12:30am, on Saturday from 6am to 12:20am, and on Sunday from 8am to 12:20am.

The most recent streetcar addition is not a newcomer at all, but is, in fact, San Francisco's beloved rejuvenated 1930s streetcars. The beautiful green-and-cream–colored F-Market line runs from downtown Market Street to the Castro and back. It's a quick and charming way to get uptown and downtown without any hassle.

**BY BART**    BART, an acronym for **Bay Area Rapid Transit (☎ 650/992-2278),** is a futuristic-looking, high-speed rail network that connects San Francisco with the East Bay—Oakland, Richmond, Concord, and Fremont. Four stations are located along Market Street (see "By Metro Streetcar," above). Fares range from $1 to $3.55, depending on how far you go. Tickets are dispensed from machines in the stations and are magnetically encoded with a dollar amount. Computerized exits automatically deduct the correct fare. Children 4 and under ride free. Trains run every 15 to 20 minutes, Monday to Friday from 4am to midnight, on Saturday from 6am to midnight, and on Sunday from 8am to midnight.

A $2.5-billion, 33-mile BART extension, currently under construction, includes a southern line that is planned to extend all the way to San Francisco International Airport. It will open, presumably, around the year 2000.

## BY TAXI

This isn't New York, so don't expect a taxi to appear whenever you need one. If you're downtown during rush hour, or leaving a major hotel, it won't be hard to hail

**Handy Driving Tips**

California law requires that both drivers and passengers wear seat belts. You may turn right at a red light (unless otherwise indicated), after yielding to traffic and pedestrians, and after making a complete stop. Cable cars always have the right-of-way, as do pedestrians at intersections and crosswalks. Pay attention to signs and arrows on the streets and roadways or you may find yourself suddenly in a lane that requires exiting or turning when you really want to go straight ahead. What's more, San Francisco's many one-way streets can drive you in circles, but most road maps of the city indicate which way traffic flows.

a cab—just look for the lighted sign on the roof that indicates if one is free. Otherwise, it's a good idea to call one of the following companies to arrange a ride: **Veteran's Cab** (☎ 415/552-1300), **Desoto Cab Co.** (☎ 415/673-1414), **Luxor Cabs** (☎ 415/282-4141), **Yellow Cab** (☎ 415/626-2345), or **Pacific** (☎ 415/986-7220). Rates are approximately $2.50 for the first mile and $1.80 for each mile thereafter.

# BY CAR

You don't need a car to explore downtown San Francisco; and in fact, in central areas, such as Chinatown, Union Square, and the Financial District, a car can be your worst nightmare. But if you want to venture outside of the city, driving is the best way to go. As a precaution, before heading outside the city, especially in winter, call for California **road conditions** (☎ **800/427-7623**).

## RENTING A CAR

All the major companies operate in the city and have desks at the airports. When we last checked, a compact car could be secured for a week for about $170, including all taxes and other charges, but prices change dramatically on a daily basis, as well as depending on which company you rent from.

Some of the national car-rental companies operating in San Francisco include: **Alamo** (☎ 800/327-9633), **Avis** (☎ 800/331-1212), **Budget** (☎ 800/527-0700), **Dollar** (☎ 800/800-4000), **Hertz** (☎ 800/654-3131), **National** (☎ 800/227-7368), and **Thrifty** (☎ 800/367-2277).

In addition to the big chains, there are dozens of regional rental places in San Francisco, many of which offer lower rates. These include **A-One Rent-A-Car,** 434 O'Farrell St. (☎ **415/771-3977**) and **Bay Area Rentals,** 229 Seventh St. (☎ **415/621-8989**).

Car-rental rates vary even more than airline fares. Prices depend on the size of the car, where and when you pick it up and drop it off, the length of the rental period, where and how far you drive it, whether you buy insurance, and a host of other factors. A few key questions could save you hundreds of dollars, because reservations agents don't often volunteer money-saving information.

- Are weekend rates lower than weekday rates? Ask if the rate is the same for pickup Friday morning, for instance, as it is for Thursday night. Reservations agents won't volunteer this information, so don't be shy about asking lots of questions.
- Does the agency assess a drop-off charge if you don't return the car to the same location where you picked it up?
- Are special promotional rates available? If you see an advertised price in your local newspaper, be sure to ask for that specific rate; otherwise you may be charged the standard cost. Terms change constantly.

# Demystifying Renter's Insurance

Before you drive off in a rental car, be sure you're insured. Hasty assumptions about your personal auto insurance or a rental agency's additional coverage could end up costing you tens of thousands of dollars—even if you are involved in an accident that was clearly the fault of another driver.

If you already hold a **private auto insurance** policy, you are most likely covered in the United States for loss of or damage to a rental car, and liability in case of injury to any other party involved in an accident. Be sure to find out whether you are covered in the area you are visiting, whether your policy extends to all persons who will be driving the rental car, how much liability is covered in case an outside party is injured in an accident, and whether the type of vehicle you are renting is included under your contract. (Rental trucks, sports utility vehicles, and luxury vehicles such as the Jaguar may not be covered.)

Most **major credit cards** provide some degree of coverage as well—provided they were used to pay for the rental. Terms vary widely, however, so be sure to call your credit card company directly before you rent.

If you are **uninsured,** your credit card provides primary coverage as long as you decline the rental agency's insurance. This means that the credit card will cover damage or theft of a rental car for the full cost of the vehicle. (In a few states, however, theft is not covered; ask specifically about state law where you will be renting and driving.) If you already have insurance, your credit card will provide secondary coverage—which basically covers your deductible.

Credit cards **will not cover liability,** or the cost of injury to an outside party and/or damage to an outside party's vehicle. If you do not hold an insurance

- Are discounts available for members of AARP, AAA, frequent-flyer programs, or trade unions? If you belong to any of these organizations, you may be entitled to discounts of up to 30%.
- How much tax will be added to the rental bill? Local tax? State use tax?
- How much does the rental company charge to refill your gas tank if you return with the tank less than full? Though most rental companies claim these prices are "competitive," fuel is almost always cheaper in town. Try to allow enough time to refuel the car yourself before returning it.

Some companies offer "refueling packages," in which you pay for an entire tank of gas up front. The cost is usually fairly competitive with local prices, but you don't get credit for any gas remaining in the tank. If a stop at a gas station on the way to the airport will make you miss your plane, then by all means take advantage of the fuel-purchase option. Otherwise, skip it.

A minimum-age requirement—usually 25—is set by most car-rental agencies. If you are between 21 and 24, some agencies will rent to you, but will tack on an extra fee of $10 to $25 a day. Some agencies also have a maximum-age limit. If you're concerned that these limits may affect you, ask about rental requirements at the time of booking to avoid problems later.

Most rental firms pad their profits by selling an additional **Collision Damage Waiver** (CDW), which can cost an extra $10 or more per day. Before agreeing to this, check with your insurance carrier and credit card company. Many people don't realize that they are already covered by either one or both. If you're not, the CDW is a wise investment.

policy, you may seriously want to consider purchasing additional liability insurance from your rental company. Be sure to check the terms, however: Some rental agencies cover liability only if the renter is not at fault; even then, the rental company's obligation varies from state to state.

Bear in mind that each credit card company has its own peculiarities. Most American Express Optima cards, for instance, do not provide any insurance. American Express does not cover vehicles valued at over $50,000 when new, luxury vehicles such as the Porsche, or vehicles built on a truck chassis. Master-Card does not provide coverage for loss, theft, or fire damage, and only covers collision if the rental period does not exceed 15 days. Call your own credit card company for details.

The basic insurance coverage offered by most car rental companies, known as the **Loss/Damage Waiver (LDW)** or **Collision Damage Waiver (CDW),** can cost as much as $20/day. It usually covers the full value of the vehicle with no deductible if an outside party causes an accident or other damage to the rental car. In all states *except California,* you will probably be covered in case of theft as well. Liability coverage varies according to the company policy and state law, but the minimum is usually at least $15,000. If you are at fault in an accident, however, you will be covered for the full replacement value of the car but not for liability. Some states allow you to buy additional liability coverage for such cases. Most rental companies will require a police report in order to process any claims you file, but your private insurer will not be notified of the accident.

## PARKING

If you want to have a relaxing vacation here, don't even attempt to find street parking in Nob Hill, North Beach, Chinatown, by Fisherman's Wharf, or on Telegraph Hill. Park in a garage or take a cab or a bus. If you do find street parking, pay attention to street signs that will explain when you can park and for how long. Be especially careful not to park in zones that are tow areas during rush hours.

Curb colors also indicate parking regulations. *Red* means no stopping or parking; *blue* is reserved for drivers with disabilities who have a California-issued disabled plate or a placard; *white* means there's a 5-minute limit; *green* indicates a 10-minute limit; and *yellow* and *yellow-black* curbs are for commercial vehicles only. Also, don't park at a bus stop or in front of a fire hydrant, and watch out for street-cleaning signs. If you violate the law, you may get a hefty ticket or your car may be towed. To get your car back, you must obtain a release from the nearest district police department, then go to the towing company to pick up the vehicle.

When parking on a hill, apply the hand brake, put the car in gear, and *curb your wheels*—toward the curb when facing downhill, away from the curb when facing uphill. Curbing your wheels will not only prevent a possible "runaway," but will also keep you from getting a ticket—an expensive fine that is aggressively enforced.

## BY FERRY

**TO/FROM SAUSALITO** The **Golden Gate Ferry Service** fleet (☎ **415/ 923-2000**) shuttles passengers daily between the San Francisco Ferry Building, located at the foot of Market Street, and downtown Sausalito. Service is frequent,

# Cheap Parking Garages Around the City

Forget Donkey Kong and Pac Man—if you really want to play a fast and furious game, try searching for the cheapest parking in the city. "*What?*" you ask. "Cheap parking in San Francisco? No way!"

Yes, Virginia, we do have inexpensive parking lots, but there are only 10 of them, and unless you know where to go (or get lucky), you won't find them. They're cheap because they're owned by the city, which charges a measly $1 an hour for the first 3 hours, and slightly more after 4 hours. Compare that to most private garages in the downtown area that charge up to $2.75 for the first 20 *minutes,* or the Pier 39 lot that charges $5 per hour. Heck, that's a steak dinner for an afternoon's outing.

One thing to remember: After you park, take your ticket with you, because you'll have to pay (via automatic tellers or live ones) before you start searching for your car. Here's the skinny on cheap parking in San Francisco, including the rates as of press time:

In **Chinatown,** try the **Portsmouth Square Garage,** with an entrance on Kearny between Washington and Clay (504 spaces; $1 per hour for the first 4 hours), or the **Golden Gateway Garage,** with an entrance on both Washington and Clay streets between Battery and Davis (1,000 spaces; $3 per hour for the first 4 hours).

In the **Nob Hill/Union Square** area, there's **St. Mary's Square Garage,** with entrances on Pine, Kearny, and California, bordered by Grant (828 spaces; $1 per hour for the first 4 hours on weekends, $4 per hour for the first 4 hours on weekdays), or the **Sutter-Stockton Garage,** with entrances on Stockton and Bush, bordered by Grant and Sutter (1,865 spaces; $1 per hour for the first 4 hours). Right in Union Square, try the **Union Square Garage,** with an entrance on Geary Street, bordered by Powell, Post, and Stockton (1,100 spaces; $1 per hour for the first 4 hours), or the **Ellis-O'Farrell Garage,** with entrances on O'Farrell and Ellis, bordered by Powell and Stockton (1,263 spaces; $1 per hour for the first 4 hours).

If you're hanging out in **SoMa** or near the **MOMA,** we'd recommend the **Fifth & Mission Garage,** with entrances on Mission or Minna, bordering 4th and 5th streets (2,622 spaces; $1 per hour for the first 4 hours), and the **Moscone Center Garage,** with an entrance on 3rd Street, between Howard and Folsom (732 spaces; $1 per hour for the first 4 hours).

Finally, two cheap garages near the **Civic Center and Hayes Valley** are the **Civic Center Garage,** with an entrance on McAllister between Polk and Larkin (840 spaces; $1 per hour for the first 4 hours), and the **Performing Arts Garage,** with an entrance on Grove between Gough and Franklin (612 spaces; $1 per hour for the first 4 hours).

departing at reasonable intervals every day of the year except New Year's Day, Thanksgiving Day, and Christmas Day. Phone for exact schedule. The ride takes a half hour, and one-way fares are $4.75 for adults and $3.55 for kids 6 to 12. Senior and disabled passengers ride for $2.35; children 5 and under ride free. Family rates are also available on weekends.

Ferries of the **Blue & Gold Fleet** (recorded info: ☎ **415/773-1188;** tickets: ☎ **415/705-5555**) also provide round-trip service to downtown Sausalito, leaving from Fisherman's Wharf at Pier 41. The cost is $11 round-trip, half price for kids 5 to 11. Boats run on a seasonal schedule; phone for departure information.

**TO/FROM LARKSPUR**   The **Golden Gate Ferry Service** fleet (☎ **415/923-2000**) also shuttles passengers daily between the San Francisco Ferry Building, located at the foot of Market Street, and downtown Larkspur. The Larkspur ferry is primarily a commuter service during the week, with frequent departures around the rush hours and limited service on weekends. Boats make the 13-mile trip in about 45 minutes and cost $2.75 for adults, $2.05 for kids ages 6 to 12, and $1.35 for seniors and passengers with disabilities; on weekends, prices rise to $4.70 for adults, and $2.35 for seniors and passengers with disabilities; children 12 and under ride free.

**TO/FROM ANGEL ISLAND & TIBURON**   Ferries of the **Blue & Gold Fleet** (recorded info: ☎ **415/773-1188;** tickets: ☎ **415/705-5555**) leave from Pier 43½ (Fisherman's Wharf) and travel to both Angel Island and Tiburon. Boats run on a seasonal schedule; phone for departure information. The round-trip fare is $10 to Angel Island, $11 to Tiburon; half price for kids 5 to 11.

# Fast Facts: San Francisco

**Airports**   See "Getting There," in chapter 2.

**American Express**   For travel arrangements, traveler's checks, currency exchange, and other member services, American Express has an office at 560 California St., at Battery Street (☎ **415/536-2686**), open Monday to Friday from 9am to 5pm, and at 455 Market St., at First Street (☎ **415/536-2600**), in the Financial District, open Monday to Friday from 8:30am to 5:30pm and Saturday from 9am to 2pm. To report lost or stolen traveler's checks, call ☎ **800/221-7282.** For American Express Global Assist, call ☎ **800/554-2639.**

**Area Code**   The area code for San Francisco is **415;** Oakland, Berkeley, and much of the East Bay use the 510 area code, and the peninsula is generally 650. Most phone numbers in this book are in San Francisco's 415 area code, but there's no need to dial it if you're within city limits.

**Baby-Sitters**   Hotels can often recommend a baby-sitter or child-care service. If yours can't, try **Temporary Tot Tending** (☎ **650/355-7377,** or 650/871-5790 after 6pm), which offers child care by licensed teachers by the hour for children from 3 weeks to 12 years of age. It's open Monday to Friday from 6am to 7pm (weekend service is available only during convention times).

**Business Hours**   Most banks are open Monday to Friday from 9am to 3pm. Several stay open until about 5pm at least 1 day a week. Many banks also feature ATMs for 24-hour banking (see "Visitor Information," in chapter 2).

Most stores are open Monday to Saturday from 10am or 11am to at least 6pm, with restricted hours on Sunday. But there are exceptions: Stores in Chinatown, Ghirardelli Square, and Pier 39 stay open much later during the tourist season; and large department stores, including Macy's and Nordstrom, keep late hours.

Most restaurants serve lunch from about 11:30am to 2:30pm and dinner from 5:30 to 10pm. You can sometimes get served later on weekends. Nightclubs and bars are usually open daily until 2am, when they are legally bound to stop serving alcohol.

**Car Rentals**   For car-rental information, see "Getting Around," in this chapter.

**Climate**   See "When to Go," in chapter 2.

**Dentist**   In the event of a dental emergency, see your hotel concierge or contact the **San Francisco Dental Society** (☎ 415/421-1435) for a referral to a specialist. The **San Francisco Dental Office,** 132 The Embarcadero (☎ 415/777-5115), between Mission and Howard streets, offers emergency service and comprehensive dental care Monday, Tuesday, and Friday from 8am to 4:30pm, Wednesday and Thursday from 10:30am to 6:30pm.

**Doctor**   **Saint Francis Memorial Hospital,** 900 Hyde St., between Bush and Pine streets on Nob Hill (☎ 415/353-6000), provides emergency-care service 24 hours; no appointment is necessary. The hospital also operates a **physician-referral** service (☎ 800/333-1355).

**Driving Rules**   See "Handy Driving Tips," earlier in this chapter.

**Drugstores**   There are **Walgreens** pharmacies all over town, including one at 135 Powell St. (☎ 415/391-4433). The store is open Monday to Saturday from 8am to midnight and on Sunday from 9am to 9pm, but the pharmacy has more limited hours: Monday to Friday they're open from 8am to 9pm, Saturday from 9am to 5pm, and Sunday from 10am to 6pm. The branch on Divisadero Street at Lombard (☎ 415/931-6415) has a 24-hour pharmacy. **Merrill's** pharmacy, 805 Market St. (☎ 415/431-5466), is open Monday to Saturday from 8:30am to 6:30pm, while the rest of the drugstore is open Monday to Friday from 7am to 9pm, Saturday from 9am to 7pm, and Sunday from 9:30am to 6pm. Both chains accept MasterCard and Visa.

**Earthquakes**   There will always be earthquakes in California, most of which you'll never notice. However, in case of a significant shaker, there are a few basic precautionary measures you should know. When you are inside a building, seek cover; do not run outside. Stand under a doorway or against a wall and stay away from windows. If you exit a building after a substantial quake, use stairwells, not elevators. If you are in your car, pull over to the side of the road and stop—but not until you are away from bridges, overpasses, telephone poles, and power lines. Stay in your car. If you're out walking, stay outside and away from trees, power lines, and the sides of buildings. If you're in an area with tall buildings, find a doorway in which to stand.

**Emergencies**   Dial ☎ 911 for police, an ambulance, or the fire department; no coins are needed from a public phone. Emergency hot lines include the **Poison Control Center** (☎ 800/523-2222) and **Rape Crisis** (☎ 415/647-7273).

**Liquor Laws**   Liquor and grocery stores, as well as some drugstores, can sell packaged alcoholic beverages between 6am and 2am. Most restaurants, nightclubs, and bars are licensed to serve alcoholic beverages during the same hours. The legal age for purchase and consumption is 21; proof of age is required.

**Newspapers & Magazines**   The city's two main dailies are the *San Francisco Chronicle* and the *San Francisco Examiner;* both are distributed throughout the city. The two papers combine for a massive Sunday edition that includes a pink "Datebook" section—an excellent preview of the week's upcoming events. The free weekly *San Francisco Bay Guardian,* a tabloid of news and listings, is indispensable for nightlife information; it's widely distributed through street-corner dispensers and at city cafes and restaurants.

Of the many free tourist-oriented publications, the most widely read are *Key* and *San Francisco Guide.* Both of these handbook-size weeklies contain maps and information on current events. They can be found in most hotels, shops, and restaurants in the major tourist areas.

**Pharmacies**    See "Drugstores," above.

**Police**    For emergencies, dial ☎ **911** from any phone; no coins are needed. For other matters, call ☎ **415/553-0123.**

**Post Office**    There are dozens of post offices located all around the city. The closest office to Union Square is inside Macy's department store, 170 O'Farrell St. (☎ **800/275-8777**). You can pick up mail addressed to you and marked "General Delivery" (Poste Restante), at the **Civic Center Post Office Box Unit,** P.O. Box 429991, San Francisco, CA 94142-9991 (☎ **800/275-8777**).

**Safety**    Few locals would recommend that you walk alone late at night in certain areas, particularly the Tenderloin, between Union Square and the Civic Center. Compared with similar areas in other cities, however, even this section of San Francisco is relatively tranquil. Other areas where you should be particularly alert are the Mission District, around 16th and Mission streets; the lower Fillmore area, around lower Haight Street; and the SoMa area south of Market Street.

Keep in mind that there are a substantial number of homeless people throughout the city with concentrations in and around Union Square, the Theater District, the Tenderloin, and Haight Street, so don't be alarmed if you're approached for spare change. Basically, just use common sense.

For additional crime-prevention information, phone **San Francisco SAFE** (☎ **415/553-1984**).

**Smoking**    If San Francisco is the state's most European city, the comparison stops here. Each year smoking laws are becoming more and more strict. As of January 1, 1998, smoking is prohibited from restaurants and bars. Although there's been argument against it, so far the new law's been enforced in most establishments. Hotels are also offering more non-smoking rooms, which is often leaving those who like to puff out in the cold—literally.

**Taxes**    An 8.5% sales tax is added at the register for all goods and services purchased in San Francisco. There is no sales tax on hotel rooms, but the city hotel tax is a whopping 14%.

**Taxis**    See "Getting Around," earlier in this chapter.

**Television**    In addition to cable stations, available in most hotels, all the major networks and several independent stations are represented. They include: Channel 2, KTVU (FOX); Channel 4, KRON (NBC); Channel 5, KPIX (CBS); Channel 7, KGO (ABC); and Channel 9, KQED (PBS).

**Time Zone**    San Francisco is in the Pacific standard time zone, which is 8 hours behind Greenwich mean time and 3 hours behind eastern standard time. To find out what time it is, call ☎ **415/767-8900.**

**Transit Information**    The San Francisco Municipal Railway, better known as Muni, operates the city's cable cars, buses, and Metro streetcars. For customer service, call **Muni** at ☎ **415/673-6864** during the week between 7am and 5pm and on the weekends between 9am and 5pm. At other times, recorded information is available.

**Useful Telephone Numbers**    Tourist information (☎ **415/391-2001**); highway conditions (☎ **800/427-7623**); KFOG Entertainment Line (☎ **415/777-1045**); Movie Phone Line (☎ **415/777-FILM**); Grateful Dead Hot Line (☎ **415/457-6388**).

**Weather**    Call the National Weather Service, ☎ **650/364-7974,** to find out when the next fog bank is rolling in.

# 5 Accommodations You Can Afford

Aside from airfare, the bulk of your vacation money will probably be spent on accommodations. The bad news is that, as of press time, the average room rate in San Francisco was hovering around $135 a night, which would most certainly blow your $60-a-day budget. The good news is that, with a whole lot of research and running around, we actually managed to find lodgings that were both inexpensive enough to justify the title of this guidebook and decent enough that snobs like us would be willing to stay there ourselves. In short, we found the city's best hotels in every reasonable price range.

Of course, there's a catch. You can kiss the mints-on-your-pillow luxuries good-bye, because most budget hotels keep their prices down by offering only the bare essentials—phone, TV, bed, and bath—and in the high-rent zones even a bathroom is considered an upgrade. The trick is to avoid the heavily concentrated areas such as Union Square and Fisherman's Wharf, and instead park your bags at the city's outlying districts such as the Marina or the Haight and take a bus into town. Not only are the room rates far lower (and the chances of having your own bathroom doubled), but the clientele is usually more, shall we say, "refined" as well.

**TIPS ON FINDING REASONABLE RATES** Hunting for hotels in San Francisco can be a tricky business, particularly if you're not a seasoned traveler. What you don't know—and the reservation agent may not tell you—may very well ruin your vacation, so keep the following pointers in mind when it comes time to book a room:

- The prices listed below do not include the city's 14% hotel tax. Other hidden extras may include parking fees and hefty surcharges—up to $1 per local call—for telephone use.
- Some hotels entice you with complimentary continental breakfast, which can be a real money-saver. But beware: Sometimes a big promise translates to just coffee and a croissant.
- If a hotel is listed under "Super-Cheap," don't be surprised if your room is on the funky side (though we 86ed the real dives). Nothing's free, mate.
- San Francisco is Convention City, so if you wish to secure rooms at a particular hotel during high season—roughly April to September—book well in advance.
- Be sure to have a credit or charge card in hand when making a reservation, and don't be surprised if you're asked to pay for at least 1 night in advance (this doesn't happen often, though).

- Reservations are usually held until 6pm. If you don't tell the hotel you'll be arriving late, you may lose your room.
- Almost every hotel in San Francisco requires a credit or charge card imprint for "incidentals" (and to prevent walkouts). If you don't have a credit or charge card, be sure to make special arrangements with the management before you hang up the phone, and take down names.

**HOW WE'VE ORGANIZED THIS CHAPTER**    The hotels listed below are classified first by area and then by price, using the following categories: Our general Frommer's recommendations range in price from a bit under $80 per night to $140 a night. **Super-Cheap Sleeps** are classified as those under $40 a night (essentially hostels), the **Worth a Splurge** category features hotels that cost more than $140 per night. These categories reflect the price of an average double room—*not including the 14% hotel tax*—during the high season, which, again, runs approximately from April to September. Keep in mind that prices listed are the hotel's "rack rates" (the published rates for walk-ins) and you should always ask for special discounts or, even better, vacation packages. It's possible that you could get the room you want for $20 to $40 a night less than what's quoted here, except in summer when the hotels are packed and bargaining is close to impossible. Also note that we don't list rates for singles. However, some hotels, particularly more budget-oriented establishments, do offer lower rates for singles, so be sure to ask about these if you're traveling alone. And if you're an AAA member, be sure to order the free guide to California's hotels and motels, which not only supplies readers with further options, but also ranks them from one to five diamonds. It also has discount coupons and quotes special member rates.

In general, hotel rates in San Francisco are rather inelastic; they don't vary much during the year because the city is so popular year-round. You should always ask about weekend discounts, corporate rates, and family plans; most larger hotels offer them, but many don't mention these discounts unless you make a specific inquiry. You'll find no-smoking rooms available in all the larger hotels and many of the smaller hotels; establishments that are entirely no-smoking are listed as such. Nowadays, the best advice for smokers is to confirm a smoking-permitted room in advance.

Most larger hotels will also be able to accommodate guests confined to wheelchairs or those who have other special needs. Ask when you make a reservation to ensure that your hotel of choice will be able to accommodate your needs, especially if you're interested in a bed-and-breakfast.

Pay close attention to the hotels that we've awarded stars to. These are the ones that are exceptional, the ones that offer above-average accommodations at below-average rates.

**AFFORDABLE HOTEL CHAINS**    The reason we avoid reviewing chain hotels and motels is probably the very same reason you may want to consider staying in one: Every outpost is a veritable clone, hence you always know what you're going to get. But if all our recommendations in your price range are booked or if you just don't mind going generic, you can always try one of the following chains, which all have hotels either in the city or nearby: **Best Western** (☎ 800/528-1234), **Comfort Inn** (☎ 800/228-5150), **Days Inn** (☎800/325-2525), **Doubletree Hotels** (☎800/222-TREE), **Econo Lodges** (☎800/55-ECONO), **Holiday Inn** (☎ 800 /HOLIDAY), **Howard Johnson** (☎ 800/654-2000), **La Quinta Motor Inns** (☎800/531-5900), **MOTEL6** (☎ 800/466-8356), **Ramada** (☎ 800/ 2-RAMADA), **Rodeway Inns** (☎800/228-2000), **SUPER8** (☎ 800/800-8000), **Travelodge** (☎800/255-3050), and **Vagabond Inns** (☎800/522-1555).

# Reservation Services

Having reservations about your reservations? Then leave it up to the pros:

**Bed-and-Breakfast California,** 12711 McCartysville Place, Saratoga, CA 95070 (☎ **800/872-4500** or 408/867-9662; fax 408/867-0907; www.bbintl.com; E-mail info@bbintl.com), offers a selection of B&Bs ranging from $60 to $140 per night (2-night minimum). Accommodations range from simple rooms in private homes to luxurious, full-service carriage houses, houseboats, and Victorian homes.

**San Francisco Reservations,** 22 Second St., San Francisco, CA 94105 (☎ **800/677-1500** or 415/227-1500), arranges reservations for more than 300 of San Francisco's hotels and often offers discounted rates. Ask about their Events and Hotel Packages that include VIP or discount admissions to various San Francisco museums. This service also has a nifty Web site that allows Internet users to make their reservations online. Plug in at **www.hotelres.com**.

## 1 Union Square/Nob Hill

**Adelaide Inn.** 5 Isadora Duncan Court (formerly Adelaide Place, off Taylor St., between Post and Geary sts.), San Francisco, CA 94102. ☎ **415/441-2261.** Fax 415/441-0161. 18 units, all with shared bathroom. TV. $52–$58 double with shared bathroom. AE, MC, V. Rates include continental breakfast. Bus: 2, 3, 4, 27, 38, or 76.

They say San Francisco is America's most European city, and if you're into the facade, the Adelaide will definitely complete the illusion. The last of the true old-style *pensiones,* this three-level building tucked in a surprisingly quiet cul-de-sac is bright, cheery, and decorated in long-forgotten ornamentation (remember textured wallpaper?). Colors and furniture hark back to the 1960s not because the owner's gone retro, but probably because he hasn't changed the furnishings since then. But in an inexplicably quaint way, the atmosphere works. Perhaps its the sunny and funky rooms; the small, bright breakfast room; the stairway skylight; or the shared fridge in the kitchen (it certainly isn't the spongy mattresses or the tiny bathrooms and old, wet-smelling showers). Whatever it is, this place does feel a lot like home. Services include morning complimentary coffee and rolls, and on-the-premises pay phones. *Note:* This place may not appeal to older travelers—it has steep stairs and no elevators.

**Amsterdam Hotel.** 749 Taylor St. (between Sutter and Bush sts.), San Francisco, CA 94108 ☎ **800/637-3444** or 415/673-3277. Fax 415/673-0453. 34 units. TV TEL. $99–$139 double (including continental breakfast). AE, MC, V. Parking $13. Bus: 2, 3, 4, or 76.

This small hotel doesn't have the grand feeling that comes with larger properties, but it still offers pleasant accommodations at a very reasonable price. All guest rooms have been newly redecorated—some with Jacuzzi tubs and others with curiously out-of-

## Dial Direct

When booking a room in a chain hotel, call the hotel's local line, as well as the toll-free number, and see where you'll get the best deal. A hotel makes nothing on a room that stays empty. The clerk who runs the place is more likely to know about vacancies and will often grant deep discounts in order to fill up.

place marble or black-lacquer bathrooms (for a $100 room?). On sunny days most guests prefer to enjoy their free continental breakfasts at the small dining patio out back.

**Andrews Hotel.** 624 Post St. (between Jones and Taylor sts.), San Francisco, CA 94109. ☎ **800/926-3739** or 415/563-6877. Fax 415/928-6919. www.sftrips.com. 48 units. TV TEL. $85–$135 double; $125–$142 petite suite. Rates include continental breakfast and evening wine. AE, DC, JCB, MC, V. Self-parking $15. Cable car: Powell-Hyde and Powell-Mason lines (3 blocks east). Bus: 2, 3, 4, 30, 38, or 45.

Two blocks west of Union Square, the Andrews was formerly a Turkish bath before its conversion in 1981. As is fitting with Euro-style hotels, the well-maintained rooms are small but comfortable, and include voice mail, irons and ironing boards; white lace curtains and fresh flowers in each room add a light touch. Some rooms have shower only, and bathrooms in general tend to be tiny, but for the location—a few blocks from Union Square—and price, the Andrews is a safe bet for an enjoyable stay in the city. An added bonus is the adjoining Fino Bar and Ristorante, which offers complimentary wine to its hotel guests in the evening.

**Beresford Arms.** 701 Post St. (at Jones St.), San Francisco, CA 94109. ☎ **800/533-6533** or 415/673-2600. Fax 415/929-1535. 148 units. MINIBAR TV TEL. $125 double; $145 Jacuzzi suite; $180 parlor suite. Rates include continental breakfast and afternoon wine and tea. Extra person $10. Children under 12 stay free in parents' rm. Senior-citizen and AAA discounts available. AE, CB, DC, DISC, MC, V. Valet parking $16, self-parking $13. Cable car: Powell-Hyde line (3 blocks east). Bus: 2, 3, 4, 27, or 38.

Its excellent prices are the main reason we recommend this dependable, though slightly unfashionable hotel. On the plus side, many rooms have Jacuzzi whirlpool bathtubs and bidets, and a choice of wet bar or fully equipped kitchen—a key for families. All have VCRs and honor bars, and there's a "Manager's Social Hour" with free wine and snacks. The downside is the common areas' painfully red carpeting, gloomy lobby, and occasionally old mattresses. Modest business services are available, as is valet or self-parking. The hotel's location, sandwiched between the Theater District and Union Square in a quieter section of San Francisco, is ideal for car-free visitors. *Tip:* Post side accommodations may be a bit noisier, but they're also larger, sunnier and some have window seats.

**Beresford Hotel.** 635 Sutter St. (near Mason St.), San Francisco, CA 94102. ☎ **800/533-6533** or 415/673-9900. Fax 415/474-0449. 114 units. MINIBAR TV TEL. $109–$129 double. Rates include continental breakfast. Extra person $10. Children under 12 stay free in parents' rm. Senior citizen and AAA discounts available. Ask for special rates. AE, CB, DC, DISC, MC, V. Self parking $16. Cable car: Powell-Hyde line (1 block east). Bus: 2, 3, 4, 30, 38, or 45.

Small and friendly, the seven-floor Beresford Hotel is a decent, moderately priced choice near Union Square. Rooms have a mish-mash of furniture and stocked fridges, and to block out the street noise, they've recently installed soundproof windows. Everything's well kept, but don't expect much more than a clean place to rest. The adjacent White Horse Tavern, an attractive replica of an old English pub, serves a complimentary continental breakfast, as well as lunch and dinner.

**Best Inn and Suites.** 415 O'Farrell St. (between Taylor and Jones sts.), San Francisco, CA 94102. ☎ **800/BEST-INN** or 415/928-6800. www.bestinn.com. 50 units, all with bathroom. TV TEL. $95–$175 double. Rates include buffet breakfast. Inquire about discounts. AE, DC, DISC, JCB, MC, V. Parking across the street $16. Bus: 2, 3, 4, 28, 37, or 76.

The Best Inn and Suites is anything but the best, but if all you're looking for is downtown lodging that is clean, safe, and relatively inexpensive, this will do. It's on the edge of a sketchy neighborhood, but it's also within throwing distance of Union Square. The rooms, which were entirely redecorated in 1998 with brand-new

# Accommodations Near Union Square & Nob Hill

Adelaide Inn 18
Amsterdam Hotel 28
Andrews Hotel 21
Atherton Hotel 35
AYH Hostel at Union Square 8
Beresford Arms 25
Best Inn & Suites 17

Cartwright Hotel 4
Clarion Bedford Hotel 26
Commodore International 27
Cornell Hotel 11
Dakota Hotel 19
Essex Hotel 34
Fitzgerald 20

Golden Gate Hotel 12
Grant Plaza Hotel 2
Hotel Astoria 3
Hotel Halcyon 24
Beresford Hotel 15
Hotel David
   Bed & Breakfast 16
Hotel Rex 10

The Maxwell **9**

Monticello Inn **7**

Nob Hill Inn **30**

Nob Hill Hotel **32**

Pensione International **33**

Petite Auberge **29**

Savoy Hotel **23**

Shannon Court **22**

The Sheehan **14**

The Stratford Hotel **5**

Temple Hotel **1**

Villa Florence **6**

White Swan Inn **13**

York Hotel **31**

furnishings, are tidy and no-nonsense, and come with coffeemakers, big color TVs, and clean bathrooms. There's a wide array of room, bathroom, and bed sizes—including family suites—so when you book your room be sure to haggle with the clerk for the best deal. Mind you, the rooms facing O'Farrell are the noisiest. If you're not picky about your morning meal, you'll probably enjoy the free morning buffet, which includes eggs, bacon, toast, and so forth, Served from 7 to 11am.

**Cartwright Hotel.** 524 Sutter St. (at Powell St.), San Francisco, CA 94102. ☎ **800/ 227-3844** or 415/421-2865. Fax 415/983-6244. 114 units. TV TEL. $129–$169 double or twin; $199–$259 family suite sleeping 4. Rates include continental breakfast and evening wine. AE, CB, DC, DISC, MC, V. Self parking $18, valet parking $24. Cable car: Powell-Hyde and Powell-Mason lines (direct stop). Bus: 2, 3, 4, 30, or 45.

Diametrically opposed to the hip-hop, happenin' Hotel Triton down the street, the Cartwright Hotel is geared toward the "older, mature traveler" (as hotel marketers like to put it). The hotel management takes pride in its reputation for offering clean, comfortable rooms at fair prices, which explains why most of its guests have been repeat customers for a long time. Remarkably quiet despite its convenient location near one of the busiest downtown corners, the eight-story hotel looks not unlike it did some 80 years ago when it first opened. High-quality antiques collected during its decades of faithful service furnish the lobby, as well as each of the individually decorated rooms. A nice perk usually reserved for fancier hotels are the fully equipped bathrooms, all of which have tubs, shower massages, thick fluffy towels, and terry-cloth robes. Guests have access to a nearby health club; complimentary wine, tea, and cookies are served in the small library adjacent to the lobby from 5 to 6pm on weekends. *Tip:* Request a room with a view of the backyard; they're the quietest.

**Clarion Bedford Hotel.** 761 Post St. (between Leavenworth and Jones sts.), San Francisco, CA 94109. ☎ **800/252-7466** or 415/673-6040. Fax 415/563-6739. 144 units. MINIBAR TV TEL. $129–$179 double; from $175 suite. Continental breakfast $8.50 extra. AE, CB, DC, DISC, JCB, MC, V. Parking $20. Cable car: Powell-Hyde and Powell-Mason lines (4 blocks east). Bus: 2, 3, 4, or 27.

For the price and location (3 blocks from Union Square) the 17-story Bedford offers a darn good deal. Your hard-earned dollars will get you a large, spotless, recently renovated room with flowery decor that's not exactly en vogue but definitely in fine taste, as well as service from an enthusiastic, attentive, and professional staff. Each accommodation is well furnished with king, queen, or two double beds, writing desk, armchair, in-room coffeemakers, and a well-stocked honor bar with plenty of munchies. Big closets are a tradeoff for the small bathrooms. Most rooms are sunny and bright and have priceless views of the city (the higher the floor, the better the view). The hotel's bistro, Crushed Tomato's, has a small, beautiful mahogany bar opposite the registration desk. There's also room service (for breakfast only), dry cleaning, laundry, secretarial services, and valet parking.

✪ **Commodore International.** 825 Sutter St. (at Jones St.), San Francisco, CA 94109. ☎ **800/338-6848** or 415/923-6800. Fax 415/923-6804. 113 units. TV TEL. $99–$139 double or twin. AE, DC, MC, V. Parking $15. Bus: 2, 3, 4, 27, or 76.

If you're looking to pump a little fun and fantasy into your vacation, this is the place. Before its new owners revamped the aging Commodore from top to bottom, it . . . well, okay, it sucked. Then along came San Francisco hotelier Chip Conley who instantly recognized this dilapidated eyesore's potential, added it to his collection, then let his hip-hop decor designers do their magic. The result? One groovy hotel. Stealing the show is the Red Room, a Big Apple–style bar and lounge that reflects no other color of the spectrum but ruby red (you gotta see this one). The stylish lobby comes in a close second, followed by the adjoining Titanic Café, a cute little diner serving griddlecakes, Vietnamese tofu sandwiches, and dragon-fire salads. Appealing to the masses, Chip left the first four floors as standard no-frills—though quite clean and comfortable—rooms, while decking out the top two floors in neo-deco overtones (well worth the extra $10 per night).

**Cornell Hotel.** 715 Bush St. (between Powell and Mason sts.), San Francisco, CA 94108. ☎ **800/232-9698** or 415/421-3154. Fax 415/399-1442. 60 units. TV TEL. $100–$150 double. Rates include full breakfast. Weekly package including 7 breakfasts and 5 dinners, $875 double per week. AE, CB, DC, MC, V. Parking $13. Cable car: Powell-Hyde and Powell-Mason lines. Bus: 2, 3, 4, 30, or 45.

It's the quirks that make this hotel more charming than many in its price range. You'll be greeted by Rameau, the house golden retriever, when you enter this small French-style hotel. Pass the office, where a few faces will glance up in your direction and smile, and embark on a ride in the old-fashioned elevator to get to your room. Each floor is dedicated to a French painter and is decorated with reproductions. The comfortable rooms are individually decorated in a simple modern style, and come with a desk and chairs. No smoking is allowed in any of them. A full breakfast is included in the cavernlike provincial basement dining room, Jeanne d'Arc, and Union Square is a few blocks away.

**Dakota Hotel.** 606 Post St. (at Taylor St.), San Francisco, CA 94109. ☎ **415/931-7475.** Fax 415/931-7486. 45 units. TV TEL. $70–$125 double. Rates include continental breakfast. MC, V. Parking across the street $15 per day. BART: Powell. Cable car: Powell-Mason line. Bus: 2, 3, 4, 27, 30, 38, 76, and all Market St. buses and Muni Metros.

When we stumbled upon this place a few years back, it gave us the creeps. Part hotel, part residence, it had a flophouse feel and downtrodden appearance. But it seems that those days are behind the European-style Dakota Hotel. New owners took over, brightened up the small lobby, booted out the long-term residents, and renovated the rooms. Of this eight-story hotel's 27 available rooms, the most attractive are those on the upper floors, especially the ones ending in "02"—almost all windows, they're bright and cheery and have decent views of the surrounding street action. Unfortunately, they're also on the corner of Post and Taylor streets, which means that unless you're a heavy sleeper you'll be cursing us for recommending them. It has all the usual perks, including cable TV, private bathrooms (with claw-foot tubs!), and microwaves and refrigerators on request. For the money, you'd be better off staying at the Commodore, but this is still a decent choice, particularly when considering its prime downtown location.

**The Fitzgerald.** 620 Post St. (between Jones and Taylor sts.), San Francisco, CA 94109. ☎ **800/334-6835** or 415/775-8100. Fax 415/775-1278. 39 units. TV TEL. $79–$155 double. Rates include continental breakfast. Extra person $10. Lower rates in winter. AE, CB, DC, DISC, JCB, MC, V. Self-parking $16. Bus: 2, 3, 4, or 27.

If you think the guy at the front desk looks cramped in his nook of a lobby, wait till you get to your room. The Fitzgerald's 47 guest accommodations may be outfitted with newish furniture that's accented with bright bedspreads and patterned carpet, but some of the rooms are really small (one that we saw had a dresser less than a foot from the bed). Ask for a larger room. If you can live without a sizable closet (read: tiny), the price, breakfast, and newness of this hotel make it a good value. Families will especially appreciate the two-bedroom suites, which offer one queen- and one full-size bed. Breakfasts include home-baked breads, scones, muffins, juice, tea, and coffee, while amenities include a concierge, dry cleaning, laundry service, in-room massage, complimentary coffee in the lobby, and free access to a nearby off-premises indoor pool and health club.

*Note:* The view of the Golden Gate that's printed on the brochure is not actually visible from the hotel.

**Golden Gate Hotel.** 775 Bush St. (between Powell and Mason sts.), San Francisco, CA 94108. ☎ **800/835-1118** or 415/392-3702. Fax 415/392-6202. 23 units, 14 with bathroom. TV. $72 double without bathroom, $109 double with bathroom. Rates include continental breakfast and afternoon tea. AE, CB, DC, MC, V. Self parking $12. Cable car: Powell-Hyde and Powell-Mason lines (1 block east). Bus: 2, 3, 4, 30, 38, or 45. Powell & Market BART.

Among San Francisco's small hotels occupying historic turn-of-the-century buildings are some real gems, and the Golden Gate Hotel is one of them. It's 2 blocks north of Union Square and 2 blocks down (literally) from the crest of Nob Hill, with cable-car stops at the corner for easy access to Fisherman's Wharf and Chinatown (the city's theaters and best restaurants are also within walking distance). But the best thing about the Golden Gate Hotel is that this is a family-run establishment: John and Renate Kenaston are hospitable innkeepers who take obvious pleasure in making their guests comfortable. Each individually decorated room has handsome antique furnishings (plenty of wicker) from the early 1900s, quilted bedspreads, and fresh flowers (request a room with a clawfoot tub if you enjoy a good, hot soak). All rooms have phones, and complimentary afternoon tea is served daily from 4 to 7pm.

**Hotel Astoria.** 510 Bush St. (at Grant Ave.), San Francisco, CA 94108. ☎ **800/666-6696** or 415/434-8889. Fax 415/434-8919. 70 units. TV, TEL. $47 double without bathroom, $72 double with bathroom. AE, MC, V. BART: Montgomery. Bus: 2, 3, 4, 9X, 27, 30, 38, 45, 76, and all Market St. buses and Muni Metros.

If you're a sensitive traveler who needs lots of TLC from your hotel, don't book a room here. The Chinese staff is very matter of fact, and will do little more than take you're credit card and point toward the elevator. But if you can get beyond that, you'll be joining the predominantly Asian clientele who enjoy the very clean and adequate Astoria. Pass the lobby—more of a meeting mecca than a leisure lounge—take the small elevator, and you'll find the rooms are simple, with lovely bedspreads, color TV, and in-room safes. Those looking onto Bush and Grant are noisier, but downtown gets pretty quiet at night anyway, so unless you're a late sleeper, they should do the trick. Unless you're staying at the Grant Plaza, you can't get any closer to Chinatown and its world of dim sum, vegetable markets, and trinket shops. Non-smokers should be sure to request properly; there's plenty of puffing going on here.

**✪ Hotel David Bed & Breakfast.** 480 Geary St. (between Taylor and Mason sts.), San Francisco, CA 94102. ☎ **800/524-1888** or 415/771-1600. Fax 415/931-5442. 42 units. TV TEL. $119 double. AE, DISC, MC, V. Rates include full breakfast. Valet parking $20.

No hotel in the area offers so many amenities for so little money as Hotel David. So what if entering this small, *pensione*-like hotel via the adjoining large, kosher deli is a little odd. That's the beauty of this place; it's so well hidden that no one knows it's there (not to mention the fact that there's easy access to decent matzoh-ball soup and hot pastrami on rye). But even beyond that, Hotel David's full of surprises. Whether you come in through the street-side entrance or the restaurant, step off the elevator and you'll find immaculate, smallish rooms, with chic-moderne decor, streamlined maple furnishings, and colorful accents. Expect often-overlooked extras like an AM/FM radio, hot towel racks, voice mail, and soundproofed walls. And there's more: free transportation from the S.F. airport (for guests staying 2 or more nights), valet parking (currently $20 per night), and a free full and hearty breakfast—served at David's Deli, of course. *Note:* If your hotel experience is heightened by entering and lingering in a grand, proper lobby, look elsewhere.

⚙ **Hotel Halcyon.** 649 Jones St. (between Geary and Post sts.), San Francisco, CA 94102. ☎ **800/627-2396** or 415/929-8033. Fax 415/441-8033. www.bradyacres.com. 25 units. TV TEL. $75–$95 double per day May–Sept with special weekly rates. Available only by the week Oct–Apr; special weekly rates. MC, V. Parking garage nearby for $14–$16 per day. Bus: 2, 3, 4, 27, or 38.

Inside this small, four-story brick building is a penny-pincher's dream come true, the kind of place where you'll find everything you need, yet won't have to pay through the nose to get it. The small but very clean rooms have all been newly renovated and are equipped with microwave ovens, small refrigerators, toasters, and coffeemakers; hair dryers and alarm clocks; phones (with free local calls) and answering machines; color cable TVs and radio/cassette players. The bathrooms were recently renovated as well, and a coin-operated washer and dryer are located in the basement, along with free laundry soap and irons. The owners are usually on hand to offer friendly, personal service, making this option all in all an unbeatable deal. Be sure to ask about special rates for weekly stays.

**Monticello Inn.** 127 Ellis St. (between Mason and Powell sts.), San Francisco, CA 94102. ☎ **800/669-7777** or 415/392-8800. Fax 415/398-2650. 91 units. A/C MINIBAR TV TEL. From $125–$185 double; from $155–$240 suite. Rates include continental breakfast, coffee and tea in the lobby, and evening wine. Extra person $15. AE, CB, DC, DISC, MC, V. Valet parking $18. Cable car: Powell-Hyde and Powell-Mason lines (direct stop). Muni Metro: All Market St. metros. Bus: All Market St. buses.

Okay, we'll admit it: We didn't know Monticello was the estate of Thomas Jefferson, and we also didn't know that the Monticello mansion is on the tail side of the nickel (Tom's noggin is on the front.) Why the history lesson? In addition to the moniker, "Monticello" is also the hotel's theme. Federal-style decor, Chippendale furnishings, grandfather clocks, Revolutionary War paintings, a toasty, brass-mantled fireplace, and various other old stuff scattered around the lobby in an attempt to create a colonial milieu. Though it makes for a pleasant entrance, unfortunately the period effect doesn't quite follow through to the rooms. Though the rooms are comfortable, spacious, and reasonably attractive, the stark blue carpets and floral upholstery don't have the same faux-Federal theme (certainly the homely air conditioners recessed into the walls don't help). If you can live with this, however, you'll be quite content here, especially considering the little extras—bathrobes, umbrellas, voice mail, modem/data port, Nintendo, and a morning ride to the Financial District. The service is wonderful, the downtown location is primo, parking comes with in-out privileges, and there's even access to a great fitness club around the block (for a $15 fee).

The hotel's restaurant, Puccini & Pinetti, features modern Italian cuisine; it's located next door, at the corner of Ellis and Cyril Magnin streets.

**Nob Hill Hotel.** 835 Hyde St. (between Bush and Sutter sts.), San Francisco, CA 94109. ☎ **877/NOBHILL** or 415/885-2987. Fax 415/921-1648. www.nobhillhotel.com. 53 units. TV TEL. $125–$300 double. Rates include continental breakfast. AE, DISC, MC, V. Bus: 2, 3, or 4.

If you can scrape together $125 for the tariff, the Nob Hill Hotel is actually quite an amazing deal for such a ritzy environment. Whoever renovated the lobby—it used to be real dumpy—did a smashing job restoring it to its original "Old San Francisco" splendor. Though the rooms are somewhat small, they are all handsomely decorated with old-fashioned furnishings such as Victorian antique armoires, marble bathrooms,

# Accommodations with Free Parking

Despite our exhortations to leave the driving to locals and use the public transportation system to get around, we know that some of you will still want to drive the crazy streets of San Francisco. But with parking fees averaging $20 a night at most hotels (talk about a monopoly), the extra charges can really add up for visitors with wheels. So if you're going to rent a car or bring your own, you might want to consider staying at one of the following affordable choices, which all offer free parking (some even offer free covered parking):

- **Bay Bridge Inn,** 966 Harrison St., between 5th and 6th streets (☎ **415/397-0657**). *See page 75.*
- **Beck's Motor Lodge,** 2222 Market St., at 15th Street (☎ **800/227-4360** or 415/621-8212). *See page 90.*
- **Bel Aire Travelodge,** 3201 Steiner St., at Greenwich Street (☎ **800/280-3242** or 415/921-5162). *See page 80.*
- **Chelsea Motor Inn,** 2095 Lombard St., between Fillmore and Webster streets (☎ **415/563-5600**). *See page 81.*
- **Cow Hollow Motor Inn & Suites,** 2190 Lombard St., between Steiner and Fillmore streets (☎ **415/921-5800**). *See page 81.*
- **Dolores Park Inn,** 3641 17th St. (☎ **415/621-0482**). *See page 90.*
- **Fort Mason Youth Hostel,** Building 240, Fort Mason (☎ **415/771-7277**). *See page 83.*
- **Lombard Motor Inn,** 1475 Lombard St., at Franklin Street (☎ **800/835-3639** or 415/441-6000). *See page 81.*
- **Marina Motel,** 2576 Lombard St., between Divisadero and Broderick streets (☎ **800/346-6118** or 415/921-9406). *See page 82.*
- **Motel Capri,** 2015 Greenwich St., at Buchanan Street (☎ **415/346-4667**). *See page 82.*
- **Phoenix Hotel,** 601 Eddy St., at Larkin St. (☎ **800/248-9466** or 415/776-1380). *See page 87.*
- **Seal Rock Inn,** 545 Point Lobos Ave., at 48th Avenue (☎ **415/752-8000**). *See page 89.*
- **Vagabond,** 2550 Van Ness Ave., at Filbert Street (☎ **800/522-1555** or 415/776-7500). *See page 83.*
- **The Wharf Inn,** 2601 Mason St., at Beach Street (☎ **800/548-9918** or 415/673-7411). *See page 77.*

brass beds with comforters, and carved-wood nightstands. A pleasant oxymoron: All the rooms are also equipped with such high-tech amenities as microwaves, DSL (high-speed Internet) lines, personal voice mail, and copy, fax, and e-mail services. Complimentary pastries and coffee are served each morning, and there's even free evening wine tasting. The adjacent La Capella restaurant is a good place to refuel on fine Italian food before venturing down the street to Union Square. Parking and complimentary 24-hour Nautilus machines are also available.

✪ **Nob Hill Inn.** 1000 Pine St. (at Taylor St.), San Francisco, CA 94109. ☎ **415/673-6080.** Fax 415/673-6098. 21 units. TV TEL. $99–$169 double; $219–$249 suite. Rates include afternoon tea/sherry. AE, CB, DC, DISC, MC, V. Cable car: California St. line. Bus: 1.

Though most of the rooms at the luxurious Nob Hill Inn are well out of budget range, their three "Gramercy" rooms are among the most opulent you will find in the city for under $100. Built in 1907 as a private home, the four-story inn has been masterfully refurbished with Louis XV antiques, expensive fabrics, museum-quality artwork, and a magnificent etched-glass European-style lift. Yet even their lowest priced rooms are given equal attention: large bathrooms with marble sinks and clawfoot tubs, antique furnishings, faux-antique phones and discreetly placed televisions, a comfortable full-size bed, and pin-drop silence. Granted, the Gramercy rooms are small, but so utterly charming that it's difficult to complain, especially when you consider that it comes with complimentary afternoon tea and sherry, nightly turndown service, and the distinction of being among the city's most prestigious hotels.

**Pensione International.** 875 Post St. (at Hyde St.), San Francisco, CA 94109. ☎ **415/775-3344.** 46 units. TV TEL. $75 without bathroom, $90 with bathroom. Rates include continental breakfast. AE, MC, V. Bus: 2, 3, or 4.

Fashion is given a backseat to low rates at this European-style hotel located 5 blocks west of Union Square. Though the rooms are oddly decorated, they're all outfitted with the standard amenities, including phones, TVs, double beds, a small dresser, and a closet; the rooms with baths also come with a small refrigerator. If you can get past the mismatched furniture and mosaic of mixed carpets, you're bound to admit that this isn't a bad deal for $75 (or $90 if you abhor the thought of sharing a shower with strangers). The hotel caters mostly to foreign travelers, and though the minimally trained staff isn't exactly at the forefront of hotel hospitality, they're a friendly bunch nonetheless.

✪ **Petite Auberge.** 863 Bush St. (between Taylor and Mason sts.), San Francisco, CA 94108. ☎ **415/928-6000.** Fax 415/775-5717. 26 units. TV TEL. $120–$175 double; $245 petite suite. Rates include full breakfast. AE, DC, MC, V. Parking $19. Cable car: Powell-Hyde and Powell-Mason lines. Bus: 2, 3, 4, 30, 38, or 45.

The Petite Auberge is so cute we can't stand it. We want to say it's overdone, that any hotel that's filled with teddy bears is absurd, but we can't. Bribed each year with fresh-baked cookies from their never-empty platter, we make our rounds through the rooms and ruefully admit to ourselves that we're just going to have to use that word we loath to hear: adorable. Nobody does French country like the Petite Auberge. Handcrafted armoires, delicate lace curtains, cozy little fireplaces, adorable (there's that word again) little antiques and knickknacks—no hotel in Provence ever had it this good. Honeymooners should splurge on the Petite suite, which has its own private entrance, deck, spa tub, refrigerator, and coffeemaker. The breakfast room, with its mural of a country market scene, terra-cotta tile floors, French-country decor, and gold-yellow tablecloths, opens onto a small garden. There are complimentary California wines, tea, and hors d'oeuvres served each afternoon.

**Savoy Hotel.** 580 Geary St. (between Taylor and Jones sts.), San Francisco, CA 94102. ☎ **800/227-4223** or 415/441-2700. Fax 415/441-0124. 83 units. MINIBAR TV TEL. $115–$145 double; from $205 suite. Ask about package, government, senior, and corporate rates. AE, CB, DC, DISC, MC, V. Parking $18. Bus: 2, 3, 4, 27, or 38.

When the Savoy opened, it was deemed by travelers and *Travel & Leisure* as one of the sweetest affordable options off Union Square. While that's still the case, unfortunately the hotel hasn't kept up with the wear and tear associated with brisk business. However, rooms, which can be small, are still cozy French provincial, with 18th-century period furnishings, featherbeds, and goose-down pillows—plus modern conveniences such as hair dryers and remote-control color TVs. Not all rooms are alike, but each has beautiful patterned draperies, triple sheets, turndown service, full-length mirrors, and two-line telephones. Guests also enjoy concierge service and overnight shoeshine free of charge. Rates include late-afternoon cookies, sherry, and tea, served in the Brasserie Savoy, an excellent seafood restaurant.

**The Shannon Court.** 550 Geary St. (between Jones and Taylor sts.), San Francisco, CA 94102. ☎ **800/228-8830** or 415/775-5000. Fax 415/928-6813. 173 units. TV TEL. $129–$159 double or twin; from $350 suite. Extra person $15. Continental breakfast $9.75, full breakfast $14. Senior, government, AAA, group, and promotional rates available. AE, CB, DC, MC, V. Valet parking $18. Cable car: Powell-Hyde and Powell-Mason lines (3 blocks east). Bus: 2, 3, 4, 30, 38, or 45.

Spacious rooms rarely come as cheaply as they do here, but you'll be trading a little ambiance for the few dollars you save. The Shannon Court's 1929 landmark building maintains some of its original Spanish flavor, with gracefully curved arches, white stucco walls, and brass fixtures in the lobby. When you head off for your room, however, the cheery atmosphere disappears in the dark, cold hallways. But don't turn and head for the nearest motel yet. You'll be pleasantly surprised at how large, quiet (especially in the back portion of the building), and sunny the rooms are. Because all the rooms' carpeting, bedspreads, and drapes were replaced in 1997, rooms are looking especially dapper, and most have either a sitting area or an extended bathroom. Extras include a small, unstocked fridge, voice mail, data ports, Nintendo, and many rooms have couches and writing desks. The hotel's five suites are on the 16th floor; two have rooftop terraces. Regardless of the upkeep, the building is almost 70 years old, so expect to see some age. Complimentary morning coffee and afternoon tea are available in the lobby. The City of Paris restaurant, which is popular with the theater crowd, adjoins the hotel and is open daily for breakfast, lunch, and dinner; aside from decent fare at affordable prices, there's also an oyster bar, a good wine list, and a full bar that remains open until 2am.

**The Sheehan.** 620 Sutter St. (near Mason St.), San Francisco, CA 94102. ☎ **800/848-1529** or 415/775-6500. Fax 415/775-3271. www.citysearch.com/sfo/sheehanhotel. 65 units; 3 without bathroom. TV TEL. $89–$99 double without bathroom, $99–$149 double with bathroom. Rates include continental breakfast. AE, DISC, MC, V. Parking $16. Cable car: Powell-Hyde and Powell-Mason lines (2 blocks east). Bus: 2, 3, 4, 30, 38, or 45.

Formerly a YWCA hotel, the Sheehan is dirt cheap considering its location 2 blocks from Union Square. Of course, this isn't the Ritz—some walls could use a little paint and there are plenty of areas that would benefit from a little TLC, but ask for one of the remodeled rooms and you'll do just fine. The clean rooms are simply furnished and come with cable TV, and the bathrooms are brand new and include hair dryers. The hotel has a clean, pleasant lobby and an indoor, heated lap pool and workout area.

**☺ Stratford Hotel.** 242 Powell St. (between Geary and O'Farrell sts.), San Francisco, CA 94102. ☎ **888/50-HOTEL** or 415/397-7080. Fax 415/397-7087. 105 units. TV TEL. $105–$109 double. Rates include continental breakfast. AE, CB, DC, DISC, MC, V. Garage parking nearby. BART: Powell. Cable car: Powell-Hyde line. Bus: 2, 3, 4, 27, 30, 38, 76, and all Market St. buses and Muni Metros.

Renovation fever has hit the ever-touristy downtown, and the Stratford is the latest to get the bug. Until now, no one ever noticed there are actually hotels along the noisiest, most densely-tourist-populated section of Union Square. But the Stratford's colorful facelift is turning eyes—and hotel reservations—to the southern corner of the area. The resurrection of this large 1907 building includes the addition of colorfully painted hallways and rooms with new carpeting, textiles,

TVs, and cheery bedspreads (which currently hide old, scratchy motel blankets). Accommodations vary tremendously, so be sure and request what you want; some can be small, some dark; those that face Powell have more noise (clanging cable cars are far less cute when you're trying to sleep).

**Villa Florence.** 225 Powell St. (between Geary and O'Farrell sts.), San Francisco, CA 94102. ☎ **800/553-4411** or 415/397-7700. Fax 415/397-1006. 183 units. A/C MINIBAR TV TEL. $115–$185 double; $165–$225 studio king. AE, CB, DC, DISC, MC, V. Valet parking $24. Cable car: Powell-Hyde and Powell-Mason lines (direct stop). Bus: 2, 3, 4, 30, 38, or 45.

Located half a block south of Union Square and fronting the Powell Street cable car line, the seven-story Villa Florence is parked in one of the liveliest sections of the city (no need to drive, 'cause you're already here). A recent—and sorely needed–renovation has brightened up the rooms considerably. Essentially it's a lower-end replica of the spectacular rooms at the Hotel Monaco (which is owned by the same company), with lots of bold stripes and vibrant colors. You'll like the large, comfortable bed and the bathroom equipped with hand-milled soap and hair dryers. But never mind the rooms: It's the hotel's restaurant that makes it a worthy contender among Union Square's medium-priced inns. As if the location alone weren't reason enough to book a room.

   **Dining/Diversions:** Adjoining the hotel is Kuleto's, one of San Francisco's most popular and stylish Italian restaurants (trust us, you'll want to make a reservation for dinner along with your room). See chapter 6, "Great Deals on Dining," for complete information.

**York Hotel.** 940 Sutter St. (between Hyde and Leavenworth sts.), San Francisco, CA 94109. ☎ **415/885-6800.** Fax 415/885-2115. 96 units, 5 suites. MINIBAR TV TEL. $129–$220 double. Rates include continental breakfast. Extra person $15. AE, DC, DISC, MC, V. Valet parking $16. Bus: 2, 3, or 4.

If this place gives you a sense of déjà vu, it's because this hotel is where Kim Novak stayed in the Alfred Hitchcock classic *Vertigo.* Of course that was a long time ago; things have changed some. Though far from glamorous, the York's rooms are clean and basic, and provide a few extra amenities, such as in-room coffeemakers, walk-in closets, and voice mail. The hotel has a fitness center and a bar, but its most charming feature is the Plush Room, a small cabaret theater where you might catch some of San Francisco's finest talent.

## SUPER-CHEAP SLEEPS

**AYH Hostel at Union Square.** 312 Mason St. (between Geary and O'Farrell sts.), San Francisco, CA 94102. ☎ **415/788-5604.** Fax 415/788-3023. 260 beds. $17–$19 for hosteling members, $20–$22 for non-members. Half price for children under 12 when accompanied by a parent. Maximum stay 14 nights per year. MC, V. No parking on premises. A public parking lot on Mission between 4th and 5th sts. charges $12 per 24-hr. period. Cable car: Powell-Mason line. Bus: 7B or 38.

For around $20 per night you can relive college-dorm life in an old San Francisco–style building right in the heart of Union Square. Occupying five sparsely decorated floors, rooms here are simple and clean, each with two or three bunk beds, its own sink, and a closet; best of all, you can lock your door and take the key with you. Although private rooms share hallway bathrooms, a few have private facilities. Suite rooms are reserved for families. Freshly painted hallways are adorned with laminated posters, and there are several common rooms, including a reading room, a smoking room, and a large kitchen with lots of tables, chairs, and refrigerator space. There are laundry facilities nearby, and a helpful information desk offering tour reservations and sightseeing trips. The hostel is open 24 hours, and reservations are essential during the summer. Persons under 18 may not stay without a parent unless they have a notarized letter, and then they must pay the adult rate.

## WORTH A SPLURGE

**Hotel Rex.** 562 Sutter St. (between Powell and Mason sts.), San Francisco, CA 94102. ☎ **800/433-4434** or 415/433-4434. Fax 415/433-3695. 94 units. MINIBAR TV TEL. $155–$295 double; $575 suite. AE, CB, DC, MC, V. Self parking $19, valet parking $25. Cable car: Powell-Hyde and Powell-Mason lines (1 block east). Bus: 2, 3, 4, 30, 38, or 45.

Joie de Vivre, the most creative hotel group in the city, recently acquired this historic building (formerly the Orchard Hotel), which is situated near several fine galleries, theaters, and restaurants. They've kept some of the hotel's imported furnishings the European boutique hotel ambiance, but they gave the lobby and rooms a $2-million facelift, adding a decorative flair that makes their hotels among the most popular in town. The clublike lobby lounge is modeled after a 1920s library and is, like all their properties, cleverly stylish. Joie de Vivre is positioning the Rex as a hotel for the arts and literary community (not unlike the Algonquin Hotel in New York City), and in that spirit an antiquarian bookstore adjoins the lobby. The renovated rooms, which are all above average in size, feature two-line telephones with voice mail and data port, CD players, and a new electronic key-card system. If you have one of the rooms in the back, you'll look out over a shady, peaceful courtyard (that's something you won't get in New York City). Attention to the details makes Hotel Rex one of the better choices in this price range downtown.

**Amenities:** Concierge, room service, same-day laundry/dry cleaning, complimentary newspaper, coffee, evening wine hour, and morning car service to the Financial District.

✪ **The Maxwell.** 386 Geary St. (at Mason St.), San Francisco, CA 94102. ☎ **888/734-6299** or 415/986-2000. Fax 415/397-2447. 153 units. A/C TV TEL. $155–$215 double; $295–$595 suite. $15 extra person. Corporate discounts available. AE, CB, DC, DISC, MC, V. Parking $18. Cable car: Powell-Hyde and Powell-Mason lines (1 block east). Bus: 2, 3, 4, 30, 38, or 45.

What was once an old, somewhat rundown hotel in an excellent location (1 block from Union Square) is now an incredibly chic-boutique experience that was created in 1997. Rooms blend velvets, brocades, stripes, plaids, rich color, and handcrafted artistic accents into what the management calls "Theatre deco" fused with Victorian decor (a sort of smoking club/study atmosphere). Ambers, reds, greens, and browns dominate the color scheme, and rooms come with upholstered chairs, hand-painted bedside lamps, luxurious pillows, boldly tiled sinks, and respectable prints hanging on the walls. Other plusses are writing desks, hair dryers, iron and ironing boards, Nintendo, three phones, and data ports. The suites, which are more like rich personal penthouse apartments, are some of the most stunning in town; unfortunately, from their location you can hear the old elevator kick into gear every time it's beckoned.

**Dining:** Adjoining Max's On The Square Restaurant looks great but its American fare and service are nothing to write home about. It does, however, do the trick if you're looking for a decent bite.

**Services:** Limited room service, concierge, meeting facilities.

✪ **White Swan Inn.** 845 Bush St. (between Taylor and Mason sts.), San Francisco, CA 94108. ☎ **800/999-9570** or 415/775-1755. Fax 415/775-5717. 26 units. MINIBAR TV TEL. $165–$185 double; $195 romance suite; $250 2-room suite. $15 extra person. Rates include full breakfast and afternoon wine and hors d'oeuvres. AE, DC, MC, V. Parking $20. Cable car: California St. line (1 block north). Bus: 1, 2, 3, 4, 27, or 45.

From the moment you are buzzed in to this well-secured inn, you'll know you're not in a generic bed-and-breakfast. Close to 50 teddy bears grace the lobby, and if that doesn't cure homesickness, complimentary homemade cookies, tea, and coffee will. The romantically homey rooms are warm and cozy—the perfect place to snuggle up with a good book. They're also quite big, with hardwood entryways, rich, darkwood furniture, working fireplaces, and an assortment of books tucked in nooks (in case you forgot one). The decor is English elegance at its best, if not to excess, with floral prints almost everywhere. Wine and hors d'oeuvres are served every evening. The Romance suites are not much better than regular rooms, just a little bigger with the addition of chocolates, champagne, and a VCR. Its location—2½ blocks from Union Square—makes this 1900s building a charming and serene choice with service and style the most discriminating traveler.

**Dining:** Each morning a generous breakfast is served in a common room just off a tiny garden. Afternoon tea is also served, with hors d'oeuvres, sherry, wine, and home-baked pastries. You can have your sherry in front of the fireplace while you browse through the books in the library. Note that there's no smoking.

**Amenities:** Concierge, laundry, overnight shoe shine, morning newspaper, evening turndown. Guests have access to an off-premises health club for an extra $15 per day.

## 2 South of Market (SoMa)

**Bay Bridge Inn.** 966 Harrison St. (between 5th and 6th sts.), San Francisco, CA 94107. ☎ **415/397-0657.** Fax 415/495-5117. 22 units. TV TEL. $89 double. AE, CB, DC, DISC, MC, V. Free parking. Bus: 10, 20, 30, 42, 45, 50, 60, 70, or 80.

The South of Market region is woefully short on budget hotels, which is why we give the Bay Bridge Inn only a nominal recommendation. The only reason you might want to stay in this part of town is if you're here for a convention (the Moscone Convention Center is 2½ blocks away), or you're a serious party hound who prefers to stay within stumbling distance of SoMa's club scene. The rooms score zero points for character, but they're quite clean and in very good condition. Queen-size beds are standard, and rooms with king-size beds run an extra $20. Parking is free (though it's not too congested around here anyway), and buses to nearly every corner of the city depart from the nearby Transbay Terminal.

### WORTH A SPLURGE

**Harbor Court.** 165 Steuart St. (between Mission and Howard sts.), San Francisco, CA 94105. ☎ **800/346-0555** in the U.S., or 415/882-1300. Fax 415/882-1313. 131 units. A/C MINIBAR TV TEL. $175–$325 double. Continental breakfast $8 extra. AE, CB, DC, MC, V. Parking $24. Muni Metro: Embarcadero. Bus: 14, 32, or 80x.

When the Embarcadero Freeway was torn down after the Big One in 1989, a major benefactor was the Harbor Court hotel; its backyard view went from a wall of cement to a dazzling view of the Bay Bridge (be sure to request a bay-view room, which is $50 extra). Located just off the Embarcadero at the edge of the Financial District, this former YMCA books a lot of corporate travelers, but anyone who prefers stylish, high-quality accommodations—half-canopy beds, large armoires, writing desks, soundproof windows—with a superb view and lively scene will be perfectly content here. A major bonus for health nuts is the free use of the adjoining top-quality fitness club with indoor, Olympic-size swimming pool.

**Dining:** In the evening, the hotel's dark, velvety restaurant, Harry Denton's, transforms into the Financial District's hot spot for hungry singles.

**Amenities:** Concierge, limited room service, dry cleaning, laundry, secretarial services, newspaper delivery, express checkout, excellent fitness club, valet, courtesy car, free refreshments in lobby.

# 3 Chinatown

**Grant Plaza Hotel.** 465 Grant Ave. (at the corner of Pine St.), San Francisco, CA 94108. ☎ **800/472-6899** or 415/434-3883. Fax 415/434-3886. E-mail: grantplaza@worldnet. att.net. 72 units. TV TEL. $62–$89 double. AE, CB, DC, MC, V. Nearby parking $11.50. Cable car: Powell-Hyde and Powell-Mason lines (2 blocks west).

You won't find any free little bottles of shampoo here. What you will find are cheap accommodations and basic—and we mean basic—rooms right in the middle of Union Square/Chinatown action. Many of the small, well-kept rooms in this six-story building overlook Chinatown's main street, and all of them had new bed-spreads, draperies, and hair dryers added in 1997. The downside is the minuscule bathrooms and small shower (most don't have tubs). Corner rooms on higher floors are both larger and brighter. Ask for a room on the top floor—they're the newest and are substantially nicer than the older rooms.

**Temple Hotel.** 469 Pine St. (at Kearny St.), San Francisco, CA 94104. ☎ **415/781-2565.** 88 units. TV. $57 double without bathroom, $67 double with bathroom. No credit cards. BART: Montgomery. Bus: 2, 3, 4, 9X, 15, 30, 45, and all Market St. buses and Muni Metros.

Ignore the unimpressive entrance and the receptionist behind glass and prepare yourself for super-funky decor. Now you're ready to appreciate some of the best ultra-cheap rooms in the entire downtown area. The archaic elevator, the old-fashioned kind with the double doors you pull closed yourself, leads to dark rooms containing a well-polished dresser and bedside tables, decorative tchotchkes straight out of the 1970s, ancient TVs, and groovy 1960s brown carpeting. Beds are a bit hard, but the clawfoot tubs add charm to the bathrooms. The shared showers are sparse and old, but very, very clean. While you're only a few blocks from Union Square, you're steps away from hoppin' Belden Lane and the martini-and-cigar Occidental Grill restaurant. It ain't heaven, but for $57 for downtown digs it doesn't get much better than this.

# 4 North Beach/Fisherman's Wharf

✪ **Hotel Bohème.** 444 Columbus St., (between Vallejo and Green sts.), San Francisco, CA 94133. ☎ **415/433-9111.** Fax 415/362-6292. 15 units. TV TEL. $139 double. AE, CB, DISC, DC, JCB, MC, V. Parking $23 at nearby public garage. Cable car: Powell-Mason line. Bus: 12, 15, 30, 41, 45, or 83.

North Beach romance awaits you at the Bohème. Although located on the busiest strip in North Beach, this recently renovated hotel's style and demeanor are more reminiscent of a prestigious home in upscale Nob Hill. The decor is reminiscent of the beat generation, which flourished here in the 1950s; rooms are small but hope-lessly romantic, with gauze-draped canopies and walls artistically accented with lavender, sage green, black, and pumpkin. The staff is ultra hospitable, and bonuses include hair dryers and complimentary sherry in the lobby each afternoon. Outside the front door, it's a few steps to some of the greatest cafes, restaurants, bars, and shops in the city, and Chinatown and Union Square are within walking distance. *Take note:* While the bathrooms are sweet, they're also absolutely tiny. *Tip:* Request a room off the street side; they're quieter.

**☉ San Remo Hotel.** 2237 Mason St. (at Chestnut St.) San Francisco, CA 94133. ☎ **800/ 352-REMO** or 415/776-8688. Fax 415/776-2811. www.sanremohotel.com. E-mail: info@ sanremohotel.com. 63 units, 1 with bathroom. $60–$85 double; $125 suite. AE, CB, DC, JCB, MC, V. Parking $10–$12. Cable car: Powell-Mason line. Bus: 15, 22, 30, or 42.

This small, European-style *pensione* is one of the best budget hotels in San Francisco. Located in a quiet North Beach neighborhood and within walking distance of Fisherman's Wharf, the San Remo originally served as a boardinghouse for dockworkers displaced by the great fire of 1906. As a result, the rooms are small and bathrooms are shared, but all is forgiven when it comes time to pay the bill. Rooms are decorated in a cozy country style with brass and iron beds, oak, maple or pine armoires, and wicker furnishings; most have ceiling fans. The shared bathrooms, each one immaculately clean, feature clawfoot tubs and brass pull-chain toilets with oak tanks and brass fixtures. If the penthouse is available, book it: You won't find a more romantic place to stay in San Francisco for so little money (it's got it's own bathroom, TV, fridge, and patio).

**Washington Square Inn.** 1660 Stockton St. (between Filbert and Union sts.), San Francisco, CA 94133. ☎ **800/388-0220** or 415/981-4220. Fax 415/397-7242. 15 units, 2 with bathroom across from the rm. TV TEL. $125–$210 double. Rates include continental breakfast. AE, CB, DC, DISC, MC, V. Valet parking $20. Bus: 15, 30, 41, or 45.

Reminiscent of a traditional English inn right down to the cucumber sandwiches served during the afternoon tea, wine-and-cheese hour, this small, comely bed-and-breakfast is ideal for older couples who prefer a more quiet, subdued environment than the commotion of downtown San Francisco. It's located across from Washington Square in the North Beach District—a coffee addict's haven—and within walking distance of Fisherman's Wharf and Chinatown. Each room is decorated in English floral fabrics with quality European antique furnishings and plenty of fresh flowers; all have private bathrooms and data ports. A continental breakfast is included, as are afternoon tea, wine, and hors d'oeuvres. Fax and VCRs are available upon request.

**The Wharf Inn.** 2601 Mason St. (at Beach St.), San Francisco, CA 94133. ☎ **800/ 548-9918** or 415/673-7411. Fax 415/776-2181. 51 units. TV TEL. $98–$165 double; penthouse $270–$370. AE, CB, DC, DISC, MC, V. Free parking. Cable car: Powell-Mason. Bus: 15, 32, or 42.

Our top choice for budget lodging at Fisherman's Wharf, The Wharf Inn offers above-average accommodations amidst one of the most popular tourist attractions in the world. The recently refurbished rooms, done in handsome tones of forest green, burgundy, and pale yellow, come with all the standard amenities, including complimentary coffee and tea. Its main attribute, however, is its location—right smack dab in the middle of the wharf, 2 blocks away from Pier 39 and the cable-car turnaround, and within walking distance of the Embarcadero and North Beach. The inn is ideal for car-bound families because parking is free (there's $25-a-day saved) and there's no charge for packing along an extra person.

## WORTH A SPLURGE

**Tuscan Inn.** 425 North Point St. (at Mason St.), San Francisco, CA 94133. ☎ **800/ 648-4626** or 415/561-1100. Fax 415/561-1199. 221 units. A/C MINIBAR TV TEL. $148–$218 double; $188–$268 suite. Rates include coffee, tea, and evening fireside wine reception. AE, DC, DISC, MC, V. Parking $18. Cable car: Powell-Mason line. Bus: 42, 15, or 32.

The Tuscan Inn is, in our opinion, the best hotel at Fisherman's Wharf. Like an island of respectability in a sea of touristy schlock, the Tuscan exudes a level of style

# Accommodations Around Town

Abigail Hotel **8**
Archbishop's Mansion **30**
Art Center Bed & Breakfast **16**
Bay Bridge Inn **7**
Beck's Motor Lodge **35**
Bed & Breakfast Inn **17**
Bel Aire Travelodge **21**
Best Western Miyako Inn **27**
Castillo Inn **33**
Chelsea Motor Inn **20**
Cow Hollow Motor Inn & Suites **20**
Dolores Park Inn **38**
Edward II Inn & Pub **22**
Fort Mason Youth Hostel **15**
Harbor Court **6**
Herb 'n Inn **39**
Hotel Bohème **5**
Hotel Majestic **28**
Inn on Castro **36**
Jackson Court **25**
Lombard Motor Inn **13**
Marina Inn **14**
Marina Motel **23**
The Metro Hotel **31**
Monte Cristo **26**
Motel Capri **18**
Nob Hill Motel **11**
Parker House **36**
Pensione San Francisco **32**
Phoenix Hotel **10**
Queen Anne Hotel **28**
Red Victorian Bed, Breakfast & Art **40**
San Francisco Central YMCA Hotel **9**
San Remo Hotel **3**
Seal Rock Inn **29**      **2**
Stanyan Park Hotel **40**
Tuscan Inn **41**
24 Henry **34**
Union Street Inn **24**
Vagabond Inn **12**
Washington Square Inn **4**
The Wharf Inn **1**
The Willows Bed & Breakfast Inn **34**

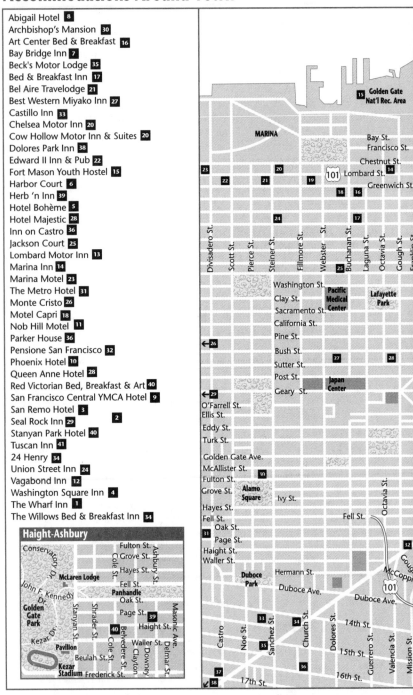

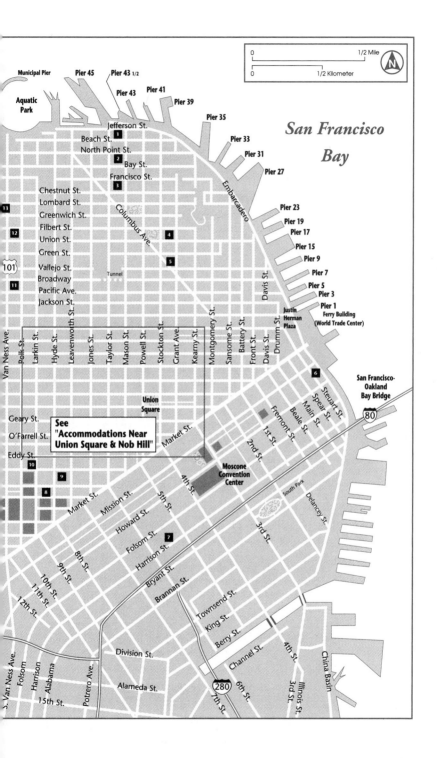

Municipal Pier    Pier 45    Pier 43 1/2
                              Pier 43        Pier 41
Aquatic                                              Pier 39
Park                                                        Pier 35
                    Jefferson St.                                  Pier 33
              Beach St.                                      Pier 31
          North Point St.                                 Pier 27
                    Bay St.
              Francisco St.                                     Pier 23
      Chestnut St.                                        Pier 19
      Lombard St.                                         Pier 17
      Greenwich St.                                       Pier 15
      Filbert St.                                         Pier 9
      Union St.                                           Pier 7
      Green St.                                           Pier 5
      Vallejo St.                        Tunnel          Pier 3
      Broadway                                           Pier 1
      Pacific Ave.                                      Ferry Building
      Jackson St.                                       (World Trade Center)

San Francisco
Bay

Columbus Ave.
Embarcadero
Davis St.

Van Ness Ave.
Polk St.
Larkin St.
Hyde St.
Leavenworth St.
Jones St.
Taylor St.
Mason St.
Powell St.
Stockton St.
Grant Ave.
Kearny St.
Montgomery St.
Sansome St.
Battery St.
Front St.
Davis St.
Drumm St.

Justin
Herman
Plaza

San Francisco-
Oakland
Bay Bridge

Union
Square

Geary St.

See
"Accommodations Near
Union Square & Nob Hill"

O'Farrell St.

Market St.

Eddy St.

Steuart St.
Spear St.
Main St.
Beale St.
Fremont St.
1st St.

Moscone
Convention
Center

Market St.

Mission St.
Howard St.
Folsom St.
Harrison St.

4th St.
5th St.
2nd St.
3rd St.

South Park

Delancey St.

8th St.
9th St.
10th St.
11th St.
12th St.

Bryant St.
Brannan St.

Townsend St.

King St.

Berry St.

4th St.
China Basin

S. Van Ness Ave.
Folsom
Harrison
Alabama

Potrero Ave.

Division St.

Channel St.

6th St.
7th St.
Illinois St.
3rd St.

Alameda St.

15th St.

0    1/2 Mile
0    1/2 Kilometer

N

79

and comfort far beyond its neighboring competitors. Splurge on parking—cheaper than the wharf's outrageously priced garages—then saunter your way toward the plush lobby warmed by a grand fireplace. Even the rooms, each equipped with writing desks and armchairs, are a definite cut above competing Fisherman's Wharf hotels. The only caveat is the lack of scenic views; a small price to pay for a good hotel in a great location.

**Dining:** The adjoining Cafe Pescatore, open for breakfast, lunch, and dinner, serves standard Italian fare in an airy, partial alfresco setting. (See chapter 6, "Great Deals on Dining," for complete information.)

**Amenities:** Concierge, room service, laundry service

## 5 Marina District/Cow Hollow

**Art Center Bed & Breakfast.** 1902 Filbert St. (at Laguna St.), San Francisco, CA 94123. ☎ **415/567-1526.** 4 units, 1 suite. $105–$125 double; $145 suite. Rates include continental breakfast. AE, DISC, MC, V. Bus: 28, 43, or 76.

If there was ever an antithesis to the chain motel, this is it. Decorated with a bewildering array of original artwork—ranging from oil paintings and pastels to sculptures and model ships—this 1857 French provincial residence is one of the more unusual places to stay in San Francisco. It's like staying in some eclectic artist's home, where everything from breakfast to books and phone messages is shared by all. Granted, there's a bit of hippie-era funk to the place, but the overall esprit de corps is contagiously pleasing. There are only five units, ranging from a three-room suite with a full kitchen and hide-a-bed in the living room to our favorite, the Gaviota—a large, sunny studio with its own private entry, two beds, a Jacuzzi tub, and a soothing mural of the bay painted on the wall. A no-host breakfast is served in the communal kitchen, which is connected by a plant-filled atrium to a small, sunny back porch. The Cow Hollow neighborhood is quiet and safe, and within walking distance of numerous restaurants, shops, and galleries.

✪ **Bed & Breakfast Inn.** 4 Charlton Court (off Union St., between Buchanan and Laguna sts.), San Francisco, CA 94123. ☎ **415/921-9784.** Fax 415/921-0544. 13 units, 4 with shared bathroom. $80–$100 double without bathroom; $150 double with bathroom; $250–$300 suite. Rates include continental breakfast. AE, CB, DC, DISC, MC, V. Parking $11 a day at nearby garage. Bus: 41 or 45.

San Francisco's first bed-and-breakfast is composed of a trio of Victorian houses all gussied up in "English country" style, hidden in a cul-de-sac just off Union Street. While it doesn't have quite the casual ambiance of the neighboring Union Street Inn, the Bed & Breakfast Inn is loaded with charm. Each room is uniquely decorated with family antiques, original art, and a profusion of fresh flowers. The Garden Suite—highly recommended for families or groups of four—comes with a fully stocked kitchen, a living room with fireplace, two bedrooms, two bathrooms (one with a Jacuzzi tub), a study, and French doors leading out into the sun room and garden. Breakfast (freshly baked croissants; fresh fruit; orange juice; and coffee, tea, or cocoa) is either brought to your room on a tray with flowers and a morning newspaper, or served in a sunny Victorian breakfast room with antique china.

**Bel Aire Travelodge.** 3201 Steiner St. (at Greenwich St.), San Francisco, CA 94123. ☎ **800/280-3242** or 415/921-5162. Fax 415/921-3602. 32 units. TV TEL. $96–$103 double. AE, CB, DC, DISC, MC, V. Bus: 28, 43, or 76.

What separates this Travelodge from all the rest is its superb location. It's in the heart of Cow Hollow, one of San Francisco's safest and most schlock-free districts, with many of our favorite restaurants and shops (if you hate Fisherman's Wharf, you'll like Cow Hollow). Okay, so the salmon-pink and copper paint scheme is a bit grandma-ish. But just as you'd expect from a Travelodge, everything works; the rooms are spotless, and the prices are very reasonable—particularly when you factor in the free parking, free local phone calls, free morning newspaper, and free shuttle service from SFO. Character? Not a drop. Class? Nope. A haven for the budget traveler? You bet.

**Chelsea Motor Inn.** 2095 Lombard St. (between Fillmore and Webster sts.), San Francisco, CA 94123. ☎ **415/563-5600.** Fax 415/567-6475. 60 units. A/C TV TEL. $96 double. $10 extra person. AE, CB, DC, MC, V. Free parking. Bus: 22, 28, 30, or 76.

This member of the "motel strip" that stretches from the Golden Gate Bridge to Van Ness Avenue is perfectly located for a stroll along Union Street. Expect generic, clean motel accommodations, with coffeemakers in each room. No breakfast is offered.

**Cow Hollow Motor Inn & Suites.** 2190 Lombard St. (between Steiner and Fillmore sts.), San Francisco, CA 94123. ☎ **415/921-5800.** Fax 415/922-8515. 130 units. A/C TV TEL. $96 double, $10 extra per person; from $195 suite, $10 extra person. AE, DC, MC, V. Free parking. Bus: 28, 43, or 76.

If you're less interested in being downtown, and more into playing in and around the beautiful bay-front Marina, check out this modest brick hotel smack in the middle of busy Lombard Street. There's no fancy theme here; but each room comes loaded with such amenities as cable TV, free local phone calls, free covered parking, and in-room coffeemakers. All the rooms were renovated in 1996, so you'll be sure to sleep on a nice firm mattress surrounded by clean, new carpeting and drapes. Families will appreciate the one- and two-bedroom suites, which have full kitchens and dining areas.

✪ **Edward II Inn & Pub.** 3155 Scott St. (at Lombard St.), San Francisco, CA 94123. ☎ **800/473-2846** or 415/922-3000. Fax 415/931-5784. 32 units, 11 with shared bathroom. TV TEL. $75 double with shared bathroom; $99 double with private bathroom; $165–$225 suite/cottage. Rates include continental breakfast and evening sherry. AE, MC, V. Self-parking $10 across the street. Bus: 28, 43, or 76.

This self-styled three-story "English country" inn has a room for almost anyone's budget, ranging from pension rooms with shared bathrooms to luxuriously appointed suites and cottages with living rooms, kitchens, and whirlpool bathtubs. Originally built to house guests who attended the 1915 Pan-Pacific Exposition, it's now run by innkeepers Denise and Bob Holland, who have done a fantastic job maintaining its worldly charm. Regardless of their rate, all rooms are spotlessly clean and comfortably appointed with cozy antique furnishings and plenty of fresh flowers. The only caveat is that its Lombard Street location is usually congested with traffic, although nearby Chestnut and Union Streets offer some of the best shopping and dining in the city. Complimentary breakfast and evening drinks are served in the adjoining pub.

**Lombard Motor Inn.** 1475 Lombard St. (at Franklin St.)., San Francisco, CA 94123. ☎ **800/835-3639** or 415/441-6000. Fax 415/441-4291. 48 units. A/C TV TEL. $96 double. $10 extra person. AE, CB, DC, MC, V. Bus: 42, 47, 49, 76, or 82X.

The Lombard Motor Inn is one of the many big motels along Highway 101's approach to the Golden Gate Bridge, and a fine option if you're looking for a clean, decent-sized room in the beautiful Marina District. Accommodations are clean, spacious, and a step above standard motel style—"with three-star AAA ratings," the manager reminds us. The immediate vicinity is not exactly charming, but with the neighborhoods of Pacific Heights and Cow Hollow, as well as the Palace of Fine

Arts and the Marina promenade nearby, you'll be one of the lucky few who can park and meander around this crowded and popular area. Extra bonuses include free parking, local calls, in-room coffeemakers (with coffee and tea), and baby cribs on request. Upon arrival, ask for a room in the back, if available, to avoid traffic noise, and be forewarned: Large vans won't fit in the covered parking area.

✪ **Marina Inn.** 3110 Octavia St. (at Lombard St.), San Francisco, CA 94123. ☎ **800/ 274-1420** or 415/928-1000. Fax 415/928-5909. 40 units. TV TEL. Nov 1–Feb 29 $65–$105 double, Mar 1–May 31 $75–$115 double, June 1–Oct 31 $85–$125 double. Rates include continental breakfast, afternoon sherry, and turndown service. AE, MC, V. Bus: 28, 30, 43, or 76.

The Marina Inn is, without question, the best low-priced hotel in San Francisco. How they offer so much for so little is mystifying. Each guest room within this 1924 four-story Victorian looks as if it has been culled from a Country Furnishings catalog, complete with rustic pine-wood furnishings, a four-poster bed with silk-soft comforter and new mattress, pretty wallpaper, and soothing tones of rose, hunter green, and pale yellow. There's even high-class touches that many of the city's expensive hotels don't include, such as new remote-control televisions discreetly hidden in pine cabinetry, full bathtubs with showers, and nightly turndown service with chocolates on your pillow—all for as little as *$65 a night*. Combine that with complimentary continental breakfast, afternoon sherry, friendly service, and an armada of shops and restaurants within easy walking distance, and there you have it: Our no. 1 choice for Best Overall Value.

**Marina Motel.** 2576 Lombard St. (between Divisadero and Broderick sts.), San Francisco, CA 94123. ☎ **800/346-6118** or 415/921-9406. Fax 415/921-0364. 38 units. TV TEL. $99–$119 double; $176 suite. Lower rates in winter. MC, V. Free covered parking. Bus: 23, 43, or 76.

Established in 1939, the Marina Motel is one of San Francisco's first motels, built for the opening of the Golden Gate Bridge. The same family has owned this peach-colored, Spanish-style stucco building for three generations, and has taken exquisite care of it. The courtyard is awash with beautiful flowering plants. Though the rooms show minor signs of wear and tear (a ding here, a chip there), they're all quite clean, bright, quiet, and pleasantly decorated with framed lithographs of Old San Francisco—a thoughtful touch that adds to the motel's old-fashioned character, which makes this budget accommodation stand out from all the rest along busy Lombard Street. Kitchens and two-bedroom suites are also available. Location-wise, the Presidio and Marina Green are mere blocks away, and you can easily catch a bus downtown.

**Motel Capri.** 2015 Greenwich St. (at Buchanan St.), San Francisco, CA 94123. ☎ **415/ 346-4667.** Fax 415/346-3256. 42 units, 4 suites. TV, TEL. $70 double; $100 suite. AE, CB, DISC, JCB, MC, V. Free parking. Bus: 22, 41, or 45.

Of the Marina's motel selections, being one block off Lombard (Hwy. 101) makes all the difference when it comes to a quiet night's rest. Here the decor is anything but up-to-date (read: unintentionally retro 1970s), but the place is squeaky clean and the beds are comfy. Plus you get free parking (a valuable commodity in the crowded Marina District) and complimentary coffee, tea, and hot chocolate in the lobby. A few bucks extra will get you a more modern hotel along Lombard; but if all you require is a quiet crash pad, this is the place. Families should consider a suite, which has four beds and a kitchenette.

**Nob Hill Motel.** 1630 Pacific Ave. (between Van Ness Ave. and Polk St.), San Francisco, CA 94109. ☎ **800/343-6900** or 415/775-8160. Fax 415/673-8842. 29 units. A/C TV TEL. $115–$145 double. Rates include continental breakfast. AE, DISC, MC, V. Free parking. Bus: 12, 42, 47, 49, or 83.

A short walk from decent nightlife and great restaurants, and a 20-minute stroll from Fisherman's Wharf, is the Nob Hill Motel, a quintessential motel that more than aims to please. The Astroturf may throw you off at first, but trust us—once you open the shiny wooden door to your room, you'll find spotless rooms that are freshly decorated in lush carpeting, mauves, and florals. All the rooms have large TVs, hair dryers, big closets, and homey touches; some even have a VCR, a microwave, and a fridge. Their claim to be one of the quietest motels in the area is true, and the only drawback we can find is they are a little overpriced for the area.

✪ **Union Street Inn.** 2229 Union St. (between Fillmore and Steiner sts.), San Francisco, CA 94123. ☎ **415/346-0424.** Fax 415/922-8046. www.unionstreetinn.com. 5 units, 1 cottage. TV TEL. $135–$245 standard double; $245 cottage. Rates include breakfast, hors d'oeuvres, and evening beverages. AE, MC, V. Parking $15. Bus: 22, 28, 41, 45, or 47.

Who would have guessed that one of the most delightful B&Bs in California would be in San Francisco? This two-story Edwardian may front the perpetually busy (and trendy) Union Street, but it's quiet as a church on the inside. All individually decorated rooms are comfortably furnished, and most come with canopied or brass beds with down comforters, fresh flowers, bay windows (beg for one with a view of the garden), and private bathrooms (a few even have Jacuzzi tubs). An extended continental breakfast is served either in the parlor, in your room, or on an outdoor terrace overlooking a lovely English garden. The ultimate honeymoon retreat is the private carriage house behind the inn, but any room at this warm, friendly inn is guaranteed to please.

**Vagabond.** 2550 Van Ness Ave. (at Filbert St.), San Francisco, CA 94109. ☎ **800/522-1555** or 415/776-7500. Fax 415/776-5689. 132 units, 10 suites. TV TEL. May–Nov $99–$150 double, Dec–Apr $79–$130 double. Rates include continental breakfast. Children 17 and under stay free in parents' room. AE, DC, DISC, MC, V. Free parking (limited). Bus: 41, 42, 47, 49, or 76.

We rarely bother to plug chain motels, but this five-story courtyard building's slew of amenities make it worth mentioning. Its location, on busy Van Ness Avenue, makes it less charming than many other options, but few places in the city offer always-available coffee and tea; complimentary doughnuts, fruit, and pastries for breakfast; free local phone calls, weekday newspaper, incoming fax documents, and HBO; *and* a clean outdoor heated pool (surrounded by Astroturf) at this price. The rooms, which have basic motel-style furnishings (a bit worn in some suites), vary substantially. Those facing the courtyard have minuscule balconies; a few have decent views of the Golden Gate Bridge, and the ones above Van Ness are noisier. Families will appreciate the kitchenette suites, which have more elbow room and up to three beds. Unfortunately, the bathrooms are hopelessly small. Other bonuses include its proximity to the Marina and Fisherman's Wharf (a 20-minute walk), an accommodating staff who negotiate during the slow season (call the hotel directly to bargain), and a cocktail lounge and 24-hour restaurant on the premises, which was under renovation during our visit. Be sure to inquire about available discounts, including seniors, auto club, and corporate.

## SUPER-CHEAP SLEEPS

**Fort Mason Youth Hostel.** Fort Mason, Building 240, San Francisco, CA 94123. ☎ **415/771-7277.** Fax 415/771-1468. 170 beds. $17–$18 per night. MC, V. Reservations needed well in advance. Breakfast included in the rate.

Unbelievable but true, you can get front-row bay views for a mere $17 nightly. The hostel is on national-park property, provides dorm-style accommodations for 170 guests, and offers easy access to the Marina's shops and restaurants. Rooms sleep

2 to 12 persons, and communal space includes a fireplace, pool table, kitchen, dining room, coffee bar, complimentary movies, laundry facilities, and free parking. The complimentary breakfast alone practically makes it worth the price.

## 6  Pacific Heights

✪ **Hotel Majestic.** 1500 Sutter St. (between Octavia and Gough sts.), San Francisco, CA 94109. ☎ **800/869-8966** or 415/441-1100. Fax 415/673-7331. 60 units. TV TEL. $135–$215 double; from $325 suite. Group, government, corporate, and relocation rates available. Continental breakfast $8.50 extra. AE, CB, DC, DISC, MC, V. Valet parking $18.

Both tourists and business travelers adore the Majestic because it covers every professional need while retaining the ambiance of a luxurious old-world hotel. It was built in 1902, and thankfully retains its original integrity—the lobby alone will sweep guests into another era with an overabundance of tapestries, tasseled brocades, Corinthian columns, and intricate, lavish detail. Rooms are furnished with French and English antiques, including a large four-poster canopy bed; you'll also find custom-made, mirrored armoires and antique reproductions. All drapes, fabrics, carpet, and bedspreads were replaced in 1997; and half the bathrooms and guest rooms went under a $2-million renovation in 1999, which ensures you'll rest not only in style, but in freshness as well. Conveniences include a full-size, well-lit desk and clock-radio; extra bathroom amenities include bathrobes. Some rooms also have fireplaces.

**Dining:** Café Majestic and Bar serves California/Asian fare in a romantic setting and continues to intrigue a local clientele. Cocktails are offered in the adjacent bar complete with French mahogany marble-topped bar and a collection of African butterflies.

**Amenities:** Concierge, 24-hour room service, valet, dry cleaning, laundry service, complimentary newspaper, in-room massage, baby-sitting, secretarial service, courtesy car on weekdays, and afternoon sherry and fresh-baked cookies from 6 to 8pm nightly.

**Monte Cristo.** 600 Presidio (at Pine St.), San Francisco, CA 94115. ☎ **415/931-1875.** Fax 415/931-6005. 15 units, 10 with bathroom; 1 suite. $73 double without bathroom, $98 double with bathroom; $118 suite. Rates include buffet breakfast. AE, DC, DISC, MC, V. Street parking is usually abundant. Bus: 1, 2, 4, 31BX, or 43.

Built in 1875, the Monte Cristo was once a bordello, a refuge after the 1906 earthquake, and a speakeasy; it's now one of the cutest old-style B&Bs in town. Located near Sacramento Street's quaint shopping stretch, the Monte Cristo seems a colorful mirage in a desert of gray concrete. Its elegant exterior (richly painted red, black, and cream) encloses equally exuberant accommodations reminiscent of Old San Francisco. Every nook of the inn is adorned with period furnishings, antique wallpaper, cozy sitting areas, and sweet touches, such as the velvet curtains that frame each guest room's door. Heck, even the pay-phone booth is so attractive that you'll think of someone to call just to hang out in it. Bathrobes, stacks of newspapers, a sweet breakfast room, a full buffet breakfast—even the fact that some of the tasteful furniture is worn—make this place feel more like a stay at an old relative's house than at a hotel. *Note:* The front rooms are noisier, but the street quiets down at night; five rooms have telephones; many rooms share the small, clean bathrooms.

**Queen Anne Hotel.** 1590 Sutter St. (between Gough and Octavia sts.), San Francisco, CA 94109. ☎ **800/227-3970** or 415/441-2828. Fax 415/775-5212. www.queenanne.com. 44 units. TV TEL. $130–$180 double; $185–$295 suite. $10 extra person. Rates include continental breakfast. AE, CB, DC, DISC, MC, V. Parking $12. Bus: 2, 3, or 4.

This majestic 1890 Victorian, which was once a grooming school for upper-class young women, is today a stunning hotel. Restored in 1981 and renovated in 1995, the four-story building remains true to its heritage and emulates San Francisco's golden days. Walk under rich, red drapery to the immaculate and lavish "grand salon" lobby complete with English oak-paneling and period antiques. Rooms follow suit with antiques—armoires, marble-top dressers, and other Victorian pieces. Some have corner turret bay windows that look out on tree-lined streets, as well as separate parlor areas and wet bars; others have cozy reading nooks and fireplaces. All rooms have a telephone in the bathroom, and a computer hookup. Guests can relax in the parlor, with fluted columns and an impressive floor-to-ceiling fireplace, or in the hotel library. There's a complimentary continental breakfast. Services include room service, concierge, morning newspaper, and complimentary afternoon tea and sherry. There's also access to an off-premises health club with a lap pool. If you're not partial to Union Square, this hotel comes highly recommended.

## WORTH A SPLURGE

**Jackson Court.** 2198 Jackson St. (at Buchanan St.) San Francisco, CA 94115. ☎ **415/929-7670.** Fax 415/929-1405. 10 units. TV TEL. $150–$205 double. Rates include continental breakfast. AE, MC, V. Parking on street only.

The Jackson Court, a stately three-story brownstone Victorian mansion, is located in one of San Francisco's most exclusive neighborhoods, Pacific Heights. Its only fault—that it's far from the action—is also its blessing: If you crave a blissfully quiet vacation while swathed in elegant surroundings, this is the place. Each newly renovated room is individually furnished with superior-quality antique furnishings; two have wood-burning fireplaces (*de rigueur* in the winter). The Blue Room, for example, features a brass-and-porcelain bed and an inviting window seat, while the Garden Suite has handcrafted wood paneling and a large picture window looking out at the private garden patio. After breakfast, spend the day browsing the shops along nearby Union and Fillmore streets, then return in time for afternoon tea.

## 7 Japantown

**Best Western Miyako Inn.** 1800 Sutter St. (at Buchanan St.), San Francisco, CA 94115. ☎ **415/921-4000.** Fax 415/923-1064. 123 units, 2 suites. A/C TV TEL. $115 double; $275 suite. AE, DC, JCB, MC, V. Parking $10. Bus: 2, 3, 4, or 22.

Because this eight-story hotel is tucked between Japantown and upper Fillmore, it's an equal dash to a sushi-and-shiatsu-massage afternoon and a stretch of town that's perfect for snacking, shopping, and strolling. Though the 125 rooms are typically modern and unremarkable, they are certainly clean and comfortable. There's a restaurant on the premises, but with a worldly array of options within a few blocks' radius, it would be foolish to fill up here.

## 8 Civic Center & Environs

**Abigail Hotel.** 246 McAllister St. (between Hyde and Larkin sts.), San Francisco, CA 94102. ☎ **800/243-6510** or 415/861-9728. Fax 415/861-5848. 60 units. TV TEL. $79 double standard; $89 deluxe; $149 suite. $10 extra person. Rates include continental breakfast. AE, CB, DC, DISC, MC, V. Valet parking $16. Muni Metro: All Market St. trams. Bus: All Market St. buses.

The Abigail is one of San Francisco's rare sleeper hotels: Though it doesn't get much press, this is one of the better medium-priced hotels in the city. Built in 1925 to

---

### ℹ️  Affordable Family-Friendly Hotels

**Hotel Halcyon** *(see p. 69)*   Not only is this one of the city's best budget hotels, it's also a great place for families; rooms come with microwaves, refrigerators, and other lifesaving amenities, and weekly rentals are available.

**Stanyan Park Hotel** *(see p. 89)*   A great moderately priced choice for families, the Stanyan Park is ideally located across from Golden Gate, where kids can let off some steam at the nearby playground and ride on an authentic carousel.

**The Wharf Inn** *(see p. 77)*   No whining about when you'll get there 'cause you're already there—right smack dab in the middle of Fisherman's Wharf. Parking is free, and there's no charge for packing along an extra pint-sized monster.

---

house celebrities performing at the world-renowned Fox Theater, what the Abigail lacks in luxury it more than makes up for in charm. The rooms, while on the small side, are clean, cute, and comfortably furnished with cozy antiques and down comforters. Morning coffee, pastries, and complimentary newspapers greet you in the beautiful faux-marble lobby designed by Shawn Hall, while dinner is served downstairs in the "organic" restaurant, Millennium (see chapter 6, "Great Deals on Dining," for complete information).

**Atherton Hotel.** 685 Ellis St. (at Larkin St.), San Francisco, CA, 94109. ☎ **800/474-5720** in the U.S., or 415/474-5720. Fax 415/474-8256. 75 units. TEL TV. $79–$129 double. Continental breakfast $5 extra. AE, DC, MC, V. BART: Civic Center. Bus: 19, 27, 31, 38, or 72.

Contrary to the shady Tenderloin neighborhood just a few blocks away, the Atherton is a safe and cheery hotel. The well-maintained 1927 building offers old-world charm and small tidy rooms with tasteful motel-like decor and nice toiletries. The rooms look newer than those at the neighboring Essex, and all guests have access to complimentary morning coffee, dry cleaning, laundry, a fax, and the bar and ground-floor restaurant, which serves breakfast and dinner. While there's no parking on the premises, there's a lot 2 blocks up on Van Ness Avenue. *Note:* The only major downside to staying here is the surrounding neighborhood. We don't recommend walking to downtown from here, especially at night; there are some rough streets in between.

**Essex Hotel.** 684 Ellis St. (between Larkin and Hyde sts.), San Francisco, CA 94109. ☎ **800/443-7739** in the U.S., 800/443-7739 in Canada, or 415/474-4664. Fax 415/441-1800. 100 units. TEL TV. $89 double. AE, MC, V. Bus: 19, 27, 31, or 38.

As at the neighboring Atherton, once you're inside the Essex you leave the gloomy neighborhood behind. This hotel, too, has European-style charm, makes every effort to please its guests, and is a fine option as long as you avoid the neighboring Tenderloin district (the staff will point you in the right direction). Overall it's a fine, affordable option for a downtown hotel.

**Pensione San Francisco.** 1668 Market St. (between Gough and Franklin sts.), San Francisco, CA 94102. ☎ **415/864-1271.** Fax 415/861-8116. 36 units, none with bathroom. $79 double. AE, MC, V. Bus: 6, 7, 8, 21, 66, or 71.

If only the rooms were as tastefully decorated as the entranceway and common room, then we'd give the Pensione San Francisco high praise. But, alas, they aren't. Rather, the guest rooms look like an exercise in minimalism, equipped with only the bare necessities—double bed with drab spread, dresser, chair, lamp, sink, a small closet, and, if you're lucky, a view of Market Street. Notice that we didn't mention a toilet or bath; bathrooms are shared, European style. Obviously, you'll want to spend as little time in your room as possible, which is easy to do since you're already on San Francisco's busiest thoroughfare. So why would you stay here? Because it's safe, clean, very inexpensive (especially considering the central location), run by a friendly and knowledgeable staff, and frequented by an eclectic mix of high-spirited Europeans. If you can live with the bare-bones rooms, it's otherwise a fine budget choice (and, surprisingly enough, voted *The New York Times* Budget Choice for Accommodations in 1993).

✪ **Phoenix Hotel.** 601 Eddy St. (at Larkin St.), San Francisco, CA 94109. ☎ **800/ 248-9466** or 415/776-1380. Fax 415/885-3109. 44 units. TV TEL. $119–$129 double; $159–$179 suite. Rates include continental breakfast. AE, DC, MC, V. Free parking. Bus: 19, 31, 38, 42, or 47.

If you'd like to tell your friends back home that you've stayed in the same hotel as Linda Ronstadt, Arlo Guthrie, and the Red Hot Chili Peppers, this is the place. Situated on the fringes of San Francisco's less-than-pleasant Tenderloin District, this retro 1950s-style hotel has been described by *People* as the hippest hotel in town, a gathering place for visiting rock musicians, writers, and filmmakers who crave a dose of Southern California—hence the palm trees and pastel colors—on their trips to San Francisco. The focal point of the Palm Springs–style hotel is a small, heated outdoor pool adorned with a paisley mural by artist Francis Forlenza and ensconced by a modern-sculpture garden.

The rooms, while far from plush, were upgraded in 1998, and are comfortably equipped with bamboo furnishings, potted plants, and original local art. In addition to the usual amenities, the inn offers VCRs and movies upon request. Services include an on-call massage therapist, concierge, laundry/valet, and—whoo hoo!— free parking. Adjoining the hotel is Backflip (formerly Miss Pearl's Jam House), a superhip and oh-so-blue cocktail lounge serving tapas and Caribbean-style appetizers and a heck of a lot of San Francisco attitude.

## SUPER-CHEAP SLEEPS

**San Francisco Central YMCA Hotel.** 220 Golden Gate Ave. (between Hyde and Leavenworth sts.), San Francisco, CA 94102. ☎ **415/885-0460.** 105 units. $51–$55 double. Rates include use of facilities and continental breakfast. MC, V. Bus: 5, 8, 9, or 19.

The YMCA Hotel is about a half step up from a hostel, offering guests four walls instead of four bunks. It's what you'd expect for about $50 a night: a bed, a sink, and if you're unlucky, a view of the Tenderloin, San Francisco's seediest neighborhood. Take our advice and—even if there's just two of you—request one of the larger corner rooms, which have a fairly large private bathroom. You can't complain about the perks, however: 24-hour desk services, airport shuttle, on-site parking, free coffee and muffins, TV room, lock boxes, short-term storage, free maps, laundry facilities, maid service, and—best of all—free use of the fitness center, swimming pool, garden roof deck, and sauna. *Safety Note:* If you're venturing out after dark, call a cab; the Tenderloin is not a safe place to walk through at night.

## WORTH A SPLURGE

**The Archbishop's Mansion.** 1000 Fulton St. (at Steiner St.), San Francisco, CA 94117. ☎ **800/543-5820** or 415/563-7872. Fax 415/883-3193. 15 units. TEL TV. $139–$385 double. Rates include continental breakfast. AE, CB, DC, MC, V. Limited free parking. Bus: 5 or 22.

One thing is for certain: The archbishop who built this 1904 belle-epoque beauty was no Puritan. Drippingly romantic, the Archbishop's Mansion is one of the most opulent and fabulously adorned B&Bs you could possibly hope to stay in. The Don Giovanni suite—larger than most San Francisco houses—comes with a huge, cherub-encrusted four-poster bed imported from a French castle, a palatial fireplace, elaborately embroidered linens, and a seven-head shower that you'll never want to leave. Slightly closer to earth is the Carmen suite, which has a deadly romantic combination of a clawfoot bathtub fronting a toasty, wood-burning fireplace. In the morning, breakfast is delivered to the guest rooms, and in the evening, complimentary wine is served in the elegant parlor.

**Amenities:** Concierge, limited room service, laundry/valet, complimentary morning newspaper, limousine service.

## 9　Haight-Ashbury

**The Herb 'n Inn.** 525 Ashbury St. (between Page and Haight sts.), San Francisco, CA 94117. ☎ **415/553-8542.** Fax 415/553-8541. 4 units. TV (upon request). $70–$85 double. 2-night minimum. MC, V. Parking with advance notice. Bus: 6, 7, 33, 43, 66, or 71.

For those of you who want to immerse yourself in the sights and sounds of San Francisco's legendary Haight-Ashbury District without compromising on high-quality (and low-cost) accommodations, there's The Herb 'n Inn. Run by sister/brother duo Pam and Bruce Brennan—who know the history and highlights of the Haight better than anyone—this modernized Victorian inn consists of four attractive guest rooms, a huge country-style kitchen, a sunny back garden, and the beginnings of Bruce's Psychedelic History Museum (a.k.a. the dining room). Top choice among the guest rooms is the Cilantro Room, which, besides being the largest, has the only private bathroom and a view of the garden—all for only $10 extra per night. The Tarragon Room has two small beds and a private deck (optimal for smokers, who aren't allowed to fire up inside the house), while the large Coriander Room faces the near-mythical intersection of Haight and Ashbury streets, where there's always something going on. A hearty full breakfast—such as waffles, crepes, popovers, or potato pancakes—is included, as well as office services (including forwarded e-mail), personal city tours à la Bruce, and plenty of free advice on how to spend your day in the city. Kids and gay couples are welcome.

**Metro Hotel.** 319 Divisadero St. (between Oak and Page sts.), San Francisco, CA 94117. ☎ **415/861-5364.** Fax 415/863-1970. 23 units. TV TEL. $59 double with a double bed, $69 double with a queen-size bed; $89–$109 suite. AE, DC, DISC, MC, V. Bus: 6, 7, 16, 24, 66, or 71.

It's not exactly in the heart of the Haight, but from this remodeled Victorian you can walk to the Castro, Golden Gate Park, or upper or lower Haight in under 30 minutes. Buses stop a block away and blast downtown and to the Haight every few minutes (a 10-minute trip once on board). The neighborhood isn't the best in town, but it beats Civic Center by a long shot and has plenty of cheap restaurants nearby. The high-ceilinged hotel is reminiscent of a European pensione—smallish rooms, nothing too fancy, but clean and friendly with everything you need to get by. There's a garden out back, too. *Take note:* Parking is free in the evenings, but you'll have to find your own during the day.

**Red Victorian Bed, Breakfast, & Art.** 1665 Haight St. (between Cole and Belvedere sts.), San Francisco, CA 94117. ☎ **415/864-1978.** Fax 415/863-3293. 18 units, 4 with bathroom; 1 suite. TEL. $86–$96 double without bathroom; $120–$126 double with bathroom; $160 suite. Rates include continental breakfast and afternoon tea. Rates decrease based on length of stay. AE, DISC, MC, V. Guarded parking lot nearby. Muni Metro: N line. Bus: 7, 66, 71, or 73.

Still having flashbacks from the 1960s? Or want to? No problem. A room at the Red Vic, located in the heart of the Haight, will throw you right back into the Summer of Love (minus, of course, the free-flowing LSD). Owner Sami Sunchild, a confessed former flower child, has re-created this historic hotel and Peace Center as a living museum honoring the bygone era and Golden Gate Park. The rooms are inspired by San Francisco's sights and history, and are decorated accordingly—psychedelic posters and all. The Flower Child Room has a sun on the ceiling and a rainbow on the wall, while the bed sports a hand-crocheted shawl headboard. The Peacock Suite, though pricey, is one funky and colorful room, with red beads, a canopy bed, and multicolored patterns throughout. The clincher is its bedroom bathtub, which has a circular pass-through looking into the sitting area. Four guest rooms have private baths; the remaining accommodations share four bathrooms down the hall. In general, the rooms and baths are clean and the furnishings lighthearted. This hotel isn't for conservatives, but if you're into it, it's pretty groovy. Rates for longer stays are a great deal. A family-style continental breakfast is a gathering place for a worldly array of guests, and there's a gift shop called the Meditation Room and Peace Center.

**Stanyan Park Hotel.** 750 Stanyan St. (at Waller St.), San Francisco, CA 94117. ☎ **415/ 751-1000.** Fax 415/668-5454. www.stanyanpark.com. 36 units. TV TEL. $110–$160 double; from $250 suite. Rates include continental breakfast. Rollaway bed $20; free cribs. AE, CB, DC, DISC, MC, V. Off-site parking $5. Muni Metro: N line. Bus: 7, 33, 43, 66, 71, or 73.

Considering this small inn is the only real hotel on the east end of Golden Gate Park, it's your only real option if you want to stay in Haight-Ashbury. The Victorian has operated as a hotel under a variety of names since 1904, is on the National Register of Historic Places, and is a charming, three-story establishment decorated with antique furnishings, Victorian wallpaper, and pastel quilts, curtains, and carpets. Tub/shower bathrooms come complete with massaging showerhead, shampoos, and fancy soaps.

There are one- and two-bedroom suites. Each has a full kitchen and formal dining and living rooms, and can sleep up to six comfortably; they're ideal for families. There's a complimentary tea service each afternoon and evening. Continental breakfast is served in a pleasant room off the lobby. All rooms are non-smoking.

## 10  Richmond District

**Seal Rock Inn.** 545 Point Lobos Ave. (at 48th Ave.), San Francisco, CA 94121. ☎ **415/ 752-8000.** Fax 415/752-6034. 27 units. TV TEL. $86–$112 double. AE, MC, V. Bus: 38 or 38L.

You would think that a city surrounded on three sides by water would have a slew of seaside hotels. Oddly enough, it only has one: the **Seal Rock Inn.** It's about as far from Union Square and Fisherman's Wharf as you can place a hotel in San Francisco, but that just makes it all the more unique. The hotel fronts Sutro Heights park, which in turn fronts Ocean Beach. Most rooms in the four-story structure have at least partial views of the ocean; at night, guests are lulled to sleep by the sound of the surf and distant foghorns. The rooms, though large and spotless, obviously haven't been redecorated since the Nixon administration; a monotone hue of beige, brown, and gray make you feel as if you're colorblind. Amenity options range from kitchenettes to two-room suites with wood-burning fireplaces; phones, TVs, covered parking, and free use of the enclosed patio and pool area are standard. Adjacent to the inn is a small cafe serving breakfast and lunch. Golden Gate Park and the Presidio are both nearby, and the Geary bus—which snails its way to Union Square and Market Street—stops right out front.

## 11 The Castro

Though everyone is welcome, hotels in the Castro mainly cater to a gay and lesbian clientele. The options listed below are safe choices in the heart of the Castro, but it's the location that is the real reason to stay here—pick any of the following choices and you'll be in the center of one of the most liberated gay environments in the world.

**24 Henry.** 24 Henry St. (at Noe St.), San Francisco, CA 94114. ☎ **800/900-5686** or 415/864-5686. Fax 415/864-0406. E-mail: HenryST24@aol.com. 9 units, 2 with bathroom. $80–$95 double; $95 suite. $25 extra person. Rates include continental breakfast. AE, MC, V. Muni Metro: J, F, K, L, M, or N. Bus: 8, 22, or 37.

This charming 123-year-old Victorian, located on a serene side street in the Castro District, is popular among gay travelers. Each of the inn's five guest rooms has high ceilings, antique furnishings, and private phone lines with voice mail. After a day of exploring the Castro on foot, guests can watch TV or read in the double parlor (where breakfast is also served). The apartment suite sleeps three comfortably, and includes a parlor, separate entrance, phone, and TV. Two rooms have full kitchens, and all are nonsmoking.

**Beck's Motor Lodge.** 2222 Market St. (at 15th St.), San Francisco, CA 94114. ☎ **800/227-4360** in the U.S., except CA; 415/621-8212 (if in CA, call collect to make reservations). Fax 415/241-0435. 57 units. TV TEL. $75–$125. Rates include parking. AE, CB, DC, DISC, MC, V. Metro: F. Bus: 8 or 37.

In a town where DINK (double income, no kids) tourists happily spend fistfuls of money, you'd think someone would create a gay luxury hotel—or even a moderate hotel for that matter. But absurdly, the most commercial and modern accommodation in the ever-touristy Castro District is this run-of-the-mill motel. Standard, but contemporary, the ultra-tidy rooms include coffeemakers, refrigerators, free HBO, and access to coin-operated washing machines, a sundeck overlooking upper Market Street, and free parking. Unless you're into the homey B&Bs, this is really your only choice in the area—fortunately, it's very well maintained.

**Castillo Inn.** 48 Henry St., San Francisco, CA 94114. ☎ **800/865-5112** or 415/864-5111. Fax 415/641-1321. 5 units, none with bathroom. $75 double; $160 suite. Suite rate negotiable depending on season and number of guests. Rates include a continental breakfast. AE, MC, V. Muni Metro: F, K, L, or M. Bus: 8, 22, 24, or 37.

Just 2 minutes from the heart of the Castro District, this charming little house provides a safe, quiet, and clean environment for its clientele. Catering mostly to gay men (though anyone is welcome), the Castillo makes its clientele feel at home while away. Hardwood floors decorated with throw rugs aid in the warmth. Bedrooms are small yet cozy, and phone messages via voice mail are collected at the front desk. The Castillo also provides the shared usage of a large refrigerator and microwave oven in the kitchen. One enormous, two-bedroom suite that sleeps four comfortably has a full kitchen, VCR, parking, and a deck.

**Dolores Park Inn.** C/o Bernie H. Vielwerth, 3641 17th St., San Francisco, CA 94114. ☎ **415/621-0482.** Fax is the same; please call before faxing. 3 units, none with bathrooms; 1 suite (with kitchenette). TV $119–$199 double; $179 suite; MC, V. Free parking. Muni Metro: F, J, K, L, or M. Bus: 22 or 24.

Conveniently located in the Castro, this inn is within easy walking distance to many shops and clubs, and it's a quick jaunt to downtown. Each bedroom is individually decorated with beautiful antiques and a queen-size bed. Rumor has it celebrities (Tom Cruise, members of the *Sister Act* cast, Robert Downey Jr., and others) have stayed here to avoid hype. The owner takes special care in providing a warm, hospitable, and romantic environment with helpful service. The suite has a 20-foot sundeck looking up at Twin Peaks, kitchen, cable TV/VCR, and a four-poster bed, while the Carriage House offers a heated marble floor, kitchen, washer/dryer, fireplace, Jacuzzi, and VCR. A 2-night minimum stay is required (4 nights in the Carriage House), and there is no smoking allowed.

**Inn on Castro.** 321 Castro St. (at Market St.), San Francisco, CA 94114. ☎ **415/861-0321.** 8 units. TEL. $95–$108 double; from $120–$140 suite. Rates include full breakfast and evening brandy. AE, MC, V. Muni Metro: Castro.

One of the better choices in the Castro, half a block away from all the action, is this Edwardian-style inn decorated with contemporary furnishings, original modern art, and fresh flowers throughout. Almost all rooms have private bathrooms, direct-dial phones, and color TVs. Most rooms share a small back patio, and the suite has its own private outdoor sitting area. There's also a two-bedroom apartment available for $140 to $200.

**☉ The Parker House.** 520 Church St. (between 17th and 18th sts.), San Francisco, CA 94114. ☎ **888/520-PARK** or 415/621-3222. Fax 415/621-4139. Members.aol.com/ parkerhse/sf.html. E-mail: parkerhse@aol.com. 8 units. $99–$199 double. Rates include complimentary breakfast. AE, MC, V. Self-parking $15.

This is the best B&B option in the Castro. The neighborhood's "newest and grandest guest house" is a 5,000-square-foot, 1909 Edwardian located in a cheery neighborhood a few blocks from the heart of the action and half a block from grassy Dolores Park. It also happens to be the best choice in the area. Along with a well-decorated common library with fireplace and piano, breakfast room, formal dining room, and garden with patio, there's a lawn, "fern den," fountains, spa and steam room. Each room features a private bathroom, voice mail, cable TV, and modem hookups.

**The Willows Bed & Breakfast Inn.** 710 14th St. (between Church and Market sts.), San Francisco, CA 94114. ☎ **415/431-4770.** Fax 415/431-5295. www.WillowsSF.com. 13 units, all with shared bathroom. TEL. $90–$108 double; $120–$140 suite. Rates include continental breakfast. AE, DISC, MC, V. Limited on-street parking. Muni Metro: Church St. Station (across the street) or F. Bus: 22 or 37.

Right in the heart of the gay Castro District, The Willows Inn employs a staff eager to greet and attend to visitors to San Francisco. The inn's willow furnishings, antiques, and Laura Ashley prints add a touch of romantic elegance. After a long and eventful day of sightseeing and shopping, followed by a night of dancing and cruising, you will be tucked in with a "sherry-and-chocolate turndown." The staff will appear the next morning with your personalized breakfast delivered with a freshly cut flower and the morning newspaper. The place has simple elegance and quality and is eagerly sought out by discriminating gay visitors to San Francisco. Extra amenities include direct-dial phones, alarm-clock radios, and kimono bathrobes.

# 12  Near the Airport

**Embassy Suites.** 250 Gateway Blvd., South San Francisco, CA 94080. ☎ **800/362-2779** or 650/589-3400. Fax 650/876-0305. www.embassy-suites.com. 312 units. A/C MINIBAR TV TEL. $119–$209 double. AE, DC, MC, V.

Your best pick—and most expensive—of the airport chain hotels is Embassy Suites, which does its darndest to make you forget you're in the middle of drab south San

Francisco. The property's got an indoor pool, whirlpool, sauna, courtyard with a fountain, palm plants, and bar/restaurant and the tastefully decorated two-room suites have wet bar, fridge, microwave, coffeemaker, hair dryer, iron et al., two TVs, and two phones. A cooked-to-order breakfast comes with the cost of the room, which you can have delivered to your door before you're whisked to the airport via their free shuttle.

**Holiday Inn.** San Francisco International Airport North, 275 S. Airport Blvd. (off Hwy. 101), South San Francisco, CA 94080. ☎ **800/HOLIDAY** or 650/873-3550. Fax 650/873-4524. 224 units. A/C TV TEL. $85–$169 double. AE, CB, DC, DISC, MC, V.

Considering all the free amenities—health spa, movie channels, 24-hour airport shuttle, guest parking—a room at this Holiday Inn is surprisingly reasonable, starting at $85 per night. Granted, there's nary a thing to see or do within a 10-mile radius, but as a layover for next morning's flight out of San Francisco, the Holiday Inn is always a safe bet because the airport is a mere 5 minutes away via the hotel's complimentary shuttle. The rooms are classic Holiday Inn: large, clean, and inoffensively dull, with the usual amenities such as coffeemakers, hair dryers, and minibars. To keep you occupied before your flight departs, the hotel has a gym, sauna, Jacuzzi, and tanning bed, as well as full business services, a gift shop, and Rookie's Sports Bar & Grill, which does a brisk bar business most evenings (the smaller City Café serves American-style breakfast, lunch, and dinner as well).

**San Francisco Airport North Travelodge.** 326 S. Airport Blvd. (off Hwy. 101), South San Francisco, CA 04080. ☎ **800/578-7878** or 650/583-9600. Fax 650/873-9392. 200 units. A/C TV TEL. $90–$99 double. AE, CB, DC, DISC, MC, V.

The Travelodge is a good choice for families, mainly due to the hotel's large heated pool, which allows the kids to let off some steam while the parents bask in South San Francisco's typically balmy weather. Yes, the rooms are as ordinary as you'd expect from a Travelodge, but they're quite clean and comfortable, and each comes with complimentary HBO, in-room coffee and tea, voice mail, a complimentary copy of *USA Today*, and free toll-free, and credit card calls. The clincher, however, is the 24-hour complimentary shuttle, which makes the 2-mile trip to SFO in a mere 5 minutes. A 24-hour restaurant serving standard American grub is nearby, as is Rookie's Sports Bar & Grill, at the Holiday Inn down the street.

# Great Deals on Dining

## 6

**R**estaurants are to San Franciscans as bagels are to New Yorkers: indispensable. At last count, city residents had more than 3,300 reasons to avoid cooking at home, and actually spent more money on dining out than natives of any other U.S. city. Afghan, Cajun, Burmese, Jewish, Moroccan, Persian, Cambodian, Vegan—whatever cuisine you're in the mood for tonight, this town has got it covered. All you need is a little money and an adventurous palate, because half the fun of visiting San Francisco is the rare opportunity to sample the flavors of the world in one fell swoop. In fact, some of the city's best eating experiences are its small, affordable neighborhood haunts, the kind you'll never find unless someone (like us) let's you in on San Francisco's savory secrets.

To help you decide which restaurants are in your neighborhood and price range, we've categorized the restaurants by area and by price (for a dinner) as follows: Super-Cheap Eats (most main courses for $10 or less); For a Few Bucks More (most main courses $11 to $15); Moderately Priced Options (most main courses $16 to $20); and Worth a Splurge (most main courses more than $20). These categories reflect the cost per person for a main course and a beverage—which means you *can* get away with spending that amount, but of course you can easily blow your budget if you go crazy on appetizers, cocktails, coffee, and dessert.

*Note:* For the ultimate in budget dining, check out the "Hog Heaven Happy Hours" box on page 112, which lists plenty of festive bars throughout the city that will fill you up for next to nada.

While dining in San Francisco is almost always a hassle-free experience, there are a few things you should keep in mind the next time you eat out:

- When choosing a restaurant, keep in mind that there are ways to eat in places beyond your budget. If you want the experience without the expense, read our tips in the restaurant reviews below. Also consider heading to the pricier restaurants for lunch.
- If you want a table at the more expensive restaurants with the best reputations, you'll need to book 6 weeks ahead for weekends and several weeks ahead for a table during the week.
- If there's a long wait for a table, ask if you can order at the bar, which is often faster, more affordable, and more fun.
- Don't leave *anything* valuable in your car while you're dining (particularly in or near high-crime areas), and only give the valet the car key, *not* the key to your hotel room or house.

- Remember that it's against the law to smoke in any bar or restaurant in San Francisco, though you're welcome to smoke outside the front door.

# 1  Restaurants by Cuisine

## AMERICAN
Balboa Café (Marina District/
  Cow Hollow)
Beach Chalet Brewery & Restaurant
  (Sunset District)
Bitterroot (Mission District)
Boulevard (SoMa)
Café de la Presse (Union Square)
Chow (The Castro)
Doidge's (Marina District/Cow
  Hollow)
Dottie's True Blue Café (Union
  Square)
Family Inn Coffee Shop (Union
  Square)
Fizz Supper Club
  (Financial District)
Hamburger Mary's (SoMa)
Hard Rock Cafe (Nob Hill/Russian
  Hill)
Hot 'n' Hunky (The Castro)
Mad Dog in the Fog (Haight-
  Ashbury)
Mel's Diner (Marina District/Cow
  Hollow)
Mo's Gourmet Burgers (North Beach)
Patio Café (The Castro)
Planet Hollywood (Union Square)
Postrio (Union Square)
Salmagundi (Union Square)
Sears Fine Foods (Union Square)
Spaghetti Western (Haight-Ashbury)
Tommy's Joynt (Civic Center &
  Environs)
Universal Café (Mission District)

## ARGENTINEAN
Il Pollaio (North Beach)

## BASQUE
Des Alpes (North Beach)

## BREAKFAST
Home Plate (Marina District/
  Cow Hollow)

## CAFE FARE
Caffe Centro (SoMa)
The Grove (Marina District/Cow
  Hollow)
Mad Magda's Russian Tearoom &
  Café (Civic Center & Environs)
Tassajara (Haight-Ashbury)

## CAJUN/CRÉOLE
The Elite Café (Pacific Heights)

## CALIFORNIA
AsiaSF (SoMa)
Café Flore (The Castro)
Cafe Kati (Pacific Heights)
Café Metropol (Financial District)
California Pizza Kitchen (Union
  Square)
Cliff House (Richmond District)
Gordon Biersch Brewery Restaurant
  (SoMa)
Grand Cafe (Union Square)
PlumpJack Café (Marina
  District/Cow Hollow)
Pluto's (Marina District/
  Cow Hollow)
Rumpus (Union Square)
2223 (The Castro)

## CARIBBEAN
Cha Cha Cha (Haight-Ashbury)

## CHINESE/DIM SUM
Brandy Ho's Hunan Food
  (Chinatown)
Eliza's (Civic Center & Environs)
Great Eastern (Chinatown)
Hong Kong Flower Lounge
  (Richmond District)
House of Nanking (Chinatown)
Hunan Home's (Chinatown)
The Mandarin (Fisherman's Wharf)
Oriental Pearl (Chinatown)
Sam Woh (Chinatown)
Yank Sing (Financial District)

## CONTINENTAL
LuLu (SoMa)

## CRÊPES
Cafe Bastille (Financial District)
Crepes on Cole (Haight-Ashbury)
Ti Couz (Mission District)

## DELIS
Boudin Sourdough Bakery & Café
(Fisherman's Wharf)
David's Delicatessen (Union Square)
San Francisco Art Institute Cafe
(North Beach)

## ENGLISH PUB GRUB
Mad Dog in the Fog (Haight-
Ashbury)

## FRENCH
Bizou (SoMa)
Cafe Bastille (Financial District)
Café Claude (Union Square)
Café de la Presse (Union Square)
Des Alpes (North Beach)
Flying Saucer (Mission District)
Fringale Restaurant (SoMa)
Grand Cafe (Union Square)
PlumpJack Café (Marina
District/Cow Hollow)
Scala's Bistro (Union Square)
South Park Café (SoMa)
YOYO Bistro (Japantown)

## FUSION
Eos (Haight-Ashbury)
YOYO Bistro (Japantown)

## INDIAN
North India Restaurant (Marina
District/Cow Hollow)

## INTERNATIONAL
World Wrapps (Marina District/
Cow Hollow)

## ITALIAN
Bizou (SoMa)
Café Metropol (Financial District)
Cafe Pescatore (Fisherman's Wharf)
Cafe Tiramisu (Financial District)
Caffè Freddy's (North Beach)

Caffè Macaroni (North Beach)
Capp's Corner (North Beach)
Crab Cake Lounge (Fisherman's
Wharf)
E'Angelo Restaurant (Marina
District/Cow Hollow)
Emporio Armani Cafe
(Union Square)
Gira Polli (North Beach)
Golden Boy Pizza (North Beach)
The Gold Spike (North Beach)
Hyde Street Bistro (Nob Hill/
Russian Hill)
Il Fornaio (Fisherman's Wharf)
Il Pollaio (North Beach)
Jackson Fillmore (Pacific Heights)
Kuleto's (Union Square)
L'Osteria del Forno (North Beach)
Lou's Pier 47 (Fisherman's Wharf)
Marcello's Pizza (The Castro)
Mario's Bohemian Cigar Store
(North Beach)
Nob Hill Café (Nob Hill/Russian Hill)
Original Joe's (Civic Center &
Environs)
Pane e Vino (Pacific Heights)
Pasta Pomodoro (North Beach)
Puccini & Pinetti (Union Square)
Rose Pistola (North Beach)
Scala's Bistro (Union Square)
Steps of Rome Café (North Beach)
Stinking Rose (North Beach)
Tommaso's (North Beach)
Zinzino (Marina District/Cow Hollow)

## JAPANESE
Ace Wasabi's (Marina District/
Cow Hollow)
Isobune (Japantown)
Kabuto Sushi (Richmond District)
Mifune (Japantown)
Nanbantei (Union Square)
Nippon Sushi (The Castro)
Osome (Pacific Heights)
Sanppo (Japantown)
Sushi-A (Japantown)
Yum Yum Fish (Sunset District)

## MEDITERRANEAN
Bruno's (Mission District)
Enrico's (North Beach)

Firewood Café (The Castro)
Fizz Supper Club (Financial District)
La Méditerranée (Pacific Heights)
Mecca (The Castro)
PlumpJack Café (Marina District/Cow Hollow)
Truly Mediterranean (Mission District)
Zuni Café (Civic Center & Environs)

## MEXICAN
Andalé Taqueria (Marina District/Cow Hollow)
Café Marimba (Marina District/Cow Hollow)
Campo Santo (North Beach)
La Canasta (Marina District/Cow Hollow)
Puerto Alegre Restaurant (Mission District)
Roosevelt Tamale Parlor (Mission District)
Sweet Heat (Marina District/Cow Hollow)
Taquerias La Cumbre (Mission District)
Zona Rosa (Haight-Ashbury)

## MIDDLE EASTERN/PERSIAN
Maykadeh (North Beach)

## NOODLES
Long Life Noodle Company & Jook Joint (SoMa)

## PIZZA
California Pizza Kitchen (Union Square)
Golden Boy Pizza (North Beach)
L'Osteria del Forno (North Beach)
Marcello's Pizza (The Castro)
Nob Hill Café (Nob Hill/Russian Hill)
Pauline's (Mission District)
Tommaso's (North Beach)

## SEAFOOD
Cliff House (Richmond District)
Crab Cake Lounge (Fisherman's Wharf)

Hayes Street Grill (Civic Center & Environs)
Lou's Pier 47 (Fisherman's Wharf)
Plouf (Financial District)
Swan Oyster Depot (Nob Hill/Russian Hill)

## SINGAPOREAN
Straits Café (Richmond District)

## SPANISH
Thirsty Bear Brewing Company (SoMa)
Zarzuela (Nob Hill/Russian Hill)

## SUSHI
Ace Wasabi's (Marina District/Cow Hollow)
Isobune (Japantown)
Kabuto Sushi (Richmond District)
Nippon Sushi (The Castro)
Osome (Pacific Heights)
Sushi-A (Japantown)
Yum Yum Fish (Sunset District)

## THAI
Cha Am (SoMa)
Cha Am Express (Financial District)
Khan Toke Thai House (Richmond District)
Manora's (SoMa)
Neecha Thai (Japantown)
Thep Phanom (Haight-Ashbury)

## VEGETARIAN
Greens Restaurant (Marina District/Cow Hollow)
Millennium (Civic Center & Environs)

## VIETNAMESE
Golden Turtle (Nob Hill/Russian Hill)
Saigon Saigon (Mission District)
The Slanted Door (Mission District)
Tú Lan (SoMa)

## 2  Union Square

**Café Claude.** 7 Claude Lane. ☎ **415/392-3515.** www.cafeclaude.com. Reservations recommended. Main courses $7–$13. AE, DC, DISC, MC, V. Mon–Sat 11am–11:30pm. Cable car: Powell-Mason and Powell-Hyde lines. FRENCH.

Euro-transplants love Café Claude, a crowded and lively restaurant tucked in a narrow lane near Union Square. Seemingly everything—every table, every spoon, every saltshaker, and every waiter—is imported from France. There is live jazz Thursday through Saturday from 8 to 10:30pm. Outdoor seating is available when weather permits. With prices topping out at about $13 for main courses such as *cassoulet* (white beans with duck confit and sausage), *poussin rôti* (roast Cornish hen with potatoes and aioli), French shepherd's pie, or the *poisson du jour* (fish of the day), Café Claude is a good value.

**Café de la Presse.** 352 Grant Ave. (at Bush St.). ☎ **415/398-2680.** Breakfast $6.25–$10; lunch and dinner main courses (other than fish and meat) $9–$13; fish and meat main courses $15–$20. AE, DC, DISC, MC, V. Daily 7am–11pm. Bus: 9X, 15, 30, or 45. FRENCH/AMERICAN.

Europeans won't find a place more comforting than this bright corner cafe with lots of foreign magazines, books, travel information, coffee drinks, and sidewalk seating. But you don't have to be a foreigner to enjoy this place: Its location, directly across from the Chinatown gates, makes it one of the best spots to pull up a chair and watch downtown bustle with life. The menu offers affordable, light fare—sandwiches, burgers, quiches, pastas, and salads—though the main courses get a bit more pricey (around $15 for salmon or lamb). But the reason to come here is not to indulge, but to "cafe it," so arrive ready to rest your weary shopping feet, get amped on java, snack on a pastry, and soak up the streetside scene.

**Café Metropol.** 168 Sutter St. (between Montgomery and Kearny sts.). ☎ **415/732-7777.** Salads and sandwiches $6.50–$8; main courses $9–$13. AE, DC, MC, V. Mon–Fri 7:30am–9pm, Sat 11am–4pm. Bus: 2, 3, 4, 9X, 15, 30, or 45. CALIFORNIA/ITALIAN.

A highly designed interior and full bar make the Metropol immediately alluring, but it's the colorful, flavorful, and fresh salads and other healthy, produce-oriented dishes that keep loyal locals coming back for more. The bean salad, for example, is no plain old green, garbonzo, and kidney mix, but rather black and whites tossed with mango, tomatoes, and cilantro. Beet salads have been in fashion recently, so you can bet on finding one here too—with pears, red onions, herbs, and lemon vinaigrette. (In case you're the kind who needs visual inspiration, most salads are temptingly displayed behind glass.) Sandwiches are of the gourmet variety: roast pork loin, grilled eggplant, and roast beef on brioche with horseradish sauce and pickled onions. Most dishes are available in half portions—great for grazers. But if you must go hearty, the rosemary chicken with goat cheese mashed potatoes or one of the pasta dishes will do you right. There's also a splendid selection of housemade sweets. *Tip:* Come for lunch, when the place is at its liveliest.

**California Pizza Kitchen.** 438 Geary St. (Mason and Taylor sts.). ☎ **415/563-8911.** Pizzas $7.50–$10; main courses $7–$10.50. AE, DC, DISC, MC, V. Mon–Thurs 11:30am–10pm, Fri–Sat 11:30am–11pm, Sun noon–10pm. Bus: 2, 3, 7, 27, or 38. CALIFORNIA/PIZZA.

There's nothing unique about this particular outpost of the trendy pizza chain—just more of its trademark neon and black-and-yellow 1980s-style decor and blaring retro-pop music. But while "CPK" is hardly cutting-edge contemporary, it is a revolutionary diversion, both visually and culinarily, from yesterday's fast-food pizza joint. The 1990s California-style selection of pies may send a toppings traditionalist into a tantrum, but those ready for a twist on the standard crusty disc will welcome the unusual wood-fired–oven combinations—shrimp scampi, kung-pao chicken, goat cheese, grilled burrito, even a BLT version, to name just a few. The soups, nine types of salads (by the half or full order), pastas, and sandwiches on the menu ensure that there's something for everybody. And yes, you can get a good old pepperoni pizza here, too.

# Union Square & Financial District Dining

Cafe Bastille 21
Cafe Claude 17
Cafe de la Presse 16
Cafe Metropol 18
Cafe Tiramisu 21
California Pizza Kitchen 6
Cha Am Express 19

David's Delicatessen 5
Dottie's True Blue Cafe 9
Emporio Armani Cafe 14
Family Inn Coffeeshop 8
Fizz Supper Club 21
Grand Cafe 7
Kokkari 23

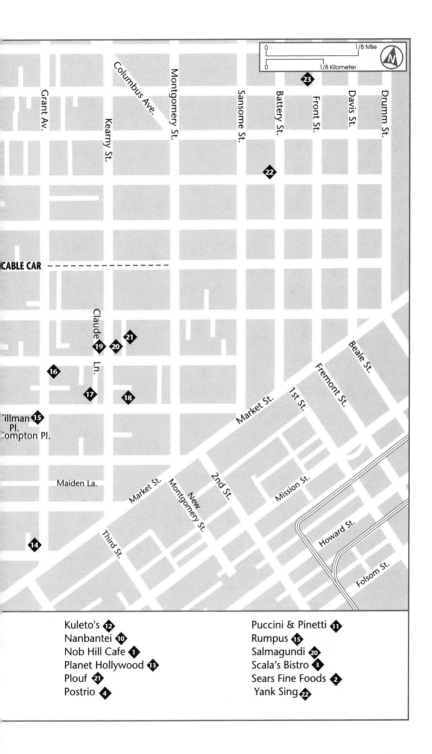

0                    1/8 Mile
0              1/8 Kilometer

Columbus Ave.
Montgomery St.
Grant Av.
Kearny St.
Sansome St.
Battery St.
Front St.
Davis St.
Drumm St.

**23**

**22**

CABLE CAR

Claude Ln.

**19** **20** **21**

**16**

**17** **18**

Tillman Pl. **15**
Compton Pl.

Beale St.

Fremont St.

Market St.
1st St.

Maiden La.

Market St.
New Montgomery St.
2nd St.
Mission St.

Third St.

Howard St.

**14**

Folsom St.

Kuleto's **12**
Nanbantei **10**
Nob Hill Cafe **1**
Planet Hollywood **13**
Plouf **21**
Postrio **4**

Puccini & Pinetti **11**
Rumpus **15**
Salmagundi **20**
Scala's Bistro **3**
Sears Fine Foods **2**
Yank Sing **22**

99

✪ **Emporio Armani Cafe.** 1 Grant Ave. (at O'Farrell St., off Market St.). ☎ **415/677-9010.** Main courses $6–$13. AE, DC, DISC, MC, V. Mon–Sat 11:30am–4:30pm, Sun noon–4:30pm. Bus: All Union Square buses. ITALIAN.

All the hobnobbing of an elite dining club comes cheaply at the counter of the Armani Cafe. It's nothing more than a circular counter located in the middle of Armani's ever-fashionable (and expensive) clothing store. But the fare and the upscale/casual atmosphere are enough to lure folks who only have lunch, not a new designer suit, on their minds. Local favorites include a homemade antipasto misto, artichoke-heart salad with baby greens and shaved Parmesan, and penne with smoked salmon, tomato, vodka, mascarpone cheese, and chives. There's also a nice variety of sandwiches and, as always, a large dose of attitude. Although there are some dishes that cost more than $10, you can snack well on a 10-spot here. Outside seating is available when weather permits.

**Kuleto's.** 221 Powell St. (between Geary and O'Farrell sts., in the Villa Florence Hotel). ☎ **415/397-7720.** Reservations recommended. Breakfast $5–$10; main courses $8–$22. AE, CB, DC, DISC, MC, V. Mon–Fri 7–10:30am; Sat and Sun 8–10:30am; daily 11:30am–11pm. Cable car: Powell-Mason and Powell-Hyde lines. Muni Metro: Powell. Bus: 2, 3, 4, or 38. ITALIAN.

Kuleto's is a beautiful place filled with beautiful people who are here to see and be seen (don't come under- or overdressed). The best plan of action is to skip the wait for a table, muscle a seat at the antipasto bar, and fill up on appetizers (which are often better than the entrees). For a main course, try the penne pasta drenched in a tangy lamb-sausage marinara sauce, the clam linguini (generously overloaded with fresh clams), or any of the fresh-fish specials grilled over hardwoods. If you don't arrive by 6pm, expect to wait—this place fills up fast.

**Nanbantei.** 115 Cyril Magnin St. (at Ellis St.). ☎ **415/421-2101.** Main courses $4–$6. AE, DC, MC, V. Lunch Mon–Fri 11:30am–2pm, dinner Mon–Thurs 5–10:30pm, Fri–Sun 5–11:30pm. Bus: 27 or 38. JAPANESE.

This flashy San Francisco branch of the original in Tokyo serves only yakitori, those savory skewered and grilled meats and veggies that we can never seem to get enough of. It's all prepared Benihana style, with acrobatic chefs whirling knives around and making lots of "Hi!," "ahhh," "ooohh" sounds to everyone's amusement. Choices range from Japanese eggplant and grilled octopus dumplings to duck breast with onions, marinated beef tongue, and prawns. Our favorites are the asparagus spears wrapped in thinly sliced pork, and the grilled shiitake mushrooms. A few tables are perched beside windows overlooking downtown San Francisco, but the best seats are at the long, arched yakitori bar, where the deft chefs spear together nearly 30 versions of the meal-on-a-stick. You can order either one pair at a time if you like the show, or all at once for a feast; about a half dozen make a meal. The terminally indecisive can opt for the Yakitori Dinner Set for $19.95: 12 sticks of yakitori (vegetable, pork, beef, and chicken), along with miso soup, steamed rice, pickles, and dessert.

**Planet Hollywood.** 2 Stockton St. (at Market St.). ☎ **415/421-7827.** Reservations accepted only for parties of 20 or more. Main courses $8.50–$18.95. AE, DC, DISC, MC, V. Sun–Thurs 11am–11am, Fri–Sat 11am–midnight. Muni Metro: All lines. Bus: 38 or any Market St. bus. AMERICAN.

You won't find any locals here (or movie stars, for that matter), but for some reason visitors can't help but flock to Planet Hollywood. Similar to the Hard Rock Cafe (though the food's not as good), this is a theme-restaurant chain that exhibits movie—instead of music—memorabilia. Expect plenty of wide-eyed tourists and a large menu featuring salads, sandwiches, pastas, burgers, pizzas, fajitas, and a few grilled meat items.

**Puccini & Pinetti.** 129 Ellis St. (at Cyril Magnin St.). ☎ **415/392-5500.** Reservations recommended. Main courses $7.95–$14.95. AE, CB, DC, DISC, MC, V. Mon–Thurs 11:30am–10pm, Fri–Sat 11am–11pm, Sun 5–10pm. Cable car: Powell-Mason line. Bus: 27 or 38. ITALIAN.

It takes some buco bravado to open an Italian restaurant in San Francisco, but partners Bob Puccini and Steve Pinetti obviously did their homework—this trendy little trattoria has been packed since the day it opened. The formula isn't exactly unique: good food at fair prices. What really makes it work, though, is the upbeat yet casual ambience, the colorful decor, a good location, and a very "in" crowd. The menu doesn't take any chances. Italian standbys—pastas, salads, wood-fired-oven pizzas, grilled meats—dominate the menu. The grilled pork loin served over polenta and topped with grilled asparagus and a balsamic reduction sauce has been well received. The fresh-baked focaccia sandwiches do well during lunch, as does the grilled portobello mushrooms with fresh mozzarella, roasted peppers, and baby mixed greens. The creamy tiramisu makes for a proper finish.

**Rumpus.** 1 Tillman Place (off Grant Ave., between Sutter and Post sts.). ☎ **415/421-2300.** Reservations recommended. Main courses $11.95–$19.95. AE, DC, MC, V. Mon–Sat 11:30am–2:30pm; Sun–Thurs 5:30–10pm; Fri–Sat 5:30–11pm. Bus: 2, 3, 4, 30, 45, or 76. Cable car: Powell-Hyde and Powell-Mason lines. CALIFORNIA.

Tucked into a small cul-de-sac off Grant Avenue you'll find Rumpus, a fantastic restaurant serving well-prepared California fare at reasonable prices. The perfect place for a business lunch, shopping break, or dinner with friends, Rumpus is architecturally playful, colorful, and buzzing with conversation. The menu is affordable, offering a delight of flavorful options, such as the pan-roasted chicken whose crispy and flavorful crust is almost as delightful as the perfectly cooked chicken and mashed potatoes beneath it; and the quality cut of New York steak comes with savory mashed potatoes. If nothing else, make sure to stop in for one of the best desserts we've ever had: the puddinglike chocolate brioche cake. (We've introduced it to out-of-town guests, and they've cursed us ever since because they now know it exists and can't get it at home.)

**Scala's Bistro.** 432 Powell St. (at Sutter St.). ☎ **415/395-8555.** Reservations recommended. Breakfast $7–$10; lunch and dinner main courses $9–$18. AE, CB, DC, DISC, MC, V. Mon–Fri 7am–midnight; Sat–Sun 8am–midnight. Cable car: Powell-Hyde line. Bus: 2, 3, 4, 30, 45, or 76. FRENCH/ITALIAN.

We had heard so much hype about Scala's Bistro when it first opened that we were sure it wouldn't live up to our expectations. Let's just say we were happily mistaken. Firmly entrenched at the base of the refurbished Sir Francis Drake Hotel, this latest venture by husband-and-wife team Giovanni (the host) and Donna (the chef) is one of the better restaurants in the city. The Parisian-bistro/old-world atmosphere blends just the right balance of elegance and informality, which means it's perfectly okay to have some fun here (and apparently most people do).

Drawing from her success at Bistro Don Giovanni in Napa, Donna has put together a fantastic array of Italian and French dishes that are priced surprisingly low. Start with the Earth and Surf calamari appetizer (better than anything we've sampled along the Mediterranean) or the grilled portobello mushrooms. The Golden Beet salad and Anchor Steam mussels are also good bets. Generous portions of the moist, rich duck-leg confit will satisfy hungry appetites, but if you can only order one thing, make it Scala's signature dish: the seared salmon. Resting on a bed of creamy buttermilk mashed potatoes and ensconced with a tomato, chive, and white-wine sauce, it's one of the best salmon dishes we've ever tasted. Finish with the creamy Bostini cream pie, a dreamy combo of vanilla custard and orange chiffon cake with a warm chocolate glaze.

**Sears Fine Foods.** 439 Powell St. (between Post and Sutter sts.). ☎ **415/986-1160.** Reservations for parties of 6 or more. Breakfast $3–$8; salads and soups $3–$18; main courses $6–$10. No credit cards. Thurs–Mon 6:30am–2:30pm. Cable car: Powell-Mason and Powell-Hyde lines. Bus: 2, 3, 4, or 38. AMERICAN.

Sears would be the perfect place for breakfast on the way to work, but you can't always guarantee you'll get in the door before 9am. It's not just another pink-tabled diner run by motherly matrons—it's an institution, famous for its crispy, dark-brown waffles, light sourdough French toast, and Swedish, silver-dollar-sized pancakes. As the story goes, Sears was founded in 1938 by Ben Sears, a retired clown, but it was his Swedish wife, Hilbur, who was responsible for the legendary pancakes, which are still whipped up according to her family's secret recipe. Keeping up with the 1990s trend, the menu also offers a "healthy-heart menu."

## SUPER-CHEAP EATS

**David's Delicatessen.** 474 Geary St. (between Mason and Taylor sts.). ☎ **415/276-5950.** Soups $3–$6; most sandwiches $3–$8; most main courses $8–$12. AE, DISC, MC, V. Mon–Fri 7am–midnight, Sat–Sun and major holidays 8am–midnight. Closed Jewish holidays. Cable car: Powell-Hyde or Powell-Mason line. Bus: 2, 3, 4, or 76. JEWISH DELI.

You might wonder what's so special about this old kosher deli, which looks as if it's right out of the 1960s. Well, for one thing, in the 1960s it was *the* dining hot spot for theatergoers, so for many longtime San Franciscans, years of memories were made here. Nowadays there's far less hoopla and fanfare, so what's left is the food: breakfast (including eggs, pancakes, and blintzes), soups (like cabbage borscht, split pea, and matzoh ball), sandwiches (egg and onion, meatball, chopped liver, and brisket, among many others), and such standards as meatloaf, stuffed cabbage, burgers, chicken, and blintzes, which are all fine and served in large portions, but not fantastic. However, with designer diners and restaurant chains snuffing out good old American tradition everywhere you look, there's something soothing about grabbing a stool and eating the plain, old-fashioned way.

**✪ Dottie's True Blue Café.** 522 Jones St. (at O'Farrell St.). ☎ **415/885-2767.** Reservations not accepted. Breakfast $4.25–$8; main courses $4–$8. DISC, MC, V. Wed–Mon 7:30am–2pm. Cable car: Powell-Mason line. Bus: 2, 3, 4, 27, or 38. AMERICAN.

This family-owned breakfast restaurant within the Pacific Bay Inn is our favorite downtown diner. It's the kind of place you'd expect to see off Route 66, where most customers are on a first-name basis with the staff and everyone is welcomed with a hearty hello and steaming mug of coffee. Dottie's serves above-average American morning fare (big portions of French toast, pancakes, bacon and eggs, omelets, and the like) delivered to blue-and-white checkerboard tablecloths on rugged, diner-quality plates. Whatever you order arrives with delicious homemade bread, muffins, or scones. There are also daily specials and vegetarian dishes.

**Family Inn Coffee Shop.** 505 Jones St. (at O'Farrell St.). ☎ **415/771-5995.** Main courses $4–$6. No credit cards. Tues–Fri 7am–6pm, Sat 7am–4:30pm. Bus: 2, 3, 4, or 38. AMERICAN.

If you want a really inexpensive, hearty meal, it's hard to top the Family Inn. The menu varies daily, but homemade soups are featured at lunch, along with a special main course served with mashed potatoes, a vegetable, bread, and dessert that costs less than $6. It's not the least bit fancy—just counter seats in front of a hard-working kitchen—but the food is wholesome and good, and the price is right.

**Haute Cuisine Hint**

So you want to dine in high San Francisco style but can't afford the experience. Well, my friend, here's the inside scoop: Both Postrio and the Grand Café, two of the city's primo restaurants, have small "open kitchens" in their stylish cocktail lounges, serving cuisine on par with their main menu at about half the price (and the tip). What's more, you don't need a reservation.

---

**Salmagundi.** 308 Kearny St. (at Bush St.). ☎ **415/981-SOUP.** Soups and salads $3.50–$8.50. AE, MC, V. Mon–Fri 8am–4pm. Bus: 15. AMERICAN.

If you're pinching pennies on this trip, there's no better deal on a meal near Union Square than at Salmagundi. Bright, pleasant, and sparkling clean, this cafeteria-style restaurant offers a variety of soups, salads, sandwiches, and the occasional special. Among the more unusual soup choices are Hungarian goulash, North Beach minestrone, and their most popular—sopa de tortilla.

## WORTH A SPLURGE

✪ **Grand Cafe.** 501 Geary St. (at Taylor St., adjacent to the Hotel Monaco). ☎ **415/292-0101.** Reservations accepted. Main courses $15–$27. AE, CB, DC, DISC, MC, V. Mon–Fri breakfast 7am–10:30am, lunch 11:30am–2:30pm, dinner 5:30–11pm; Sat breakfast 7–10:30am, lunch 11:30am–2:30pm, dinner 5:30–11pm; Sun breakfast 8–10:30am, brunch 11:30am–2:30pm, dinner 5:30–10pm. Valet parking $7 for 3 hr, $3 each additional 1/2 hour. Bus: 2, 3, 4, 27, or 38. CALIFORNIA/FRENCH.

With the exception of Farallon restaurant, the Grand Cafe has the most, well, grand dining room in San Francisco. The cocktail area alone is impressive, but the *pièce de résistance* is the enormous turn-of-the-century grand ballroom, a magnificent combination of old Europe and art nouveau. From every angle you'll see playful sculptures, original murals, and a cadre of dazzling deco chandeliers. Until recently, the fare had never quite lived up to the view, but chef Denis Soriano and his crew have finally worked out the kinks and are now enjoying that most coveted of clientele: the repeat customer. On a recent visit, seated in a plush booth with deep brown velvet and framed in walnut, we feasted on rich and decadent polenta soufflé, tender, pan-seared duck leg confit with cabbage-walnut dressing and a delicate baby-spinach salad with sliced pears, feta, walnuts, and fresh raspberry vinaigrette. Recommended entrees are the roasted duck breast with mission figs and huckleberry sauce, and the grilled filet mignon in a mushroom-shallot sauce—the most tender cut of meat we've ever encountered. Service was both friendly and prompt, making the entire dining experience a pleasure. *Note:* The bar area has it's own exhibition kitchen and menu, offering similar dishes for about half the price. The pizzas from the wood-burning oven are excellent, as is the grilled marinated skirt steak with whipped potatoes and red-wine sauce.

✪ **Postrio.** 545 Post St. (between Mason and Taylor sts.). ☎ **415/776-7825.** Reservations recommended. Main courses $6–$15 breakfast, $14–$15 lunch, $19–$30 dinner. AE, CB, DC, DISC, MC, V. Mon–Wed 7–10am, 11:30am–2pm, and 5:30–10pm; Thurs–Fri 7–10am, 11:30am–2pm, and 5:30–10:30pm; Sat 11:30am–2pm and 5:30–10:30pm; Sun 9am–2pm and 5:30–10pm; bar daily 11:30am–2am. Cable car: Powell-Mason and Powell-Hyde lines. Bus: 2, 3, 4, or 38. AMERICAN.

They say the higher you climb, the longer it takes to fall, and that's certainly the case with Postrio. Celebrated chefs Anne and David Gingrass left the kitchen long ago, but owner Wolfgang Puck knows how to pick his chefs and all's still well in the glamorous dining room. In fact, it's a rare night when brother chefs Mitchell and Steven Rosenthal don't perform to a full house. But eating, however, is only half the reason one comes to Postrio. After squeezing through the perpetually swinging bar—which, in its own right, dishes out excellent pizzas from a wood-burning oven in the corner—guests are forced to make a grand entrance down the antebellum staircase to the cavernous dining room below (it's everyone's 15 seconds of fame, so make sure your fly is zipped). Pure Hollywood for sure, but fun.

The menu combines Italian, Asian, French, and California styles with mixed results. When we last visited Postrio, the sautéed salmon, for example, was a bit overcooked, but the accompanying plum glaze, wasabi mashed potatoes, and miso vinaigrette were outstanding. The desserts, each artistically sculpted by pastry chef Susan Brinkley, were the highlight of the evening. Despite the prime-time rush, service was friendly and infallible, as was the presentation.

## 3 Financial District

Finding cheap eats (particularly for dinner) in the Financial District can be challenging, since most diners in this neighborhood are footing the bill with corporate credit cards or expense accounts. Nevertheless, we've scouted out some affordable options.

**Yank Sing.** 427 Battery St. (between Clay and Washington sts.). ☎ **415/781-1111.** Dim sum $2.65–$3.40 for 3 to 4 pieces. AE, DC, MC, V. Mon–Fri 11am–3pm, Sat–Sun 10am–4pm. Cable car: California St. line. Bus: 1 or 42. CHINESE/DIM SUM.

Loosely translated as "a delight of the heart," Yank Sing is the best dim sum restaurant in the Downtown/Financial District area. Poor quality of ingredients has always been the shortcoming of all but the most expensive Chinese restaurants, but Yank Sing manages to be both affordable and excellent. Confident, experienced

---

# Budget Dining at Belden Place

As cosmopolitan as San Francisco claims to be, it's woefully lacking in alfresco dining options compared to most European cities. One pocket of exceptions, however, is Belden Place, an adorable little brick alley in the heart of the Financial District that is closed to everything but foot traffic. When the weather is agreeable, the restaurants that line the alley break out the big umbrellas, tables, and chairs à la Boulevard Saint-Michel, and voilà—a bit of Paris just off Pine Street. Prices are reasonable, too, with most dinner dishes ranging from $12 to $15.

The four cafes that line Belden Place offer a wide variety of cuisines. From south to north, they are **Cafe Bastille,** 22 Belden Place (☎ **415/986-5673**), your classic French bistro and fun speakeasy basement serving excellent crepes, mussels, and French onion soup along with live jazz on weekends; **Cafe Tiramisu,** 28 Belden Place (☎ **415/421-7044**), a stylish Italian hot spot serving additive risottos and gnocchi; **Plouf,** 40 Belden Place (☎ **415/986-6491**), which specializes in big bowls of mussels slathered in a choice of seven sauces as well as fresh seafood; and **Fizz Supper Club,** 471 Pine St. (☎ **415/421-3499**), a chic American-Mediterranean bistro serving such entrees as Andouille-stuffed quail with saffron risotto cake and braised rabbit with jalapeño peach chutney. There's also live jazz nightly at Fizz, but it's a cloudless San Francisco day that draws the city's sun-starved culinary cognoscenti to all four of these chic little cafes.

---

# Food Courts

Catering to the dense population of downtown white-collar workers, the **Rincon Center's Food Court,** 101 Spear St., at Mission Street (☎ **415/777-4100**), has about a dozen to-go places serving cheap, respectable fare ranging the gastronomic gamut: Korean, American, Mexican, pizza, coffee and cookies, Indian, Thai, sandwiches, Middle Eastern, and Chinese. You can't eat where you buy, but there's a sea of tables dispersed throughout the indoor courtyard. Most of the restaurants are open Monday to Friday from 11am to 3pm, but some remain open until early evening.

Similar eats, though not as good or as cheap, can be found at the base of **Embarcadero Four's Justin Herman Plaza,** located at the foot of Market Street at the Embarcadero. It's a great place to catch a few rays when the sun is shining.

---

servers take the nervousness out of novices—they're good at guessing your gastric threshold. Most dim-sum dishes are dumplings, filled with tasty concoctions of pork, beef, fish, or vegetables. *Congees* (porridges), spareribs, stuffed crab claws, scallion pancakes, shrimp balls, pork buns, and other palate-pleasers complete the menu. Like most good dim-sum meals, at Yank Sing you choose the small dishes from carts continually wheeled around the dining room. While the food is delicious, the location makes this the most popular tourist spot; locals generally head to Ton Kiang way out in the Richmond District. A second location is at 49 Stevenson St., off First Street (☎ **415/541-4949**).

## SUPER-CHEAP EATS

**Cha Am Express.** 307 Kearny St. (at Bush St.). ☎ **415/956-8241.** Main courses $3–$6. No credit cards. Mon–Fri 10:30am–4pm. Cable car: California St. line. Bus: 9X, 15, or 38. THAI.

With only three bar tables and a cafeteria-style counter, this no-frills eatery is hardly the place to come for a relaxing and atmospheric meal. However, as far as fast food goes, Cha Am is an excellent option. An offspring of Berkeley's and SoMa's popular Cha Am restaurants, this one offers such saucy specials as cashew chicken, pork eggplant, roast duck, sweet beef and peanut curry, and sautéed mixed vegetables—each served fresh and with rice—for less than $4.

## WORTH A SPLURGE

✪ **Kokkari.** 200 Jackson St. (at Front St.). ☎ **415/981-0983.** Reservations recommended. Main courses $14.95–$24. AE, DC, MC, V. Mon–Fri 11:30am–2:30pm lunch; Mon–Thurs 5–11pm, Fri–Sat 5pm–midnight dinner. Valet parking: $6. Bus: 41, 15, 12, 42, or 83. GREEK.

Greek food has never blown our minds before, but a night at Kokkari quickly did just that. The hottest new restaurant in town (dubbed by food critic Michael Bauer as one of the best in the States) comforts the crowds in two dining rooms. The first is a beautifully rustic living room with a huge fireplace, oversized furnishings and an air of home. Past the bar, generally two-deep with yuppies, the other main room is more casual with exposed wood beams, pretty standing lamps, and a view of the glass-enclosed private dining room where during our dinner guests attempted a drunken rendition of Greek dancing. Executive chef Jean Alberti, however, gives everyone reason to celebrate with his traditional Aegean dishes. A great way to start the meal is with *Pikilia,* a sampling of traditional Greek spreads served with *dolmathes.* There are excellent soups and salads, too, but try not to fill up on starters.

The moussaka (eggplant, lamb, potato, and bechamel) is to die for and the quail, stuffed with winter greens served on oven-roasted leeks, orzo, and wild rice *pilafi*, is phenomenal. In fact, the only complaint we have is the valet parking situation: The wait at the end of the meal can be tediously long.

## 4 Nob Hill/Russian Hill

**The Golden Turtle.** 2211 Van Ness Ave. (between Broadway and Vallejo St.). ☎ **415/441-4419.** Main courses $8–$12. AE, CB, DC, DISC, MC, V. Tues–Sun 5–11pm. Bus: 38 or 45. VIETNAMESE.

The Golden Turtle is widely regarded as one of the city's finest Vietnamese restaurants, a far cry better than the typical *pho* noodle houses that have recently sprung up all over the place. Located in a converted Victorian home on a busy stretch of Van Ness, the restaurant's elaborate carved-wood paneling creates a soothing, romantic ambiance. Recommended dishes are the five-spice roasted chicken, marinated barbecued quail, imperial rolls with minced pork, prawn, and crab; and any of the seasonal crab dishes.

**Hard Rock Cafe.** 1699 Van Ness Ave. (at Sacramento St.). ☎ **415/885-1699.** Reservations accepted for groups of 15 or more. Main courses $6–$16. AE, DC, DISC, MC, V. Sun–Thurs 11:30am–11pm; Fri–Sat 11:30am–midnight. Valet $4.25 for 2 hr. Cable car: California St. line. Bus: 1. AMERICAN.

We hate to plug chains, and this loud, rock nostalgia-laden place would be no exception if it didn't serve a fine burger and decent heaping plates of food at such moderate prices. Music blares to an almost exclusively tourist clientele and for many the real draw is the merchandise shop, which often has as long a line as the restaurant.

The menu offers burgers, fajitas, baby-back ribs, grilled fish, chicken, salads, and sandwiches; we usually go for the chicken sandwich with a side of onion rings, both of which are pretty darn good. Although it's nothing unique to San Francisco, the Hard Rock is a fine place to bring the kids and grab a bite.

✪ **Nob Hill Café.** 1148 Taylor St. (between Sacramento and Clay sts.). ☎ **415/776-6500.** Reservations not accepted. Main courses $7–$11.75. DC, MC, V. Daily 11:30am–10pm. Bus: 1. ITALIAN/PIZZA.

Considering the cost and formality of most meals on ultra-elite Nob Hill, it's no wonder that neighborhood residents don't mind waiting around for a table to open up at the Nob Hill Café. This is the kind of place where you can come wearing jeans, relax over a large bowl of pasta and a glass of merlot, and leave fulfilled without blowing a wad of dough. The dining room is split into two small, simple rooms, with windows looking onto Taylor Street and bright local art on the walls. Service is friendly, and one of the owners is almost always on hand to satisfy your every need. When the kitchen is "on," expect fare worth at least twice its price; on off days, it's still decent. Start with a salad or the decadent polenta with tomato sauce. Then fill up on the veal picatta, any of the pastas or pizzas, or petrole sole. It also serves the best french fries we've ever had—period!

**Zarzuela.** 2000 Hyde St. (at Union St.). ☎ **415/346-0800.** Main courses $8.95–$13.95. DISC, MC, V. Tues–Sat 5:30–11pm. Cable car: Powell-Hyde line. Bus: 41 or 45. SPANISH.

Cashing in on the tapas craze is Zarzuela, a relative newcomer to the Russian Hill dining scene. You can't miss the blazing yellow awning at the corner of Hyde and Union. Inside, Spanish music bounces off tiled flooring and sandy-colored walls adorned with hand-painted plates. The table settings are rather formal: Wine glasses are standard issue, as are white tablecloths covered with butcher paper. Good bread and a small dish of olives are brought immediately by oh-so-polite waiters, which is a good thing considering that the kitchen takes its sweet time preparing your meal. Aside from a superb version of Paella Valenciana (which is only prepared for two or more and takes 30 minutes), the menu lists a wide array of hot and cold tapas as well as classic Spanish plates such as grilled lamb, oxtail casserole, and zarzuela (seafood stew) at reasonable prices. *Note:* Parking is a nightmare in Russian Hill, so you might want to take a cab.

## SUPER-CHEAP EATS

✪  **Swan Oyster Depot.** 1517 Polk St. (between California and Sacramento sts.). ☎ **415/673-1101.** Reservations not accepted. Seafood cocktails $5–$8; clams and oysters on the half shell $6–$7.50 per half dozen. No credit cards. Mon–Sat 8am–5:30pm. Bus: 27. SEAFOOD.

Pushing 90 years of faithful service to Bay Area chowder-heads, the Swan Oyster Depot is classic San Francisco; a unique dining experience you shouldn't miss. Opened in 1912, this tiny hole in the wall run by the city's friendliest and vivacious servers is little more than a narrow fish market that decided to slap down some bar stools. There are only 20 or so seats jammed cheek by jowl along a long marble bar. Most patrons come for a quick cup of chowder or a plate of half-shelled oysters that arrive chilling on crushed ice. The menu is limited to fresh crab, shrimp, oyster, and clam cocktails, Maine lobster, and Boston-style clam chowder, all of which are exceedingly fresh. *Note:* Don't let the lunchtime line dissuade you—it moves fast.

## 5 South of Market (SoMa)

✪  **AsiaSF.** 201 9th St. (at Howard St.). ☎ **415/255-2742.** Reservations accepted for large parties. Main courses $6–$14. AE, DC, MC, V. Wed–Sun 5–10pm. Bus: 9, 12, 42, or 47. CALIFORNIA-ASIAN.

Who knows what took so long for San Francisco to follow New York's lead and open a great restaurant featuring "gender illusionists?" But it's now the rage and at AsiaSF you'll be entertained by Asian men—dressed as women—who lip-sync to show tunes as they dish out an excellent grilled shrimp and herb salad, Asian-influenced hamburger, pot stickers, duck quesadillas, and chicken sate. Fortunately, the food and the atmosphere are as colorful as the staff, which means a night here is more than a meal, it's a very happening event.

**Bizou.** 598 Fourth St. (at Brannan St.). ☎ **415/543-2222.** Reservations recommended. Main courses $12.50–$21. AE, MC, V. Mon–Fri 11:30am–2:30pm; Mon–Thurs 5:30–10pm; Fri–Sat 5:30–10:30pm. Closed Sunday. Bus: 15, 30, 32, 42, or 45. FRENCH/ITALIAN.

Bizou is a quaint neighborhood-style restaurant serving wonderfully flavorful food at very reasonable prices. The restaurant's golden-yellow walls and terra-cotta ceiling are warmly lit by antique light fixtures and art-deco wall sconces, and provide an atmosphere perfect for a first date, or an evening out with Mom. The wait staff is friendly and professional, and all the ingredients are fresh and in creative combinations. Our only complaint is that on our last visit literally every dish was rich and powerfully flavorful (including the salads), it was a bit of a sensory overload. The menu's starters include an Italian flat bread with caramelized onions, fresh herbs, and Parmesan cheese, Sonoma duck-liver terrine, and baked shrimp with white beans, tomato, and feta. The main courses may include a grilled veal chop with broccoli-rabe potato gratin or stuffed chicken with celeriac, apple, and goat cheese. All main-course portions are substantial here, so don't overindulge on appetizers.

# Dining Around Town

Ace Wasabi's 10
Andalé Taqueria 9
Asia SF 47
Balboa Cafe 13
Beach Chalet 31
Betelnut 19
Bizou 78
Boudin Sourdough
  Bakery & Cafe 63
Boulevard 69
Caffé Centro 75
Cafe Flore 38
Cafe Kati 28
Cafe Marimba 3
Cafe Pescatore 64
Caffé Freddy's 66
Caffé Luna Piena 36
Cha Am 74
Cha Cha Cha 80
Chow 40
Cliff House 30
Crab Cake Lounge at
  McCormick & Kuleto's 60
Crêpes on Cole 82
Doidge's 18
E'Angelo Restaurant 5
Elite Cafe 23
Eliza's 49
Eos 83
Firewood Cafe 35
Fog City Diner 68
Fringale 77
Golden Turtle 58
Gordon Biersch
  Brewery 71
The Grove 6
Greens Restaurant
  Fort Mason 1
Hamburger Mary's 46
Hard Rock Cafe 57
Hayes Street Grill 51
Home Plate 8
Hong Kong Flower
  Lounge 30
Hot 'n' Honky 47
Il Fornaio 68
Isobune 27
Jackson Fillmore 21
Kabuto Sushi 30
Khan Toke Thai House 30
La Canasta 12
La Méditerranée 22

Long Life Noodle Co. 70
Lou's Pier 47 62
LuLu 73
Mad Dog in the Fog 33
Mad Magda's Russian
  Tea Room & Cafe 50
The Mandarin 61
Manora's 45
Marcello's 36
Mecca 42
Mel's Diner 15 & 30
Mifune 27
Millennium 52
Neecha Thai 29
Nippon Sushi 41
North India
  Restaurant 16
Original Joe's 54
Osome 24
Pane e Vino 17
Patio Cafe 36
Pauline's 44
Plumpjack Cafe 14
Pluto's 4
Prego 20
The Ramp 79
San Francisco
  Art Institute Cafe 66
Sanppo 50
South Park Cafe 76
Spaghetti Western 32
Straits Cafe 30
Sushi-A 25
Swan Oyster
  Depot 56
Sweet Heat 11
Tassajara 84
Thep Phanom 34
Thirsty Bear Brewing
  Company 72
Tommy's Joynt 55
Ton Kiang 30
Truly Mediterranean 43
Tú Lan 53
2223 39
World Wrapps 7
YOYO Bistro 26
Yum Yum Fish 81
Zarzuela 59
Zinzino 2
Zona Rosa 80
Zuni Cafe 48

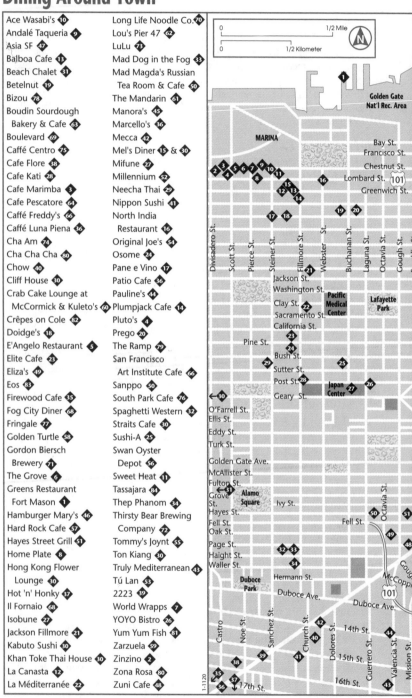

**Haight-Ashbury**

Conservatory D.
Fulton St.
McLaren Lodge
Grove St.
Cole St.
Hayes St.
Ashbury St.
Fell St.
Panhandle
John F. Kennedy Dr.
Oak St.
Golden Gate Park
Stanyan St.
Page St.
Shrader St.
Haight St.
Masonic Ave.
Kezar Dr.
86
Belvedere St.
Waller St.
Delmar St.
Pavilion
Clayton
Downey
Kezar Stadium
Beulah St.
Frederick St.
81
Carl St.
82 83
Parnassus Ave.
84

Municipal Pier
Pier 45
Pier 43 1/2
Pier 43
Pier 41
Pier 39
Pier 35
Aquatic Park
Jefferson 63 St.
Beach St. 64
62
Pier 33
60 61
North Point St.
Pier 31
Bay St.
Pier 27
Francisco St.
Chestnut St. 65
Embarcadero
Pier 23
Lombard St. 66
Columbus Ave.
68
Pier 19
Greenwich St.
67
Pier 17
Filbert St.
59
Pier 15
Union St.
Pier 9
Green St.
Pier 7
01
Vallejo St.
Davis St.
Pier 5
Broadway
Tunnel
Pier 3
58
Pacific Ave.
Pier 1
Jackson St.
Justin Herman Plaza
Ferry Building (World Trade Center)

*San Francisco Bay*

7
56
Larkin St.
Hyde St.
Leavenworth St.
Jones St.
Taylor St.
Mason St.
Powell St.
Stockton St.
Grant Ave.
Kearny St.
Montgomery St.
Sansome St.
Battery St.
Front St.
Davis St.
Drumm St.
69
70
San Francisco-Oakland Bay Bridge
Polk
71
80

Union Square

Geary St.
See also "Union Square & Financial District Dining"
Market St.
O'Farrell St.
1st St.
Fremont St.
Beale St.
Main St.
Spear St.
Steuart St.
2nd St.
Eddy St.
54
Moscone Convention Center
72
52
Market St.
Mission St.
4th St.
74
73
South Park
Howard St.
5th St.
75
Delancey St.
Folsom St.
76
3rd St.
8th St.
Harrison St.
77
78
9th St.
47
Bryant St.
Brannan St.
10th St.
11th St.
46
Townsend St.
12th St.
45
King St.
Berry St.
Division St.
Channel St.
4th St.
China Basin
Alameda St.
280
6th St.
7th St.
Illinois St.
3rd St.
79
Ness Ave.
Folsom
Harrison
Alabama
Potrero Ave.
15th St.

**109**

And save a little room for dessert—the meringue covered in chocolate and topped with coffee ice cream and candied almonds is quite a treat.

**Cha Am.** 701 Folsom St. (at 3rd St.). ☎ **415/546-9711.** Reservations recommended for parties of three or more. Main courses $5.95–$6.95 at lunch, $6.95–$14.95 at dinner. AE, DC, MC, V. Daily 11am–3pm, 5–10pm. (Happy hour, Mon–Fri 3–7pm.) Bus: 9 or 15. THAI.

Cha Am is one of those sleeper restaurants you'd never find unless someone told you about it. Hidden behind the Moscone Convention Center, this wonderful little Thai restaurant does a brisk lunch business when large conventions are in town (how conventioneers know about this place, we have no idea). A good opener is the Cha Am prawn appetizer: stuffed, grilled prawns layered with a spicy tamarind sauce. Other favorites are mu yang (marinated sweet-and-sour pork chops) and pla sam rod, a whole striped bass that's deboned and deep fried until crispy, then topped with a spicy sweet-and-sour sauce. Service by the mostly Thai staff is efficient and friendly (be sure to ask them about the daily specials), and prices are surprisingly reasonable.

✪ **Fringale Restaurant.** 570 4th St. (between Brannan and Bryant sts.). ☎ **415/543-0573.** Reservations recommended. Main courses $4–$12 at lunch, $11–$19 at dinner. AE, MC, V. Mon–Fri 11:30am–3pm; Mon–Sat 5:30–10:30pm. Bus: 30 or 45. FRENCH.

One of San Francisco's best restaurants for the money, Fringale—French colloquial for "sudden urge to eat"—has enjoyed a weeklong waiting list since the day chef/co-owner Gerald Hirigoyen first opened this small SoMa bistro. Sponged, eggshell-blue walls and other muted sand and earth tones provide a serene dining environment, which is all but shattered when the 18-table room inevitably fills with Hirigoyen's fans. For starters, try the steamed mussels with fried garlic vinaigrette, or the sheep's-milk cheese and prosciutto tureen with figs and greens. Among the dozen or so main courses on the seasonally changing menu you might find rack of lamb with potato gratin or pork tenderloin confit with onion and apple marmalade. Desserts are worth savoring, too, particularly the hazelnut-and-roasted-almond mousse cake or the signature crème brûlée with vanilla bean. The mostly French waiters provide uncharacteristically charming service, and prices are surprisingly reasonable for such high-quality cuisine. It's one of our favorites.

**Gordon Biersch Brewery Restaurant.** 2 Harrison St. (on the Embarcadero). ☎ **415/243-8246.** Reservations recommended. Main courses $7.50–$17. AE, DC, DISC, MC, V. Lunch Mon–Fri 11:30am–3pm; Sat–Sun 11:30am–4pm. Dinner Sun–Mon 5–9pm; Tues–Thurs 5–10pm; Fri–Sat 5–10:30pm (bar stays open later). Bus: 32. CALIFORNIA.

Popular with the young Republican crowd (loose ties and tight skirts predominate), this modern, two-tiered brewery and restaurant eschews the traditional brew-pub fare—no spicy chicken wings on this menu—in an attempt to attract a more upscale clientele. And it works. The baby-back ribs with garlic fries is their best seller, followed by the lemon roasted half chicken with garlic mashed potatoes. Start with the delicate and crunchy calamari fritti appetizer or, if you're garlic hounds like us, the tangy Caesar salad. Most dishes can be paired with one of the brewery's lagers. *Note:* Couples bent on a quiet, romantic dinner can skip this one; when the lower-level bar fills up, you practically have to shout to be heard. But beer lovers who want to pair their suds with decent grub will be quite content.

**Hamburger Mary's.** 1582 Folsom St. (at 12th St.). ☎ **415/626-5767.** Reservations recommended. Breakfast $5–$9; main courses $6–$10. AE, DC, DISC, MC, V. Tues–Thurs 11:30am–1am; Fri 11:30am–2am; Sat 10am–2am; Sun 10am–1am; closed Monday. Bus: 9, 12, 42, or 47. AMERICAN.

San Francisco's most . . . alternative burger joint, Hamburger Mary's is a popular hangout for gays, lesbians, and just about everyone else eschewing society's norms.

The restaurant's kitsch decor includes thrift-shop floral wallpaper, family photos, garage-sale prints, stained glass, religious drawings, and Oriental screens. You'll get to know the bar well—it's where you'll stand with the tattooed masses while you wait for a table. Don't despair: They mix a good drink, and people watching is what you're here for anyway. Sandwiches, salads, and vegetarian dishes provide an alternative to their famous greasy burgers, served on healthful nine-grain bread (like it makes a difference). *Tip:* Go with the home fries over the french fries. In the morning, Hamburger Mary's doubles as a breakfast joint, a good stop for a three-egg omelet or French toast.

**LuLu.** 816 Folsom St. (at 4th St.). ☎ **415/495-5775.** Reservations recommended. Main courses $7–$13 lunch, $10–$18 dinner. AE, DC, MC, V. Sun–Thurs 11:30am–10:30pm; Fri–Sat 11:30am–11pm. Bus: 15, 30, 32, 42, or 45. CONTINENTAL.

Famed chef Reed Hearon put this place on the map, but long after his departure LuLu is still an excellent place for a very San Francisco dining experience.

The energy within the enormous dining room still radiates as the cadre of cooks, communicating via headsets, slide bubbling plates of pizza and shellfish in and out of the open kitchen's wood-fired ovens. Watching the carefully orchestrated chaos makes dining here something of an event. The main room seats 170 and has a crowded bar that overlooks the cavernous room, but even as you sit amidst a sea of stylish diners, the room somehow feels warm and convivial. And then there's the food, which is consistently delicious. Locals return again and again for the roasted mussels piled high on an iron skillet; the chopped salad with lemon, anchovies, and tomatoes; the pork loin with fennel, garlic, and olive oil; and any of the other wonderful dishes. Everything is served family style and is meant to be shared. Save room for dessert; opt for the gooey chocolate cake, which oozes with chocolate to be scooped up with the side of melting ice cream.

✪ **Manora's.** 1600 Folsom St. (at 12th St.). ☎ **415/861-6224.** Main courses $5.95–$11.95. MC, V. Mon–Fri 11:30am–2:30pm and 5:30–10:30pm; Sat 5:30–10:30pm; Sun 5:30–10pm. Bus: 9, 12, or 47. THAI.

Manora's cranks out some of the best Thai in town, and is well worth a jaunt to its SoMa location. But this is no relaxed dining affair. It's perpetually packed (unless you come early), and you'll be seated sardinelike at one of the cramped but well-appointed tables. During the dinner rush, the noise level can make conversation almost impossible among larger parties, but the food is so darn good, you'll probably prefer to turn your head toward your plate and stuff your face. Start with a Thai iced tea or coffee and one of the tangy soups or the chicken satay, which comes with a decadent peanut sauce. Follow up with any of the wonderful dinner dishes—which should be shared—and a side of rice. There are endless options, including a vast array of vegetarian plates. Every remarkably flavorful dish arrives seemingly seconds after you order it, which is great if you're hungry, a bummer if you were planning a long, leisurely dinner. Come before seven or after nine if you don't want a loud, rushed meal.

✪ **South Park Café.** 108 South Park. (between 2nd and 3rd Sts and Brannan and Bryant sts.). ☎ **415/495-7275.** Reservations recommended during dinner. Main courses $12.50–$17.50. AE, MC, V. Mon–Fri 7:30am–10pm; Sat 6–10pm. Bus: 15, 30, 32, 42, 45, or 76. FRENCH.

Whenever we get the urge to dump everything and fly to Paris (which is about every day), we head to South Park Café—it's not quite the same thing as a bistro on Boulevard Montparnasse—it's in a newly hip and well-hidden SoMa locale, but it's close. Usually we're content with an espresso and pastry; a splurge involves the white-wine mussels or roasted duck breast with lavender sauce. For the ultimate

# Hog Heaven Happy Hours

It doesn't matter what your budget is—everybody appreciates happy hour. Low prices, free-flowing drinks, and a lively bar put everyone in the mood to party. And with the money you'll save on free (or super-cheap) food available at the following places, you may even feel sporting enough to buy a round or two. The following are a few of the most popular happy hours in the city that double as an early-bird dinner house:

If barbecue, cold beer, and alternative rock are your kind of Sunday afternoon, wind your way to **Bottom of the Hill,** 1233 17th St., at Missouri (☎ 415/ 626-4455), and fork over $4 for the all-you-can-eat feast, which includes chicken, sausages, and a selection of salads. Drinks will cost you a little extra (though not much), but the music is free. This deal is on Sunday only, from 4 to 7pm.

Thank goodness there's an alternative to the pot of processed pink Cheddar cheese and all-you-can-eat Ritz crackers that **Eddie Richenbacker's,** 133 2nd St., between Howard and Mission streets (☎ 415/543-3498), otherwise always has on hand. Show up weekdays between 5 and 7pm (the earlier the better), elbow your way through the crowd of white collars, and indulge in the feast of freebies, which includes a selection of fresh seafood, pâté, sweet-and-sour pork, meatballs, and more. There's also a cool old train set overhead and a bunch of other knick-knacks to peruse as you munch. Drinks range from $3 to $6.

The party on the patio is always in fashion at **El Rio,** 3158 Mission St., at Army Street (☎ 415/282-3325), the Mission District's favorite dive. Every Friday from 5 to 7pm the place fills with the young and the thirsty, who come for seriously cheap and *muy fuerte* (strong) margaritas and the all-you-can-eat oyster bar, which costs $10. Drinks run $2 to $3.50.

The yuppified **Holding Company,** 2 Embarcadero Center (☎ 415/ 986-0797), offers 21 on-tap beers, as well as barbecued beef, assorted veggies, and platters of fruit and cheese, Monday to Friday from 5 to 7pm. Folks also love the interactive televised trivia games.

Single professionals mingle with free, juicy baby-back ribs (quickly clamor for them or miss out) along with an array of vegetables, chips and dip, and chicken wings at **MacArthur Park,** 607 Front St., at Jackson (☎ 415/398-5700), Monday to Friday from 5 to 7pm. *Hint:* The singles scene reaches its height on Friday.

Last but not least, the **Tonga Room,** 950 Mason St., at California Street (☎ 415/772-5278), is the Fairmont's version of an old-fashioned Disneyland attraction, complete with Polynesian theme and fruity cocktails. Happy hour is Monday to Friday from 5 to 7pm and features a $5 all-you-can-eat dim sum spread, as well as fruit and cheese and half-price cocktails.

romantic intention, bring a blanket and dine *sur l'herbe* at the adorable park across the street. Beware of the midweek lunch rush, though.

**Thirsty Bear Brewing Company.** 661 Howard St. (1 block east of the Moscone Center). ☎ **415/974-0905.** Reservations recommended. Main courses $12–$18. AE, DC, MC, V. Mon–Fri 11:30am–11pm, Sat noon–11pm, Sun 4:30–11pm. Bus: 12, 15, 30, 45, or 76. SPANISH.

Despite the dumb name, the Thirsty Bear Brewing Company quickly became a favorite of the Financial District/SoMa crowd, who come for the excellent house-made brews and Spanish food. The Paella Valenciana—a sizzling combo of chicken, shrimp, sausage, shellfish, and saffron-laden rice served in a cast-iron skillet, is a must-order. Upscale pub grub includes a variety of hot and cold tapas, a few of our favorites being the Escalivada (roasted vegetables—spicy caramelized onions are wild—served at room temperature) and the Espinacas à la Catalana (spinach sautéed with garlic, pine nuts, and raisins). Ask the waiter which brews best accompany the dishes. The house's signature dessert is La Sagrada Familia—twin towers of sugar cones (fans of Gaudí will recognize them immediately) filled with chocolate mousse that rest upon a bed of Chantilly cream and fresh berries. Almost as impressive as the food is the costly conversion from a high-ceilinged brick warehouse to a two-level industrial-chic brew pub complete with pool tables, and dart boards.

## SUPER-CHEAP EATS

✪ **Caffe Centro.** 102 South Park (between 2nd and 3rd sts. and Bryant and Brannan sts.). ☎ **415/882-1500.** Main courses under $6. AE, MC, V. Mon–Fri 7am–6:30pm, Sat 8am–4pm. Bus: 9, 15, 30, 45, 76, or 81X. CAFE.

If it's a sunny day and you're in the mood for a little SoMa adventure, you'll find no place as relaxing as this hidden cafe retreat. Caffe Centro's limited kitchen and dining room inhibits it from becoming a destination restaurant, but its simple, cozy space, too-quaint sidewalk seating, and view of a grassy minipark and lovely, Old San Francisco–style homes make it the perfect place to catch a few rays, read the paper, and simply exist. The only reminder that you're in a big city is the hip, high-tech–industry professionals who come in for a dose of high-octane java and a lunch of delicious bread, salad, and sandwiches, or a breakfast of pastries, fruit, granola, and poached eggs.

**Long Life Noodle Company & Jook Joint.** 139 Steuart St. (near Mission St.). ☎ **415/281-3818.** Main courses $5.50–$8.50. MC, V. Mon–Thurs 11:30am–10pm; Fri 11:30am–11pm; Sat 5pm–11am; Sun 5–10pm. Bus: 15, 30, 32, 42, or 45. NOODLES.

Asian noodles are all the rage these days, so it comes as no surprise that big-time restaurateurs such as George Chen of Betelnut are willing to invest big bucks in what has traditionally been a small-change business. The concept at Long Life is to offer a wide range of unfamiliar noodle dishes gleaned from China, Korea, Japan, and other Asian lands and serve them in a familiar Westernized setting (in this case, a sleek, supermodern interior with lots of neon and Plexiglas). The problem is choosing from the 30 or so noodle dishes, all of which are wildly different. Do you go with Buddha's Bliss (ramen noodles in miso broth with smoked trout, tofu, and endoki mushrooms) or the Enchanted Heat (a "Chinese hangover cure" comprised of whole-wheat noodles, lily pods, tree ears, and secret healing ginseng herbs)? We recommend you try the Ghengis' Buns, crisp sesame biscuits filled with Chinese roast beef, cucumber, cilantro, and hoisin sauce, and wash it all down with either the Cool Cucumber Juice or Ginseng Ginger Ale.

**Tú Lan.** 8 6th St. (at Market St.). ☎ **415/626-0927.** Main courses $3.50–$7. No credit cards. Mon–Sat 11am–9pm. Bus: 6, 7, 27, 31, 66, or 71. Cable car: Powell-Mason and Powell-Hyde lines. Muni Metro: F, J, K, L, M, N. VIETNAMESE.

You'll have to walk past the winos, weirdos, and street stench to get to this total dive Vietnamese restaurant bordering on Union Square and SoMa, but we do it happily to get our hands on the best imperial rolls on the planet. Daily crowds, and even

Julia Child (whose face graces the greasy old menus), have been known to pull up a chair at this shack of a restaurant to feast on such goodies as the out-of-this-world imperial rolls on a bed of rice noodles, lettuce, peanuts, and mint (under $5), and other regional dishes.

## WORTH A SPLURGE

✪ **Boulevard.** 1 Mission St. (at Embarcadero and Steuart St.). ☎ **415/543-6084.** Reservations recommended. Main courses $19–$30. AE, CB, DC, DISC, MC, V. Mon–Fri 11:30am–2pm; bistro 2:15–5:15pm; dinner Mon–Wed and Sun 5:30–10pm, Thurs–Sat 5:30–10:30pm. Bus: 15, 30, 32, 42, or 45. Valet parking $8. AMERICAN.

Master restaurant designer Pat Kuleto and chef Nancy Oaks teamed up to create one of San Francisco's most exciting restaurants, and though it debuted in 1993, it's still one of our—and the city's—all-time favorites.

The dramatically artistic belle-epoch interior with vaulted brick ceilings, floral-design banquettes, a mosaic floor, and fluid, tulip-shaped lamps combined with Oaks's equally impressive sculptural and mouth-watering dishes. Starters alone could make a perfect meal, especially if you indulge in the sweetbreads wrapped in prosciutto on watercress and Lola Rose lettuce with garlic croutons and a whole-grain mustard vinaigrette; Sonoma foie gras with Elderberry syrup, toast, and Bosc pear salad; or Maine sea scallops on garlic mashed potato croustade with truffle and portobello mushroom relish. The nine or so main courses are equally revered and creative, and might include pan roasted miso glazed sea bass with asparagus salad, Japanese rice, and shiitake mushroom broth or spit-roasted cider-cured pork loin with sweet potato–swirled mashed potatoes and sautéed baby red chard. Vegetarian items, such as wild-mushroom risotto with fresh chanterelles and Parmesan, are also offered. Three levels of formality—bar, open kitchen, and main dining room—keep things from getting too snobby. Though steep prices prevent most from making Boulevard a regular gig, you'd be hard-pressed to find a better place for a special, fun-filled occasion. And cocktailers: Do ask the bartender about their special martinis—they're some of the best in town.

# 6 Chinatown

**Brandy Ho's Hunan Food.** 217 Columbus Ave. (at Pacific Ave.). ☎ **415/788-7527.** Reservations accepted. Main courses $8–$13. AE, DC, DISC, MC, V. Sun–Thurs 11:30am–11pm; Fri–Sat 11:30am–midnight. Bus: 15 or 41. CHINESE.

Fancy black-and-white granite tabletops and a large, open kitchen give you the first clue that the food here is a cut above the usual Hunan fare. Take our advice and start immediately with the fried dumplings (in the sweet-and-sour sauce) or cold chicken salad. Next, move on to the fish-ball soup with spinach, bamboo shoots, noodles, and other goodies. The best main course is Three Delicacies, a combination of scallops, shrimp, and chicken with onion, bell pepper, and bamboo shoots, seasoned with ginger, garlic, and wine, and served with black-bean sauce. Most dishes here are quite hot and spicy, but the kitchen will adjust the level to meet your specifications. There is a small selection of wines and beers, including plum wine and sake.

**Great Eastern.** 649 Jackson St. (between Kearny St. and Grant Ave.). ☎ **415/986-2500.** Most main courses $8–$13. AE, MC, V. Daily 11–1am. Bus: 15, 30, 41, or 45. CHINESE.

Great Eastern is famous for its fresh and hard-to-find seafood, pulled straight from the myriad of tanks that line the walls. Rock cod, steelhead, sea chochs, sea bass, shrimp, frogs, softshell turtle, abalone—if it's even remotely aquatic and edible, it's

# Dining Near North Beach & Chinatown

Black Cat Cafe 17
Brandy Ho's Hunan Food 20
Caffe Macaroni 22
Campo Santo 19
Capp's Corner 2
Des Alpes 1
Enrico's 16
Gira Polli 3
The Gold Spike 9
Golden Boy Pizza 10
Great Eastern 24
House of Nanking 21
Hunan Home's 23
Il Pollaio 7

L'Osteria del Forno 8
Mario's Bohemian Cigar Store 5
Maykadeh 11
Mo's Gourmet Burgers 12
Oriental Pearl 25
Pasta Pomodoro 4
Rose Pistola 6
Sam Woh 24
Steps of Rome Cafe 14
Stinking Rose 15
Tavolino 12
Tommaso's 17

See also the "Dining Around Town" map to locate North Beach restaurants.

on the menu at this hugely popular Hong Kong-style dinner house. The day's catch, sold by the pound, is listed on a board. Both upper- and lower-level dining rooms are rather stylish, with shiny black and emerald furnishings.

**Hunan Home's.** 622 Jackson St. (between Kearny St. and Grant Ave.). ☎ **415/982-2844.** Main courses $6.95–$9.75. AE, CB, DISC, MC, V. Daily 11:30am–9:30pm. Bus: 15, 30, 41, or 45. CHINESE.

One of Chinatown's best Hunan restaurants, Hunan Home's is a real feast for the eyes—ubiquitous pink-and-white walls lined with big wall-to-wall mirrors that reflect armies of fish tanks and tacky chandeliers—as well as the palate. The rule of thumb here is not to put anything in your mouth until you're armed with a glass of water, because most every dish is ooooweeeee hot! Start with Home's excellent hot-and-sour soup (the acid test of every Chinese restaurant) or wonton soup (chock full of shrimp, chicken, barbecued pork, squid, and vegetables), followed by the Succulent Bread appetizer, a platter of prawns with bean curd and straw mushrooms, and the scallops à la Hunan (sautéed along with snow peas, baby corn, celery, and mushrooms). Photographs of the more popular dishes are posted out front, though it's hard to tell which ones will singe your nose hairs.

**Oriental Pearl.** 788 Clay St. (between Kearny St. and Grant Ave.). ☎ **415/433-1817.** Main courses $8.25–$9.50. AE, CB, DC, MC, V. Daily 11am–3pm and 5–9:30pm. Bus: 15, 30, 41, or 45. CHINESE/DIM SUM.

Wherever the Chiu Chow region in southern China is, one thing's for sure: They're eating well there. Oriental Pearl specializes in regional Chiu Chow cuisine, a variation of Cantonese that's unlike anything you've ever seen or tasted, such as the house special chicken meatball—a delicate mix of shrimp, chicken, water chestnuts, and ham wrapped in a thin veneer of egg whites. Other recommended choices are the pei pa tofu with shrimp, seafood chow mein, and spicy braised prawns, all served by spiffy waiters wearing white shirts and black bow ties that go well with the sedate gray-and-white interior (though the pink napkins have got to go). The roomy, spotless restaurant is so obscurely located on the second floor of a business complex that it must rely almost exclusively on repeat and word-of-mouth clientele; but the word must be spreading, because it's usually packed. Unlike most other restaurants in Chinatown, dim sum is ordered via a menu, which isn't as fun but guarantees freshness (the steaming baskets of shrimp and scallop dumplings are excellent). Prices are slightly higher than average, but most definitely worth the extra money.

## SUPER-CHEAP EATS

✪ **House of Nanking.** 919 Kearny St. (at Columbus Ave.). ☎ **415/421-1429.** Reservations accepted for 6 or more. Main courses $4.95–$8.95. No credit cards. Mon–Fri 11am–10pm; Sat noon–10pm; Sun 4–10pm. Bus: 9, 12, 15, or 30. CHINESE.

To the unknowing passerby, the House of Nanking has "greasy dive" written all over it. To its legion of fans, however, the wait—sometimes up to an hour—is worth what's on the plate. Located on the edge of Chinatown just off Columbus Avenue, this inconspicuous little diner is one of San Francisco's worst-kept secrets. When the line is reasonable, we drop by for a plate of pot stickers (still some of the best we've ever tasted) and chef/owner Peter Fang's signature shrimp-and-green-onion pancake served with peanut sauce. Trust the waiter when he recommends a special, or simply point to what looks good on someone else's table. Even with an expansion that's doubled the elbow room, seating is tight, so prepare to be bumped around a bit, and don't expect good service—it's all part of the Nanking experience.

**Sam Woh.** 813 Washington St. (by Grant Ave.). ☎ **415/982-0596.** Reservations not accepted. Main courses $3.50–$6. No credit cards. Mon–Sat 11am–3am. Bus: 15, 30, 41, or 45. CHINESE.

Very handy for late-nighters, Sam's is a total dive that's well known and often packed. The restaurant's two pocket-size dining rooms are located on top of each other, on the second and third floors—take the stairs past the first-floor kitchen. You'll have to share a table, but this place is for mingling almost as much as for eating. The house specialty is *jook* (known as congee in its native Hong Kong)—a thick rice gruel flavored with fish, shrimp, chicken, beef, or pork; the best is Sampan, made with rice and seafood. Try sweet-and-sour pork rice, wonton soup with duck, or a roast-pork/rice-noodle roll. More traditional fried noodles and rice plates are available, too; our favorites are the tomato beef with noodles and the house special chow mein.

# 7  North Beach

✪ **Black Cat Cafe.** 501 Broadway (at Kearny St.). ☎ **415/981-2233.** Reservations highly recommended. Main courses $8.75–$25, $6–$11 lunch. Credit AE, DC, MC, V. Daily 11:30am–4pm; 5:30pm–2am. Valet parking: $6 day, $8 night. Bus 12, 15, 30, or 83. SAN FRANCISCAN.

With Reed Hearon's latest sexy brasserie, he again proves he knows how to give the people what they want, which in this case is local nostalgia contrived to perfection.

The ambiance is early-century Parisian brasserie meshed with classic San Francisco, and though the concept is as highly produced as a Hollywood feature film (and we all know how San Franciscans loathe any comparison), the place definitely works. Inside, the dining room is designed for optimum people watching with high ceilings, bright lighting, red low leather booths, and strategically placed mirrors. Classic San Francisco shines in the menu, which features cuisines honoring North Beach (Italian), Chinatown, Fisherman's Wharf (seafood) and the Barbary Coast (old-fashioned grill). Executive chef Scott Warner presides over the well-organized, extensive menu, which features appetizers such as a savory fritto misto of artichokes and mushrooms, soups, salads, and clay pots (excellent beef short ribs with carrots and turnips). Main courses ranging from a giant T-bone steak for four to grilled sea bass with herb butter and french fries (or for the late-night set, perhaps one of the few all-day breakfast options). There's also a section highlighting lobster, crab and shrimp served by the pound and prepared in any of five ways (black bean, grilled with garlic and hot pepper, and so on). If you order an array of small, delicious plates you can snack your way through a perfect San Francisco dining experience. Wash it all down with a wicked Black Cat Martini (with a sake kick) and slink downstairs to the Blue Bar live jazz club where a limited menu satisfies the lounge lizards, and you'll see why this new hot spot is truly the cat's meow.

**Caffè Freddy's.** 901 Columbus Ave. (corner of Lombard St.). ☎ **415/922-0151.** Reservations accepted. Main courses $2–$8 brunch, $4–$11.75 lunch, $5–$13.75 dinner. AE, MC, V. Tues 5pm–9:30pm; Wed–Thurs 11am–9:30pm; Fri 11am–10:30pm; Sat 10am–10:30pm; Sun 10am–4pm. Bus: 15 or 41. ITALIAN.

Recognizable by the large, painted palms that frame the doorway, Caffè Freddy's attracts a young, hungry, and low-budgeted clientele that comes for the generous servings at generous prices. Pizzas, pastas, sandwiches, salads, and a large assortment of appetizers line the menu—try the antipasto plate of bruschetta, fresh melon, ham, sun-dried tomatoes, and pesto. Start with the warm cabbage salad with goat cheese, currants, walnuts, rosemary, and spinach, then move on to the restaurant's specialty: fresh seafood dishes such as mixed fish soup, steaming bowls of mussels, or thick cuts of Atlantic salmon for under $14. Granted, it's not the best Italian food you'll ever eat, but it's good, cheap, and plentiful.

**Caffè Macaroni.** 59 Columbus Ave. (at Jackson St.). ☎ **415/956-9737.** Reservations accepted. Main courses $6.95–$13.95. No credit cards. Mon–Sat 5–10pm. Bus: 15 or 41. ITALIAN.

You wouldn't know it from the looks (or name) of it, but this tiny, funky restaurant on busy Columbus Avenue is one of the best southern Italian restaurants in the city. It looks as if it can only hold two customers at a time, and if you don't duck your head when entering the upstairs dining room you might as well ask for one lump or two. Fortunately, the kitchen also packs a wallop, dishing out a large variety of antipasti and excellent pastas. The spinach-and-cheese ravioli with wild-mushroom sauce is outstanding, and the gnocchi is probably the best you'll find outside Italy. The owners and staff are always vivacious and friendly, and young ladies in particular will enjoy the attentions of the charming Italian men manning the counter.

**Capp's Corner.** 1600 Powell St. (at Green St.). ☎ **415/989-2589.** Reservations recommended. Main courses $13–$15. AE, CB, DISC, MC, V. Mon–Thurs 4:30–10pm; Fri–Sat 4:30–11pm; Sun 4–10pm. Bus: 15 or 41. ITALIAN.

This funky old family-style Italian restaurant on the corner of Powell and Green streets is one of our favorite places to take a group of friends and pig out on hearty Italian fare. Capp's is a place of givens: It's a given that there's always some high-spirited regulars hunched over the bar; that Frank Sinatra's singing on the jukebox; and that you'll always be served huge portions at low prices in a raucous atmosphere that goes on until the wee hours. The waitresses, who have worked here since the Truman administration, are usually brusque and bossy, but always with a wink. Long tables are set up for family-style dining: bread, soup, salad, choice of main dish (herb-roasted leg of lamb, veal tortellini with sun-dried tomato sauce, osso buco with fresh polenta, fettuccine with rock shrimp), and dessert—all for under $15 per person, $10 for kids. You may have to wait an hour for a table, but you won't get bored if the old cronies at the bar take a liking to you.

**Des Alpes.** 732 Broadway (between Stockton and Powell sts.). ☎ **415/391-4249.** Seven-course meal $13.50 ($7.50 for children 9 and under). MC, V. Tues–Thurs and Sun 5–9:30pm; Fri–Sat 5:30–10pm. Cable car: Powell-Mason line. Bus: 12, 15, 30, 41, 45, or 83. FRENCH/BASQUE.

Founded in 1904, Des Alpes is one of the few Basque restaurants in the city, and one of the few bastions left for authentic family-style dining. Dozens of boisterous diners pack long rows of tables with checked cloths, feasting on big platters of meats and huge bowls of soups and stews. These hearty seven-course dinners are dirt cheap—about $14 per person, and half that amount for kids 9 and under—but the caveat is that they tell you *what* you're going to eat, *when* you're going to eat it, and often *who* you're going to eat it with (though meeting your new neighbor is often the best part of your evening). The menu changes daily: On our last visit, Tuesday was fillet of sole or sweetbreads appetizer, roast beef or chicken main course; Wednesday was fish in green sauce or beef tongue appetizer, pork chops or roast lamb main course; and so on. The only alternative to the day's menu is a $17 side order of New York steak or lamb chops. If you've never had the opportunity to dine Basque style, now's your chance, and Des Alpes is the perfect place to start.

**Enrico's.** 504 Broadway (at Kearny St.). ☎ **415/982-6223.** Reservations recommended. Main courses $8–$13 lunch, $13–$19 dinner. AE, DC, DISC, MC, V. Mon–Sun 11:30–11pm;

Fri–Sat 11:30–midnight; bar daily noon–2am. Valet parking $5–$10. Bus: 12, 15, 30, or 83.
MEDITERRANEAN.

Though North Beach's Broadway has only recently began shirking its bawdy rep, Enrico's has remained the hip glitzy sidewalk restaurant/supper club that was *the* place to hang out before Broadway took its seedy downward spiral. Families may want to skip this one, but anyone with an appreciation for live jazz (played nightly), late-night noshing, and weirdo watching from the outdoor patio would be quite content spending an alfresco evening under the heat lamps. Chewy brick-oven pizza, a handful of pastas, zesty tapas, and thick steaks are hot items on the monthly changing menu. The best part? No cover charge, killer burgers served until midnight on weekends, and valet parking.

**Gira Polli.** 659 Union St. (at Columbus Ave.). ☎ **415/434-4472.** Reservations recommended. Main courses $7.50–$12.50. AE, MC, V. Daily 4:30–9:30pm. Bus: 15, 30, 39, 41, or 45. ITALIAN.

I used to live 3 blocks from Gira Polli, and man oh man do I miss it. Whenever I'd rent a video, I'd drop by here for the Gira Polli special: a foil-lined bag filled with half a wood-fired chicken (scrumptious), Palermo potatoes (the best in the city), a fresh garden salad, perfectly cooked vegetables, and a soft roll—all for less than 10 bucks. Next, I'd nab a bottle of good, cheap wine from the liquor store next door, take my goodies home, disconnect the phone, and love life for a while. *Tip:* On sunny days there's no better place in North Beach for a picnic lunch than Washington Square, right across the street.

**The Gold Spike.** 527 Columbus Ave. (between Green and Union sts.). ☎ **415/421-4591.** Main courses $10–$16.50. AE, CB, DISC, MC, V. Mon, Tues, Thurs 5–10pm, Fri–Sat 5–11pm, Sun 4:30–9:45pm. Bus: 15 or 41. ITALIAN.

This dusty, dark, funky, cavelike restaurant has endured a love-hate relationship with San Francisco since 1920. Over the decades, San Franciscans have learned to either love the Gold Spike or hate it. (Food critics Don and Betty Martin hit the nail on the head when they described it as "a pioneer museum that exploded.) Thousands of yellowing business cards plaster the walls alongside war memorabilia, stuffed moose heads, and an endless array of knickknacks that have accumulated since the place opened. Dinner consists mainly of Italian-American standards such as osso buco and veal parmigiana, all served family style at small booths opposite the bar. Recommended dishes are the eggplant parmigiana, chicken marsala, and Italian pot roast, served either à la carte or as part of a six-course dinner for an extra $3.50. A Crab Cioppino Feed is held every Friday night. Is it good food? Not particularly, but it's filling and fairly inexpensive, and the ambience is undeniably unique.

**Il Pollaio.** 555 Columbus Ave. (between Green and Union sts.). ☎ **415/362-7727.** Main courses $6.75–$12.50. AE, MC, V. Mon–Sat 11:30am–9pm. Cable car: Powell-Mason line. Bus: 15, 30, 39, or 41. ITALIAN/ARGENTINEAN.

Simple, affordable, and consistently delicious is a winning combination at Il Pollaio. The dining room is casual, the menu simple, and the fresh-from-the-grill chicken is so moist it practically falls off the bone (you'll love the tangy lemon flavor). Each meal is served with a choice of salads, and if you're not in the mood for chicken, you can opt for rabbit, lamb, pork chop, or Italian sausage.

✪ **L'Osteria del Forno.** 519 Columbus Ave. (between Green and Union sts.). ☎ **415/982-1124.** Sandwiches $5.50–$6.50; pizzas $11–$15; main courses $6–$9.75. No credit cards. Mon–Wed 11:30am–10pm; Fri–Sat 11:30am–10:30pm; Sun 1–10pm. Bus: 15 or 41. ITALIAN.

L'Osteria del Forno may only be slightly larger than a walk-in closet, but it's one of the top-three Italian restaurants in North Beach. Peer in the window facing Columbus Avenue, and you'll probably see two Italian women with their hair up, sweating from the heat of their brick-lined oven that cranks out the best focaccia (and focaccia sandwiches) in the city. There's no pomp or circumstance involved: Locals come here strictly to eat. The menu features a variety of superb pizzas and fresh pastas, plus a few daily specials (pray for the roast pork braised in milk). Small baskets of warm focaccia bread keep you going until the entrees arrive, which should always be accompanied by a glass of Italian red.

**Maykadeh.** 470 Green St. (between Kearny St. and Grant Ave.). ☎ **415/362-8286.** Reservations recommended. Main courses $10–$18. MC, V. Mon–Thurs 5–10:30pm; Fri–Sat 11:45am–11pm; Sun 11:45am–10pm. Bus: 15 or 41. PERSIAN/MIDDLE EASTERN.

If you're looking to add a little exotic adventure to your evening dinner plans, this is the place. Surrounded by a sea of Italian bistros, Maykadeh is one of San Francisco's best and most elegant Persian restaurants. The Middle East may no longer be the culinary capital of the world, but at Maykadeh you can still sample the exotic flavors that characterize Persian cuisine. Of the dozen or so appetizers offered on the menu, some of the best are the eggplant with mint garlic sauce, the stuffed grape leaves, and the lamb tongue with lime juice, sour cream, and saffron (c'mon, live a little). About eight mesquite-grilled items are offered, including fillet of lamb marinated in lime, homemade yogurt, saffron, and onions. House specialties include half a dozen vegetarian dishes, such as the eggplant braised with saffron, fresh tomato, and dried lime.

**Mo's Gourmet Burgers.** 1322 Grant Ave. (Vallejo and Green sts.). ☎ **415/788-3779.** Main courses $4.95–$12. MC, V. Mon–Thurs 11am–10:30pm; Fri 11am–11:30pm; Sat 9am–11:30pm; Sun 9am–10:30pm. Bus: 9X, 15, 30, 39, 41, or 45. AMERICAN/BURGERS.

The best and juiciest burgers in town are at this simple North Beach diner. Mo's offers a simple but winning combination: big, thick grilled patties of fresh-ground, best-quality, center-cut chuck; fresh french fries; cabbage slaw, sautéed garlic mushrooms, or beans and rice—violà! You've got the city's burger of choice (Zuni's is an easy contender, but almost twice the price). The other food—spicy chicken sandwich; steak with veggies, garlic bread, and potatoes ($12.50); and token veggie dishes—is also up to snuff, but it's that messy and memorable burger that keeps the carnivores captivated (not to mention the sinisterly sweet shakes).

✪ **Rose Pistola.** 532 Columbus Ave. (at Union and Green sts.). ☎ **415/399-0499.** Reservations highly recommended. Main courses $6.95–$18.50 lunch; most dishes $9–$24 dinner. AE, DC, MC, V. Sun–Thurs 11:30am–10:30pm with late-night menu until midnight; Fri–Sat 11:30am–11:30pm with late-night menu until 1am. Valet parking $10. Bus: 15, 30, 41, or 45. ITALIAN.

The hottest new restaurant in 1997 is still going strong under the watchful eye of restaurateur extraordinaire Reed Hearon. Like its North Beach neighborhood, the atmosphere is smart at this bustling bistro with divided dining areas and cramped tables next to the bar. Sidewalk seating is favored on sunny afternoons, but inside there's plenty to see as chefs crank out the eclectic food from the open kitchen. Fare here is meant to be shared, and aside from sandwiches, comes à la carte. The appetizer list features a barrage of hot and cold antipasti, which are reasonably priced between $2.75 and $7.50, but tend to be in small portions. We opted for fried chickpeas, an innovative and tasty new way to enjoy the seed; lemon, prosciutto, sweet pea, and mozzarella risotto fritters, which were wonderful but pricey for four golf-ball–size morsels ($4.75); and a boring—and again pricey—chopped salad ($5.50).

Along with meats and foul, you'll find a variety of fish choices on the menu. We tried mussels in a rich tomato broth, which was so flavorful we kept it around to soak up our bread long after the shellfish had been devoured. Our favorite dish, however, was the whole Arctic char, which came bathing in fennel and tapenade in a big iron skillet. The fish was crispy and perfectly seasoned on the outside, tender and juicy on the inside—definitely worth writing home about. The "flaming cream" dessert, three fried crème-brûlée–type diamonds that arrived afire with a Bacardi-and-apricot sauce, was creative and very tasty, but not worth the $7.50 asking price. Still, overall, we agree that Rose Pistola is hot for the right reasons: It's the place to be, the food is great, and the menu is varied enough for all tastes and budgets.

**Stinking Rose.** 325 Columbus Ave. (between Vallejo and Broadway). ☎ **415/781-7673.** Reservations accepted. Main courses $12–$18. AE, DC, JCB, MC, V. Sun–Thurs 11am–11pm; Fri–Sat 11am–midnight. Bus: 15, 30, 41, or 45. ITALIAN.

Garlic, of course, is the "flower" from which this restaurant gets its name. From soup to ice cream, the supposedly healthful herb is a star ingredient in most every dish. ("We season our garlic with food," exclaims the menu.) From a strictly gourmet point of view, the Stinking Rose is unremarkable. Pizzas, pastas, and meats smothered in simple, overpowering garlic sauces are tasty, but memorable only for their singular garlicky intensity. That said, this is a fun place; the restaurant's lively atmosphere and odoriferous aroma combine for good entertainment. Black-and-white floors, gray marble tables, and large windows overlooking the street help maintain the high energy. The best dishes here include garlic-steamed clams and mussels, garlic pizza, and 40-clove garlic chicken (served with garlic mashed potatoes, of course).

✪ **Tavolino.** 401 Columbus Ave. (at Vallejo St.). ☎ **415/392-1472.** Reservations recommended. Dishes $3.25–$13.50. AE, DISC, MC, V. Daily 11:30am–1am. Valet parking: $5. Bus: 15, 30, 41, or 45. VENETIAN/ITALIAN.

This casual bright restaurant, which opened in May 1998, is serving the city's finest (and perhaps only) *cicchetti,* or Venetian tapas. With sidewalk tables surrounding the corner restaurant and prices topping out at around $10, it's the perfect place for an afternoon drink or snack, but that's not to say dinner is any less enticing. The dining room—a tasteful combination of arches, columns, mahogany, and mosaic tile—is a jovial place for a supper splurge. Our favorite type of dining is sampling lots of little plates, and that's exactly what you'll do here. Fried olives stuffed with anchovy or almonds are the way to start, then go with anything from the cold bar (such as delicious oysters, octopus and mussel salad, and chilled shrimp) to steamed mussels, room-temperature sea bass with pine nuts and marinated onions, soft-shell crab with lemon aioli, seafood bolognese with penne pasta; and their signature sturgeon Saltimboca (pan fried, wrapped in proscuitto di Parma, and served with fig vinaigrette and crisp-fried sage). The specialty cocktails and moderately priced wine list are two more reasons why the restaurant is a very good addition to North Beach.

**Tommaso's.** 1042 Kearny St. (at Broadway). ☎ **415/398-9696.** Reservations not accepted. Pasta and pizza $9–$22; main courses $9–$15. AE, DC, MC, V. Tues–Sat 5–10:30pm; Sun 4–9:30pm. Closed Dec 15–Jan 15. Bus: 15 or 41. ITALIAN.

From the street, Tommaso's looks wholly unappealing; a drab, windowless brown facade sandwiched between sex shops. Then why are people always waiting in line to get in? Because everyone knows that Tommaso's bakes one of San Francisco's best traditional-style pizzas, and has for decades. The center of attention in the downstairs dining room is the chef, who continuously tosses huge hunks of garlic and mozzarella onto pizzas before sliding them into the oak-burning brick oven. Nineteen different toppings make pizza the dish of choice, even though Italian classics such as veal marsala, chicken cacciatore, and a superb lasagna are also available (they have wonderful calzones, too). Half bottles of house wines are sold, as are homemade cannoli and good Italian coffee. If you can overlook the seedy surroundings, this fun, boisterous restaurant is a great place to take the family.

## SUPER-CHEAP EATS

**Campo Santo.** 240 Columbus Ave. (between Pacific Ave. and Broadway). ☎ **415/ 433-9623.** Main courses $5.95–$8.95. MC, V. Lunch Mon–Fri 11:30am–2:30pm, dinner Tues–Sat 6–10pm. Bus: 12, 15, 30, 41, 45, or 83. MEXICAN.

Campo Santo looks a bit out of place in the heavily Italianate North Beach, but it would look a bit out of place just about anywhere in the city. Part restaurant, part Hispanic folk-art museum, the entire cafe is festooned with a dazzling riot of colorful candles, masks, icons, sculptures, and shrines celebrating the dead. The menu's imaginative entrees range from a Vera Cruz quesadilla filled with oven-roasted prawns, tomatoes, cactus nopales, and panela cheese (only $6.95) to a chicken breast sautéed in a mole sauce of dried apricots, oranges, acho chiles, and a hint of chocolate. There are also several vegetarian dishes. Prices are so low it's almost worth eating here just to admire the artwork.

**Golden Boy Pizza.** 542 Green St. (between Stockton St. and Grant Ave.). ☎ **415/ 982-9738.** Pizza slice $2–$3. No credit cards. Sun–Thurs 11:30am–11pm, Fri–Sat 11:30am–1am. Bus: 15, 30, 45, 39, or 41. ITALIAN/PIZZA.

Pass by Golden Boy when the bars are hopping in North Beach and you'll find a crowd of inebriated sots savoring steamy slices of darn good pizza. But you don't have to be bombed to enjoy the big, doughy squares of Italian-style pizzas, each enticingly placed in the front windows (the aroma alone is deadly). Locals have flocked here for years to fill up on one of the cheapest and cheesiest meals in town. Expect to take your feast to go on busy nights, as there are only a few bar seats inside.

**Mario's Bohemian Cigar Store.** 566 Columbus Ave. ☎ **415/362-0536.** Sandwiches $5–$6.25. No credit cards. Daily 10am–midnight. Closed Dec 24–Jan 1. Bus: 15, 30, 41, or 45. ITALIAN.

Across the street from Washington Square is one of North Beach's most popular neighborhood hangouts: Mario's. The century-old bar—small, well worn, and perpetually busy—is best known for its focaccia sandwiches, including meatball or eggplant. Wash it all down with an excellent cappuccino or a house Campari as you watch the tourists stroll by. And yes, they do sell cigars.

*Note:* A newer, larger location with live jazz Wednesday and Sunday nights is at 2209 Polk St., between Green and Vallejo streets (☎ **415/776-8226**).

**Pasta Pomodoro.** 655 Union St. (at Columbus Ave.). ☎ **415/399-0300.** Main courses $4.60–$8.95. MC, V. Mon–Fri 11am–11pm; Sat noon–midnight; Sun noon–11pm. Cable car: Mason St. Bus: 15, 30, 41, or 45. ITALIAN.

If you're looking for a good, cheap meal in North Beach, or anywhere else in town, for that matter, this S.F. chain can't be beat. There's usually a 20-minute wait for a table, but after you're seated you'll be surprised at how promptly you're served. Every dish is fresh and sizable, and best of all, they cost a third of what you'll pay elsewhere. Winners include the spaghetti *frutti di mare* made with calamari, mussels, scallops, tomato, garlic and wine, or *cavatappi pollo* with roast chicken, sundried tomatoes, cream, mushrooms, and Parmesan—both are under $7. Avoid the

*[San Francisco is] the city that knows how.*

—President William Howard Taft

*[San Francisco is] the city that knows chow.*

—Trader Vic, restaurateur

cappellini Pomodoro or ask for extra sauce—it tends to be dry. Of their 12 other locations a few are at 2027 Chestnut St., at Fillmore (☎ **415/474-3400**); 2304 Market St., at 16th Street (☎ **415/558-8123**); 3611 California St. (☎ **415/831-0900**); and 816 Irving St., between 9th and 10th streets (☎ **415/566-0900**).

**San Francisco Art Institute Cafe.** 800 Chestnut St. (at Jones and Leavenworth sts.). ☎ **415/749-4567.** Main courses $3–$5. No credit cards. Fall–spring, Mon–Fri 8am–9pm, Sat 9am–2pm; summer, Mon–Fri 9am–2pm. Cable car: Powell-Hyde or Powell-Mason line. Bus: 30. DELI.

One of the best-kept secrets in San Francisco, this cafe offers fresh, affordable fare for in-the-know residents and visitors as well as Art Institute students. You may have seen this place in the movie *Copycat* (its exterior served as the outside of Sigourney Weaver's ridiculously chic apartment). Though the food is tasty, it's the view that's actually the draw: From here get a bird's-eye view of the San Francisco Bay and a meal for around $5.

**Steps of Rome Café.** 348 Columbus Ave. (between Grant Ave. and Vallejo St.). ☎ **415/397-0435.** Most main courses $5–$10. AE, DC, DISC, MC, V. Wed–Mon 5:30–1am. Bus: 9X, 15, 30, 41, or 45. ITALIAN.

It's a funny thing: Name a San Francisco restaurant after one of Italy's famed hangouts and, as if transported from the ancient steps themselves, youthful Europeans swarm the place. Even the waiters speak English as a second language, if at all. But the Euro-scene adds to the vibe of this loud coffeehouse-like restaurant. The large storefront windows of the bright, split-level, simply decorated room look onto bustling Columbus Avenue. While many linger over coffee and conversation, some stay long enough to enjoy a grilled focaccia sandwich (very simply Italian), pasta (11 fettuccine choices for a mere $6 or so), or the roasted meat dish of the day, which comes with roasted potatoes for about $8 to $10. It won't be the absolute best Italian you ever had, but the pasta's respectable, and the young, lively atmosphere and prices make this a fine choice for a quick bite (as long as you're not looking for a tranquil environment, that is). Next door is the ever-lively cafe.

# 8 Fisherman's Wharf

**Cafe Pescatore.** 2455 Mason St. (at North Point St.). ☎ **415/561-1111.** Reservations recommended. Main courses $3.95–$8.95 breakfast, $10–$18 lunch or dinner. AE, DC, DISC, MC, V. Sun–Thurs 7am–10pm, Fri–Sat 7am–10:30pm; Sat–Sun 7am–3pm brunch, 3–5pm cafe menu. Cable car: Powell-Mason line. Bus: 42, 15, or 39. ITALIAN.

Though locals are a rarity at Cafe Pescatore, most agree that if they had to dine at Fisherman's Wharf, this cozy trattoria would be their first choice. Two walls of sliding glass doors offer pseudo-sidewalk seating when the weather's warm, although heavy vehicular traffic can detract from the alfresco experience. The general consensus is to order anything that's cooked in the open kitchen's wood-fired oven, such as the pizzas and roasts. A big hit with tourists is the *polenta al forno*—oak-roasted cheese polenta with marinara sauce and fresh pesto. The huge roast chicken is also a safe bet.

**✪ Crab Cake Lounge at McCormick and Kuleto's.** 900 North Point St. (at Beach and Larkin sts.). ☎ **415/929-1730.** Main courses $6–$11. AE, CB, DC, DISC, MC, V. Mon–Sat 11:30am–11pm, Sun 10:30am–11pm. Cable car: Powell-Hyde line. Bus: 19, 30, or 42. SEAFOOD/ITALIAN.

On the upper level of this glamorous (and expensive) multi-tiered restaurant is a small seafood counter called the Crab Cake Lounge, which offers huge selections of shellfish, sandwiches, and light entrees at very reasonable prices. Case in point: The calzone, made with fresh spinach, mushrooms, tomatoes, and ricotta cheese and baked in their wood-fired brick oven, goes for a mere $7. Twice the price, but worth every penny, is the heaping pile of clams, mussels, crayfish, and Dungeness crab in a garlicky broth that's perfect for dipping the crusty French bread (easily a meal for two). Other menu items range from fresh oysters on the half shell to salmon sandwiches, blackened catfish, and an array of soups and salads. Just about everything served at the lounge is under $11, though you still get a slice of the million-dollar view of the bay.

**Fog City Diner.** 1300 Battery St. (at Lombard St.). ☎ **415/982-2000.** Reservations accepted. Main courses $7.50–$19. CB, DC, DISC, MC, V. Sun–Thurs 11:30am–11pm; Fri–Sat 11:30am–midnight. Bus: 42. AMERICAN.

More popular because of its Visa commercial than its food, Fog City is a tourist destination, with a few locals straggling in for business lunches. The restaurant looks like a genuine American metallic diner, but only from the outside. Inside, dark polished woods, inspired lighting, and a well-stocked raw bar tell you this is no hash-slinger.

Dressed-up dinner dishes include gourmet chili dogs, salads, sandwiches, burgers, cioppino, and pot roast. Fancier fish and meat meals include grilled catches of the day and thick-cut steaks. Lighter eaters can make a meal out of the long list of "small plates" that include crab cakes or quesadilla with chili peppers and almonds. The place is cute and the food is fine, but if your heart is set on coming here, do so at lunch—you'll be better off elsewhere if you want a special dinner.

**Il Fornaio.** Levi Plaza, 1265 Battery St. (bounded by Sansome, Battery, Union, and Greenwich sts.). ☎ **415/986-0100.** Main courses $9–$18. AE, DC, MC, V. Mon–Thurs 7am–11pm; Fri 7am–midnight; Sat–Sun 9am–11pm. Bus: 12, 32, or 42. Valet parking $5. ITALIAN.

This trattoria is one of our favorite standbys, producing consistently good Italian fare at decent prices. The large split dining room in Levi Plaza a few minutes away from Pier 39 has lively atmosphere and smart Italian decor. By day, it is buzzing with Financial District types and socialites, by night, with couples and gathering friends.

If you don't have a reservation and can't wait to eat, pull up a stool at the marble-topped bar, where the view of the open kitchen and dining room is unobstructed. On a sunny day, grab a patio table that looks onto Levi Plaza's fountain.

Once situated, the first of many delights is the basket of fresh-baked breads, breadsticks, and a dipping dish of olive oil. Complement them with any of the delicious salads or the daily soup (especially if it's carrot), then venture onward to any of the pastas, pizzas, or main courses. Our favorite is the rotisserie duck in balsamic vinegar, which Il Fornaio somehow serves without all the fat you'd expect from duck and all the crispy skin you wish for. Parents especially appreciate the "bambini" menu, which features pint-size fare for under $6. Desserts are decadent and wonderful. Try the tiramisu and a glass of rose grappa—a perfect way to end the meal. Breakfasts here are a treat as well.

**Lou's Pier 47.** 300 Jefferson St. (near Pier 47). ☎ **415/771-5687.** Main courses $11–$18. AE, DC, MC, V. Daily 11am–11pm (club remains open until 2am). Cable car: Powell-Hyde line. Bus: 32. STEAK/SEAFOOD/CAJUN.

This popular restaurant and blues club is one of the few establishments on Fisherman's Wharf that locals will admit they've been to. The bottom floor consists of a bar and bistro-style dining room, while the upstairs hosts blues bands every night of the week, with the occasional Motown, country, and R&B act thrown in for variety. Lunch and dinner items range from a variety of Cajun classics such as gumbo ya ya, jambalaya and shrimp creole to baby-back ribs, steamed Dungeness crab, blackened swordfish, and Big Robbie's New York steak. There's only a lengthy starters menu if you just want to nosh on a Jamaica jerk salad, Louisiana crawfish bowl, or "peel 'em and eat" shrimp. *Budget Tip:* There's no cover charge until 8pm to get into the blues club.

## SUPER-CHEAP EATS

**Boudin Sourdough Bakery & Café.** 157 Jefferson St. (between Mason and Taylor sts.). ☎ **415/928-1849.** Sandwiches, soups, salads $5–$6. AE, MC, V. Mon–Thurs 7:30am–9pm, Fri–Sun 7:30am–10pm. Cable car: Powell-Mason line. Bus: 15, 32, 39, 42, or 82X. DELI.

If your only taste of the crusted, tangy, and moist loaf known as sourdough has been store-bought outside the Bay Area, you've really never experienced this delicious bread. Though locals will argue that smaller bakeries such as East Bay's Acme and Semifreddi are the real breadmasters, Boudin ("Bo-deen") does a darn good job, plus it serves sandwiches so hearty that it takes two hands to tame it. Bakery outposts are scattered throughout town and offer similar menus: turkey, ham, tuna, and roast beef sandwiches; salads; clam chowder; and other simple fare. At this location, seating is outdoors, but you can easily order your food to go (not advisable for the soup in a bread bowl, however, which gets soggy almost instantly) and head for any of the infinite open-air vista points. Of course, you can also grab a few loaves to go. (Buy it fresh on the day you're leaving if you want to take some home with you.) There are dozens of locations throughout the city, including 2890 Taylor St., at Jefferson Street (☎ **415/776-1849**), and in the basement at Macy's downtown, at O'Farrell and Stockton streets (☎ **415/296-4740**).

## WORTH A SPLURGE

**The Mandarin.** At Ghirardelli Sq., 900 North Point St. ☎ **415/673-8812.** Reservations accepted. Main courses $15–$45; fixed-price dinners $35–$45. AE, CB, DC, MC, V. Daily 11:30am–11pm. Cable car: Hyde St. line. Bus: 19, 30, 42, 47, or 49. CHINESE.

Created by Madame Cecilia Chiang in 1968, The Mandarin is meant to feel like a cultured, northern Chinese home; fine furnishings, silk-covered walls, and good-quality Asian art create one of the most elegant Chinese restaurants in the city. Tables are spaced comfortably apart, and the better of two softly lit dining rooms offers matchless views of the bay. True to its name, The Mandarin offers exceptional northern Chinese cuisine. Take our advice and start with the sesame prawns or minced squab appetizer, then follow through with either the smoked tea duck (their version of Beijing duck, but smoked over burning tea leaves until crispy) or—if you have a party of two or more and call a day in advance—the Beggar's Chicken, which is encased in clay and cooked to slow perfection.

## 9 Marina District/Cow Hollow

If you find yourself in this neck of the woods around lunchtime, you might opt for a picnic at the Marina Green, a popular recreational park with fantastic front-row bay views. The **Marina Safeway,** 15 Marina Blvd. (☎ **415/563-4946**), is the perfect place to pick up fresh-baked breads, gourmet cheeses, and other foodstuffs (including fresh cracked crab when in season). It's open 24 hours.

**Ace Wasabi's Rock 'n' Roll Sushi.** 3339 Steiner St. (at Chestnut St.). ☎ **415/567-4903.** Reservations not accepted. Main courses $4–$9. AE, MC, V. Mon–Thurs 5:30–10:30pm, Fri–Sat 5:30–11pm, Sun 5–10pm. Bus: 30. JAPANESE/SUSHI.

Yeah, more sushi, but this time with a twist. What differentiates this Marina hot spot (formerly known as Flying Kamikazes) from the usual sushi joints around town is its unique combinations, the varied menu, and the young, hip atmosphere. Ace Wasabi's innovative rolls are a nice welcome to those bored with the traditional styles, though they may be too much adventure for some (don't worry, there's plenty of non-sea and non-raw items on the menu). Don't miss the rainbow "Three Amigos" roll or the "Rock and Roll" with cooked eel, avocado, and cucumber. The buckwheat-noodle-and-julienne-vegetable salad is also a treat. The service could be improved—on busy nights you'll wait forever for your server to pour your Sapporo— but the staff is friendly and the atmosphere is fun, so nobody seems to mind.

**Balboa Café.** 3199 Fillmore St. (at Greenwich St.). ☎ **415/921-3944.** Reservations for 6 or more only. Main courses $7–$12 at lunch, $7–$21 at dinner, $7–$10 at weekend brunch. AE, DC, MC, V. Daily 11am–11pm; bar daily 11am–2am. Bus: 22. AMERICAN.

Back in the 1980s, the Balboa Café was San Francisco's main "meet market," filled each week with the young and the restless. Though things bottomed out in the early 1990s, the wheel is turning once again for this trendy, stylish Cow Hollow hangout since the crew at the wildly popular PlumpJack Café took over (in fact, patrons put on hold at PlumpJack are usually sent here for a pre-dinner cocktail). Though Balboa isn't nearly of the caliber as its around-the-corner cousin, you'll probably be forced to mingle with the Marina "pretty people" crowd at the bar until a table frees up. The limited menu offers some upscale options, such as cabernet braised short ribs with mashed potatoes and roasted root vegetables, but it's the Balboa Burgers and Caesar salads that get the most requests.

**Betelnut.** 2030 Union St. (at Buchanan St.). ☎ **415/929-8855.** Reservations recommended. Main courses $9–$16. CB, DC, DISC, MC, V. Sun–Thurs 11:30am–11pm; Fri–Sat 11:30am–midnight. Bus: 22, 41, or 45. SOUTHEAST ASIAN.

While San Francisco is teeming with Asian restaurants, few offer the posh, fashionable dining environment of this restaurant on upscale Union Street. As the menu explains, the restaurant is themed after "Pejui Wu," a traditional Asian beer house offering local brews and savory dishes. But with the bamboo paneling, red Formica countertops, and low-hanging lamps, the place feels less like an authentic harbor restaurant and more like a set out of Madonna's movie *Shanghai Surprise*. Still, the atmosphere is en vogue, with dimly lit booths, ringside seating overlooking the bustling stir-fry chefs, sidewalk tables (weather permitting), and body-to-body flirting at the cramped but festive bar. Starters include sashimi and tasty salt-and-pepper whole gulf prawns; main courses offer wok-seared Mongolian beef and Singapore chili crab (seasonal). While prices seem reasonable, it's the incidentals such as white rice ($1.60 per person) and tea ($4 per pot) that rack up the bill. Whatever you do, order their heavenly signature dessert: a mouth-watering tapioca pudding with sweet red adzuki beans.

**Café Marimba.** 2317 Chestnut St. (between Scott and Divisadero sts.). ☎ **415/776-1506.** Main courses $7–$14. AE, MC, V. Mon 5:30–10pm; Tues–Thurs and Sun 11:30am–10pm; Fri–Sat 11:30am–11pm. Bus: 30. MEXICAN.

As much as we hate to plug the yuppified Marina District, we have to admit that we're completely addicted to Café Marimba's grilled Yucatan-spiced snapper and grilled chicken tacos. Add just the right amount of guacamole and pineapple salsa, and *acheewahwah* that's good! The *shrimp mojo de ajo* (shrimp seared along with onions, garlic and jalapeño) is also a knockout (heck, even the chips and guac are the best in town). For parties of three or more, order the family-style platter of grilled meats and vegetables and prepare to do battle. We're obviously not the only ones who fancy this fun, festive cafe, so expect a long wait during peak hours (our M.O. is to sneak seats at the bar and order there). But we say *hasta mañana* to the margaritas—*muy màl.* (Hint: don't come for lunch; it's not nearly as festive as dinnertime.)

✪ **Doidge's.** 2217 Union St. (between Fillmore and Steiner sts.). ☎ **415/921-2149.** Reservations accepted and essential on weekends. Breakfast $4.50–$10; lunch $5.25–$10. MC, V. Mon–Fri 8am–1:45pm; Sat–Sun 8am–2:45pm. Bus: 41 or 45. AMERICAN.

Doidge's is sweet, small, and always packed, serving up one of the better breakfasts in San Francisco since 1971. The restaurant's fame is based on eggs Benedict; eggs Florentine, prepared with thinly sliced Motherlode ham, runs a close second. Invariably, the menu includes a gourmet omelet packed with luscious combinations, and to delight the kid in you, hot chocolate comes in your very own teapot. Lunch also puts a gourmet spin on such favorites as cobb salad, a lean ground chuck burger, grilled portobello mushroom sandwich, and the good ol' BLT. The six seats at the original mahogany counter are still the most coveted by locals.

**E'Angelo Restaurant.** 2234 Chestnut St. (between Pierce and Scott sts.). ☎ **415/567-6164.** No reservations. Main courses $7.50–$12.45. No credit cards. Tues–Sun 5–11pm. Bus: 22, 28, 30, 30X, 43, or 76. ITALIAN.

Back when I was barely making enough to cover my rent, I would often treat myself to a night out at E'Angelo. All the house specialties, pastas, and pizzas cost less than $13, the atmosphere is casual and fun, the gingham-covered tables are cozy-cramped, and the Italian staff is friendly. For me, the combination made not only for a hearty meal, but also for an opportunity to mingle with San Francisco: to live a little, eavesdrop on our neighbors' conversation, and perhaps even run into local celebrities such as Robin Williams with his family. While years have passed, not much has changed at this traditional Italian hot spot. The place still won't take reservations or credit cards, but it does serve decent portions of pastas, veal, lamb, chicken, and fish; a carafe of red or white wine for about 10 bucks (thrifty by-the-bottle prices, too); and one heck of a rich eggplant parmigiana. And unlike most of the neighboring restaurants, desserts are between $3 and $4.

**Greens Restaurant, Fort Mason.** Building A, Fort Mason Center (enter Fort Mason opposite the Safeway at Buchanan and Marina sts.). ☎ **415/771-6222.** Reservations recommended 2 weeks in advance. Lunch main courses: $8–$12; dinner main courses $11–$16; fixed-priced dinner $40; brunch $8–$11. DISC, MC, V. Mon 5:30–9:30pm; Tues–Fri 11:30am–2pm and 5:30–9:30pm; Sat 11:30am–2:30pm and 5:30–9pm; Sun brunch

**Budget Tip**

If you like Indian food and you're partial to dining early, consider the $12.95 fixed-price dinner available from 5 to 7pm at **North India Restaurant** (see below).

10am–2pm. Greens To Go Mon–Fri 8am–9:30pm; Sat 8am–3:30pm; Sun 9am–3:30pm. Bus: 28 or 30. VEGETARIAN.

Knowledgeable locals swear by Greens, where executive-chef Annie Somerville (author of *Fields of Greens*) cooks with the seasons, using produce from Green Gulch Farm and other local organic farms. Located in an old warehouse, with enormous windows overlooking the bridge and the bay, the restaurant is both a pioneer and a legend. A weeknight dinner may feature such appetizers as tomato, white-bean, and sorrel soup, or grilled asparagus with lemon, Parmesan cheese, and watercress, followed by such choices as spring-vegetable risotto with asparagus, peas, shiitake and crimini mushrooms, and Parmesan cheese, or Sri Lankan curry made of new potatoes, cauliflower, carrots, peppers, and snap peas stewed with tomatoes, coconut milk, ginger, and Sri Lankan spices.

A special four-course dinner is served on Saturday only. A recent example began with grilled asparagus, yellowfin potatoes, and peppers with blood-orange beurre blanc, followed by shiitake and crimini mushroom lasagna with leeks and mushroom port sauce. Desserts are equally adventuresome; try the chocolate pave with mint crème anglaise or the espresso ice cream with chocolate sauce (*Insider tip:* A "Late Evening Desert" is served Mon to Sat from 9:30 to 11pm.). Lunch and brunch are somewhat simpler, but equally as inventive.

Like the restaurant, the adjacent Greens To Go bakery is also operated by the Zen Center. It sells homemade breads, sandwiches, soups, salads, and pastries to take home.

**North India Restaurant.** 3131 Webster St. (at Lombard St.). ☎ **415/931-1556.** Reservations recommended. Main courses $14.50–$19.95; fixed-price dinner $12.95. AE, DC, MC, V. Mon–Fri 11:30am–2:30pm; daily 5–10:30pm. Bus: 41 or 45. INDIAN.

While many Indian establishments lack atmosphere, chef Parvesh Sahi's full Indian menu is served in a plush, dimly lit dining room, providing the perfect ambiance for an intimate evening out with some ethnic flair. As you settle into a maroon velvet chair and browse the menu, soft Indian music reminds you what part of the world your taste buds will venture to. Start by ordering a cup of the sweet and spicy chai tea, and the oversized, moist samosas (spiced potatoes and green peas served in a crisp pocket), then venture onward with any of the tandoori specials, such as the mixed seafood dish with sea bass, jumbo prawns, and calamari. There are plenty of vegetarian dishes as well, ranging from *aloo gobi* (cauliflower and potatoes in curry sauce) to *baingan aloo masala* (eggplant, potatoes, tomatoes, ginger, garlic, green onions, and spices). All these tasty feasts are accompanied by bottomless pots of delicious mango chutney and cucumber-dill sauce. Anything you order here will be fresh, well prepared, and served by courteous waiters wearing vests adorned with Indian-style mirrors and gold embroidery. Although expensive for Indian food, it's worth the extra bucks if you want to be ensured good quality and atmosphere. Arrive between 5 and 7pm and you can opt for the very affordable fixed-price dinner for $12.95.

✪ **Pane e Vino.** 3011 Steiner St. (at Union St.). ☎ **415/346-2111.** Reservations recommended. Main courses $8.50–$19.95. AE, MC, V. Mon–Thurs 11:30am–5pm and 5–10:30pm; Fri–Sat 11:30am–10:30pm; Sun 5–10pm. Valet parking Wed–Sat: $8. Bus: 41 or 45. ITALIAN.

Pane e Vino is one of San Francisco's top and most authentic Italian restaurants, as well as our personal favorite. The food is consistently excellent (careful not to fill up on the outstanding breads served upon seating), the prices reasonable, and the mostly Italian-accented staff always smooth and efficient under pressure (you'll see). The two small dining rooms, separated by an open kitchen that emanates heavenly aromas, offer only limited seating, so expect a wait even if you have a reservation. The menu offers a wide selection of appetizers, including a fine carpaccio, *vitello tonnato* (sliced roasted veal and capers in a lemony tuna sauce), and the hugely popular chilled artichoke stuffed with bread and tomatoes and served with vinaigrette. Our favorite, the antipasti of mixed grilled vegetables, always spurs a fork fight. A similar broad selection of pastas is available, including a flavorful *pennette alla boscaiola* with porcini mushrooms and pancetta in a tomato cream sauce. Other specialties are grilled fish and meat dishes, including a chicken breast marinated in lime juice and herbs. Top dessert picks are any of the Italian ice creams, the crème caramel, and (but, of course) the creamy tiramisu.

**PlumpJack Café.** 3127 Fillmore St. (between Filbert and Greenwich sts.). ☎ **415/ 563-4755.** Reservations recommended. Main courses $15–$22. AE, DC, DISC, MC, V. Mon–Fri 11:30am–2pm; Mon–Sat 5:30–10:30pm. Bus: 41 or 45. CALIFORNIA/FRENCH/ MEDITERRANEAN.

Wildly popular among San Francisco's style-setters, this small Cow Hollow restaurant is one of the neighborhood's most "in" place to dine. This is partly due to the fact that it's run by one of the Getty clan (as in J. Paul), but mostly because Chef Maria Helm's food is just plain good and the whimsical decor is a veritable work of art.

Though the menu changes weekly, you might find such appetizers as grilled day boat scallops wrapped in pancetta on shaved fennel with citrus vinaigrette and herb scented Roquefort soufflé. Main dishes range from risotto or sweet potato, wild mushrooms, proscuitto, and Grana Parmesan to duck confit and roasted breast with potato rosti, dried sour cherries, and port glaze. Top it off with bittersweet chocolate soufflé or cinnamon-scented Alsatian apple cake. The extraordinarily extensive California wine list—gleaned from the PlumpJack wine shop down the street—is sold at next to retail, with many wines available by the glass.

**Prego.** 2000 Union St. (at Buchanan St.). ☎ **415/563-3305.** Reservations accepted. Pasta and pizza $9–$13; main courses $13–$20. AE, DC, MC, V. Daily 11:30am–midnight. Bus: 22, 41, or 45. ITALIAN.

A light and airy trattoria, frequented by an upscale clientele, Prego is a place to be seen or people-watch as you dine beyond the windows facing Union Street. Specialties include thin-crust, oak-fired pizzas, pasta, and grilled fish and meats. Spit-roasted, free-range chicken is prepared on a rotisserie and served with potatoes and vegetables. A good selection of wine is also available by the glass or bottle.

✪ **Zinzino.** 2355 Chestnut St. (at Divisadero St.). ☎ **415/346-6623.** Reservations accepted. Main courses $9.50–$18.50. AE, DC, MC, V. Tues–Thurs 6–10pm; Fri–Sat 5:30–11pm; Sun 5:30–9:30pm. Bus: 22 or 30. ITALIAN.

Owner Ken Zankel and Spago-sired chef Andrea Rappaport have combined forces to create one of the city's top Italian restaurants. Zinzino may look like a tiny trattoria from the outside, but you could fit a small nuclear sub in the space from the sun-drenched facade to the shaded back patio of this former Laundromat.

Italian movie posters, magazines, antiques, and furnishings evoke memories of past vacations, but we rarely recall the food in Italy being this good (and certainly not this cheap). Start off with the crispy calamari with a choice of herbed aioli or tomato sauces (second only to Scala's Earth and Surf), the roasted jumbo prawns wrapped in crisp pancetta and bathed in a tangy balsamic reduction sauce, or the peculiar-tasting shaved-fennel-and-mint salad—or try them all. Rappaport is giving Zuni Café a run for its money with her version of roasted half chicken, the most tender bird we've ever tasted ("It's all the wood-fired oven," she admits); the accompanying goat cheese salad and potato frisee were also superb. New to the menu are Rappaport's weekly rotating specials, such as her roasted shellfish platter, oven-roasted half lobster, or baby lamb chops.

## SUPER-CHEAP EATS

✪ **Andalé Taqueria.** 2150 Chestnut St. (between Steiner and Pierce sts.). ☎ **415/ 749-0506.** Most dishes $5.25–$7. No credit cards. Mon–Thurs 11am–10pm; Fri–Sat 11am–11pm; Sun 11am–9pm. Bus: 22, 28, 30, 30X, 43, 76, or 82X. MEXICAN.

Andalé (Spanish for "hurry up") offers incredible high-end, fast food for the health-conscious eater. As the long menu explains, this small California chain prides itself on using all fresh ingredients and low-cal options: no lard or preservatives and no canned items; salad dressings made with cholesterol-free double virgin olive oil; whole vegetarian beans (not refried); skinless chicken; salsas and aguas frescas made from fresh fruits and veggies; and mesquite-grilled meats—heck, even the chips are fried in cholesterol-free Canola oil. Add the location (situated on the sunny shopping stretch of Chestnut), sophisticated decor, a full bar, and check-me-out patio seating (complete with corner fireplace), and it's no wonder the good-looking, fitness-fanatic Marina District considers this place home. Prices are kept low by serving the fare cafeteria style. *Bargain tips:* No one can complain about a quarter of a mesquite-roasted chicken with potatoes, salsa, and tortillas for $5.95. But if you want to go traditional, stick with the giant burritos or the fantastic $2.75 tacos—a nibbler's dream.

**The Grove.** 2250 Chestnut St. (between Scott and Pierce sts.). ☎ **415/474-4843.** Most main courses $6–$7. MC, V. Mon–Fri 7am–midnight, Sat–Sun 8am–midnight. Bus: 22, 28, 30, 30X, 43, 76, or 82X. CAFE.

The Grove is the kind of place you go just to hang out and enjoy the fact that you're in San Francisco. That the heaping salads, lasagne, pasta, sandwiches, and daily specials are wholesome is an added bonus. It's the easy-going vibe that's the real attraction: the old, large, family-style tables along the scuffed hardwood floor; huge, open windows where inside diners scope those at the sidewalk seats; a casual, attractive, sociable crowd; and Nina Simone or some other fabulous blues CD playing overhead. It's the perfect place to read the newspaper, meet up with friends, or sip an enormous cup of coffee, an espresso, a glass of wine, or a beer.

**Home Plate.** 2274 Lombard St. (at Pierce St.). ☎ **415/922-HOME.** Main courses $3.75–$6.50. MC, V. Daily 7am–4pm. Bus: 28, 30, 43, or 76. BREAKFAST.

Dollar for dollar, Home Plate just may be the best breakfast place in San Francisco. Many Marina residents kick off their hectic weekends by carbo-loading here on big piles of buttermilk pancakes and waffles smothered with fresh fruit, or hefty omelets stuffed with everything from apple-wood–smoked ham to spinach. You'll always start off with a coveted plate of freshly baked scones, best eaten with a bit of butter and a dab of jam. Be sure to look over the daily specials scrawled on the little green chalkboard before you order. And as every fan of this tiny cafe knows, it's best to call ahead and ask to have your name put on the waiting list before you slide into Home Plate.

✪ **La Canasta.** 3006 Buchanan St. (at Union St.). ☎ **415/921-3003.** Main courses $2.80–$6.15. No credit cards. Mon–Sat 11am–10pm. Bus: 22, 41, or 45. MEXICAN.

Unless you head to the Mission District, you won't find a better (or bigger) burrito than those served at this tiny take-out establishment, where you can stuff yourself with a huge chicken burrito for around $5 (the meat's grilled fresh to order). Best of all, the beautiful Marina Green is a short walk away and offers a million-dollar view that no Marina restaurant can match.

**Mel's Diner.** 2165 Lombard St. (at Fillmore St.). ☎ **415/921-3039.** Reservations accepted. Main courses $4–$5.50 breakfast, $6–$8 lunch, $8–$12 dinner. No credit cards. Sun–Thurs 6am–3am; Fri–Sat 24 hr. (Lombard location only). Bus: 22, 43, or 30. AMERICAN.

Sure, it's contrived, touristy, and nowhere near healthy, but when you get that urge for a chocolate shake and banana cream pie at the stroke of midnight, no other place in the city comes through like Mel's Diner. Modeled after a classic 1950s diner, right down to the nickel jukebox at each table, Mel's harks back to the halcyon days when cholesterol and fried foods didn't stroke your guilty conscience with every greasy, wonderful bite. Too bad the prices don't reflect the 1950s; a burger with fries and a coke runs about $8, and they don't take credit. There's another Mel's at 3355 Geary at Stanyan Street (☎ **415/387-2244**).

**Pluto's.** 3258 Scott St. (at Chestnut St.). ☎ **415/7-PLUTOS.** Main courses $3.50–$5.75. MC, V. Daily Mon–Thurs 11:30am–10pm; Fri 11:30am–10pm; Sat 9:30am–11pm; Sun 9:30am–10pm. Bus: 28, 30, 42, or 76. CALIFORNIA.

Catering to the Marina District's underpaid and overworked DINKS (double income, no kids), Pluto's combines assembly-line efficiency with three-star quality. The result is cheap, fresh, high-quality fare ranging from humungous salads with a dozen choices of toppings to oven-roasted poultry and grilled meats (the flank steak is great), sandwiches, and a wide array of sides like crispy garlic potato rings, seasonal veggies, and barbecued chicken wings. There are cappuccinos, tea, sodas, bottled brews, and Napa wines to drink, as well as homemade desserts. The ordering system is bewildering to newcomers; first grab a checklist and hand it to the food servers who check off your order and relay it to the cashier. Odd, yes, but fast and efficient. Seating is limited during the rush, but the turnover is fairly fast.

**Sweet Heat.** 3324 Steiner St. (between Lombard and Chestnut sts.). ☎ **415/474-9191.** www.citysearch.com. Reservations not accepted. All entrees less than $8. MC, V. Daily 11am–11pm. MEXICAN.

If you're shopping on Chestnut Street and looking for a flavorful and light lunch, check out this casual place offering "healthy Mexican food to die for." Far from traditional Mexican food, Sweet Heat has capitalized on California's love affair with old-style food prepared in new ways—and the results are impressive. Prices are as low as $4.50 for a veggie burrito with grilled zucchini, red pepper, and roasted corn, or $5.95 for a tasty scallop burrito with green chili chutney. On a sunny day, the back patio is a great place to sun while you eat. Both locations have a tequila bar with 40 variations. Two other locations—at 1725 Haight St. (☎ **415/387-8845**) and 2141 Polk St. (☎ **415/775-1055**)—are equally popular and delicious.

**World Wrapps.** 2257 Chestnut St. (between Pierce and Scott sts.). ☎ **415/563-9727.** Wraps $2.50–$7. MC, V. Daily 11am–11pm. Bus: 22, 28, 30, 43, or 76. INTERNATIONAL.

You'll know you've found World Wrapps when you come upon the trendy, health-conscious crowd standing in line on yuppified Chestnut Street. There are hardly any tables here and plenty of other eateries nearby, so what's the big deal? It's yet another version of San Franciscans' beloved burrito, only this time it's not Mexican-influenced, but rather a tortilla filled with your choice of cuisine from around the world (hence the name). Fresh ingredients, cheap prices, and the love affair Marina residents have with hanging out on this street make World Wrapps the place to grab a bite. A second location is at 2227 Polk St., between Green and Vallejo streets (☎ **415/931-9727**).

# 10  Pacific Heights

**The Elite Café.** 2049 Fillmore St. (between Pine and California sts.). ☎ **415/346-8668.** Reservations not accepted. Main courses $12–$24. AE, DC, DISC, MC, V. Mon–Sat 5–11pm; Sun 10am–3pm and 5–10pm. Bus: 41 or 45. CAJUN/CREOLE.

Some habits do indeed die hard, and the Elite is one of them. This place is always bustling with Pacific Heights's beautiful people who come for fresh oysters, blackened beef fillet with Cajun butter, jambalaya, Grandad's chicken and dumplings, or any of the other well-spiced Cajun dishes. The high-backed booths provide more intimate dining than the crowded tables and bar. Brunch is good, too, when all kinds of egg dishes—Benedict, sardou, Hangtown fry, and many more—are offered along with such goodies as cornbread, bagels and lox, and smoked chicken sausage.

**Jackson Fillmore.** 2506 Fillmore St. (at Jackson St.). ☎ **415/346-5288.** Main courses $10–$17. AE, DC, MC, V. Mon–Thurs 5:30–10pm, Fri–Sat 5:30–11pm, Sun 5–10pm. Bus: 3, 12, 22, or 24. ITALIAN.

One of the most popular cafes in Pacific Heights, this cozy, boisterous neighborhood trattoria consists of eight tables covered in blue-and-white-checked cloths and a long black bar overlooking the antipasto table. It's attractive without being overdone, which can also be said for the rustic Italian fare: simple preparations of top-quality ingredients, such as fresh portobello mushrooms grilled with olive oil and garlic and served on a bed of arugula, or ricotta ravioli with pesto and mozzarella. Prices are moderate enough to maintain a regular clientele. One of the best things about Jackson Fillmore, though, is the complimentary (and highly addictive) warm bruschetta that's placed on your table the moment you're seated.

**Osome.** 3145 Fillmore St. (between Filbert and Greenwich sts.). ☎ **415/346-2311.** Sushi $3–$7.50 apiece; main courses $8.95–$14.20. AE, MC, V. Mon–Sat 5:30–11pm, Sun 5–10:30pm. Bus: 41 or 45. JAPANESE/SUSHI.

What this neighborhood restaurant lacks in decor, it more than makes up for in fresh, well-presented Japanese cuisine. There are fewer than a dozen tables for large parties, but the best seats are definitely at the bar, where sushi chefs slice and roll *maguro* (tuna), *unagi* (eel), and close to 40 other savory rice-and-fish combinations. Many of our friends fill up before going out for sushi so they won't spend a fortune satisfying their hunger. There's no need to do that here because there's also a full, and reasonably priced, dinner menu with tempura, teriyaki, and sukiyaki. Start with the surprisingly sculptural spinach goma ae, a skyline of spinach towers bathing in a tangy sesame-seed sauce. From there, let your taste buds be your guide.

## SUPER-CHEAP EATS

**La Méditerranée.** 2210 Fillmore St. (at Sacramento St.). ☎ **415/921-2956.** Main courses $6.50–$8. MC, V. Mon–Thurs 11am–10pm, Fri–Sat 11am–11pm. Bus: 1, 1BX, 22, or 24. MEDITERRANEAN.

With an upscale-cafe ambience and quality food, La Méditerranée has long warranted its reputation as one of the cheaper, and quainter, restaurants on upper Fillmore. Here you'll find freshly prepared traditional Mediterranean food that's worlds apart from the Euro-eclectic fare many restaurants now call "Mediterranean." Baba ghanoush, tabuleh, dolma, and hummus start out the menu. But, more importantly, it continues to offer one very tasty chicken Cilicia, a phyllo-dough dish that's hand-rolled and baked with cinnamony spices, almonds, chickpeas, and raisins; as well as zesty chicken pomegranate drumsticks on a bed of rice. Both come with salad, potato salad, or soup for around $8. Ground-lamb dishes, quiches, and

Middle Eastern combo plates round out the very affordable menu, and wine comes by the glass and in half- or full liters. Other locations: 288 Noe St., at Market Street (☎ **415/431-7210**), and 2936 College Ave., at Ashby Street (☎ **510/540-7773**).

## WORTH A SPLURGE

✪ **Cafe Kati.** 1963 Sutter St. (between Fillmore and Webster sts.). ☎ **415/775-7313.** Reservation recommended. Main courses $16–$20. MC, V. Tues–Sun 5:30–10pm. Bus: 2, 3, or 4. CALIFORNIA/EAST-WEST.

Chef Kirk Webber works small wonders in an even smaller kitchen at this diminutive yet distinctive restaurant just off Fillmore Street. The menu highlights California-style dishes spiced with a dash of the Orient and Italy, all of which are presented in high form, such as the signature Caesar salad sculpted into a towering monument of germane romaine. The seasonally changing menu offers such cross-cultural creations as pancetta-wrapped pork tenderloin bathed in a ragu of baby artichokes; miso-marinated Chilean sea bass saddled with tempura kabocha squash and chanterelle mushrooms; and crispy duck confit with sweet-potato gnocchi and wild mushrooms. When making a reservation, request a table in the front room—far more appealing—and don't make any plans for afterwards as the kitchen takes its sweet time preparing your object d'art.

# 11 Japantown

**Isobune.** In the Japan Center, 1737 Post St. ☎ **415/563-1030.** Sushi $1.20–$2.95 apiece. MC, V. Daily 11:30am–10pm. Bus: 2, 3, 4, 22, or 38. SUSHI.

Unless you arrive early, there's almost always a short wait to pull up a chair around this enormous oval sushi bar. But once you're seated, the wait is over. Right before your eyes, plates and plates of sushi pass by on a circling sushi tugboat floating in a minuscule canal that encircles the bar. If you see something you like, just grab it off the boat and enjoy; the service staff will tally up the damages at the end. (They can tell how much you've eaten by the number of empty plates.) It's not the best sushi in town, but it's relatively cheap and the atmosphere is fun.

**Mifune.** In the Japan Center, 1737 Post St. ☎ **415/922-0337.** Main courses $4–$16.50. AE, DC, DISC, MC, V. Daily 11am–10pm. Bus: 2, 3, 4, 22, or 38. JAPANESE.

Mifune has been serving traditional Japanese food for 15 years and has a steady clientele of folks who are happy with the fare, and ecstatic about the prices. Slide into one of the Japanese-style booths and order the house specialty, a homemade udon and soba noodles dinner. You might go for one of the donburi dishes or a full-blown tempura dinner.

**Sanppo.** 1702 Post St. (at Laguna St.). ☎ **415/346-3486.** Reservations not accepted. Main courses $6–$15; combination dishes $10–$17. MC, V. Mon–Sat 11am–10pm; Sun 11:30am–10pm. Bus: 2, 3, 4, or 38. JAPANESE.

Simple and unpretentious though it is, Sanppo, across from the Japan Center, serves excellent, down-home Japanese food. You may be asked to share one of the few tables that surround a square counter in the small dining room. Lunches and dinners all include miso soup, rice, and pickled vegetables. At lunch, you might have an order of fresh, thick-cut sashimi, teriyaki, tempura, beef donburi, or an order of *gyoza* (dumplings filled with savory meat and herbs) for $5 to $12. The same items are available at dinner for about $1 additional. Combination dishes, including tempura, sashimi, and gyoza, or tempura and teriyaki, are also available. Beer, wine, and sake are also served.

**Sushi-A.** 1737 Buchanan St. (at Sutter St.). ☎ **415/931-4685.** Main courses $8.95–$15.95. AE, MC, V. Thurs–Mon 11:30am–2:30pm and 5–10pm. Bus: 2, 3, 4, 22, or 38. JAPANESE/ SUSHI.

Ensconced in a Japantown mini-mall is this little—and little-known—restaurant that serves exceptional Japanese cuisine in a subdued and intimate environment. Sushi-A eschews flashy presentation and boisterous atmosphere and instead focuses its energy on producing top-quality preparations. For the perfect three-course dinner, start with a bowl of mild miso soup and an unagi appetizer, followed by a kaiseki sampler comprised of an array of small meat, seafood, and vegetable dishes that vary with each season. Particularly good are Sushi-A's clay-pot seafood dishes, brimming with noodles, fresh vegetables, and tofu in a light, flavorful broth. The standard teriyaki, sukiyaki, and tempura dinners are also available, or if you prefer, order a combo plate of all three. Seating is limited, as there are only 10 tables and a six-stool sushi bar, so be sure to make reservations.

## SUPER-CHEAP EATS

**Neecha Thai.** 2100 Sutter St. (at Steiner St.). ☎ **415/922-9419.** Reservations accepted only for large parties. Most dishes $5–$8. AE, MC, V. Mon–Fri 11am–3pm and 5–10pm, Sat–Sun 5–10pm. Bus: 2, 4, or 38. THAI.

We've been coming here for many years for very simple reasons: The food's consistently good, the ambience homey, and the prices low. Changes have occurred recently, but not necessarily for the worst; the old, dark, decor was replaced by a brighter but not-quite-harmonious moderne style (unfortunately, they kept the ugly fake-brick paneling). The original oil paintings on the walls are still created by one of the waiters, but apparently he's been "discovered"; so while the pieces used to go for a few hundred bucks, they're now several thousand. The fare is standard but well-prepared Thai, with over 70 choices, including satay; salads; lemongrass soup; coconut-milk curries; and exotic meat, chicken, seafood, and vegetable dishes—and yes, the ever-popular pad Thai, too.

## WORTH A SPLURGE

**YOYO Bistro.** In the Miyako Hotel, 1611 Post St. (at Laguna St.). ☎ **415/922-7788.** Reservations not necessary. Main courses $9–$14. AE, CB, DC, JCB, MC, V. Daily 6:30am–11am and 5:30–10pm. Validated parking in Japan Center garage. Bus: 2, 3, 22, or 38. ASIAN/FRENCH.

You'd be wise to venture out of downtown for dinner in YOYO's dark, 50-person dining room, which is surrounded by authentic shoji screens. Previously Elka, the restaurant changed hands in 1996, and is now run by ex-Elka employees who have put a great deal of care into creating a quality dining experience. The room and the food combine contemporary and ancient, Asian and French. One of the best times to come is between 5:30 and 10pm for *tsumami* (Japanese tapas) where you can order à la carte or choose four dishes for $14. These scrumptious little creations are anything from fresh oysters to pork ribs, and all come with outstanding sauces. Main courses from the dinner menu will include fresh fish, duck, and chicken—all very well prepared.

## 12 Civic Center & Environs

✪ **Eliza's.** 205 Oak St. (at Gough St.). ☎ **415/621-4819.** Main courses $4.50–$5.15 at lunch, $5.25–$9 at dinner. MC, V ($10 minimum). Mon–Fri 11am–3pm and 5–9pm; Sat 11am–9pm. Bus: 6, 7, 21, 66, or 71. CHINESE (HUNAN/MANDARIN).

Eliza's serves some of the freshest, best-tasting, cheap Chinese in town. But unlike most comparable options, here the atmosphere and presentation parallel the food.

The fantastically fresh soups, salads, seafood, pork, chicken, duck, and such specials as spicy eggplant are outstanding and served on beautiful Italian plates. Large windows flank the front and allow natural light to warm the room, while the modern colorful decor and art keep the place attractive throughout the evening. We often come at midday and order the wonderful kung-pao chicken lunch special: a mixture of tender chicken, peanuts, chili peppers, a subtly hot sauce, and perfectly crunchy vegetables. It's only one of 21 main-course choices that come with rice and soup for around $5. But the place is also jumping at night with the opera- and symphony-going crowd.

**Hayes Street Grill.** 320 Hayes St. (near Franklin St.). ☎ **415/863-5545.** Reservations recommended. Main courses $9.25–$18.75. AE, DC, DISC, MC, V. Mon–Thurs 11:30am–2pm and 5–9:30pm; Fri 11:30am–2pm and 5–10:30pm; Sat 6–10:30pm; Sun 5–8:30pm. Bus: 19, 31, or 38. SEAFOOD.

For well over a decade this small, no-nonsense seafood restaurant has maintained a solid reputation among San Francisco's picky epicureans for its impeccably fresh and straightforwardly prepared fish. Choices ranging from Hawaiian swordfish to Puget Sound salmon—cooked to perfection, naturally—are matched with your sauce of choice (Szechuan peanut, tomatillo salsa, shallot butter) and a side of their signature french fries. Fancier seafood specials are available too, such as paella with clams, mussels, scallops, calamari, chorizo, and saffron rice, as well as an impressive selection of garden-fresh salads and local grilled meats. Finish with the outstanding crème brûlée.

**Millennium.** In the Abigail Hotel, 246 McAllister St. (between Hyde St. and Larkin St.). ☎ **415/487-9800.** Reservations recommended. Main courses $11–$16. DC, MC, V. Daily 5–9:30pm. Bus: 5, 9, or 71. VEGAN.

Banking on the trend toward lighter, healthier cooking, chef Eric Tucker and his band of merry waiters set out to prove that a meatless menu doesn't mean you have to sacrifice taste. Set in a narrow, handsome Parisian-style dining room with checkered tile flooring, French windows, and sponge-painted walls, Millennium has had nothing but favorable reviews for its egg-, butter-, and dairy-free creations since the day it opened. Granted, it can be a hit-or-miss experience for nonvegans like ourselves, but we've also had some fantastic dishes (particularly the soups). Favorites include the sweet-and-spicy plantain torte served over a wonderful papaya and black-bean salsa appetizer and main courses such as the filo purse filled with a ragout of wild mushrooms, leeks, and butternut squash, or the warm Yukon Gold potato salad with sautéed portobello mushrooms. Even the wine-and-beer list has a good selection of organic labels.

**Original Joe's.** 144 Taylor St. (between Turk and Eddy sts.). ☎ **415/775-4877.** Main courses $6.50–$19. DC, MC, V. Daily 10:30am–12:30am. Bus: 6, 7, 8, 9, 31, 66, 71, or 76. ITALIAN/BURGERS.

In continuous operation since 1937, this family-owned and operated Italian restaurant has won the hearts and hardened the arteries of every old-time San Franciscan from the late Herb Caen to Mayor Willie Brown. The menu tells it all: "the biggest and best hamburger this side of Texas" served by the "oldest waiters this side of Medicare," offering "the best value for the money anywhere in the area." And that's no hyperbole, particularly the burger part—a three-quarter-pound patty of coarsely chopped ground chuck studded with onions and stuffed into a hollowed-out quarter loaf of French bread (no "Where's the beef?" uttered here). The dimly lit dining room equipped with a sea of cushy red vinyl booths doesn't look quite the same without a haze of lingering smoke, but otherwise Original Joe's is the same as it ever was, serving hearty Italian food at extremely reasonable prices.

---

### 🏫 Affordable Family-Friendly Restaurants

**Caffè Freddy's** *(see p. 117)*   This longtime family favorite will please not only the kids but their parents as well, especially with its low prices. But the food is good, too: an array of gourmet pizzas, pastas, sandwiches, and unusual salads along with main-dish specialties.

**Hard Rock Cafe** *(see p. 106)*   Like its affiliates around the world, this loud, nostalgia-laden place offers big portions of decent food at moderate prices, and plenty of blaring music to an almost exclusively tourist clientele. Although it's nothing unique to San Francisco, the Hard Rock is a fine place to bring the kids and grab a bite.

**Mel's Diner** *(see p. 131)*   This retro-style burger-slinging joint is not only neat to look at (it was the diner that starred in the movie American Graffiti), it also caters to kids. Youngsters get their own color-in menu (crayons are already on the table), and some meals are served in boxes shaped like classic American cars. Jukeboxes at each table will keep the whole family busy figuring out which oldie to select.

---

✪ **Zuni Café.** 1658 Market St. (at Franklin St.). ☎ **415/552-2522.** Reservations recommended. Main courses $15–$22.50. AE, MC, V. Tues–Sat 11:30am–midnight; Sun 11am–11pm. Valet parking $5. Muni Metro: All Market St. trams. Bus: 6, 7, 71, or 75. MEDITERRANEAN.

Even factoring in the sometimes snotty wait staff, Zuni Café is still one of our favorite places in the city to have lunch. Its expanse of windows and prime Market Street location guarantee good people watching—a favorite San Francisco pastime—and chef Judy Rodgers's Mediterranean-influenced menu is wonderfully diverse and satisfying. For the full effect, sit at the bustling, copper-topped bar and peruse the foot-long oyster menu (a dozen or so varieties are on hand at all times); you can also sit in the stylish, exposed-brick dining room or on the outdoor patio. Though the changing menu always includes meat, such as New York steak with Belgian endive gratin, and fish—either grilled or braised in the kitchen's brick oven—the proven winners are Rodgers's brick-oven–roasted chicken for two with Tuscan-style bread salad, the polenta appetizer with mascarpone, and the hamburger on grilled rosemary focaccia bread (a strong contender for the city's best burger). Whatever you decide, be sure to order a side of the shoestring potatoes.

## SUPER-CHEAP EATS

**Mad Magda's Russian Tearoom & Café.** 579 Hayes St. (between Octavia and Laguna sts.). ☎ **415/864-7654.** Reservations not accepted. Soups, salads, sandwiches 75¢–$6.95. No credit cards. Mon–Tues 8am–9pm, Wed–Fri 8am–midnight, Sat 9am–midnight, Sun 9am–7pm. Bus: 21. CAFE (SOUPS/SALADS/SANDWICHES).

Set in a late 19th-century Victorian house, this small and mysterious cafe located in Hayes Valley (between the Civic Center and the Western Addition) is a charmingly fun place for a light meal if you're strolling the nearby shops—and everything costs less than $10. Its guardian spirit is that of Magda, a long-dead relative of the owners who is said to have an ongoing relationship with the staff here. In her honor, the floor is decorated with numerological and tarot symbols, the walls with an imitation of cloud-covered skies and imperial Russian decorations that include a large and extraordinary rendering, in wood and fabric, of the onion domes in Moscow. Munch on a Catherine the Great (tuna with Swiss cheese), the Czar sandwich (with chicken salad), or a Russian blintz (served only on weekends). Other specialties include homemade piroshkis, Russian savory pie baked with homemade stuffing, and borscht. Cough up some spare cash for a 15-minute session with one of the in-house tarot and tea-leaf readers who'll divine your future—if you dare to know.

**Tommy's Joynt.** 1109 Geary St. (at Van Ness Ave.). ☎ **415/775-4216.** Reservations not accepted. Main courses $4–$7. No credit cards. Daily 10am–2am. Bus: 2, 3, 4, or 38. AMERICAN.

With its colorful mural exterior, it's hard to miss Tommy's Joynt, a late-night favorite for those in search of a cheap and hearty meal. The interior of Tommy's looks like a Buffalo Bill museum that imploded, a wild collage of stuffed birds, a mounted buffalo head, an ancient piano, rusty firearms, fading prints, a beer-guzzling lion, and Santa Claus masks. The Hofbrau-style buffet offers a cornucopia of rib-clinging à la carte dishes such as their signature buffalo stew, ham sandwiches, sloppy joes, oxtails, corned beef, meatballs, and mashed potatoes. There's also a slew of seating and almost 100 varieties of beer.

# 13  Haight-Ashbury

✪ **Cha Cha Cha.** 1801 Haight St. (at Shrader St.). ☎ **415/386-5758.** Reservations not accepted. Tapas $4.50–$7.75; main courses $9–$13. MC, V. Daily 11:30am–4pm; Sun–Thurs 5–11pm; Fri–Sat 5–11:30pm. Muni Metro: N. Bus: 6, 7, 66, 71, or 73. CARIBBEAN.

This is one of our all-time favorite places to come for dinner, but it's not for everybody. Cha Cha Cha is not a meal, it's an experience. Put your name on the mile-long list, crowd into the minuscule bar, and drink sangria while you wait (and try not to spill when you get bumped by all the young, attractive patrons who are also waiting). When you do finally get seated (it usually takes at least an hour), you'll dine in a loud—and we mean loud—dining room with Santeria altars, banana trees, and plastic tropical tablecloths. The best thing to do is order from the *tapas* menu and share the dishes family-style. The fried calamari, fried new potatoes, Cajun shrimp, and mussels in saffron broth are all bursting with flavor and are accompanied by rich, luscious sauces, but whatever you choose, you can't go wrong. This is the kind of place where you take friends in a partying mood, let your hair down, and make an evening of it. If you want the flavor without the festivities, come during lunch. A second, larger location opened in the Mission at 2327 Mission St. (between 19th and 20th streets) ☎ **415/648-0504.**

✪ **Eos.** 901 Cole St. (at Carl St.). ☎ **415/566-3063.** Reservations recommended. Main courses $16–$26. AE, MC, V. Mon–Sat 5:30–11pm; Sun 5–11pm. Muni Metro: N. Bus: 6, 33, or 43. EAST-WEST FUSION.

Named after the Greek goddess of dawn, Eos is certainly basking in the spotlight thanks to chef/proprietor Arnold Wong, a master of texture and taste who perfected his craft while working at Masa's and Silks. With a twinge of guilt you'll dig into the artistic presentation of each dish, such as the tender breast of Peking duck, smoked in ginger-peach tea leaves and served with a plum-kumquat chutney, or the blackened Asian catfish atop a bed of lemongrass risotto. For starters, try the almond-encrusted soft-shell crab dipped in spicy plum ponzu sauce. Unfortunately, the stark, industrial-deco decor does little to dampen the decibels, making a romantic outing nearly impossible unless you're into shouting. There is, however, a quiet, casual wine bar around the corner (same name) which stocks more than 400 vintages from around the globe.

✪ **Thep Phanom.** 400 Waller St. (at Fillmore St.). ☎ **415/431-2526.** Reservations recommended. Main courses $6.95–$11.95. AE, CB, DC, DISC, MC, V. Daily 5:30–10:30pm. Bus: 6, 7, 22, 66, or 71. THAI.

By successfully incorporating flavors from India, China, Burma, Malaysia, and more recently the West, Thep Phanom rose the heady ranks to become one of the best Thai restaurants in San Francisco. Case in point: There's almost always a line out the front door. Start with the signature dish, *ped swan*—boneless duck in a light honey sauce served on a bed of spinach. The *larb ped* (minced duck salad), velvety basil-spiked seafood curry served on banana leaves, and spicy *yum plamuk* (calamari salad) are also recommended. Its Haight Street location attracts an eclectic crowd and informal atmosphere, though the decor is actually quite tasteful. Reservations are advised, and don't leave anything even remotely valuable in your car.

## SUPER-CHEAP EATS

**Crepes on Cole.** 100 Carl St. (at Cole St.). ☎ **415/664-1800.** Reservations not accepted. No prices over $6. No credit cards. Sun–Thurs 7am–11pm, Fri–Sat 7am–midnight. Muni Metro: N Judah. Bus: 6, 7, 66, or 71. CREPES.

Every few years, a new food trend becomes really hot in the city. Cajun, sushi, Thai—just when you thought restaurateurs had thought of everything, enter the crepe. These paper-thin, egg-based pancakes usually encase a glob of goodies and can be served as a main course or a dessert. If you're in the Cole Valley or Haight-Ashbury area and you're looking for a hearty, casual, and affordable meal, this is the place to try them. Build your own or order from choices such as the Florentine crepe made with Cheddar cheese, onions, spinach, and cottage cheese, or the Mediterranean crepe with Cheddar, onion, eggplant, pesto, tomato, and roasted peppers. All options, including the less-celebrated omelets, come with a heaping pile of house potatoes. You can also order one of the simple sandwiches, bagels, or an enormous Caesar salad, all for under $8.

**Mad Dog in the Fog.** 530 Haight St. (between Fillmore and Steiner sts.). ☎ **415/626-7279.** Main courses $4–$7. No credit cards. Mon–Fri 11:30am–2am, Sat–Sun 10am–2am. Bus: 6, 7, 22, 66, or 71. BRITISH/AMERICAN.

When there's a big soccer game on the telly, San Francisco's die-hard soccer fans (most of whom are British) make a beeline for Mad Dog, a homey and refreshingly attitude-free Haight Street hangout that's known for its cheap beer and pub grub. If you're short on cash, keep this in mind: imported beer, $2.50 a pint, weekdays from 11:30am to 7pm and on weekends from 10am to 7pm. But wait, it gets better: Weekdays from 11:30am to 2:30pm you get a free pint of beer (from some 20 brews on tap) with your lunch, whether it's steak-and-mushroom pie, bangers and mash, a housemade chicken-and-veggie pie, roast beef, Jamaican chicken, or simply a garden burger and salad. The only drawback is the sketchy neighborhood, where there's a lot of hustling for change going on, but that's life in the Haight.

✪ **Spaghetti Western.** 576 Haight St. (between Fillmore and Steiner sts.). ☎ **415/864-8461.** Most main courses $4–$7. No credit cards. Mon–Fri 8am–3pm, Sat–Sun 8am–4pm. Bus: 6, 7, 22, 66, or 71. AMERICAN.

Freaks and eggs aren't on the actual menu, but they've made Spaghetti Western a favorite lower Haight breakfast spot for years now. The heaping Spuds-o-Rama (fried potatoes topped with cheese, salsa, and sour cream), a hearty breakfast burrito (with eggs, cheese, and black beans), pancakes, and other morning munchies are dished out to a young, eccentric clientele by the tatooed, bald, or otherwise-ornamented service staff. The vibe is dive and the food is good, just the way the neighborhood likes it.

**Tassajara.** 1000 Cole St. (at Parnassus St.). ☎ **415/664-8947.** Pastries $1.30–$3.25; sandwiches $4.25. MC, V. Mon–Thurs 7am–9pm; Fri–Sat 7am–10pm; Sun 8am–9pm. Muni Metro: N. Bus: 6, 37, or 43. SOUPS/SALADS/SANDWICHES.

Once owned and operated by a Zen center of the same name, Tassajara may have been bought out by the local Just Desserts chain a few years back, but apparently the deal included the recipe for the best bear claws in town, and that's all we needed to know. Decor is not earthy, but rather bright and clean with vibrant original art and large windows. The vibe, however, is still mellow and vegetarian, though there's more sugar behind the glass to amp you up. Soups, sandwiches, breakfast pastries, and heavenly breads are interspersed with carrot, poppy-seed, and one helluva chocolate cake.

**Zona Rosa.** 1797 Haight St. (at Shrader St.). ☎ **415/668-7717.** Burritos $4.50–$5.75. No credit cards. Daily 11am–11pm. Muni Metro: N. Bus: 6, 7, 66, 71, or 73. MEXICAN.

This is a great place to stop and get a cheap (and healthful) bite. The most popular items here are the burritos, which are made to order and include your choice of beans (refried, whole pinto, or black), meats, or vegetarian ingredients. You can sit on a stool at the window and watch all the Haight Street freaks strolling by, relax at one of five colorful interior tables, or take it to go and head to Golden Gate Park (it's just 2 blocks away). Zona Rosa is one of the best burrito stores around.

# 14  Richmond District

**Cliff House.** 1090 Point Lobos (at Merrie Way). ☎ **415/386-3330.** Two dining areas: upstairs and main room. Reservations recommended for upstairs and brunch only. Main courses $7–$12 upstairs breakfast; $7–$12 upstairs lunch, $9–$22 main lunch; $12–$22 main and upstairs dinner. AE, DC, MC, V. Upstairs: Mon–Fri 9am–3:30pm and 5–10pm; Sat–Sun 8:30am–4pm and 5–10pm. Main room: Mon–Sat 11am–10:30pm; Sun 9am–2pm and 3:30–10:30pm. Bus: 38 or 18. SEAFOOD/CALIFORNIA.

Back in the old days (we're talking way back) the Cliff House was the place to go for a romantic night on the town. Nowadays, this aging San Francisco landmark caters mostly to tourists who arrive by the busloads to gander at the Sutro Bath remains next door.

Three restaurants in the main two-story building give diners a choice of how much they wish to spend. Phineas T. Barnacle is the least expensive; sandwiches, salads, soups and such are served Hofbrau-style across from the elaborate saloon-style bar, after which you can seat yourself at the windowside tables overlooking the shore or beside the fireplace if you're chilled. A step up from the P.T.B. (literally) is Upstairs at the Cliff House, a slightly more formal setting that's best known for its breakfast omelets, and the main room, known as the Seafood and Beverage Co., the fanciest of the lot. Refurbished back to its glory days near the turn of the century, it offers superb ocean views, particularly at sunset, when the fog lets up; unfortunately, the food is a distant second to the scenery. Your best option is to arrive before dusk, request a window seat, order a few appetizers and cocktails, and enjoy the view, or opt for the elaborate Sunday brunch served from 10am to 3pm in the newly renovated Terrace Room.

✪ **Hong Kong Flower Lounge.** 5322 Geary Blvd. (between 17th and 18th aves.). ☎ **415/668-8998.** Most main dishes $7.95–$14.95; dim-sum dishes $1.80–$3.50. Mon–Fri 11am–2:30pm; Sat–Sun 10am–2:30pm; daily 5–9:30pm. Bus: 1, 2, or 38. CHINESE/DIM SUM.

You know you're at a good Chinese restaurant when most people waiting for a table are Chinese. And if you come for dim sum, be prepared to stand in line because you're not the only one who's heard this is one of the better spots in town. The Hong Kong Flower Lounge has been one of our very favorite restaurants for years now. It's not the pink and green decor or the live fish swimming in the tank, or even the beautiful marble bathrooms; it's simply that every little dish that comes our way is so darn good. Don't pass up taro cake, salt-fried shrimp, shark-fin soup, and shrimp or beef crepes.

✪ **Kabuto Sushi.** 5116 Geary Blvd. (at 15th Ave.). ☎ **415/752-5652.** Sushi $3–$8; main courses $11–$18. MC, V. Tues–Sat 5:30–11pm. Bus: 2, 28, or 38. JAPANESE/SUSHI.

For a town overflowing with seafood and pretentious taste buds, you'd think it'd be easier to find great sushi. But the truth is, finding an outstanding sushi restaurant in San Francisco is more challenging than spotting a parking space in Nob Hill. Still, chop-sticking these fish-and-rice delicacies is one of the most joyous and adventurous ways to dine, and Kabuto is one of the best (and most expensive) places to do it. Chef Sachio Kojima, who presides over the small, ever-crowded sushi bar, constructs each dish with smooth, lightning-fast movements known only to master chefs. Last time we were here, we were lucky enough to sit next to some businessmen visiting from Japan who were ordering things we'd never seen before. We followed their lead and had perhaps the best sushi dinner to date. If you're big on wasabi, ask for the stronger stuff Kojima serves on request.

**Khan Toke Thai House.** 5937 Geary Blvd. ☎ **415/668-6654.** Reservations recommended. Main courses $6–$12; fixed-price dinner $17.95. AE, MC, V. Daily 5–10pm. Bus: 38. THAI.

Khan Toke Thai is so traditional you're asked to remove your shoes before being seated. Popular for special occasions, this Richmond Distinct fixture is easily the prettiest Thai restaurant in the city; lavishly carved teak interiors evoke the ambiance of a Thai temple.

To start, order the tom yam gong lemongrass shrimp with mushroom, tomato, and cilantro soup. Follow with such well-flavored dishes as ground pork with fresh ginger, green onion, peanuts, and lemon juice; prawns with hot chilies, mint leaves, lime juice, lemongrass, and onions; or the chicken with cashew nuts, crispy chilies, and onions. For a real treat, have the deep-fried pompano topped with sautéed ginger, onions, peppers, pickled garlic, and yellow-bean sauce; or deep-fried red snapper with "three-flavors" sauce and hot basil leaves. A complete dinner including appetizer, soup, salad, two main courses, dessert, and coffee is a great value.

**Straits Café.** 3300 Geary Blvd. (at Parker St.). ☎ **415/668-1783.** Reservations recommended. Main courses $6.95–$17.95. AE, DC, MC, V. Sun–Thurs 11:30am–10pm; Fri–Sat 11:30am–11pm. Bus: 2, 3, 4, or 38. SINGAPOREAN.

Straits Café is what we like to call "adventure dining," because you never know quite what you're going to get. Burlap palm trees, pastel-painted trompe l'oeil houses, faux balconies, and clotheslines strung across the walls evoke a surreal image of a Singaporean village at this Richmond District restaurant; the cuisine, however, is the real thing. Among chef Chris Yeo's spicy Malaysian/Indian/Chinese offerings there's *murtabak* (stuffed Indian bread), chili crab, basil chicken, *nonya daging rendang* (beef simmered in lime leaves), *ikan pangang* (fish stuffed with a chili paste), and hottest of all, *sambal udang* (prawns sautéed in a chili shallot sambal sauce). For dessert try the sago pudding or the *bo bo cha cha* (taro root and sweet potato in sweetened coconut milk).

**Ton Kiang.** 5821 Geary Blvd. (between 22nd and 23rd aves.). ☎ **415/387-8273.** Reservations accepted for parties of 8 or more. Dim sum $1.80–$4.50. Daily 10:30am–10pm. AE, MC. V. Bus: 38. DIM SUM.

We still love the Hong Kong Flower Lounge, but Ton Kiang is justifiably the number-one place in the city to do dim sum. Wait in the never-ending line (which is out the door anytime between 11am and 1:30pm), get a table on either the first or second floor, and get ready to party with your palate. From stuffed crab claws, roast Peking duck, and a gazillion dumpling selections (including scallop and vegetable, shrimp, and beef) to the delicious and hard-to-find "doa miu" (a.k.a. snow pea sprouts, which are flash sautéed with garlic and peanut oil), shark-fin soup, and a mesmerizing mango pudding, every tray of morsels coming from the kitchen is an absolute delight. This is definitely one of our favorite places to do lunch, and it happens to have an unusually friendly staff.

## 15  Sunset District

**Beach Chalet Brewery & Restaurant.** 1000 Great Hwy. (at the west end of Golden Gate Park near Fulton St.). ☎ **415/386-8439.** Reservations accepted. Lunch appetizers $5–$7.50; main courses $8–$12.75 at lunch, $12.50–$189.50 at dinner. MC, V. Mon–Thurs 11:30am–10pm (bistro menu 3–5:30pm); Fri–Sat 11:30am–11pm (bistro menu 3–5:30pm); Sun 10am–10pm. (Bar open until midnight Sunday through Thursday, 2am Friday and Saturday.) Bus: 18, 31, or 38. Metro: N. AMERICAN.

Since reopening on New Year's Eve 1996, the Beach Chalet has been one of the most popular reasons to make it out to the breakers. The restaurant occupies the upper floor of a historic public lounge that originally opened in 1900, was rebuilt in 1925, and, after being closed for more than 15 years, was recently renovated. Today, the main floor's wonderful restored WPA frescoes and historical displays on the area are enough to lure tourists and locals, but upstairs is something altogether different. The only thing harking back to yesteryear is the timeless view of the great Pacific Ocean. While the place is bright and cheery, we agree with the critics: The restaurant should have been more reminiscent of its heritage. Dinner is pricey and the view disappears with the sun, so come for lunch or bistro snacks, when you can eat your Niman-Schell burger, rock shrimp quesadilla, or chopped vegetable and romaine salad with one of the best vistas around. After dinner, it's a more local thing, especially on Tuesday, Friday, and Saturday when live blues accompany the cocktails and housemade brews. *Note:* Be careful getting into the parking lot (only accessible from the northbound side of the highway); it's a quick, sandy turn.

### SUPER-CHEAP EATS

**Yum Yum Fish.** 2181 Irving St. (between 22nd and 23rd aves.). ☎ **415/566-6433.** Main courses $6–$20. No credit cards. Daily 10:30am–7:30pm. Bus: 71. SUSHI.

Sure, Yum Yum Fish smells like a fish market, but that's only because it *is* a fish market. But those-in-the-know also come here for the freshest cheap sushi in the city, served at a little counter in the back and eaten at a folding table with two garage-sale/giveaway chairs. How cheap is cheap? The seven-piece inari combo (California, tofu, and mixed veggie) runs about $12 at most sushi restaurants—here, it's $4. If you want to be the life of the next potluck party (or hate to cook), order the $39 party platter, which comes loaded with various rolls and nigiri. The staff here is super friendly, and once you get used to the smell you're bound to stay a while, stuffing yourself on top-notch sushi.

# Low-Price Lunching Near Golden Gate Park

Curiously (and happily) there are no restaurants other than museum cafes in Golden Gate Park, but that doesn't mean your choices are limited to the hot-dog cart. In the newly chic neighborhood of Inner Sunset, there is a handful of excellent restaurants, all of which are open for lunch, are very moderately priced, and are a block outside of the park along 9th Avenue. One of our favorites is **Park Chow** (1240 9th Ave., between Lincoln and Irving, ☎ 415/665-9912). Its rambling wood frame house and roof garden are a casual venue for Italian-inspired eclectic fare such as burgers, Asian noodles, grills, and roasts—all at serious bargain prices for such high-quality dining. Brunch goes until 2:30pm on weekends. In addition, some of the city's best sushi, sashimi, and Japanese fare is served at bare-bones traditional **Ebisu** (1283 9th Ave., between Lincoln and Irving, ☎ **415/556-1770**) a neighborhood favorite for 17 years. At **Avenue 9,** at 1243 9th Ave. ☎ **415/664-6999,** the creative kitchen cooks up fabulous gourmet cheese burgers, flat-iron steaks, fries, spinach and prawn salad, and butternut squash pancakes with pear preserves in a colorful retro-modern setting. Brunch is offered on Sundays from 10am to 3pm. Another design-conscious restaurant, **House on 9th,** at 1269 9th Ave. ☎ **415/682-3898,** serves great noodle dishes and curries in an architecturally playful neighborhood room. It's only open for lunch, however, Tuesday through Friday. And for something totally different, head to **Organica The Living Cuisine** (1224 9th Ave., ☎ **415/665-6519**), an entirely raw, organic, vegan restaurant that's critically acclaimed and worlds more tasty and creative than you could possibly imagine. They're closed on Monday. (Chef/owner/wildman Juliano recently published a fab cookbook.)

## 16  The Castro

While you'll see gay and lesbian singles and couples at almost any restaurant in San Francisco, the following spots cater particularly to the San Francisco gay community, though being gay is certainly not a requirement for enjoying them.

**2223.** 2223 Market St. (between Sanchez and Noe sts.). ☎ **415/431-0692.** Reservations recommended. $12.95–$19.95. AE, MC, V. Sat–Sun 10am–2pm; Sun–Thurs 5:30–10pm; Fri–Sat 5:30–11pm. Muni Metro: F, L, K, or M. Bus: 8, 22, 24, or 37. CALIFORNIA.

Surrounded by hardwood floors, candles, streamlined modern light fixtures and loud music, festive gays and straights come here to cocktail on the heavy-handed specialty drinks and dine on grilled pork chops or the ever-popular roasted chicken with garlic mashed potatoes. Along with Mecca, this is currently the dining and schmoozing spot in the area.

**Café Flore.** 2298 Market St. (at Noe St.). ☎ **415/621-8579.** Reservations not accepted. American breakfast $5.95; main courses $4.50–$10. No credit cards. Sun–Thurs 7am–11:30pm; Fri–Sat 7am–midnight. Muni Metro: F. Bus: 8. CALIFORNIA.

Sheathed with glass on three sides, and overlooking Market Street, Noe Street, and a verdant patio in back, Café Flore attracts young, bright, and articulate members of the gay (mostly male) community. Local wits refer to it as a place where body piercing is encouraged but not mandatory, although this kind of exhibitionism tends to be more prevalent in the evening rather than during the day.

Many of the menu items are composed of mostly organic ingredients, and include a succulent version of roasted (sometimes free-range) chicken, soups, pastas, and steaks. Café latte costs $2 a cup. Plan on hearing a lot of noise and possibly seeing a handsome young man sending not particularly furtive glances your way. Those with late-night munchies take heed: While the place stays open later, the kitchen closes at 10pm.

**Caffè Luna Piena.** 558 Castro St. (between 18th and 19th sts.). ☎ **415/621-2566.** Reservations recommended for brunch. Main courses $9–$17. AE, DC, DISC, MC, V. Mon–Fri 11am–3pm; Sat–Sun 9am–3pm; Tues–Sun 5:30–10:30pm. Muni Metro: F, K, L, or M. Bus: 24, 35, or 37. ITALIAN.

This venue is one of the Castro's most warm and sophisticated dining environments, complete with rich yellow, brush-painted walls adorned with local artwork. The room stretches all the way back to the outdoor dining patio (yes, there are heat lamps) and a lush Japanese garden. The fare is contemporary American with Italian and Mediterranean influences. Lunch offers soups, salads, sandwiches (with a choice of garlic fries or a green salad), such as the grilled eggplant with roasted red pepper and smoked mozzarella on pane integrale; or main lunch courses that may include blanched vegetables, and a lemon caper vinaigrette. Dinner features such dishes as lamb shanks braised with rosemary and garlic and served with soft polenta or roasted vegetable lasagna with sweet-potato sauce. Desserts follow city folks' favorites: crème brûlée and a dose of chocolate with the chocolate budino. Counter diners can watch chefs at work in the partially open kitchen. If you come for Saturday or Sunday brunch, reserve in advance or be prepared to wait in line for a yeast-raised waffle with strawberries, poached eggs with soft polenta, smoked salmon and shrimp cream, or any of the other breakfast treats.

✪ **Chow.** 215 Church St. (near Market St.). ☎ **415/552-2469.** Main courses $4.95–$7.50. MC, V. Sun–Thurs 11am–11pm, Fri–Sat 11am–midnight. Muni Metro: F, J, K, L, or M line. Bus: 8 or 37. AMERICAN.

Chow actually claims to serve American cuisine, but the management must be thinking of today's America, because the menu is not exactly baseball and apple pie. But that's just fine with us. If we can't decide between a burger, Italian, or Asian-influenced fare, we just come here. Mixed in with the expected cobb salad, fresh-fish dish, and grilled rosemary-lemon chicken are such exotic twists as noodles with peanut sauce; fuji apples and cucumber; an array of innovative pastas (starting at $4!); grilled meats, veggies, and fish; and wood-fired-oven pizzas. More traditional are the budget-efficient daily sandwich specials, which range from a scrambled egg, ham, Cheddar, and asparagus variety (Sun) to a chicken salad with bleu cheese, bacon, and apple selection (Thurs); both come with salad, soup, or fries for less than $7. While the food and prices alone would be a good argument for coming here, beer on tap, a great inexpensive wine selection, and a fun, tavernlike environment clinch the deal. However, if you're on the run, you can grab a pizza slice ($1.50) and other quick bits for a mere pittance. A second location, Park Chow, is at 1240 9th Ave., ☎ **415/665-9912.**

**Nippon Sushi.** 314 Church St. (at 15th St.). No phone. Sushi $2.05–$4.15 apiece. No credit cards. Mon–Sat noon–10pm. Bus: 8, 22, or 37. JAPANESE/SUSHI.

The lack of exterior signage inspired the locals to call this small, plain sushi restaurant "No Name." But even with its intentionally low profile, for over 10 years the tiny room has had a line out the door. What's the big deal? Since its beginnings it's been one of the cheapest sushi houses in town. How cheap? Try a vegetable roll for $2.05, a California roll for $3.60, or a melt-in-your-mouth tekka maki for $3.40.

It ain't the best in town by far, but for the price, you can't beat it. *Note:* It has fewer than 30 seats, so be prepared to wait for a table, and don't expect to wash your fish down with sake or beer—Nippon has no liquor license.

**Patio Café.** 531 Castro St. (at 18th St.). ☎ **415/621-4640.** Reservations not accepted. Main courses $4.75–$8.95 at lunch, $6.95–$12.50 at dinner. AE, MC, V. Sun–Thurs 8am–10:30pm, Fri–Sat 8am–11pm. Bus: 24 or 33. AMERICAN.

Since the early 1970s, this Castro Street bar and restaurant has served as the rendezvous point for uncounted numbers of trysts and peccadilloes, and love affairs of all kinds that have blossomed within its confines. Originally established as the Baker's Café, it retains the original ovens that contributed to its early reputation, though today they're purely decorative. Set in the backyard of a cluster of shops and ringed with trellises and greenery, the patio features a glass roof (whose entertainment value derives from the heft and brawn of the staff, who climb skyward to manually crank it open in good weather). Menu items include virtually any drink you can think of and such dishes as Caesar salads, Chinese chicken salad (laced with fresh ginger), prime rib, and grilled salmon with Cajun-hollandaise sauce. The most popular drinks include a Melon Margarita and a Patio Mai Tai. Weekend breakfasts are especially happening.

## SUPER-CHEAP EATS

✪ **Firewood Café.** 4248 18th St. (at Diamond St.). ☎ **415/252-0999.** Main courses $5.25–$7.95. MC, V. Daily 11am–11pm. Muni Metro: F, K, L, or M line. Bus: 8, 33, 35, or 37. ITALIAN/AMERICAN.

It shouldn't take a genius to realize that aesthetics count even in cheap restaurants. But apparently it did, because until just recently, finding budget gourmet food and attractive decor together was about as likely as seeing Newt Gingrich dancing through the Castro wearing chaps. But times they are a-changin', and this restaurant is setting the standard. One of the sharpest rooms in the neighborhood, the colorful Firewood put its money in the essentials and eliminated extra overhead. There are no waiters or waitresses here; everyone orders at the counter, then relaxes at either the single, long family-style table, one of the small tables facing the huge street-side windows, or seating in the cheery back dining room.

What they didn't skimp on is the cozy-chic atmosphere and inspired-but-limited menu: The fresh salads, which are $6.25, come with a choice of three "fixin's" ranging from caramelized onions to spiced walnuts and three gourmet dressing options. Then there's the pastas—three tortellini selections, such as roasted chicken and mortadella—and gourmet pizzas: the calamari with lemon-garlic aioli is a winner. Or how about an herb-roasted half or whole chicken ($6.25 or $12.50, respectively) with roasted new potatoes? Wines cost $3.95 to $4.95 by the glass and a reasonable $16.95 to $19.95. Draft and bottled beers are also available, and desserts top off at $2.25. (Thank goodness someone realized that $6 for an after-dinner treat borders on the ridiculous.)

✪ **Hot 'n' Hunky.** 4049 18th St. (at Hartford St.). ☎ **415/621-6365.** Burgers and sandwiches $4.50–$6. No credit cards. Sun–Thurs 11am–midnight, Fri–Sat 11am–1am. AMERICAN/BURGERS.

The name may reflect the neighborhood preference (it's in the heart of the Castro, after all), but late hours, hefty portions, juicy burgers, and painless prices bring all walks of life to this small, straightforward eatery. Order at the counter, grab one of the few tables, and grub out. With a burger, fries, and a shake topping off at around $7 (the combo special), you can't go wrong.

# A Hidden Treasure

Lucky enough to be in San Francisco on one of those rare hot days? Well, don't waste those fleeting sunny moments lunching inside. Call for directions and head to **The Ramp,** 855 China Basin St., at the end of Mariposa Street (☎ **415/ 621-2378**), a favorite bayside hangout among in-the-know locals. The fare is of the basic-lunch variety: burgers, sandwiches, salads, and soups for $4 to $10. But the boatyard environment and patio seating make this an excellent place to dine in the sun (if you're especially ambitious you can head here for breakfast, too). In summer, the place really rocks when live bands perform and tanned, cocktailing singles prowl the area. American Express, MasterCard, and Visa are accepted. Food is served daily from 8am to 4pm, with live music and appetizers later in the day Friday to Sunday. The bar is open Sunday to Thursday from 8am to 8pm and on Friday and Saturday from 8am to 1:30am. Take bus no. 22 or 48.

**Marcello's Pizza.** 420 Castro St. (at Market St.). ☎ **415/863-3900.** Pizza slices $1.90–$2.80; pies $9.20–$21.50. No credit cards. Sun–Thurs 11am–1am; Fri–Sat 11am–2am. Muni Metro: L, M, or N to Castro St. Station. PIZZA.

Marcello's isn't a fancy place, just a traditional pizza joint with a couple of tables and tasty pizza by the slice and a few other basic dishes. Weekend nights there's a line out the door of drunk and/or stoned Castro Street partiers with the late-night munchies.

## WORTH THE SPLURGE

✪ **Mecca.** 2029 Market St. (between Duboce and Church sts.). ☎ **415/621-7000.** www.sfmecca.com. Reservations recommended. Main courses $15–$25. AE, DC, MC, V. Mon–Wed 5pm–midnight; Thurs–Sat 5pm–1:30am; Sun 4–11pm;. Valet parking $8. Muni Metro: F, K, L, or M. Bus: 8, 22, 24, or 37. AMERICAN.

In 1996, Mecca entered the scene in a decadent swirl of chocolate-brown velvet, stainless steel, cement, and brown Naugahyde, unveiling the kind of industrial-chic supper club that makes you want to order a martini just so you'll match the ambiance. And cocktail they do—that eclectic city clientele (with a heavy dash of same-sex couples) who mingle at the oval centerpiece bar. A night here promises a live DJ spinning hot grooves, and a fine California meal, served at tables tucked into several dining nooks. Menu options include such classic starters as Osetra caviar, oysters on the half shell, and Caesar salad, as well as more creative dishes such as stir fried clams with garlic and minced pork in a black-bean sauce. Main courses include shrimp and lemongrass crusted Chilean sea bass, rosemary grilled rack of lamb, and soft-shell crabs with white corn salsa and Creole mustard vinaigrette. The food is very good, but it's that only-in-San-Francisco vibe that makes this place the smokin' hot spot in the Castro.

## 17 Mission District

**Bitterroot.** 3122 16th St. (at Valencia St.). ☎ **415/626-5523.** Most main courses $4–$6.50 at breakfast, $4–$6.75 at lunch, $6.25–9.75 at dinner. ATM, MC, V. Mon and Wed–Thurs 7am–5pm and 6–10pm, Tues 7am–5pm, Fri 7am–5pm and 6–11pm, Sat 8am–4pm and 6–11pm, Sun 8am–4pm and 6–10pm. BART: Mission. Bus: 14, 22, 33, 49, or 53. AMERICAN.

In a part of town where folks are most likely to party all night, it's appropriate that Bitterroot serves breakfast until 3 or 4pm. But that's not all that draws in the wild assortment of locals. The Old West comfy-casual environment, good draft beers, low prices, and red Naugahyde set the scene for good ol' American grub served to an undeniably San Franciscan clientele. At any given moment—but especially on weekends—you're likely to find the whole range of neighborhood folk, from tattooed grungers to young lesbian, gay, and straight folks who've come to graze. But almost anytime is fine to stop by for a hearty helping of potato cakes with applesauce and sour cream, housemade raisin French toast (with housemade syrup), or eggs any way you like 'em. Poverty-stricken pockets will appreciate the "pickin's": fruit, biscuits and gravy, oatmeal, bagel, or potatoes for less than $4. Lunch here satisfies those hankerin' for a hunk-a-sandwich, which come in 10 variations including the favored roast turkey, and still more pickin's: soup, chili, fries, onion rings, and slaw. Dinner rounds out the menu with more traditional American favorites: pork chops and hominy grits, Hangtown fry (sautéed oyster and bacon omelet), pasta, and turkey pot pie.

✪ **Pauline's.** 260 Valencia St. (between 14th St. and Duboce Ave.). ☎ **415/552-2050.** Reservations recommended. Main courses $10.50–$21.50. MC, V. Tues–Sat 5–10pm. Bus: 14, 26, or 49. PIZZA.

The perfect pizza? Quite possibly. At least it's the best we've ever had. Housed in a cheery double-decker yellow building that stands out like a beacon in a somewhat seedy neighborhood, Pauline's only does two things—pizzas and salads—but does them better than any other restaurant in the city. It's worth running the gauntlet of panhandlers for a slice of Pauline's Italian sausage pizza on handmade thin-crust dough. The eclectic toppings range from house-spiced chicken to French goat cheese, roasted eggplant, Danish fontina cheese, and tasso (spiced pork shoulder). The salads are equally amazing: certified organic, hand-picked by California growers, and topped with fresh and dried herbs (including edible flowers) from Pauline's own gardens in Berkeley. The wine list offers a smart selection of low-priced wines, and service is excellent. Yes, prices are a bit steep (small pizzas start at $10.50), but what a paltry price to pay for perfection.

**Saigon Saigon.** 1132–1134 Valencia St. (at 22nd St.). ☎ **415/206-9635.** Reservations accepted only for large parties. Main courses $6–$8. AE, MC, V. Mon–Fri 11:30am–2:30pm and 5:30–10pm, Sat 5:30–10pm, Sun 5:30–9:30pm. Bus: 14, 26, or 49. VIETNAMESE.

The decor here is half ambivalent, half interesting, with old phone boxes gracing the otherwise bare walls. But low prices, an eclectic Mission District clientele, and seating for large parties make this neighborhood restaurant a fine option for a satisfying—if not exactly memorable—meal. The menu features a variety of salads, soups, fowl, meats, vegetable and rice dishes, and seafood, most of which are accompanied by very fresh veggies. Wine served by the liter will remind you that you're not in a fancy spot, but it'll also keep the bill down. Lunch plates are an especially good deal—soup, salad, rice, and one of 15 vegetarian, seafood, and meat options for under $7. *Tips:* If you're famished, avoid ordering the seafood (other options come in larger portions), and if you arrive late, be sure to ask when the kitchen closes (the waiter didn't tell us, so we were unable to order dessert).

✪ **The Slanted Door.** 584 Valencia St. (at 17th St.). ☎ **415/861-8032.** Reservations strongly recommended. Lunch main courses $5.25–$16.50; most dinner dishes $5.75–$16.50. MC, V. Daily 11:30am–3pm; Sun–Thurs 5:30pm–10pm; Fri–Sat 5:30pm–10:30pm. Valet parking: $7. Bus: 22, 26, 33, 49 or 53; BART: 16th St. station. VIETNAMESE.

# Mission District Dining

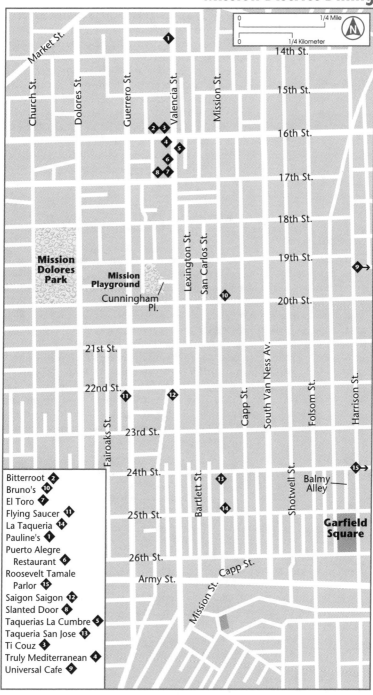

Bitterroot 2
Bruno's 10
El Toro 7
Flying Saucer 11
La Taqueria 14
Pauline's 1
Puerto Alegre
  Restaurant 6
Roosevelt Tamale
  Parlor 15
Saigon Saigon 12
Slanted Door 8
Taquerias La Cumbre 5
Taqueria San Jose 13
Ti Couz 3
Truly Mediterranean 4
Universal Cafe 9

In the last edition of this guide, we said that we didn't understand the hoopla surrounding Slanted Door, but our last few visits clarified why this superpopular restaurant turns away up to 100 diners a day. Despite the sometimes aloof staff, the colorful industrial chic warehouse of a dining room serves up incredibly fresh and flavorful Vietnamese food at excellent prices. Pull up a modern, color-washed chair, as Mick Jagger did during a recent visit, and order anything from clay-pot catfish or the amazing green papaya salad to one of the inexpensive lunch rice dishes, which come in a large ceramic bowl and are topped with such options as grilled shrimp, curry chicken, or stir-fried eggplant. Dinner items, which change seasonally, may range from steamed chicken with black-bean sauce, long beans with shrimp to vegetarian noodles sautéed with mushrooms, lily buds, tofu, bamboo, and shiitake mushrooms. Whatever you order it's bound to be clean and wholesome, but flavorful and outstanding. There's also an eclectic collection of teas, which come by the pot for $3 to $5.

**Ti Couz.** 3108 16th St. (at Valencia St.). ☎ **415/252-7373.** Crepes $1.95–$8.25. MC, V. Mon–Fri 11am–11pm; Sat 10am–11pm; Sun 10am–10pm. BART: 16th & Mission. Bus: 14, 22, 33, 49, or 53. CREPES.

With fierce culinary competition around every corner, many restaurants try to invent new gourmet gimmicks to hook the hungry. Unfortunately, the results are often creative concoctions that verge on palate pandemonium. Not true for Ti Couz (say "Tee Cooz"), one of the most architecturally stylish and popular restaurants in the Mission. Here the headliner is simple: a delicate, paper-thin crepe. And while its fillings aren't exactly original, they're excellently executed and infinite in their combinations. The menu advises how to enjoy these wraps: Order a light crepe as an appetizer, a heftier one as a main course, and a drippingly sweet one for dessert. Recommended combinations are listed, but you can build your own from the 15 main-course selections (such as smoked salmon, mushrooms, sausage, ham, scallops, and onions) and 19 dessert options (caramel, fruit, chocolate, Nutella, and more). Soups and salads solicit the less adventurous palate but are equally stellar; the sensational seafood salad, for example, is a compilation shrimp, scallops, and ahi tuna with veggies and five kinds of lettuce. Ciders and beer complement the cuisine.

✪ **Universal Café.** 2814 19th St. (at Bryant St.). ☎ **415/821-4608.** Reservations recommended for dinner. Main courses $2–$8 at breakfast (full on weekends, continental on weekdays), $5–$12 at lunch, $8–$20 at dinner. AE, MC, V. Tues–Thurs 7:30am–2:30pm and 6–10pm; Fri 9am–11:30pm; Sat 9am–2:30pm and 6–10pm; Sun 9am–2:30pm and 5:30–9:30pm. Bus: 27. AMERICAN/FRENCH.

It was love at first sight (as well as bite) at this small restaurant in the middle of a drab part of inner Mission. Not only does the place look good—suave and stylish with thick floor-to-ceiling windows and a profusion of sculptured metal and marble—it also attracts a nightly gaggle of locals who come for the phenomenal focaccia sandwiches (go for the moist and memorable salmon), inventive thin-crust pizzas, and gourmet salads for lunch, and superb dinner dishes such as braised duck leg on a bed of creamy polenta, sea bass served with risotto, spinach, and caramelized onions, or hearty pot roast with lumpy mashed potatoes and fresh veggies. Granted, it's on the way to nowhere, but if you're near the Mission and have a few minutes to spare, it's well worth the detour.

## SUPER-CHEAP EATS

**Puerto Alegre Restaurant.** 546 Valencia St. (between 16th and 17th sts.). ☎ **415/255-8201.** Reservations accepted only for parties of five or more. Main courses $3.85–$6.35.

MC, V. Mon 11am–10pm, Tues–Sun 11am–11pm. BART: Mission. Bus: 14, 22, 33, 49, or 53.
MEXICAN.

This would hardly be a popular spot were it not for two critical factors: Pitchers of
margaritas are a mere $11, and the dive-restaurant prices come with a more festive
and intimate atmosphere than other Mexican restaurants in the 'hood. This is not
a place for wolfing down a quick burrito; this is the kind of joint where you gather
with friends, suck back a few slushy 'ritas, and get loose amid the plastic-covered
seats and tables. And you order a burrito or combination plate not because it's the
best in town but because it's *good enough* and dirt cheap, and because you're bound
to get snockered if you don't soak up that tequila with something.

**Roosevelt Tamale Parlor.** 2817 24th St. (between Bryant and York sts.). ☎ **415/550-
9213.** Full meals $2.20–$8.25. No credit cards. Tues–Sun 10am–9:45pm. Bus: 9, 27, 33, or
48. MEXICAN.

Open since 1922, Roosevelt's may be the budget traveler's ultimate dream come
true. As far as tamales (and other Mexican dishes) go, the food here is nothing fancy,
but it's certainly good. Best of all, you can fill yourself to the brim for under $8.
The restaurant is dark, a little divelike, and filled with an eclectic mix of the young
and the groovy, regular folks, and longtime customers.

✪ **Taquerias La Cumbre.** 515 Valencia St. (between 16th and 17th sts.). ☎ **415/863-
8205.** Tacos and burritos $2–$4.25; dinner plates $5–$7. No credit cards. Mon–Sat
11am–10pm; Sun noon–9pm. BART: Mission. Bus: 14, 22, 33, 49, or 53. MEXICAN.

If San Francisco commissioned a flag honoring its favorite food, we'd probably all
be waving a banner of the Golden Gate Bridge bolstering a giant burrito—that's
how much we love these mammoth tortilla-wrapped meals. And while most restaurants gussy up their gastronomic goods with million-dollar decor and glamorous
gimmicks, the burrito needs only to be craftily constructed of fresh pork, steak,
chicken, or vegetables, plus cheese, beans, rice, salsa, and maybe a dash of guacamole or sour cream, and practically the whole town will drive to the remotest corners to taste it. In this case, the fact that it's served in a cafeteria-like brick-lined
room with overly shellacked tables and chairs is all the better: There's no mistaking
the attraction here.

There are plenty of fabulous burrito options in the Mission, as well as
throughout town, and La Cumbre is definitely one of them. Other great Mission
choices are **El Toro,** 3071 17th St., at Valencia Street (☎ **415/431-3351**), which
holds its simple bean- and rice-filled wrapper high; **La Taqueria,** 2889 Mission St.,
at 25th Street (☎ **415/285-7117**), a top contender in tacos (and burritos); and
**Taqueria San Jose,** 2830 Mission St., at 24th Street (☎ **415/282-0203**), which is
well favored with aficionados.

**Truly Mediterranean.** 3109 16th St. (at Valencia St.). ☎ **415/252-7482.** Fare
$3.50–$5.25. No credit cards. Mon–Sat 11am–midnight, Sun 11am–10pm. BART: Mission.
Bus: 14, 22, 33, 49, or 53. MEDITERRANEAN.

Hankering for tasty, fresh traditional Mediterranean food, but only have about five
bucks to spare? Well, break out the bill and wind your way to this Mission District
shack of a restaurant. With four stools, a small countertop, and two sidewalk tables,
the place is about as charming (and as crowded) as a Muni bus. But the falafels,
kebabs, baba ghanoush, and stuffed pitas are worth the trip. You can't go wrong
with the combo plate: falafel, hummus, baba, tabbouleh, cucumber salad, dolmas,
feta cheese, onions, tahini sauce, and pita bread (whew!)—all for $5.50. The other
location is 1724 Haight St., at Cole Street (☎ **415/751-7482**).

# WORTH A SPLURGE

**Bruno's.** 2389 Mission St. (between 19th and 20th sts.). ☎ **415/550-7455.** Reservations recommended. Main courses $14–$21. DC, MC, V. Tues–Thurs 6:30–11pm; Fri–Sat 6:30pm–midnight. Parking in back lot $5. ECLECTIC.

When the new owners scraped 60 years worth of grease and cigar smoke from the wood-paneled bar, added live music, and began serving flavorful fare in the 1950s-style dining room, the hipsters came in droves. But even 3 years after its opening, crowds are still coming to this Mission District restaurant. The reason? Aside from people watching, the food here actually competes with the ambiance. House specialties include apple salad, grilled boneless quail, and oxtail with mashed potatoes. After dinner, meander into the bar and beyond, where bands entertain the crowd. *Note:* While the dining room is closed on Monday, you can still order appetizers and desserts at the bar.

**Flying Saucer.** 1000 Guerrero St. (at 22nd St.). ☎ **415/641-9955.** Reservations recommended. Main courses $15–$26. AE, MC, V. Tues–Sat 5:30–9:30pm. Bart: 24th St. Station. Bus: 14 or 26. FRENCH.

Outrageously, yet artfully, presented food is the hallmark of this Mission District fixture. Peering into the glass-walled kitchen, diners can catch the kitchen staff leaning over plates, carefully standing a jumbo prawn on its head atop a baked column of potato polenta. Fish, beef, and fowl dishes are competently grilled, baked, or flamed before being surrounded by a flurry of sauces and garnishes. While the pricey food is certainly intense and flavorful, the overwhelming sensation at this bistro is visual. The party extends from the plate to the decor, where plastic flying saucers mingle with colorful murals and creative lighting. The menu changes frequently and there are almost always specials. If you ask your waiter to bring you the chef's most flamboyant offering, chances are you won't be disappointed. Reservations are essential, as is a blind eye to the sometimes infuriatingly snotty service.

# Exploring the City

**O**kay—so you've finally made it to San Francisco, checked into your hotel room, had lunch, and are ready to hit the town. You don't have a ton of cash, so you're pretty much limited to walking and looking around, right? Wrong! San Francisco may be one of the most expensive places in the world to live, but when it comes to seeing the city's sights and playing with all of its toys, you can have a ball for mere dollars a day. Case in point: Of our favorite things to do in and around the city (see "Frommer's Favorite (& Mostly Free) San Francisco Experiences" in chapter 1), nine are free, two cost $3, and the other two are less than $12—that's $30 for 4 days of nonstop fun. Not bad.

But wait, there's more. Listed below are dozens and dozens of cool places and activities to see and experience—from mind-broadening Sunday sermons to romantic rowboats for rent in Golden Gate Park—all of which have been given our stamp of approval (that means we've weaned out the weenies). Stick with our recommendations—particularly the starred ✪ attractions—and you're guaranteed an awesome stay in San Francisco without blowing your budget.

## 1 Famous San Francisco Sights

✪ **Alcatraz Island.** Pier 41, near Fisherman's Wharf. ☎ **415/773-1188** (for info only; no ferry reservations accepted at this number). Admission (includes ferry trip and audio tour) $11.25 adults, $9.50 seniors 62 and older, $6 children 5–11. Winter daily 9:30am–2:15pm; summer daily 9:15am–4:15pm. Advance purchase advised. Ferries depart every half hour, at 15 and 45 min. after the hour on the weekends, and every 45 min. throughout the week. Arrive at least 20 min. before sailing time.

Visible from Fisherman's Wharf, Alcatraz Island (a.k.a. "The Rock") has seen a checkered history. It was discovered in 1775 by Juan Manuel Ayala, who named it after the many pelicans that nested on the island. From the 1850s to 1933, when the army vacated the island, it served as a military post protecting the bay shoreline. In 1934, the buildings of the military outpost were converted into a maximum-security prison. Given the sheer cliffs, treacherous tides and currents, and frigid temperatures of the waters, it was believed to be a totally escape-proof prison. Among the famous gangsters who were penned in cell blocks A through D were Al Capone; Robert Stroud, the so-called Birdman of Alcatraz (because he was an

# Cheap Thrills: What to See & Do for Free
## (or Almost) in San Francisco

In addition to our "Frommer's Favorite (& Mostly Free) San Francisco Experiences" (see chapter 1), here are more fun and (mostly) free things to do:

- **Riding the Outdoor Elevators at the Westin St. Francis Hotel,** 335 Powell St., at Union Square. Your heart may skip a beat as you race skyward at 1,000 feet per minute. The view, as you'd expect, is dazzling, and you don't have to be a guest at the Westin to take a ride. Almost as thrilling is the glass elevator at the **Fairmont Hotel,** 950 Mason St., at California Street. The finale is a 360° view—the best in the city—from the Crown Room restaurant and lounge.

- **Skating Golden Gate Park on a Weekend Day.** If you've never tried in-line skating before, there's no better place to learn than on the wide, flat street through Golden Gate Park, which is closed to vehicles on weekends. **Skates on Haight,** 1818 Haight St. (☎ 415/752-8376), is the best place to rent in-line skates, and it's only 1 block away from the park. Protective wrist guards and knee pads are included in the cost: $8 per hour for in-line or conventional skates. A major credit/charge card and ID are required for rentals. The shop is open Monday to Friday from 11am to 7pm, and Saturday and Sunday from 10am to 6pm.

- **Riding on the Powell-Hyde or Powell-Mason Cable Car.** It's the most fun you can have in San Francisco for only a few dollars. Start on Market Street, then hang on to the brass rail for dear life as you whiz through the city toward Fisherman's Wharf.

- **Climbing the Filbert Street Steps.** San Francisco is a city of stairs, and the crème de la crème of steps is on Filbert Street between Sansome Street and the eastern side of Telegraph Hill. The terrain is so steep here that Filbert Street becomes Filbert Steps, a 377-step descent that wends its way through verdant

expert in ornithological diseases); Machine Gun Kelly; and Alvin Karpis. It cost a fortune to keep them imprisoned here because all supplies, including water, had to be shipped in. In 1963, after an apparent escape in which no bodies were recovered, the government closed the prison, and in 1972 it became part of the Golden Gate National Recreation Area. The wildlife that was driven away during the military and prison years has begun to return—the black-crested night heron and other seabirds are nesting here again—and a new trail has been built that passes through the island's nature areas. Tours, including an audio tour of the prison block and a slide show, are given by the park's rangers, who entertain their guests with interesting anecdotes.

It's a popular excursion and space is limited, so purchase tickets as far in advance as possible. The tour is operated by **Blue & Gold Fleet** (☎ 415/705-5555) and can be charged to American Express, MasterCard, or Visa ($2.25 per ticket service charge on phone orders). Tickets may also be purchased in advance from the Blue & Gold ticket office on Pier 41.

Wear comfortable shoes and take a heavy sweater or windbreaker because even when the sun's out, it's cold. The National Parks Service also notes that there are a lot of steps to climb on the tour.

flower gardens and some of the city's oldest and most varied housing. It's a beautiful walk down, and great exercise going up.

- **Enjoying a Coke-on-the-Rocks at the Marriott Hotel's Atrium Lobby Lounge.** It takes a few stiff sodas to get the nerve to peer 40 stories straight down from the Marriott's Atrium Lounge, 777 Market St., at Grant Avenue, where the only thing between you and the pavement is a pane of glass.

- **Strolling Haight Street Between Stanyan and Masonic Streets.** The San Francisco Zoo pales in comparison to some of the wildlife you'll see along lower Haight Street (don't worry, they won't bite). You'll also find plenty of colorful characters on Castro Street between Market and 19th streets.

- **Taking a "Magical Mysteries Explained" Tour Through the Exploratorium.** Both kids and adults can spend the entire day at this huge, hands-on science museum and never get bored. And don't miss the incredible antique amusement machines at the Musée Méchanique inside the Cliff House.

- **Pondering the Mission District Murals.** The Mission is one of the most ethnically colorful parts of the city. You could easily spend a day here seeking out the hundreds of vibrant murals. On Saturday, you can take an hour-long tour ($4) which highlights more than 70 murals. Contact the **Precita Eyes Mural Arts Center,** at 348 Precita Ave., at Folsom Street (☎ **415/285-2287**).

- **Catching Some Air in Your Car.** It's *The Streets of San Francisco* relived as you careen down the center lane of Gough Street between Ellis and Eddy streets, screaming out "Whooooeee!" as you feel the pull of gravity leave you momentarily, followed by the requisite thump of the shocks bottoming out. Wimpier folk can settle for the steepest street in San Francisco: Filbert Street, between Leavenworth and Hyde streets.

For those who want to get a closer look at Alcatraz without going ashore, two boat-tour operators offer short circumnavigations of the island (see "Self-Guided & Organized Tours," below, for complete information).

✪ **Cable Cars.** The Powell-Hyde and Powell-Mason lines begin at the base of Powell and Market sts.; the California St. line begins at the foot of Market St.

Although they may not be San Francisco's most practical means of transportation, cable cars are certainly the best loved. Designated official historic landmarks by the National Parks Service in 1964, they clank up and down the city's steep hills like mobile museum pieces, tirelessly hauling thousands of tourists each day to nowhere in particular.

San Francisco's cable cars were invented in 1869 by London-born engineer Andrew Hallidie, who got the idea by way of serendipity. As the story goes, Hallidie was watching a team of overworked horses haul a heavily laden carriage up a steep San Francisco slope. As he watched, one horse slipped and the car rolled back, dragging the other tired beasts with it. At that moment, Hallidie resolved that he would invent a mechanical contraption to replace such horses, and just 4 years later, in 1873, the first cable car made its maiden run from the top of Clay Street. Promptly

# Major San Francisco Sights

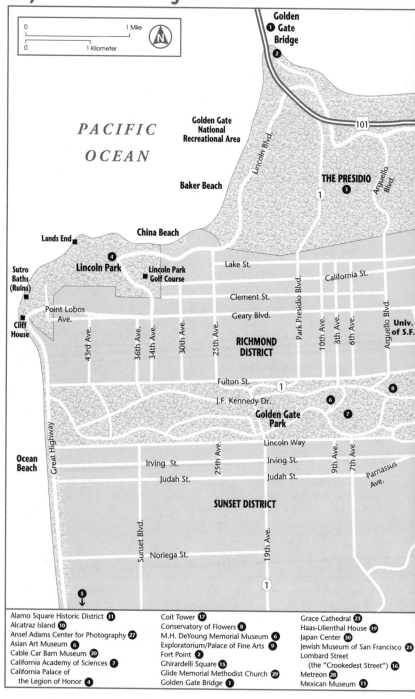

0 [_____] 1 Mile
0 [_____] 1 Kilometer

**PACIFIC OCEAN**

Golden Gate National Recreational Area

Baker Beach

Lands End

Sutro Baths (Ruins)

Cliff House

Point Lobos Ave.

Lincoln Park

China Beach

Lincoln Park Golf Course

**THE PRESIDIO** ❸

Lincoln Blvd.

Arguello Blvd.

Lake St.

California St.

Clement St.

Geary Blvd.

Park Presidio Blvd.

10th Ave.

3th Ave.

6th Ave.

Arguello Blvd.

**Univ. of S.F.**

Fulton St.

J.F. Kennedy Dr.

**Golden Gate Park**

Lincoln Way

Irving St.

Judah St.

**SUNSET DISTRICT**

**RICHMOND DISTRICT**

43rd Ave.

36th Ave.

34th Ave.

30th Ave.

25th Ave.

Irving St.

Judah St.

9th Ave.

7th Ave.

Parnassus Ave.

Ocean Beach

Great Highway

Sunset Blvd.

25th Ave.

19th Ave.

Noriega St.

❻ ❼ ❽ ❹ ❺

Golden Gate Bridge ❶ ❷

101

1

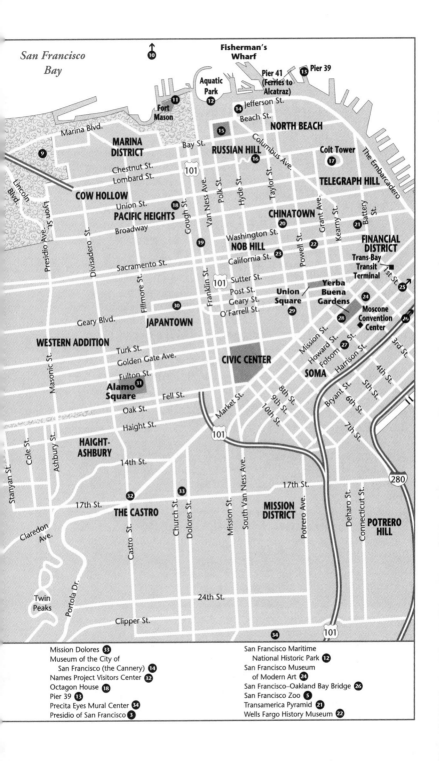

San Francisco Bay

San Francisco Bay

10

Fisherman's Wharf

Pier 41 (Ferries to Alcatraz)

Pier 39 13

Aquatic Park 12

Jefferson St. 14

Beach St.

NORTH BEACH

Fort Mason 11

Marina Blvd.

MARINA DISTRICT

Bay St. 15

RUSSIAN HILL 16

Columbus Ave.

Coit Tower 17

Chestnut St.

Lombard St.

101

COW HOLLOW

Union St. 18

PACIFIC HEIGHTS

Broadway

TELEGRAPH HILL

The Embarcadero

CHINATOWN 20

Battery St. 21

FINANCIAL DISTRICT

Washington St.

NOB HILL

Grant Ave.

Kearny St.

Powell St. 22

California St. 23

Trans-Bay Transit Terminal

1st St. 25

Sacramento St.

101

Sutter St.

Post St.

Union Square

Yerba Buena Gardens 24

Moscone Convention Center 26

Geary St.

O'Farrell St. 29

28

Geary Blvd. 30

JAPANTOWN

Mission St. 27

Howard St.

Folsom St.

Harrison St.

SOMA

3rd St.

WESTERN ADDITION

Turk St.

Golden Gate Ave.

CIVIC CENTER

8th St.

9th St.

Bryant St.

5th St.

6th St.

7th St.

Fulton St.

Alamo Square 31

Fell St.

Oak St.

Haight St.

Market St.

101

HAIGHT-ASHBURY

14th St.

280

17th St.

32

33

17th St.

THE CASTRO

Church St.

Dolores St.

Mission St.

South Van Ness Ave.

MISSION DISTRICT

Potrero Ave.

Deharo St.

Connecticut St.

POTRERO HILL

Twin Peaks

Portola Dr.

24th St.

Clipper St.

34

101

Mission Dolores 33
Museum of the City of
   San Francisco (the Cannery) 14
Names Project Visitors Center 32
Octagon House 18
Pier 39 13
Precita Eyes Mural Center 34
Presidio of San Francisco 3

San Francisco Maritime
   National Historic Park 12
San Francisco Museum
   of Modern Art 24
San Francisco–Oakland Bay Bridge 26
San Francisco Zoo 5
Transamerica Pyramid 21
Wells Fargo History Museum 22

155

ridiculed as "Hallidie's Folly," the cars were slow to gain acceptance. One early onlooker voiced the general opinion by exclaiming, "I don't believe it—the damned thing works!"

Even today, many visitors have difficulty believing that these vehicles, which have no engines, actually work. The cars, each weighing about 6 tons, are hauled along by a steel cable, enclosed under the street in a center rail. You can't see the cable unless you peer straight down into the crack, but you'll hear its characteristic clickity-clanking sound whenever you're nearby. The cars move when the gripper (not the driver) pulls back a lever that closes a pincerlike "grip" on the cable. The speed of the car therefore is determined by the speed of the cable, which is a constant 9½ miles per hour—never more, never less.

The two types of cable cars in use hold, respectively, a maximum of 90 and 100 passengers, and the limits are rigidly enforced. The best views are had from the outer running boards, where you have to hold on tightly when taking curves. Everyone, it seems, prefers to ride on the running boards.

Often imitated but never duplicated, similar versions of Hallidie's cable cars have been used throughout the world, but all have been replaced by more efficient means of transportation. San Francisco planned to do so, too, but the proposal was met with so much opposition that the cable cars' perpetuation was actually written into the city charter in 1955. This mandate cannot be revoked without the approval of a majority of the city's voters—a distant and doubtful prospect.

San Francisco's three existing lines comprise the world's only surviving system of cable cars, which you can experience for yourself should you choose to wait in the endless boarding line (up to a 2-hour wait in summer). For more information on riding them, see "Getting Around" in chapter 4, "Getting to Know San Francisco."

**The Cannery.** 2801 Leavenworth St. ☎ **415/771-3112.** www.thecannery.com.

The Cannery was built in 1894 as a fruit-canning plant and converted in the 1960s into a mall containing 50-plus shops, a paint-it-yourself ceramic studio, a comedy club, and several restaurants and galleries, including **Jack's Cannery Bar** (☎ **415/ 931-6400**), which features 110 beers on tap (the most anywhere in the country). Vendors' stalls and sidewalk cafes are set up in the courtyard amid a grove of century-old olive trees, and on summer weekends street performers are out in force entertaining tourists. **The Museum of the City of San Francisco** (☎ **415/ 928-0289**), which traces the city's development with displays and artifacts, is on the third floor. The museum is free and is open Wednesday to Sunday from 10am to 4pm.

**Coit Tower.** Atop Telegraph Hill. ☎ **415/362-0808.** Admission (to the top of the tower) $3.75 adults, $2.50 seniors, $1.50 children 6–12. Daily 10am–6pm. Bus: 39 ("Coit").

In a city known for its great views and vantage points, Coit Tower is tops. Located atop Telegraph Hill, just east of North Beach, the round, stone tower offers panoramic views of the city and the bay.

Completed in 1933, the tower is the legacy of Lillie Hitchcock Coit, a wealthy eccentric who left San Francisco a $125,000 bequest "for the purpose of adding beauty to the city I have always loved" and also as a memorial to its volunteer firemen. She had been saved from a fire as a child and thereafter held the city's firefighters in particularly high esteem.

Inside the base of the tower are the impressive murals titled *Life in California, 1934,* which were completed under the WPA during the New Deal. They were completed by more than 25 artists, many of whom had studied under Mexican muralist Diego Rivera.

# Funky Favorites at Fisherman's Wharf

The following sights are all clustered on or near Fisherman's Wharf. To reach this area by cable car, take the Mason line to the last stop and walk to the wharf; by bus, take no. 30, 32, or 42. If you're arriving by car, park on adjacent streets or on the wharf between Taylor and Jones streets.

The popular battle-scarred World War II fleet submarine **USS *Pampanito,*** Pier 45, Fisherman's Wharf (☎ **415/775-1943**), saw plenty of action in the Pacific. It has been completely restored, and visitors are free to crawl around inside. An audio tour is included with admission, which runs $5 for adults, $3 for children 13 to 17, and free for seniors and children under 12; there is also a family pass for $15 (two adults, up to four kids). The *Pampanito* is open daily 9am to 8pm.

**Ripley's Believe It or Not! Museum,** 175 Jefferson St. (☎ **415/771-6188; www.ripleysf.com**), has been drawing curious spectators through its doors for over 30 years. Inside, you'll experience the extraordinary world of improbabilities: a one-third scale match-stick cable car, a shrunken human torso once owned by Ernest Hemingway, a dinosaur made from car bumpers, a walk through a kaleidoscope tunnel, and video displays and illusions. Robert LeRoy Ripley's infamous arsenal may lead you to ponder whether truth is in fact stranger than fiction. Admission is $8.50 for adults, $7 for seniors over 60, $5.50 for children 5 to 12, and free for children under 5. From June 15 through Labor Day it is open Sunday to Thursday from 9am to 11pm, until midnight on Friday and Saturday; the rest of the year it is open Sunday to Thursday from 10am to 10pm, until midnight on Friday and Saturday. Call for special hours on major holidays.

Conceived and executed in the Madame Tussaud mold, San Francisco's **Wax Museum,** 145 Jefferson St. (☎ **415/202-0400**), has long been a kitchy harborside tourist trap. But in 1999, with the closing of adjoining Haunted Goldmine, the museum is expanding and undergoing a $15-million tear-down and renovation. It is scheduled to re-open at the end of 1999 as a huge complex that includes national retail and restaurant chains. (Not any less of a tourist trap, mind you, only a newer, slicker one.) Surely they will spiff up the museum's 250 lifelike figures including singer Michael Jackson, Marilyn Monroe, John Wayne, former president George Bush, and "Feared Leaders" such as Fidel Castro. They'll also reintroduce the Chamber of Horrors, which features Dracula, Frankenstein, and a werewolf, along with bloody victims hanging from meat hooks. But the clinchers will be the addition of 1990s pop icons such as Leonardo DiCaprio and Will Smith. Admission is likely to change with the reopening, but before the renovations, prices were $11.95 for adults, $9.95 for teens 13 to 17, $8.95 for seniors over 60, $5.95 for children 6 to 12, and free for children under 6. Call for re-opening schedule and new hours.

**Fisherman's Wharf & Pier 39.** Cable Car: Powell-Mason line (last stop; then walk to the wharf). Bus: 30, 32, or 42.

Few cities in America are as adept at wholesaling their historical sites as San Francisco, which has converted Fisherman's Wharf into one of the most popular tourist destinations in the world. Unless you come really early in the morning, you won't find any traces of the traditional waterfront life that once existed here; the only fishing going on around here is for tourists' dollars.

Originally called Meigg's Wharf, this bustling strip of waterfront got its present moniker from generations of fishers who used to base their boats here. Today, the bay has become so polluted with toxins that bright yellow placards warn against eating fish from these waters. A small fleet of fewer than 30 boats still operates from here, but basically Fisherman's Wharf has been converted into one long shopping mall stretching from Ghirardelli Square at the west end to Pier 39 at the east. Some people love it, others can't get far enough away from it, but most agree that Fisherman's Wharf, for better or for worse, has to be seen at least once in your life.

**Ghirardelli Square,** at 900 N. Point, between Polk and Larkin streets (☎ 415/775-5500), dates from 1864 when it served as a factory making Civil War uniforms, but it's best known as the former chocolate-and-spice factory of Domingo Ghirardelli (say "Gear-a-deli"). The factory has been converted into a 10-level mall containing 50-plus stores and 20 dining establishments. Scheduled street performers play regularly in the West Plaza. The stores generally stay open from 10am to 9pm in the summer and until 6 or 7pm in the winter. Incidentally, the Ghirardelli Chocolate Company still makes chocolate, but its factory is located in a lower-rent district in the East Bay.

**Pier 39,** on the waterfront at Embarcadero and Beach Street (☎ **415/981-8030;** shops are open daily from 10:30am to 8:30pm), is a 4½-acre, multi-level waterfront complex a few blocks east of Fisherman's Wharf. Constructed on an abandoned cargo pier, it is, ostensibly, a re-creation of a turn-of-the-century street scene, but don't expect a slice of old-time maritime life. This is the busiest mall of the lot and, according to the *London Observer,* the third most visited attraction in the world, behind Disney World and Disneyland—with more than 100 stores, 10 bay-view restaurants (including the Bubba Gump Shrimp Co., an over-buttered spin-off from the *Forrest Gump* movie), a two-tiered Venetian carousel, and a new big-screen Cinemax Theater showing the *Secret of San Francisco.*

The latest major addition to Fisherman's Wharf is **Underwater World,** a $38-million, 707,000-gallon marine attraction filled with sharks, stingrays, and more, all witnessed via a moving footpath that transports visitors through clear acrylic tunnels.

Accommodating a total of 350 boats, two marinas flank the pier and house the Blue & Gold bay-sightseeing fleet. In recent years, some 600 California sea lions have taken up residence on the adjacent floating docks. Until they abandon their new playground, which seems more and more unlikely, these playful, noisy creatures (some nights you can hear them all the way from Washington Square) create one of the best free attractions on the wharf. Ongoing docent-led programs are offered at Pier 39 on weekends from 11am to 5pm that teach visitors about the range, habitat, and adaptability of the California sea lion.

## ✪ Golden Gate Bridge

1996 marked the 60th birthday of what is possibly the most beautiful, and certainly the most photographed, bridge in the world. Often half-veiled by the city's trademark rolling fog, San Francisco's Golden Gate Bridge spans tidal currents, ocean waves, and battering winds to connect the City by the Bay with the Redwood Empire to the north.

With its gracefully swung single span, spidery bracing cables, and sky-zooming twin towers, the bridge looks more like a work of abstract art than the practical engineering feat that it is, among the greatest of this century. Construction began in May 1937 and was completed at the then-colossal cost of $35 million.

The mile-long steel link (longer if you factor in the approach), which reaches a height of 746 feet above the water, is an awesome bridge to cross. Traffic usually

# Fisherman's Wharf & Vicinity

San Francisco Bay

Pier 39 Yacht Harbor

Grant Ave.
Midway St.
Bellair
Pfeiffer St.
Edgardo Pl.
Edith St.
Stockton St.
Worden St.
Powell St.
Beach St.
North Point St.
Bay St.
Vandewater St.
Chestnut St.
Newell St.
Jansen St.
Mason St.
Francisco St.
Water St.
Fielding St.
The Embarcadero
Jefferson St.
Taylor St.
Powell-Mason Line
Jones St.
Columbus Ave.
Houston St.
Lombard St.
Bret Harte Ter.
SF Art Institute
Leavenworth St.
Montclair Ter.
"Crookedest Street"
Fisherman's Wharf
Hyde St.
Powell-Hyde Line
Beach St.
North Point St.
Russian Hill Park
Larkin St.
Angel Island & Tiburon Ferries
Hyde Street Pier
Victorian Park
Ghirardelli Square
Bay St.
Municipal Pier
Aquatic Park
Polk St.
Chestnut St.
Van Ness Ave.
Francisco St.

1/8 Mile
1/8 Kilometer
N

**LEGEND**
Cable Car – – –

Alma **12**
Alcatraz Ferry **2**
Aquatic Park **15**
Balclutha **13**
The Cannery **8**
C.A. Thayer **14**
Eureka **10**
Fisherman's Wharf **7**
Ghirardelli Square **17**
Hercules **11**
Maritime Historical Park & Museum **16**
Pier 39 **1**
Powell-Hyde Cable Car Turnaround **9**
Powell-Mason Cable Car Turnaround **6**
Ripley's "Believe It Or Not!" Museum **5**
U.S.S. Pampanito **3**
The Wax Museum at Fisherman's Wharf **4**

159

# A Room with a View

Few sights are more spectacular than gazing down upon a city from the top of a skyscraper. In San Francisco, the best place to go for an awesome aerial view is the **SkyDeck,** located on the 41st floor of the Embarcadero Center. Granted, it's no Empire State Building, but the view of the city and surrounding bay is far, far prettier than dirty ol' NYC. In addition to the sky-high scenery, the SkyDeck also features interactive kiosks that explore San Francisco's colorful history and neighborhoods (this is the home of Silicon Valley, after all).

The entrance and ticket booth to the SkyDeck are on the lobby level of One Embarcadero Center (those four slender, identical buildings with small rectangular windows), located between Battery and Front and Sacramento and Clay streets. It's open Memorial Day to Labor Day from 9:30am to sunset and Labor Day to Memorial Day Saturday through Wednesday from noon to 9pm, Thursday and Friday from 10am to 9pm. Admission is $6 for adults, $4 for students and seniors 62 and older, $3.50 for children 5 to 12, and free for kids under 5. Complimentary docent-led tours are also available, starting at 12:30pm. Parking is available below all Embarcadero Center buildings, and is only $1 per hour on weekends and evenings. For more information, call the SkyDeck at ☎ **888/737-5933** or 415/772-0555.

moves quickly, so crossing by car won't give you too much time to see the sights. If you drive ($3 toll, payable southbound) from the city, park in the lot at the foot of the bridge on the city side and make the crossing by foot. Back in your car, continue to Marin's Vista Point, at the bridge's northern end. Look back and you'll be rewarded with one of the greatest views of San Francisco.

Millions of pedestrians walk or bike across the bridge each year, gazing up at the tall red towers, out at the vistas of San Francisco and Marin County, and down into the stacks of oceangoing liners. You can walk out onto the span from either end, but be prepared—it's usually windy and cold, and the bridge vibrates. Still, walking even a short way is one of the best ways to experience the immense scale of the structure.

Bridge-bound **Golden Gate Transit buses** (☎ **415/923-2000**) depart every 30 to 60 minutes during the day for Marin County, starting from the Transbay Terminal at Mission and First streets and making convenient stops at Market and Seventh streets, at the Civic Center, and along Van Ness Avenue and Lombard Street.

**Lombard Street.** Between Hyde and Leavenworth sts.

Known as the "crookedest street in the world," the whimsically winding block of Lombard Street draws thousands of visitors each year (much to the chagrin of neighborhood residents, most of whom would prefer to block off the street to tourists). The angle of the street is so steep that the road has to snake back and forth to make a descent possible. The brick-lined street zigzags around the residences' bright flower gardens that explode with color during warmer months. This short stretch of Lombard Street is one way, downhill, and fun to drive. Take the curves slowly and in low gear, and expect a wait during the weekend. Save your film for the bottom, where, if you're lucky, you can find a parking space and take a few snapshots of the silly spectacle. You can also walk the block, either up or down, via staircases (without curves) on either side of the street.

# 2  Museums

*Note:* For additional museums within Golden Gate Park, see section 4, below.

**Ansel Adams Center for Photography.** 250 Fourth St. ☎ **415/495-7000.** Admission $5 adults, $3 students, $2 seniors and children 13–17, free for children 12 and under. Daily 11am–5pm; until 8pm the 1st Thurs of each month. Muni Metro: Powell St. lines. Bus: 30, 45, or 9X.

This popular SoMa museum features five separate galleries for changing exhibitions of contemporary and historical photography. One area is dedicated solely to displaying the works and exploring the legacy of Ansel Adams.

**Cable Car Barn Museum.** Washington and Mason sts. ☎ **415/474-1887.** Free admission. Apr–Oct daily 10am–6pm; Nov–Mar daily 10am–5pm. Cable car: Both Powell St. lines stop by the museum.

If you've ever wondered how cable cars work, this nifty museum will explain (and demonstrate!) it all to you. Yes, this is a museum, but the Cable Car Barn is no stuffed shirt. It's the living powerhouse, repair shop, and storage place of the cable-car system and is in full operation. Built for the Ferries and Cliff House Railway in 1887, the building underwent an $18-million reconstruction to restore its original gaslight-era look, install an amazing spectators' gallery, and add a museum of San Francisco transit history.

The exposed machinery, which pulls the cables under San Francisco's streets, looks like a Rube Goldberg invention. Stand in the mezzanine gallery and become mesmerized by the massive groaning and vibrating winches as they thread the cable that hauls the cars through a huge figure eight and back into the system via slack-absorbing tension wheels. For a better view, move to the lower-level viewing room where you can see the massive pulleys and gears operating underground.

Also on display here is one of the first grip cars developed by Andrew S. Hallidie, operated for the first time on Clay Street on August 2, 1873. Other displays include an antique grip car and trailer that operated on Pacific Avenue until 1929, and dozens of exact-scale models of cars used on the various city lines. There's also a shop where you can buy a variety of cable-car gifts.

✪ **California Palace of the Legion of Honor.** In Lincoln Park (at 34th Ave. and Clement St.). ☎ **415/750-3600** or 415/863-3330 (for recorded information). Admission (including the Asian Art Museum and M. H. De Young Memorial Museum) $7 adults, $5 seniors 65 and over, $4 youths 12–17, free for children 11 and under (fees may be higher for special exhibitions); free the 2nd Wed of each month when hours are 9:30am–8:45pm. Open Tues–Sun 9:30am–5pm. Bus: 38 or 18.

Designed as a memorial to California's World War I casualties, the neoclassical structure is an exact replica of the Legion of Honor Palace in Paris, right down to the inscription "*Honneur et Patrie*" above the portal.

The Legion of Honor re-opened in late 1995 after a 2-year, $34.6-million renovation and seismic upgrading that was stalled by the discovery of almost 300 turn-of-the-century coffins. The exterior's grassy expanses, cliff-side paths, and incredible view of the Golden Gate make this an absolute must-visit attraction before you even get in the door. But the inside is equally impressive. The museum's permanent collection covers 4,000 years of art and includes paintings, sculpture, and decorative arts from Europe, as well as international tapestries, prints, and drawings. The chronological display of more than 800 years of European art includes one of the world's finest collections of Rodin's sculptures.

# Free Culture

Almost all art galleries and museums are open free to the public one day of the month. The following list will help you learn how to plan your week around museums' free-day schedules (refer to the individual attractions listings for complete information on each museum).

**First Monday**
• The Jewish Museum San Francisco

**First Tuesday**
• Museum of Modern Art

**First Wednesday**
• Exploratorium
• M. H. De Young Memorial Museum and Asian Art Museum
• California Academy of Sciences
• Mexican Museum

**Second Wednesday**
• California Palace of the Legion of Honor

**First Thursday**
• Center for the Arts at Yerba Buena Gardens (from 6 to 8pm)

**Always Free**
• The Names Project AIDS Memorial Quilt Visitors Center
• Cable Car Barn Museum
• San Francisco Maritime National Historical Park and Museum (there is a fee to board ships)
• Wells Fargo History Museum

**Yerba Buena Center for the Arts.** 701 Mission St. ☎ **415/978-2700,** or box office 415/978-ARTS. Admission $5 adults, $3 seniors and students; free every 1st Thurs of the month from 6–8pm. Tues–Sun 11am–6pm. Muni Metro: Powell or Montgomery. Bus: 30, 45, or 9X.

Cutting-edge computer art and multimedia shows are on view in the high-tech galleries. The initial exhibition, "The Art of Star Wars," featured the special effects created by George Lucas for the film.

✪ **The Exploratorium.** 3601 Lyon St., in the Palace of Fine Arts (at Marina Blvd.). ☎ **415/563-7337** or 415/561-0360 (for recorded information). Admission $9 adults, $7 senior citizens and college students with ID, $5 children 6–17, $2.50 children 3–5, free for children under 3; free for everyone 1st Wed of each month. MC, V. Summer (Memorial Day–Labor Day) and holidays, Mon–Tues and Thurs–Sun 10am–6pm; Wed 10am–9pm. Rest of the year Tues and Thurs–Sun 10am–5pm; Wed 10am–9pm. Closed Thanksgiving Day, and Christmas Day. Free parking. Bus: 30 from Stockton St. to the Marina stop.

*Scientific American* magazine rates the Exploratorium as "the best science museum in the world"—pretty heady stuff for this exciting hands-on science fair that contains more than 650 permanent exhibits that explore everything from giant bubble blowing to Einstein's theory of relativity. It's like a mad scientist's penny arcade, an educational fun house, and an experimental laboratory all rolled into one. Touch a tornado, shape a glowing electrical current, finger-paint via computer, or take a sensory journey in total darkness in the Tactile Dome—you could spend all day here and still not see everything. Every exhibit at the Exploratorium is designed to be interactive, educational, safe, and most important, fun. And don't think this is just for kids; parents inevitably end up being the most reluctant to leave. On the way out, be sure to stop in the wonderful gift store, which is chock-full of affordable brain candy.

The museum is located in San Francisco's Marina District at the beautiful Palace of Fine Arts, the only building left standing from the Panama-Pacific Exposition of 1915, which celebrated the opening of the Panama Canal. The adjoining park and lagoon—the perfect place for an afternoon picnic—is home to ducks, swans, seagulls, and grouchy geese, so bring bread.

**Haas-Lilienthal House.** 2007 Franklin St. (at Washington St.). ☎ **415/441-3004.** Admission $5 adults, $3 children 6–12 and seniors. Wed noon–3:15pm; Sun 11am–4:15pm. Cable car: California St. line. Bus: 1, 12, 19, 27, 42, 47, 49, or 83.

Of the city's many gingerbread Victorians, this handsome Queen Anne house is one of the most flamboyant. The 1886 structure features all the architectural frills of the period, including dormer windows, flying cupolas, ornate trim, and wistful turrets. The elaborately styled house is now a museum, its rooms fully furnished with period pieces. The house is maintained by the Foundation for San Francisco's Architectural Heritage, which offers tours 2 days a week. A new Costume Exhibit has been added, which features such themes as ragtime-era costumes, artifacts, and accessories.

**The Jewish Museum San Francisco.** 121 Steuart St. (between Mission and Howard sts.). ☎ **415/543-8880.** Admission $5 adults, $2.50 students and seniors; free the 1st Mon of each month. Sun–Wed 11am–5pm; Thurs 11am–8pm. Closed Fri–Sat. Bus: 14 or 32.

The Jewish Museum San Francisco was inaugurated in 1984 to educate the community about Jewish history, traditions, and values. The museum hosts a variety of shows that concentrate on the themes of immigration, assimilation, and identity of the Jewish community in the United States and around the world. They are illustrated by paintings, sculptures, and photographs, as well as educational programs involving nonsectarian schools and summer camps. In 2000, they're beginning renovations on a new location at Jesse and Mission streets, but the move isn't scheduled until 2002.

**Mexican Museum.** Bldg. D, Fort Mason, Marina Blvd. (at Laguna St.). ☎ **415/202-9700.** Admission $3 adults, $2 children. Free 1st Wed of the month. Wed–Fri noon–5pm; Sat–Sun 11am–5pm. Bus: 76 or 28.

The first museum in the nation dedicated to the work of Mexican and other Latino artists, the Mexican Museum maintains an impressive collection of art covering pre-Hispanic, colonial, folk, Mexican fine art, and Chicano/Mexican-American art. Revolving art shows range from the art of New Mexican women to such subjects as Mexican surrealism. *Note:* The museum is expected to relocate to the Yerba Buena neighborhood at the end of 2001; its phone numbers are expected to remain the same.

**Octagon House.** 2645 Gough St. (at Union St.). ☎ **415/441-7512.** Free admission (donation suggested). Open only on the 2nd Sun and 2nd and 4th Thurs of each month (except January), noon–3pm. Closed Jan and holidays. Bus: 41 or 45.

This unusual, eight-sided, cupola-topped house dates from 1861 and is maintained by the National Society of Colonial Dames of America. The architectural features are extraordinary, and from the second floor it is possible to look up into the cupola, which is illuminated at night. Now a small museum, you'll find Early American furniture, portraits, silver, pewter, looking glasses, and English and Chinese ceramics. There are also some historic documents, including the signatures of 54 of the 56 signers of the Declaration of Independence. Even if you're not able to visit during opening hours, this strange structure is worth a look.

**San Francisco Maritime National Historical Park.** At the foot of Polk St. (near Fisherman's Wharf). ☎ **415/556-3002.** Museum free; ships $4 adults, $2 children 12–17, free for children 11 and under and seniors over 62. Museum daily 10am–5pm. Ships on Hyde St. Pier May 31–Sept 1 daily 10am–6pm; Sept 2–May 30 daily 9:30am–5pm. Closed Thanksgiving Day, Christmas Day, and New Year's Day. Cable car: Hyde St. line to the last stop. Bus: 19, 30, 32, 42, or 47.

Shaped like an art-deco ship, the Maritime Museum is filled with sailing, whaling, and fishing lore. Remarkably good exhibits include intricate model craft, scrimshaw, and a collection of shipwreck photographs and historic marine scenes, including an 1851 snapshot of hundreds of abandoned ships, deserted en masse by crews dashing off to participate in the gold rush. The museum's walls are lined with beautifully carved, brightly painted wooden figureheads from old windjammers.

Two blocks east, at the park's Hyde Street Pier, are several historic ships, now moored and open to the public.

The *Balclutha*, one of the last surviving square-riggers and the handsomest vessel in San Francisco Bay, was built in Glasgow, Scotland, in 1886, and used to carry grain from California at a near-record speed of 300 miles a day. The ship is now completely restored. Visitors are invited to spin the wheel, squint at the compass, and imagine they're weathering a mighty storm. Kids can climb into the bunking quarters, visit the "slop chest" (galley to you, matey), and read the sea chanteys (clean ones only) that decorate the walls.

The 1890 *Eureka* still carries a cargo of nostalgia for San Franciscans. It was the last of 50 paddle-wheel ferries that regularly plied the bay; it made its final trip in 1957. Restored to its original splendor at the height of the ferryboat era, the sidewheeler is loaded with deck cargo, including antique cars and trucks.

The black-hulled, three-masted *C. A. Thayer*, built in 1895, was crafted for the lumber trade and carried logs felled in the Pacific Northwest to the carpentry shops of California.

Other historic ships docked here include the tiny two-masted *Alma*, one of the last scow schooners to bring hay to the horses of San Francisco; the *Hercules*, a huge 1907 oceangoing steam tug; and the *Eppleton Hall*, a side-wheel tugboat built in England, in 1914, to operate on London's River Thames.

At the pier's small-boat shop, visitors can follow the restoration progress of historic boats from the museum's collection. It's located behind the maritime bookstore on your right as you approach the ships.

**San Francisco Museum of Modern Art (MOMA).** 151 Third St. (2 blocks south of Market St., across from Yerba Buena Gardens). ☎ **415/357-4000.** Admission $8 adults, $5 senior citizens, $4 for students 14–with ID, free for children 12 and under; half price for everyone Thurs 6–9pm, and free for everyone the 1st Tues of each month. Labor Day–Memorial Day Thurs 11am–9pm; Fri–Tues 11am–6pm. Memorial Day–Labor Day Thurs 10am–9pm; Fri–Tues 10am–6pm. Closed Wed and major holidays. Muni Metro: J, K, L, or M to Montgomery Station. Bus: 15, 30, or 45.

Swiss architect Mario Botta, in association with Hellmuth, Obata, and Kassabaum, designed the $62-million museum, which opened in SoMa in January 1995. The building is the most welcomed new development in years and has made SoMa one of the more popular areas to visit for tourists and residents alike. The museum's collection consists of more than 15,000 works, including close to 5,000 paintings and sculptures by artists such as Henri Matisse, Jackson Pollock, and Willem de Kooning. Other artists represented include Diego Rivera, Georgia O'Keeffe, Paul Klee, the Fauvists, and exceptional holdings of Richard Diebenkorn. MOMA was also one of the first to recognize photography as a major art form; its extensive collection includes more than 9,000 photographs by such notables as Ansel Adams, Alfred Stieglitz, Edward Weston, and Henri Cartier-Bresson. Docent-led tours are offered daily. Times are posted at the museum's admission desk. Phone for current details of upcoming special events.

The Caffè Museo, located to the right of the museum entrance sets a new precedent for museum food with flavorful and fresh soups, sandwiches, and salads that are as respectable as those served in many local restaurants.

No matter what, don't miss the MuseumStore, which carries a wonderful array of architectural gifts, books, and trinkets. It's one of the best stores in town.

**Wells Fargo History Museum.** 420 Montgomery St. (at California St.). ☎ **415/396-2619.** Free admission. Mon–Fri 9am–5pm. Closed bank holidays. Muni Metro: Montgomery St. Bus: any to Market St.

Wells Fargo, one of California's largest banks, got its start in the Wild West. Its history museum, at the bank's head office, houses hundreds of genuine relics from the company's whip-and-six-shooter days, including pistols, photographs, early banking articles, posters, and mining equipment.

# 3  Neighborhoods Worth a Visit

To really get to know San Francisco, break out of the downtown and Fisherman's Wharf areas to explore the ethnically and culturally diverse neighborhoods. Walk the streets, browse the shops, grab a bite at a local restaurant; you'll find that San Francisco's beauty and charm is around every corner, not just at the popular tourist destinations.

*Note:* For information on Fisherman's Wharf, see "Famous San Francisco Sights," above. (For information on other San Francisco neighborhoods and districts that aren't discussed here, see the "Neighborhoods & Districts in Brief" section in chapter 4.)

## NOB HILL

When the cable car was invented in 1873, this hill became the exclusive residential area of the city. The "Big Four" and the "Comstock Bonanza kings" built their mansions here, but they were all destroyed by the earthquake and fire in 1906. The only two surviving buildings were the Flood Mansion, which serves today as the Pacific Union Club, and the Fairmont Hotel, which was under construction when the earthquake struck. Today, the burned-out sites of former mansions are occupied by the city's luxury hotels—the Mark Hopkins, the Stanford Court, the Fairmont, and the Huntington—as well as spectacular Grace Cathedral, which stands on the Crocker mansion site. A visit to Nob Hill is worth your time, if only to stroll around Huntington Park, attend a Sunday service at the cathedral, or ooh and aah your way around the Fairmont's spectacular lobby.

## SOUTH OF MARKET (SOMA)

From Market Street to Townsend and the Embarcadero to Division Street, SoMa has become the city's newest cultural and multimedia center. The process started when alternative clubs began opening in the old warehouses in the area nearly a decade ago, followed by a wave of entrepreneurs seeking to start new businesses in what was once an extremely low-rent district compared to the neighboring Financial District. Today, gentrification and high rents are well underway, spurned by a building boom that started with the Moscone Convention Center and continues today with the Center for the Arts at Yerba Buena Gardens and the San Francisco Museum of Modern Art, all of which continue to be supplemented by other institutions, businesses, and museums that are moving into the area daily. A substantial portion of nightlife also takes place in warehouse spaces throughout the district.

## NORTH BEACH

In the late 1800s, an enormous influx of Italian immigrants into North Beach firmly established this aromatic area as San Francisco's "Little Italy." Today, dozens of Italian restaurants and coffeehouses continue to flourish in what is still the center of the city's Italian community. Walk down Columbus Avenue any given morning and you're bound to be bombarded with the wonderful aromas of roasting coffee and savory pasta sauces. Though there are some interesting shops and bookstores in the area, it's the dozens of eclectic little cafes, delis, bakeries, and coffee shops that give North Beach its Italian-bohemian character.

For a proper perspective of North Beach, follow the detailed walking tour in chapter 8, "City Strolls," or sign up for a guided Javawalk with coffee-nut Elaine Sosa (see "Walking Tours" in this chapter).

## ✪ CHINATOWN

The first Chinese came to San Francisco in the early 1800s to work as servants. By 1851, there were 25,000 Chinese working in California, most of whom had settled in San Francisco's Chinatown. Fleeing famine and the Opium Wars, they had come seeking the promise of good fortune in the "Gold Mountain" of California, hoping to return with that prosperity to their families back in China. For the vast majority, the reality of life in California did not live up to the promise. First employed as workers in the gold mines during the gold rush, they were later used to build the railroads, working as little more than slaves and facing constant prejudice. Yet the community, segregated in the Chinatown ghetto, thrived. Growing prejudice led to the Chinese Exclusion Act of 1882, which halted all Chinese immigration for 10 years and limited it severely thereafter; the Chinese Exclusion Act was not repealed until 1943. The Chinese were also denied the opportunity to buy homes outside of the Chinatown ghetto until the 1950s.

Today, San Francisco has the second largest community of Chinese in the United States (about 33% of the city's population is Chinese). More than 80,000 people live in Chinatown, but the majority of Chinese have moved out into newer areas such as the Richmond and Sunset districts. Though frequented by tourists, the area continues to cater to the Chinese community who crowd the vegetable and herbal markets, restaurants, and shops. Tradition still runs deep here, too, and if you're lucky, through an open window you might hear women mixing mahjong tiles as they play the century-old game.

The gateway at Grant and Bush marks the entry to Chinatown. The **Chinese Historical Society of America,** at 650 Commercial St. (☎ **415/391-1188**), has a small but interesting collection relating to the Chinese in San Francisco, which can be viewed for free anytime Monday from 1pm to 4pm and Tuesday to Friday from 10:30am to 4pm. The heart of Chinatown is at Portsmouth Square where you'll find Chinese locals playing board games (often gambling) or just sitting quietly.

On Waverly Place, a street where the Chinese celebratory colors of red, yellow, and green are much in evidence, you'll find three temples, Jeng Sen at no. 146, Tien Hou at no. 125, and Norras at no. 109.

A block north of Grant, Stockton from 1000 to 1200 is the main shopping street of the community lined with grocers, fishmongers, tea sellers, herbalists, noodle parlors, and restaurants. Here, too, is the Kon Chow Temple at no. 855, above the Chinatown post office. Explore at your leisure. A Chinatown walking tour is outlined in chapter 8.

## JAPANTOWN

Today, more than 12,000 citizens of Japanese descent live in San Francisco, or Soko, as it is often called by the Japanese who first emigrated here. Initially, they settled in Chinatown and also South of Market along Stevenson and Jessie streets from Fourth to Seventh. After the earthquake in 1906, SoMa became a light industrial and warehouse area and the largest Japanese concentration took root in the Western Addition between Van Ness Avenue and Fillmore Street, the site of today's Japantown. By 1940, it covered 30 blocks.

In 1913, the Alien Land Law was passed, depriving Japanese-Americans of the right to buy land. From 1924 to 1952, Japanese immigration was banned by the United States. During World War II, the U.S. government froze Japanese bank accounts, interned community leaders, and removed 112,000 Japanese-Americans—two-thirds of them citizens—to camps in California, Utah, and Idaho. Japantown was emptied of Japanese, and their place was taken by war workers. Upon their release in 1945, the Japanese found their old neighborhood occupied. Most of them resettled in the Richmond and Sunset districts; some did return to Japantown but it had shrunk to a mere 6 or so blocks. Among the community's notable sights are the Buddhist Church of San Francisco at 1881 Pine St. at Octavia; the Konko Church of San Francisco at 1909 Bush at Laguna; the Sokoji-Soto Zen Buddhist Temple at 1691 Laguna St. at Sutter; and Nihonmachi Mall, 1700 block of Buchanan Street between Sutter and Post, which contains two steel fountains by Ruth Asawa; and the Japan Center.

Japan Center is an Asian-oriented shopping mall occupying 3 square blocks bounded by Post, Geary, Laguna, and Fillmore streets. At its center stands the five-tiered Peace Pagoda, designed by world-famous Japanese architect Yoshiro Taniguchi "to convey the friendship and goodwill of the Japanese to the people of the United States." Surrounding the pagoda, in a network of arcades, squares, and bridges, are dozens of shops and showrooms featuring everything from TVs and *tansu* chests to pearls, *bonsai* (dwarf trees), and kimonos. When it opened in 1968, the complex seemed as modern as a jumbo jet. Today, the concrete structure seems less impressive, but it still holds some interesting surprises. The **Kabuki Springs & Spa,** at 1750 Geary Blvd. (☎ **415/922-6002**), the center's most famous tenant, was an authentic traditional Japanese bathhouse, but was recently purchased and renovated by Joie de Vivre hotel group, and is now more pan-Asian spa with a focus on wellness. The deep ceramic communal tubs, private baths, and shiatsu massages remain, but joining them are an array of massages and Ayurvedic treatments, body scrubs, wraps, and facials. The Japan Center also houses numerous restaurants, teahouses, shops, and the Asian-inspired 14-story Radisson Miyako Hotel.

There is often live entertainment on summer weekends, including Japanese music and dance performances, tea ceremonies, flower-arranging demonstrations, martial-arts presentations, and other cultural events. The Japan Center is open Monday to Friday from 10am to 10pm, Saturday and Sunday from 9am to 10pm. It can be reached by the no. 2, 3, or 4 bus (exit on Buchanan and Sutter sts.); or nos. 22 or 38 (exit on the northeast corner of Geary Boulevard and Fillmore St.).

## HAIGHT-ASHBURY

Few of San Francisco's neighborhoods are as varied—or as famous—as the Haight-Ashbury. Walk along Haight Street and you'll encounter everything from drug-dazed drifters begging for change to an armada of the city's most counterculture (read: cool) shops, clubs, and cafes. Yet turn anywhere off Haight, and instantly you're among the clean-cut, young urban professionals who are the only ones who can afford the steep rents in this hip 'hood. The result is an interesting mix of well-to-do and well-screw-you lifestyles rubbing shoulders with aging flower children, former Deadheads, homeless people, and the throngs of tourists who try not to stare as they wander through this most human of zoos. Some find it depressing, others find it fascinating, but everyone agrees that it ain't what it was in the free-lovin' psychedelic Summer of Love. Is it still worth a visit? Absolutely, if only to enjoy a cone of Cherry Garcia at the now-famous Ben & Jerry's ice cream shop on the corner of Haight and Ashbury streets, then wander and gawk at the exotic people of the area.

## THE CASTRO

Castro Street, between Market and 18th, is the center of the city's gay community, as well as a lovely strolling neighborhood teeming with shops, restaurants, bars, and other institutions that cater to the area's colorful clientele. Among the landmarks are Harvey Milk Plaza, the Names Project quilt, and the Castro Theatre, a 1930s movie palace with a Wurlitzer. The gay community began to move here in the late 1960s and early 1970s from the earlier gay neighborhood called Polk Gulch, which still has a number of gay-oriented bars and stores. Castro is one of the most lively streets in the city, and the perfect place to shop for gifts and revel in how free spirited this town is.

## THE MISSION DISTRICT

Once inhabited almost entirely by Irish immigrants, the Mission District is now the center of the city's Latino community, an oblong area stretching roughly from 14th to 30th streets between Potrero Avenue in the east and Dolores on the west. In the outer areas, many of the city's finest Victorians still stand, though many seem strangely out of place in the mostly lower-income neighborhoods. The heart of the community lies along 24th Street between Van Ness and Potrero, where dozens of excellent ethnic restaurants, bakeries, bars, and specialty stores attract people from all over the city. The area surrounding 16th Street and Valencia is now a hotbed for impressive—and impressively cheap—restaurants and bars catering to the city's hip crowd. The Mission District at night isn't exactly the safest place to be, and walking around the area should be done with caution, but it's usually quite safe during the day and highly recommended.

For an even better insight into the community, go to the **Precita Eyes Mural Arts Center,** 348 Precita Ave., at Folsom Street (☎ **415/285-2287**), and take one of the 1-hour-and-45-minute tours conducted on Saturday at 11am and 1:30pm, which cost $7 for adults, $4 for seniors, and $1 for under-18s. You'll see 85 murals in an 8-block walk. Every year they also hold a Mural Awareness Week (usually the 2nd week in May) when tours are given daily. All tours leave from their second and newer location is at 2981 24th St. (at Harrison St.), ☎ **415/285-2287.** Other signs of cultural life include a number of progressive theaters—Eureka, Theater Rhinoceros, and Theater Artaud, to name only a few.

At 16th and Dolores is the Mission San Francisco de Assisi (better known as Mission Dolores), which is the city's oldest surviving building (see the separate listing below) and the district's namesake.

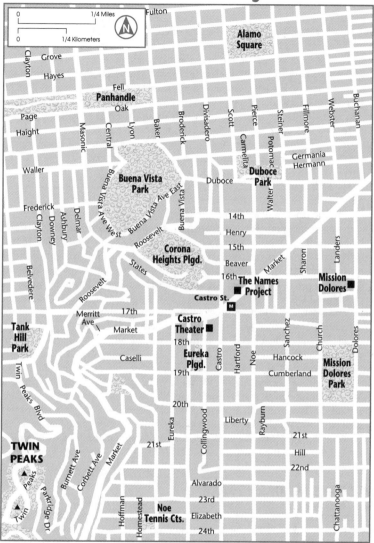

## 4 Golden Gate Park

Everybody loves Golden Gate Park: people, dogs, birds, frogs, turtles, bison, trees, bushes, and flowers. Literally everything feels unified here in San Francisco's enormous arboreal front yard. But this great city landmark wasn't always a favorite place to convene. It was conceived in the 1860s and 1870s, but took its current shape in the 1880s and 1890s thanks to the skill and effort of John McClaren, a Scot who arrived in 1887 and began the landscaping of the park. Totaling 1,017 acres, the park is a narrow strip that stretches from the Pacific coast inland. No one had thought about the challenge the sand dunes and wind would present to any land-scape artist. McClaren developed a new strain of grass called "sea bent," which he had planted to hold the sandy soil along the Firth of Forth, and he used this to anchor the soil here too. He also built the two windmills that stand on the western edge of the park to pump water for irrigation. Every year the ocean eroded the western fringe of the park, and ultimately he solved this problem too. It took him 40 years to build a natural wall, putting out bundles of sticks, which were then cov-ered with sand by the tides. Under his brilliant eye, the park took shape.

Today's Golden Gate Park is a truly magical place. Spend one sunny day stretched out on the grass along JFK Drive, have a good read in Shakespeare Garden, or stroll around Stow Lake, and you too will understand the allure. It's an interactive botanical symphony, and everyone is invited to play in the orchestra.

The park is made up of hundreds of gardens and attractions attached by wooded paths and paved roads. While many stop-worthy sites are clearly visible, there are infinite hidden treasures, so pick up information if you want to find the more obscure, quaint spots. For information on the park, head first to the **McClaren Lodge and Park Headquarters,** which is open Monday to Friday (☎ **415/831-2700**). Of the dozens of special gardens in the park, most recognized are the Rhododendron Dell, the Rose Garden, the Strybing Arboretum, and at the western edge of the park a springtime array of thousands of tulips and daffodils around the Dutch windmill.

In addition to the highlights below, the park contains several recreational facili-ties: tennis courts, baseball, soccer and polo fields, golf course, riding stables, fly-casting pools, and boat rentals at the Strawberry Hill boathouse. It is also the home of three major museums: the M. H. De Young Memorial Museum, the Asian Art Museum, and the California Academy of Sciences (see their separate listings below). *Note:* There's talk of moving the De Young to an undetermined location, and the Asian Art Museum is moving to the old Main Library site in the Civic Center around 2001. If you plan to visit all the park's attractions, consider buying the **Explorer Pass,** which enables you to visit the three museums and the Japanese Tea Garden for $14. Passes are available at each site and at the Visitor Information Center. For further information, call ☎ **415/391-2000.** Enter the park at Kezar Drive, an extension of Fell Street. Bus: 16AX, BX, 5, 6, 7, 66, or 71.

## MUSEUMS INSIDE THE PARK

**Asian Art Museum.** In Golden Gate Park, near 10th Ave. and Fulton St. ☎ **415/379-8800;** 415/752-2635 for the hearing impaired. Admission (including the M. H. De Young Memorial Museum and California Palace of the Legion of Honor) $7 adults, $5 seniors 65 and over, $4 youths 12–17, free for children 11 and under (fees may be higher for special exhibitions); free admission for everyone the 1st Wed (all day) of each month. Tues–Sun 9:30am–4:45pm; 1st Wed each month 10am–8:45pm. Bus: 5, 44, or 71.

Adjacent to the M. H. De Young Museum and the Japanese Tea Garden, this exhi-bition space, opened in 1966, can only display about 1,800 pieces from the museum's vast collection of 12,000. About half of the works on exhibit are in the ground-floor Chinese and Korean galleries and include world-class sculptures, paintings, bronzes, ceramics, jades, and decorative objects spanning 6,000 years of history. There is also a wide range of exhibits from more than 40 Asian countries—Pakistan, India, Tibet, Japan, Southeast Asia—including the world's oldest-known "dated" Chinese Buddha. The museum's free daily guided tours are highly infor-mative and sincerely recommended. Call for times.

# Golden Gate Park

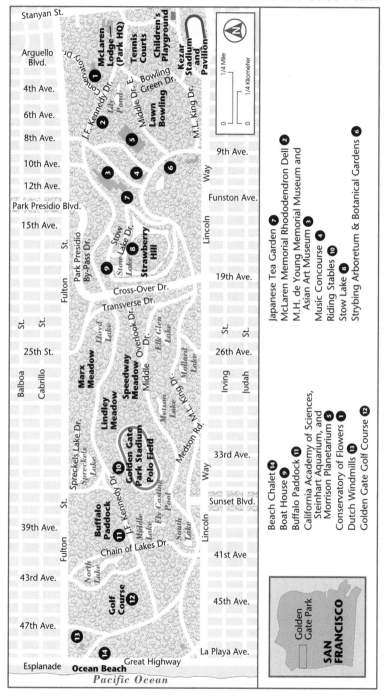

Japanese Tea Garden **7**

McLaren Memorial Rhododendron Dell **2**

M.H. de Young Memorial Museum and Asian Art Museum **3**

Music Concourse **4**

Riding Stables **10**

Stow Lake **8**

Strybing Arboretum & Botanical Gardens **6**

Beach Chalet **14**

Boat House **9**

Buffalo Paddock **11**

California Academy of Sciences, Steinhart Aquarium, and Morrison Planetarium **5**

Conservatory of Flowers **1**

Dutch Windmills **13**

Golden Gate Golf Course **12**

Golden Gate Park

SAN FRANCISCO

**California Academy of Sciences.** On the Music Concourse of Golden Gate Park. ☎ **415/ 750-7145** for recorded information. Admission (aquarium and Natural History Museum) $8.50 adults, $5.50 students 12–17 and seniors 65 and over, $2 children 4–11, free for children under 4; free for everyone the 1st Wed of every month. Planetarium shows $2.50 adults, $1.25 children under 18 and seniors 65 and over. Labor Day–Memorial Day daily 10am–5pm; Memorial Day–Labor Day daily 9am–6pm; 1st Wed of every month 10am–9pm. Muni Metro: N to Golden Gate Park. Bus: 5, 71, or 44.

Clustered around the Music Concourse in Golden Gate Park are three outstanding world-class museums and exhibitions that are guaranteed to entertain every member of the family. The **Steinhart Aquarium,** for example, is the most diverse aquarium in the world, housing some 14,000 specimens, including amphibians, reptiles, marine mammals, penguins, and much more, in 189 displays. A huge hit with the youngsters is the California tide pool and a "hands-on" area where children can touch starfish and sea urchins. The living coral reef is the largest display of its kind in the country and the only one in the West. In the Fish Roundabout, visitors are surrounded by fast-swimming schools of fish kept in a 100,000-gallon tank. Seals and dolphins are fed every 2 hours, beginning at 10:30am; the penguins are fed at 11:30am and 4pm.

The **Morrison Planetarium** presents sky shows as well as laser-light shows. Its sky shows offer guided tours through the universe projected onto a 65-foot domed ceiling. Approximately four major exhibits, with titles such as "Star Death: The Birth of Black Holes" and "The Universe Unveiled," are presented each year. Related cosmos exhibits are located in the adjacent Earth and Space Hall. Sky shows are featured at 2pm on weekdays and hourly every weekend and holiday (☎ **415/ 750-7141** for more information). **Laserium laser-light shows** are also presented in the planetarium Thursday through Sunday nights (☎ **415/750-7138** for more information).

The **Natural History Museum** includes several halls displaying classic dioramas of fauna in their habitats. The Wattis Hall of Human Cultures traces the evolution of different human cultures and how they adapted to their natural environment; the "Wild California" exhibition in Meyer Hall includes a 14,000-gallon aquarium and seabird rookery, life-size battling elephant seals, and two larger-than-life views of microscopic life forms; in McBean-Peterson Hall, visitors can walk through an exhibit tracing the course of 3½ billion years of evolution from the earliest life forms to the present day; in the Hohfeld Earth and Space Hall visitors can experience a simulation of two of San Francisco's biggest earthquakes, determine what their weight would be on other planets, see a real moon rock, and learn about the rotation of the planet at a replica of Foucault's Pendulum (the real one is in Paris).

**M. H. De Young Memorial Museum.** In Golden Gate Park (near 10th Ave. and Fulton St.). ☎ **415/750-3600** or 415/863-3330 (for recorded information). Admission (including the Asian Art Museum and California Palace of the Legion of Honor) $7 adults, $5 seniors over 65, $4 youths 12–17, free for children 11 and under (fees may be higher for special exhibitions); free the 1st Wed of each month. Wed–Sun 9:30am–5pm (1st Wed of the month until 8:45pm). Bus: 44.

One of the city's oldest museums, it's best known for its American art dating from colonial times to the 20th century, and includes paintings, sculptures, furniture, and decorative arts by Paul Revere, Winslow Homer, John Singer Sargent, and Georgia O'Keeffe. Special note should be taken of the American landscapes, as well as the fun trompe l'oeil and still-life works from the turn of the century.

Named after the late 19th-century publisher of the *San Francisco Chronicle,* the museum also possesses an important textile collection, with primary emphasis on rugs from central Asia and the Near East. Other collections on view include decorative art from Africa, Oceania, and the Americas. Major traveling exhibitions are equally eclectic, including everything from ancient rugs to great Dutch paintings. Call the museum to find out what's on. Tours are offered daily; call for times.

The museum's Café De Young is exceptional, serving daily specials that might include Peruvian stew, Chinese chicken salad, and Italian vegetables in tomato-basil sauce. In summer, visitors can dine in the garden, among bronze statuary. The cafe is open Wednesday through Sunday from 10am to 4pm.

## OTHER HIGHLIGHTS

**CONSERVATORY OF FLOWERS** (1878)   Built for the 1894 Midwinter Exposition, this striking assemblage of glass architecture usually exhibits a rotating display of plants and shrubs at all times of the year. Unfortunately, recent years' rough weather has damaged the already-delicate structure and renovations aren't scheduled to be complete until 2004. Still, the exterior, which is modeled on the famous glass house at Kew Gardens in London, is indeed grand.

**JAPANESE TEA GARDEN** (1894)   McClaren hired the Hagiwara family to care for this garden developed for the 1894 Midwinter Exposition. It's a quiet place with cherry trees, shrubs, and bonsai crisscrossed by winding paths and high-arched bridges crossing over pools of water. Focal points and places for contemplation include the massive bronze Buddha that was cast in Japan in 1790 and donated by the Gump family, the Shinto wooden pagoda, and the Wishing Bridge, which reflected in the water looks as if it completes a circle. The garden is open daily October through February from 8:30am to 6pm (with the teahouse only open until 5:30pm), and March through September from 9am to 6:30pm. For **information** on admissions, call ☎ **415/752-4227.** For the **teahouse,** call ☎ **415/752-1171.**

**STRYBING ARBORETUM & BOTANICAL GARDENS**   Six thousand plant species grow here; among them some very ancient plants in a special "primitive garden," rare species, and a grove of California redwoods. Docent-led tours are given at 1pm daily during operating hours, which are Monday to Friday from 8am to 4:30pm and Saturday and Sunday from 10am to 5pm. For more information, call ☎ **415/753-7089.**

✪ **STRAWBERRY HILL/STOW LAKE**   Rent a paddleboat, rowboat, or motor-boat here and cruise around the circular lake as painters create still lifes and joggers pass along the grassy shoreline. Ducks waddle around waiting to be fed, and turtles bathe on rocks and logs. Strawberry Hill, the 430-foot-high artificial island that lies at the center of Stow Lake, is a perfect picnic spot and boasts a bird's-eye view of San Francisco and the bay. It also has a waterfall and peace pagoda. To reach the **boathouse,** call ☎ **415/752-0347.** Boat rentals are available daily from 9am to 4pm.

## 5 The Presidio & Golden Gate National Recreation Area

### THE PRESIDIO

In October 1994, the Presidio was transferred from the U.S. Army to the National Park Service and became one of a handful of urban national parks that combines historical, architectural, and natural elements into one giant arboreal expanse. The 1,480-acre area incorporates a variety of terrain—coastal scrub, dunes, and prairie grasslands that shelter many rare plants and more than 150 species of birds, some of which nest here.

This military outpost has a 220-year history, stretching from its founding in September 1776 by the Spanish under José Joaquin Moraga to its closure in 1995. From 1822 to 1835, the property was in Mexican hands.

# Golden Gate National Recreation Area & The Presidio

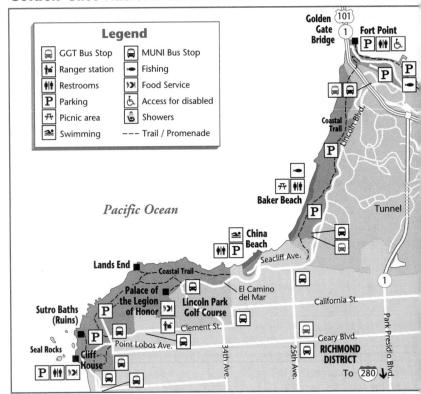

During the war with Mexico, American forces occupied the fort, and in 1848, when California became part of the Union, it was formally transferred to the United States. When San Francisco suddenly became an important urban area during the gold rush, the U.S. government installed battalions of soldiers, built Fort Point to protect the entry to the harbor, and expanded the post during the Civil War and later during the Indian Wars of the 1870s and 1880s. By the 1890s, it was no longer a frontier post, but a major base for American expansion into the Pacific. During the war with Spain in 1898, thousands of troops camped in tent cities awaiting shipment to the Philippines, and the sick and wounded were treated at the Army General Hospital. By 1905, 12 coastal defense batteries were built along the headlands. In 1914, troops under the command of Gen. John Pershing left here to pursue Pancho Villa and his men. The Presidio expanded during the 1920s when Crissy Army Airfield (the first airfield on the West Coast) was established, but the major action was seen during World War II after the attack on Pearl Harbor. Soldiers dug foxholes along nearby beaches, and the Presidio became the headquarters for the Western Defense Command. Some 1.6 million men shipped out from nearby Fort Mason to fight in the Pacific and many returned to the hospital, whose capacity peaked one year at 72,000 patients. In the 1950s, the Presidio served as the headquarters for the Sixth U.S. Army and a missile defense post, but its role was slowly reduced. In 1972, it was included in new legislation establishing the Golden Gate National Recreation Area; in 1989, the Pentagon decided to close the post and transfer it to the National Park Service.

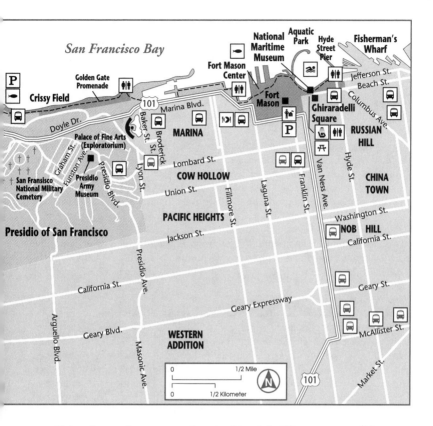

Today, the area features more than 510 historic buildings, a scenic golf course, a national cemetery, and a variety of terrain and natural habitats. The National Park Service offers a variety of walking and biking tours around the Presidio; reservations are suggested. The **Presidio Museum,** located at the corner of Lincoln Boulevard and Funston Avenue (open noon to 5pm Wed to Sun), tells its story in dioramas, exhibitions, and photographs. For more information, call the **Visitor Information Center** at ☎ **415/561-4323.** Take the 82X, 28, or 76 bus.

**San Francisco Zoo & Children's Zoo.** Sloat Blvd. and 45th Ave. ☎ **415/753-7080.** www.sfzoo.org. Main zoo $9 adults, $6.50 seniors and youths 12–17, $3 for children 3–11, and free for children 2 and under if accompanied by an adult; free to everyone the 1st Wed of each month. Carousel $2. Main zoo daily 10am–5pm. Children's zoo Mon–Fri 11am–4pm; Sat–Sun 10:30am–4:30pm. Muni Metro: L from downtown Market St. to the end of the line.

Located between the Pacific Ocean and Lake Merced, in the southwest corner of the city, the San Francisco Zoo is among America's highest-rated animal parks. Begun in 1889 with a grizzly bear named Monarch donated by the *San Francisco Examiner,* the zoo now sprawls over 65 acres and is growing. It attracts up to a million visitors each year. Most of the 1,000-plus inhabitants are contained in landscaped enclosures guarded by concealed moats. The innovative Primate Discovery Center is particularly noteworthy for its many rare and endangered species. Expansive outdoor atriums, sprawling meadows, and a midnight world for exotic nocturnal primates house such species as the owl-faced macaque, ruffed-tailed lemur, black-and-white colobus monkeys, patas monkeys, and emperor tamarins—pint-size primates distinguished by their long, majestic mustaches.

Other highlights include Koala Crossing, which is linked to the Australian Walk-About exhibit that opened in 1995, housing kangaroos, emus, and wallaroos; Gorilla World, one of the world's largest exhibits of these gentle giants; and Penguin Island, home to a large breeding colony of Magellanic penguins. The new Feline Conservation Center is a wooded sanctuary and breeding facility for the zoo's endangered snow leopards, Persian leopards, and other jungle cats. Musk Ox Meadow is a 2½-acre habitat for a herd of rare white-fronted musk oxen brought from Alaska. The Otter River exhibit features waterfalls, logs, and boulders for the North American otters to climb on. And the Lion House is home to rare Sumatran and Siberian tigers, Prince Charles (a rare white Bengal tiger), and the African lions (you can watch them being fed at 2pm Tues to Sun).

The Children's Zoo, adjacent to the main park, allows both kids and adults to get close to animals. The barnyard is alive with strokable domestic animals such as sheep, goats, ponies, and a llama. Also of interest is the Insect Zoo, which showcases a multitude of insect species, including the hissing cockroach and walking sticks.

A free, informal walking tour of the zoo is available on weekends at 11am. The Zebra Zephyr train tour takes visitors on a 30-minute "safari" daily (only on weekends in winter). The tour is $2.50 for adults, $1.50 for children 15 and under and seniors.

## GOLDEN GATE NATIONAL RECREATIONAL AREA

The largest urban park in the world, the GGNRA makes New York's Central Park look like a putting green, covering three counties along 28 miles of stunning, condo-free shoreline. Run by the National Parks Service, the Recreation Area wraps around the northern and western edges of the city, and just about all of it is open to the public with no access fees. The Muni bus system provides transportation to the more popular sites, including Aquatic Park, the Cliff House, Fort Mason, and Ocean Beach. For more information, contact the **National Park Service** (☎ **415/556-0560**). For more detailed information on particular sites, see the "Staying Active" section at the end of this chapter.

Here is a brief rundown of the salient features of the park's peninsula section, starting at the northern section and moving westward around the coastline:

**Aquatic Park,** adjacent to the Hyde Street Pier, has a small swimming beach, although it's not that appealing (and darn cold). Far more entertaining is a visit to the ship-shaped museum across the lawn that's part of the San Francisco Maritime National Historical Park (see above for more information).

**Fort Mason Center** occupies an area from Bay Street to the shoreline and consists of several buildings and piers that were used during World War II. Today, they are occupied by a variety of museums, theaters, and organizations, as well as by Greens vegetarian restaurant, which affords views of the Golden Gate Bridge (see chapter 6 for more information). For information about Fort Mason events, call ☎ **415/441-5706.** The park headquarters is also at Fort Mason.

Farther west along the bay at the northern end of Laguna Street is **Marina Green,** a favorite local spot for kite flying, jogging, and walking along the Promenade. The St. Francis Yacht Club is also located here.

From here begins the 3½-mile paved **Golden Gate Promenade,** San Francisco's best and most scenic biking, jogging, and walking path, which runs along the shore past Crissy Field (be sure to stop and watch the gonzo windsurfers) and ends at Fort Point under the Golden Gate Bridge.

**Fort Point** (☎ **415/556-1693**) was built in 1853 to protect the narrow entrance to the harbor. It was designed to house 500 soldiers manning 126 muzzle-loading cannons. By 1900, the fort's soldiers and obsolete guns had been removed, but the formidable brick edifice still remains. Fort Point is open Wednesday to Sunday from 10am to 5pm, and guided tours and cannon demonstrations are given at the site once or twice daily, depending on the time of year.

Lincoln Boulevard sweeps around the western edge of the bay to Baker Beach, where the waves roll ashore—a fine spot for sunbathing, walking, or fishing. Hikers can follow the Coastal Trail from Fort Point along this part of the coastline all the way to Lands End.

A short distance from Baker, China Beach is a small cove where swimming is permitted. Changing rooms, showers, a sundeck, and rest rooms are available.

A little farther around the coast appears Lands End looking out to Pyramid Rock. A lower and an upper trail provide a hiking opportunity amid windswept cypresses and pines on the cliffs above the Pacific.

Still farther along the coast lies Point Lobos, the Sutro Baths, and the Cliff House. The latter has been serving refreshments to visitors since 1863, and providing views of Seal Rocks, home to a colony of sea lions and many marine birds. There's an **information center** here (open daily from 10am to 5pm; ☎ **415/ 556-8642**) as well as the incredible Musée Mecanique, an authentic old-fashioned arcade with 150 coin-operated amusement machines. Only traces of the Sutro Baths remain today to the northeast of the Cliff House. This swimming facility was a major summer attraction that could accommodate up to 24,000 people before it burned down in 1966.

A little farther inland at the western end of California Street is Lincoln Park, which contains a golf course and the spectacular Palace of the Legion of Honor museum.

At the southern end of Ocean Beach, 4 miles down the coast, is another area of the park around Fort Funston, where there's an easy loop trail across the cliffs (**ranger office:** ☎ **415/239-2366**). Here, too, you can watch the hang gliders taking advantage of the high cliffs and strong winds.

Farther south along route 280, Sweeney Ridge, which can only be reached by car, affords sweeping views of the coastline from the many trails that crisscross this 1,000 acres of land. It was from here that the expedition led by Don Gaspar de Portolá first saw San Francisco Bay in 1769. It's located in Pacifica and can be reached via Sneath Lane off Route 35 (Skyline Blvd.) in San Bruno.

The GGNRA also extends into Marin County, where it encompasses the Marin Headlands, Muir Woods National Monument, and the Olema Valley behind the Point Reyes National Seashore. See chapter 11 for information on these areas.

## 6  Churches & Religious Buildings

Some of San Francisco's churches and religious buildings are worth checking out.

✪ **Glide Memorial United Methodist Church.** 330 Ellis St. (west of Union Sq.). ☎ **415/ 771-6300.** Services held Sun at 9 and 11am. Muni Metro: Powell. Bus: 37.

Reverend Williams's enthusiastic and uplifting preaching and singing with homeless and poor people of the neighborhood has attracted nationwide fame to Glide Memorial. In 1994, during the pastor's 30th-anniversary celebration, singers Angela Bofill and Bobby McFerrin joined with comedian Robin Williams, author Maya Angelou, and talk-show queen Oprah Winfrey to honor him publicly. Williams's nondogmatic, fun Sunday services attract a diverse audience that crosses all socioeconomic boundaries. Go for an uplifting experience. *Note:* Reverend Williams is considering retiring and may not be present by the time you get there, but his high-spirited, hand-clapping, roof-raising spiritual love-in is guaranteed to continue.

⭐ **Grace Cathedral.** California St. (between Taylor and Jones sts.). ☎ **415/749-6300.**

Although this Nob Hill cathedral, designed by architect Lewis P. Hobart, looks like it is made of stone, it is in fact constructed of reinforced concrete, beaten to achieve a stonelike effect. Construction began for this cathedral on the site of the Crocker mansion in 1928, but it was not completed until 1964. Among the more interesting features of the building are its stained-glass windows, particularly those by the French Loire studios, depicting such modern figures as Thurgood Marshall, Robert Frost, and Albert Einstein; the replicas of Ghiberti's bronze *Doors of Paradise* at the east end; the series of religious frescoes completed in the 1940s by Polish artist John de Rosen; and the 44-bell carillon.

**Mission Dolores.** 16th St. (at Dolores St.). ☎ **415/621-8203.** Donations appreciated. May–Oct daily 9am–4:30pm; Nov–Apr daily 9am–4pm; Good Friday 10am–noon. Closed Thanksgiving Day and Christmas Day. Muni Metro: J line to the corner of Church and 16th sts. Bus: 22.

San Francisco's oldest standing structure, the Mission San Francisco de Assisi (a.k.a. Mission Dolores) has withstood the test of time, as well as two major earthquakes, relatively intact. In 1776, at the behest of Franciscan Missionary Junípero Serra, Father Francisco Palou came to the Bay Area to found the sixth in a series of missions that dotted the California coastline. From these humble beginnings grew what was to become the city of San Francisco. The mission's small, simple chapel, built solidly by Native Americans who were converted to Christianity, is a curious mixture of native construction methods and Spanish-colonial style. A statue of Father Serra stands in the mission garden, although the portrait looks somewhat more contemplative, and less energetic, than he must have been in real life. An audio tour is available, too, which lasts 45 minutes and costs $5 for adults, $4 for children, and is available during open hours.

## 7  Architectural Highlights

### MUST-SEES FOR ARCHITECTURE BUFFS

**ALAMO SQUARE HISTORIC DISTRICT**   San Francisco's collection of Victorian houses, known as "Painted Ladies," is one of the city's most famous assets. Most of the 14,000 extant structures date from the second half of the 19th century and are private residences. Spread throughout the city, many have been beautifully restored and ornately painted. The small area bordered by Divisadero Street on the west, Golden Gate Avenue on the north, Webster Street on the east, and Fell Street on the south—about 10 blocks west of the Civic Center—has one of the city's greatest concentrations of these Painted Ladies. One of the most famous views of San Francisco—seen on postcards and posters all around the city—depicts sharp-edged Financial District skyscrapers behind a row of Victorians. This fantastic juxtaposition can be seen from Alamo Square, in the center of this historic district, at Fulton and Steiner streets.

**CITY HALL & CIVIC CENTER**   Built in 1915 in the classic French Renaissance style, San Francisco's magnificent City Hall has recently undergone a multi-million-dollar earthquake-proof renovation that has restored it to its original splendor, making it well worth a tour. The exterior, which is composed of stately granite columns and brick and ceramic veneer, is topped by a gilded copper dome that is 90 feet in diameter and rises to a height of 302 feet (even higher than the nation's capitol, thank you very much). The interior rotunda soars 112 feet and is finished in oak, marble, and limestone, and features a monumental marble staircase

# The Civic Center

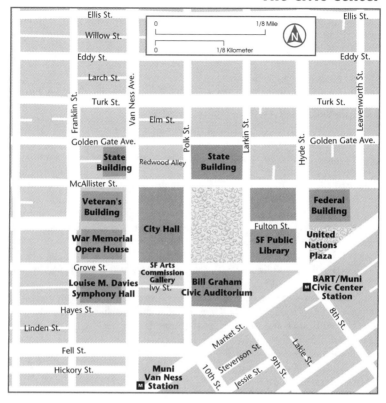

leading to the second floor. It's truly an impressive piece of architecture. It's located directly in the middle of the city between Polk Street and Van Ness Avenue, and Grove and McAllister streets.

✪ **YERBA BUENA GARDENS AND CENTER**   Between Mission and Howard streets at Third Street, the Yerba Buena Center (☎ **415/978-2787**), which opened in 1993 adjacent to the Moscone Convention Center, is the city's new cultural facility, similar to New York's Lincoln Center. It stands on top of the northern extension of the underground Moscone Convention Center. The Center for the Arts presents music, theater, dance, and visual arts. It consists of two buildings, a 755-seat theater designed by James Stewart Polshek, and the Galleries and Arts Forum designed by Fumihiko Maki, which features three galleries and a space designed specially for dance. The complex also includes a 5-acre garden featuring several artworks. The most dramatic outdoor art piece is an emotional mixed-media memorial to Martin Luther King Jr. Created by sculptor Houston Conwill, poet Estella Majozo, and architect Joseph de Pace, it features 12 panels, each inscribed with quotations from King, sheltered behind a 50-foot-high waterfall. The new children's addition, called Zeum, (☎ **415/777-2800**) includes a cafe, an interactive cultural center, an ice skating rink, a fabulous 1906 historic carousel, and an interactive play and learning garden. Sony's new Metreon Entertainment Center (☎ **415/537-3400**), is a 350,000-square-foot complex housing movie theaters, an IMAX Theatre, small restaurants, interactive attractions (including one that features Maurice Sendak's *Where the Wild Things Are*), and shops. Also in the Yerba

Buena Center is a bowling alley, a child-care center, an ice-skating rink, and an IMAX Theatre. As part of the plan to develop this area as the city's cultural hub, the California Historical Society opened at 678 Mission in late 1995 and the Mexican Museum will relocate to the area in 2000. For recorded information and tickets, call ☎ **415/978-ARTS.**

Take the Muni Metro to Powell or Montgomery, or the 30, 45, or 9X bus.

## OTHER ARCHITECTURAL HIGHLIGHTS

San Francisco is a center of many architecturally striking sights. This section concentrates on a few highlights.

Around Union Square and the Financial District is the now-closed **Circle Gallery** at 140 Maiden Lane. (Hopefully another business will have opened in the space by the time you get there so you can tour the interior.) It's the only building in the city designed by Frank Lloyd Wright (in 1948) and was the prototype for the seashell-shaped circular gallery space of the Guggenheim, even though it was meant to serve as a retail space for V. C. Morris, a purveyor of glass and crystal. Note the arresting exterior, a solid wall with a circular entryway to the left. Maiden Lane is just off Union Square between Geary and Post.

The **Hallidie Building,** at 130–150 Sutter St., which was designed by Willis Polk in 1917, is an ideal example of a glass-curtain building. The vast glass facade is miraculously suspended between the two cast-iron cornices. The fire escapes that course down each side of the building complete the stage-like theatrical effect.

The **Medical Dental Building,** at 450 Sutter St., is a steel-frame structure beautifully clad in terra-cotta. It was designed by Miller and Pflueger in 1929. The entrance and the window frames are elaborately ornamented with Mayan relief work; the lobby ceiling is similarly decorated with additional gilding. Note the ornate elevators, too.

Two prominent pieces of San Francisco's skyline are in the Financial District. The **TransAmerica Pyramid,** at 600 Montgomery St. between Clay and Washington streets, is one of the tallest structures in San Francisco. This corporate headquarters was completed in 1972, stands 48 stories tall, and is capped by a 212-foot spire. The former **Bank of America World Headquarters,** at 555 California St., was designed by Wurster, Bernardi, and Emmons in conjunction with Skidmore, Owings, and Merrill. This carnelian-marble–covered building dates from 1969. Its 52 stories are topped by a panoramic restaurant and bar, the Carnelian Room (see chapter 10, "San Francisco After Dark," for complete information). The focal point of the building's formal plaza is an abstract black granite sculpture, known locally as the "Banker's Heart," which was designed by Japanese architect Masayuki Nagare.

At the foot of Market Street you will find the **Ferry Building.** Built between 1895 and 1903, it served as the city's major transportation hub before the Golden Gate and Bay bridges were built, and some 170 ferries docked here daily, unloading Bay Area commuters until the 1930s. The tower that soars above the building was inspired by the Campanile of Venice and the Cathedral Tower in Seville. Plans are afoot to restore the building to its former glory, opening up the soaring galleries to the sky again. If you stop by the Ferry Building, you might also want to go to **Rincon Center,** at 99 Mission St. to see the WPA murals painted by the Russian artist Refregier in the post office that is located here.

Several important buildings can be found on or near Nob Hill. The **Flood Mansion,** at 1000 California St. at Mason Street, was built between 1885 and 1886 for James Clair Flood, who, thanks to the Comstock Lode, rose from being a bartender to being one of the city's wealthiest men. He established the Nevada bank that later

# Yerba Buena Gardens

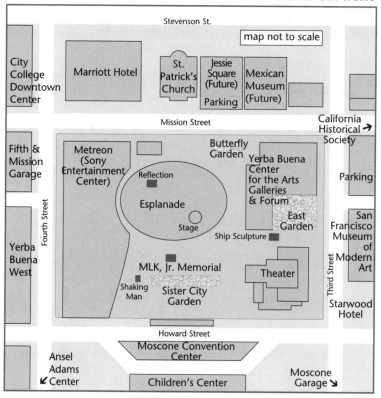

merged with Wells Fargo. The house cost $1.5 million; the fence alone cost $30,000. It was designed by Augustus Laver and modified by Willis Polk after the earthquake to accommodate the Pacific Union Club.

Built by George Applegarth in 1913 for the sugar magnate Adolph Spreckels, the **Spreckels Mansion,** at 2080 Washington St., is currently home to romance novelist Danielle Steele (don't even try to get in to see her!). The extraordinary building has rounded-arch French doors on the first and second floors and curved balconies on the second floor. Inside, the original featured an indoor pool in the basement, Adamesque fireplaces, and a circular Pompeian room with fountain.

Finally, one of San Francisco's most ingenious architectural accomplishments is the **San Francisco–Oakland Bay Bridge.** Although it's visually less appealing than the nearby Golden Gate Bridge, the Bay Bridge is in many ways more spectacular. The silvery giant that links San Francisco with Oakland is 8¼ miles long and is one of the world's longest steel bridges. It opened in 1936, 6 months before the Golden Gate. Each of its two decks contains five automobile lanes. The Bay Bridge is not a single bridge at all, but a superbly dovetailed series of spans joined in midbay, at Yerba Buena Island, by one of the world's largest (in diameter) tunnels. To the west of Yerba Buena, the bridge is really two separate suspension bridges, joined at a central anchorage. East of the island is a 1,400-foot cantilever span, followed by a succession of truss bridges. And it looks even more complex than it sounds. You can drive across the bridge (the toll is $2, paid westbound), or you can catch a bus at the Transbay Terminal (Mission at First Street) and ride to downtown Oakland.

## 8 Especially for Kids

The following San Francisco attractions have major appeal to kids of all ages:
- Alcatraz Island *(see p. 151)*
- Cable cars *(see p. 153)*
- Cable Car Barn Museum *(see p. 161)*
- California Academy of Sciences, including Steinhart Aquarium *(see p. 172)*
- The Exploratorium *(see p. 162)*
- Golden Gate Bridge *(see p. 158)*
- Golden Gate Park (including the Children's Playground, Bison Paddock, and Japanese Tea Garden) *(see above and p. 169)*
- National Maritime Museum and the historic ships anchored at Hyde Pier *(see p. 164)*
- The San Francisco Zoo *(see p. 175)*

In addition to the sights listed above, the following attractions are of particular interest to kids:

**Metreon.** 701 Mission St. (at Fourth St., adjacent to Yerba Buena Gardens). ☎ **415/369-6000.** Movie Times and Imax Schedule ☎ 415/369-6200. Admission to Metreon mall is free. Daily 10am–10pm. Muni Metro: J, K, L, M or N to Montgomery Station. Bus: 15, 30, or 45.

Metreon is Sony's hip new high-tech megamall, a four-story, 350,000-square-foot, $85-million temple to every audio and video gadget Sony makes (which is a heckuva lot of gadgets). If your kid's into video games, music videos, movies, computers, and other assorted electronic paraphernalia, he'll go bug-eyed the second he (or she) steps into this highly energized cybernetic theme park. Among the venues designed to get a hold of a child's attention and a parent's credit card are: The Way Things Work, a multimedia attraction that uses gears and levers to teach children about physics and technology; Hear Music, which allows patrons to listen to thousands of CDs at listening stations throughout the store; a futuristic arcade called Airtight Garage (which uses debit cards instead of quarters); high-tech interactive attractions such as Maurice Sendak's *Where the Wild Things Are;* 15 cinemas showing all the latest movie releases; and a Sony IMAX Theatre sporting a 100-foot screen. There are also restaurants, bars, numerous shops, an elevated outdoor deck overlooking Yerba Buena (parents gotta smoke somewhere), and several nervous Sony executives who are banking on Metreon to be a big success.

### CHILDREN'S PLAYGROUNDS

One of the most enormous and fun playgrounds for kids is in Golden Gate Park. In addition, there are several others. The **Cow Hollow Playground,** on Baker Street between Greenwich and Filbert streets, is surrounded by apartment buildings on three of four sides. This landscaped playground features a bi-level play area fitted with well-conceived, colorful play structures including a tunnel, slides, swings, and a miniature cable car. **Huntington Park,** on Taylor Street, between Sacramento and California streets, sits atop Nob Hill. This tiny play area contains several small play structures that are particularly well suited to children under 5. **Julius Kahn Playground,** on West Pacific Avenue at Spruce Street, is a popular playground situated inside San Francisco's great Park Presidio. Larger play structures and forested surroundings make this ground attractive to children and adults alike.

# 9  Self-Guided & Organized Tours

## THE 49-MILE SCENIC DRIVE

The self-guided, 49-mile "Scenic Drive" is an easy way to orient yourself, and to grasp the beauty of San Francisco and its extraordinary location. Beginning in the city, it follows a rough circle around the bay and passes virtually all the best-known sights from Chinatown to the Golden Gate Bridge, Ocean Beach, Seal Rocks, Golden Gate Park, and Twin Peaks. Originally designed for the benefit of visitors to San Francisco's 1939 and 1940 Golden Gate International Expositions, the route is marked with blue-and-white seagull signs. Although it makes an excellent half-day tour, this mini-excursion can easily take longer if you decide, for example, to stop to walk across the Golden Gate Bridge or to have tea in Golden Gate Park's Japanese Tea Garden.

The **San Francisco Visitor Information Center,** at Powell and Market streets (see "Visitor Information" in chapter 4), distributes free route maps. Since a few of the Scenic Drive marker signs are missing, the map will come in handy. Try to avoid the downtown area during the weekday rush hours from 7 to 9am and 4 to 6pm.

## A BART TOUR

One of the world's best commuter systems, **Bay Area Rapid Transit (BART)** runs along 71 miles of rail, linking eight San Francisco stations with Daly City to the south and 25 stations in the East Bay. Under the bay, BART runs through one of the longest underwater transit tubes in the world. This link opened in September 1974, 2 years behind schedule, and 6 months after the general manager resigned under fire. The train cars are 70 feet long and are designed to represent the last word in public transport luxury. Twenty years later they no longer seem futuristic, but they're still attractively modern, with carpeted floors, tinted picture windows, automatic air-conditioning, and recessed lighting. The trains can hit a top speed of 80 miles per hour; a computerized control system monitors and adjusts their speed.

The people who run BART think so highly of their trains and stations that they sell a $3.80 **"Excursion Ticket,"** which allows you, in effect, to "sightsee" the BART system. Tour the entire system as much as you like for up to 3 hours as long as you exit from the same station you entered (if you get out anywhere along the line, the fare gate will instantly compute the normal fare). For more information, call ☎ **650/992-BART** (2278).

## BOAT TOURS

One of the best ways to look at San Francisco is from a boat bobbing on the bay. There are several cruises to choose from, many of which start from Fisherman's Wharf. There is now only one major company.

**Blue & Gold Fleet,** at Pier 39, Fisherman's Wharf (☎ **415/773-1188**), tours the bay year-round in a sleek, 400-passenger sightseeing boat, complete with food and beverage facilities. The fully narrated, 1¼-hour cruise passes beneath the Golden Gate and Bay bridges, and comes within yards of Alcatraz Island. Frequent daily departures from Pier 39's West Marina begin at 10am during summer and 11am in winter. Tickets cost $17 for adults, $13 for juniors 5 to 17 and seniors over 62, $9 for children 5 to 11, and children under 5 sail free (an additional $2.25 is charged for ordering tickets via phone).

The **Red & White Fleet,** at Pier 43-1/2 (☎ **415/447-0597;** www.redandwhite.com) offers daily Bay Cruises tours that leave from pier 43½ and cruise under the Golden Gate Bridge, past the Marin Headlands, Sausalito, Tiburon, Angel Island, and Alcatraz. Prices are $17 for adults, $13 seniors, $13 for teens 12 to 18, and $9 for children 6 to 11.

## BUS TOURS

**Gray Line,** with offices in the Transbay Terminal, First and Mission streets, Pier 39, and Union Square (☎ 800/826-0202 or 415/558-9400), is San Francisco's largest bus-tour operator. They offer several itineraries on a daily basis. There is a free pickup and return service between centrally located hotels and departure locations. Reservations are required for most tours, which are available in several foreign languages including French, German, Spanish, Italian, Japanese, and Korean.

## WALKING TOURS

**Javawalk** is a 2-hour walking tour by self-described "coffeehouse lizard" Elaine Sosa. As the name suggests, it's loosely a coffee walking tour through North Beach, but there's a lot more going on than drinking cups of brew. Javawalk also serves up a good share of historical and architectural trivia, offering something for everyone. The best part of the tour, however, may be the camaraderie that develops among the tour-goers. Sosa keeps the tour interactive and fun, and it's obvious that she knows a profusion of tales and trivia about the history of coffee and its North Beach roots. It's a guaranteed good time, particularly if you're addicted to caffeine. Javawalk is offered Tuesday to Saturday at 10am. The price is $20 per person, with kids 12 and under at half price. For information and reservations, call ☎ 415/673-WALK (9255).

**Cruisin' the Castro** (☎ 415/550-8110) is an informative historical tour of San Francisco's most famous gay quarter and will give you a totally new insight into the contribution of the gay community to the political maturity, growth, and beauty of San Francisco. Tours are personally conducted by Trevor Hailey, who was involved in the development of the Castro in the 1970s. She knew Harvey Milk, the first openly gay politician elected to office in the United States. You'll learn about Milk's rise from shopkeeper to city supervisor and visit Harvey Milk Plaza, where most marches, rallies, and protests begin. In addition, you'll explore the Names Project visitors center, Castro Theatre, and side streets lined with beautifully restored Victorians, as well as the plethora of community-oriented stores on the Castro—gift shops, bookstores, restaurants, jewelers—whose owners Hailey knows personally. Tours are conducted Tuesday to Saturday from 10am to 2pm, and begin at Harvey Milk Plaza, atop the Castro Street Muni station. The cost includes lunch at Caffè Luna Piena (see page 143 in chapter 6 for a complete review). Reservations are required. The tour, with lunch, costs $40 for adults, $35 for seniors 62 and over, and children's prices are negotiable.

The **Haight-Ashbury Flower Power Walking Tour** (☎ 415/863-1621) is for you if Woodstock 2 made you nostalgic for the 1960s, or if you want to tour the hippie haunts with Pam and Bruce Brennan and revisit in 3 short hours the Grateful Dead's crash pad, Janis Joplin's house, and other reminders of the Summer of Love. Tours begin at 9:30am Tuesday and Saturday. The cost is $15 per person. Reservations are required.

San Francisco's Chinatown is always fascinating, but for many visitors with limited time it's hard to know where to search out the "non-touristy" shops, restaurants, and historical spots in this microcosm of Chinese culture. **Wok Wiz Chinatown Walking Tours & Cooking Center** (654 Commercial St. between Kearny and Montgomery sts; ☎ 800/281-9255 or 415/981-8989; www.wokwiz. com; e-mail: wokwiz@aol.com), founded 13 years ago by author, TV personality,

# The Names Project AIDS Memorial Quilt

The Names Project began in 1987 as a memorial for people who have died from AIDS. The idea was to direct grief into positive action and to help the world understand the devastating impact of AIDS. Sewing machines and fabric were acquired, and the public was invited to make coffin-sized panels for a giant memorial quilt. More than 40,000 individual panels now commemorate the lives of those who have died of complications related to AIDS. Each has been uniquely designed and sewn by the victims' friends, lovers, and family members.

The AIDS Memorial Quilt, which would cover 24 football fields if laid out end to end, was first displayed on the Capitol Mall in Washington, D.C., during a 1987 national march on Washington for lesbian and gay rights. Although sections of the quilt are often on tour throughout the world, portions of the largest community art project in the world are on display at **The Names Project AIDS Memorial Quilt Visitors Center & Panelmaking Workshop,** 2362-A Market St. (☎ **415/863-1966**). The center is open Monday to Friday noon to 7pm and Sunday from noon to 6pm. To get there, take the Muni Metro K, L, or M line to the Castro Street station, or the F line to Church and Market streets; bus no. 24, 33, or 35 will also get you there. A sewing machine and fabrics, along with assistance from trained volunteers, are available for those interested in making a quilt panel for someone lost to AIDS.

cooking instructor, and restaurant critic Shirley Fong-Torres, is the answer. The Wok Wiz tours take you into nooks and crannies not usually seen by tourists. Most of her guides are Chinese, speak fluent Cantonese or Mandarin, and are intimately acquainted with all of Chinatown's alleys and small enterprises, as well as Chinatown's history, folklore, culture, and food.

Tours are conducted daily from 10am to 1:30pm and include dim sum (Chinese lunch). There's also a less expensive tour that does not include lunch. It's an easy walk, fun and fascinating, and you're bound to make new friends. Groups are generally held to a maximum of 12, and reservations are essential. Prices (including lunch) are $37 for adults, $35 for seniors 60 and older, and $30 for children under 12.

Shirley Fong-Torres also operates an **I Can't Believe I Ate My Way Through Chinatown** tour that starts with a Chinese breakfast in a noodle house, moves to a wok shop, and then makes further stops for nibbles at a vegetarian restaurant, rice-noodle factory, and a supermarket before taking a break for a sumptuous luncheon (most Saturdays; $65 per person), as well as a **Walk & Wok** tour that includes shopping for food in Chinatown, then cooking (and eating) it together at Shirley's Cooking Center (most Saturdays; $75 per person).

Jay Gifford, founder of **Victorian Homes Historical Walking Tour** (☎ **415/ 252-9485**) and San Francisco resident for two decades, portrays his enthusiasm and love of San Francisco throughout this highly entertaining walking tour. The 2½-hour tour, set at a very leisurely place, incorporates a wealth of interesting knowledge about San Francisco's Victorian architecture, as well as the city's storied history—particularly the periods just before and after the great earthquake and fire of 1906. You'll stroll through the neighborhoods of Japantown, the Western Addition (where you can take a break to cruise the trendy shops on Fillmore Street), and onward to Pacific Heights and Cow Hollow. In the process you'll see more than 200 meticulously restored Victorians, including the one where Mrs. Doubtfire was filmed. Jay's guests often find they are the only ones on the quiet neighborhood streets, where tour buses are forbidden. The tour ends with a trolley bus ride back to Union Square, passing though North Beach and Chinatown.

Tours, which start at Union Square at 11am, are offered daily year-round and cost $20 per person. Reservations are required. You can preview his tour at his Web site: **www.victorianwalk.com**.

# 10  Staying Active

Half the fun in San Francisco takes place outdoors. If you're not in the mood to trek it, there are other things to do that will allow you to enjoy the surroundings.

## BALLOONING

Though it'll take you a 1-hour drive to get there, hot-air ballooning is an ethereal and silent flight over the Wine Country.

**Adventures Aloft.** P.O. Box 2500, Vintage 1870, Yountville, CA 94599. ☎ **800/944-4408** or 707/944-4408. www.nvaloft.com. $185 per person. Flights daily 6–7am (weather permitting).

The Napa Valley's oldest hot-air balloon company is staffed with full-time professional pilots. Groups are small, and the flight will last about an hour. The cost of $185 per person includes a post-adventure champagne brunch, and a framed "first-flight" certificate.

## BEACHES

For beach information, call ☎ **415/391-2000.** Most days it's too chilly to hang out at the beach. But when the fog evaporates and the wind dies down, one of the best ways to spend the day is ocean-side in the city. On any truly hot day, thousands flock to worship the sun, build sandcastles, and throw the ball around. Without a wetsuit, swimming is a fiercely cold endeavor and there are only two beaches considered safe for swimming: **Aquatic Park** is adjacent to the Hyde Park Pier; and **China Beach** is a small cove on the western edge of the South Bay. But dip at your own risk—there are never lifeguards on duty.

Also on the South Bay, **Baker Beach** is ideal for picnicking, sunning, walking, or fishing against the backdrop of the Golden Gate.

**Ocean Beach,** at the end of Golden Gate Park, on the westernmost side of the city, is San Francisco's largest beach—4 miles long. Just offshore, at the northern end of the beach in front of Cliff House, are the jagged Seal Rocks inhabited by various shore birds and a large colony of barking sea lions (bring binoculars for a close-up view). To the left, Kelly's Cove is one of the more challenging surf spots in town. Ocean Beach is ideal for strolling or sunning, but don't swim here—tides are tricky, and each year bathers drown in the rough surf.

Stop by Ocean Beach bus terminal at the corner of Cabrillo and La Playa to learn about San Francisco's playful history in local artist Ray Beldner's whimsically historical sculpture garden. Then hike up the hill to explore the Cliff House and the ruins of Sutro Baths. These baths, able to accommodate 24,000 bathers, were lost to fire in 1966.

## OTHER MUNICIPAL PARKS

In addition to **Golden Gate Park** and the **Golden Gate National Recreation Area** discussed above, San Francisco boasts more than 2,000 additional acres of parkland, most of which is perfect for picnicking or throwing around a Frisbee.

Smaller city parks include: **Buena Vista Park** (Haight Street between Baker and Central streets), which affords fine views of the Golden Gate and is also a favored lounging ground for gay lovers; **Ina Coolbrith Park** (Taylor Street between Vallejo and Green streets), offering views of the Bay Bridge and Alcatraz; and **Sigmund Stern Grove** (at 19th Avenue and Sloat Boulevard) in the Sunset District, which is the site of the famous free summer music festival.

One of our personal favorites is **Lincoln Park,** a 270-acre green on the northwestern side of the city at Clement Street and 34th Avenue. The California Palace of the Legion of Honor is here (see "Museums," above), as is a scenic 18-hole municipal golf course (see "Activities," below). But the best things about this park are the 200-foot cliffs that overlook the Golden Gate Bridge and San Francisco Bay. To get to the park, take bus no. 38 from Union Square to 33rd and Geary streets, then walk a few blocks to the park.

## ACTIVITIES

**BICYCLING**    Two city-designated bike routes are maintained by the Parks and Recreations department. One winds 7½ miles through Golden Gate Park to Lake Merced; the other traverses the city, starting in the south, and follows a route over the Golden Gate Bridge. These routes are not dedicated to bicyclists, and caution must be exercised to avoid crashing into pedestrians. Helmets are recommended for adults, and required by law for kids under 18. A bike map is available from the San Francisco Visitor Information Center, at Powell and Market streets (see "Visitor Information" in chapter 4), and from bicycle shops all around town.

Ocean Beach has a public walk- and bikeway that stretches along 5 waterfront blocks of the Great Highway between Noriega and Santiago streets. It's an easy ride from Cliff House or Golden Gate Park.

**Park Cyclery,** at 1749 Waller St. (☎ **415/751-7368**), is a shop in the Haight that rents bikes. Located next to Golden Gate Park, the cyclery rents mountain bikes exclusively, along with helmets. The charge is $5 per hour, $25 per day, and it's open daily from 10am to 6pm.

**BOATING**    At the **Golden Gate Park Boat House** (☎ **415/752-0347**) on Stow Lake, the park's largest body of water, you can rent a rowboat or pedal boat by the hour and steer over to Strawberry Hill, a large, round island in the middle of the lake, for lunch. There's usually a line on weekends. The boat house is open daily, June through September from 9am to 5pm, and the rest of the year daily from 9am to 4pm.

**Cass Marina,** 1702 Bridgeway, in Sausalito (☎ **800/472-4595** or 415/332-6789), rents sailboats measuring 22 to 101 feet. Sail under the Golden Gate Bridge on your own or with a licensed skipper. In addition, large sailing yachts leave from San Francisco and Sausalito on a regularly scheduled basis. Call for schedules, prices, and availability of sailboats or check them out on the Web at **www. cassmarina.com**. The marina is open daily from 9am to sunset.

**CITY STAIR-CLIMBING**    Many U.S. health clubs now have stair-climbing machines and step classes, but in San Francisco, you need only to go outside. The following city stair climbs will provide you not only with a good workout, but with great sightseeing, too.

**Filbert Street Steps,** between Sansome Street and Telegraph Hill, are a particular challenge. Scaling the sheer eastern face of Telegraph Hill, this 377-step climb wends its way through verdant flower gardens and charming 19th-century cottages.

Napier Lane, a narrow wooden plank walkway, leads to Montgomery Street. Turn right, and follow the path to the end of the cul-de-sac where another stairway continues to Telegraph's panoramic summit.

The **Lyon Street Steps,** between Green Street and Broadway, were built in 1916. This historic stairway street contains four steep sets of stairs totaling 288 steps in all. Begin at Green Street and climb all the way up, past manicured hedges and flower gardens, to an iron gate that opens into the Presidio. A block east, on Baker Street, another set of 369 steps descends to Green Street.

**CROQUET**   The **San Francisco Croquet Club** (☎ 415/776-4104) offers free public lessons (by reservation) from 10am to 1pm on the first Saturday of each month (or anytime by reservation for parties of four or more). The game is taught according to international six-wicket rules at the croquet lawns in Stern Grove, at 19th Avenue and Wawona Street.

**FISHING   New Easy Rider Sport Fishing,** at 225 University Ave. in Berkeley (☎ 415/285-2000), makes daily trips from Fisherman's Wharf for ling cod, rock fish, and many other types of game fish all year-round, as well as salmon runs from June through October. Fishing equipment is available; the cost of $55 per person includes bait; $60 during winter when it's a crab and fish combo. Reservations are required, as are licenses for adults (1-day licenses can be purchased before departure). Departures are daily at 6am, returning at 4pm. Fish are cleaned, filleted, and bagged on the return trip for a small fee.

**GOLF**   San Francisco has a few beautiful golf courses. At press time, one of the most lavish, the **Presidio Golf Course** (☎ 415/561-4664), had just opened up to the public for the first time (greens fees $35 Mon to Thurs, $45 Fri, and $55 Sat and Sun). There are also two decent municipal golf courses in town if you're itching to put on your golf shoes and swing some clubs.

**Golden Gate Park Course.** 47th Ave. and Fulton St. ☎ **415/751-8987.** Greens fees $10 per person Mon–Fri; $13 Sat–Sun. Daily 6am–dusk.

This small 9-hole course covers 1,357 yards and is par 27. All holes are par 3, tightly set, and well trapped with small greens. The course is a little weathered in spots, but it's a casual, fun, and inexpensive place to tee off, local style.

**Lincoln Park Golf Course.** 34th Ave. and Clement St. ☎ **415/221-9911.** Greens fees $23 per person Mon–Fri; $27 Sat–Sun. Daily 6:30am–dusk.

San Francisco's prettiest municipal course has terrific views and fairways lined with Monterey cypress trees. Its 18 holes encompass 5,081 yards, for a par 68, and the 17th hole has a glistening ocean view. This is the oldest course in the city and one of the oldest in the West.

**Mission Bay Golf Center.** Sixth St. at Channel St. (from downtown San Francisco, take Fourth St. south to Channel St. and turn right). ☎ **415/431-7888.** Bucket of balls $7. Mon 11:30am–11pm; Tues–Sun 7am–11pm. Last bucket sold at 10pm.

San Francisco's most popular driving range, the Mission Bay Golf Center is an impeccably maintained 7-acre facility that consists of a double-decker steel and concrete arc containing 66 covered practice bays. The grass landing area extends 300 yards, has nine target greens, and is lit for evening use. There's also a putting green, as well as a chipping and bunker practice area.

**HANDBALL**   The city's best handball courts are in Golden Gate Park, opposite Seventh Avenue, south of Middle Drive East. Courts are available free, on a first-come, first-served basis.

---

# Work It Out

While San Francisco has plenty to offer in the way of outdoor exercise and activities, there are plenty of indoor places to relieve stress, work up a sweat, or treat your body to a little TLC.

The **San Francisco Bay Club,** located at 150 Greenwich St., at Battery Street (☎ **415/433-2200**), is one of the most exclusive and extensive gym-turned-spas in the Bay Area. Celebrities such as Tom Cruise, Cindy Crawford, and Hugh Grant have flexed a few muscles here when on location, and regular members include the city's old and new elite. The club takes up almost a full block and offers three floors filled with health equipment, including two pools (one's heated); tennis, squash, racquetball, and basketball courts; aerobics and yoga; free weights, cardiovascular, and Nautilus equipment; a sundeck; sauna, steam room, and whirlpool; and a cafe. Although walk-in guests are not permitted, sign up for any of the luxurious spa treatments and you're extended full workout privileges for the day. Services include massage, facials, manicures, and pedicures.

A more spiritual workout can be found at **The Mindful Body,** a center for movement, body, and personal inner work. It is located at 2876 California St., between Broderick and Divisadero (☎ **415/931-2639** for class schedules). After an intense yoga or stretch class, guided meditation, or massage, you'll be a new person.

Adventurers can hone their skills at **Mission Cliffs Rock Climbing Center** at 2295 Harrison, at 19th Street (☎ **415/550-0515**). For $16, or $8 if you come before 3pm on a weekday (plus $6 if you need rental equipment), you can climb 14,000 feet of terrain and 2,000 square feet of boulders. Lessons, which cost extra and include children's and outdoor programs, can be arranged. Once you're worn out, relax in the sauna.

If getting your heart rate up seems like a chore, take a less painful approach at the **Metronome,** which offers ballroom, swing, Latin, nightclub, and salsa dance classes for individuals and groups. Call for information on class times, package deals, and weekend dance parties (☎ **415/252-9000**).

**RUNNING**   The **Bay to Breakers Foot Race** is an annual 7½-mile fun from downtown to Ocean Beach. About 80,000 entrants gather—many dressed in wacky, innovative, and sometimes X-rated costumes—for what's considered one of San Francisco's favored trademark events. The event is sponsored by the *San Francisco Examiner* and is held the third Sunday of May. Call ☎ **415/777-7770** or check out **www.baytobreakers.com** for details.

The San Francisco Chronicle Marathon is held annually in the middle of July. For further information, contact **West End Management** (☎ **415/284-9492**).

**SKATING (Conventional & In-Line)**   Although people skate in Golden Gate Park all week long, Sunday is best, when JFK Drive between Kezar Drive and Transverse Road is closed to automobiles. A smooth "skate pad" is located on your right, just past the Conservatory. **Skates on Haight,** at 1818 Haight St. (☎ **415/752-8376**), is the best place to rent either in-line or conventional skates, and is located only 1 block from the park. Protective wrist guards and knee pads are included free. The cost is $8 per hour for in-line or "conventional" skates, $28 for all-day use. Major credit card and ID deposit are required. The shop is open

Monday to Friday from 11am to 7pm, and Saturday and Sunday from 10am to 6pm.

**TENNIS**    More than 100 courts throughout the city are maintained by the **San Francisco Recreation and Parks Department** (☎ 415/753-7001). All are available free, on a first-come, first-served basis. The exceptions are the 21 courts in Golden Gate Park; a $4-to-$6 fee is charged for their use, and courts must be reserved in advance for weekend play. Call the number above on Wednesday between 7 and 9pm, or on Thursday and Friday from 9am to 5pm. For weekend reservations call ☎ 415/753-7101.

**WALKING & HIKING**    The **Golden Gate National Recreation Area** offers plenty of opportunities for walking and hiking. One pleasant walk, or bike ride for that matter, is along the Golden Gate Promenade, from Aquatic Park to the Golden Gate Bridge. The 3½-mile paved trail leads along the northern edge of the Presidio, out to Fort Point. You can also hike along the Coastal Trail all the way from near Fort Point to the Cliff House. The park service maintains several other trails in the city. For more information or to pick up a map of the Golden Gate National Recreation Area, stop by the park service headquarters at Fort Mason at the north end of Laguna Street (☎ 415/556-0560).

Though most drive to this spectacular vantage point, a more rejuvenating way to experience Twin Peaks is to walk up from the back roads of U.C. Medical Center (off Parnassus) or from either of the two roads that lead to the top (off Woodside or Clarendon aves.). Early morning is the best time to trek, when the city is quiet, the air is crisp, and the sightseers haven't crowded the parking lot. Keep an eye out for cars, since there's no real hiking trail, and be sure to walk beyond the lot and up to the highest vantage point.

# 11  Spectator Sports

The Bay Area's sports scene includes several major professional franchises, including football, baseball, and basketball. Check the local newspapers' sports sections for daily listings of local events.

Baseball is represented by the **San Francisco Giants,** who play at 3Com/ Candlestick Park, Giants Drive and Gilman Avenue (☎ 415/467-8000). From April through October, the National League Giants play their home games at Candlestick Park, off U.S. 101 about 8 miles south of downtown. Tickets are usually available up until game time, but seats can be dreadfully far from the action. You can get tickets through **BASS Ticketmaster** (☎ 510/762-2277). Special express bus service is available from Market Street on game days; call **Muni** (☎ 415/ 673-6864) for pickup points and schedule information. Bring a coat; this 60,000-seat stadium is known for its chilly winds.

The Bay Area's other team is the 1989 world-champion **Oakland Athletics,** who play across the bay at the Oakland Coliseum Complex, at the Hegenberger Road exit from I-880, in Oakland (☎ 510/430-8020). The stadium holds close to 50,000 spectators and is serviced by BART's Coliseum station. Tickets are available from the Coliseum box office or by phone through **BASS Ticketmaster** (☎ 510/ 762-2277).

Pro basketball is represented by the **Golden State Warriors,** who play at the Oakland Coliseum Complex, at the Hegenberger Road exit from I-880, in Oakland (☎ 510/986-2200). The NBA Warriors play basketball in the 15,025-seat Oakland Coliseum Arena. The season runs from November through April, and most games are played at 7:30pm. Tickets are available at the arena, and by phone through BASS Ticketmaster (☎ **510/762-2277**).

As of 1995, the Bay Area once again plays home to two professional football teams. The **San Francisco 49ers** play at 3Com/Candlestick Park (Giants Dr. and Gilman Ave.) (☎ **415/468-2249**). Games are played on Sundays from August through December; kickoff is usually at 1pm. Tickets sell out early in the season, but are available at higher prices through ticket agents beforehand and from scalpers at the gate. Ask your hotel concierge or visit **City Box Office,** 153 Kearny St., Suite 302 (☎ **415/392-4400**). Special express bus service is available from Market Street on game days; call **Muni** (☎ **415/673-6864**) for pickup points and schedule information.

Also back in the Bay Area are the 49ers' archenemy, the **Oakland Raiders.** Their home turf is the Oakland Alameda County Coliseum, off the 880 Freeway (Nimitz) (☎ **800/949-2626** for ticket information).

The **University of California Golden Bears** play in Memorial Stadium at 61 Harmon Gym, University of California, Berkeley (☎ **800/GO-BEARS** or 510/642-3277), on the university campus across the bay. Tickets are usually available at game time. Phone for schedules and information.

Fans can see horse racing at **Golden Gate Fields,** located on Gilman Street, off I-80, in Albany, 10 miles northeast of San Francisco (☎ **510/559-7300**). Scenic thoroughbred races are held here from January through March and from April to the end of June. The park is located on the seashore. Call for admission prices and post times.

The nearest autumn racing takes place at **Bay Meadows,** 2600 S. Delaware St., off U.S. 101, in San Mateo (☎ **650/574-7223**). This thoroughbred and quarter-horse track, on the peninsula about 20 miles south of downtown San Francisco, hosts races 4 or 5 days each week from September through January. Call for admission and post times.

# 8 City Strolls

**D**espite a handful of killer hills, San Francisco is a city best explored on foot. Best of all, these self-guided tours won't cost you a dime and will give you some interesting insights—both historic and contemporary—into two of San Francisco's most popular and unique neighborhoods: Chinatown and North Beach. For guided walking tours of San Francisco's other neighborhoods, such as Haight-Ashbury and the Castro, see "Self-Guided & Organized Tours" in chapter 7, or check out *Frommer's Memorable Walks in San Francisco,* available at most major bookstores.

*Budget Tip:* Free neighborhood tours are offered by **City Guides,** an affiliate of the San Francisco Library. Call ☎ **415/557-4266** for schedules, or pick a self-guided one up at the San Francisco Visitor Information Center, on the lower level of Hallidie Plaza, 900 Market St., at Powell Street (☎ **415/391-2000**), or any San Francisco Public Library.

## Walking Tour 1— Chinatown: History, Culture, Dim Sum & Then Some

**Start:** Corner of Grant Avenue and Bush Street.
**Public Transportation:** 2, 3, 4, 9X, 15, 30, 38, 45, or 76 bus.
**Finish:** Commercial Street, between Montgomery and Kearny streets.
**Time:** 2 hours, not including museum or shopping stops.
**Best Times:** Daylight hours when there's the most action.
**Worst Times:** Too early or too late because shops will be closed and no one will be milling around.
**Hills That Could Kill:** None.

This tiny section of San Francisco, bounded loosely by Broadway, Stockton, Kearny, and Bush, is said to harbor one of the largest Chinese populations outside of Asia. Daily proof is the crowds of Chinese residents who shop the plethora of herbal stores, vegetable markets, and Chinese restaurants and businesses. Chinatown also marks the spot where the city began its development in the mid-1800s. Embark on this walk and you'll learn why Chinatown

# Walking Tour—Chinatown

0 | 1/8 Mile
0 | 1/8 Kilometer

Jackson St.

Ross Alley

Portsmouth Square

Washington St.

Merchant St.

Clay St.

Stockton St.

Waverly Pl.

Grant Av.

Walter U. Lum Pl.

Kearny St.

Commercial St.

20

finish here

Montgomery St.

Sacramento St.

California St.

St. Mary's Square

Pine St.

Bush St.

start here

Sutter St.

Columbus Av.

Take-a-Break

1. Chinatown Gateway Arch
2. Grant Avenue
3. St. Mary's Square
4. Old St. Mary's Church
5. Canton Bazaar
6. Bank of America
7. Chinatown Kite Shop
8. The Wok Shop
9. The original street of "American" California
10. Bank of Canton
11. Ten Ren Tea Co., Ltd.
12. Ross Alley
13. Golden Gate Fortune Cookie Company
14. Stockton Street
15. Great China Herb Co.
16. Waverly Place
17. Tin How Temple
18. Portsmouth Square
19. Chinese Cultural Center
20. Chinese Historical Society of America Museum

remains intriguing to all who traverse its narrow and crowded streets, and how its origins are responsible for the town as we know it.

To begin the tour, make your way to the corner of Bush Street and Grant Avenue where you can't miss the:

1. **Chinatown Gateway Arch.** It is traditional in China that villages have ceremonial gates like this one. This gate is a lot less formal than those in China, built here more for the benefit of the tourist industry than anything else.

Once you cross the threshold you'll be at the beginning of Chinatown's portion of:

2. **Grant Avenue,** a.k.a. the mecca for tourists who wander in and out of gift shops that offer a variety of unnecessary junk interspersed with quality imports, decent restaurants, and grocery stores frequented by Chinese residents ranging from children to the oldest living people you've ever seen.

Tear yourself away from the shops, go right at the corner of Pine Street, crossing to the left side of Pine, and on your left you'll come to:

3. **St. Mary's Square,** where you'll find a huge metal-and-granite statue of Dr. Sun Yat-sen, the founder of the Republic of China. A native of Guandong (Canton) Province, Sun Yat-sen's goal was to overthrow the Qing Dynasty.

Note also the second monument in the square, which honors Chinese-American victims of both world wars. (An added bonus: A pay toilet is strategically placed here for visitors in need.)

Walk to the other end of the square toward California Street, cross California and you'll be standing in front of:

4. **Old St. Mary's Church.** The first Catholic cathedral in San Francisco, and the site of the Chinese community's first English-language school, St. Mary's was built primarily by Chinese laborers and dedicated on Christmas Day, 1854.

Step inside to find a written history of the church and turn-of-the-century photos of San Francisco. Stop in on a Tuesday or Thursday at 12:30pm and you'll be privy to the free half-hour classical music performance.

Upon leaving the church, take a right and walk to the corner of Grant and California, then go right on Grant. Here you'll find a shop called the:

5. **Canton Bazaar,** at 616 Grant Ave. Of the barrage of knickknack and import shops lining Grant Avenue, this is one of the most popular.

Continue in the same direction on Grant Avenue, cross Sacramento Street and Grant Avenue to arrive at the northwest corner and the doorstep of:

6. **Bank of America,** which is in the traditional Chinese architectural style. Notice dragons subtly portrayed on many parts of the building.

Heading in the same direction (north) on Grant, a few doors down at 717 Grant is the:

7. **Chinatown Kite Shop.** This store's assortment of flying objects includes attractive fish kites, windsock kites in nylon or cotton, hand-painted Chinese paper kites, wood-and-paper biplanes, and pentagonal kites.

Other take-home treasures of a more functional kind can be found across the street at:

8. **The Wok Shop** at 718 Grant Ave., where you can purchase just about any utensil, cookbook, or vessel you might need to do Chinese-style cooking in your own kitchen.

When you come out of the Wok Shop, go right; walk past Commercial Street and you'll arrive at the corner of Grant Avenue and Clay Street; cross Clay and you'll be standing on the:

**9. Original street of "American" California.** Here the first tent was set up by an English seaman named William Richardson in 1835.

Continue north on Grant to Washington Street. Go right, and at 743 Washington you will be standing in front of the:

**10. Bank of Canton,** which boasts the oldest (1909) Asian-style edifice in Chinatown. This three-tiered temple-style building once housed the China Telephone Exchange, known as "China-5" until 1945.

You're probably getting thirsty by now, so follow Washington a few doors down (east) and on your right-hand side you will come upon:

☕ **TAKE A BREAK   Washington Bakery & Restaurant.** No need to actually have a full meal here—the service can be abrupt and the food, mediocre. Do stop in, however, for a little potable adventure: snow red bean with ice cream. The sugary-sweet drink mixed with whole beans and ice cream is not something you're likely to have tried elsewhere and it happens to be quite tasty. Whatever you do, don't fill up—a few sites away some wonderfully fresh dim sum awaits you.

Go back to Grant Avenue, cross Washington and then Grant, and follow the western side of Grant 1 block to no. 949, the location of:

**11. Ten Ren Tea Co., Ltd.** In this amazing shop you can sample whatever freshly brewed variation they're offering and check out the dozens of drawers and canisters labeled with over 40 varieties of tea.

When departing Ten Ren, take a left, and when you reach Jackson Street, make another left. On the left-hand side at 735 Jackson, through the storefront window you'll notice stacks of steaming wooden baskets manned by a Chinese cook. You've reached your snacking destination.

☕ **TAKE A BREAK**   It's the **House of Dim Sum**—nothing fancy, for sure, but the dumplings are fresh, cheap, and delicious, and the staff is friendly. Order at the counter: pork, chive and shrimp, and shark-fin dumplings; sweet buns; turnip cake; or sweet rice with chicken wrapped in a lotus leaf. Unless they're taken, it's best to sit at one of the two tables to enjoy your feast.

As you leave the House, turn left up the hill and make another left on:

**12. Ross Alley.** As you walk along the narrow street, it's not difficult to imagine that this block was once rife with gambling dens.

As you follow the alley south, on the left-hand side of the street you'll encounter:

**13. Golden Gate Fortune Cookie Company,** at 56 Ross St. It's just a tiny place where one woman sits at a conveyer belt, folding messages into warm cookies as the manager calls out to tourists to buy a big bag of the fortune-telling treats.

Sometimes the staff pushes a purchase, while at other times they might hand you a free warm cookie.

As you exit the alley, take a right on Washington and follow it up to:

**14. Stockton Street.** From Broadway to Sacramento Street, Stockton is where most of the residents of Chinatown do their daily shopping.

A good stop if you're in the market for some jewelry is at Jade Galore (1000 Stockton St. at the corner of Stockton and Washington streets).

You might want to wander up Stockton Street to absorb the atmosphere and street life of this less-tourist-oriented Chinese community before doubling back to Washington Street.

Once back at Stockton and Washington, turn left down Washington and head back toward Grant Avenue. On the right side of the street you will stumble upon the:

**15. Great China Herb Co.** at 857 Washington (Stockton and Grant). Chinese and holistic Westerners come to shops like this one—full of exotic herbs, roots, and other natural substances—to buy what they believe cures all types of ailments and ensures good health and long life. Thankfully, unlike many similar shops in the area, owners Mr. and Mrs. Ho speak English, so you will not be met with a blank stare as you inquire what exactly is in each box, bag, or jar arranged along dozens of shelves.

Continue back toward Grant Avenue, and take a right on:

**16. Waverly Place,** or "The Street of Painted Balconies." This is probably China-town's most popular side street or alleyway because of its painted balconies and colorful architectural details, a sort of Chinese-style New Orleans street.

Most buildings aren't open to the public, but one temple you can visit (but make sure it's open before you go climbing up the long narrow stairway) is the:

**17. Tin How Temple,** at 125 Waverly Place. Accessible via a narrow stairway four floors up, this incense-laden sanctuary decorated in traditional black, red, and gold lacquered wood is a house of worship. Chinese Buddhists come here to pray, meditate, and send offerings to their ancestors and to Tin How, the Queen of the Heavens and Goddess of the Seven Seas. When you visit, try to be as unobtrusive as possible. It is customary to give a donation or buy a bundle of incense during your visit.

Once you've finished exploring Waverly Place, walk down Clay Street past Grant Avenue and continue until you come upon the block-wide urban playground that is also the most important site in San Francisco's history:

**18. Portsmouth Square.** This very spot was the center of the region's first township, which was called Yerba Buena before it was renamed San Francisco in 1847.

Around 1846, before any semblance of a city had taken shape, this plaza was at the foot of the eastern shoreline of the bay. There were less than 50 non-Indian residents, no substantial buildings to speak of, and the few boats that pulled into the cove did so less than a block from where you're standing.

In 1846, when California was claimed as American territory, the marines who landed here named the square after their ship, the USS *Portsmouth*. (Today, there's a bronze plaque that marks the spot where they raised the American flag.)

Yerba Buena briefly remained a modest township until the gold rush of 1849. Immediately following the rush, the population would grow from under 1,000 to over 19,000 as gold-seekers from around the world made their way here.

When the square became crowded, long wharves were constructed to support new buildings above the bay. Eventually, the entire area would become landfill.

That was almost 150 years ago, but today the square still serves as an important meeting place for neighborhood Chinese as a sort of communal outdoor living room. Some practice tai chi here in the early morning; children play and elderly men gamble over Chinese cards.

It is said that Robert Louis Stevenson also used to love to sit on a bench here and watch life going on all around him. (You'll find a monument to his memory at the northeast corner of the square.)

Cross the bridge leading from Portsmouth Square over the traffic and across the street to The Holiday Inn at 750 Kearny. Cross the street, enter the hotel, and take the elevator to the third floor where you'll find the:

**19.** **Chinese Cultural Center,** which is oriented toward both the community and tourists, offering lectures, films, and seminars; there are also interesting display cases housing Chinese art and a gallery with rotating exhibits of Asian art and writing.

When you leave the Holiday Inn, take a left on Kearny and go 3 short blocks to Commercial Street. Halfway down this street on the left is the:

**20.** **Chinese Historical Society of America Museum,** founded in 1963. Head downstairs to this basement-cum-museum and you'll find a small but fascinating collection of gold-rush relics, photos, and artifacts that illuminates the role of Chinese immigrants in American history, particularly in San Francisco and California. Admission is free, but the museum appreciates any donation you can give. It's open from about noon to 4pm Tuesday through Saturday. The curator sometimes closes early if there are no visitors, so be sure to get there well before 4pm.

## Walking Tour 2—Noshing Through North Beach

**Start:** Intersection of Montgomery Street, Columbus Avenue, and Washington Street.

**Public Transportation:** 15, 30X, 41, or 42 bus as near as you can get to the intersection of Montgomery Street, Columbus Avenue, and Washington Street.

**Finish:** Washington Square.

**Time:** 3 hours, including a stop for lunch.

**Best Times:** Start the tour Monday to Saturday anytime between 11am and 4pm.

**Worst Times:** Sunday when shops are closed.

**Hills That Could Kill:** The Montgomery Street hill that runs from Broadway to Vallejo Street; otherwise, this is a very easy walk.

Along with Chinatown, North Beach is one of the city's oldest neighborhoods. Originally the city's Latin Quarter, it became the city's Italian Quarter when Italian immigrants moved "uphill" in the early 1870s, crossing Broadway from the Jackson Square area and settling in. They quickly set up restaurants, cafes, bakeries, and other businesses familiar to them from their homeland. The "Beat Generation" helped put North Beach on the map, with the likes of Jack Kerouac and Allen Ginsberg holding court in the area's cafes during the 1950s. Although most of the original beat poets are gone, their spirit lives on in North Beach, which is still a haven for bohemian artists and writers. The neighborhood, thankfully, still retains the Italian village feel, where residents from all walks of life enjoy taking time for conversation over a pastry and a frothy cappuccino.

If there's one landmark you can't miss, it's the familiar looking building on the corner of Montgomery Street and Columbus Avenue, the:

**1.** **TransAmerica Pyramid.** Noted for its spire (which rises 212 ft. above the top floor) and its "wings" (which begin at the 29th floor and stop where the spire begins), the pyramid is San Francisco's tallest building and an identifying landmark of the city's skyline. You may wish to take a peek at one of the rotating art exhibits in the lobby, or go around to the right and into the half-acre Redwood Park, which is part of the TransAmerica Center.

The site occupied by the TransAmerica Pyramid, in addition to the rest of the 600 block of Montgomery Street, was once occupied by a historic building called:

2. **The Montgomery Block.** Originally four stories high, it was the tallest building in the West when it was built in 1853. San Franciscans called it "Halleck's Folly" because it was built on a raft of redwood logs that had been bolted together and floated at the edge of the ocean (which was right at Montgomery Street at that time). The building was demolished in 1959, but is fondly remembered for its historic importance as the power center of the city, whose tenants also included artists and writers of all kinds, among them Jack London, George Sterling, Ambrose Bierce, Bret Harte, and Mark Twain.

From the southeast corner of Montgomery and Washington streets, look across Washington to the corner of Columbus Avenue, and you'll see the:

3. **Original TransAmerica Building,** across the street at 4 Columbus Ave. (now Sanwa Bank). A beaux-arts flat-iron building covered in white terra-cotta, it was also the home of the old Fugazi Bank. Built for the Banco Populare Italiano Operaia Fugazi in 1909, it was originally a two-story building, but a third floor was added in 1916. In 1928, Fugazi merged his bank with the Bank of America, which was started by A. P. Giannini, who also created the TransAmerica Corporation.

Cross Washington Street and continue north on Montgomery Street to no. 730, the:

4. **Golden Era Building,** erected in about 1852. The building is named after the literary magazine, the *Golden Era,* which was published here. Part of the group of young writers who worked on the magazine were known as the Bohemians, and they included Samuel Clemens (a.k.a. Mark Twain) and Bret Harte (who began as a typesetter here). Backtrack a few dozen feet and stop for a minute to admire the annex, located at no. 722 (marked by a faded black-and-white-striped awning). The Belli Annex, as it is currently known, is registered as a Historic Landmark.

Continue north again and take the first right onto Jackson Street. Now you're in the:

5. **400 block of Jackson Square,** where you'll find some of the only commercial buildings to survive the 1906 earthquake and fire. 415 Jackson served as the headquarters for the Ghirardelli Chocolate Company from 1855 to 1894, and was built around 1853. The Hotaling Building (no. 451) was built in 1866. At no. 472 is another of the buildings that survived the disaster of 1906.

Continue toward the intersection of Columbus Avenue and Jackson Street, turn right on Columbus and look across the street for the small triangular building at the junction of Kearny and Columbus, the:

6. **Columbus Tower (a.k.a. Sentinel Building).** If you walk up a little farther and then turn around and look back down Columbus, you'll be able to get a better look at this flat-iron—a building shaped to a triangular site—beauty erected between 1905 and 1907, which was bought and restored by movie director and producer Francis Ford Coppola in the mid-1970s and is now home to his film production company, American Zoetrope Studios. As this book goes to press the first floor is undergoing construction with the intention of opening a Niebaum-Coppola cafe, shop, and wine bar. This is one of the few pre-1906 earthquake buildings in the city center.

Across the street from the Tower on Columbus Avenue is the:

7. **Purple Onion,** at 140 Columbus Ave. Many famous headliners have played here (often before they were famous), including Phyllis Diller (now so big that she's famous for something as simple as her laugh), who was still struggling when she played a 2-week engagement here in the late 1950s.

# Walking Tour—North Beach

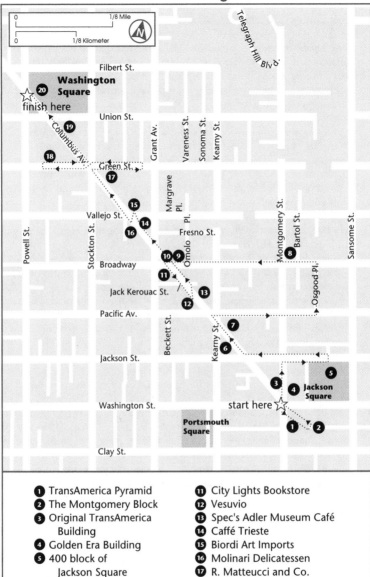

1 TransAmerica Pyramid
2 The Montgomery Block
3 Original TransAmerica Building
4 Golden Era Building
5 400 block of Jackson Square
6 Columbus Tower
7 Purple Onion
8 1010 Montgomery Street
9 hungry i
10 Former site of the Condor Club
11 City Lights Bookstore
12 Vesuvio
13 Spec's Adler Museum Café
14 Caffé Trieste
15 Biordi Art Imports
16 Molinari Delicatessen
17 R. Matteucci and Co. four-faced clock
18 Club Fugazi
19 Mario's Bohemian Cigar Store
20 Washington Square

Turn right on Pacific Avenue, and just after you cross Montgomery Street you'll be at brick-lined Osgood Place on the left, which is now registered as a Historic Landmark and, as a result, is one of the few quiet—and car-free—little alleyways left in the city. Stroll up Osgood and go left on Broadway to:

8. **1010 Montgomery St.** (at the corner of Montgomery and Broadway). This is where Allen Ginsberg lived during the time he wrote his legendary poem *Howl,* first performed on October 13, 1955, in a converted auto-repair shop at the corner of Fillmore and Union streets. By the time Ginsberg finished reading, he was crying and the audience was going wild. Jack Kerouac proclaimed, "Ginsberg, this poem will make you famous in San Francisco." Continue along Broadway toward Columbus Avenue. This particular stretch of Broadway is San Francisco's answer to New York's Times Square, complete with strip clubs and peep shows. Currently it's among the most sought-after locations in the city as more and more highly profitable restaurants and clubs continue to spring up.

Along the way, on the right side of the street, you'll come to Columbus Books, 540 Broadway, which sells new and used discount books and is worth a quick trip inside for a good, cheap read.

A few dozen yards further up Broadway is the current location of the:

9. **hungry i,** 546 Broadway. Now a seedy strip club, the original "hungry i" (which was located at 599 Jackson St.) was owned and operated by the vociferous "Big Daddy" Nordstrom. If you had been here while Banducci was in charge, you would have found only a plain room with an exposed brick wall and director's chairs around small tables, but a who's who of nightclub entertainers fortified their careers at the original hungry i, including Lenny Bruce, Billie Holiday (who first sang "Strange Fruit" here), Bill Cosby, Richard Pryor, Woody Allen, and Barbra Streisand.

When you get to the corner of Broadway and Columbus Avenue, you will also see the:

10. **Former site of the Condor Club,** 300 Columbus Ave., where Carol Doda scandalously bared her breasts and danced topless for the first time in 1964 (note the bronze plaque claiming the Condor Club as "Birthplace of the world's first topless & bottomless entertainment"). Go inside what is now the Condor Bistro and have a look at the framed newspaper clippings that hang around the dining room. From the elevated back room, you can see Doda's old dressing-room, and, on the floor below, an outline of the piano that would descend from the second floor with her atop it.

When you leave the Condor Bistro, cross to the south side of Broadway. Note the mural of jazz musicians painted on the whole side of the building directly across Columbus. Across Columbus Avenue, diagonally across the intersection from the Condor Bistro, is the:

11. **City Lights Bookstore,** at 261 Columbus Ave. Owned by one of the first Beat poets to arrive in San Francisco, Lawrence Ferlinghetti, City Lights is now a city landmark and literary mecca—one of the last of the Beat-era hangouts in operation. As an active member in the Beat movement, Ferlinghetti established his shop as a meeting place where writers and bibliophiles could (and still do) attend poetry readings and other events. It's still a vibrant part of the literary scene in San Francisco; a well-stocked bookshop prides itself on its collection of art, poetry, and political paperbacks.

Upon exiting the City Lights Bookstore, turn right, cross aptly named Jack Kerouac Street, and stop by the bar named:

**12. Vesuvio,** 255 Columbus Ave. (at Broadway). Because of its proximity to City Lights Bookstore, Vesuvio became a favorite hangout of the Beats. Originally opened in 1949, Dylan Thomas used to drink here, as did Jack Kerouac, Ferlinghetti, and Ginsberg. Even today, Vesuvio still maintains its original bohemian atmosphere. The building itself dates from 1913, and is an excellent example of pressed-tin architecture.

Facing Vesuvio across Columbus Avenue are two other favorite spots of the Beat Generation:

**13. Spec's Adler Museum Café,** 12 Saroyan Place, is one of the city's funkiest bars, a small, dimly-lit watering hole with ceiling-hung maritime flags and exposed brick walls crammed with a hodgepodge of memorabilia. Within the bar is a minimuseum that consists of a few glass cases filled with mementos brought back and dropped off by various seamen who have frequented the pub.

From here, go up Columbus across Broadway to Grant Avenue, where you should turn right, walking until you come to Vallejo Street. At 606 Vallejo St. (at the corner of Vallejo Street and Grant Avenue) is:

**14. Caffe Trieste,** yet another favorite spot of the Beats, that was founded by Gianni Giotta in 1956 and is still run by his family members. The quintessential San Francisco coffeehouse, Trieste features opera on the jukebox and the real thing, performed by the Giottas, on Saturday afternoons. Any day of the week is a good one to stop in for a cappuccino or espresso, since the beans are roasted right next door.

Go left out of Caffe Trieste onto Vallejo Street, turn right on Columbus Avenue, and bump into the loveliest shop in all of North Beach:

**15. Biordi Art Imports,** at 412 Columbus Ave. The shopkeepers have been importing hand-painted Majolica pottery from the hill towns of central Italy for more than 50 years. Some of the colorful patterns date from the 14th century. Biordi hand-picks its artisans, and in their catalog you'll find biographies of those who are currently represented.

Across Columbus Avenue at the corner of Vallejo is:

**16. Molinari Delicatessen,** 373 Columbus Ave. (☎ **415/421-2337**), which has been selling pungent, air-dried salamis since 1896. They still make their own ravioli and tortellini in the back of the shop, but it's the mouthwatering selection of cold salads, cheeses, and marinades up front that captures the attention of most folks. The Italian subs are big enough for two hearty appetites.

Continue up Columbus Avenue about half a block, and across the street you'll see the:

**17. R. Matteucci and Co. four-faced clock.** Located directly in front of the R. Matteucci jewelry store at 450 Columbus Ave., the ornate clock, which dates from 1908, is the only four-faced clock in working order in San Francisco and one of the few fine-quality old street clocks left in the city. It's a spring-wound clock manufactured by Seth Thomas, and the proprietor of the jewelry store, Matteo Ciuffreda, dutifully wound it every Saturday morning until the winding mechanism was stolen 21 years ago (it's now electric). Legend has it that it kept excellent time until its owner, jeweler Rocco Matteuchi, died, after which it stopped for a week of mourning and began again.

Walk back to the lively intersection of Columbus, Green, and Stockton, cross Columbus Avenue, and continue west on Green to:

**18. Club Fugazi,** at 678 Beach Blanket Babylon Blvd. (an extension of Green Street, between Columbus and Powell streets). It doesn't look like much from the outside, but Fugazi Hall stages San Francisco's legendary musical revue "Beach Blanket Babylon." The show evolved from Steve Silver's Rent-a-Freak service, which consisted of a group of party-goers who would attend parties dressed as any number of characters in outrageous costumes. The fun caught on, and soon came Beach Blanket Babylon. You'll love this supercharged show, which is definitely worth the price of admission.

On the way back to Columbus Avenue, be sure to stop in at O'Reilly's Irish Pub (622 Green St.) to see the mural of Irish authors that peer out from the back wall (How many can you name?). As you come out of O'Reilly's, turn left, cross Columbus Avenue, and proceed 1 block northwest on Columbus to:

**19. Mario's Bohemian Cigar Store.** Located across the street from Washington Square at 566 Columbus Ave. is one of North Beach's most popular neighborhood hangouts: Mario's. This historic, tiny, and charmingly threadbare bar has long been a popular meeting place for aged Sicilians and Beat poets, though nowadays it attracts all types, including the occasional tourist in search of a cigar (of which none are sold nor welcome in this former cigar store). Oddly enough, they don't serve regular ol' coffee, though the hot focaccia sandwiches are superb.

Our next stop, directly across Union Street, is:

**20. Washington Square,** one of the oldest parks in the city. This land was designated a public park in 1847 and has undergone many changes since then. Its current landscaping dates from 1955. Even though it's called a "square," this little oasis in the middle of such a bustling neighborhood sort of lost its square status when Columbus Avenue was laid out and one of its four corners was lopped off. Why isn't it named Columbus Square? Because the park was named in the 1850s before Montgomery Avenue was changed to Columbus Avenue.

# Shopping 9

Like its population, San Francisco's shopping is both worldly and intimate. Every persuasion, style, era, fetish, and financial status is represented here—not in big, tacky shopping malls, but in hundreds of quaint and dramatically diverse boutiques scattered throughout the city. Whether it's a Chanel knockoff or Chinese herbal medicine you're looking for, San Francisco's got it. Just pick a shopping neighborhood and give yourself a spending budget, and you're sure to end up with at least a few affordable take-home treasures. For those of you who travel cheaply so you can blow your wad on expensive mementos—or at least like to pretend you can—we've also included a few of San Francisco's more costly but noteworthy shops, as well as the best of the city's discount shopping scene.

## 1 The Shopping Scene

### MAJOR SHOPPING AREAS

San Francisco has many shopping areas, but the following places are where you'll find most of the action:

**Union Square & Environs** San Francisco's most congested and popular shopping mecca is centered around Union Square and enclosed by Bush, Taylor, Market, and Montgomery streets. Most of the big department stores and many high-end specialty shops are in this area. Be sure to venture to Grant Avenue, Post and Sutter streets, and Maiden Lane.

**Chinatown** When you pass under the gate to Chinatown on Grant Avenue, say good-bye to the world of fashion and hello to a swarm of cheap tourist shops selling everything from linen and jade to plastic toys and $2 slippers. But that's not all Chinatown has to offer. The real gems here are tucked on side streets or are small, one-person shops selling Chinese herbs, original art, and jewelry. Grant Avenue is the area's main thoroughfare, and side streets between Bush Street and Columbus Avenue are full of restaurants, markets, and eclectic shops. Walking is best, since traffic through this area is slow at best and parking is next to impossible. Most of the stores in Chinatown are open daily from 10am to 10pm. Serviced by bus lines 9X, 15, 30, 41, and 45.

**Union Street** Union Street, from Fillmore to Van Ness, caters to the upper–middle-class crowd. It's a great place to stroll, window-shop the plethora of boutiques, cafes, and restaurants, and watch the beautiful people parade by. Serviced by bus lines 22, 41, 42, and 45.

**Chestnut Street** Parallel to and a few blocks north of Union Street, Chestnut is a younger Union Street, with endless shopping and dining choices, and the ever-tanned, superfit population of postgraduate singles who hang around cafes and scope each other out. Serviced by bus lines 22, 28, 30, 41, 42, 43, and 76.

**Fillmore Street** Some of the best shopping in town is packed into 5 blocks of Fillmore Street in Pacific Heights. From Jackson to Sutter streets, Fillmore is the perfect place to grab a bite and peruse the high-priced boutiques, craft shops, and incredible houseware stores. Don't miss Zinc Details and Fillamento. Serviced by bus lines 1, 2, 3, 4, 12, 22, and 24.

**Haight Street** Green hair, spiked hair, no hair, or mohair—even the hippies look conservative next to Haight Street's dramatic fashion freaks. The shopping in the 6 blocks of upper Haight Street, between Central Avenue and Stanyan Street, reflects its clientele and offers everything from incense and European and American street styles to furniture and antique clothing. Bus lines 7, 66, 71, and 73 run the length of Haight Street. The Muni metro N line stops at Waller Street and at Cole Street.

**SoMa** Though this area isn't suitable for strolling, you'll find almost all the discount shopping in warehouse spaces South of Market. You can pick up a discount-shopping guide at most major hotels. Many bus lines pass through this area.

**Hayes Valley** It may not be the prettiest area in town (with some of the shadier housing projects a few blocks away), but while most neighborhoods cater to more conservative or trendy shoppers, lower Hayes Street, between Octavia and Gough, celebrates anything vintage, artistic, or downright funky. Though still in its developmental stage, it's definitely the most interesting new shopping area in town, with furniture and glass stores, thrift shops, trendy shoe stores, and men's and women's clothiers. There are also lots of great antique shops south on Octavia and on nearby Market Street. Bus lines include 16AX, 16BX, and 21.

**Fisherman's Wharf & Environs** The tourist-oriented malls run along Jefferson Street and include hundreds of shops, restaurants, and attractions. Ghirardelli Square, Pier 39, the Cannery, and the Anchorage are all outlined under "Shopping Centers & Complexes," below.

## HOURS, TAXES & SHIPPING

Store hours are generally Monday to Saturday from 10am to 6pm and Sunday from noon to 5pm. Most department stores stay open later, as do shops around Fisherman's Wharf, the most heavily visited area.

Sales tax in San Francisco is 8.5%, which is added on at the register for all goods and services purchased. If you live out of state and buy an expensive item, you may want to consider having the store ship it home for you. You will escape paying the sales tax, but will have to pay for its transport.

Most of the city's shops can wrap your purchase and ship it anywhere in the world via United Parcel Service (UPS). If they can't, you can send it yourself, either through **UPS** (☎ **800/742-5877**) or through the U.S. mail (see "Fast Facts: San Francisco" in chapter 4).

# Hitting the Outlets

There are many factory outlet stores in San Francisco, selling overstocked and discontinued fashions at bargain prices. All the following shops are located south of Market Street, in the city's warehouse district, known as SoMa.

At the **Esprit Outlet Store,** 499 Illinois St., at 16th Street (☎ **415/ 957-2550**), you'll find all the Esprit collections and Susie Tompkins merchandise at 30% or more off regular retail prices. In addition to clothes, the store sells accessories, shoes, and assorted other items. Open Monday to Friday from 10am to 8pm, Saturday from 10am to 7pm, and Sunday from 11am to 6pm.

✪ **Jeremys,** Two South Park, at 2nd Street (☎ **415/882-4929**), is a SoMa boutique offering top designer fashions from shoes to suits, all at rock-bottom prices. No cheap knockoffs here—just good men's and women's clothes and accessories. New West also has its own stylish clothing line. Open Monday to Saturday from 10am to 5pm and on Sunday from noon to 5pm.

Well known for its sporting, camping, and hiking equipment, **The North Face,** 1325 Howard St., between 9th and 10th streets (☎ **415/626-6444**), has an off-price outlet carrying a limited but high-quality selection of skiwear, boots, sweaters, and outdoor goods such as tents, packs, and sleeping bags. The North Face makes heavy use of Gore-Tex, down, and other durable, lightweight materials. Open Monday to Friday from 10am to 8pm, Saturday from 10am to 7pm, and Sunday from 11am to 6pm.

And then there are the national classics. As its name hints, the **Burlington Coat Factory,** 899 Howard St., at 5th Street (☎ **415/495-7234**), has hundreds of coats—from cheapies to designer—as well as men's and women's clothing, shoes, and accessories. But the best deal is the home section, where designer bedding, bath, and housewares go for a fraction of their normal retail prices. Open Monday to Saturday from 10am to 8pm and on Sunday from 11am to 7pm.

San Francisco's branch of **Loehmann's,** 222 Sutter St., between Kearny Street and Grant Avenue (☎ **415/982-3215**), caters to a sophisticated white-collar crowd, so you won't find as much tacky fashion as you might at more suburban locations of this discount designer chain. Many women swear that this place has the ultimate in professional clothing at bargain prices. Open Monday to Friday from 9am to 8pm, Saturday from 9:30am to 8pm, and Sunday from 11am to 6pm.

# 2 Shopping A to Z

## ANTIQUES

**Jackson Square,** a historic district just north of the Financial District's Embarcadero Center, is the place to go for the top names in fine furniture and fine art. More than a dozen dealers on the 2 blocks between Columbus and Sansome streets specialize in European furnishings from the 17th to the 19th centuries; there are many Asian-art dealers here as well. Yes, it's expensive, but it sure is fun to browse. Most shops here are open Monday to Friday from 9am to 5pm and Saturday from 11am to 4pm.

**Butterfield & Butterfield.** 220 San Bruno Ave. (at 16th St.). ☎ **415/861-7500.**

This renowned auction house holds preview weekends for upcoming auctions of furnishings, silver, antiques, art, and jewelry. It offers an opportunity to find some real deals on antiques. The office open Monday through Friday from 8:30am to 5pm.

**Fumiki Fine Asian Arts.** 272 Sutter St. (at Grant Ave.). ☎ **415/922-0573.**

Although this store moved recently, it's new, much bigger space still has one of the largest collections of antique Japanese *Imari* and Korean and Japanese *tansus* in the country, as well as an extensive collection of Asian art and antiques, including Japanese baskets and Chinese artifacts and embroidery. Open Monday to Saturday from 10am to 6pm and Sunday from noon to 5pm.

## ART

Note: *The San Francisco Gallery Guide,* a comprehensive, bimonthly publication listing the city's current shows, is available free by mail. Send a self-addressed stamped envelope to San Francisco Bay Area Gallery Guide, 1369 Fulton St., San Francisco, CA 94117 (☎ **415/921-1600**), or pick one up at the San Francisco Visitor Information Center at 900 Market St.

**Atelier Dore.** 771 Bush St. (between Mason and Powell sts.). ☎ **415/391-2423.**

Atelier Dore features American and European paintings from the 19th and 20th centuries, including some WPA art. Open Tuesday to Saturday from 11am to 5pm; Monday by appointment only.

**✪ Catharine Clark Gallery.** 49 Geary St., 2nd floor (between Kearny and Grant sts.). ☎ **415/399-1439.**

Catharine Clark's is a different kind of gallery experience. While many galleries focus on already-established artists and out-of-this world price points, Catharine's exhibits up-and-coming contemporary artists (who are mainly from California) and nurtures beginning collectors by offering an unusual purchasing plan. Almost unheard of in the art business, you can buy a piece here on layaway and take up to a year to pay for it—interest free! Prices here make art a realistic purchase for everyone for a change, but serious collectors still frequent her shows because she has such a keen eye for talent. Shows change every four to six weeks. No credit cards are accepted. Open Tuesday to Friday from 10:30am to 5:30pm and Saturday from 11am to 5:30pm; 1st Thursday of the month from 10:30am to 7:30pm.

**Eleonore Austerer.** 540 Sutter St. (between Powell and Mason sts.). ☎ **415/986-2244.**

Limited-edition graphics by modern masters like Braque, Matisse, Miró, Picasso, Calder, Chagall, and Hockney, as well as original works by European and American contemporary artists can be found at Eleonore Austerer. The gallery, located in a beautiful old building near Union Square, is open Monday to Saturday from 10am to 6pm.

**Fraenkel Gallery.** 49 Geary St., 4th floor (between Grant Ave. and Kearny St.). ☎ **415/981-2661.**

This photography gallery features works by contemporary American and European artists. Excellent shows change frequently. Open Tuesday to Friday from 10:30am to 5:30pm and Saturday from 11am to 5pm.

**Images of the North.** 1782 Union St. (at Octavia St.). ☎ **415/673-1273.**

The highlight here is one of the most extensive collections of Canadian and Alaskan Inuit art in the United States. There's also a fine collection of Native American masks and jewelry. Open Monday to Saturday from 11am to 5:30pm and Sunday from noon to 4pm.

**Maxwell Galleries.** 559 Sutter St. (between Powell and Mason sts.). ☎ **415/421-5193.**

The specialties at Maxwell Galleries are 19th- and 20th-century European and American sculpture and paintings, including works by Raphael and Butler. Open Monday to Friday from 9:30am to 5:15pm and Saturday from 11am to 5pm.

**Meyerovich Gallery.** 251 Post St., 4th floor (at Stockton St.). ☎ **415/421-7171.**

Works on paper by modern and contemporary masters here include Chagall, Matisse, Miró, and Picasso. Their new Contemporary Gallery, which is located directly across the hall, features works by Lichtenstein, Motherwell, Dine, and Hockney. Check 'em out on the Web at **www.meyerovchgallery.com**. Open Monday to Friday from 9:30am to 6pm, Saturday from 10am to 5pm, and by appointment.

## BIKER ATTIRE

**Dudley Perkins Co./Harley Davidson.** 66 Page St. (at Franklin St.). ☎ **415/703-9477.**

You may not be able to afford a hot new hog, but you can at least dress the part. You'll find all the leather biking attire and accessories you'll need at this full-service shop, which also happens to be the world's oldest Harley dealership. Open Sunday to Wednesday and Friday from 8am to 6pm, and Saturday from 9am to 5pm.

## BOOKS

**Barnes and Noble Booksellers.** 2552 Taylor St., near Fisherman's Wharf. ☎ **415/ 292-6762.**

When you've given up trying to find a parking space at Borders in Union Square, come to Barnes and Noble, which offers something few other bookstores in the city can match: free parking. The megastore carries more than 150,000 titles, including all the bestsellers, works from smaller presses, and thousands of magazines. They have a great children's department and a small cafe as well. Open daily from 9am to 11pm.

**The Booksmith.** 1644 Haight St. (between Clayton and Cole sts.). ☎ **800/493-7323** orr 415/863-8688. www.booksmith.com. E-mail: read@booksmith.com.

Haight Street's best selection of new books is housed in this large, well-maintained shop. It carries all the top titles, along with works from smaller presses, and more than 1,000 different magazines. Open Monday to Saturday from 10am to 9pm and Sunday from 10am to 6pm.

**Borders Books & Music.** 400 Post St., at Union Square (at Powell and Post sts.). ☎ **415/399-1633.**

With three stories neatly packed with books, magazines, videos, a cafe, and plenty of reading nooks, it's a good thing this megastore is open late because you could spend hours browsing the selections. Open Monday through Thursday from 9am to 11pm, Friday and Saturday from 9am to midnight, and Sunday from 9am to 9pm.

✪ **City Lights Booksellers & Publishers.** 261 Columbus Ave. (at Broadway). ☎ **415/ 362-8193.**

Brooding literary types browse this famous bookstore owned by Lawrence Ferlinghetti, the renowned Beat-Generation poet. The three-level bookshop prides itself on a comprehensive collection of art, poetry, and political paperbacks, as well as more mainstream books. Open daily from 10am to midnight.

✪ **A Clean, Well-Lighted Place for Books.** 601 Van Ness Ave. (between Turk St. and Golden Gate Ave.). ☎ **415/441-6670.**

Voted best bookstore by the *San Francisco Bay Guardian,* this independent has good new fiction and nonfiction sections and also specializes in music, art, mystery, and cookbooks. The store is very well known for its schedule of author readings and events. For a calendar of events, call the store or check their Web site at **www.bookstore.com.** Open Monday through Thursday 10am to 11pm, Friday and Saturday from 10am to midnight, and Sunday from 10am to 9pm.

✪ **Green Apple Books.** 506 Clement St. (at 6th Ave.). ☎ **415/387-2272.**

The local favorite for used books, Green Apple is crammed with titles—more than 60,000 new and 100,000 used books. Their extended sections in psychology, cooking, art, history; collection of modern first editions; and rare graphic comics are only superseded by the staff's superlative service. Open Sunday to Thursday from 10am to 10:30pm, and Friday and Saturday from 10am to 11:30pm.

## CHINA, SILVER & GLASS

**The Enchanted Crystal.** 1895 Union St. (at Laguna St.). ☎ **415/885-1335.**

This shop has an extensive collection of fine crystal, art glass, jewelry, and one-of-a-kind decorative art, including one of the largest crystal balls in the world (from Madagascar). Open Monday to Saturday from 10am to 6pm and Sunday from noon to 5pm.

✪ **Gump's.** 135 Post St. (between Kearny St. and Grant Ave.). ☎ **415/982-1616.**

Founded over a century ago, Gump's offers gifts and treasures ranging from Asian antiquities to contemporary art glass, and exquisite jade and pearl jewelry. Many items are made specifically for the store. Gump's also has one of the most revered window displays each holiday season. Open Monday to Saturday from 10am to 6pm.

## CRAFTS

**The Canton Bazaar.** 616 Grant Ave. (between Sacramento and California sts.). ☎ **415/362-5750.**

Amid a wide variety of handicrafts you'll find an excellent selection of rosewood and carved furniture, cloisonné enamelware, rose Canton chinaware, porcelain ware, carved jade, embroideries, jewelry, and antiques from mainland China. Open daily from 10am to 10pm.

**The New Unique Company.** 838 Grant Ave. (between Clay and Washington sts.). ☎ **415/981-2036.**

Primarily a calligraphy- and watercolor-supplies store, the shop also has a good assortment of books relating to these topics. In addition, there is a wide selection of carved stones for use as seals on letters and documents. The store will carve seals to order should you want a special design or group of initials. Open Monday to Saturday from 10:30am to 6pm and Sunday from 11am to 6pm.

**Silkroute International.** 3119 Fillmore St. (at Filbert St.). ☎ **415/563-4936.**

Owned and operated by an Afghan who offers fascinating wares—old and new—from his native country, the shop sells Oriental and tribal rugs, kilims, dhurries, textiles, jewelry, clothing, pillows, arts, and antiques. Open Monday to Saturday from 11am to 6pm.

## DEPARTMENT STORES

**Macy's.** Corner of Stockton and O'Farrell sts., Union Sq. ☎ **415/397-3333.**

The seven-story Macy's West features contemporary fashions for women and juniors, including jewelry, fragrances, cosmetics, and accessories. The third floor offers a "hospitality suite" where visitors can leave their coats and packages, grab a cup of coffee, or find out more about the city from the concierge. The top floors contain home furnishings, while the Cellar sells kitchenware and gourmet foods. You'll even find a Boudin Cafe (great sandwiches!) and Wolfgang Puck Cafe on the premises. Across the street, Macy's East has five floors of men's and children's fashions, as well as the recently added, largest Men's Polo by Ralph Lauren shop in the country, and the Fresh Choice cafe. Macy's most recent acquisition, the old Emporium building at 835 Market (between Fourth and Fifth streets), is now temporarily a Macy's Home Store. A remodeling of the women's store will be complete at the end of 1999. Now if only the service were better. Open Monday to Saturday from 10am to 8pm and Sunday from 11am to 7pm.

**Neiman Marcus.** 150 Stockton St., Union Sq. ☎ **415/362-3900.**

Some call this unit of the Texas-based chain "Needless Mark-up." But if you've got the cash, the men's and women's clothes, precious gems, and conservative formal wear here are some of the most glamorous in town. The Rotunda Restaurant, on the top floor, is a beautiful, relaxing place for lunch and afternoon tea. Open Monday through Wednesday and Friday and Saturday from 10am to 7pm, Thursday 10am to 8pm, and Sunday from noon to 6pm.

**Nordstrom.** 865 Market St. (in the San Francisco Shopping Centre). ☎ **415/243-8500.**

Renowned for its personalized service, this is the largest member of the Seattle-based fashion department-store chain. Nordstrom occupies the top five floors of the San Francisco Shopping Centre (see "Shopping Centers & Complexes," below) and is that mall's primary anchor. Equally devoted to women's and men's fashions, the store has one of the best shoe selections in the city, and thousands of suits in stock. The Nordstrom Café, on the fourth floor, has a panoramic view and is an ideal place for an inexpensive lunch or light snack. The fifth floor is occupied by the Nordstrom Spa, the perfect place to relax after a hectic day of bargain hunting. Open Monday to Saturday from 9:30am to 9pm and Sunday from 10am to 7pm.

## FABRICS

**Britex Fabrics.** 146 Geary St. (between Stockton and Grant sts.). ☎ **415/392-2910.**

A San Francisco institution since 1952, Britex offers an absurd amount and variety of fabrics, not to mention over 30,000 button selections. Open Monday to Wednesday and Saturday from 9:30am to 6pm, and Thursday and Friday from 9:30am to 7pm. Closed Sunday.

## FASHIONS

**Grand Women's Boutique.** 1435 Grant Ave. (between Green and Union sts.). ☎ **415/951-0131.**

Invited to an underground club and forgot your funky rave attire? Grand's North Beach shop features the latest in fashion-forward street wear by local designers. Garb comes both baggy and tight; the style is club, and the price is right. Open daily from noon to 7pm.

**Gucci America.** 200 Stockton St. (between Geary and Post sts.). ☎ **415/392-2808.**

Donning Gucci's golden Gs is not a cheap endeavor. But if you've got the cash, you'll find all the latest lines of shoes, leather goods, scarves, and pricey accessories, such as a $7,000 handmade crocodile bag. Open Monday to Saturday 10am to 6pm and on Sunday noon to 5pm.

**Niketown.** 278 Post St. (at Stockton St.). ☎ **415/392-6453.**

Here it's not "I can," but "I can spend." At least that's what the kings of sportswear were banking on when they opened this megastore in 1997. As you'd expect, inside the doors it's Nike's world, offering everything the merchandising team could create. Open Monday to Friday from 10am to 8pm, Saturday from 10am to 7pm, and Sunday from 11am to 6pm.

**Three Bags Full.** 2181 Union St. (at Fillmore). ☎ **415/567-5753.** www.threebagsfull.com.

Snuggling up in a cozy sweater can be a fashionable event if you do your shopping at this pricey boutique, which carries the gamut in handmade and one-of-a-kind playful and extravagant knitwear. Open daily from 10:30am to 5pm. Other city locations are 500 Sutter St. and 3314 Sacramento St.

## MEN'S FASHIONS

**All American Boy.** 463 Castro St. (between Market and 18th sts.). ☎ **415/861-0444.**

Long known for setting the mainstream style for gay men, All American Boy is the quintessential Castro clothing shop. Open Monday to Thursday and Sunday from 10am to 7pm and Friday and Saturday from 10am to 8pm.

**Citizen Clothing.** 536 Castro St. (between 18th and 19th sts.). ☎ **415/558-9429.**

The Castro has some of America's best men's casual clothing stores, and this is one of them. Stylish (but not faddish) pants, tops, and accessories are sold here. Open Monday to Saturday from 10am to 8pm and Sunday from 11am to 7pm.

**MAC.** 5 Claude Lane (off Sutter St. between Grant Ave. and Kearny St.). ☎ **415/837-0615.**

The more-classic-than-corporate man shops here for imported tailored suits in new and intriguing fabrics. Lines include London's Katherine Hamnett, Belgium's SO, Italy's Alberto Biani, New York's John Bartlett, and one of our personal favorites, San Francisco's Lat Naylor. Open Monday to Saturday from 11am to 6pm and Sunday from noon to 5pm. Their women's store is located at 1543 Grant Ave. (between Filbert and Union streets; ☎ **415/837-1604**).

## WOMEN'S FASHIONS

**Bella Donna.** 539 Hayes St. (between Laguna and Octavia sts.). ☎ **415/861-7182.**

Another blessing to the small but growing Hayes Valley alternative shopping mecca is this expensive but quality boutique offering luxurious women's clothing, such as hand-knit sweaters, silky slip dresses, and fashionable knit hats. There's also a wonderful (albeit expensive) collection of vases and other household trinkets, as well as a small selection of remainder fabrics. Upstairs, the wedding and bridal section focuses on the vintage look. Open Tuesday through Saturday from 11am to 7pm and Sunday from 11am to 5pm; bridals by appointment only.

**The Chanel Boutique.** 155 Maiden Lane (between Stockton St. and Grant Ave.). ☎ **415/981-1550.**

Ever fashionable and expensive, Chanel is appropriately located on Maiden Lane, the quaint downtown side street where the most exclusive stores and spas cluster.

You'll find what you'd expect from Chanel: clothing, accessories, scents, cosmetics, and jewelry. Open Monday to Saturday from 10am to 6pm and Sunday from noon to 5pm.

⊙ **Métier.** 355 Sutter St. (between Grant and Stockton sts.). ☎ **415/989-5395.**

The classic, sophisticated, and expensive creations for women found here include European ready-to-wear lines and designers Peter Cohen, Georgina Von Etzdorf, Alberto Biani, and local Lat Naylor, as well as a distinguished collection of antique-style, high-end jewelry from LA's Kathie Waterman. Open Monday to Saturday from 10am to 6pm. Closed Sunday.

**Solo Fashion.** 1599 Haight St. (at Clayton St.). ☎ **415/621-0342.**

While strolling upper Haight, stop in here for a good selection of upbeat, contemporary, English-style streetwear, along with a collection of dresses designed exclusively for this shop. Open daily from 11am to 7pm.

## CHILDREN'S FASHIONS

**Minis.** 2042 Union St. (between Webster and Buchanan sts.). ☎ **415/567-9537.**

Christina Profili, a San Francisco native who used to design for Banana Republic, opened this children's clothing store selling her own creations. Every piece, from shirts to pants and dresses, is made from cotton or organic cotton. Every outfit perfectly coordinates with everything else in the store. Minis also offers educational and creative toys and storybooks with matching dolls, and most recently, maternity wear. Open daily from 10:30am to 6:30pm.

## VINTAGE CLOTHING

**Aardvark's.** 1501 Haight St. (at Ashbury St.). ☎ **415/621-3141.**

One of San Francisco's largest secondhand clothing dealers, Aardvark's has seemingly endless racks of shirts, pants, dresses, skirts, and hats from the last 30 years. Open daily from 11am to 7pm.

**Buffalo Exchange.** 1555 Haight St. (between Clayton and Ashbury sts.). ☎ **415/ 431-7733.**

This large storefront on upper Haight Street is crammed with racks of antique and new fashions from the 1960s, 1970s, and 1990s. It stocks everything from suits and dresses to neckties, hats, handbags, and jewelry. Buffalo Exchange anticipates some of the hottest new street fashions. Open Monday to Saturday from 11am to 7pm and Sunday from noon to 6pm. A second shop is located at 1800 Polk St. (at Washington St.; ☎ **415/346-5726**).

**Crossroads Trading Company.** 2231 Market St. (between Noe and Sanchez sts.). ☎ **415/ 626-8989** and 1901 Fillmore St. (at Bush St.; ☎ **415/775-8885**).

Vintage clothing used to imply used, cool, and cheap. Yet, in San Francisco, the motto is often "The older it is, the more it costs." Luckily, we found this gem in the Castro. It's the perfect spot to score killer finds for men, women, or "others." The top-quality merchandise is sold at the kinds of low, low prices that made this genre of boutique so irresistible in the first place. Open Monday to Saturday from 11am to 7pm and Sunday from noon to 6pm.

⊙ **Good Byes.** 3464 Sacramento St. and 3483 Sacramento St. (between Laurel and Walnut sts.). ☎ **415/346-6388.**

One of the best new- and used-clothes stores in San Francisco, Good Byes carries only high-quality clothing and accessories, including an exceptional selection of men's fashions at unbelievably low prices (for example, $350 pre-owned shoes for $35). Women's wear is in a separate boutique across the street. Open Friday to Wednesday from 10am to 6pm, and Thursday from 10am to 8pm.

**La Rosa.** 1711 Haight St. (at Cole). ☎ **415/668-3744.**

On a street packed with vintage-clothing shops, this is one of the more upscale options, featuring a selection of high-quality, dry-cleaned secondhand goods. Formal suits and dresses are its specialty, but you'll also find sport coats, slacks, and shoes. You may also want to visit its more moderately priced sister store, Held Over, on Haight near **Ashbury.** Open daily from 11am to 7pm.

**Wasteland.** 1660 Haight St. (at Cole St.). ☎ **415/863-3150.**

The enormous art-filled exterior fronts a large collection of vintage and contemporary clothes for men and women. Leathers, natural fibers, and dark colors predominate. Grandma's furniture is also for sale. Open daily from 11am to 7pm.

## FLEA MARKETS

**Alemany Flea.** 100 Alemany (off U.S. 101 in Bernal Heights).

Held beneath the ramps of the U.S. 101 and I-280 interchange, this market is a great place to pick up inexpensive collectibles, antiques, appliances, and all sorts of bric-a-brac, both new and old. On Saturday mornings, this is the same site as the Certified Farmers Market. Open Sunday from 8am to 3pm.

**Pier 29 Antique and Collectible Market.** Pier 29 (on the Embarcadero at Sansome and Chestnut sts.).

Dozens of serious dealers of collectible antiques, books, jewelry, furniture, clothing and such display their wares in this huge dock house (key on cold and rainy days). Open Sunday from 9:30am to 5pm.

**San Francisco Flea Market.** 1651 Mission St. (where Mission St. and S. Van Ness Ave. intersect near 12th St.).

Antiques, toys, appliances, jewelry, junk, and gems both new and used are displayed from early morning until late afternoon in a large parking lot on the edge of the SoMa district. It's far more unorthodox than the Pier 29 Market, and a whole lot easier to get to than Alemany Flea. Open Saturday and Sunday from 6am to 4:30pm.

## FOOD

**Golden Gate Fortune Cookies Co.** 56 Ross Alley (between Washington and Jackson sts.). ☎ **415/781-3956.**

This tiny, touristy factory sells fortune cookies hot off the press. You can purchase them in small bags or in bulk, and if your order is large enough, you may even be able to negotiate your own message. Even if you're not buying, stop in to see how these sugary treats are made (although the staff can get pushy for you to buy). Open daily from 10am to 7pm.

✪ **Joseph Schmidt Confections.** 3489 16th St. (at Sanchez St.). ☎ **800/861-8682** or 415/861-8682.

Chocolate takes the shape of exquisite sculptural masterpieces, such as long-stemmed tulips and heart-shaped boxes, that are so beautiful, you'll be hesitant to bite the head off your adorable chocolate panda bear. But once you do, you'll know why this is the most popular chocolatier in town. Prices are also remarkably reasonable. Open Monday to Saturday from 10am to 6:30pm.

✪ **Ten Ren Tea Company.** 949 Grant Ave. (between Washington and Jackson sts.). ☎ **415/362-0656.**

At the Ten Ren Tea Company you will be offered a steaming cup of roselle tea, made of black tea and hibiscus. In addition to a selection of almost 50 traditional and herbal teas, the company stocks related paraphernalia, such as pots, cups, and infusers. If you can't make up your mind, take home a mail-order form. Open daily from 9am to 9pm.

## GIFTS

**Art of China.** 839–843 Grant Ave. (between Clay and Washington sts.). ☎ **415/981-1602.**

Amid a wide variety of collectibles, this shop features exquisite, hand-carved Chinese figurines. You'll also find a lovely assortment of ivory beads, bracelets, necklaces, and earrings. Pink-quartz dogs, jade figurines, porcelain vases, cache pots, and blue-and-white barrels suitable for use as table bases are just some of the many collectibles on offer. Open daily from 10am to 6pm.

**Babushka.** 333 Jefferson St. (at Leavenworth St.). ☎ **415/673-6740.**

Located near Fisherman's Wharf, adjacent to the Anchorage Shopping Center, Babushka sells only Russian products, most of which are wooden or papier-mâché nesting dolls. Open Monday to Friday 9am to 10pm, Saturday and Sunday from 9am to 10:30pm.

**Cost Plus Imports.** 2552 Taylor St. (between North Point and Bay sts.). ☎ **415/928-6200.**

At the Fisherman's Wharf cable-car turntable, Cost Plus is a vast warehouse crammed to the rafters with Chinese baskets, Indian camel bells, Malaysian batik scarves, and innumerable other items from Algeria to Zanzibar. More than 20,000 items from 40 nations are purchased directly from their country of origin and packed into this well-priced warehouse. They also have a decent wine shop. Open daily from 9am to 9pm.

✪ **Dandelion.** 55 Potrero Ave. (at Alameda St.). ☎ **415/436-9500.**

Many locals were dismayed when, after almost 20 years in business, Dandelion closed its doors on California Street a few years back. But owners Steve, Del, and Carl weren't finished for good. Their new location is larger and even more packed with the most wonderful collection of gifts, collectibles, and furnishings. There's something for every taste and budget here, ranging from an excellent collection of teapots, decorative dishes, and gourmet foods, to silver, books, cards, and picture frames. Don't miss the Zen-like second floor, with its variety of peaceful furnishings in Indian, Japanese, and Western styles. Open Tuesday through Saturday from 10am to 6pm; closed Sunday and Monday.

**Distractions & Euphoria.** 1552 Haight St. (between Ashbury and Clayton sts.). ☎ **415/252-8751.**

This is the best of the Haight Street shops selling pseudo-1960s memorabilia, street fashion, ravewear, and underground electronica CDs. You'll find retro hippie clothes, pipes, toys, and stickers are liberally intermixed with tie-dyed Grateful Dead paraphernalia and lots of cool stuff to look at. Open daily from 10:30am to 7:30pm.

**Flax.** 1699 Market St. (at Valencia and Gough sts.). ☎ **415/552-2355.** www.flaxart.com.

If you're the type of person who goes into an art store for a special pencil and comes out $300 later, don't go near this shop. Flax has everything you can think of in art and design supplies, along with an amazing collection of locals' arts and crafts, blank bound books, children's art supplies, frames, calendars, you name it. There's a gift for every type of person here, especially you. If you can't stop by, call for a mail-order catalog. Open Monday to Saturday from 9:30am to 6pm.

✪ **Good Vibrations.** 1210 Valencia St. (at 23rd St.). ☎ **800/BUY-VIBE,** or 415/974-8980 for mail order. www.goodvibes.com.

A layperson's sex-toy, book, and video emporium, Good Vibrations is specifically designed (but not exclusively) for women. Unlike most sex shops, it's not a back-alley business, but rather a straightforward shop with healthy and open attitudes about human sexuality. They also have a vibrator museum. Open Sunday to Thursday from 11am to 7pm and Friday and Saturday from 11am to 8pm. A second location is in Berkeley at 2504 San Pablo Ave.

**Quantity Postcards.** 1441 Grant St. (at Green St.). ☎ **415/986-8866.**

You'll find the perfect postcard for literally everyone you know here, as well as some depictions of old San Francisco, movie stars, and Day-Glo posters featuring concert-poster artist Frank Kozik. Prices range from 35¢ to $2 per card, and even if you don't need any cards, you'll enjoy browsing the eclectic collection of mailables. Open Sunday to Thursday from 11am to 11pm and Friday to Saturday from 11am to 12:30am.

✪ **SFMOMA MuseumStore.** 151 Third St. (2 blocks south of Market St., across from Yerba Buena Gardens). ☎ **415/357-4035.** www.sfmoma.org.

With an array of artistic cards, books, jewelry, housewares, knickknacks, and creative tokens of San Francisco, it's virtually impossible not to find something you'll consider a must-have. (Check out the Fog Dome!) Aside from being one of the locals' favorite shops, it also offers far more tasteful mementos than most Fisherman's Wharf options. Open daily from 10:30am to 6:30pm. You can request a catalog via e-mail at museumstore@sfmoma.org.

**Smile.** 500 Sutter St. (between Powell and Mason sts.). ☎ **415/362-3436.**

Need a little humor in your life? Smile specializes in whimsical art, furniture, clothing, jewelry, and American crafts guaranteed to make you grin. Open Monday to Saturday from 9:30am to 5:30pm.

## HOUSEWARES/FURNISHINGS

✪ **Biordi Art Imports.** 412 Columbus Ave. (at Vallejo St.). ☎ **415/392-8096.**

Whether it's your intention to decorate your dinner table, color your kitchen, or liven up the living room, Biordi's Italian Majolica pottery is the most exquisite and unique way to do it. The owner has been importing these hand-painted collectibles for 50 years, and every piece is a showstopper. Call for a catalog if you like. They'll ship anywhere. Open Monday to Saturday from 9:30am to 6pm. Closed Sunday.

✪ **Fillamento.** 2185 Fillmore St. (at Sacramento St.). ☎ **415/931-2224.**

The best housewares store in the city, Fillamento's three floors are always packed with shoppers searching for the most classic, artistic, and refined housewares. Whether you're looking to set a good table or revamp your bedroom, you'll find it all here. Open daily from 10am to 6pm.

**Maison Ideale.** 1501 Waller St. (at Clayton St.). ☎ **415/682-0112.**

French home furnishings are celebrated at this lovely neighborhood boutique. Here you'll find everything from armoires to kitchen and dining room accoutrements to vintage vases. If you like, the shop will custom finish your piece in a perfect faux-marble finish. Open Tuesday to Friday from 9:30am to 5pm and Saturday from 10:30am to 5pm.

**Victorian Interiors.** 575 Hayes St. (at Laguna St.). ☎ **415/431-7191.**

Draped with an array of period floral wallpapers, this little store is the perfect place to shop for any Victorian fanatic. Along with traditional Victorian housewares such as wallpapers, moldings, drapery cornices and rods, tiles, fabrics, and carpets, you'll find a great collection of old pipes and knickknacks. Open Tuesday to Saturday from 11am to 6pm and Sunday from noon to 5pm.

**The Wok Shop.** 718 Grant Ave. (at Clay St.). ☎ **888/780-7171** for mail order, or 415/ 989-3797. www.wokshop.com.

This shop has every conceivable implement for Chinese cooking, including woks, brushes, cleavers, circular chopping blocks, dishes, oyster knives, bamboo steamers, strainers—you name it. The shop also sells a wide range of kitchen utensils, baskets, handmade linens from China, and aprons. Open Sunday to Friday from 10am to 6pm and Saturday from 10am to 9pm.

✪ **Zinc Details.** 1905 Fillmore St. (between Bush and Pine sts.). ☎ **415/776-2100.**

One of our favorite stores in the city, Zinc Details has received accolades from everyone from *Elle Decor Japan* to *Metropolitan Home* for its amazing collection of locally handcrafted glass vases, pendant lights, ceramics, and furniture. Each piece is a true work of art created specifically for the store (except vintage items) and these pieces are in such high demand that the store's wholesale accounts include Barney's New York and The Guggenheim Museum Store. Open Monday to Saturday from 11am to 7pm and Sunday from noon to 6pm.

## JEWELRY

**Dianne's Old & New Estates.** 2181A Union St. (at Fillmore St.). ☎ **888/346-7525** or 415/346-7525.

Buy yourself a bauble, or treat yourself to a trinket at this shop featuring top-of-the-line antique jewelry—pendants, diamond rings, necklaces, bracelets, and natural pearls. For a special gift, check out the collection of platinum wedding and engagement rings and vintage watches. Don't worry if you can't afford it now—this shop offers 1-year interest-free layaway. Open Thursday to Tuesday from 11am to 6pm.

**Jerusalem Shoppe.** 313 Noe St. (at Market St.). ☎ **415/626-7906.**

Known for its extensive collection of silver and gold gemstone jewelry by more than 300 local and international artists, this shop also displays other unique treasures, from clothing and accessories to imported antique Indian quilts. Open Monday to Saturday from 11am to 9pm and Sunday from 11am to 7pm.

**The Magical Trinket.** 524 Hayes St. (between Laguna and Octavia sts.). ☎ **415/ 626-0764.**

Do-it-yourself jewelry makers beware. This store, brimming with beads, baubles, and bangles, will inspire you to make your own knickknacks and kick yourself for the prices you've been paying for costume jewelry in retail stores. If you're overwhelmed by all the bead options, colors, shapes, and styles, owner Eve Blake calmly

---

# A New 'Do for a 10-Spot or Two

While the car you drive defines you in Los Angeles, it's the hair you wear that defines you in San Francisco—and it's a lot cheaper and easier to upgrade. Cutting-edge color and cuts can cost a small fortune here, but if you simply must join the chic-sheered ranks, you don't have to pay top dollar. Call **Architects & Heroes,** 2239 Fillmore St. (☎ **415/921-8383**), one of the premier salons in the city, and find out if there's an opening with one of the trainees. Each Monday, licensed cosmetologists who are participating in an 18-month apprenticeship program use volunteers to hone their skills on specific cuts and/or colors. Don't worry: Their work is supervised by an Architects & Heroes staff member, and during the times we've participated, we never left with a bag over our heads. *A word of caution:* You cannot select the treatment you want—you have to go with whatever style they're studying at the time (they'll tell you when you call to make a reservation). You only have to pay for materials used, which usually cost only $15. Book well in advance.

---

explains how to create your wearable masterpiece and offers more extensive classes for those who are really bead-dazzled. Open Monday from noon to 6pm, Tuesday to Saturday from 11am to 7pm, and Sunday from noon to 5pm.

**Pearl & Jade Empire.** 127 Geary St. (between Stockton St. and Grant Ave.). ☎ **415/362-0606.**

The Pearl & Jade Empire has been importing jewelry from all over the world since 1957. They are specialists in unusual pearls and jade and offer restringing on the premises. Open Monday to Saturday from 9:30am to 5:30pm. They have an additional location at 427 Post St. (at Powell St.), ☎ **415/362-0606.**

**Tiffany & Co.** 350 Post St. (at Powell St.). ☎ **415/781-7000.**

Even if you don't have lots of cash to buy an exquisite bauble that comes in Tiffany's famous light-blue box, enjoy this renowned store à la Audrey Hepburn in *Breakfast at Tiffany's.* The designer collection features Paloma Picasso, Jean Schlumberger, and Elsa Peretti in both silver and 18-karat gold, and there's an extensive gift collection in sterling, china, and crystal. Open Monday to Saturday from 10am to 6pm.

**Union Street Goldsmith.** 1909 Union St. (at Laguna St.). ☎ **415/776-8048.**

A showcase for Bay Area goldsmiths, this exquisite shop sells custom-designed jewelry in all karats. Many pieces emphasize colored stones in their settings. Open Monday to Saturday from 11am to 5:45pm and Sunday from noon to 4:45pm.

## MARKETS/PRODUCE

✪ **Farmers Market.** Embarcadero, at Green St. ☎ **510/528-6987.**

Every Saturday from 8am to 1:30pm, northern California fruit, vegetable, bread, and dairy vendors join local restaurateurs in selling fresh, delicious edibles. There's no better way to enjoy a bright San Francisco morning than strolling this gourmet street market and snacking your way through breakfast. You can also pick up locally made vinegars and oils—they make wonderful gifts. From April through November there's another market on Tuesday at Justin Herman Plaza (at Market St. and Embarcadero) from 10:30am to 2:30pm.

# RECORDS & CDS

**Recycled Records.** 1377 Haight St. (between Central and Masonic sts.). ☎ **415/626-4075.**

Easily one of the best used-record stores in the city, this loud shop in the Haight has a good selection of promotional CDs and cases of used "classic" rock LPs. Sheet music, tour programs, and old *TV Guides* are sold. Open Monday to Friday from 10am to 7pm, Saturday from 10am to 9pm, and Sunday from 11am to 7pm.

✪ **Streetlight Records.** 3979 24th St. (between Noe and Sanchez sts.). ☎ **415/282-3550.**

Overstuffed with used music in all three formats, this place is best known for its records and excellent CD collection. Rock music is cheap here, and a money-back guarantee guards against defects. Their second location is at 2350 Market St., between Castro and Noe streets (☎ **415/282-8000**); call for open hours. Open Monday to Saturday from 10am to 10pm and on Sunday from 10:30am to 8:30pm.

**Virgin Megastore.** 2 Stockton (at Market St.). ☎ **415/397-4525.**

With thousands of CDs, including an impressive collection of imports, videos, laser discs, a multimedia department, a cafe, and related books, any music-lover could blow his or her entire vacation fund in this enormous Union Square store. Open Sunday to Thursday from 9am to 10pm, Friday and Saturday from 9am to midnight.

# SHOES

**Birkenstock Natural Footwear.** 1815 Polk St. (between Washington and Jackson sts.). ☎ **415/989-2475.**

This relaxed store is known for its earthy California-style, form-fitting sandals. Other orthopedically correct shoes are also available, including Finn Comforts and traditional Danish clogs by Dansko. Open Monday to Saturday from 10am to 6pm and Sunday from noon to 6pm.

**Bulo.** 437A Hayes St. (at Gough St.). ☎ **415/864-3244.**

If you have a fetish for foot fashions, you must check out Bulo, which carries nothing but imported Italian men's and women's shoes. The selection is small, but styles run the gamut, from casual to dressy, reserved to wildly funky. Since new shipments come in every 3 to 4 weeks, their selection is ever-changing, eternally hip, and unfortunately, ever-expensive, with many pairs going for close to $200. Open Monday to Saturday from 11am to 6:30pm and Sunday from noon to 6pm.

**Gimme Shoes.** 2358 Fillmore St. (at Washington St.). ☎ **415/441-3040.**

The staff is snobby, the prices are steep, and the European shoes and accessories are utterly chic.

**Kenneth Cole.** 865 Market St. (in the San Francisco Shopping Centre). ☎ **415/227-4536.**

High-fashion footwear for men and women is sold at this trendy shop. There is also an innovative collection of handbags and small leather goods and accessories. Other shops are located at 2078 Union St., at Webster Street (☎ **415/346-2161**) and 166 Grant St. at Post Street. Open Monday to Saturday from 9:30am to 8pm and Sunday from 11am to 6pm.

## SHOPPING CENTERS & COMPLEXES

**The Anchorage.** 2800 Leavenworth St. (at Beach and Jefferson sts. on Fisherman's Wharf). ☎ **415/775-6000.**

This touristy waterfront mall has close to 55 stores that offer everything from music boxes to home furnishings; street performers entertain during opening hours. Generally open daily from 10am to 9pm.

**The Cannery.** 2801 Leavenworth St. (at Jefferson St.). ☎ **415/771-3112.**

Once a Del Monte fruit-canning plant, this complex is now occupied by a score or two of shops, restaurants, and nightspots, and thankfully only a few chain stores. Shops include **Gourmet Market** (☎ 415/673-0400), selling international foods, coffees, and teas; **The Print Store** (☎ 415/771-3576), offering a well-chosen selection of fine-art prints and local original art; and the **Basic Brown Bear Factory** (☎ 415/931-6670), where you can stuff your own teddy bear. Vendors' stalls and sidewalk cafes are also set up in the courtyard, amid a grove of olive trees. On summer weekends street performers entertain. The **Museum of the City of San Francisco** (☎ 415/928-0289) is on the third floor. **Cobb's Comedy Club** (see chapter 10, "San Francisco After Dark") is also here, along with several restaurants. The Cannery is open Monday to Saturday from 10am to 6pm and Sunday from 11am to 6pm; there are extended hours during the summer and on holidays.

**Crocker Galleria.** 50 Post St. (at Kearny St.). ☎ **415/393-1505.**

Modeled after Milan's Galleria Vittorio Emanuele, this glass-domed, three-level pavilion, about 3 blocks east of Union Square, features about 40 high-end shops. Fashions include Nicole Miller, Versace, and Polo/Ralph Lauren. Open Monday to Saturday from 10am to 6pm.

**Ghirardelli Square.** 900 North Point (between North Point and Beach sts.). ☎ **415/775-5500.**

This former chocolate factory is one of the city's largest malls and most popular landmarks. It dates from 1864, when it served as a factory making Civil War uniforms, but it's best known as the former chocolate-and-spice factory of Domingo Ghirardelli (say "Gear-a-deli"). The whole complex is crowned by a clock tower that is an exact replica of the one at France's Château de Blois. Inside the tower, on the mall's plaza level, is the Ghirardelli soda fountain, where small amounts of chocolate are still made and are available for purchase, but the big draw is the old-fashioned ice-cream parlor. A free map and guide to the mall is available from the information booth, located in the center courtyard.

Many chain stores are located here, including the women's clothier **Ann Taylor** (☎ 415/775-2872), and **The Sharper Image** (☎ 415/776-1443) for unique, upscale electronics and designs.

The complex is open Sunday to Thursday from 10am to 6pm and Friday and Saturday from 10am to 9pm. Main plaza shops' and restaurants' hours vary, with extended hours during the summer. (Incidentally, the Ghirardelli Chocolate Company still makes chocolate, but it's located in a lower-rent district in the East Bay.)

**Pier 39.** Embarcadero and Beach St. (on the waterfront). ☎ **415/981-PIER.**

Its automated information voice mail boasts Pier 39 is the "third most visited attraction in the country," and in almost the same breath, reminds callers not to forget to bring along their Visa card. To residents, that pretty much wraps up Pier 39, an expensive tourist trap where out-of-towners go to waste money on worthless souvenirs and greasy fast food. For vacationers, though, Pier 39 does have some redeeming qualities—fresh crab (when in season), playful sea lions, phenomenal views, and plenty of fun for the kids. If you want to get to know the real San Francisco, skip the cheesy T-shirt shops and limit your time here to one afternoon. Some of the most interesting stores include **Puppets on the Pier** (☎ 415/781-4435), a store that sells, you guessed it, puppets; and **Kite Flight** (☎ 415/956-3181), where you can buy a fanciful creation to fly in the breezes off the bay. Open weekdays from 10:30am to 8:30pm; weekends from 10am to 8:30pm; store and restaurant hours vary; extended hours during the summer.

**San Francisco Shopping Centre.** 865 Market St. (at Fifth St.). ☎ **415/495-5656.**

Opened in 1988, this $140-million complex is one of the few vertical malls in the United States. Its most stunning features are the four-story spiral escalators that circle their way up to Nordstrom (see "Department Stores," above) and the nine-story atrium covered by a retractable skylight. More than 90 specialty shops include Adrienne Vittadini, Ann Taylor, bebe, Mondi, Benetton, Footlocker, J. Crew, and Victoria's Secret. Open Monday to Saturday from 9:30am to 8pm and on Sunday from 11am to 6pm; holiday hours may vary.

# TOYS

**The Chinatown Kite Shop.** 717 Grant Ave. (between Clay and Sacramento sts.). ☎ **415/391-8217.**

This shop's playful assortment of flying objects includes attractive fish kites, wind socks in nylon or cotton, hand-painted Chinese paper kites, wood-and-paper biplanes, pentagonal kites, and do-it-yourself kite kits, all of which make great souvenirs or decorations. Computer-designed stunt kites have two or four control lines to manipulate loops and dives. Open daily from 10:30am to 9pm.

**The Disney Store.** 400 Post St. (at Powell St.). ☎ **415/391-6866.**

Capitalizing on the world's love for The Mouse and his friends, this store offers everything Disney-oriented you could possibly want, from clothes and toys to high-end commissioned art from the Disney gallery. Those looking for a simple token can fork over $3 for a plastic character, while more serious collectors can throw down $9,000 for a Yamagata Disney lithograph. Open in winter Monday to Friday from 10am to 7pm, Saturday from 10am to 6pm, and Sunday from 11am to 5pm. Hours are extended during the summer and holiday season; call for details. Another location is at Pier 39 (☎ 415/391-4119).

**F.A.O. Schwarz.** 48 Stockton St. (at O'Farrell St.). ☎ **415/394-8700.**

The world's greatest—and most overpriced—toy store for both children and adults is filled with every imaginable plaything, from hand-carved, custom-painted carousel rocking horses, Barbie dolls, and stuffed animals, to gas-powered cars, train sets, and hobby supplies. At the entrance is a singing 22-foot clock tower with 1,000 different moving parts. Open Monday to Saturday from 10am to 7pm and on Sunday from 11am to 6pm.

# TRAVEL GOODS

**On the Road Again.** Embarcadero and Beach St. (in Pier 39). ☎ **415/434-1482.**

In addition to lightweight luggage, this smart shop sells toiletry kits, travel bottles, travel-size items, and a good selection of other related goods. Open Sunday to Thursday from 10am to 7pm, and Friday and Saturday from 10am to 8:30pm; hours vary seasonally.

**Thomas Bros. Maps & Books.** 550 Jackson St. (at Columbus Ave.). ☎ **800/969-3072** for mail order, or 415/981-7520.

The best map shop in the city, Thomas Bros. sells street, topographic, and hiking maps depicting San Francisco, California, and the world, as well as an extensive selection of travel guides and atlases. Open Monday to Friday from 9:30am to 5:30pm.

# WINE

✪ **Wine Club San Francisco.** 953 Harrison St. (between Fifth and Sixth sts.). ☎ **415/512-9086.**

The Wine Club is a discount warehouse that offers bargain prices on more than 1,200 domestic and foreign wines. Bottles cost between $4 and $1,100. Open Monday to Saturday from 9am to 7pm and Sunday from 11am to 6pm.

For a city with fewer than a million inhabitants, San Francisco's arts scene is nothing short of phenomenal. The city's opera is justifiably world renowned, the ballet is well respected, and the theaters rank high in both quantity and quality. Dozens of piano bars and top-notch lounges are augmented by one of the best dance-club cultures this side of New York, and skyscraper lounges offer some of the most dazzling city views in the world. In short, there's always something going on in the city, and, unlike in Los Angeles or New York, you don't have to pay outrageous cover charges to be a part of the scene.

Typically, cover charges at most clubs and rooftop lounges range from $5 to $10; if it's anything over that, you're probably paying too much. If you're in a financial pinch, note that most clubs waive cover charges during the week, but overall you should expect to spend at least $20 on admission and a few drinks. Opera, symphony, ballet, and major theatrical tickets are usually pricey, ranging anywhere from $25 to $140; but if you can hold out buying tickets until the night of the performance, you can usually get in for half-price (see "Getting Tickets," below).

For up-to-date nightlife information, turn to the *San Francisco Weekly* and the *San Francisco Bay Guardian,* both of which contain comprehensive current entertainment listings. They're available free at bars and restaurants, and from street-corner boxes all around the city. *Where,* a free tourist monthly, has information on programs and performance times; it's available in most of the city's finer hotels. The Sunday edition of the *San Francisco Examiner/ Chronicle* also features a "Datebook" section, printed on pink paper, with information and listings on the week's upcoming events.

**GETTING TICKETS**    Located on Stockton Street between Post and Geary streets on the east side of Union Square opposite Maiden Lane, **TIX Bay Area** (☎ **415/433-7827**) sells **half-price tickets** to theater, dance, and music performances on the day of the show only; tickets for Sunday and Monday events, if available, are sold on Saturday. They also sell advance, full-price tickets for most performance halls, sporting events, concerts, and clubs. A service charge, ranging from $1 to $3, is levied on each ticket. Only cash or traveler's checks are accepted for half-price tickets; Visa and MasterCard are accepted for full-price tickets. It's open Tuesday to Thursday from 11am to 6pm, and Friday and Saturday from 11am to 7pm.

Tickets to most theater and dance events can also be obtained through **City Box Office,** 153 Kearny St., Suite 402 (☎ **415/392-4400**). American Express, Master-Card, and Visa are accepted.

**BASS Ticketmaster** (☎ **510/762-2277**) sells (with a hefty service charge) computer-generated tickets to concerts, sporting events, plays, and special events. Downtown BASS Ticketmaster ticketing offices include Tix Bay Area (see above) and at **Warehouse** stores throughout the city. The most convenient location is at 30 Powell St.

# 1 The Performing Arts

Special concerts and performances are staged in San Francisco year-round. **San Francisco Performances,** 500 Sutter St., Suite 710 (☎ **415/398-6449**), has been bringing acclaimed artists to the Bay Area for more than 15 years. Shows run the gamut from classical chamber music to dance and jazz. Performances are in several venues, including the city's Performing Arts Center, Herbst Theater, and the Center for the Performing Arts at Yerba Buena Center. The season lasts from late September through May. Tickets cost $12 to $55, and are available through **City Box Office** (☎ **415/392-4400**). There is also a 6pm Thursday after-work concert series at the EC Cabaret, 3 Embarcadero Center, in fall and winter; $6 admission at the door (☎ **415/398-6449** for information).

## CLASSICAL MUSIC

In addition to two world-class groups, described below, visitors might also be interested in the **San Francisco Contemporary Music Players** (☎ **415/252-6235**), whose concerts are held at the Center for the Arts at Yerba Buena Gardens; they play modern chamber works by international artists. Tickets, available by phone (☎ **415/978-ARTS**), cost $14 for adults, $10 for seniors, and $6 for students. Another commendable group is the **Women's Philharmonic** (☎ **415/437-0123**). For more than 15 years, this critically acclaimed orchestra has been playing works by historical and contemporary women composers. Most performances, at least for the next season, are held at Herbst Theater. Phone for dates, programs, and ticket prices.

**Philharmonia Baroque Orchestra.** Performing in the Herbst Theater, 401 Van Ness Ave. ☎ **415/392-4400** (box office) or 415/495-7445. www.philparmonia.org. E-mail: info@ philharmonia.org. Tickets $30–$42.

Acclaimed by the *New York Times* as "the country's leading early music orchestra," Philharmonia Baroque performs in San Francisco and all around the Bay Area. The season lasts from September through April. The company's administrative offices can be reached at ☎ **415/495-7445.**

**San Francisco Symphony.** Performing at Davies Symphony Hall, 201 Van Ness Ave. (at Grove St.). ☎ **415/864-6000** (box office). Tickets $12–$73.

Founded in 1911, the internationally respected San Francisco Symphony has long been an important part of this city's cultural life under such legendary conductors as Pierre Monteux and Seiji Ozawa. In 1995, Michael Tilson Thomas took over from Herbert Blomstedt, and has already led the orchestra to new heights and crafted an exciting repertoire of classical and modern music. The season runs from September through June. Summer symphony activities include a Composer Festival and a Summer Pops series.

## OPERA

In addition to San Francisco's major opera company, you might also check out the amusing **Pocket Opera,** 44 Page St., Suite 200 (☎ **415/575-1100**). From mid-February to mid-June, this comic company stages farcical performances in English of well-known operas accompanied by a chamber orchestra. The staging is intimate and informal, without lavish costumes and sets. The cast ranges from 3 to 16 players, and is supported by a chamber orchestra. The rich repertoire includes such works as *Don Giovanni* and *The Barber of Seville.* Performances are on Friday, Saturday, or Sunday. Call the box office (☎ **415/575-1102**) for complete information and show times. Tickets cost $10 (students) to $25.

**San Francisco Opera.** Performing at newly refurbished War Memorial Opera House, 301 Van Ness Ave. (at Grove St.). ☎ **415/864-3330** (box office). Tickets $10–$140.

The San Francisco Opera was the United States' first municipal opera, and is one of the city's cultural icons. Brilliantly balanced casts may feature celebrated stars like Frederica Von Stade and Placido Domingo, along with promising newcomers and the regular members, in productions that range from traditional to avant-garde. All productions have English supertitles. The opera season starts in September and lasts just 14 weeks. Performances are held most evenings, except Monday, with matinees on Sundays. Tickets go on sale as early as June, and the best seats sell out quickly. Unless Pavarotti or Domingo is in town, some less-coveted seats are usually available until curtain time.

## THEATER

After 12 successful years, **Climate,** 252 Ninth St., at Folsom Street (☎ **415/978-2345**), is still showcasing avant-garde and experimental works in a casual and intimate atmosphere. **Eureka Theatre Company,** 330 Townsend, Suite 210, at Fourth Street (☎ **415/243-9899**), produces contemporary plays. The season runs from September through June, and performances are usually presented Wednesday to Sunday. Tickets cost $16 to $22, with discounts for students and seniors (call for specific theater location). **Theatre Rhinoceros,** 2926 16th St. (☎ **415/861-5079**), founded in 1977, was America's first (and still the foremost) theater ensemble devoted solely to works addressing gay and lesbian issues. The company presents five main stage shows and a dozen studio productions of new and classic works each year. The theater is located 1 block east of the 16th Street/Mission BART station.

✪ **American Conservatory Theater (A.C.T.).** Performing at the Geary Theater, 415 Geary St. (at Mason St.). ☎ **415/749-2228.** Tickets $14–$55.

American Conservatory Theater (A.C.T.) made its debut in 1967 and quickly established itself as the city's premier resident theater group. The troupe is so venerated that A.C.T. has been compared to the superb British National Theatre, the Berliner Ensemble, and the Comédie Française. The A.C.T. season runs from September through July and features both classical and experimental works.

A.C.T. recently returned to its home, the fabulous **Geary Theater** (1910), a national historic landmark, after the theater sustained severe damage in the 1989 earthquake and was closed for renovations. Now it's fully refurbished, and has been modernized to such an extent that it is regarded as one of America's finest performance spaces.

**Lorraine Hansberry Theatre.** Performing at 620 Sutter St. ☎ **415/474-8800.**

San Francisco's top African-American theater group performs in a 300-seat theater off the lobby of the Sheehan Hotel, near Mason Street. Special adaptations from literature are performed along with contemporary dramas, classics, and world premieres. Tickets range from $15 to $25. Phone for dates and programs.

**The Magic Theatre.** Performing at Bldg. D, Fort Mason Center, Marina Blvd. (at Buchanan St.). ☎ **415/441-8822.** Tickets $18–$32. Discounts for students and seniors.

The highly acclaimed Magic Theatre continues to be a major West Coast company dedicated to presenting the works of new playwrights; over the years it has nurtured the talents of such luminaries as Sam Shepard and Jon Robin Baitz. Shepard's Pulitzer prize–winning play *Buried Child* premiered here. More recent productions have included works by Athol Fugard, Claire Chafee, and Nilo Cruz. The season usually runs from September through July; performances are offered Wednesday to Sunday.

## DANCE

In addition to the local companies, top traveling troupes like the Joffrey Ballet and the American Ballet Theatre make regular appearances. Primary modern dance spaces include the **Theatre Artaud,** 450 Florida St., at 17th Street (☎ **415/621-7797**); the **Cowell Theater,** at Fort Mason Center, Marina Boulevard, at Buchanan Street (☎ **415/441-3400**); **Dancer's Group/Footwork,** 3221 22nd St., at Mission Street (☎ **415/824-5044;** www.dancersgroup.org); and the **ODC Theatre,** 3153 17th St., at Shotwell in the Mission District (☎ **415/863-9834**). Check the local papers for schedules or contact the theater box offices directly.

**San Francisco Ballet.** Performances at War Memorial Opera House, 301 Van Ness Ave. (at Grove St.). ☎ **415/865-2000.** Tickets and information. Tickets $7–$100.

Founded in 1933, the San Francisco Ballet is the oldest professional ballet company in the United States, and is regarded as one of the country's finest, performing an eclectic repertoire of full-length, neoclassical, and contemporary ballets. Even the *New York Times* proclaimed, "The San Francisco Ballet under Helgi Tomasson's leadership is one of the spectacular success stories of the arts in America." The 1998/1999 Repertory Season runs from February through June. All performances are accompanied by the San Francisco Ballet Orchestra.

## 2 Comedy & Cabaret

**Bay Area Theatresports (BATS).** Center for Improvisational Theatre at the Fort Mason Center, Bldg. B, 3rd floor. ☎ **415/474-8935.** Tickets $5–$15.

Combining improvisation with competition, Bay Area Theatresports (BATS) operates an improvisational tournament, in which four-actor teams compete against each other, taking on hilarious improvisational challenges from the audience. Judges then good-naturedly flash scorecards, or honk a horn for scenes that just aren't working. Shows are staged on Monday only. Phone for reservations.

✪ **Beach Blanket Babylon.** At Club Fugazi, 678 Green St./Beach Blanket Babylon Blvd. (between Powell St. and Columbus Ave.). ☎ **415/421-4222.** Tickets $20–$55.

Now a San Francisco tradition, Beach Blanket Babylon evolved from Steve Silver's Rent-a-Freak service—a group of party-givers extraordinaire who hired themselves out as a "cast of characters" to entertain, complete with fabulous costumes and sets, props, and gags. After their act caught on, it moved into the Savoy-Tivoli, a North Beach bar. By 1974, the audience had grown too large for the facility, and Beach Blanket has been at the 400-seat Club Fugazi ever since.

The show is a comedic musical send-up that is best known for its outrageous costumes and oversized headdresses. It's been playing almost 22 years now, and almost every performance sells out. The show is updated often enough that locals still attend. Those under 21 are welcome at Sunday matinees at 3pm when no alcohol is served; photo ID is required for evening performances. It's wise to call for tickets at least 3 weeks in advance for weekend-performance tickets, or to obtain them through Tix (see above). *Note:* When you purchase tickets, they will be within a specific section depending upon price; however, seating is still first-come/first-seated within that section. Performances are given on Thursday through Saturday at 8pm, and on Sunday at 7pm.

**Cobb's Comedy Club.** 2801 Leavenworth St. (at Beach St.) ☎ **415/928-4320.** Cover $5 Mon–Wed, $10–$13 Fri–Sat, $10 Thurs and Sun (plus a 2-beverage minimum nightly). Validated parking.

Located in the Cannery at Fisherman's Wharf, Cobb's features such national headliners as Pam Stone, Brian Regan, and Jake Johannsen. There is comedy every night, including a 15-comedian All-Pro Monday showcase (a 3-hr. marathon). Cobb's is open to those 18 and over, and occasionally to kids ages 16 and 17 if they are accompanied by a parent or legal guardian (call ahead first). Food is served from adjoining Belle Roux Louisiana Kitchen. Shows Monday through Wednesday at 8pm, Thursday and Sunday at 9pm, and Friday and Saturday at 8 and 10pm.

**Finocchio's.** 506 Broadway (at Kearny St.). ☎ **415/982-9388.** Cover $14.50 (2-drink minimum).

For more than 50 years, this family-run cabaret has showcased the best female impersonators in a funny, kitschy show. Three different revues are presented nightly (usually Thurs to Sat at 8:30, 10, and 11:30pm), and a single cover is good for the entire evening. Parking is available next door at the Flying Dutchman.

**Punch Line.** 444 Battery St., plaza level (between Washington and Clay sts.). ☎ **415/ 397-4337** or 415/397-7573 for recorded information. Cover $5 Sun, $8–$15 Tues–Sat (plus a 2-drink minimum nightly).

Adjacent to the Embarcadero One office building, this is the largest comedy nightclub in the city. Three-person shows with top national and local talent are featured Tuesday to Saturday. Showcase night is Sunday, when 15 to 20 rising stars take the mike. There's an all-star showcase or a special event on Monday nights. Buy tickets in advance (if you don't want to wait in line) from **BASS** outlets (☎ **510/ 762-2277**). Shows are Tuesday to Thursday and Sunday at 9pm, and on Friday and Saturday at 9 and 11pm.

# 3  The Club & Music Scene

The greatest legacy from the 1960s is the city's continued tradition of live entertainment and music, which explains the great variety of clubs and music scenes available in a city of this size. The hippest dance places are located South of Market Street (SoMa), in former warehouses, the artsy bohemian scene centers around the Mission, and most popular cafe culture is still centered in North Beach.

*Note:* The club and music scene is always changing, often outdating recommendations before the ink can dry on a page. Most of the venues below are promoted as different clubs on various nights of the week, each with its own look, sound, and style. Discount passes and club announcements are often available at hip clothing stores and other shops along upper Haight Street.

If you prefer to let someone else take the lead (and the driver's seat) for a night out, give a call to **3 Babes and a Bus** (☎ 415/552-2582). This nightclub tour company (the head babe is a stockbroker by day) will take you and a gaggle of 20- to 40-something partiers (mostly single women) out on the town, skipping lines and cover charges, for $30 per person.

Drink prices at most bars, clubs, and cafes range from about $3.50 to $6, unless otherwise noted.

**DIAL-A-SCENE**   The local newspapers won't direct you to the city's underground club scene, nor will they advise you which of the dozens of clubs are truly hot. To get dialed in, do what the locals do—turn to the **Be-At Line** (☎ 415/626-4087) for its daily recorded update on the town's most hoppin' hip-hop, acidjazz, and house clubs. The scene is reported by one of its coolest residents, Mayor Brown's street-suave son, Michael. For the grooviest message and inside scoop on the feel-good, underground party scene, tune in to the **Bug Out Line** (☎ 415/437-6905). **Housewares Rave** (☎ 415/281-0125) highlights the heavy techno scene. The far more commercial **Club Line** (☎ 415/979-8686) offers up-to-date schedules for the city's larger dance venues.

## ROCK & BLUES CLUBS

In addition to the following listings, see "Dance Clubs," below, for (usually) live, danceable rock.

**Biscuits and Blues.** 401 Mason (at Geary St.). ☎ **415/292-2583.** Cover (during performances) $5–$25.

With a crisp, blow-your-eardrums-out sound system, New Orleans–speakeasy (albeit commercial) appeal, and nightly line-up of live entertainment, there's no better place to muse the blues than at this basement-cum-nightclub. During performances there can be hefty ticket prices (up to $25), but entrance is free during happy hour (Mon to Fri from 5 to 7pm) when there's usually recorded music, drink specials, and inexpensive snacks—not to mention the only opportunity to socialize: once the bands get going, it's so loud you can't even hear yourself holler. *Note:* There's a full dinner menu here, but the only notable treat is the moist and flaky biscuits.

**The Fillmore.** 1805 Geary Blvd. (at Fillmore St.). ☎ **415/346-6000.** www.thefillmore.com. Tickets $9–$25.

Re-opened after years of neglect, The Fillmore, made famous by promoter Bill Graham in the 1960s, is once again attracting big names. Check the local listings in magazines, or call the theater for information on upcoming events.

**Grant & Green.** 1371 Grant Ave. (at Green St.). ☎ **415/693-9565.** No cover.

The atmosphere at this North Beach dive rockery is not that special, but the local bands are pretty good. Look for daytime shows on the weekends.

**Lou's Pier 47 Club.** 300 Jefferson St. (at Jones St). ☎ **415/771-5687.** Cover $5 to $10.

There's few locals in the place, but Lou's happens to be good, old-fashioned fun and a casual spot where you can let your hair down with Cajun seafood (downstairs), live jazz, blues, rock and country bands (upstairs). Major happy hour specials (Monday through Friday 4 to 7pm) and a vacation attitude make the place one of the more, um, jovial spots near the Wharf. There's no cover for the first band, which plays nightly from 4 to 8pm, but it will cost you for the second, which comes on at 9pm.

**The Saloon.** 1232 Grant Ave. (at Vallejo St.). ☎ **415/989-7666.** Cover $4–$5 Fri–Sat.

An authentic gold rush survivor, this North Beach dive is the oldest extant bar in the city. Popular with both bikers and daytime pinstripers, there's live blues nightly.

**Slim's.** 333 11th St. (at Folsom St.). ☎ **415/522-0333.** Cover free to $20 (plus a 2-drink minimum when seated at table).

Co-owned by musician Boz Scaggs, who sometimes takes the stage under the name "Presidio Slim," This glitzy restaurant/bar seats 300, serves California cuisine, and specializes in excellent American music—homegrown rock, jazz, blues, and alternative music—almost nightly. Menu items range from $3 to $8.50.

## JAZZ & LATIN CLUBS

✪ **Cafe du Nord.** 2170 Market St. (at Sanchez St.). ☎ **415/861-5016.** Cover charge $3 to $10.

Although it's been around since 1907, this basement-cum-jazz-supper club has finally been recognized as a respectable jazz, swing, and salsa music venue. With a younger generation now appreciating the music, the place is often packed from the 40-foot mahogany bar to the back room with a pool table. *Notes:* If Lavay Smith and The Red Hot Skillet Lickers are in the house, definitely stop by; du Nord puts out its own compilation CDs, which are definitely worth purchasing.

**Jazz at Pearl's.** 256 Columbus Ave. (at Broadway). ☎ **415/291-8255.** No cover, but there is a 2-drink minimum.

This is one of the best venues for jazz in the city. Ribs and chicken are served with the sounds, too, with prices ranging from $4 to $8.95. The live jams last until 2am nightly.

**Rasselas.** 2801 California St. (at Divisadero St.). ☎ **415/567-5010.** No cover, but there is a 2-drink minimum.

Large, casual, and comfortable, with couches and small tables, this is a favorite spot for hearing local jazz and R&B combos. The adjacent restaurant serves Ethiopian cuisine under an elegant Bedouin tent. Menu items range from $3 to $10.75.

**Up & Down Club.** 1151 Folsom St. (between 7th and 8th sts.). ☎ **415/626-2388.** Cover varies.

One of the original homes for SoMa's now-familiar new-jazz scene, the Up & Down jazz supper club attracts a trendy crowd to both its restaurant and dance floor. Dinner's at 8pm (reservations required), the music starts at 9:30pm, and dancing begins at 10pm.

## DANCE CLUBS

While a lot of clubs around town allow dancing, the following clubs are the places to go if all you want to do is shake your groove thang.

**Club Ten 15.** 1015 Folsom St. (at Sixth St.). ☎ **415/431-1200.** Cover $5–$15.

Get decked out and plan for a late-nighter if you're headed to this enormous party warehouse. Three levels, a full-color laser system, and 4,000 feet of dance floor make for an extensive variety of dancing venues, complete with a 20- and 30-something gyrating mass who live for the DJs' pounding house, disco, and acid-jazz music. Each night is a different club that attracts its own crowd that ranges from yuppie to hip-hop. With a $1.5-million renovation through 1999, which included the addition of 6,000 more square feet of dance floor and a new VIP area, this place only keeps getting wilder. Call ☎ **415/431-1200** for a complete schedule of events.

# Salsa!

Okay you wallflowers, no more excuses for not hitting the dance floor. It's silly to let money repress your inner rhythm, particularly when San Francisco offers so many venues for dance lessons at such teensy prices. The hot new dance these days is salsa, and more and more clubs are drumming up (pun intended) business by offering **free salsa lessons** a few hours before the band begins. It's loads of fun, and one of the cheapest duos of instruction and entertainment you'll find in the city (or anywhere else, for that matter). Schedules at many of the clubs tend to change, so be sure to call ahead. We think your best bet is the **Cafe du Nord,** 2170 Market St., between Church and Sanchez streets (☎ 415/861-5016), which usually offers free salsa lessons on Tuesday from 9 to 10pm.

**The EndUp.** 401 Sixth St. (at Harrison St.). ☎ **415/357-0827.** Cover varies.

For over a decade, this place has thrown some of the most kickin' parties in town. Here it's a different theme every night: Monday and Wednesday are Reggae with Club Dread; Thursday sets swinging singles loose at the Kit Kat Club; Fag Friday is just what it sounds like, plus lots of throw-down dancing; Saturday is the very festive lesbian club The G Spot; and Sunday is ever-popular with the sleepless dance-all-day crowd who come here after the other clubs close (it opens at 5:30am). Call to confirm nights—venues change from time to time.

**HiFi.** 2125 Lombard St. (at Fillmore St.). ☎ **415/345-8663.** Cover $3–$6.

Previously a small, dark blues bar, it's latest incarnation is a 1950s and 1960s "jet-set lounge" perfectly poised to attracted the partying yuppie set. Most nights a DJ spins house, Latin, soul, and disco while live bands rock the place on Sundays.

**Nickie's Bar-be-cue.** 460 Haight St. (between Fillmore and Webster sts.). ☎ **415/621-6508.** www.nickies.com. Cover $3–$5.

Don't show up here for dinner; the only hot thing you'll find here is the small, crowded dance floor. But don't let that stop you from checking it out—Nickie's is a sure thing. Every time we come here, the old-school disco hits are in full-force, casually dressed dancers lose all their inhibitions, and the crowd is mixed with all types of friendly San Franciscans. This place is perpetually hot, so dress accordingly, and you can always cool down with a pint from the wine-and-beer bar. Keep in mind, lower Haight is on the periphery of a shady neighborhood, so don't make your rental car look tempting, and stay alert as you walk through the area.

**Paradise Lounge.** 1501 Folsom St. (at 11th St.). ☎ **415/861-6906.** Cover $3–$15.

Labyrinthine Paradise features three dance floors simultaneously vibrating to different beats. Smaller, auxiliary spaces include a pool room with a half dozen tables. Poetry readings are also fairly common here.

**Sound Factory.** 525 Harrison St. (at First St.). ☎ **415/243-9646.** Cover $10 Fri, $15 Sat.

Herb Caen dubbed this disco theme park the "mother of all discos." The maze of rooms and nonstop barrage of house, funk, lounge vibes, and club classics attracts swarms of young urbanites looking to rave it up until sometimes as late as 6am. Management tries to eliminate the riffraff by enforcing a dress code (no sneakers, hooded sweatshirts, or sports caps).

## SUPPER CLUBS

If you can eat dinner, listen to live music, and dance (or at least wiggle in your chair) in the same room, it's a supper club—that's our criteria.

✪ **Blue Bar.** Below the Black Cat Café, 501 Broadway (at Kearny St.). ☎ **415/981-2233.** Cover Wed–Sun $5.

Whether you're passing by North Beach or finishing a night at Reed Hearon's Black Cat Cafe (see review in chapter 6 for complete details) you should drop into this chic-cozy live jazz/blues venue with cushy couches and a laid-back atmosphere. The restaurant's full menu is available here—a plus for late-night eaters, and a bummer for those who come exclusively for the music.

**Harry Denton's.** 161 Steuart St. (between Mission and Howard sts.). ☎ **415/882-1333.** $10 cover after 10pm Thurs–Sat, $15 cover after 10pm (free other times).

Early evening it's filled with "suits" and secretaries on the prowl. But weekend nights reflect the restaurant owner, Harry Denton, who, although now sober, is known for getting himself and his guests intoxicated and dancing on tables, and being the all-around wildest party host in town. When the stately restaurant with mahogany bar, red-velvet furnishings, and chandeliers, clears away dining utensils and turns up the music, a glitzy crowd pulls up to the valet with their boogie shoes on. In the front lounge, R&B or jazz performers usually play loud enough to drown out the disco and pop dancing in the back room. But that's where all the action is, so head back there and join the 30- and 40-something yuppie masses flailing to pop and disco hits. Eat dinner at neighboring Boulevard first; the food here is not memorable.

✪ **Harry Denton's Starlight Room.** Atop the Sir Francis Drake Hotel, 450 Powell St., 21st floor. ☎ **415/395-8595.** Cover $5 Wed–Thurs after 8pm, $10 Fri–Sat after 8pm.

Come dressed to the nines or in casual attire to this celestial cocktail-lounge-cum-nightclub. It's located atop a highrise, and both tourists and locals come here to watch the sunset at dusk, and to boogie down to live swing and big-band tunes after dark. The room is classic 1930s San Francisco, with red-velvet banquettes, chandeliers, and fabulous views. But what really attracts flocks of all ages is a night of Harry Denton–style fun, which usually includes plenty of drinking and unrestrained dancing. The full bar stocks a decent collection of single-malt scotches and champagnes, and you can snack from the pricey Starlight appetizer menu. Like Harry's SoMa dance club, early evening is more relaxed, but come the weekend, this place gets loose.

**Julie's Supper Club.** 1123 Folsom St. (at Seventh St.). ☎ **415/861-0707.** No cover.

Julie's is a longtime standby for cocktailing and late dining. Divided into two rooms, the vibe is very 1950s cartoon, with a space-aged "Jetsons" appeal. Good-looking singles prowl, cocktails in hand, as live music plays by the front door. The food is hit-and-miss, but the atmosphere is definitely a casual and playful winner with a little interesting history; this building is one location where the Symbionese Liberation Army held Patty Hearst hostage back in the 1970s. Menu items range from $7.50 to $16.

✪ **Mercury.** 540 Howard St. (between 1st and 2nd Sts.). ☎ **415/777-1419.** Cover (without dinner) to downstairs club Wed–Sat $20.

Celebrated nightclub master Dr. Winkie has revamped the long-closed, multi-level DV8 club space into a sexy visual wonder well worth a visit. The glittering and glamorous retro-modern interior is one of San Francisco's swankiest (to match the equally image-conscious clientele) with supper-club dining and jazz leading to basement disco dancing. The wildly silver Mirror Bar mimics the bubbly and other libations served there. The Pearl Bar looks like it sounds, and the dining room is an elegant diversion. Plainly put, this is a must-see and with jazz and disco and an eclectic clientele, you're sure to find action to your liking.

**330 Ritch.** 330 Ritch (between 3rd and 4th sts. off Townsend). ☎ **415/541-9574,** or 415/522-9558 for recorded band information. Cover $3–$10.

If you can find the place, you must be cool. It's located on a 2-block alley in SoMa, and even locals have a hard time remembering how to get there. But head there Wednesday through Sunday (it's closed the rest of the week) and you'll find happy-hour cocktails (specials on a few select mixed drinks and draft brews), pool tables, and a hip, young crowd at play. On weekends, the place really livens up when bands take center stage on Fridays, and the Latin lovers salsa all night to the spicy beat. Free swing-dancing lessons (with $5 cover charge) are offered every Wednesday to the Bay Area's best swing bands. A "hearty American" dinner is served Wednesday to Saturday from 6 to 10pm.

## RETRO CLUBS

Well, daddyo, we hope you didn't throw out your old hep duds, because America's halcyon days are back. So don your fedora and patent leather shoes, cause you don't mean a thing if you ain't got that swing.

**Bruno's.** 2389 Mission St. (at 20th St.). ☎ **415/550-7455.** Cover $3–$7 after 9:30pm.

Before its recognition (and a later denunciation) as a destination restaurant, Mission District hipsters were already keen on this retro hot spot. There's live music nightly in the back lounge, and the long, 1950s-style full bar is almost always crowded with a mixture of wannabes, the cool, and the curious. Appetizers and desserts are served until 1am.

**Club Deluxe.** 1511 Haight St. (at Ashbury St.). ☎ **415/552-6949.** Cover $2 to $10.

Before the recent 1940s trend hit the city, Deluxe and its fedora-wearing clientele had been celebrating the bygone era for years. Fortunately, even with all the retro-hype, the vibe here hasn't changed. Expect an eclectic mix of throw-backs and generic San Franciscans in the intimate, smoky bar and adjoining lounge, and live jazz or blues most nights. Although many regulars dress the part, there's no attitude here; so come as you like.

✪ **HiBall Lounge.** 473 Broadway (between Kearny and Montgomery sts.). ☎ **415/397-9464.** Cover $2–$8.

Retro-jazz is in full swing in the city, and one of the most popular places to hear it—and dance to it—is at this North Beach joint. Harking back to Broadway at its best, the vibe is full-on 1940s/1950s, from the red banquettes and stage curtains, to the small, dark, room. Live bands perform nightly to a young, swingin' crowd. There's also a swing-dance class Thursday through Sunday. The kitchy-fun adjoining Bamboo Hut lounge celebrates classic tiki cocktailing. A dress code denounces baseball caps, tennis shoes, T-shirts, and ripped jeans.

## 4 The Bar Scene

Finding your idea of a comfortable bar has a lot to do with picking a neighborhood filled with your kind of people and investigating that area. There are hundreds of bars throughout San Francisco, and although many are obscurely located and can't be classified by their neighborhood, the following is a general description of what you'll find and where:

- **Chestnut and Union Street** bars attract a post-collegiate crowd.
- **Mission District** haunts are frequented by young alternatives.
- **Upper Haight** caters to eclectic neighborhood cocktailers.
- **Lower Haight** is skate-/snowboarder grungy.
- **Downtown** pubs mix tourists with theatergoers and thirsty businesspeople.
- **North Beach** serves all types.
- **Castro** caters to gay locals and tourists.
- **South of Market** (SoMa) offers an eclectic mix.

The following is a list of a few of San Francisco's more interesting bars.

**Albion.** 3139 16th St. (between Valencia and Guerrero sts.). ☎ **415/552-8558.**

This Mission District club is a grit-and-leather in-crowd place packed with artistic types and various SoMa hipsters. Live music plays Sunday between 4 and 7pm and ranges from ragtime and blues to jazz and swing.

**Backflip.** 601 Eddy St. (at Larkin St.). ☎ **415/771-FLIP.**

Adjoining the funky Phoenix Hotel, this shimmering aqua-blue cocktail lounge—designed to induce the illusion that you're carousing in the deep end—serves tapas and Caribbean-style appetizers to a mostly young, fashionable crowd, so please don't order a Cosmopolitan. While the scene continues to change, on Thursday the crowd seems to be young and gay/alternative; weekends, wannabe-cool yuppies tend to pack the place. Regardless, if you're headed here, you can expect the unexpected, kick back with a martini, and enjoy the city's varied eye candy.

✪ **Bottom of the Hill.** 1233 17th St. (at Missouri St.). ☎ **415/621-4455.** Cover $4–$10.

Voted one of the best places to hear live rock in the city by the *San Francisco Bay Guardian,* this popular neighborhood club attracts an eclectic crowd ranging from rockers to real-estate salespeople. The main attraction is live music every night of the week, but it also offers pretty good burgers and kebabs, outdoor seating on the back patio, and an awesome $4 all-you-can-eat barbecue on Sunday from 4 to 7pm. There's also a happy hour Monday to Friday from 4 to 7pm.

**Caribbean Zone.** 55 Natoma St. (between 1st and 2nd sts.). ☎ **415/541-9465.** No cover.

Not just another restaurant bar, this is a visual Disneyland, jam-packed with a cluttered, tropical decor that includes a full-size airplane fuselage. It's been around a little too long, but tourists seem to love it. Dinner ranges from $14 to $19.

**Chalkers Billiard Club.** One Rincon Center, 101 Spear St. (at Mission St.). ☎ **415/512-0450.** www.chalkers.com. E-mail: chalkerssb@aol.com.

Pool hall meets men's smoking club at this enormous, classy billiards joint. Food and drinks are delivered to the 30 cherry-wood tables, which you can rent by the hour. Pool sharks especially appreciate the custom cue shop, where savvy sticks can go for up to $25,000. Happy hour on weekdays from 5 to 7pm offers more beer for your buck.

**Edinburgh Castle.** 950 Geary St. (between Polk and Larkin sts.). ☎ **415/885-4074.**

Since 1958, this legendary Scottish pub has been known for unusual British ales on tap and the best selection of single-malt scotches in the city. The huge pub, located near Polk Street, is decorated with Royal Air Force mementos, horse brasses, steel

# San Francisco Happy Hours

If you're like us, one if the fastest ways you blow your budget is having a good time at the bars. Like everything else in San Francisco, drinks tend to be expensive, so it's definitely worth your while to search out the best happy hours in the city and start your night-on-the-town a bit early. Here's a sampling our neighborhood favorites, but be sure to call ahead and make sure they're still offering specials before you go, since they change often:

**Lower Haight**    Join the young and the grungy at **Mad Dog in the Fog,** 530 Haight St., at Fillmore Street (☎ **415/626-7279**), from 11am to 7pm for $2.50 pints and $8 pitchers of beer; or at the nearby **Noc Noc,** 557 Haight St., at Fillmore Street (☎ **415/861-5811**), where you'll find $2.50 drafts (15 selections) from 5 to 7pm daily.

**The Mission**    One of the coolest bars in the Mission, **Dalva,** 3121 16th St., at Valencia Street (☎ **415/252-7740**), offers $2 well drinks, sangría, and beer daily from 4 to 7pm. Another option is the garagelike **Shotwell 59,** 3349 20th St., at Shotwell Street (☎ **415/647-1141**), where a young neighborhood crowd comes for $8 pitchers of beer from 5 to 7pm nightly.

**Union Square**    At **Biscuits & Blues,** 410 Mason St., at Geary Street (☎ **415/292-BLUE**), you can down $2.50 martinis and margaritas, $2 drafts, and discounted featured drinks while listening to live or recorded blues. The party happens Monday to Friday from 5 to 7pm. Call for special promotions and/or performances.

**Financial District    Perry's Downtown,** 185 Sutter St., between Montgomery and Kearny streets (☎ **415/989-6895**), offers sporty business-crowd flirting, $2 Rolling Rock beers, $1.50 sliders (miniburgers), drink specials, and seven televisions featuring all major sports events from 3 to 6pm Monday to Friday. At the Financial District's **Fizz,** 471 Pine St., at Kearny Street (☎ **415/421-3499**), you can chow on the killer $2 appetizer menu (pasta, penne, polenta, mussels, and so on), and drink the $2 draft beer, and $3 martinis Monday to Friday from 5 to 7:30pm.

**The Castro**    Chill out with jazz and pool at the **Cafe du Nord,** 2170 Market St., between Sanchez and Church streets (☎ **415/861-7244**), where $2 martinis and manhattans and $2.50 well drinks and beer bring in an eclectic group from 4 to 7pm daily. (The music starts at 7pm, just when you're getting *real* happy.)

helmets, and an authentic Ballantine caber used in the annual Scottish games. Fish-and-chips and other traditional foods are available until 11pm.

**The Great Entertainer.** 975 Bryant (at Eighth St.). ☎ **415/861-8833.**

This is a glorified pool hall with 50 pool tables, plus five private billiard suites, snooker, shuffleboard, darts, table tennis, and a video arcade. Drinks, pizza, and other dishes accompany the games. Menu items range $2 to $20.

**Li Po Cocktail Lounge.** 916 Grant Ave. (between Washington and Jackson sts.). ☎ **415/982-0072.**

A divey Chinese bar, Li Po is made special by a clutter of dusty Asian furnishings and mementos that include an unbelievably huge rice-paper lantern hanging from the ceiling, and a glittery golden shrine to Buddha behind the bar.

**Perry's.** 1944 Union St. (at Laguna St.). ☎ **415/922-9022.**

If you read *Tales of the City*, you already know that this bar and restaurant has a colorful history as a pickup place for Pacific Heights and Marina singles. Though the times are not as wild, locals still come to casually check out the happenings at the dark mahogany bar. A separate dining room offers breakfast, lunch, dinner, and weekend brunch at candlelit tables. It's a good place for hamburgers, simple fish dishes, and pasta. Menu items range from $7 to $20.

**Persian Aub Zam Zam.** 1633 Haight St. (at Clayton St.). ☎ **415/861-2545.**

If you make it through the forbidding metal doors you'll feel as if you're in Casablanca, but unfortunately, most people don't get that far. The owner/bartender, Bruno, who has poured here for over 40 years, opens the place when he wants some company and arbitrarily chooses who's allowed to join him at the bar. If you meet his random requirements, play it safe and order a martini, a drink Bruno likes to serve (we've been ousted for ordering a Coors Light). Along with the challenge of getting in, locals love Bruno's ne'er-changing rituals: yesteryear's prices, a classic martini, and 50¢ pieces as change. Strategic tips to better your chances at entering and being allowed to stay: Don't come with a large party (he never lets anyone sit at the tables, and there are very limited bar seats); don't wear unusual attire (backward baseball hats are definitely out of the question!); drink beer from a glass, not the bottle; and don't order fancy cocktails. Then just sit back and enjoy watching everyone else get kicked out.

**Pied Piper Bar.** In the Sheraton Palace Hotel, 2 New Montgomery (at Market St.). ☎ **415/ 512-1111.**

The huge Pied Piper mural by Edwardian illustrator Maxfield Parrish steals the show at this historic mahogany bar, where high stakes were once won and lost on the roll of the dice.

**The Red Room.** In the Commodore Hotel, 827 Sutter St. (at Jones St.). ☎ **415/346-7666.**

At one time the hottest cocktail lounge in town (though it's cooled off a bit), this ultramodern, Big Apple–style bar and lounge reflects no other spectrum but ruby red. Really, you gotta see this one.

**The Savoy-Tivoli.** 1434 Grant Ave. (at Green and Union sts.). ☎ **415/362-7023.**

Euro-trash (and wannabes) crowd the few pool tables and indoor and patio seating to smoke cigarettes and look cool at this popular, trendy bar. It's mostly tourists and newcomers who frequent here because posing gets tiring after a while, and there are far cooler bars in town. But a sidewalk-facing table in the heart of North Beach allows for great people watching, and the high-profile clientele does create an entertaining atmosphere. Take heed of the waitresses, who have been known to overcharge for drinks, which are supposed to range from $3.50 to $6.

✪ **Spec's.** 12 Saroyan Place (off Columbus Ave.). ☎ **415/421-4112.**

Spec's incognito locale on Saroyan Place, a tiny alley at 250 Columbus Ave., makes it less of a walk-in bar and more of a lively locals' hangout. Its funky decor—maritime flags that hang from the ceiling, exposed brick walls lined with posters, photos, and various oddities—gives it character that intrigues every visitor. A "museum," displayed under glass, contains memorabilia and items brought back by seamen who drop in between sails, and the clientele is funky enough to keep you preoccupied while you drink a beer.

**Toronado.** 547 Haight St. (at Fillmore St.). ☎ **415/863-2276.**

Lower Haight isn't exactly a charming street, but there's plenty of nightlife here catering to an artistic/grungy/skateboarding 20-something crowd. While Toronado definitely draws in the young'uns, its 40-plus microbrews on tap and 60 bottled beers also entice a more eclectic clientele in search of beer heaven. The brooding atmosphere matches the surroundings: an aluminum bar, a few tall tables, dark lighting, and a back room packed with tables and chairs. A DJ picks up the pace on Friday and Saturday nights.

✪ **Tosca.** 242 Columbus Ave. (between Broadway and Pacific Ave.). ☎ **415/986-9651.**

Open daily from 5pm to 2am, Tosca is a popular watering hole for local politicos, writers, media types, and similar cognoscenti of unassuming classics. Visiting celebrities have been known to drop in as impromptu bartenders, serving martinis in chilled long-stemmed glasses. Equipped with dim lights, red leather booths, and the requisite vintage jukebox spilling out Italian arias, it's everything you'd expect an old North Beach legend to be.

✪ **Vesuvio.** 255 Columbus Ave. (at Broadway). ☎ **415/362-3370.** www.vesuvio@vesuvio.com.

Situated along Jack Kerouac Alley across from the famed City Lights Bookstore is this renowned literary beatnik hangout that's not just riding its historic coattails. The atmosphere is way cool, as are the people who frequent it. Bring a chess board, borrow a game here, or write in a notebook, but whatever you do, make sure you look brooding and intense. Popular with neighborhood writers, artists, songsters, and wannabes, Vesuvio is crowded with self-proclaimed philosophers, and everyone else ranging from longshoremen and cab drivers to businesspeople. The convivial space is two stories of cocktail tables, complemented by a changing exhibition of local art and an ongoing slide show. In addition to drinks, Vesuvio features an espresso machine. No credit cards are accepted.

## BREW PUBS

**Gordon Biersch Brewery.** 2 Harrison St. (on the Embarcadero). ☎ **415/243-8246.**

Gordon Biersch Brewery is San Francisco's largest brew-restaurant, serving decent food and tasty brew to an attractive crowd of mingling professionals. There are always several beers to choose from, ranging from light to dark. Menu items range from $3.50 to $17. (See the review in chapter 6 for more information.)

**San Francisco Brewing Company.** 155 Columbus Ave. (at Pacific St.). ☎ **415/434-3344.** www.sfbrewing.com.

Surprisingly low key for an ale house, this cozy brew pub serves its brew along with burgers, fries, and the like. The bar is one of the city's few remaining old saloons, aglow with stained-glass windows, tile floors, skylit ceiling beveled glass, a mahogany bar, and a massive overhead fan running the full length of the bar—a bizarre contraption crafted from brass and palm fronds. The handmade copper brew kettle is visible from the street. There's music most evenings. Darts, chess, backgammon, cards, and dice are all available. Menu items range from $3.25 to $16. The happy-hour special, a dollar per 10-ounce microbrew beer (or $1.75 a pint), runs daily from 4 to 6pm and midnight to 1am.

**Thirsty Bear Brewing Company.** 661 Howard St. (1 block east of the Moscone Center). ☎ **415/974-0905.**

# Midnight or Midday Mochas

If you happen to be wandering around North Beach past your bedtime and need to satisfy your caffeine fix, these cafes offer not only excellent espresso, but also a glimpse into what it must have been like back in the days of the beatniks, when nothing was as crucial as a strong cup of coffee, a good smoke, and a stimulating environment.

Doing the North Beach thing is little more than hanging out in a sophisticated but relaxed atmosphere over a well-made cappuccino. You can do it at **Caffè Greco,** 423 Columbus Ave., between Green and Vallejo streets (☎ **415/397-6261**), and grab a bite, too. The affordable fare includes beer, wine, a good selection of coffees, focaccia sandwiches, and desserts (try the gelato or homemade tiramisu).

**Caffè Trieste,** 601 Vallejo St., at Grant Avenue (☎ **415/392-6739**), is one of San Francisco's most beloved cafes—very down-home Italian, with only espresso drinks, pastries, and indoor and outdoor seating. Opera is always on the jukebox, unless its Saturday afternoon, when the family and their friends break out in operatic arias from 2 to 5pm.

Seven superb, handcrafted varieties of brew, ranging from a fruit-flavored Strawberry Ale to a steak-in-a-cup stout, are always on tap at this stylish high-ceilinged brick edifice. Excellent Spanish food, too (see chapter 6). Pool tables and dart boards are upstairs, and live music (jazz, flamenco, blues, alternative, and classical) can be heard most nights.

**20 Tank Brewery.** 316 11th St. (at Folsom St.). ☎ **415/255-9455.**

Right in the heart of SoMa's popular strip, this huge, come-as-you-are bar is known for serving good beer at fair prices. Pizzas, sandwiches, chilies, and assorted appetizers are also available. Menu items range from $3.25 to $12.95. Pub games include darts, shuffleboard, and dice.

## COCKTAILS WITH A VIEW

**The Carnelian Room.** 555 California St., in the Bank of America Building (between Kearny and Montgomery sts.). ☎ **415/433-7500.**

On the 52nd floor of the Bank of America Building, the Carnelian Room offers uninterrupted views of the city. From a window-front table you feel as if you can reach out, pluck up the TransAmerica Pyramid, and stir your martini with it. In addition to cocktails, "Discovery Dinners" are offered for $39 per person. Jackets and ties are required for men. *Note:* The restaurant has the most extensive wine list in the city—1,275 selections to be exact.

**Cityscape.** Atop Hilton Tower I, 333 O'Farrell St. (at Mason St.), 46th floor. ☎ **415/923-5002.**

When you sit under the glass roof and sip a drink here, it's as if you're sitting out under the stars and enjoying views of the bay. There's dinner available and nightly dancing to a DJ's picks from 10pm. The mirrored columns and floor-to-ceiling draperies help create an elegant and romantic ambiance.

**Crown Room.** In the Fairmont Hotel, 950 Mason St., 24th floor. ☎ **415/772-5131.**

Of all the bars listed here, the Crown Room is definitely the plushest. Reached by an external glass elevator, the panoramic view from the top will encourage you to linger. In addition to drinks (steep at $7 to $9), dinner buffets are served for $36.50.

**Equinox.** In the Hyatt Regency Hotel, 5 Embarcadero Center. ☎ **415/788-1234.**

The sales "hook" of the Hyatt's rooftop Equinox is a revolving floor that gives each table a 360° panoramic view of the city every 45 minutes. In addition to cocktails, dinner is served daily.

✪ **Harry Denton's Starlight Room.** Atop the Sir Francis Drake Hotel, 450 Powell St., 21st floor. ☎ **415/395-8595.**

See "Supper Clubs," above, for a full review.

✪ **Top of the Mark.** In the Mark Hopkins Intercontinental, 1 Nob Hill (California and Mason sts.). ☎ **415/616-6916.**

This is one of the most famous cocktail lounges in the world and for good reason—the spectacular glass-walled room features an unparalleled view. During World War II, it was considered de rigueur for Pacific-bound servicemen to toast their good-bye to the States here. Live entertainment is offered at 8:30 nightly, but there is a $6 to $10 cover charge these nights, too. There's afternoon tea service from 3 to 5pm Monday to Friday, and Sunday brunch, which is served from 10am to 2pm, costs $39 without champagne, $55 with. Drinks are also pricey, ranging from $6 to $8.

## PIANO BARS

San Francisco is lucky to have several lively piano bars. As in other cities, these specialized lounges are perfectly suited to the grand hotels in which they are usually located.

**Nob Hill Terrace.** In the Mark Hopkins Intercontinental, 1 Nob Hill (California and Mason sts.). ☎ **415/392-3434.**

Drinks ($5 to $10) are served nightly in a delightfully intimate, skylit room with hand-painted murals. It's located just off the lobby.

✪ **The Redwood Room.** In the Clift Hotel, 495 Geary St. ☎ **415/775-4700.**

A true art-deco beauty, this ground-floor lounge is one of San Francisco's most comfortable and nostalgic piano bars. Its gorgeous redwood interior was completely built from a single 2,000-year-old tree. It's further enhanced by the large, brilliantly colored Gustav Klimt murals. Drinks go for $6 to $9.

## SPORTS BARS

**Bayside Sports Bar and Grill.** 1787 Union St. (at Octavia St.). ☎ **415/673-1565.**

This is easily one of the largest sports bars in the city, equipped with a state-of-the-art super-large-screen television, 30 smaller ones, 19 beers on tap, and two pool tables. The crowd is mainly Marina yuppies (lots of baseball caps, sweatshirts, and Lycra shorts), which is made bearable by the fast, friendly food service (mostly burgers, sandwiches, and such) and the myriad of sports channels. Happy hour is Monday to Friday from 4 to 6pm.

**Greens Sports Bar.** 2239 Polk St. (at Green St.). ☎ **415/775-4287.** www.citysearch.com/sfo/greenssportsbar.

If you think San Francisco sports fans aren't as enthusiastic as those on the East Coast, we dare you to try to get a seat (or even get in) at Green's during a 49ers game. It's a classic old sports bar, with lots of polished dark wood and windows that open out onto Polk Street, but it's loaded with modern appliances, including a large-screen television, 10 smaller ones, 18 beers on tap, and a pool table. They don't serve food here, but you can bring in grub for the game. A late-night happy hour runs Sunday to Wednesday from 10pm to 2am.

## WINE/CHAMPAGNE BARS

**The Bubble Lounge.** 714 Montgomery St. (at Colombus). ☎ **415/434-4204.**

San Francisco nightlife is in full swing, and toasting the town is a nightly event, at this relatively new champagne bar. With 300 champagnes, with around 30 by the glass, brick walls, couches, velvet curtains, and a pool table within its two levels, there's plenty of pop in this fizzy lounge.

**Eos.** 101 Carl St. (at Cole St.). ☎ **415/566-3063.**

If you're downtown, London Wine Bar. If you're around the Civic Center, Hayes and Vine. For anything west of these two, your top choice is Eos, a fairly new and highly successful restaurant and wine bar in Cole Valley (near the Haight). Around the corner from the restaurant is this chic, lively wine bar filled mostly with a young Cole Valley clientele who dabble among the 400 vintages from around the world.

**Hayes and Vine.** 377 Hayes St. (at Gough St.). ☎ **415/626-5301.**

Choose among 750 wines (with over 50 by the glass!) from around the world at this unpretentious wine bar staffed by true cognoscenti of fine wine (which is a good thing, since you'll probably have never heard of 90% of these wines). Be sure to ask about taking a "flight," where you can try several different wines for a fixed price. Cheese, breads, and desserts are also served.

**London Wine Bar.** 415 Sansome St. (between Sacramento and Clay sts.). ☎ **415/788-4811.**

This British-style wine bar and store is a popular after-work hangout among Financial District suits. It's more of a place to drink and chat than to admire fine wines. Usually two to three dozen wines are open at any given time, mostly from California. It's a great venue for sampling local Napa Valley wines before you buy.

## 5  Gay & Lesbian Bars & Clubs

As with straight establishments, gay and lesbian bars and clubs target varied clienteles. Whether you're into leather or Lycra, business or bondage, there's gay nightlife here just for you.

Check the free weeklies, the *San Francisco Bay Guardian* and *San Francisco Weekly,* for listings of events and happenings. The *Bay Area Reporter* is a gay paper with comprehensive listings, including a weekly community calendar. All the above papers are free and are distributed weekly on Wednesday or Thursday. They can be found stacked at the corner of 18th and Castro streets, and Ninth and Harrison streets, as well as in bars, bookshops, and stores around town. To find out what's up with lesbian events in San Francisco ranging from women's golf to nightlife, call **Girl Spot** (☎ 415/337-4962). There are also a number of gay and lesbian guides to San Francisco. See "For Gay & Lesbian Travelers," in Chapter 2, "Planning a Trip to San Francisco," for further details.

Listed below are some of the city's more established, mainstream gay hangouts.

**Alta Plaza.** 2301 Fillmore St. (at Clay St.). ☎ **415/922-1444.** www.altaplaza.com. No cover.

Pacific Heights's wealthy gays flock to this classy Fillmore establishment, with both bar and restaurant. Cocktail hour, from 4 to 7pm nightly, offers $3 well and call drinks, and is especially festive on Friday and Saturday. Later in the evening, the restaurant fills with yuppie diners who come for the Northern California cuisine with Pacific Rim and Italian influences or to hang at the bar area and check out the hotties. There's live jazz Sunday to Thursday and a DJ on weekend nights.

**Badlands.** 4121 18th St. (at Castro St.). ☎ **415/626-9320.** No cover.

This popular hangout is decorated with license plates from practically everywhere, and a bar that stretches the length of the place. A pool table and pinball machine offer entertainment, but so do the Levi's-clad clientele for that matter.

✪ **The Café.** 2367 Market St. (at Castro St.). ☎ **415/861-3846.**

When this place first got jumping, it was the only predominantly lesbian dance club on Saturday nights in the city. But once the guys found out how much fun the girls were having, they joined the party. Today, it's still a very happening mixed gay and lesbian scene with two bars, a steamy, free-spirited dance floor, and a small patio.

**Castro Station.** 456B Castro St. (between 17th and 18th sts.). ☎ **415/626-7220.** No cover.

A well-known gay hangout in the Castro District, this bar is popular with the leather and Levi's crowd, as well as trendy boys from around the country who come here looking for action. Drinks range from $2.25 to $6.

**The Cinch Saloon.** 1723 Polk St. (near Washington St.). ☎ **415/776-4162.** No cover.

Among the popular attributes of this cruisy neighborhood bar are the outdoor patio, Sunday barbecue or buffet, and progressive music and videos. Forty-niner fans also gather here for televised games. Decorated in a Southwestern theme ("down home in Arizona"), the bar attracts a mixed crowd of gays, lesbians (now that there are almost no exclusively lesbian bars left in San Francisco), and gay-friendly straight folk. There are "beer busts" or theme drink nights weekly. The nominal charge for barbecues and buffets is donated entirely to various AIDS organizations.

**Detour.** 2348 Market St. (near Castro St.). ☎ **415/861-6053.** No cover.

Right in the heart of gay San Francisco, this bar attracts a young, often hot crowd of boys, with its low lighting and throbbing house music. Chain-link fences seem to hold in the action while a live DJ spins a web of popular hits. Special events, including the Saturday go-go dancers, keep this place jumping.

**The Eagle.** 398 12th St. (at Harrison St.). ☎ **415/626-0880.** www.sfeagle.com.

One of the city's most traditional Levi-leather bars, The Eagle boasts a heated outdoor patio, a happy hour Monday to Friday from 5 to 8pm, and a popular Sunday-afternoon beer fest.

**The EndUp.** 401 Sixth St. (at Harrison St.). ☎ **415/357-0827.** Cover varies.

It's a different nightclub every night of the week, but regardless of who's throwing the party, the place is always jumping with the DJ's blasting tunes. There are two pool tables, a flaming fireplace, outdoor patio, and a mob of gyrating souls on the dance floor. Some nights are straight, so call for gay nights.

**Giraffe Lounge.** 1131 Polk St. (near Sutter St.). ☎ **415/474-1702.** No cover.

Favored by a younger, action-seeking crowd, this video bar, with its 15 ceiling-mounted monitors, is a good place for cruising or shooting pool. It's a friendly neighborhood hangout during the week and livens up on weekends.

**Kimo's.** 1351 Polk St. (at Pine St.). ☎ **415/885-4535.** Free to nominal cover.

This neighborhood bar located in the seedier gay section of town is a friendly oasis, decorated with plants, pictures, and "gay banners." The bar provides a relaxing venue for chatting, drinking, and quiet cruising, and things occasionally liven up when drag shows preside.

**Lone Star Saloon.** 1354 Harrison St. (between 9th and 10th sts.). ☎ **415/863-9999.** No cover.

Expect dykes and a heavier, furrier motorcycle crowd (both men and women) most every night. The Sunday-afternoon beer bust on the patio is especially popular.

**Metro.** 3600 16th St. (at Market St.). ☎ **415/703-9750.** No cover.

With modern art on the walls and much use of terra-cotta, the Metro provides the gay community with high-energy dance music and the best view of the Castro District from its large balcony. The bar seems to attract people of all ages who enjoy the friendly bartenders and the highly charged, cruising atmosphere. There's also a Chinese restaurant on the premises if you get hungry.

**The Mint.** 1942 Market St. (at Laguna St.). ☎ **415/626-4726.** No cover.

Come out of the shower and into The Mint, where every night you can sing show tunes at this gay and lesbian karaoke bar. Along with song, you'll encounter a mixed 20- to 40-something crowd who like to combine cocktails with do-it-yourself cabaret.

**Rawhide II.** 280 Seventh St. (at Folsom St.). ☎ **415/621-1197.** Weekend cover charge ($5) includes 1 free drink.

Gay or straight, this is one of the city's top country-western dance bars, patronized by both men and women. $5 dance lessons are offered Tuesday to Friday from 7:30 to 9:30pm.

**The Stud.** 399 Ninth St. (at Harrison St.). ☎ **415/863-6623.** Cover $2–$6 weekends.

The Stud has been around for 30 years, is one of the most successful gay establishments in town, and is mellow enough for straights as well as gays. The interior has an antique-shop look and a miniature train circling over the bar and dance floor. Music here is a balanced mix of old and new, and nights vary from cabaret and oldies to disco. Call in advance for the evening's venue. Drink prices range from $2 to $6.

**The Swallow.** 1750 Polk St. (between Clay and Washington sts.). ☎ **415/775-4152.** No cover.

Some consider this classy piano bar for the middle-age-and-up crowd the best gay bar on Polk.

**Twin Peaks Tavern.** 401 Castro St. (at 17th and Market sts.). ☎ **415/864-9470.** No cover.

Right at the intersection of Castro, 17th, and Market streets is one of the Castro's most famous gay hangouts, which caters to an older crowd and is considered the first gay bar in America. Because of its relatively small size and desirable location, the place becomes fairly crowded and convivial by 8pm, earlier than many neighboring bars.

## 6 Film

The **San Francisco International Film Festival,** held in March of each year, is one of America's oldest film festivals. Tickets are relatively inexpensive. Entries include new films by beginning and established directors. For a schedule or information, call ☎ **415/931-FILM;** www.sfiff.org. Tickets can be charged by phone through **BASS Ticketmaster** (☎ **510/762-2277**).

Even if you're not here in time for the festival, don't despair. The classic, independent, and mainstream cinemas in San Francisco are every bit as good as the city's other cultural offerings.

### REPERTORY CINEMAS

**Castro Theatre.** 429 Castro St. (near Market St.). ☎ **415/621-6120.**

Built in 1922, the beautiful Castro Theatre is known for its screenings of classic cinema and for its Wurlitzer organ, which is played before each show. There's a different feature here almost nightly, and more often than not it's a double feature. Bargain matinees are usually offered on Wednesday, Saturday, Sunday, and holidays. Phone for schedules, prices, and show times.

**Red Vic.** 1727 Haight St. (between Cole and Shrader sts.). ☎ **415/668-3994.**

The worker-owned Red Vic movie collective recently moved from the Victorian building that gave it its name. The theater specializes in independent releases and contemporary cultish hits. Prices are $6 for adults ($4.50 during matinees), $3 for seniors and kids 12 and under. Tickets go on sale 20 minutes before each show. Phone for schedules and show times.

**Roxie.** 3117 16th St. (at Valencia St.). ☎ **415/863-1087.**

The Roxie consistently screens the best new alternative films anywhere. The low-budget contemporary features shown here are largely devoid of Hollywood candy coating; many are West Coast premieres. Films change weekly, sometimes sooner. Phone for schedules, prices, and show times.

# Side Trips from San Francisco

**11**

San Francisco may be one of the world's most captivating cities, but don't let it monopolize your time to the point of ignoring its environs, which contain a multitude of natural wonders such as Mount Tamalpais and Muir Woods, scenic communities such as Tiburon, Sausalito, Half Moon Bay, and bustling Bay Area cities such as Oakland and Berkeley.

Most of the attractions at these destinations are either free or very inexpensive: Hiking will cost you no more than a parking pass, and strolling the shorelines and boutique-filled streets doesn't cost a thing (until you invariably slap down your credit card for a bayside lunch or a souvenir). From San Francisco, you can reach any of these points in less than an hour by car or public transport. Budget accommodations and dining are available in most areas.

## 1 Berkeley

10 miles NE of San Francisco

Berkeley is famous for its University of California at Berkeley, which is world-renowned for its first-rate academic standards, its 16 Nobel Prize winners, and the protests that led to the most renowned student riots in U.S. history. Today, there's still hippie idealism in the air, but the radicals have aged; the sixties are only present in tie-dye and paraphernalia shops, and the students have less angst. But the biggest change the town is facing is yuppification; as San Francisco's rent and property prices have maxed out, everyone with less than a small fortune is seeking shelter elsewhere, and Berkeley is one of the top picks. Still, it's a charming town teeming with all types of people, a beautiful campus, vast parks, great shopping, and some incredible restaurants.

### ESSENTIALS

The Berkeley **BART** station is 2 blocks from the university. The fare from San Francisco is under $3.

If you are coming **by car** from San Francisco, take the Bay Bridge (go during evening commute and you'll think Los Angeles's traffic is a breeze), follow I-80 east to the University Avenue exit, and follow University until you hit the campus. Parking is tight near the campus, so either leave your car at the Sather Gate parking lot on Telegraph and Durant or expect to fight for a spot.

---

**Travel Tip**

Half- and full-day trips to Muir Woods, Sausalito, Napa, and Sonoma are also available via **Tower Tours** (☎ 415/434-8687), which runs regularly scheduled tours by microbus to San Francisco's neighboring towns and countryside. Excursions to Yosemite and the Monterey Peninsula are available as well. Phone for price and departure information.

---

Phone the **Visitor Hot Line** (☎ 510/549-8710) for automated information on events and happenings in Berkeley.

## WHAT TO SEE & DO

Hanging out is the preferred Berkeley pastime, and the best place to do it is on Telegraph Avenue, the street that leads to the campus's southern entrance. Most of the action lies between Bancroft Way and Ashby Avenue, where coffeehouses, restaurants, shops, great book and record stores, and craft booths swarm with life. Pretend you're local: Plant yourself at a cafe, sip a latte, and ponder something intellectual or survey the town's unique residents bustling by.

Bibliophiles must stop at **Cody's Books,** at 2454 Telegraph Ave., ☎ 510/845-7852, to peruse their gargantuan selection of titles, independent-press books, and magazines. The avenue is also packed with street vendors selling everything from T-shirts and jewelry to I Ching and tarot-card readings.

### UC BERKELEY CAMPUS

The University of California at Berkeley itself is worth a stroll as well. It's a beautiful old campus with plenty of woodsy paths, architecturally noteworthy buildings, and, of course, many of the 31,000 students scurrying to and from classes. Among the architectural highlights of the campus are a number of buildings by Bernard Maybeck, Bakewell and Brown, and John Galen Howard.

Contact the **Visitor Information Center** at 101 University Hall, 2200 University Ave. (at Oxford Street) (☎ 510/642-5215), to join a free, regularly scheduled campus tour (Mon through Sat at 10am, Sun at 1pm; no tours offered from mid-Dec to mid-Jan); or stop by the office and pick up a self-guided walking-tour brochure.

You'll find the university's southern entrance at the northern end of Telegraph, at Bancroft Way. Walk through the main entrance into Sproul Plaza, and when school is in session you'll encounter the gamut of Berkeley's inhabitants here: colorful street people, rambling political zealots, chanting Hare Krishnas, and ambitious students. You'll also find the Student Union, complete with a bookstore, cafes, and an information desk on the second floor where you can pick up a free map of Berkeley, as well as the local student newspaper (also found in dispensers throughout campus).

You might be lucky enough to stumble upon some impromptu musicians or a heated, and sometimes absurd, debate. There's always something going on, so stretch out on the grass for a few minutes and take in the Berkeley vibe.

For viewing more traditional art forms, there are some noteworthy museums here, too. The **Lawrence Hall of Science** (☎ 510/642-5132), offering hands-on science exploration, is open from 10am to 5pm daily and is a wonderful place to watch the sunset. Admission is $6 for adults, $4 for seniors and children 7 to 18, $2 for children 3 to 6, free for kids under 3. The **University Art Museum** (☎ 510/642-0808) is open from 11am to 5pm on Wednesday and Friday through

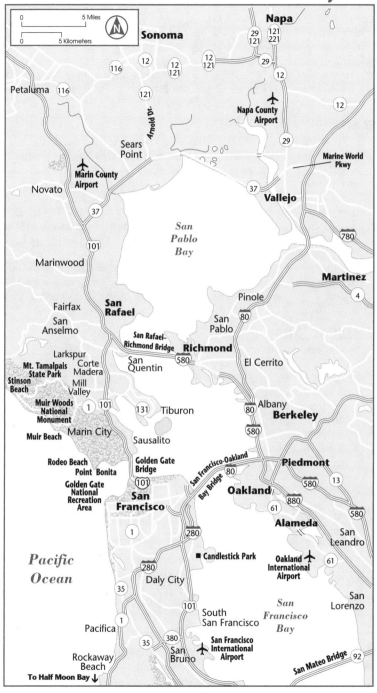

Sonoma

Napa

Petaluma

Sears Point

Marin County Airport

Novato

Marinwood

Fairfax

San Anselmo

San Rafael

Larkspur

Mt. Tamalpais State Park

Corte Madera

Stinson Beach

Mill Valley

Muir Woods National Monument

Muir Beach

Marin City

San Quentin

Tiburon

Sausalito

Rodeo Beach    Point Bonita

Golden Gate Bridge

Golden Gate National Recreation Area

San Francisco

Pacific Ocean

Daly City

Pacifica

Rockaway Beach

To Half Moon Bay ↓

San Bruno

Napa County Airport

Marine World Pkwy

Vallejo

San Pablo Bay

Martinez

Pinole

San Pablo

Richmond

El Cerrito

San Rafael–Richmond Bridge

Albany

Berkeley

San Francisco-Oakland Bay Bridge

Piedmont

Oakland

Alameda

San Leandro

Candlestick Park

Oakland International Airport

San Lorenzo

San Francisco Bay

South San Francisco

San Francisco International Airport

San Mateo Bridge

Arnold Dr.

Sunday, and Thursday from 11am to 9pm. Admission is $6 for adults, $4 for seniors and children 12 to 17, and free for kids under 12. This museum includes a substantial collection of Hans Hofmann paintings, a sculpture garden, and the Pacific Film Archive.

If you're interested in notable off-campus buildings, contact the **Berkeley Convention and Visitors Bureau** (☎ 510/549-7040) for an architectural walking tour brochure.

## PARKS

Unbeknownst to many travelers, Berkeley has some of the most extensive and beautiful parks around. If you want to wear out the kids or enjoy hiking, swimming, or just getting a breath of California air and sniffing a few roses, jump in your car and make your way to **Tilden Park.** On the way, stop at the colorful terraced Rose Garden, located in north Berkeley on Euclid Avenue between Bay View and Eunice Street. Then head high into the Berkeley hills to Tilden, where you'll find plenty of flora and fauna, hiking trails, an old steam train and merry-go-round, farm and nature area for kids, and a chilly tree-encircled lake (☎ 510/843-2137 for further information).

Another worthy nature excursion is the **University of California Botanical Garden,** which features a vast collection of herbage ranging from cacti to redwoods; it's located in Strawberry Canyon on Centennial Drive (☎ 510/642-3343 for details).

## WHERE TO SHOP

If you're itching to exercise your credit cards, head to one of two places. College Avenue from Dwight all the way down to the Oakland border is crammed with eclectic boutiques, antique shops, and restaurants. The other option is Fourth Street, in west Berkeley just 2 blocks north of the University Avenue exit. This 2-block expanse is the perfect place to go on a sunny morning. Grab a cup of java, read the paper at a patio table, and then hit the **Crate and Barrel Outlet** (where prices are 30% to 70% off retail) at 1785 Fourth St., between Hearst and Virginia (☎ 510/528-5500), which is open Monday to Saturday from 10am to 6pm and Sunday from 11am to 6pm, or any of the small, wonderful stores crammed with imported and locally made housewares. Nearby is **REI,** the Bay Area's favorite outdoor outfitters at 1338 San Pablo Ave., near Gilman Street (☎ 510/527-4140).

## WHERE TO STAY

**Bed and Breakfast California,** 12711 McCartysville Place, Saratoga, CA 95070 (☎ 800/872-4500 or 408/867-9662; fax 408/867-0907; www.bbintl.com; e-mail: info@bbintl.com), accommodates visitors in more than 150 private homes and apartments in the San Francisco–Berkeley area. The cost ranges from a reasonable $65 to $300 per night, and there's a 2-night minimum. The **Berkeley Convention and Visitors Bureau,** 2015 Center St., Berkeley, CA 94704 (☎ 800/847-4823, 510/549-7040, or the hot line 510/549-8710), can also find accommodations for you, as well as provide free visitor guides, maps, and area literature. It's staffed Monday to Friday from 9am to 5pm.

### SUPER-CHEAP SLEEPS

**Campus Motel.** 1619 University Ave. (between McGee Ave. and California St.), Berkeley, CA 94703. ☎ 510/841-3844. 23 units. TV TEL. $60 double. AE, DISC, MC, V.

You won't be pampered with imported soaps or extra-fluffy towels, but this basic motel only 5 blocks from the south end of campus offers clean, well-kept rooms

# Berkeley

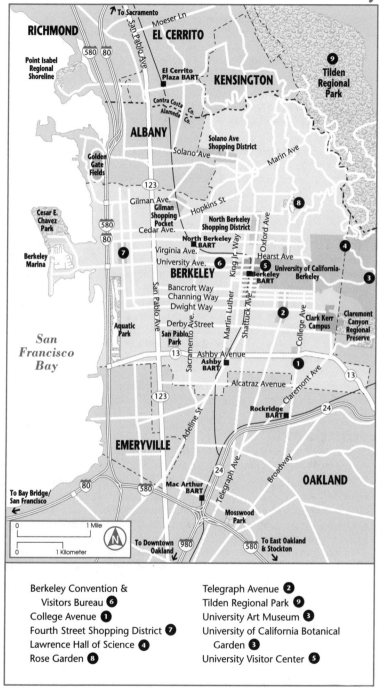

RICHMOND

To Sacramento

Moeser Ln

EL CERRITO

Point Isabel
Regional
Shoreline

El Cerrito
Plaza BART

KENSINGTON

Tilden
Regional
Park **9**

San Pablo Ave

580 80

Contra Costa Co.
Alameda Co.

ALBANY

Solano Ave
Shopping District

Golden
Gate
Fields

Solano Ave

Marin Ave

Cesar E.
Chavez
Park

123

Gilman Ave.

Gilman
Shopping
Pocket

Hopkins St

Cedar Ave.

North Berkeley
Shopping District

580
80

North Berkeley
BART

Oxford Ave

**8**

Berkeley
Marina

Virginia Ave.

**7**

University Ave.

**6**

Hearst Ave

BERKELEY

King Jr. Way

University of California-
Berkeley

Berkeley
BART

**5**

Aquatic
Park

Bancroft Way

Channing Way

Dwight Way

Martin Luther

Shattuck Ave

**2**

College Ave

Clark Kerr
Campus

**4**

**3**

San Pablo Ave

Derby Street

San Pablo
Park

Sacramento Ave

13

Ashby Avenue

Claremont
Canyon
Regional
Preserve

San
Francisco
Bay

Ashby
BART

**1**

Alcatraz Avenue

Claremont Ave

13

123

Adeline St

Rockridge
BART

24

To Bay Bridge/
San Francisco

80

580

Mac Arthur
BART

Telegraph Ave

Broadway

OAKLAND

24

EMERYVILLE

Mosswood
Park

To Downtown
Oakland

980

To East Oakland
& Stockton

580

0          1 Mile

0          1 Kilometer

| | | |
|---|---|---|
| Berkeley Convention & Visitors Bureau **6** | Telegraph Avenue **2** | |
| College Avenue **1** | Tilden Regional Park **9** | |
| Fourth Street Shopping District **7** | University Art Museum **3** | |
| Lawrence Hall of Science **4** | University of California Botanical Garden **3** | |
| Rose Garden **8** | University Visitor Center **5** | |

245

with a full bath and coffeemaker at an almost unbeatable price. It's located on a busy strip that leads to the west end of campus and is surrounded by cheap ethnic restaurants. You probably won't want to hang around here during the day (there's not much to see), but with the campus and north Berkeley nearby, you won't miss out on anything if you stay here.

✪ **Golden Bear Motel.** 1620 San Pablo Ave. (between University and Cedar sts.), Berkeley, CA 94702. ☎ **800/525-6770** or 510/525-6770. 42 units. TEL TV. Doubles $54–$64; cottages $120–$135. AE, DC, DISC, MC, V. Pets okay ($5 1-time fee).

The price is right, the rooms are surprisingly attractive and clean, and the staff is congenial at this comfortable, 1950s Spanish-style motor lodge near Cafe Fanny and the new hip Fourth Street shops. Each room comes with either a queen or two twin beds, a dresser, a night stand, and a desk—all of which have been recently renovated. For a few extra dollars you can opt for one of the three cottages, which are perfect for families and have two bedrooms, a living room, and a full kitchen. Guests also enjoy free local calls and voice mail. All in all, an excellent deal.

## WHERE TO DINE

East Bay dining is a relaxed alternative to the city's gourmet night out; there are plenty of ambitious Berkeley restaurants worth foraging and, unlike San Francisco, plenty of parking.

If you want to do it student-style, eat on campus Monday to Friday. Buy something at any of the sidewalk stands or in the building directly behind the Student Union. The least-expensive food is available downstairs in the **Cafeteria,** on Lower Sproul Plaza. There's also the **Bear's Lair Pub and Coffee House,** the **Terrace,** and the **Golden Bear Restaurant.** All the university eateries have both indoor and outdoor seating.

Telegraph Avenue has an array of small, ethnic restaurants, cafes, and sandwich shops. Follow the students: if the place is crowded, it's either good, super cheap, or both.

### SUPER-CHEAP EATS

**Blue Nile.** 2525 Telegraph Ave. ☎ **510/540-6777.** Reservations required Fri–Sat. Main courses $7.50–$8.95. MC, V. Tues–Sat 11:30am–10pm, Sun 5–10pm. ETHIOPIAN.

Step through the beaded curtains into the Blue Nile, and the African paintings and music will summon your appetite to other parts of the world. But the journey doesn't end there—be prepared to savor the flavorful specialties such as *doro wat* (a spiced stew of beef, lamb, or chicken, served with a fluffy crepe injera) or *gomen wat* (mustard greens sautéed in cream) with no utensils other than your fingers. Sure, you could convince the wait staff to drum up a fork or two, but don't bother. After all, when in Africa. . . No appetizers are served, but meals come with a small salad.

**Cambodiana's.** 2156 University Ave. (between Shattuck and Oxford). ☎ **510/843-4630.** Reservations recommended on Fri–Sat. Main courses $7.50–$13; fixed-price dinner $11.25. AE, CB, DC, JCB, MC, V. Mon–Fri 11:30am–3pm; Mon–Thurs and Sun 5–9:30pm, Fri–Sat 5–10:30pm. CAMBODIAN.

For those who relish the spicy cuisine of Cambodia, this is quite a find. The decor is as colorful as the fare; amidst brilliant blue, yellow, and green walls with Breuer-style chairs set at tables, you can feast on a variety of dishes. Especially tasty is the curry or *naga* dishes with a sauce of tamarind, turmeric, lemongrass, shrimp paste, coconut-milk galinga, shallot, lemon leaf, sugar, and green chili. This sauce may smother salmon, prawns, chicken, or steak. Another tempting dish is the chicken *chaktomuk* prepared with pineapple, red peppers, and zucchini in soy and oyster

# People's Park/People's Power

In late 1967, the university demolished an entire block of buildings north of Telegraph Avenue. The destruction, which forced hippies and other "undesirables" from the slum housing that stood there, was done under the guise of university expansion and urban renewal—good liberal causes. But after the lot lay vacant for almost 2 years, a group of Berkeley radicals whose names read like a who's who of 1960s leftists, including Jerry Rubin, Bobby Seale, and Tom Hayden, decided to take the land for "the people."

On April 29, 1969, hundreds of activists invaded the vacant lot with gardening tools and tamed the muddy ground into a park. One month later, Berkeley's Republican mayor sent 250 police officers into the park, and 4,000 demonstrators materialized to challenge them. A riot ensued, the police fired buckshot at the crowd, and one rioter was killed and another blinded. Governor Ronald Reagan sent in the National Guard, and for the next 17 days the guardsmen repeatedly gassed innocent students, faculty, and passersby. Berkeley was a war zone, and People's Park became the most important symbol of "people power" during the 1960s.

People's Park once again sparked controversy in 1992 when university officials decided to build volleyball courts there. In August of that year, a park activist broke into the campus home of the university's chancellor. When a police officer arrived, the activist lunged at him with a machete and was shot dead. On the victim's body was a note with the message: "We are willing to die for this land. Are you?" On news of the contemporary radical's death, more than 150 of her supporters rioted. Ironically, the nets didn't get much use and now basketball courts have taken their place.

sauce. There are plenty of vegetarian and low-cal options, and the three-course, fixed-price dinner is an excellent value.

✪ **Cafe Fanny.** 1603 San Pablo Ave. (at Cedar St.). ☎ **510/524-5447.** Most breakfast items $5, lunch $5–$7. MC, V. Mon–Fri 7am–3pm, Sat 8am–4pm, Sun 8am–3pm. Breakfast is served until 11am except for Sun when it's an all-day thing. Closed major holidays. FRENCH/ITALIAN.

Alice Waters' (of Chez Panisse fame) cafe is one of those local must-do breakfast traditions. Grab the morning paper, put on your Birkenstocks, and head here to wait in line for a simple, but masterfully prepared stand-up French breakfast. The menu offers such items as a soft-boiled farm egg with levain toast and house jam, buckwheat crepes with jam), and an assortment of sweet pastries. Lunch is more of an Italian experience featuring seasonal selections. Sandwiches, such as baked ham and watercress on focaccia; roasted eggplant with red peppers, mozzarella, aioli, and tapenade on a baguette; and grilled chicken breast wrapped in prosciutto, sage, and aioli on an Acme bread might convince you that you've never really had a sandwich before. There's also a selection of pizzettas, salads, and soup. Eat inside at the stand-up food bar (one bench), or outside (virtually in the parking lot) at one of the cafe tables.

## MODERATELY PRICED OPTIONS

✪ **Cafe Rouge.** 1782 4th St. (between Delaware and Hearst). ☎**510/525-1440.** Main courses $9.50–$20. MC, V. Mon 11:30am–3pm; Tues–Sat 11:30am–3pm, interim menu 3–5pm, dinner 5:30–9:30pm; Sun 5–9pm. BISTRO.

After cooking at San Francisco's renowned Zuni Cafe for 10 years, chef/owner Marsha McBride launched her own restaurant, a sort of Zuni east. She brought ex-Zuni staff and some of the restaurant's flavor with her, and now the sparse, loftlike dining room is serving salads, rotisserie chicken with oil and thyme, grilled lamb chops, steaks, and homemade sausages. East Bay carnivores are especially happy with the burger; just like Zuni's, it's top notch.

✪ **Rivoli.** 1539 Solano Ave. ☎ **510/526-2542.** Reservations recommended. Main courses $10.25–$15.75 MC, V. Mon–Thurs 5:30–9:30pm, Fri 5:30–10pm, Sat 5–10pm, Sun 5–9pm. CALIFORNIA.

One of the favored dinner destinations in the East Bay, Rivoli's winning combination is top-notch food at amazingly reasonable prices. The owners have done the most with an otherwise uninteresting space by creating a warm, intimate dining environment, which overlooks a sweet little garden with visiting raccoons and possums. Aside from a few house favorites, the menu changes entirely every three weeks in order to serve whatever's freshest and in season. While many love it, we weren't thrilled with the portobello mushroom fritter, which in our mind was a glorified variation on the fried zucchini stick. However, we did have an absolute A+ dish here (*very* rare): the hearty oven braised pork ragout with butternut squash and dandelion greens intermingled with tender and crispy semolina gnocchi. Perfection at this price ($13.50 for the ragout) is enough to put most high-end San Francisco restaurants to shame. Finish the evening with the Meyer lemon cheesecake; it's a decadent sour-cream-like affair with a subtle pistachio crust.

## 2  Oakland

10 miles E of San Francisco

Though it's less than a dozen miles from San Francisco, the city of Oakland is worlds apart from its sister city across the bay. Originally little more than a cluster of ranches and farms, Oakland's size and stature exploded practically overnight as the last mile of transcontinental railroad track was laid down. Major shipping ports soon followed, and to this day Oakland has retained its hold as one of the busiest industrial ports on the West Coast.

The price for all this economic success, however, is Oakland's lowbrow reputation for being a predominantly working-class city, forever in the shadow of San Francisco's chic spotlight. But with all its shortcomings and bad press, Oakland still manages to offer a few pleasant surprises for the handful of tourists who venture this way. Rent a sailboat on Lake Merritt, stroll along the waterfront, explore the fantastic Oakland Museum: They're all great reasons to hop the bay and spend a fog-free day exploring one of California's largest and most ethnically diversified cities.

### ESSENTIALS

**Bay Area Rapid Transit (BART)** makes the trip from San Francisco to Oakland through one of the longest underwater transit tunnels in the world. Fares range from $1 to $4, depending on your station of origin; children 4 and under ride free. BART trains operate Monday to Friday from 4am to midnight, Saturday from 6am to midnight, and on Sunday from 8am to midnight. Exit at the 12th Street station for downtown Oakland.

**By car** from San Francisco, take I-80 across the San Francisco–Oakland Bay Bridge and follow the signs to downtown Oakland. Exit at Grand Avenue South for the Lake Merritt area.

Downtown Oakland is bordered by Grand Avenue on the north, I-980 on the west, Inner Harbor on the south, and Lake Merritt on the east. Between these landmarks are three BART stations (12th St., 19th St., and Lake Merritt), City Hall, the Oakland Museum, Jack London Square, and several other sights.

## WHAT TO SEE & DO

Lake Merritt is Oakland's primary tourist attraction along with Jack London Square (see below). Three and a half miles in circumference, the tidal lagoon was bridged and dammed in the 1860s and is now a wildlife refuge that is home to flocks of migrating ducks, herons, and geese. It's surrounded on three sides by the 122-acre **Lakeside Park,** a popular place to picnic, feed the ducks, and escape the fog. At the **Sailboat House** (☎ **510/444-3807**), in Lakeside Park along the north shore, you can rent sailboats, rowboats, pedal boats, or canoes for $6 to $12 per hour.

Another site worth visiting is Oakland's **Paramount Theatre** (☎ **510/ 893-2300**), an outstanding example of art-deco architecture and decor. Built in 1931, and authentically restored in 1973, it now functions as the city's main performing-arts center. Guided tours of the 3,000-seat theater are given the first and third Saturday of each month, excluding holidays. No reservations are necessary; just show up at 10am at the box office entrance on 21st Street at Broadway. Cameras are allowed, and admission is $1.

If you take pleasure from strolling sailboat-filled wharves or are a die-hard fan of Jack London, you might actually enjoy a visit to **Jack London Square.** Oakland's only patent tourist area, this low-key version of San Francisco's Fisherman's Wharf shamelessly plays up the fact that Jack London spent most of his youth along this waterfront. The square fronts the harbor, housing a tourist-tacky complex of boutiques and eateries that are about as far away from the "call of the wild" as you can get. Most are open Monday to Saturday from 10am to 7pm (some restaurants stay open later). One of the best venues is catching live jazz at Yoshi's restaurant and club. In the center of the square is a small reconstructed Yukon cabin in which Jack London lived while prospecting in the Klondike during the gold rush of 1897.

In the middle of Jack London Square, you'll find a more authentic memorial, **Heinold's First and Last Chance Saloon**—a funky, friendly little bar and historic landmark that's worth a visit. This is where London did some of his writing, and most of his drinking; the corner table he used has remained exactly as it was nearly a century ago. Also in the square are the mast and nameplate from the USS *Oakland,* a ship that saw extensive action in the Pacific during World War II, and a wonderful museum filled with interesting London memorabilia.

The square is located at Broadway and Embarcadero. Take I-880 to Broadway, turn south, and go to the end. BART: 12th Street station; then walk south along Broadway (about half a mile); Monday through Friday they offer a free shuttle 11am to 2pm; or take bus no. 51a to the foot of Broadway.

**Oakland Museum of California.** 1000 Oak St. ☎ **888/625-6873** or 510/238-2200 for recorded information. Admission $6 adults, $4 students and seniors, free for children 5 and under. Wed–Sat 10am–5pm; Sun noon–5pm. Closed Thanksgiving Day, Christmas Day, New Year's Day, and July 4. From I-880 north, take the Oak St. exit; the museum is 5 blocks east at Oak and 10th sts. Alternatively, take I-580 to I-980 and exit at the Jackson St. ramp. BART: Lake Merritt station (1 block south of the museum).

Located 2 blocks south of the lake, the Oakland Museum of California includes just about everything you'd want to know about the state, its people, history, culture, geology, art, environment, and ecology. Inside a low-swept, modern building set down among sweeping gardens and terraces, it's actually three museums in one:

## The USS *Potomac:* FDR's Floating White House

It took the Potomac Association's hundreds of volunteers more than 12 years—at a cost of $5 million—to restore the 165-foot presidential yacht *Potomac,* President Franklin D. Roosevelt's beloved "Floating White House." Now a proud and permanent memorial berthed at the Port of Oakland's FDR Pier at Jack London Square, the revitalized *Potomac* is open to the public for dockside tours, as well as 2-hour public education cruises along the San Francisco waterfront and around Treasure Island. Prior to departure, a 15-minute video, shown at the nearby Potomac Visitor Center, provides background on FDR's presidency and FDR's legacy concerning the Bay Area.

Dockside tours are available April through October on Wednesdays and Fridays from 10am to 2pm and Sundays from 11am to 3pm, November through March on Sundays from 11am to 3pm. Admission is $5 for families with children under 18, $3 for adults, $2 for seniors, $1 for children ages 6 to 17, and free for children age 5 and under. Due to popularity of the cruises, advance purchase is strongly recommended. Hours and days open are subject to change, so be sure to call the 24-hour information line (☎ **510/839-8256**). Tickets can be purchased in advance by calling the Potomac Association office (☎ **510/839-7533,** ext. 1). The **Potomac Visitor Center** is located at 540 Water St., at the corner of Clay and Water streets adjacent to the FDR pier at the north end of Jack London Square.

exhibitions of works by California artists from Bierstadt to Diebenkorn; collections of artifacts from California's history, from Pomo Indian basketry to Country Joe McDonald's guitar; and re-creations of California habitats from the coast to the White Mountains. The museum holds major shows of California artists and shows dedicated to major California movements, such as an "Awakening From The California Dream: An Environmental History." The museum also frequently shows photography from its huge collections.

There are 45-minute guided tours leaving the gallery information desks on request or by appointment. There is a fine cafe, a **gallery** (☎ **510/834-2329**) selling works by California artists, and a book and gift shop. The cafe is open Wednesday to Saturday from 10am to 4pm, and on Sunday from noon to 5pm.

## WHERE TO DINE
### SUPER-CHEAP EATS

**Barney's Gourmet Hamburgers.** 4162 Piedmont Ave. (at Pleasant Hill Rd.). ☎ **510/655-7180.** Main courses $4–$7. No credit cards. Mon–Thurs 11am–9:30pm, Fri 11am–10pm, Sat–Sun 10am–10pm. HAMBURGERS.

If you're like us and on a perpetual quest for the best burger in America, a mandatory stop is Barney's Gourmet Hamburgers in Oakland. Beneath a replica of Michelangelo's Sistine Chapel you have a mind-boggling 21 burgers to choose from, any of which can have the beef patty replaced with a chicken breast, and at least a dozen are offered with tofu patties. The ultimate combo is a humungous basket of fries (enough for a party of three), 1/3-pound burger, and thick shake. Popular versions are the California Burger with jack cheese, bacon, ortega chiles, and sour cream, or the Popeye Burger made with chicken, sautéed spinach and feta cheese. You can even dine alfresco in the Roman-style courtyard in back, complete with a fountain and trees.

✪ **Caffe 817.** 817 Washington St. (between Eighth and Ninth Sts.). ☎ **510/271-7965.** Main courses $5–$7.50. AE, MC, V. Mon–Fri 7:30am–5pm, Sat 9:30am–4pm. ITALIAN.

After a career as an electrical engineer, Alessandro Rossi decided to go into the restaurant business, and Oakland residents have been ever-so-grateful for his decision. Rossi hired local craftspeople to fashion the avant-garde furnishings for his high-ceilinged space, yet despite its fashionable decor, the menu is very modestly priced (particularly considering the quality of ingredients, all of which are organically grown). Pastries cappuccino and are the mainstays in the morning, and simple salads, Italian sandwiches (favorites are the grilled mozzarella with artichokes and prosciutto with herb butter and pears), and freshly made soups and stews are on the midday menu. Trust us, you'll love this place.

## MODERATELY PRICED OPTIONS

**Citron.** 5484 College Ave. (off the northeastern end of Broadway between Taft and Lawton sts.). ☎ **510/653-5484.** Reservations accepted. 3-course fixed-price menu Sun–Wed $20; main courses $15–$21. AE, DC, DISC, MC, V. Mon–Thurs 5:30–9:30pm; Fri 5:30–10pm; Sat 5–10pm; Sun 5–9pm. FRENCH/MEDITERRANEAN.

This petite, adorable French bistro was an instant smash when it first opened in 1992, and it continues to draw raves for its small yet enticingly eclectic menu. Chef Chris Rossi draws the flavors of France, Italy, and Spain together with fresh California produce for Chez Panisse–like results. Though the menu changes every few weeks, dishes range from grilled Colorado lamb sirloin with wild-mushroom spoon bread and rosemary jus, to osso buco of lamb on a bed of flageolet beans and sun-dried tomato ragout and sprinkled with a pistachio gremolata garnish. The fresh salads and Citron "40-clove" chicken are also superb.

# 3  Angel Island & Tiburon

8 miles N of San Francisco

A federal and state wildlife refuge, Angel Island is the largest of the San Francisco Bay's three islets (the others being Alcatraz and Yerba Buena). The island has been, at various times, a prison, a quarantine station for immigrants, a missile base, and even a favorite site for duels. Nowadays though, most of the people who visit here are content with picnicking on the large green lawn that fronts the docking area; loaded with the appropriate recreational supplies, they claim a barbecue, plop down on the lush green grass, and while away an afternoon free of phones, televisions, and traffic. Hiking, mountain biking, and guided tram tours are also popular options.

Tiburon, situated on a peninsula of the same name, looks like a cross between a fishing village and a Hollywood western set—imagine San Francisco reduced to toy dimensions. This seacoast town rambles over a series of green hills and ends up at a spindly, multicolored pier on the waterfront, like a Fisherman's Wharf in miniature. But in reality it's an extremely plush patch of yacht-club suburbia, as you'll see by both the marine craft and the homes of their owners. Main Street is lined with ramshackle, color-splashed old frame houses that shelter chic boutiques, souvenir stores, antique shops, and art galleries. Other roads are narrow, winding, and hilly, and lead up to dramatically situated homes. The view of San Francisco's skyline and the islands in the bay is a good enough reason to pay the precious price to live here.

## ESSENTIALS

Ferries of the **Blue & Gold Fleet** (☎ 415/705-5555) leave from Pier 41 (Fisherman's Wharf) and travel to both Angel Island and Tiburon. Boats run on a

seasonal schedule; phone for departure information. The round-trip fare is $10 to
Angel Island, $11 to Tiburon; half price for kids 5 to 11, and free for kids under 5.

**By car** from San Francisco, take U.S. 101 to the Tiburon/Highway 131 exit,
then follow Tiburon Boulevard all the way into downtown, a 40-minute drive from
San Francisco. Catch the **Tiburon-Angel Island Ferry** (☎ 415/435-2131) to
Angel Island from the dock located at Tiburon Boulevard and Main Street. The 15-
minute round-trip, which only runs on weekends, costs $6 for adults, $4 for children 5 to 11, and $1 for bikes. One child under 5 is free per each paying adult.

## WHAT TO SEE & DO ON ANGEL ISLAND

Passengers disembark from the ferry at Ayala Cove, a small marina abutting a huge
lawn area equipped with tables, benches, barbecue pits, and rest rooms. Also at
Ayala Cove is a small store, gift shop, cafe (with surprisingly good grub), and overpriced mountain-bike rental shop (helmets included).

Among the 12 miles of Angel Island's hiking and mountain-bike trails is the
**Perimeter Road,** a partly paved path that circles the island and winds its way past
disused troop barracks, former gun emplacements, and other military buildings;
several turnoffs lead up to the top of Mount Livermore, 776 feet above the bay.
Sometimes referred to as the "Ellis Island of the West," from 1910 to 1940, Angel
Island was used as a holding area for Chinese immigrants awaiting their citizenship
papers. You can still see some faded Chinese characters on the walls of the barracks
where the immigrants were held. During the warmer months you can camp at a
limited number of sites; reservations are required.

Also offered at Angel Island are guided sea-kayak tours. The all-day trips, which
include a catered lunch, combine the thrill of paddling stable two-, or three-person
kayaks with an informative, naturalist-led tour that encircles the island (conditions
permitting). All equipment is provided, kids are welcome, and no experience is necessary. Rates run about $100 per person. For more information, call **Sea Trek** at
☎ 415/332-8494.

A recently added tour is the 1-hour Angel Island Tram Tour (☎ 925/426-3058,
which costs $10 for adults, $6 children 9 to 12, and $9 for seniors; children under
9 are free.

For recorded information about **Angel Island State Park,** call ☎ 415/435-
1915.

## WHAT TO SEE & DO IN TIBURON

The main thing to do in Tiburon is stroll along the waterfront, pop into the stores,
and spend an easy $50 on drinks and appetizers before heading back to the city. For
a taste of the wine country, stop in at **Windsor Vineyards,** 72 Main St. (☎ 800/
214-9463 or 415/435-3113); their Victorian tasting room dates from 1888.
Thirty-five choices are available for a free tasting with a wine purchase. Wine accessories and gifts—glasses, cork pullers, gourmet sauces, posters, and maps—are also
available. Carry-packs are available (they hold six bottles). Ask about personalized
labels for your own selections. The shop is open Sunday to Thursday from 10am to
6pm and Friday to Saturday till 7pm.

### WHERE TO DINE IN TIBURON

**Guaymas.** 5 Main St. ☎ **415/435-6300.** Reservations recommended. Main courses
$12–$18. AE, CB, DC, DISC, MC, V. Mon–Thurs 11:30am–10pm; Fri–Sat 11:30am–11pm; Sun
10:30am–10pm Ferry: Walk about 10 paces from the landing. From U.S. 101, exit at
Tiburon/Hwy. 131; follow Tiburon Blvd. 5 miles and turn right onto Main St. The restaurant is
situated directly behind the bakery. MEXICAN.

# Marin Headlands

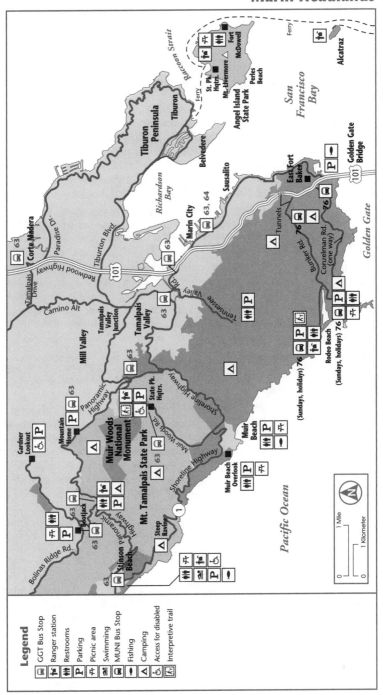

**Legend**

- GGT Bus Stop
- Ranger station
- Restrooms
- Parking
- Picnic area
- Swimming
- MUNI Bus Stop
- Fishing
- Camping
- Access for disabled
- Interpretive trail

Raccoon Strait

Ferry

St. Pk. Hqtrs.
Mt. Livermore
Fort McDowell
Perles Beach

Angel Island State Park

Alcatraz

San Francisco Bay

Tiburon Peninsula

Tiburon

Belvedere

Richardson Bay

Paradise Dr.

Corte Madera

63

Tiburton Blvd

Sausalito

Marin City

63, 64

East Fort Baker

Golden Gate Bridge

101

Tamalpais Drive

Redwood Highway

101

Camino Alt

Tunnels

Bunker Rd.

76

76

Conzelman Rd. (one way)

Golden Gate

Tamalpais Valley Junction

Tamalpais Valley

Tennessee Valley Rd.

Mill Valley

63

63

Rodeo Beach

76

(Sundays, holidays) 76

(Sunday, holidays) 76

(Sundays, holidays) 76

Panoramic Highway

Gardner Lookout

Mountain Home

State Pk. Hqtrs.

Muir Woods National Monument

Mt. Tamalpais State Park

Muir Woods Rd.

63

Shoreline Highway

Shoreline Highway

Muir Beach

Muir Beach Overlook

Bootjack

63

Panoramic Highway

Steep Ravine

Stinson Beach

63

Bolinas Ridge Rd.

1

Pacific Ocean

N

1 Mile

1 Kilometer

0

0

Guaymas offers authentic Mexican regional cuisine and a spectacular panoramic view of San Francisco and the bay. In good weather, the two outdoor patios are almost always packed with diners soaking in the sun and scene. Inside, beige walls are hung with colorful Mexican artwork, illuminated by modern track lighting. Should you be feeling chilled, to the rear of the dining room is a beehive-shaped adobe fireplace.

Guaymas is named after a fishing village on Mexico's Sea of Cortez, and both the town and the restaurant are famous for their *camarones* (giant shrimp). In addition, the restaurant features *ceviche,* handmade tamales, and charcoal-grilled beef, seafood, and fowl. Save room for dessert, especially the outrageously scrumptious fritter with "drunken" bananas and ice cream. In addition to a good selection of California wines, the restaurant offers an exceptional variety of tequilas, Mexican beers, and mineral waters flavored with flowers, grains, and fruits.

✪ **Sam's Anchor Café.** 27 Main St. ☎ **415/435-4527.** Main courses $8–$16. AE, DC, DISC, MC, V. Mon–Thurs 11am–10pm; Fri 11am–10:30pm; Sat 10am–10:30pm; Sun 9:30am–10pm. Ferry: Walk from the landing. From U.S. 101, exit at Tiburon/Hwy. 131, follow Tiburon Blvd. 4 miles and turn right onto Main St. SEAFOOD.

Summer Sundays are liveliest in Tiburon, when weekend boaters tie up to the docks at waterside restaurants like this one, the kind of place where you and your cronies can take off your shoes and have a fun, relaxed time eating burgers and drinking margaritas outside on the pier. The fare is pretty typical—sandwiches, salads, and seafood such as deep-fried oysters—but the quality and selection of the food is inconsequential: Beers, burgers, and a designated driver are all you really need.

## 4 Sausalito

5 miles N of San Francisco

Just off the northern end of the Golden Gate Bridge is the eclectic little town of Sausalito, a slightly bohemian, nonchalant, and studiedly quaint adjunct to San Francisco. With approximately 7,500 residents, Sausalito feels rather like St. Tropez on the French Riviera—minus the starlets and the social rat race. It has its quota of paper millionaires, but they rub their permanently suntanned shoulders with a good number of hard-up artists, struggling authors, shipyard workers, and fishers. Next to the swank restaurants, plush bars, and antique shops and galleries, you'll see hamburger joints, beer parlors, and secondhand bookstores. Sausalito's main touring strip is Bridgeway, which runs along the water, but those in the know make a quick detour to Caledonia Street 1 block inland; not only is it less congested, there's a far-better selection of cafes and shops.

## ESSENTIALS

The **Golden Gate Ferry Service** fleet, Ferry Building (☎ 415/923-2000), operates between the San Francisco Ferry Building, at the foot of Market Street, and downtown Sausalito. Service is frequent, departing at reasonable intervals every day of the year except New Year's Day, Thanksgiving Day, and Christmas Day. Phone for exact schedule. It's a 30-minute ride, and one-way fares are $4.75 for adults and $3.55 for kids 6 to 12. Seniors and passengers with disabilities ride for $2.35; children 5 and under ride free. Family rates are available on weekends.

Ferries of the **Blue & Gold Fleet** (☎ 415/705-5555) leave from Pier 41 (Fisherman's Wharf) and cost $11 round-trip; half price for kids 5 to 11. Boats run on a seasonal schedule; phone for departure information.

**By car** from San Francisco, take U.S. 101 north, then the first right after the Golden Gate Bridge (Alexander exit). Alexander becomes Bridgeway in Sausalito.

# WHAT TO SEE & DO

Above all, Sausalito has scenery and sunshine, for once you cross the Golden Gate Bridge, you're out of the San Francisco fog patch and under blue California sky (we hope). The town's steep hills are covered with houses that overlook a forest of masts on the waters below, but almost all the tourist action, which is almost singularly limited to window shopping and eating, takes place at sea level on Bridgeway.

**Bay Model Visitors Center.** 2100 Bridgeway ☎ **415/332-3871.** Free admission. Labor Day–Memorial Day Tues–Sat 9am–4pm; Memorial Day–Labor Day Tues–Fri 9am–4pm, Sat–Sun and holidays 10am–5pm.

The U.S. Army Corps of Engineers uses this high-tech, 1½-acre model of San Francisco's bay and delta to resolve problems and observe what impact any changes in water flow will have. The model reproduces (in scale) the rise and fall of tides, the flows and currents of water, and the mixing of fresh- and saltwater, and indicates trends in sediment movement. There's a 10-minute film that explains it all and a tour, but the most interesting time to visit is when it's actually being used, so call ahead.

# WHERE TO SHOP

Sausalito is a mecca for shoppers seeking handmade, original, and offbeat clothes and footwear, as well as arts and crafts. The town's best shops are found in the alleys, malls, and second-floor boutiques reached by steep, narrow staircases on and off Bridgeway. Additional shops are found on Caledonia Street, which runs parallel to and one block inland from Bridgeway. **Village Fair,** at 777 Bridgeway (☎ **415/ 332-1902**), is Sausalito's closest approximation to a mall. It's a complex of 30 shops, souvenir stores, coffee bars, and gardens. The complex is open daily from 10am to 6pm; restaurants stay open later.

# WHERE TO DINE
## SUPER-CHEAP EATS

**Caledonia Kitchen.** 400 Caledonia St. ☎ **415/331-0220.** No credit cards. Sun–Thurs 8am–8pm; Fri–Sat 8am–9pm.

Caledonia Kitchen is the sort of place you wish were just around the corner from your house—a beautiful little cafe serving a huge assortment of fresh salads, soups, chili, gourmet sandwiches, and inexpensive entrees like herbed roast chicken or vegetarian lasagna for only $4.95. Continental-style breakfast items and good coffee and espresso drinks are also on the menu.

**Hamburgers.** 737 Bridgeway. ☎ **415/332-9471.** No credit cards. Daily 11am–5pm.

Like the name says, the specialty at this tiny, narrow cafe is juicy flame-broiled hamburgers, arguably Marin County's best. Look for the rotating grill in the window off Bridgeway, then stand in line and salivate with the rest (chicken burgers are a slightly healthier option). Order a side of fries, grab a bunch of napkins, then head over to the park across the street.

## MODERATELY PRICED OPTIONS

**Guernica.** 2009 Bridgeway. ☎ **415/332-1512.** Reservations recommended. Main courses $10–$17. AE, MC, V. Daily 5–10pm. From U.S. 101 north, take the first right after the Golden Gate Bridge (Alexander exit); Alexander becomes Bridgeway in Sausalito. FRENCH/BASQUE.

---

## A Picnic Lunch, Sausalito Style

If the crowds are too much or the prices too steep at Sausalito's bayside restaurants, grab a bite to go for an impromptu picnic in the park fronting the marina. It's one of the best ways to spend a warm, sunny day in Sausalito. Here are two excellent sources for some inexpensive eats à la carte:

Small, clean, cute, and cheap, **Café Soleil,** 37 Caledonia St. (☎ **415/331-9355**), whips up some good soups, salads, and sandwiches along with killer smoothies. Order to go at the counter, then take your goods a block over to the marina for a dockside lunch.

Classic, European-style **Venice Gourmet Delicatessen,** 625 Bridgeway (☎ **415/332-3544**), has all the makings for a superb picnic: wines, cheeses, fruits, stuffed vine leaves, salads, quiche, delicious sandwiches (made to order on sourdough bread), and fresh-baked pastries.

---

Established in 1976, Guernica is one of those funky old kinds of restaurants that you'd probably pass up for something more chic and modern down the street if you didn't know better. What? You don't know about Guernica's legendary Paella Valenciana? Well now you do, so be sure to call ahead and order it in advance, and bring a partner 'cause it's served for two but will feed three. Begin with an appetizer of artichoke hearts or escargots. Other main courses range from grilled rabbit with a spicy red diablo sauce to a hearty Rack of Lamb Guernica and medallions of pork loin with baked apples and Calvados. Rich desserts include such in-season specialties as strawberry tart, peach Melba, and Basque-style rice pudding.

**Horizons.** 558 Bridgeway. ☎ **415/331-3232.** Reservations accepted weekdays only. Main courses $9–$21; salads and sandwiches $6–$11. AE, MC, V. Mon–Fri 11am–11pm; Sat–Sun 10am–11pm. Valet parking: $4. SEAFOOD/AMERICAN.

Eventually, every San Franciscan ends up at Horizons to meet a friend for Sunday Bloody Marys. It's not much to look at from the outside, but it gets better as you head past the funky dark-wood interior toward the waterside terrace. On warm days it's worth the wait for alfresco seating if only to watch dreamy sailboats glide past San Francisco's distant skyline. The food here can't touch the view, but it's well portioned and satisfying enough. Seafood dishes are the main items, including steamed clams and mussels, freshly shucked oysters, and a variety of seafood pastas. In fine Marin tradition, Horizons has an "herb tea and espresso" bar, and is a totally nonsmoking restaurant. The restaurant is scheduled to close for 2 months in January 2000 for renovations.

## 5 Muir Woods & Mount Tamalpais

12 miles N of the Golden Gate Bridge

While the rest of Marin County's redwood forests were being devoured to feed the building spree in San Francisco around the turn of the century, the trees of Muir Woods, in a remote ravine on the flanks of Mount Tamalpais, escaped destruction in favor of easier pickings.

### MUIR WOODS

Although the magnificent California redwoods have been successfully transplanted to five continents, their homeland is a 500-mile strip along the mountainous coast of southwestern Oregon and northern California. The coast redwood, or *Sequoia sempervirens,* is the tallest tree in the immediate region, and the largest-known specimen (located in the Redwood National Forest) towers 367.8 feet. It has an even larger relative, the *Sequoiadendron giganteum* of the California Sierra Nevada, but the coastal variety is stunning enough. Soaring toward the sky like a wooden cathedral, it is unlike any other forest in the world, and an experience you won't soon forget.

Granted, Muir Woods is tiny compared to the Redwood National Forest farther north, but you can still get a pretty good idea of what it must have been like when these redwood giants dominated the entire coastal region. What is truly amazing is that they exist a mere 6 miles (as the crow flies) from San Francisco; close enough, unfortunately, that tour buses arrive in droves on the weekends. You can, however, avoid the masses by hiking up the Ocean View Trail and returning via the Fern Creek Trail; a moderately challenging hike that shows off the woods' best sides and leaves the lazy-butts behind.

To reach Muir Woods from San Francisco, cross the Golden Gate Bridge heading north on Highway 101, take the Stinson Beach/Highway 1 exit heading west and follow the signs (and the traffic). The park is open daily from 8am to sunset, and there's an admission price of $2 per person 17 or older. There's also a small gift shop, educational displays, and docent-led tours that you're welcome to stand in on. For more information, call the **Muir Woods information line** (☎ **415/388-2595**).

If you don't have a car, you can book a bus trip with the **Red & White Fleet,** which takes you straight to Muir Woods via the Golden Gate Bridge, and on the way back makes a short stop in Sausalito. The 3½-hour tours run several times daily, and costs $30 for adults, $14 for children. Call for more information and specific departure times (☎ **800/229-2784** or 415/447-0597).

## MOUNT TAMALPAIS

The birthplace of mountain biking, Mount Tam—as the locals call it—is the Bay Area's favorite outdoor playground and the most dominant mountain in the region. Most every local has his or her secret trail and scenic overlook, as well as an opinion on the dilemma between mountain bikers and hikers (a touchy subject around here). The main trails, mostly fire roads, see a lot of foot and bicycle traffic on the weekends, particularly on clear, sunny days when you can see a hundred miles in all directions, from the foothills of the Sierra to the western horizon. It's a great place to escape from the city for a leisurely hike and to soak in the breathtaking views of the bay.

To get to Mount Tamalpais **by car,** cross the Golden Gate Bridge heading north on Highway 101, take the Stinson Beach/Highway 1 exit. Follow the shoreline highway about 2½ miles and turn into Pantoll Road and continue for about to Ridgecrest Boulevard. Ridgecrest winds to a parking lot below East Peak. From there, it's a 15-minute hike up to the top.

## 6  Point Reyes National Seashore

35 miles N of San Francisco

The National Seashore system was created to protect rural and undeveloped stretches of the coast from the pressures brought on by soaring real-estate values and increasing population. Nowhere is the success of the system more evident than at Point Reyes. Residents of the surrounding towns—Inverness, Point Reyes Station, and Olema—have steadfastly resisted runaway development. You won't find any strip malls or fast-food joints here, just a laid-back coastal town with cafes and country inns, where gentle living prevails.

Though the peninsula's people and wildlife live in harmony above the ground, the situation beneath the soil is much more volatile. The infamous San Andreas Fault separates Point Reyes, the northernmost land mass on the Pacific Plate, from the rest of California, which rests on the North American Plate. Point Reyes is making its way toward Alaska at a rate of about 2 inches per year, but there have been times when it has moved much faster. In 1906, Point Reyes jumped north almost 20 feet in an instant, leveling San Francisco and jolting the rest of the state. The half-mile Earthquake Trail, near the Bear Valley Visitor Center, illustrates this geological drama with a loop through an area torn by the slipping fault. Shattered fences, rifts in the ground, and a barn knocked off its foundation by the quake illustrate how alive the earth is here. If that doesn't convince you, a seismograph in the visitor center will.

## ESSENTIALS

Point Reyes is only 30 miles northwest of San Francisco, but it takes at least 90 minutes to reach by car (it's all the small towns, not the topography, that slows you down). The easiest route is via Sir Francis Drake Boulevard from Highway 101 south of San Rafael; it takes its bloody time getting to Point Reyes, but does so without any detours. For a much longer but more scenic route, take the Stinson Beach/Highway 1 exit off Highway 101 just south of Sausalito and follow Highway 1 north.

As soon as you arrive at Point Reyes, stop at the **Bear Valley Visitor Center** on Bear Valley Road (look for the small sign posted just north of Olema on Highway 1) and pick up a free Point Reyes trail map. The rangers here are extremely friendly and helpful, and can answer any questions you have about the National Seashore. Be sure to check out the great natural history and cultural displays as well. It's open weekdays from 9am to 5pm and weekends from 8am to 5pm (☎ **415/663-1092**).

Entrance to the park is free. **Camping** is $10 per site, per night, and permits are required (reservations can be made up to 2 months in advance by calling ☎ **415/663-8054** Mon to Fri from 9am to 2pm).

## WHAT TO SEE & DO

When headed out to any part of the Point Reyes coast, expect to spend the day surrounded by nature at its finest. But bear in mind that as beautiful as the wilderness can be, it's also untamed. Waters in these areas are not only bone-chilling cold and home to a vast array of sea life, including sharks, but are also unpredictable and dangerous. There are no lifeguards on duty and waves and riptides make swimming strongly discouraged. Pets are not permitted on any of the area's trails.

By far the most popular—and crowded—attraction at Point Reyes National Seashore is the venerable **Point Reyes Lighthouse,** located at the westernmost tip of Point Reyes (Visitor Center ☎ **415/669-1534**). Even if you plan to forego the 308 steps to the lighthouse, it's still worth the visit to marvel at the dramatic scenery, which includes thousands of common murres and prides of sea lions that bask on the rock far below (binoculars come in real handy).

The lighthouse is also the top spot on the California Coast to observe **gray whales** as they make their southward and northward migration along the coast January through April. The annual round-trip is 10,000 miles—one of the longest mammal migrations known. The whales head south in December and January, and return north in March. *Note:* If you plan to drive out to the lighthouse to whale watch, arrive early because parking is limited. If possible, come on a weekday. On a weekend or holiday from December through April, it's wise to park at the Drake's

# A Pearl on Point Reyes: Johnson's Oyster Farm

If you want to escape the crowds and have some stinky man-made entertainment, head to Johnson's Oyster Farm. Located right on the edge of Drakes Estero (a large saltwater lagoon within the Point Reyes peninsula that produces nearly 20% of California's commercial oyster yield), Johnson's may look and smell like a dump, but those tasty bivalves don't come any fresher or cheaper. Granted, it doesn't look like much—a cluster of trailer homes, shacks, and oyster tanks surrounded by huge piles of oyster shells—but that certainly doesn't detract from the taste of fresh-out-of-the-water oysters dipped in Johnson's special sauce. The popular modus operandi is 1) to buy a couple dozen, 2) head for an empty campsite along the bay, 3) fire up the barbecue pit (don't forget the charcoal), 4) split and 'cue the little guys, 5) slather them in Johnson's special sauce, then 6) slurp 'em down. Johnson's is located off Sir Francis Drake Boulevard, about 6 miles west(ish) of Inverness (☎ **415/669-1149**). Open Tuesday to Sunday from 8am to 4pm.

Beach Visitor Center and take the shuttle bus (weather permitting) to the lighthouse and on to Chimney Rock to watch elephant seals. Prices are $3 for adults, free for children under 13. Dress warmly—it's often quite cold and windy—and bring binoculars.

Whale watching is far from being the only activity offered at the Point Reyes National Seashore. On weekends, rangers conduct many different tours: You can walk along the **Bear Valley Trail,** spotting the wildlife at the ocean's edge; see the waterfowl at **Fivebrooks Pond;** explore tide pools; view some of North America's most beautiful ducks in the wetlands of **Limantour;** hike to the promontory overlooking **Chimney Rock** to see the sea lions, harbor seals, elephant seals, and seabirds; or take a guided walk along the **San Andreas Fault** to observe the site of the epicenter of the 1906 earthquake and learn about the regional geology. And this is just a sampling. Since tours vary seasonally, you can either call the **Bear Valley Visitors Center** (☎ **415/663-1092**) or request a copy of *Park Paper,* which includes a schedule of activities and other useful information. Many of the tours are suitable for travelers with disabilities.

Some of the park's best—and least crowded—highlights, however, can only be approached on foot, such as **Alamere Falls,** a freshwater stream that cascades down a 40-foot bluff onto Wildcat Beach, or **Tomales Point Trail,** which passes through the **Tule Elk Reserve,** a protected haven for roaming herds of tule elk that once numbered in the thousands. Hiking most of the trails usually ends up being an all-day outing, however, so it's best to split a 2-day trip within Point Reyes National Seashore into a "by-car" day and a "by-foot" day.

If you're into bird watching, you'll definitely want to visit the **Point Reyes Bird Observatory** (☎ **415/868-1221**), one of the few full-time ornithological research stations in the United States, located at the southeast end of the park on Mesa Road. This is where ornithologists keep an eye on more than 400 feathered species. Admission to the visitor center and nature trail is free, and visitors are welcome to observe the tricky process of catching and banding the birds. (Open daily 15 min. after sunrise to sunset. Banding hours vary, call for exact times: ☎ **415-868-0655**.)

One of our favorite things to do in Point Reyes is paddling through placid **Tomales Bay,** a haven for migrating birds and marine mammals. Kayak trips, including 3-hour sunset outings, 3½-hour full-moon paddles, yoga tours, day trips, and longer excursions, are organized by **Tamal Saka Tomales Bay Kayaking.** Instruction, clinics, and boat delivery are available, and all ages and levels are welcome. Prices start at $45 for tours. Rental begin at $25 for one person, $35 for two. Don't worry, the kayaks are very stable and there are no waves to contend with. The launching point is located on Highway 1 at the Marshall Boatworks in Marshall, 8 miles north of Point Reyes Station. Open Friday to Sunday from 9am to 6pm, and by appointment (☎ **415/663-1743;** www.tamalsaka.com).

## WHERE TO STAY
### BARGAIN BUNKS

**Point Reyes Hostel.** Off Limantour Rd. (P.O. Box 247), Point Reyes Station, CA 94956. ☎ **415/663-8811.** 44 bunks, 1 private rm. $15 per person. Maximum stay 3 nights. MC, V.

Located deep inside Point Reyes National Seashore, this beautiful old ranch-style complex has 44 dormitory-style accommodations, plus one room that's reserved for families (though at least one child must be 5 years old or younger). There are also two common rooms, each warmed by wood-burning stoves on chilly nights, as well as a fully equipped kitchen, barbecue (BYO charcoal), and patio. If you don't mind sharing your sleeping quarters with strangers, this is a deal that can't be beat. Reservations (and earplugs) are strongly recommended. Reception hours are 7:30 to 9:30am and 4:30 to 9:30pm daily.

### MODERATELY PRICED OPTIONS

**Bear Valley Inn.** 88 Bear Valley Rd., Olema, CA 94950. ☎ **415/663-1777.** No fax. 3 units, all with shared bathroom. $75–$135 double. AE, DISC, MC, V. Rates include breakfast.

Ron and JoAnne Nowell's venerable two-story 1899 Victorian has survived everything from a major earthquake to a recent forest fire, which is lucky for you because you'll be hard pressed to find a better B&B for the price in Point Reyes. Granted, the Bear Valley Inn isn't perfect, the rooms lack private bathrooms and the main highway is a tad too close, but it's loaded with Victorian charm, right down to the profusion of flowers and vines outside and comfy chairs fronting a toasty-warm woodstove inside. It's in a great location, too, with three good restaurants only a block away, and the entire National Seashore at your doorstep. Ron, who also runs a mountain-bike rental shop next door, can set you up wheel-wise for about $25 a day and point you in the right direction.

**Point Reyes Country Inn & Stables.** 12050 Calif. 1, P.O. Box 501, Point Reyes Station, CA 94956. ☎ **415/663-9696.** Fax 415/663-8888. 10 units. $75–$275. $10–$15 per horse, but no dogs. MC, V. Rates include breakfast.

Are you and your horse dreaming of a country getaway? Then book a room at Point Reyes Country Inn & Stables, a five-bedroom, ranch-style home on 4 acres that offers pastoral accommodations for two- and four-legged guests (horses only) plus access to plenty of hiking and riding trails. Each room has a private bathroom and either a balcony or a garden. The innkeepers have also added two studios (with kitchens) above the stables, and rent out two cottages on Tomales Bay equipped with decks, stocked kitchens, fireplaces, and a shared dock.

## WHERE TO DINE
### SUPER-CHEAP EATS

**The Gray Whale.** 12781 Sir Francis Drake Blvd., Inverness. ☎ **415/669-1244.** Main courses $6–$10. MC, V. Daily 11am–8pm. ITALIAN.

For more than a decade, The Gray Whale cafe has been another popular pit stop for Bay Area natives heading to the lighthouse at Point Reyes. Why so popular? First off, it's cheap: Sandwiches, such as the roasted eggplant with pesto and mozzarella, are only $5, as are most of the salads and pastas. Second, it's pretty good: Our personal favorites are the specialty pizzas, such as the Californian (artichoke hearts, fresh basil, and tomatoes) and the Vegetarian (baked eggplant, roasted onions and romas, broccoli, and piles of freshly grated Parmesan cheese). Veteran hikers and mountain bikers stop by for an espresso booster, sipped on the small patio overlooking the block-long town of Inverness.

**Taqueria La Quinta.** 11285 Hwy. 1 (at Third and Main sts.), Point Reyes Station. ☎ **415/663-8868.** Main courses $4–$6. No credit cards. Wed–Mon 11am–9pm. MEXICAN.

Fresh, good, fast, and cheap: What more could you ask for in a restaurant? Taqueria La Quinta has been one of our favorite lunch stops in downtown Point Reyes for years and years. A huge selection of Mexican-American standards are posted above the counter, but those-in-the-know inquire about the seafood specials. Since it's all self-serve, you can skip the tip, but watch out for the salsa—that sucker's hot.

## MODERATELY PRICED OPTIONS

**Station House Café.** Main St., Point Reyes Station. ☎ **415/663-1515.** Reservations recommended. Breakfast $4.45–$7.50; main courses $9–$20. DISC, MC, V. Sun–Thurs 8am–9pm; Fri–Sat 8am–10pm. AMERICAN.

For more than two decades the Station House Café has been a favorite pit stop for Bay Area locals headed to and from Point Reyes. It's a friendly, low-key establishment with a cozy fireplace, an open kitchen, an outdoor-garden dining area (key on sunny days), and live music on weekends. Breakfast dishes range from a Hangtown fry with local oysters and bacon to two eggs with creamed spinach and mashed potato pancakes. Lunch and dinner specials might include fettuccine with fresh, local mussels steamed in white wine and butter sauce, two-cheese polenta served with fresh spinach sauté and grilled garlic-buttered tomato; or a daily fresh salmon special—all made from local produce, seafood, and organically raised Niman-Schell Farms beef. The cafe has an extensive list of fine California wines, plus local imported beers.

# 7 Half Moon Bay

28 miles SW of San Francisco

A mere 45-minute drive from the teeming streets of San Francisco lies a heavenly little seaside hamlet called Half Moon Bay, one of the finest—and friendliest—small towns on the California coast. While other coastal communities like Bolinas take strides to make tourists unwelcome, Half Moon Bay residents are disarmingly amicable, bestowing greetings to anyone and everyone who stops for a visit.

Only in the last decade has Half Moon Bay begun to capitalize on its golden beaches, mild climate, and close proximity to San Francisco, so you won't find the ultra-touristy machinations that result in gaudy theme parks and time-share condos. What you will find, however, is a peaceful, unfettered slice of textbook California: pristine beaches, redwood forests, nature preserves, rustic fishing harbors, horse ranches, organic farms, and a host of superb inns and restaurants—everything you need for the perfect weekend getaway.

## ESSENTIALS

**GETTING THERE**  There is no public transportation from San Francisco to Half Moon Bay, so it's either come **by car** or don't come. There are two ways to get here: the fast way and the scenic way. To save time, take Highway 92 West from either Highway 280 or Highway 101 out of San Francisco, which will take you over a small mountain range and drop you directly into Half Moon Bay. A better and far prettier route is via Highway 1, which technically starts at the south end of the Golden Gate Bridge and veers southwest to the shoreline a few miles south of Daly City. Both routes to Half Moon Bay are clearly marked with numerous signs, so don't worry about getting lost.

Downtown Half Moon Bay is easy to miss, however, since it is not on Highway 1. Rather, it's a few hundred yards inland, reached by heading 2 blocks up Highway 92 from the Highway 1 intersection, then turning south at the Shell gas station onto Main Street until you cross a small bridge.

**VISITOR INFORMATION**    For more information, call the **Half Moon Bay Coastside Chamber of Commerce** at ☎ **650/726-8380.**

*Note:* Temperatures rarely venture into the 70s in Half Moon Bay, so be sure to pack for cool (and often wet) weather.

## WHAT TO SEE & DO

The best things to do in Half Moon Bay are the same things the locals do. For example, there's a wonderful paved beach trail that winds 3 miles from Half Moon Bay to Pillar Point Harbor. Walking, biking, jogging, and skating are all popular, and be sure to keep a lookout for dolphins and whales. Bicycles can be rented from the Bicyclery, 101A & B Main St. (☎ **650/726-6000**), in downtown Half Moon Bay. Prices range from $8 to $12 an hour to $25 to $30 for all day.

Half Moon Bay is also known for its organically grown produce, and the best place to stock up on fruits and vegetables is the **Andreotti Family Farm** (☎ **650/726-9461** or 650/726-9151). Every Friday, Saturday, and Sunday a member of the Andreotti family slides open the door to their weathered old barn at 10am sharp to reveal a cornucopia of strawberries, artichokes, cucumbers, and the like. It's a horribly charming old-fashioned outfit that's been in business since 1926. The barn is located at 329 Kelly Ave. off Highway 1 (head toward the beach and you'll see it on your right-hand side); it's open till 6pm year-round.

A few miles up Highway 92 is the **Obester Winery,** 12341 San Mateo Rd. (☎ **650/726-9463**), a small wood shack filled with award-winning wines that are free for the tasting. It's open daily from 10am to 5pm; and exactly 3 miles up Highway 92 is **Half Moon Bay Nursery,** 11691 San Mateo Rd. (☎ **650/726-5392**), a wonderful family-owned nursery where all the serious green thumbs in the county go to get their prized perennials. It's open daily from 9am to 5pm.

If you're the adventurous type, you might want to consider a day of deep-sea fishing with **Captain John's Fishing Trips** (☎ **800/391-8787** or 650/726-2913) or **Huck Finn Sportfishing** (☎ **800/572-2934** or 650/726-7133). Either outfit will take you out for a full day's fishing for about $50. You don't need experience, tackle, or even a fishing license; they'll provide everything, as well as clean, fillet, and bag your catch. January through March they also offer whale-watching trips for $30 per adult, $20 per child (reservations recommended). Both charters depart from picturesque Pillar Point Harbor, a full-service harbor that houses over 350 commercial fishing vessels and recreational boats. Whether you plan to go fishing or not, it's worth a gander to watch the trawlers unload their daily catch.

One of the most popular activities in Half Moon Bay is horseback riding along the beach. **Sea Horse Ranch** (a.k.a. Friendly Acres Horse Ranch) offers either guided or unguided (assuming you know how to ride a horse) rides along the beach or on well-worn trails for about $35 (with early-bird special rates before 10am). It's open daily from 8am to 6pm and located on Highway 1, a mile north of Half Moon Bay (☎ 650/726-2362 or 650/726-8550). And, of course, there's the requisite golf course, **Half Moon Bay Golf Links** (2000 Fairway Dr., at the south end of Half Moon Bay adjacent to the Half Moon Bay Lodge; ☎ **650/726-6384**). Designed by Arnold Palmer, the ocean-side 18-hole course has been rated among the top-100 courses in the country, as well as no. 1 in the Bay Area. It ain't cheap, though, with greens fees ranging from $95 to $135. Make reservations as far in advance as possible.

## BEACHES & PRESERVES

The 4-mile arc of golden-colored sand that rings Half Moon Bay is broken up into three state-run beaches (Dunes, Venice, and Francis), all a part of **Half Moon Bay State Beach.** There's a $5 per-vehicle entrance fee for all three beaches, though unless you plan on camping or using the rest room often, you're better off saving your lunch money and accessing the beach farther up north via Mirada Road. Though surfing is allowed, swimming isn't a good idea unless you happen to be cold-blooded.

When the surf is really up, be sure to check out the banzai surfers at **Maverick Beach,** located just south of the radar-tracking station past Pillar Point Harbor. To get here, take Westpoint Road to the West Shoreline Access parking lot and follow the trail to the beach. (While you're there, keep a lookout for sea lions basking on the offshore rocks.) Also adjacent to the parking lot is tiny **Pillar Point Marsh,** a unique fresh- and saltwater marsh that's home and way station to nearly 20% of all North American bird species—from great blue herons to snowy egrets and red-winged black birds.

A few miles farther north on Highway 1 is the **Fitzgerald Marine Reserve,** a 35-acre tidal reef housing more than 200 species of marine animals, including starfish, snails, urchins, sponges, sea anemones, and hermit and rock crabs. In fact, it's one of the most diverse tidal basins on the West Coast, as well as one of the safest, thanks to a wave-buffering rock terrace 50 yards from the beach. Call before coming to find out when it's low tide (everything's hidden at high tide) and about the docent-led tour schedules (usually offered on Sat). No dogs are allowed, and rubber-soled shoes are recommended. It's located at the west end of California Avenue off Highway 1 in Moss Beach (☎ **650/728-3584**).

Sixteen miles south of Half Moon Bay on Highway 1 (at the turnoff to Pescadero) is the **Pescadero Marsh Natural Preserve,** one of the few remaining natural marshes left on the central California coast. Part of the Pacific flyway, it's a resting stop for nearly 200 bird species, including great blue herons that nest in the northern row of eucalyptus trees. Passing through the marsh is the mile-long **Sequoia Audubon Trail,** accessible from the parking lot at Pescadero State Beach on Highway 1 (the trail starts below the Pescadero Creek Bridge).

Starting in December and continuing through March, the **Año Nuevo State Reserve** is home to one of California's most amazing animal attractions—the hallowed breeding grounds of the **northern elephant seal.** Every winter people reserve tickets months in advance for a chance to witness a fearsome clash between the 2½-ton bulls over mating privileges among the harems of females. Reservations are required for the 2½-hour naturalist-led tours (held rain or shine Dec 15 to Mar 31). For tickets and tour information, call ☎ **800/444-4445.** Even if it's not mating season, you can still see the elephant seals lolling around the shore almost year-round, particularly between April and August when they come ashore to molt.

## WHERE TO SHOP

Half Moon Bay's Main Street is a shopper's paradise. Dozens of small stores and boutiques—ranging from chic to shit-kickin'—line the half-mile strip; you'll find everything from feed and tack stores (should you be on the lookout for a used saddle) to custom furniture and camping gear. Must-see stores (from north to south) include the **Buffalo Shirt Company,** 315 Main St. (☎ 650/726-3194), which carries a fine selection of casual wear, Indian rugs, and outdoor gear; **Cartwheels,** 330 Main St. (☎ 650/726-6060), a nifty store specializing in rustic wood furniture, rugs, and toys; and **Half Moon Bay Feed & Fuel,** 331 Main St. (☎ 650/726-4814), a great place to pick up a treat for your pet.

No country boy can survive without **Cunha's Country Store,** 448 Main St. (☎ 650/726-4071), the town's beloved grocery and general store that's a mandatory stop for regular visitors from the Bay Area. And, of course, what would Half Moon Bay be without a good bookstore like **Coastside Books,** 432 Main St. (☎ 650/726-5889), which also carries a fair selection of children's books and postcards.

End your shopping spree with a stop at **Cottage Industries,** 621 Main St. (☎ 650/712-8078), to marvel at the high-quality handcrafted furniture.

## WHERE TO STAY

**The Zaballa House.** 324 Main St. (at the north end of town), Half Moon Bay, CA 94019. ☎ **650/726-9123.** Fax 650/726-3921. 23 units. $80–$250 double. Rates include breakfast and afternoon tea/wine/hors d'oeuvres. AE, DISC, MC, V.

The oldest building in Half Moon Bay, this pale-blue Victorian is decidedly pretty and unpretentious, while its adjoining annex features brand new accommodations. The nine guest rooms in the main house are pleasantly decorated with understated wallpaper and country furniture; some have fireplaces, vaulted ceilings, or Jacuzzi tubs, and all have private bathrooms. Four years ago three newer minisuites were added behind the main house, each equipped with a kitchenette, double Jacuzzi, fireplace, TV/VCR, and private deck (our favorite is the Casablanca room, which comes with an eponymous video). The newest accommodations, above the neighboring commercial building, have fireplaces, TVs, and VCRs. Prices are quite reasonable considering the amenities and central location.

## WHERE TO DINE

**Moss Beach Distillery.** Beach St. (at Ocean St.), Moss Beach (6 miles north of Half Moon Bay off Hwy. 1). ☎ **650/728-5595.** Reservations recommended. Main courses $13–$25. AE, CB, DC, DISC, MC, V. Mon–Sat noon–10pm (closing hours vary); Sun brunch 10am–3pm (closing hours vary). CALIFORNIA/CONTINENTAL.

Ever since its Prohibition bootlegging days almost a century ago, this old stucco distillery on a cliff above Moss Beach has been a wildly popular hangout for both locals and city folk passing through. In the 1920s, silent-film stars and San Francisco politicos frequented the distillery for drinks and the bordello next door for . . . other pastimes. Time and weather have aged it considerably, but a recent renovation succeeded in sprucing things up. The food—pasta primavera, grilled pork chops, Dungeness crab cakes, chicken Marsala—has never been the main draw here; rather, it's the phenomenal view of the rugged coast from almost every window. Your best bet is to come at sunset, order off the appetizer menu (the oysters are always fresh), and snuggle with your partner in the cocktail lounge.

# Dinner at Duarte's

Always a worthy side trip from Half Moon Bay is a jaunt down the coast to Pescadero, a tiny coastal community whose nightlife centers around the **Duarte's Tavern,** 202 Stage Rd. (☎ **650/879-0464**), still owned and operated by the family that built it in 1894. The town's population literally triples on weekends as folks pile into this unassuming wood-paneled restaurant for a bowl of their legendary artichoke soup. You'll also find steak, prime rib, and plenty of fresh seafood on the menu, as well as fruits and vegetables straight from the Duartes' own gardens behind the restaurant. It's open for breakfast, lunch, and dinner every day, and reservations are recommended for dinner.

Before dinner, you might want to stop at **Phipps Ranch,** 2700 Pescadero Rd. (☎ **650/879-0787**), a sort of Knott's Berry Farm in miniature, located a few miles east of Duarte's Tavern on Pescadero Road. You'll find a huge assortment of fresh, organically grown fruits and vegetables here, as well as an amazing selection of dried beans. Green thumbs will enjoy browsing the nursery and gardens. A popular early-summer pastime is picking your own olallieberries and boysenberries in the adjacent fields. It's open daily from 10am to 7pm (in the winter from 10am to 6pm).

✪ **Pasta Moon.** 315 Main St., Half Moon Bay. ☎ **650/726-5125.** Reservations recommended. Main courses $8–$23. AE, DISC, MC, V. Mon–Fri 11:30am–2:30pm; Sat noon–3pm; Sun–Thurs 5:30–9:30pm; Fri–Sat 5:30–10pm; Sun brunch 11am–2:30pm. ITALIAN.

When visitors ask, "Where is the best place to eat around here?" the inevitable answer is Pasta Moon, a handsome nouveau-Italian restaurant in downtown Half Moon Bay that specializes in making everything from scratch and using only the freshest ingredients. Pasta dishes, which are always freshly made and perfectly cooked, earn the highest recommendations, such as the house-made black-pepper fettuccine with spicy calabrese sausage and braised winter greens or hand-cut papperdelle with sweet fennel sausage, tomatoes, and cream. Another favorite is the fresh oak-smoked pork tenderloin braised with savoy cabbage. For dessert try the wonderful tiramisu, with its layers of Marsala-and-espresso–soaked ladyfingers and creamy mascarpone.

✪ **Sushi Main Street.** 696 Mill St., Half Moon Bay. ☎ **650/726-6336.** Main courses $5–$10. MC, V. Mon–Sat 11:30am–2:30pm and 5–9pm; Sun 5–9pm. JAPANESE.

Who woulda thunk that one of the most exquisite Japanese restaurants in California would be in tiny Half Moon Bay? Chef/owner Hirohito Shigeta started out his business a decade ago in a tiny space on Main Street and kept the old name when he moved into larger digs down the street. His wife Karolynne—an interior designer with impeccable taste—in turn decorated the new space with her vast collection of museum-quality Balinese artifacts, and the result is astoundingly beautiful. But even if it looked like the inside of a trailer home, it would still be worth a visit for the exceptional sushi, tempura, and soba, prepared in part by Andrew, one of the few *gai-jin* (white man) sushi chefs on the West Coast. Adventurous sushi warriors will want to try the New Zealand roll (mussels, radish, sprouts, avocado, and teriyaki), the unagi papaya, and the marinated salmon roll with cream cheese and spinach. For a traditional shoeless Japanese meal, request the knee-high table perched in the corner.

# 12

# A Side Trip to the Wine Country

**E**ven if you're having the time of your life in downtown San Francisco, we highly recommend you consider at least a quick jaunt to the valley, an hour or so north by car. Amidst the mountains dipping into a grapevine-trellised valley, you'll experience an entirely different Northern California: fresh country air, hot weather, some of the world's finest wineries, incredible restaurants, green pastures, and virtually nothing to do but overindulge. With eating, drinking, and lounging as the encouraged attractions, there's virtually no better definition of a vacation than a few days here.

To decide which of the Wine Country's two distinct valleys (Napa and Sonoma) you'll prefer to visit, you'll need to consider their differences. The most obvious distinction between them is size—Napa Valley dwarfs Sonoma Valley both in population, number of wineries, and sheer volume of tourism (and traffic). Napa is definitely the more commercial of the two, with many more wineries to visit, spas to choose from (at far cheaper rates), and a far superior selection of inexpensive restaurants, hotels, and quintessential Wine Country activities like hot-air ballooning. Further, if your goal is to really learn about the wonderful world of wine making, Napa Valley is your choice. World-class wineries such as Sterling and Robert Mondavi offer the most interesting and edifying wine tours in North America, if not the world (though Sonoma's Benziger Winery gives them a run for their money).

If you're planning a more extensive trip to the area, consult *Frommer's Portable California Wine Country.*

## 1 Napa Valley

55 miles N of San Francisco

Napa and its neighboring towns have an overall tourist and big-business feel to them. You'll still get plenty of rolling hills, flora and fauna, and vast stretches of vineyards, but they come hand-in-hand with large, upscale restaurants; designer discount outlets; rows of hotels; and in summer, plenty of traffic. Even with hordes of visitors year-round, Napa is still pretty sleepy, focusing on daytime attractions (wine, outdoor activities, and spas) and, of course, food. Nightlife is very limited, but after indulging all day, most visitors are ready to turn in early anyway.

# The Wine Country

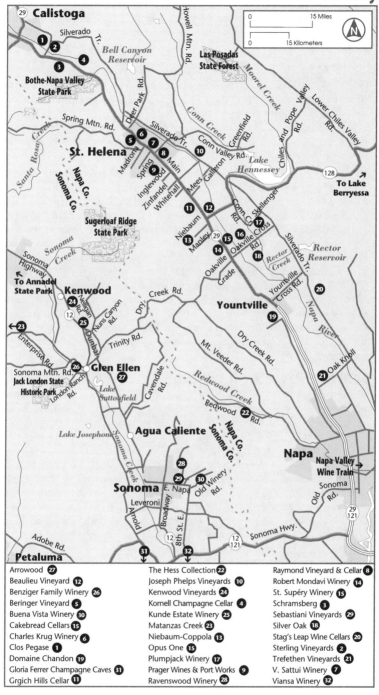

0       15 Miles

0       15 Kilometers

**Calistoga**

Silverado Tr.

Bell Canyon Reservoir

Las Posadas State Forest

Bothe-Napa Valley State Park

Howell Mtn. Rd.

Moorel Creek

Lower Chiles Valley Rd.

Chiles and Pope Valley Rd.

Spring Mtn. Rd.

Dier Park Rd.

Conn Creek

Greenfield Rd.

**St. Helena**

Madrona

Silverado Tr.

Conn Valley Rd.

Lake Hennessey

Spring

Main

Inglewood

Zinfandel

Whitehall

Mees

Galleron

Skellenger

To Lake Berryessa

Napa Co.

Sonoma Co.

Sugerloaf Ridge State Park

Sonoma Creek

Niebaum

Manley

Conn C.

Silverado Tr.

Rector Reservoir

Oakville Cross Rd.

Rector Creek

Sonoma Highway

To Annadel State Park

**Kenwood**

Nelligan

Dunbar

Dry Creek Rd.

Oakville Grade

Yountville Cross Rd.

Napa River

**Yountville**

Nuns Canyon Rd.

Trinity Rd.

Mt. Veeder Rd.

Dry Creek Rd.

Oak Knoll

Enterprise Rd.

Sonoma Mtn. Rd.

**Glen Ellen**

Jack London State Historic Park

London Ranch Rd.

Lake Suttonfield

Cavendale Rd.

Redwood Creek

Redwood Rd.

Lake Josephone

Sonoma Creek

**Agua Caliente**

Napa Co.

Sonoma Co.

**Napa**

Napa Valley Wine Train

**Sonoma**

E. Napa

Old Winery Rd.

Sonoma Rd.

Leveroni

Arnold

Broadway

8th St. E.

Old Rd.

Adobe Rd.

**Petaluma**

Sonoma Hwy.

While "Napa Valley" seems ominous on a map, it's actually relatively condensed and only 25 miles long, which means you can venture up from the town of Napa all the way to Calistoga in less than half an hour (traffic permitting).

## ESSENTIALS

**GETTING THERE**    From San Francisco, cross the Golden Gate Bridge and continue north on U.S. 101. Turn east on Calif. 37, then north on Calif. 29, the main road through the Wine Country.

California Highway 29 runs the length of Napa Valley. You really can't get lost—there's just one north-south road, on which most of the wineries, hotels, shops, and restaurants are located.

**VISITOR INFORMATION**    Get wine-country maps and brochures from the Wine Institute at 425 Market St., Suite 1000, San Francisco, CA 94105 (☎ **415/ 512-0151**). Once in the Napa Valley, stop first at **The Napa Conference & Visitors Bureau,** 1310 Town Center Mall, Napa, CA 94559 (☎ **707/226-7459**), and pick up the slick *Napa Valley Guide* or call in advance to order their $10 package, which includes the guide plus a bunch of brochures, a map, a *Four Perfect Days in The Wine Country Itinerary,* and hot-air–balloon discount coupons. If you want less to recycle, call **Vintage Publications**, 2929 Conifer Ct., Napa, CA 94558 (☎ **800/ 651-8953**) to mail-order just the guide ($6, plus $3 for shipping within the U.S.). If you don't want to pay the bucks for the official publications, point your browser to **www.napavalley.com/nvcvb.html**, the NVCVB's official site, which has lots of the same information for free. Visitors can also pick up *Wine Country Review* throughout the Napa region—it gives the most up-to-date information on wineries and related area events.

## TOURING THE VALLEY & WINERIES

Napa Valley claims 34,000 acres of vineyards, making Napa the most densely planted wine-growing region in the United States. It's an easy venture from one end to the other; you can drive it in less than half an hour (although expect it to be closer to 50 min. during high season).

Conveniently, most of the large wineries—as well as most of the hotels, shops, and restaurants—are located along a single road, Calif. 29, which starts at the mouth of the Napa River, near the north end of San Francisco Bay, and continues north to Calistoga and the top of the growing region. When planning your tour, keep in mind most wineries are closed on major holidays.

All of the Napa Valley coverage in this chapter—every town, winery, hotel, and restaurant—is organized from south to north, beginning in the village of Napa, and can be reached from this main thoroughfare.

### NAPA

The village of Napa serves as the commercial center of the Wine Country and the gateway to Napa Valley—hence the high-speed freeway that whips you right past it and on to the "tourist" towns of St. Helena and Calistoga. However, if you do veer off the highway, you'll be surprised to discover a small but burgeoning community of 63,000 residents with the most cosmopolitan (if you can call it that) atmosphere in the county—and some of the most affordable accommodations in the valley. Unfortunately, any charm Napa may exude is all but squelched by the used-car lots and warehouse superstores surrounding the quaint neighborhoods. But head even a few minutes north of the town of Napa and the real Wine Country atmosphere begins instantly with wineries, vineyards, and wide-open country views.

---

**Napa Valley Traffic Tip**

Travel the Silverado Trail as often as possible to avoid Highway 29's traffic. Avoid passing through Main Street in St. Helena during high season. While a wintertime cruise from Napa to Calistoga can take 20 minutes, in summer you can expect the trek to take you closer to 50 minutes.

---

✪ **The Hess Collection.** 4411 Redwood Rd., Napa. ☎ **707/255-1144.** Daily 10am–4pm. From Calif. 29 north, exit Redwood Rd. west, and follow Redwood Rd. for 6½ miles. No place in the valley brings together art and wine better than this combination winery/art gallery on the side of Mount Veeder. While others strive to pair wine with food, Swiss art collector Donald Hess went a different route: After acquiring the old Christian Brothers winery in 1978, he continued to produce wine while funding a huge restoration and expansion project that would honor both wine and the fine arts. The result is a working winery interspersed with gloriously lit rooms that exhibit his truly stunning art collection; the free self-guided tour takes you through these galleries as it introduces you to the wine-making process.

For a $3 fee, you can sample the winery's current cabernet and chardonnay as well as one other featured wine. If you want to take some with you, by-the-bottle prices start at $9.95 for the second-label Hess select brand, while most other selections range from $15 to $35.

**Stag's Leap Wine Cellars.** 5766 Silverado Trail, Napa. ☎ **707/944-2020.** Daily 10am–4:30pm. Tours by appointment only. From Calif. 29, go east on Trancas St. or Oak Knoll Ave., then north to the cellars. Tastings $5.

Founded in 1972, Stag's Leap shocked the oenological world in 1976 when its 1973 cabernet won first place over French wines in a Parisian blind tasting. For $5 per person, you can be the judge of the winery's current releases, or you can fork over a ten-spot for one of Stag's Leap's best-known wines, Cabernet Sauvignon Cask 23 (when available). The 1-hour tour (by appointment only) runs through everything from the vineyard to production facilities and ends with a tasting; by late 1999, it could also include their new caves, which are currently under construction.

**Trefethen Vineyards.** 1160 Oak Knoll Ave., P.O. Box 2460, Napa, CA 94558. ☎ **707/255-7700.** Daily 10am–4:30pm; tours by appointment year-round. To reach Trefethen Vineyards from Calif. 29, take Oak Knoll Ave. east.

Listed on the National Register of Historic Places, the vineyard's main building was built in 1886, and remains Napa's only wooden, gravity-powered winery. The bucolic brick courtyard is surrounded with oak and cork trees, and free wine samples are distributed in the brick-floored and wood-beamed tasting room. Although Trefethen is one of the valley's oldest wineries, it did not produce its first chardonnay until 1973—but thank goodness it did. Their whites and reds are both award-winners and a pleasure to the palate. Tours are offered by appointment only.

## YOUNTVILLE

70 miles from San Francisco

Yountville (population 3,457) was founded by the first white American to settle in the valley, George Calvert Yount. While it lacks the small-town charm of neighboring St. Helena and Calistoga—primarily because it has no rambunctious main street—it does serve as a good base for exploring the valley, and it's home to a handful of excellent wineries, inns, and restaurants, including James Beard's 1997 top dining spot in the nation, The French Laundry.

**Domaine Chandon.** 1 California Dr. (at Calif. 29), Yountville. ☎ **707/944-2280.** Nov–Dec Wed–Sun 10am–7pm, Mon–Tues 10am–6pm; Jan–Apr 10am–7pm; May–Oct Wed–Sun 10am–8pm. Free tours every hour on the hour 11am–5pm; no reservations necessary.

The valley's most renowned sparkling winery was founded in 1973 by French champagne house Möet et Chandon. The grounds suit Domaine Chandon's reputation perfectly; this is the kind of place where the world's wealthy might stroll the beautifully manicured gardens under the shade of a delicate parasol, stop at the outdoor patio for sips of the famous sparkling wine, then glide into the dining room for a world-class luncheon.

If you can pull yourself away from the bubbly (sold by the glass for $8 to $12 and served with complimentary bread and spread), the comprehensive tour of the facilities is worth the time. In addition to a shop, there's a small gallery housing artifacts from Möet et Chandon depicting the history of champagnes. The Domaine Chandon restaurant, once one of the best-known in the valley, continues to serve excellent cuisine.

## OAKVILLE
68 miles from San Francisco

Driving farther north on the St. Helena Highway (Calif. 29) brings you to Oakville, most easily recognized by Oakville Cross Road and the Oakville Grocery Café (see p. 283).

**Robert Mondavi Winery.** 7801 St. Helena Hwy. (Calif. 29), Oakville. ☎ **888/R-MONDAVI** or 707/226-1395. May–Oct daily 9:30am–5:30pm; Nov–Apr daily 9:30am–4:30pm. Reservations recommended for the guided tour (book 1 week in advance, especially for weekend tours).

If you continue on Calif. 29 up to Oakville, you'll arrive at the ultimate high-tech Napa Valley winery, housed in a magnificent mission-style facility. At Mondavi, almost every variable in the wine-making process is controlled by computer—it's absolutely fascinating to watch. After the tour, you can taste the results of all this attention to detail in selected current wines (free of charge). You can also taste without taking the tour, but it will cost you: The Rose Garden (an outdoor tasting area open in summer) offers an etched Reidel glass and three wines for $10; tastings in the ToKalon Room go from $3 for a 3-ounce taste to $15 for a rare library wine.

Fridays feature an "Art of Wine and Food" program, which includes a slide presentation on the history of wine, a tour of the winery, and a three-course luncheon with wine pairing; the cost is around $65 and you must reserve in advance. Though there's no picnicking on the grounds, Mondavi does offer gourmet picnic lunches from time to time. The Vineyard Room usually features an art show, and you'll find some exceptional antiques in the reception hall. In summer, the winery also hosts some great outdoor jazz concerts. Call to learn about upcoming events.

**Opus One.** 7900 St. Helena Hwy. (Calif. 29), Oakville. ☎ **707/944-9442.** Daily 10:30am–3:30pm. Tours by appointment only (in high season, book 3 weeks in advance).

Unlike most other vineyard experiences, a visit to Opus One is a serious and stately affair that takes after its wine and its owners: Robert Mondavi and Baroness Phillipe de Rothschild, who, after years of discussion, embarked on this state-of-the-art collaboration. Architecture buffs in particular will appreciate the tour, which takes in both the impressive Greco-Roman-meets-20th-century building and the no-holds-barred ultra–high-tech production and aging facilities.

This entire facility caters to one ultra-premium wine, which is offered here for—can you believe—$25 per 4-ounce taste (and a painful $120 per bottle). But wine-lovers happily fork over the cash: It's likely to be one of the most memorable reds you'll ever sample. Grab your glass and head to the redwood rooftop deck to enjoy the view.

## RUTHERFORD

If you so much as blink after Oakville, you're likely to overlook Rutherford, the next small town that borders on St. Helena. Still, each has its share of spectacular wineries, but you won't see most of them while driving along Highway 29.

**Silver Oak Cellars.** 915 Oakville Cross Rd. (at Money Rd.), Oakville. ☎ **800/273-8809** or 707/944-8808. Tasting room Mon–Sat 9am–4pm; closed Sunday and holiday weekends. Tours Mon–Thurs at 1:30pm, by appointment only Mon–Fri at 1:30pm. Tasting fee $5.

Twenty-seven years ago, an oil man from Colorado, Ray Duncan, and a former Christian Brothers monk, Justin Meyer, formed a partnership and a mission to create the finest cabernet sauvignon in the world. "We still haven't produced the best bottle of cabernet sauvignon of which Silver Oak is capable," admits Meyer, but this small winery is still the Wine Country's undisputed king of cabernet.

A narrow tree-lined road leads you to the handsome Mediterranean-style winery, where roughly 44,000 cases of 100% varietal cab are produced annually. The elegant tasting room is refreshingly quiet and soothing, adorned with redwood panels stripped from old wine tanks and warmed by a wood fire. Tastings and tours are $5, which include a beautiful German-made burgundy glass. At press time, only two wines were released: a 1994 Alexander Valley and a 1994 Napa Valley. If the $45-per-bottle price tag is a bit much, for half the price you can take home one of the winery's first noncab releases in 25 years—a velvety Meyer Family Port. No picnic facilities are available.

✪ **PlumpJack Winery.** 620 Oakville Cross Rd. (just west of Silverado Trail), Oakville. ☎ **707/945-1220.** Daily 10am–4:30pm.

If most wineries are like a traditional and refined Brooks Brothers suit, PlumpJack stands out as the Todd Oldham of wine tasting—chic, colorful, a little wild, and popular with a young, hip crowd. Like the franchise's PlumpJack restaurant and wine shop in San Francisco, and the resort in Tahoe, this playfully medieval winery is a welcome diversion from the same old, same old. But with Getty bucks behind what was once Villa Mount Eden winery, the budget covers far more than just atmosphere: There's some serious wine making going on here, too, and for $5 you can sample the reserve chardonnay, san giovese, and cabernet—each an impressive product from a winery that's only been open to the public since mid-1997. The few vintages for sale currently range from $15 to $32, and average around $25 per bottle. Tours are by appointment only; there are no picnic spots, but this refreshingly stylized and friendly facility will make you want to hang out for a while nonetheless.

**Cakebread Cellars.** 8300 St. Helena Hwy. (Calif. 29), Rutherford. ☎ **800/588-0298** or 707/963-5222. www.cakebread.com. Daily 10am–4:30pm. Tasting $5–$10. Tours by appointment only.

This winery's moniker is actually the owners' surname, but it suits the wines produced here, where the focus is on making wine that pairs well with food. They've done such a good job that 70% of their 65,000 annual cases go directly to restaurants, which means only a select few wine drinkers get to take home a bottle. Even if you've found their label in your local wine store, your choice has been limited: Just three varieties are distributed nationally. Here you can sample the sauvignon blanc, chardonnay, cabernet, merlot, pinot noir, the Rubaiyat blend wine, and their dry rose Vin de Porche, which are all made from Napa Valley grapes. Prices range from an affordable $14.25 for a bottle of the 1998 sauvignon blanc to a pricey $53 for the 1996 reserve cab, but the average bottle sells for just a little more than $25. In the tasting room, a large barnlike space, the hospitable hosts pour either a $5 or $10 sampling; both include a keepsake wineglass.

**St. Supéry Winery.** 8440 St. Helena Hwy. (Calif. 29), Rutherford. ☎ **800/942-0809** or 707/963-4507. www.stsupery.com. Daily 9:30am–5pm.

The outside may look like a modern corporate office building, but inside you'll find a functional and welcoming winery that encourages first-time wine tasters to learn more about oenology. On the self-guided tour, you can wander through the demonstration vineyard where you'll learn about growing techniques. Inside, kids gravitate toward "SmellaVision," an interactive display that teaches you how to identify different wine ingredients. Adjoining is the Atkinson House, which chronicles more than 100 years of wine-making history. For $3 you'll get lifetime tasting privileges, and though they probably won't be pouring their ever-popular Moscato dessert wine, the sauvignon blanc and chardonnay flow freely. Even the prices make visitors feel at home: Many bottles go for around $10, although their 1995 Meritage cabernet will set you back $40.

**Niebaum-Coppola.** 1991 St. Helena Hwy. (Calif. 29), Rutherford. ☎ **707/968-1161.** Daily 10am–5pm. Tours offered daily at 11am and 2pm.

In March 1995, Hollywood met Napa Valley when Francis Ford Coppola bought historic Inglenook Vineyards. Although the renowned film director has been dabbling in wine production for years (he's had a home in the valley for almost 25 years), Niebaum-Coppola (pronounced nee-bomb coh-pa-la) is his biggest endeavor yet. He plunked down millions to renovate the beautiful 1880s ivy-draped stone winery and restore the surrounding property to its historic dimensions, gilding it with the glitz and glamour you'd expect from Tinseltown in the process. On display are Academy Awards and memorabilia from such Coppola films as *The Godfather* and *Bram Stoker's Dracula;* the Centennial Museum chronicles the history of the estate and its wine making as well as Coppola's filmmaking.

In spite of all the Hollywood hullabaloo, wine is not forgotten. Available for tasting are a Rubicon (a blend of estate-grown cabernet, cabernet franc, and merlot, aged for more than 5 years), cabernet franc, merlot, chardonnay, zinfandel, and others, all made from organically grown grapes and ranging from around $12 to $80. There's also a wide variety of both expensive and affordable gift items. Speaking of expensive, the steep $7.50-per-person tasting fee might make you wonder whether a movie is included in the price—it's not (but you'll at least get to keep the souvenir glass). And at $20 a pop for the château-and-garden tour, you've gotta wonder whether you're funding his next film. But the grounds are indeed spectacular, and the 1¹/₂-hour journey includes private tasting and glass.

Don't let the prices deter you; if nothing else, at least visit the grounds—they're absolutely stunning and it costs nothing to stroll.

**Beaulieu Vineyard.** 1960 S. St. Helena Hwy. (Calif. 29), Rutherford. ☎ **707/967-5230.** Daily 10am–5pm. Tours daily 11am–4pm; in summer, roughly every half hour; call for winter schedule.

Bordeaux native Georges de Latour founded the third-oldest continuously operating winery in Napa Valley in 1900, and, with the help of legendary oenologist André Tchelistcheff, produced world-class, award-winning wines that have been served by every president of the United States since Franklin D. Roosevelt. The brick-and-redwood tasting room isn't much to look at, but with Beaulieu's (pronounced *bowl*-you) stellar reputation, they have no need to visually impress. They do, however, offer a complimentary glass of chardonnay the minute you walk through the door as well as a variety of bottles under $15. The Private Reserve Tasting Room offers a "flight" of reserve wines to taste for $18, but if you want to take a bottle to go, it may cost as much as $50. A free tour explains the winemaking process and the vineyard's history. No reservation is necessary.

**Grgich Hills Cellar.** 1829 St. Helena Hwy. (Calif. 29, north of Rutherford Cross Rd.), Rutherford. ☎ **707/963-2784.** Daily 9:30am–4:30pm. Free tours by appointment only, Mon–Fri 11am and 2pm; Sat–Sun 11am and 1:30pm.

Yugoslavian émigré Miljenko (Mike) Grgich made his presence known to the world when his Château Montelena chardonnay bested the top French white burgundies at the famous 1976 Paris tasting. Since then, this master vintner has teamed up with Austin Hills (of the Hills Brothers coffee fortune) and started this extremely successful and respected winery in Rutherford.

The ivy-covered stucco building isn't much to behold, and the tasting room is even less appealing, but people don't come here for the scenery: As you might expect, Grgich's (pronounced *grr*-gitch) chardonnays are legendary—and priced accordingly. The smart buys, however, are Grgich's outstanding zinfandel and cabernet sauvignon, which are very reasonably priced at around $18 and $25, respectively. The winery also produces a fantastic fumé blanc for as little as $15 a bottle. Before you leave, be sure to poke your head into the barrel-aging room and inhale the divine aroma. Tastings cost $3 on weekends, which includes the glass, and are free on weekdays. No picnic facilities are available.

## ST. HELENA

73 miles from San Francisco

Located 17 miles north of Napa on Highway 29, this former Seventh Day Adventist village manages to maintain a pseudo–Old West feel while simultaneously catering to upscale shoppers with deep pockets—hence the Vanderbilt's, purveyor of fine housewares, at 1429 Main St. It's a quiet, attractive little town hosting a slew of beautiful old homes and first-rate restaurants and accommodations.

**Raymond Vineyard & Cellar.** 849 Zinfandel Lane (off Calif. 29 or the Silverado Trail), St. Helena. ☎ **800/525-2659** or 707/963-3141. www.raymondwine.com. Daily 10am–4pm. Tours by appointment only.

As fourth-generation vintners from Napa Valley and relations of the Beringers, brothers Walter and Roy Raymond have had plenty of time to develop terrific wines—and an excellent wine-tasting experience. The short drive through vineyards to reach Raymond's friendly, unintimidating cellar is case in point: Passing the heavy-hanging grapes makes you feel you're really in the thick of things before you even get in the door. Then comes the spacious, warm room, complete with dining table and chairs—a perfect setting for sampling the four tiers of wines, most of which are free for the tasting and well priced to appeal to all levels of wine drinkers: The Amber Hill label starts at $10 a bottle for the chardonnay and $11 for the cab; the reserves are priced in the midteens, while the "Generations" cab costs $50.

Along with the overall experience, we also liked the great gift selection, which includes barbecue sauces, mustard, a chocolate wine syrup, and a gooey hazelnut merlot fudge sauce. Private reserve tastings cost $2.50. Sorry, there are no picnic facilities.

✪ **V. Sattui Winery.** 1111 White Lane (at Calif. 29), St. Helena. ☎ **707/963-7774.** www.vsattui.com. Winter daily 9am–5pm; summer daily 9am–6pm.

One of our friends has always wanted to write a guidebook on the best places for free food tastings in Northern California. If that book ever comes to be, V. Sattui (pronounced vee sa-*too*-ee) will be one of the highlights. At this combination winery-and-enormous-gourmet-deli, you can fill up on wine, pâté, and cheese samples without ever reaching for your pocketbook. The gourmet store stocks more than 200 cheeses, sandwich meats, pâtés, breads, exotic salads, and delicious desserts such as a white-chocolate cheesecake. It would be an easy place to graze were it not for the continuous mob scene at the counter.

The long wine bar in the back offers everything from chardonnay, sauvignon blanc, Riesling, cabernet, and zinfandel to a tasty Madeira and a muscat dessert wine. Their wines aren't distributed, so if you taste something you simply must have, buy it. (If you buy a case, ask to talk with a manager, who'll give you access to the less crowded, more exclusive private tasting room.) Wine prices start around $9, with many in the $13 range; reserves top out at around $95.

V. Sattui's expansive and grassy picnic facilities make this a favorite for families. This is one of the most popular stops along Highway 29, so prepare for an enormous picnic party and you won't be disappointed. *Note:* To use the facilities, food and wine must be purchased here.

✪ **Joseph Phelps Vineyards.** 200 Taplin Rd. (off the Silverado Trail), P.O. Box 1031, St. Helena. ☎ **800/707-5789.** Mon–Sat 10am–5pm; Sun 10am–4pm. Tours and tastings by appointment only.

Visitors interested in intimate, comprehensive tours and looking for a knockout tasting should schedule a tour at this stellar winery. A quick and discreet turn off the Silverado Trail in Spring Valley, Joseph Phelps was founded in 1973, and has since become a major player in both the regional and the world wine market. Phelps himself is attributed with a long list of valley firsts, including launching the syrah varietal in the valley and extending the 1970s Berkeley food revolution (led by Alice Waters) up to the Wine Country via his store, the Oakville Grocery (see p. 284).

Joseph Phelps is a favorite stop for serious wine lovers. The modern, state-of-the-art winery and big-city vibe are proof that Phelps's annual 100,000 cases prove fruitful in more ways than one. Once you pass through the wisteria-covered trellis to the entrance of the redwood building, you'll encounter an air of seriousness that hangs heavier than harvest grapes. Fortunately, the mood lightens as the well-educated tour guide explains the details of what you're tasting while pouring samples of five to six wines, which may include Riesling, sauvignon blanc, gewürztraminer, syrah, merlot, zin, and cab. (Unfortunately, some wines are so popular that they sell out quickly; come late in the season and you may not be able to taste or buy them.) The three excellently located picnic tables, on the terrace overlooking the valley, are available by reservation.

✪ **Prager Winery & Port Works.** 1281 Lewelling Lane (just west of Calif. 29, behind Sutter Home), St. Helena. ☎ **800/969-PORT** or 707/963-PORT. Daily 10:30am–4:30pm.

If you want a real down-home, off-the-beaten-track experience, Prager's can't be beat. Turn the corner from Sutter Home and roll into the small gravel parking lot; you're on the right track, but when you pull open the creaky old wooden door to this shack of a wine-tasting room, you'll begin to wonder. By all means, don't turn back! Pass the oak barrels and you'll quickly come upon the clapboard tasting room, made homey with a big Oriental rug, a cat, and, during winter, a small space heater.

Most days, your host will be Jim Prager himself, who's undeniably a sort of modern Santa Claus in both looks and demeanor. But you won't have to sit on his lap for your wish to come true: Just fork over $5 (refundable with purchase) and he'll pour you samples of his delicious $25 Madeline dessert wine, a late-harvest Johannisberg Riesling, the recently released 10-year-old port (which costs close to $50 per bottle), and a few other yummy selections like chardonnay and cab, which retail in the mid-$30s. Also available is "Prager Chocolate Drizzle," a chocolate liqueur that tops ice creams and other desserts.

We recommend tasting here even if you can't afford to purchase; if you do want to buy, this is the only place to do it, as Prager doesn't distribute. If you're looking for a special gift, Jim's daughter-in-law custom etches bottles for around $100 in the design of your choice, plus the cost of the wine.

**Beringer Vineyards.** 2000 Main St. (Calif. 29), St. Helena. ☎ **707/963-7115.** Off-season daily 9:30am–5pm (last tour 4pm); summer 9:30am–6pm (last tour 5pm). Free 45-min. tours offered every hour between 9:30am–4pm; no reservations necessary.

Follow the line of cars just north of St. Helena's business district to Beringer Vineyards, where everyone stops at the remarkable Rhine House to taste wine and view the hand-dug tunnels carved out of the mountainside. Founded in 1876 by brothers Jacob and Frederick, this is the oldest continuously operating winery in the Napa Valley; it was open even during Prohibition, when Beringer kept afloat by making "sacramental" wines. While their white zinfandel is still the winery's most popular nationwide seller, their reserve chardonnay is regularly high-ranking among top California wines. Free tastings of current vintages are conducted in the upstairs gift shop, where there's also a large selection of bottles for less than $20. Reserve wines are available in the Rhine House for a fee of $2 to $6 per taste.

**Charles Krug Winery.** 2800 St. Helena Hwy. (just north of the tunnel of trees at the northern end of St. Helena), St. Helena. ☎ **707/963-5057.** Daily 10:30am–5:30pm. Tours daily at 11:30am, 1:30, and 3:30pm.

Founded in 1861, Krug was the first winery in the valley, and is today owned by the family of Peter Mondavi (yes, Robert is his brother). It's worth paying your respects here with a $3 tour, which takes just under an hour and encompasses a walk through the historical redwood Italianate wine cellar, built in 1874, as well as the vineyards, where you'll learn more about grapes and varietals. The tour ends with a tasting in the retail center. But you don't have to tour to taste: Just stop by and fork over $3 to sip current releases, $5 to sample reserves; you'll also get a souvenir glass. On the grounds are picnic facilities with umbrella-shaded tables overlooking vineyards or the historic wine cellar.

## CALISTOGA

81 miles from San Francisco

Calistoga, the last tourist town in Napa Valley, was named by Sam Brannan, entrepreneur extraordinaire and California's first millionaire. After making a bundle supplying miners during the gold rush, he went on to take advantage of the natural geothermal springs at the north end of the Napa Valley by building a hotel and spa here in 1859. Flubbing up a speech in which he compared this natural California wonder to New York State's Saratoga Springs resort, he serendipitously coined the name "Calistoga," and it stuck. Today, this small, simple resort town with 4,713 residents and an old-time main street (no building along the 6-block stretch is more than two stories high) is popular with city folk who come here to unwind. Calistoga is a great place to relax and indulge in mineral waters, mud baths, Jacuzzis,

# The Ins & Outs of Shipping Wine Home

Perhaps the only thing more complex than that $400 case of cabernet you just purchased are the rules and regulations regarding shipping it home. Due to absurd and forever fluctuating "reciprocity laws"—which are supposedly created to protect the business of the country's wine distributors—wine shipping is limited by state regulations that vary in each of the 50 states. Shipping rules also vary from winery to winery—not to mention that, to make matters more confusing, according to at least one shipping company the list of reciprocal states (those that have agreements with Calif. that make it no problem to ship wine there) changes almost daily! Hence, depending on which state you live in, sending even a single bottle of wine can be a truly Kafkaesque experience.

If you happen to live in a reciprocal state and the winery you're buying from offers shipping, you're in luck. You buy, pay the postage, and the winery sends your purchase for you. It's as simple as that. If that winery doesn't ship, they will most likely be able to give you an easy shipping solution.

If you live in a nonreciprocal state, the winery may still have shipping advice for you, so definitely ask! Some refuse to ship at all, while others are more than accommodating ("New York has bigger fish to fry," we've been told). Do be cautious of wineries that tell you they can ship to nonreciprocal states, and make sure you get a firm commitment: When one of our New York–based editors visited Napa, a winery promised her it could, in fact, ship her purchase; but when she got home they reneged, leaving her with no way to get the wine and no potable memories of the trip.

It's possible that you'll face the challenge of finding a shipping company yourself. If that's the case, keep in mind that it's technically illegal to box your own wine and send it to a nonreciprocal state; the shippers could lose their license and you could lose your wine. However, if you do get stuck shipping illegally (not that we're recommending you do that), you might want to head to a post office, UPS, or other shipping company outside of the Wine Country area; it's less obvious that you're shipping wine from Vallejo or San Francisco than from Napa Valley.

Here are a few shippers to choose from:

**Napa Valley Shipping Companies**
**Aero Packing,** 163 Camino Dorado (off North Kelly Rd.), Napa (☎ 707/255-8025), says they'll pack and ship to anywhere in the world except Kentucky and Utah and insures the first $100 (it's 50¢ extra per hundred beyond the first). Ground shipping of one case to Los Angeles is $19 and Florida is $45.

The **St. Helena Mailing Center,** 1241 Adams St. (at Highway 29), St. Helena (☎ 707/963-2686), tells us that they will pack and ship to reciprocal states, with rates around $17 per case for ground delivery to Los Angeles. Those who live in reciprocal states are insured for up to $100. (It costs extra beyond the first $100.)

**In Sonoma Valley**
**Mail Boxes, Etc.,** 19229 Sonoma Hwy., (at Verano St.), Sonoma (☎ 707/935-3438), which has a lot of experience with shipping wine, claims it will ship your wine to any state, either via UPS (which as of now only ships to a dozen states) or Federal Express. Prices vary from $14 to LA via UPS to as much as $78 to the East Coast via FedEx or other national carriers.

massages, and, of course, wine. The vibe is more casual—and a little more groovy—than you'll find in neighboring towns to the south.

✪ **Kornell Champagne Cellars.** 1091 Larkmead Lane (just off the Silverado Trail), Calistoga. ☎ **707/942-0859.** Daily 10am–5pm.

You've gotta love this place, which used to be the Larkmead Winery. Kornell's wine dudes—Dennis, Bob, Holly, and Rich—will do practically anything to maintain their self-proclaimed reputation as the "friendliest winery in the valley." They'll serve you all the bubbly you want (four to six varieties: brut, blanc de blanc, blanc de noir, and extra dry, all ranging from $17 to $23 a bottle). They guarantee that you'll never wait more than 10 minutes to take the 20-minute tour of the oldest champagne cellar in the region, and even offer up a great story about Marie Antoinette's champagne-glass design.

Considering that the winery is owned by former Disney president Richard Frank, it's not surprising that, as one employee pointed out, the unpretentious place is a "celebrity stopover." But that's nothing new—it was once the summer home of San Francisco's renowned Lillie Hitchcock Coit (as in Coit Tower), and Marilyn used to hang out here when she was married to DiMaggio.

While the tasting room is so casual you may find yourself kicking back on a case of wine, the stone cellar (listed on the National Register of Historic Places) captures the essence of the Wine Country's history. Be sure to meander into the Back Room, where their chardonnay, zinfandel, and cabernet are poured. With a limited production of still wines each year, if you don't try (and buy) 'em here, you may never get another chance; the same goes for their motto T-shirt: "Kiss French, Drink California." Behind the tasting room is a choice picnic area, situated under the oaks and overlooking the vineyards.

✪ **Schramsberg.** 1400 Schramsberg Rd. (off Calif. 29), Calistoga. ☎ **707/942-2414** or 707/942-4558. Daily 10am–4pm. Tours and tastings by appointment only.

This 200-acre champagne estate, a landmark once frequented by Robert Louis Stevenson, has a wonderful old-world feel and is one of our all-time favorite places to explore. Schramsberg is the label that presidents serve when toasting dignitaries from around the globe, and there's plenty of historic memorabilia in the front room to prove it. But the real mystique begins when you enter the champagne caves, which wind $2^{1}/_{2}$ miles (the longest in North America, they say) and were partly hand-carved by Chinese laborers in the 1800s. The caves have an authentic Tom Sawyer ambiance, complete with dangling cobwebs and seemingly endless passageways; you can't help but feel you're on an adventure. The comprehensive, unintimidating tour ends in a charming tasting room, where you'll sit around a big table and sample several surprisingly varied selections of bubbly. Tasting prices are a bit dear at $7.50 per person, but it's money well spent. Note, however, that tastings are only offered to those who take the free tour, and you must reserve a spot in advance. They also offer a Library Tasting at $15 per glass.

✪ **Clos Pegase.** 1060 Dunaweal Lane (off Calif. 29 or the Silverado Trail), Calistoga. ☎ **707/942-4981.** Daily 10:30am–5pm. Tours daily at 11am and 2pm.

What happens when a man falls in love with art and wine making, purchases more than 450 acres of prime growing property, and sponsors a competition commissioned by the San Francisco Museum of Modern Art to create a "temple to wine?" You'll find out when you visit this magnificent winery. Renowned architect Michael Graves designed this incredible oasis, which integrates art, 20,000 square feet of aging caves, and a luxurious hilltop private home. Viewing the art here is as much the point as tasting the wines, which, by the way, don't come cheap: Prices range from $18.50 for the 1996 Mitsuko's chardonnay to as much as $50 for the 1995 Hommage Artist Series Reserve, an extremely limited blend of the winery's finest lots of cabernet sauvignon and merlot. Tasting all the current releases will cost $2.50, and reserves are $2 each. The grounds at Clos Pegase (pronounced *clo* pay-*goss*) feature an impressive sculpture garden as well as scenic picnic spots.

**Sterling Vineyards.** 1111 Dunaweal Lane (off Calif. 29, just south of Calistoga), Calistoga. ☎ **800/977-3242** or 707/942-3345. Daily 10:30am–4:30pm.

No, you don't need climbing shoes to reach this dazzling white Mediterranean-style winery, perched 300 feet up on a rocky knoll. Just fork over $6 and you'll arrive via aerial tram, which offers dazzling bucolic views along the way. Once on land, follow the self-guided tour (the most comprehensive in the entire Wine Country) of the entire wine-making process. Currently owned by the Seagram company, the winery produces more than 200,000 cases per year. Samples at the panoramic tasting room are included in the tram fare. If you can find a bottle of their 1995 Napa Valley chardonnay (currently going for about $14), buy it; it's already garnered a septuplet of awards.

## BEYOND THE WINERIES: WHAT TO SEE & DO IN NAPA VALLEY

While wine tasting is the area's undisputed main attraction, there are plenty of other things to do in Napa Valley. We've listed a few of our favorites below.

If you have time and a penchant for Victorian architecture, the **Napa Valley Conference and Visitors Bureau,** 1310 Napa Town Center Mall, off First Street (☎ **707/226-7459;** www.napavalley.com), offers self-guided walking tours of the town's historic buildings.

Anyone with an appreciation for art absolutely must visit the ✪ **di Rosa Preserve,** which until recently was closed to the public. Rene and Veronica di Rosa, who have been collecting contemporary American art for more than 40 years, converted their 53 acres of prime Wine Country property into a monument to Northern California's regional art and nature. Their world-renowned collection features 1,500 works in all media by more than 600 greater Bay Area artists. Their treasures are displayed practically everywhere, from along the shores of their 30-acre lake to each nook and cranny of their 110-year-old winery-turned-residence, adjoining building, two new galleries, and gardens. With hundreds of surrounding acres of rolling hills protected under the Napa County Land Trust, this place is truly a must-see for both art and nature lovers. It's located at 5200 Sonoma Hwy. (Highway 121/12)—look for the blue-colored gate. Visits are by appointment only, and a maximum of 25 guests is guided through the preserve. Each tour lasts 2 to 2½ hours and costs $10 per person. Call ☎ **707/226-5991** to make reservations.

**SHOPPING**　Plan to spend at least an hour if you make a visit to Red Hen's co-op collection of antiques. You'll find everything from baseball cards to living-room sets, and prices are remarkably affordable. You can't miss this enormous red barn–style building at 5091 St. Helena Hwy., on Calif. 29 at Oak Knoll Avenue West (☎ **707/257-0822**). It's open daily from 10am to 5:30pm.

St. Helena's Main Street is the best place to go if you're suffering serious retail withdrawal. Take, for example, ✪ **Vanderbilt and Company,** 1429 Main St., between Adams and Pine streets (☎ **707/963-1010**), which offers the crème de la crème of cookware, hand-painted Italian dishware, and everything else you could possibly convince yourself you need for your gourmet kitchen and dining room. Open daily from 9:30am to 5:30pm.

Shopaholics won't be able to avoid at least one sharp turn off Highway 29 for a stop at the **St. Helena Premium Outlets,** which is located 2 miles north of downtown St. Helena (☎ **707/963-7282**). Featured designers include Donna Karan, Coach, Movado, London Fog, and more. The stores are open daily from 10am to 6pm.

One last favorite stop: **Napa Valley Olive Oil Manufacturing Company,** 835 Charter Oak Rd., at the end of the road behind Tra Vigne restaurant (☎ **707/963-4173**), a tiny market that presses and bottles its own oils and sells them at a fraction of the price you'll pay elsewhere. In addition, they have an extensive selection of Italian cooking ingredients, imported snacks, and the best deals on exotic mushrooms we've ever seen. You'll also love their age-old method for totaling the bill, which you simply must find out for yourself.

**SPA TREATMENTS**    If you're sick of pampering your palate, give the rest of your body a treat with a treatment or two from either of the spas listed below. ✪ **White Sulphur Springs Retreat & Spa,** 3100 White Sulphur Springs Rd. (☎ **707/963-4361**), offers a spiritual day of cleansing and pampering. Mother Nature takes the credit for the magic here: acres of redwoods, streams, grassy fields, wooded groves, and hiking trails galore. The spa treatments, which include massages, aromatherapy treatments, seaweed or mineral mud wraps, as well as access to a pool and Jacuzzi, only make the experience that much more relaxing. Massages are given in the homey spa building or outside amidst the redwoods ($60 per hr.). A day of peaceful pampering doesn't come any cheaper, but take note: this is a casual place.

If you're a fitness freak, **Health Spa Napa Valley,** 1030 Main St. (Highway 29; ☎ **707/967-8800**), is a mandatory stop after a few days of inevitable overindulgence. You can Treadmill or Stairmaster yourself silly or you can work off that second helping of crème brûlée with a spin class, yoga, or a few laps in the outdoor pool. Then reward yourself with spa treatments: a grape-seed mud wrap, a Pancha Karma treatment (two massage therapists get out the knots with synchronized motion), or a facial. Memberships are $15 per day Monday to Thursday, $20 per day Friday to Sunday, and free with treatments and for guests of the Inn at Southbridge. Spa treatments are an additional cost.

**BICYCLING**    The quieter northern end of the valley is an ideal place to rent a bicycle and ride the Silverado Trail. **St. Helena Cyclery,** 1156 Main St. (☎ **707/963-7736**), rents bikes for $7 per hour or $25 a day, including rear rack, helmet, lock, and picnic bag.

## CALISTOGA

**NATURAL WONDERS**    **Old Faithful Geyser of California,** 1299 Tubbs Lane (☎ **707/942-6463**), is one of only three "old faithful" geysers in the world. It's been blowing off steam at regular intervals for as long as anyone can remember. The 350°F water spews out to a height of about 60 feet every 40 minutes, day and night (varying with natural influences such as barometric pressure, the moon, tides, and tectonic stresses). The performance lasts about a minute, and you can watch the show as many times as you wish. Bring along a picnic lunch to munch on between spews. An exhibit hall, gift shop, and snack bar are open daily. Admission is $6 for adults, $5 for seniors, $2 for children 6 to 12, and free for children under 6. Open daily from 9am to 6pm (to 5pm in winter). To get there, follow the signs from downtown Calistoga; it's between Calif. 29 and Calif. 128.

You won't see thousands of trees turned into stone, but you'll still find many interesting petrified specimens at the **Petrified Forest,** 4100 Petrified Forest Rd. (☎ **707/942-6667**). Volcanic ash blanketed this area after the eruption of Mount

St. Helena three million years ago. As a result, you'll find redwoods that have turned to rock through the slow infiltration of silicas and other minerals, as well as petrified seashells, clams, and marine life indicating that water covered this area even before the redwood forest. Admission is $4 for adults, $3 for seniors and children 12 to 17, $2 for children 6 to 11, and free for children under 6. Open daily from 10am to 5:30pm (to 4:30pm in winter). Heading north from Calistoga on Calif. 128, turn left onto Petrified Forest Road, just past Lincoln Street.

**CYCLING**    Cycling enthusiasts can rent bikes from **Getaway Adventures BHK** (Biking, Hiking, and Kayaking), 1117 Lincoln Ave. (☎ **800/499-BIKE** or 707/942-0332; www.getawayadventures.com). Full-day tours cost $89 and include lunch and a visit to four or five wineries; downhill cruises ($49) are available for people who hate to pedal. On weekdays, they'll even deliver bikes to you.

**HORSEBACK RIDING**    If you like horses and venturing through cool, misty forests, then $40 will seem like a bargain for a 1½-hour ride with a friendly tour guide from **Napa Valley Trail Rides** (☎ **707/996-8566;** www.thegridnet/trailrides/). After you've been saddled and schooled in the basics of horse handling at the stable, you'll be led on a leisurely stroll (with the occasional trot thrown in for excitement) through beautiful **Bothe–Napa Valley State Park,** located off Highway 29 near Calistoga. Napa Valley Trail Rides also offers a Western Barbecue Ride, Sunset Ride, Full Moon Ride, and Gourmet Boxed Lunch Ride and Winery Tour. We've taken the trip ourselves and loved every minute of it—sore butts and all.

✪ **MUD BATHS**    The one thing you should do while you're in Calistoga is what people have been doing here for the last 150 years: Take a mud bath. The natural baths are composed of local volcanic ash, imported peat, and naturally boiling mineral hot-springs water, all mulled together to produce a thick mud that simmers at a temperature of about 104°F.

Indulge yourself at any of these Calistoga spas: **Dr. Wilkinson's Hot Springs,** 1507 Lincoln Ave. (☎ 707/942-4102); **Lincoln Avenue Spa,** 1339 Lincoln Ave. (☎ 707/942-5296); **Golden Haven Hot Springs Spa,** 1713 Lake St. (☎ 707/942-6793); **Calistoga Spa Hot Springs,** 1006 Washington St. (☎ 707/942-6269); **Calistoga Village Inn & Spa,** 1880 Lincoln Ave. (☎ 707/942-0991); **Eurospa & Inn,** 1202 Pine St. (☎ 707/942-6829); **Indian Springs Resort,** 1712 Lincoln Ave. (☎ 707/942-4913); **Lavender Hill Spa,** 1015 Foothill Blvd. (☎ 800/528-4772); **Mount View Spa,** 1457 Lincoln Ave. (☎ 707/942-5789); **Nance's Hot Springs,** 1614 Lincoln Ave. (☎ 707/942-6211); or the **Roman Spa Motel,** 1300 Washington St. (☎ 707/942-4441).

## WHERE TO STAY IN THE NAPA VALLEY

Because the Napa Valley's towns are in such close proximity, it doesn't much matter which town you use as a base. Hotels in this entire region are generally expensive, so don't expect much bang for your buck. When planning your trip, keep in mind that during the high season—between June and November— hotels are usually at their most expensive, sell out completely on weekends, and many have a 2-night minimum. Off-season, you have far better bargaining power and may be able to get a room at almost half the summer rate.

If you need help organizing your Wine Country vacation, contact one of the following companies: **Accommodation Referral Bed & Breakfast Exchange** (☎ 800/240-8466, 800/499-8466 in California, or 707/963-8466), which also represents hotels and inns; **Bed & Breakfast Inns of Napa Valley** (☎ 707/

944-4444), an association of 26 Napa Valley B&Bs that provides inn descriptions and makes reservations; or **Napa Valley Reservations Unlimited** (☎ 800/251-NAPA or 707/252-1985), which is also a source for everything from hot-air balloon to glider rides.

## NAPA

**Chablis Inn.** 3360 Solano Ave., Napa, CA 94558. ☎ **800/443-3490** or 707/257-1944. Fax 707/226-6862. www.chablisinn.com. E-mail: chablisinn@aol.com. 34 units. A/C TV TEL. Early Nov to Mar $60–$95 double; Apr to early Nov $80–$130 double. AE, DC, DISC, MC, V.

There's no way around it. If you want to sleep cheaply in a town where the average room goes for upwards of $200 a night in high season, you're going to have to motel it. But look on the bright side: Since your room is likely to be little more than a crash pad after a day of eating and drinking, a clean bed and a remote control are all you'll really need. But Chablis offers much more than that. Each of the super-clean motel-style rooms has a new mattress, iron and ironing board, hair dryer, refrigerator, and coffeemaker; some even boast kitchenettes and/or whirlpool tubs. Guests have access to an outdoor heated pool and hot tub, plus a basic continental breakfast. Friendly owner Ken Patel is on hand most of the time and is constantly upgrading his tidy highway-side hostelry.

**Napa Valley Budget Inn.** 3380 Solano Ave., Napa, CA 94558. ☎ **707/257-6111.** 58 units. A/C TV TEL. Fax 707/252-2702. Mid-Nov to Mar $60–$105 double; Apr to early Nov from $90 double. Rates include continental breakfast. AE, DC, DISC, MC, V. From Calif. 29 north, turn left onto the Redwood Rd. turnoff and go 1 block to Solano Ave.; then turn left and go a half block to the motel.

This no-frills lodging offers an excellent location—close to Calif. 29—and simple, clean, and comfortable rooms. Local calls are free, and guests can enjoy the complimentary coffee in the lobby and the small pool on the premises (heated in summer only). If you reserve a room here, note that the bathrooms have showers only.

**Wine Valley Lodge.** 200 S. Coombs St. (between First and Imola sts.), Napa, CA 94559. ☎ **707/224-7911.** Fax 707/224-9152. 53 units. A/C TV TEL. $60–$94 double; $110–$165 suite. AE, CB, DC, DISC, MC, V.

Dollar for dollar, the Wine Valley Lodge offers the most for the least in all of Wine Country. Located at the south end of town in a quiet residential neighborhood, the mission-style motel is extremely well kept and accessible, just a short drive from Calif. 29 and the wineries to the north. Soft pastels dominate the color scheme, featured prominently in the matching quilted bedspreads, furniture, and objets d'art. Its decor is reminiscent of Grandma's house, to be sure, but at these prices, who cares? The clincher on the whole deal is a fetching little oasis in the center courtyard, consisting of a sundeck, barbecue, and pool flanked by a cadre of odd teacup-shaped hedges.

## YOUNTVILLE

**Napa Valley Railway Inn.** 6503 Washington St. (adjacent to the Vintage 1870 shopping complex), Yountville, CA 94599. ☎ **707/944-2000.** 9 units. A/C TV. $75–$130 double. MC, V.

This is one of our favorite places to stay in the Wine Country. Why? Because it's inexpensive and really cute. Looking hokey from the outside, the Railway Inn consists of two rows of sun-bleached cabooses and railcars sitting on a stretch of Yountville's original track and connected by a covered wooden walkway. Things get considerably better, though, as you enter your private caboose or railcar, each sumptuously appointed with comfy love seats, queen-size brass beds, and tiled full bathrooms. The coups de grâce are the bay windows and skylights, which let in plenty of California sunshine. The railcars are all suites; so if you're looking to save your pennies, opt for the cabooses. Adjacent to the inn is Yountville's main shopping complex, which includes wine tastings and some good low-priced restaurants.

## St. Helena

**El Bonita Motel.** 195 Main St. (at El Bonita Ave.), St. Helena, CA 94574. ☎ **800/541-3284** or 707/963-3216. Fax 707/963-8838. 41 units. A/C MINIBAR TV TEL. Dec–Feb $100–$150 double; Mar–Apr and Nov $120–$220; May–Oct $99–$250 double. AE, CB, DC, DISC, MC, V.

This 1930s art-deco motel was built a bit too close to Calif. 29 for comfort, but the 2½ acres of beautifully landscaped gardens behind the hotel (away from the road) help even the score. The rooms, while small, are spotlessly clean and decorated with new furnishings; all have microwaves and coffeemakers, and some have kitchens or whirlpool bathtubs. Families, attracted to the larger bungalows with kitchenettes, often consider El Bonita one of the best values in Napa Valley—especially considering the heated outdoor pool, Jacuzzi, sauna, and new massage facility.

**White Sulphur Springs Retreat & Spa.** 3100 White Sulphur Springs Rd., St. Helena, 94574. ☎ **800/593-8873** (in California and Nevada), or 707/963-8588. Fax 707/963-2890. 28 units, 9 cottages. Carriage House (shared bathroom) $95–$125 double; The Inn $115–$145 double; small Creekside Cottages $155–$185; large Creekside Cottages $185–$200. Additional person $15 extra. Discounts available during off-season and midweek. Single-night stays accepted in Carriage House rooms, but cottages require a 2-night minimum weekends from Apr–Oct and all holidays. MC, V.

If your idea of the ultimate vacation is a cozy cabin set among 330 acres of creeks, waterfalls, hot springs, hiking trails, and redwood, madrone, and fir trees, paradise is a short winding drive away from downtown St. Helena. Established in 1852, Sulphur Springs claims to be the oldest resort in California. Guests stay at the inn or in small and large creek-side cabins, which were renovated in 1998 and 1999. Each is decorated with simple but homey furnishings; some have fireplaces or wood-burning stoves, and/or kitchenettes. From here you can venture off on a hike; take a dip in the natural hot sulphur spring; lounge by the pool; sit under a tree and watch for deer, fox, raccoon, spotted owl, or woodpecker; or schedule a day of massage, aromatherapy, and other spa treatments. Note: No RVs are allowed without advance notice.

## Calistoga

**Calistoga Spa Hot Springs.** 1006 Washington St. (at Gerrard St.), Calistoga, CA 94515. ☎ **707/942-6269.** 57 units, 1 family unit. A/C TV TEL. Winter $72 double; $97 family unit; $112 suite. Summer $87 double; $112 family unit; $132 suite. MC, V.

Very few hotels in the Wine Country welcome children, which is why we strongly recommend the Calistoga Spa Hot Springs for families. Even if you don't have kids in tow, it's still a great bargain, offering unpretentious, yet clean and comfortable, rooms with kitchenettes, as well as a plethora of spa facilities ranging from exercise rooms to four naturally heated outdoor mineral pools, aerobic facilities, volcanic ash mud baths, mineral baths, steam baths, blanket wraps, massage sessions, and more. All of Calistoga's best shops and restaurants are within easy walking distance, and you can set up camp near the large pool and patio area.

# WHERE TO DINE IN THE NAPA VALLEY
## NAPA

✪ **Alexis Baking Company.** 1517 Third St. (between Main and Jefferson sts.), Napa. ☎ **707/258-1827.** Main courses: breakfast $3.25–$7.25, lunch $6–$8, dinner $6.75–$13. No credit cards. Mon–Wed 6:30am–6pm, Thur–Fri 6:30am–8pm, Sat 7:30am–3pm; Sun 8am–2pm. BAKERY/CAFE.

This bakery/restaurant is so popular, on weekend mornings there's almost always a line out the door. But once you order from the counter and find a seat in the sunny room, you can relax, enjoy the casual coffeehouse atmosphere, and start your day with spectacular pastries, coffee drinks, and breakfast goodies like pumpkin pancakes with sautéed pears. Lunch also bustles with locals who come for the daily specials like fusilli pasta with roasted pumpkin, white beans, ham, and Parmesan in a cream sauce; grilled-chicken Caesar salad; roast lamb sandwich with minted mayo and roasted shallots on rosemary bread; and lentil bulgar orzo salad. Desserts run the gamut, and include a moist and magical steamed persimmon pudding during the holiday season. This is a great stopover for vegetarians and sweet tooths.

**Bistro Don Giovanni.** 4110 St. Helena Hwy. (on Calif. 29, just north of Salvador Ave.), Napa. ☎ **707/224-3300.** Reservations recommended Fri–Sat. Main courses $11–$17. AE, DC, DISC, MC, V. Sun–Thurs 11:30am–10pm; Fri–Sat 11:30am–11pm. NORTHERN ITALIAN.

Donna and Giovanni Scala, who also run the fantastic Scala's Bistro in San Francisco, serve refined Italian fare prepared with top-quality ingredients and California flair at this large, lively, Mediterranean-style restaurant. The menu features pastas, risottos, pizzas (baked in a wood-burning oven), and a half-dozen other main courses such as braised lamb shank and Niman Schell bistro burgers. Less traditional appetizers include a grilled pear with a frisee-and-arugula salad with bleu cheese, caramelized walnuts, and bacon. Pasta-lovers should go for the farfalle with asparagus, porcini, wild mushrooms, pecorino cheese, and truffle oil. Alfresco dining among the vineyards is available—and highly recommended on a warm, sunny day.

**Downtown Joe's.** 902 Main St. (at 2nd St.), Napa. ☎ **707/258-2337.** Dinner main courses $8–$14. AE, DC, DISC, MC, V. Mon–Fri 8:30–11am (breakfast) and 11am–10pm, Sat–Sun 8:30am–2pm (brunch) and 3–10pm. AMERICAN BISTRO.

Don't let the name fool you: Downtown Joe's is anything but a greasy diner. Working from a proven formula—good food and lots of it at a fair price—Joe's has capitalized on a prime location in downtown Napa and created what's widely regarded as the best place in town to grub and groove. The menu is all over the place, offering everything from porterhouse steaks to oysters, omelets, pasta, and seafood specials. The beers, such as the tart Lickety Split Lager, are made in-house, as are the breads and desserts. If the sun's out, request a table on the outside patio adjacent to the park. Thursday through Sunday nights, rock, jazz, and blues bands draw in the locals.

Another great reason to visit Joe's is "Hoppy Hour," from 4 to 6pm Monday through Thursday, featuring $2.50 pints and free appetizers plus a drawing every half hour to win free stuff. Every Friday is TGIF, with a giveaway (appetizers, wine, and so on) every 15 minutes.

## OAKVILLE & RUTHERFORD

✪ **Oakville Grocery Café.** 7848 St. Helena Hwy. (Hwy. 29, at the Oakville Cross Rd.), Oakville. ☎ **707/944-0111.** Reservations available for parties of 8 or more. Breakfast $4–$7.50; lunch main courses $5.50–$9. AE, MC, V. Daily 7:30am–11am breakfast; 11am–4pm lunch. CALIFORNIA.

# Where to Stock Up for a Gourmet Picnic

You could easily plan your whole trip around restaurant reservations. But put together one of the world's best gourmet picnics, and the valley's your oyster.

One of the finest gourmet food stores in the Wine Country, if not all of California, is the **Oakville Grocery Co.,** 7856 St. Helena Hwy. at Oakville Cross Road (☎ **707/944-8802**). Here you can put together the provisions for a memorable picnic, or, if you give them at least 24 hours' notice, the staff can prepare a picnic basket for you. The store, with its small-town vibe and claustrophobia-inducing crowds, can be quite an experience. You'll find shelves crammed with the best breads and the choicest selection of cheeses in the northern Bay Area, as well as pâtés, cold cuts, crackers, top-quality olive oils, fresh foie gras (domestic and French, seasonally), smoked Norwegian salmon, fresh caviar (Beluga, Sevruga, Osetra), and, of course, an exceptional selection of California wines. The Grocery Co., which was launched by Joseph Phelps long before food and wine were mentioned in the same breath, is open daily from 9am to 6pm; it also has an espresso bar tucked in the corner (open daily from 7am to 3pm), offering breakfast and lunch items, house-baked pastries, and 15 wines available by the glass or for tasting.

Another of our favorite places to fill a picnic basket is New York City's version of a swank European marketplace, **Dean & DeLuca,** 607 S. Main St. (Highway 29), north of Zinfandel Lane and south of Sulphur Springs Road in St. Helena (☎ **707/967-9980**). The opening of this enormous California outpost in late 1997 offered just one more indication that the Wine Country is becoming the epicenter of palatable perfection. The ultimate gourmet grocery store is more like a world's fair of foods, where everything is beautifully displayed, and often painfully pricey. But even if you choose not to buy, this place is definitely worth a browse for the 200 domestic and imported cheeses; shelves of tapenades, pastas, oils, hand-packed dried herbs and spices, chocolates, sauces, and cookware; an espresso bar; one hell of a bakery section; and more. Head to the back where chefs prepare gourmet takeout or grab a bottle of vino with the help of wine master John Hardesty who presides over the 1,200-label collection. Hours are Monday to Saturday from 10am to 7pm (the espresso bar opens at 8am), and Sunday from 10am to 6pm.

This is one of our favorite places to come for delicious, relatively cheap food. The melt-in-your-mouth salmon, watercress, and herb aioli sandwich ($8); soups, such as a hearty vegetable barley; salads (Niçoise, goat cheese with field greens and peach-chardonnay vinaigrette, and hearts of romaine); pizzas, such as wild-mushroom; and lasagne round out the ovation-worthy lunch menu. Breakfast is celebrated with "Small Plates" such as granola ($3.75), toasted breads with house preserves ($2), and a breakfast fruit tart, and "Big Plates" of chicken hash ($7), eggs, omelets, and frittatas. Counter service keeps the prices down, thick windows keep traffic noise out, and an absolutely fab meal and sweet ambiance keep the local constituency coming back for more. In mid-1999, they're scheduled to open regularly for dinner.

## YOUNTVILLE

**The Diner.** 6476 Washington St., Yountville. ☎ **707/944-2626.** Breakfast $4–$8; lunch $6–$10; dinner $8–$13.25. No credit cards. Tues–Sun 8am–3pm and 5:30–9pm. From Calif. 29 north, take the Yountville exit and turn left onto Washington St. AMERICAN/MEXICAN.

Funky California meets traditional roadside eatery at this popular diner, decorated with a collection of vintage diner water pitchers and a rotating art exhibit. The Diner's fare is far from that of a regular greasy spoon; the "home-style" menu is extensive, portions are huge, and the food is very good. Breakfasts feature good old-fashioned omelets, French toast, and German potato pancakes. Lunch and dinner dishes include a host of Mexican and American dishes such as chicken picatta with veggies and rice, grilled fresh fish, giant burritos, and thick sandwiches made with house-roasted meats and homemade bread.

**Mustards Grill.** 7399 St. Helena Hwy. (Calif. 29), Yountville. ☎ **707/944-2424.** Reservations recommended. Main courses $11–$17. CB, DC, DISC, MC, V. Sun–Thurs 11:30am–9pm, Fri–Sat 11:30am–10pm. CALIFORNIA.

Mustards is a safe bet for anyone who is in search of quality food and a casual atmosphere but is not overly adventurous. Housed in a convivial, barn-style space, it offers an 11-page wine list and an ambitious chalkboard list of specials. We started out with a wonderfully light seared ahi tuna that melted in our mouths the way ahi should. Although the Hoisin quail with apricot sauce and bok choy and the lamb shank braised in syrah with fennel and onions were tempting, we opted for a moist, perfectly flavored grilled chicken breast with mashed potatoes and fresh herbs. The menu includes something for everyone, from gourmands and vegetarians to good old burger-lovers.

**Piatti.** 6480 Washington St. (corner of Oak Circle.), Yountville. ☎ **707/944-2070.** Reservations recommended. Main courses $11–$18. AE, DC, MC, V. Mon–Thurs and Sun 11:30am–10pm; Fri–Sat 11:30am–11pm. ITALIAN/CALIFORNIA.

This local favorite—the first (and best) of a swiftly growing Northern California chain—is known for serving excellent, reasonably priced food in a rustic Italian-style setting. Chef Peter Hall, a seasoned Napa Valley cook who honed his culinary art at Tra Vigne and Mustards before taking over the helm here, performs to a mostly sold-out crowd nightly. For the perfect meal, start with a salad of morning-cut field greens mixed with white corn and Napa Valley strawberry crostini, accompanied by a bowl of the spaghetti squash and sweet-potato soup. Though Hall offers a wide array of superb pastas and pizzas, it's the wood-oven-roasted duck—basted with a sweet cherry sauce and served over a bed of citrus risotto—that brings back the regulars. There are far fancier and more intimate restaurants in the valley, but we can't think of any that can fill you up on such outstanding fare at these prices. Note: Piatti also offers patio dining year-round, weather permitting.

## ST. HELENA

✪ **The Cantinetta At Tra Vigne Restaurant.** 1050 Charter Oak Ave., St. Helena. ☎ **707/963-8888.** Main courses $4–$8. CB, DC, DISC, MC, V. Daily 11:30am–6pm. ITALIAN.

Regardless of where we dine while in the valley, we always make a point of stopping at the Cantinetta for an espresso and a snack. Part cafe, part shop, it's a casual place with a few tables and a counter. The focaccias (we've never had better in our lives!), pasta salads, and pastries are outstanding, and there's also a selection of cookies and other wonderful treats, flavored oils (free tastings), wines, and an array of gourmet items, many of which were created here. You can also get great picnic grub to go.

**Tomatina.** At The Inn at Southbridge, 1016 Main St., St. Helena. ☎ **707/967-9999.** Pasta $6–$8; pizza $8–$19. DC, DISC, MC, V. Daily 11:30am–10pm. ITALIAN.

When we've had it up to our ears with intense eating extravaganzas, we head to Tomatina for a $3.50 chopped salad and other respites from gluttonous excess.

Families and locals come here for another reason—though the menu is limited, it's a total winner for anyone looking for freshly prepared, wholesome food at atypically cheap Wine Country prices. A Caesar salad, for example, costs a mere $4.50. "Apizzas"—pizzas folded like a soft taco—are the house specialty, and come filled with such delights as fresh Maine clams and oregano. Pizzas are of the build-your-own variety with gourmet toppings like sautéed mushrooms, fennel sausage, baby spinach, sun-dried tomatoes, and homemade pepperoni. The 26 respectable local wines are served by the glass at a toast-worthy cost of $3.75, or $18 per bottle. As for dessert, at less than $4 a pop for gelato, biscotti, or pound cake, it's an overall sweet deal. Everything is ordered at the counter and brought to the small or family-style tables in the very casual dining area or the outdoor patio. Kids especially like the pool table and big-screen TV.

## CALISTOGA

**Bosko's.** 1364 Lincoln Ave. (between Cedar and Washington sts.), Calistoga. ☎ **707/942-9088.** Main courses $6.25–$10. MC, V. Daily 11am–9:30pm. ITALIAN

It's hard not to like a place that keeps sawdust on its floors, because you immediately know that you won't encounter any snooty waiters or jacked-up prices. Bosko's formula is simple: Serve good, cheap Italian food, hot and fast, and make sure nobody leaves hungry. It's a homey place, with red-and-white-checkered tablecloths, an exposed beam ceiling, and a huge U-shaped counter that's always occupied by a least one or two locals. All sixteen versions of pasta are cooked to order, as are the ten or so pizzas and hot sandwiches. Order at the counter, scramble for a table, and then wait for your food to be delivered. The lunch special is a great deal: half a sandwich or plate of pasta, salad, and a darn good bowl of minestrone soup (needs salt, however). Even more brilliant is the method of wine selection: Simply choose a bottle from the wine rack, pay retail for it at the counter, and drink it with your meal. Why don't they all do it this way?

**Smokehouse Café.** 1458 Lincoln Ave., Calistoga. ☎ **707/942-6060.** Main courses $8–$17. MC, V. Daily 7:30am–10pm (closed Tues and only open for lunch on Wed Jan–Feb). REGIONAL AMERICAN BBQ.

Who would have guessed that some of the best spareribs and house-smoked meats in Northern California would come from this little kitchen in Calistoga? Here's the winning game plan: Start with the Sacramento delta crawfish cakes (better than any wimpy crab cakes you'll find in San Francisco) and husk-roasted Cheyenne corn, then move on to the slow pig sandwich, a half slab of ribs, or homemade sausages—all of which take up to a week to prepare (not while you wait, luckily). The clincher, though, is the fluffy all-you-can-eat cornbread dipped in pure cane syrup, which comes with every full-plate dinner. Kids are especially catered to—a rarity in these parts—and patio dining is available during the summer for breakfast, lunch, and dinner.

**Wappo Bar & Bistro.** 1226B Washington St. (off Lincoln Ave.), Calistoga. ☎ **707/942-4712.** Main courses $8.50–$14.50. AE, MC, V. Wed–Mon 11:30am–2:30pm and 6–9:30pm. INTERNATIONAL.

One of the best alfresco dining experiences in the Wine Country is under Wappo's honeysuckle-and-vine–covered arbor, but you'll also be comfortable inside this small bistro at one of the well-spaced, well-polished tables. The menu offers a wide range of choices, from Chilean sea bass with mint chutney to roast rabbit with potato gnocchi. The desserts of choice are the black-bottom coconut cream pie and the strawberry rhubarb pie.

## 2  Sonoma County

A pastoral contrast to Napa, Sonoma still manages to maintain a backcountry ambiance thanks to its far-lower density of wineries, restaurants, and hotels. Small, family-owned wineries are Sonoma's mainstay; tastings are low-key, and they come with plenty of friendly banter with the wine makers (who often will be doing the pouring themselves). Basically, this is the valley to visit if your ideal vacation includes visiting a handful of wineries along quiet, gently winding, woodsy roads, avoiding shopping outlets and Napa's high-end glitz, and simply enjoying the laid-back country atmosphere.

Truth is, even though there are far fewer wineries here, Sonoma wines have actually won more awards than any other California wine-growing region for 9 years running (much to the chagrin of Napa vintners, no doubt).

The valley itself is some 17 miles long and 7 miles wide, and is bordered by two mountain ranges: the Mayacamas to the east and Sonoma Mountains to the west. Unlike Napa Valley, you won't find palatial wineries with million-dollar art collections, aerial trams, and Hollywood ego trips (read: Niebaum-Coppola). Rather, the Sonoma Valley offers a refreshing dose of reality, where modestly sized wineries are integrated into the community rather than perched on hilltops like corporate citadels. If the Napa Valley feels more like a fantasyland, where everything exists to service the almighty grape and the visitors it attracts, then the Sonoma Valley is its antithesis, an unpretentious gaggle of ordinary towns, ranches, and wineries that welcome tourists but don't necessarily rely on them. The result, as you wind your way through the valley, is a chance to experience what Napa Valley must have been like long before the Seagrams and Möet et Chandons of the world turned the Wine Country into a major tourist destination.

As in Napa, you can also pick up *Wine Country Review* throughout Sonoma; it will give you the most up-to-date information on wineries and related area events.

### ESSENTIALS

**GETTING THERE**   From San Francisco, cross the Golden Gate Bridge and stay on U.S. 101 north. Exit at Highway 37; after 10 miles, turn north onto Highway 121. After another 10 miles, turn north onto Highway 12 (Broadway), which will take you directly into the town of Sonoma.

**VISITOR INFORMATION**   While you're in Sonoma, stop by the **Sonoma Valley Visitors Bureau,** 453 First St. E. (☎ **707/996-1090;** www.sonomavalley. com). It's open daily from 9am to 7pm in summer and from 9am to 5pm in winter. An additional **Visitors Bureau** is located a few miles south of the square at 25200 Arnold Dr. (Highway 121), at the entrance to Viansa Winery (☎ **707/996-5793**); it's open daily from 9am to 5pm. If you prefer some advance information, the free pocket-size *Sonoma Valley Visitors Guide* features almost every lodging, winery, and restaurant in the valley. Contact the Visitors Bureau on First Street, to order one, or check out their Web site at **www.sonomavalley.com**.

### TOURING THE VALLEY & WINERIES

Sonoma Valley is currently home to about 35 wineries (including California's first winery, Buena Vista, founded in 1857) and 13,000 acres of vineyards, which produce roughly 25 types of wines totaling more than five million cases a year. Cabernet is the variety for which Sonoma is most noted. Unlike the rigidly structured tours at many of Napa Valley's corporate-owned wineries, tastings and tours on the Sonoma side of the Mayacamas Mountains are usually free and low key, and come with plenty of friendly banter between the wine makers and their guests.

The towns and wineries covered below are organized geographically from south to north, starting at the intersection of Highway 37 and Highway 121 in the Carneros District and ending in Kenwood. The wineries here tend to be a little more spread out than they are in Napa, but they're easy to find. Still, it's best to decide which wineries you're most interested in and devise a touring strategy before you set out so you don't find yourself doing a lot of backtracking.

We've reviewed our favorite Sonoma Valley wineries here—more than enough to keep you busy tasting wine for a long weekend. If you'd like a complete list of local wineries, be sure to pick up one of the free guides to the valley available at the Sonoma Valley Visitors Bureau (see "Essentials," above).

## THE CARNEROS DISTRICT

As you approach the Wine Country from the south, you must first pass through the Carneros District, a cool, windswept region that borders the San Pablo Bay and marks the entrance to both Napa and Sonoma valleys. Until the latter part of the 20th century, this mixture of marsh, sloughs, and rolling hills was mainly used as sheep pasture (*carneros* means sheep in Spanish). After experimental plantings yielded slow-growing yet high-quality grapes—particularly chardonnay and pinot noir—several Napa and Sonoma wineries expanded their plantings here, eventually establishing the Carneros District as an American Viticultural Appellation. Though about a dozen wineries are spread throughout the region, there are no major towns or attractions—just plenty of gorgeous scenery as you cruise along Highway 121, the major junction between Napa and Sonoma.

✪ **Viansa Winery and Italian Marketplace.** 25200 Arnold Dr. (Calif. 121), Sonoma. ☎ **800/995-4740** or 707/935-4700. Daily 10am–5pm. Guided tours by appointment only.

The first major winery you'll encounter as you enter Sonoma Valley from the south is Viansa; this sprawling Tuscany-style villa is perched atop a knoll overlooking the entire lower valley. Viansa is the brainchild of Sam and Vicki Sebastiani, who left the family dynasty to create their own temple to food and wine (Viansa being a contraction of Vicki and Sam). While Sam, a third-generation wine maker, runs the winery, Vicki manages the marketplace, a large room crammed with a cornucopia of high-quality preserves, mustards, olive oils, pastas, salads, breads, desserts, Italian tableware, cookbooks, and such. (If you're looking for wine-related gifts, this is the place.)

The winery, which does an extensive mail-order business through its Tuscany Club (well worth joining if you love getting mail and good wine), has quickly established a favorable reputation for its cabernet, sauvignon blanc, and chardonnay, blended from premium Napa and Sonoma grapes and sold in the sexiest-shaped bottles in Sonoma. Sam is also experimenting with Italian grape varieties such as Muscat canelli, sangiovese, and nebbiolo, all of which are sold exclusively at the winery. Tastings, which are poured at the east end of the marketplace, are free, and the self-guided tour includes a trip through the underground barrel-aging cellar adorned with colorful fresco-style hand-painted murals.

Viansa is also one of the few wineries in Sonoma Valley where you can purchase deli items—the focaccia sandwiches are delicious—and dine alfresco under their grape trellis while you admire the bucolic view.

**Gloria Ferrer Champagne Caves.** 23555 Carneros Hwy. (Calif. 121), Sonoma. ☎ **707/ 996-7256.** Daily 10am–5:30pm. Tours daily; call for schedule.

When you've had it up to here with chardonnays and pinots, it's time to pay a visit to Gloria Ferrer, the grand dame of the Wine Country's sparkling wine producers. Who's Gloria, you ask? She's the wife of José Ferrer, whose family has been making sparkling wine for the past 5 centuries and whose company, Freixenet, is the largest producer of sparkling wine in the world (Cordon Negro being their most popular brand). All of which equals big bucks, and certainly a good chunk of it went into building this palatial estate. Glimmering like Oz high atop a gently sloping hill, it overlooks the verdant Carneros District. On a sunny day, it's impossible not to enjoy a glass of dry Brut while soaking-in the magnificent views of the vineyards and valley below.

If you're unfamiliar with the term *méthode champenoise,* be sure to take the free 30-minute tour of the fermenting tanks, bottling line, and caves brimming with racks of yeast-laden bottles. Afterwards, retire to the elegant tasting room for a flute-full of Brut or Cuvée ($3 to $5.50 a glass, $16 and up per bottle), find an empty chair on the veranda, and say, "Ahhh. This is the life." Yes, there are picnic tables, but it's usually too windy up here for an enjoyable experience—plus, you have to purchase a bottle of their sparkling wine to reserve a table.

## SONOMA

At the northern boundary of the Carneros District along Highway 12 is the centerpiece of Sonoma Valley, the mid-sized town of Sonoma, which owes much of its appeal to Mexican General Mariano Guadalupe Vallejo. It was Vallejo who fashioned this pleasant, slow-paced community after a typical Mexican village—right down to its central plaza, Sonoma's geographical and commercial center. The plaza sits at the top of a T formed by Broadway (Highway 12) and Napa Street. Most of the surrounding streets form a grid pattern around this axis, making Sonoma easy to negotiate. The plaza's Bear Flag Monument marks the spot where the crude Bear Flag was raised in 1846, signaling the end of Mexican rule; the symbol was later adopted by the state of California and placed on its flag. The 8-acre park at the center of the plaza, complete with two ponds populated with ducks and geese, is perfect for an afternoon siesta in the cool shade. Our favorite attraction, however, is the gaggle of brilliantly feathered chickens that roam unfettered through the streets of Sonoma—a sight you'll definitely never see in Napa.

**Sebastiani Vineyards Winery.** 389 Fourth St. E., Sonoma. ☎ **800/888-5532** or 707/938-5532. Daily 10am–5pm. Tours offered 10:30am–4pm, every half hour in summer, every 45 min. to an hr. in winter; no reservations necessary.

The name Sebastiani is practically synonymous with Sonoma. What started in 1904, when Samuele Sebastiani began producing his first wines, has, in three successive generations, now grown into a small empire and Sonoma County's largest winery. Oddly enough, the winery occupies neither the most scenic setting nor structures in Sonoma Valley, yet its place in the history and development of the region is unparalleled.

The 25-minute tour is interesting, informative, and well worth the time. You can see the winery's original turn-of-the-century crusher and press as well as the world's largest collection of oak-barrel carvings, crafted by local artist Earle Brown. If you don't want to take the tour, head straight for the charmingly rustic tasting room, where you can sample an extensive selection of wines sans tasting fee. Bottle prices are very reasonable, ranging from $5 for a 1996 white zin to $15 for a 1994 cabernet sauvignon. A picnic area is adjacent to the cellars, though a far more scenic picnic area is located across the parking lot in Sebastiani's Cherryblock Vineyards.

**Buena Vista.** 18000 Old Winery Rd. (off E. Napa St., slightly northeast of downtown), Sonoma. ☎ **800/926-1266** or 707/938-1266. Daily 10:30am–5pm. Self-guided tours only.

The patriarch of California wineries was founded in 1857 by Count Agoston Haraszthy, the Hungarian émigré who is universally regarded as the father of

# Touring the Sonoma Valley by Bike

Sonoma and its neighboring towns are so small, close together, and relatively flat that it's not difficult to get around on two wheels. In fact, if you're in no great hurry, there's no better way to tour the Sonoma Valley than via bicycle. You can rent a bike at the **Goodtime Bicycle Company,** 18503 Sonoma Hwy. (Calif. 12), Sonoma (☎ **888/525-0453** or 707/938-0453). They'll happily point you to easy bike trails, or you can take one of their organized excursions to Kenwood-area wineries or to south Sonoma wineries. Not only do they provide a gourmet lunch featuring local Sonoma products, they'll also carry any wine you purchase for you and help with shipping arrangements. Lunch rides start at 10:30am and end at around 3pm. The cost, including food and equipment, is $55 per person (that's a darn good deal). Rentals cost $25 a day or $5 per hour, and include helmets, locks, and everything else you'll need (delivery is a $25 flat day rate). Bikes are also available for rent from **Sonoma Valley Cyclery,** 20093 Broadway, Sonoma (☎ **707/935-3377**), for $20 a day, $6 per hour.

California's wine industry. A close friend of General Vallejo, Haraszthy returned from Europe in 1861 with 100,000 of the finest vine cuttings, which he made available to all winegrowers. Although Buena Vista's wine making now takes place at an ultramodern facility in the Carneros District, the winery still maintains a complimentary tasting room inside the restored 1862 Press House, a beautiful stone-crafted room brimming with wines, wine-related gifts, and accessories (as well as a small art gallery along the inner balcony).

Tastings are free for most wines, $3 for the really good stuff; bottle prices range from as low as $8.75 for a buttery 1996 sauvignon blanc to $35 for the Carneros Grand Reserve cabernet sauvignon (which was so good that we bought three). There's also a self-guided tour that you can follow any time during operating hours, and a "Historical Presentation," offered daily at 2pm, that details the life and times of the Count. After tasting, grab your favorite bottle, a selection of cheeses from the Sonoma Cheese Factory, salami, bread, and pâté (all available in the tasting room), and plant yourself at one of the many picnic tables recessed into the lush, verdant setting.

**Ravenswood Winery.** 18701 Gehricke Rd. (off Lovall Valley Rd.), Sonoma. ☎ **888/ 669-4679** or 707/938-1960. Daily 10am–4:30pm. Tours by reservation only.

Compared to old heavies like Sebastiani and Buena Vista, Ravenswood is a relative newcomer to the Sonoma wine scene, but it has quickly established itself as the sine qua non of zinfandel, the versatile grape that's quickly gaining popular ground on the rapacious cabernet sauvignon. In fact, Ravenswood was one of the first wineries in the United States to focus primarily on zins, which accounts for three quarters of its 200,000-case production. It also produces a merlot, cabernet sauvignon, and a small amount of chardonnay.

The winery is smartly designed—recessed into the Sonoma hillside to protect its treasures from the simmering summers. Tours follow the wine-making process from grape to glass, and include a visit into the aromatic oak-barrel aging rooms. A gourmet "Barbecue Overlooking the Vineyards" is held each weekend (from 11am to 4:40pm, from Memorial Day through the end of September; call for details and reservations), though you're welcome to plop your own picnic basket down at any of their tables. Tastings are free and generous, though you may not find some of the pourers to be as witty as they think they are (ours was a jerk, though we've known people who have had great experiences here). Bottle prices range from $8.50 for a 1998 light and crisp French Colombard to $31.50 for a Pickberry Proprietary Blend, but it's the kick-butt zins—priced in the mid-twenties—that you'll want to stock up on.

## GLEN ELLEN

About 7 miles north of Sonoma on Highway 12 is the town of Glen Ellen, which, though just a fraction of the size of Sonoma, is home to several of the valley's finest wineries, restaurants, and inns. Aside from the addition of a few new restaurants, this charming Wine Country town hasn't changed much since the days when Jack London settled on his Beauty Ranch, about a mile west. Other than the wineries, you'll find few real signs of commercialism; the shops and restaurants, located along one main winding lane, cater to a small, local clientele—that is, until the summer tourist season, when traffic nearly triples on the weekends. If you're as yet undecided where you want to set up camp during your visit to the Wine Country, we highly recommend this lovable little town.

**Arrowood.** 14347 Sonoma Hwy. (Calif. 12), Glen Ellen. ☎ **707/938-5170.** Daily 10am–4:30pm. Tours daily. Tasting $3.

Richard Arrowood had already established a reputation as a master wine maker at Château St. Jean before he and his wife, Alis Demers Arrowood, set out to build their own winery in 1986. Their utterly picturesque winery is perched on a gently rising hillside lined with perfectly manicured vineyards. Tastings take place in the Hospitality House, the newest of Arrowood's two stately gray-and-white buildings fashioned after a New England farmhouse, complete with wraparound porches. Richard's focus is on making world-class wine with minimal intervention, and his results are impressive: four out of his five current releases have scored over 90 points. Mind you, such excellence doesn't come cheaply: Prices start at $26 for a 1997 chardonnay and quickly climb to the mid- to high 40s. Arrowood is only one of the very few wineries in Sonoma that charge for tastings ($3); but if you're curious what near-perfection tastes like, it's well worth it. No picnic facilities are available.

✪ **The Benziger Family Winery.** 1883 London Ranch Rd. (off Arnold Dr., on the way to Jack London State Historic Park), Glen Ellen. ☎ **800/989-8890** or 707/935-3000. Tasting room daily 10am–5pm. Tram tours daily (weather permitting) at 11:30am, 12:30, 2, and 3:30pm.

When Bruno Benziger moved from New York, purchased the plot next to Jack London State Park, and started the Glen Ellen label (see above), he had no idea that he would become the valley's second-largest wine producer. After the Benziger family's fast track to the top, they sold the rights to that label in order to create lower-volume, higher-quality wines under this one.

A visit here confirms that you are indeed visiting a "family" winery; at any given time three generations of Benzigers (pronounced *ben*-zigger) may be running around tending to chores, and you're instantly made to feel as if you're part of the clan. The pastoral property has a spacious tasting room manned by an amiable staff, as well as an art gallery, beautiful gardens, and an exceptional self-guided tour ("The most comprehensive tour in the wine industry," exclaims *Wine Spectator* magazine). The free 40-minute tram tour, pulled by a beefy tractor, is both informative and fun as it winds through the estate vineyards before making a champagne-tasting pit stop on a scenic bluff. (*Tip:* Tram tickets—a hot item in the summer—are available on a limited first-come, first-served basis, so either arrive early or stop by in the morning to pick up tickets for an afternoon ride.)

Tastings of the standard release wines are free, and bottle prices range from $10.99 for a 1997 fumé blanc to $17.99 for a 1996 pinot noir. The best buy, however, is the award-winning 1996 zinfandel (Sonoma County), priced to move at $17.99 a bottle. You can also purchase a full glass of wine for $4 to $6 and tour the estate in style. The winery also offers several scenic picnic spots.

## KENWOOD

A few miles north of Glen Ellen along Highway 12 is the tiny town of Kenwood, the northernmost outpost of the Sonoma Valley. Though Kenwood Vineyards' wines are well known throughout the United States, the town itself consists of little more than a few restaurants, wineries, and modest homes recessed into the wooded hillsides. The nearest lodging, the luxurious Kenwood Inn & Spa, is located about a mile south. Kenwood makes for a pleasant day trip—lunch at Café Citti, a tour of Château St. Jean, dinner at Kenwood Restaurant—before returning to Glen Ellen or Sonoma for the night.

**Kunde Estate Winery.** 10155 Sonoma Hwy., Kenwood. ☎ **707/833-5501.** www.kunde.com. Tastings daily 11am–5pm. Cave tours Fri–Sun approximately every half hour from 11am–4pm.

Expect a friendly, sociable welcome at this scenic winery, run by four generations of the Kundes since 1904. One of the largest grape suppliers in the area, the Kunde family (pronounced *kun-dee*) has converted 800 acres of their 2,000-acre ranch for growing ultra-premium-quality grapes, which they provide to about 23 Sonoma and Napa wineries. It is this abundance that allows them to make nothing but estate wines (wines made from grapes grown on the Kunde property, as opposed to purchased from other growers).

The tasting room is located in a spiffy 17,000-square-foot wine-making facility, which features specialized crushing equipment that allows the wine maker to run whole clusters to the press—a real advantage in white-wine production. Tastings of the dozen or so releases are free; bottle prices range from $11 for a Magnolia Lane sauvignon blanc to $24 for a Reserve cabernet sauvignon; most labels sell in the mid-to-high teens. The tasting room also has a gift shop and large windows overlooking the bottling room and tank room.

The tour of the property's extensive wine caves, which is held Friday through Sunday, includes a history of the winery. Private tours are available by appointment, but most folks are happy to just stop by for some vino and to relax at one of the many picnic tables placed around the man-made pond. Animal-lovers will appreciate Kunde's preservation efforts; the property has a rare-duck estuary with more than 50 species (seen by appointment only). *Gossip note:* The Kunde Estate also happens to be where actress Geena Davis and director Renny Harlin tied the knot in 1993.

**Kenwood Vineyards.** 9592 Sonoma Hwy. (Calif. 12), Kenwood. ☎ **707/833-5891.** Daily 10am–4:30pm. Tours by appointment only.

Kenwood's history dates back to 1906, when the Pagani brothers made their living selling wine straight from the barrel and into the jug. In 1970, the property was bought by the Lee family, who dumped a ton of money into converting the aging winery into a modern, high-production facility (though they have cleverly concealed most of it within the original barnlike buildings). Since then, Kenwood's wines have earned a solid reputation for consistent quality with each of their varietals: cabernet sauvignon, chardonnay, zinfandel, pinot noir, merlot, and their most popular wine, sauvignon blanc—a crisp, light wine with hints of melon.

Though the winery looks rather modest in size, its output is staggering: 360,000 cases of ultra-premium wines fermented in 60 steel tanks and 7,000 French and American oak barrels. Popular with wine collectors is wine maker Michael Lee's Artist Series cabernet sauvignon, a limited production from the winery's best vineyards featuring labels with original artwork by renowned artists. The tasting room, housed in one of the old barns, offers free tastings of most varieties, as well as gift items for sale. Wine prices are moderate, ranging from $8 for a bottle of 1995 Vintage Red table wine to $25 for an estate organically grown merlot; the Artist Series, on the other hand, runs anywhere from $70 to $250.

## JUST UP FROM THE VALLEY: SANTA ROSA

✪ **Matanzas Creek**. 6097 Bennett Valley Rd. (off Warm Springs Rd.), Santa Rosa. ☎ **800/ 590-6464** or 707/528-6464. Daily 10am–4:30pm. Tours daily by appointment only at 10:30am, 1, and 3pm. From Hwy. 12 in Kenwood or Glen Ellen, take Warm Springs Rd. turnoff to Bennett Valley Rd.; the drive takes 15–20 min.

Okay, so it's not technically in Sonoma Valley, but if there's one winery that's worth the detour, it's Matanzas Creek. After a wonderfully scenic 20-minute drive along Bennett Valley Road you'll arrive at one of the prettiest wineries in California, blanketed by fields of lavender and surrounded by rolling hills of well-tended vineyards.

The winery itself has a rather unorthodox history. In 1978, Sandra and Bill MacIver, neither of whom had any previous experience in the worlds of wine making or business, set out with one goal in mind: to create the finest wines in the country. Actually, they've overshot their mark. With the recent release of their Journey 1990 chardonnay, they've been hailed by critics as the proud parents of the finest chardonnay ever produced in the United States, comparable to the finest white wines in the world.

This state-of-the-art, environmentally conscious winery produces only three varietals—the above-mentioned chardonnay, plus sauvignon blanc and merlot—all of which are available for tasting free of charge. Prices for current releases are, as you would imagine, at the higher end, ranging from $18 for a 1997 sauvignon blanc to $48 for the 1996 Estate merlot, but it's easily the finest merlot you'll sample in the Wine Country. Also available for purchase is culinary lavender from Matanzas (pronounced mah-tan-zas) Creek's own lavender field, the largest outside of Provence and a breathtaking sight when it's in bloom in June (*Tip:* Purchase a glass of wine and bring it outside to savor as you wander through these wonderfully aromatic gardens). Picnic tables hidden under groves of oak have pleasant views of the surrounding vineyards. On the return trip, be sure to take the Sonoma Mountain Road detour for a real backcountry experience.

## WHERE TO STAY IN SONOMA COUNTY

If you have any trouble finding a room, try calling the **Sonoma Valley Visitors Bureau** (☎ **707/996-1090**). They'll refer you to a lodging that has a room to spare, but they won't make reservations for you. The **Bed and Breakfast Association of Sonoma Valley** (☎ **800/969-4667**) will refer you to one of their member B&Bs, and can make reservations for you as well. Keep in mind, however, that most B&B rates *start* at well over $100.

**El Pueblo Inn.** 896 W. Napa St., Sonoma, CA 95476. ☎ **800/900-8844** or 707/996-3651. 38 units. A/C TEL. May–Oct, $80–$94 double. Mar–Apr and Nov, $69–$80 double. Dec–Feb, $65–$80 double. AE, DISC, MC, V.

Located on Sonoma's main east-west street 8 blocks from the center of town, this isn't Sonoma's fanciest hotel, but it offers some of the best-priced accommodations around. The rooms here are pleasant enough, with post-and-beam construction, exposed brick walls, light-wood furniture, and geometric prints. A drip coffee machine should be a comfort to early risers, and an outdoor heated pool will cool you off in hot weather. Reservations should be made at least a month in advance for the spring and summer months.

**Sonoma Chalet.** 18935 5th St. W., Sonoma, CA 95476. ☎ **707/938-3129.** 3 units, 3 cottages, 1 suite. Apr–Oct, $85–$160 double. Nov–Mar, $85–$150 double. Rates include continental breakfast. AE, MC, V.

This is one of the few accommodations in Sonoma that's truly secluded; it's on the outskirts of town, in a peaceful country setting overlooking a 200-acre ranch. The accommodations, housed in a Swiss-style farmhouse and several cottages, are all delightfully decorated by someone with an eye for color and a concern for comfort. They have clawfoot tubs, beds covered with country quilts, Oriental carpets, comfortable furnishings, and private decks; some have woodstoves or fireplaces. The two least expensive rooms share a bath, while the cottages offer the most privacy. A breakfast of fruit, yogurt, pastries, and cereal is served either in the country kitchen or in your room (and the gaggles of ducks, chickens, and ornery geese will be glad to help you finish off the crumbs). If you like country rustic (and farm animals), you'll like the Sonoma Chalet.

**Sonoma Hotel.** 110 W. Spain St., Sonoma, CA 95476. ☎ **800/468-6016** or 707/996-2996. Fax 707/996-7014. 17 units, 5 with bathroom. Summer, $75–$85 double without bathroom, $115–$125 double with bathroom. Winter, Sun–Thurs, $59 double without bathroom, $90 double with bathroom; Fri–Sat, $75 double without bathroom, $115–$125 double with bathroom. Rates include continental breakfast. AE, MC, V.

This cute little historic hotel on Sonoma's tree-lined Town Square still retains the same ambience it did over a century ago. With an emphasis on European-style elegance and comfort, each room is decorated in an early-California style, with antique furnishings, fine woods, and floral-print wallpapers. Some of the rooms feature brass beds, and all are blissfully devoid of phones and TVs. Five of the third-floor rooms share immaculate baths (and significantly reduced rates), while rooms with private baths have deep clawfoot tubs with overhead showers. Perks include continental breakfast and a bottle of wine on arrival. Also within the hotel is Le Bistro, a small restaurant serving Mediterranean cuisine for lunch, dinner, and Sunday brunch.

**Victorian Garden Inn.** 316 E. Napa St., Sonoma, CA 95476. ☎ **800/543-5339** or 707/996-5339. Fax 707/996-1689. 4 units. $95–$185 double. Rates include breakfast and afternoon wine and sherry. AE, DC, MC, V.

Proprietor Donna Lewis runs what is easily the cutest B&B in Sonoma Valley. A small picket fence and wall of trees enclose an adorable Victorian garden brimming with bowers of violets, roses, camellias, and peonies, all shaded under flowering fruit trees. It's a truly marvelous sight in the springtime. Four guest rooms—three in the century-old water tower and one in the main house, an 1870s Greek Revival farmhouse—are in keeping with the Victorian theme: white wicker furniture, floral prints, padded armchairs, clawfoot tubs. The most popular rooms are the Top o' the Tower, which has it's own entrance and view overlooking the garden, and the Woodcutter's Cottage, which also has its own entrance and garden view, plus a sofa and armchairs set in front of the fireplace. A breakfast of croissants, muffins, gourmet coffee, and fruit picked from the garden is served at the dining table, in the garden, or in your room; evening wine and sherry are served in the parlor. After a hard day's wine tasting, spend the afternoon cooling off in the swimming pool or on the shaded wraparound porch, enjoying a mellow Merlot while soaking in the sweet garden smells.

# WHERE TO DINE IN THE SONOMA VALLEY
## SONOMA

**Basque Boulangerie Cafe.** 460 First St. E., Sonoma. ☎ **707/935-7687.** Menu items $3–$7. No credit cards. Daily 7am–6pm. BAKERY/DELI.

If you want a big breakfast with eggs, sausage, and the works, head to The Feed Store down the street at 529 First St. But, if you prefer a lighter morning meal and strong coffee, stand in line with the locals at the Basque Boulangerie Cafe, the most popular gathering spot in the Sonoma Valley. Most everything—sourdough Basque breads, pastries, quiche, soups, salads, desserts, sandwiches, cookies—is made in-house, and made well. Daily lunch specials, such as a grilled veggie sandwich with smoked mozzarella cheese ($4.75), are listed on the chalkboard out front. Seating is scarce, and if you can score a sidewalk table on a sunny day, consider yourself one lucky person. A popular option is ordering to go and eating in the shady plaza across the street. The cafe sells wine by the glass, as well as a wonderful cinnamon bread by the loaf—ideal for making French toast.

**Della Santina's.** 133 E. Napa St. (just east of the square), Sonoma. ☎ **707/935-0576.** Reservations recommended. Main courses $8.95–$14.75. AE, DISC, MC, V. Daily 11:30am–3pm; 5–9:30pm. ITALIAN.

Those of you who just can't take another expensive, chichi California meal should follow the locals to this friendly, and traditional Italian restaurant. How traditional? Just ask father/son team Dan and Robert: when we last dined here they pointed out Señora Santina's hand-embroidered linen doilies as they proudly told us about her Tuscan recipes. And their pride is merited: Every dish we tried here was refreshingly authentic, in huge portions, and well flavored, without overbearing sauces or one hint of California pretentiousness. Be sure to start with traditional antipasti, especially the sliced mozzarella and tomatoes or the delicious white beans. There are nine pasta dishes that are, again, wonderfully authentic (gnocchi lovers, rejoice!). The spit-roasted meat dishes are a local favorite (though we found them to be a bit overcooked), and for those who can't choose between chicken, pork, turkey, rabbit, or duck, there's a selection that offers a choice of three. Don't worry about breaking your bank on a bottle of wine, as most of the savory choices here go for under $25. Portions are huge, but save room for dessert—they're wonderful, too.

**La Casa.** 121 E. Spain St., Sonoma. ☎ **707/996-3406.** Reservations recommended on weekends and summer evenings. Main courses $6–$11. AE, CB, DC, DISC, MC, V. Daily 11:30am–10pm (bar appetizers until midnight). MEXICAN.

This no-nonsense Mexican restaurant, on the Sonoma Plaza across from the mission, serves great enchiladas, fajitas, and chimichangas. To start, try the black-bean soup or the ceviche made of fresh snapper, marinated in lime juice with cilantro and salsa, and served on crispy tortillas. Follow that with tamales prepared with cornhusks spread with corn masa, stuffed with chicken filling, and topped with a mild red-chile sauce. Or you might opt for the delicious suiza—deep-dish chicken enchiladas—or fresh snapper Veracruz if it's available. On a sunny afternoon or a clear night, choose to dine patio style, where you can sip cerveza and under the warmth of heat lamps.

✪ **Lo Spuntino.** 400 First St. E., Sonoma. ☎ **707/935-5656.** Deli items $5–$9. AE, CB, DISC, MC, V. Sun–Thurs 10am–6pm; Fri–Sat 10am–10pm. ITALIAN DELI.

Lo Spuntino, Italian for "snack" or a tiny taste, is the sexiest thing going in Sonoma, a suave deli and wine bar owned by Sam and Vicki Sebastiani, who also run Viansa Winery. It's a visual masterpiece, with shiny black-and-white-checkered flooring, long counters of Italian marble, track lighting, and a center deli and wine bar where a crew of young men slice meats, pour wines, and scoop gelato. Start by sampling the preserves and jams at the entrance, then wander the aisle and choose among the armada of cured meats, cheese, fruit, pastas, salads, and breads lining the deli. Popular choices are the hefty sandwiches on herbed focaccia bread or the herb-marinated rotisserie chickens served by the half with your choice of pasta or salad. Roasted turkey, duck, pork, lamb, and rabbit are also available. Opposite the deli is the wine bar, featuring all of Viansa's current wine releases for both tasting and purchase, as well as a small selection of microbrewed beers on tap. On your way out, stop at the gelateria and treat yourself to some intense Italian ice cream. *Note:* Lo Spuntino also hosts live jazz bands every Friday night from 7 to 10pm.

**Piatti.** 405 First St. W., Sonoma. ☎ **707/996-2351.** Reservations recommended. Main courses $9.95–$18.95. AE, DC, MC, V. Sun–Thurs 11:30am–10pm; Fri–Sat 11:30am–11pm. ITALIAN.

Part of a Northern California chain that originated in Napa, Piatti has built a steadfast and true clientele by consistently serving large portions of good Italian food at a fair price in a fun and festive setting (got all that?). The restaurant occupies the ground floor of the El Dorado Hotel at the northwest corner of Sonoma Plaza (just follow your nose). Good-tasting pizzas and braised meats, such as the superb lamb shank flavored with a rich port-wine sauce and fresh mint, emerge from a wood-burning oven. There's also an array of satisfying pastas, our favorite being the canelloni stuffed with roasted veal, spinach, porcini mushrooms, and ricotta. Other recommended dishes include a wonderful roast-vegetable appetizer, the teeming pile of fresh mussels in a tomato-and-herb broth, the rotisserie chicken with garlic mashed potatoes, and the veal scaloppine. Granted, there are fancier and more intimate restaurants in the valley, but none that can fill you up with such good food at these prices. And if the sun is out, there's no prettier place in Sonoma to dine alfresco than Piatti's courtyard.

## GLEN ELLEN

**Jack's Village Café.** 14301 Arnold Dr., Glen Ellen. ☎ **707/939-6111.** Main courses $5.75–$9.50. AE, DISC, MC, V. Breakfast, lunch daily 8:30am–4pm; dinner Wed–Sun 6–9pm. CALIFORNIA COUNTRY.

Hidden behind the Glen Ellen Tasting Room in Jack London Village is this small café run by Debra De Martini, a pretty and vivacious woman who greets guests, waits tables, and works the grill if need be. ("All hats" is her job description.) Century-old wood beams create a rustic ambiance inside, while the outdoor patio is surrounded by trees, flowers, and soothing sounds from a nearby creek. When the weather is pleasant, there's no better place in Glen Ellen to sit outside with a good glass of wine, a bowl of steamed mussels, and a roasted eggplant and mozzarella sandwich. Other menu items range from a wild mushroom risotto with braised leeks and sun-dried tomatoes (a bargain at $9.50) to a roasted pork loin sandwich sautéed onions and Jack's special barbecue sauce. Breakfast is taken seriously here: The French toast is made with thick slices of sourdough bread sprinkled with cinnamon and nutmeg. The smoked salmon with toasted bagel and cream cheese is the perfect light breakfast for two, and the hot oatmeal and homemade granola are good choices as well. *Note:* Be sure to check the Daily Specials board above the grill before you order.

# KENWOOD

**Café Citti.** 9049 Sonoma Hwy, Kenwood. ☎ **707/833-2690.** Main courses $6–$9.50. MC, V. Lunch daily 11am–3:30pm; dinner Sun–Thur 5–8:30pm, Fri–Sat 5–9pm. ITALIAN.

If you're this far north into the Wine Country, then you're probably doing some serious wine tasting. If that's the case, then you don't want to spend half the day at a fancy, high-priced restaurant. What you need is Café Citti (pronounced CHEAT-ee), a roadside do-it-yourself Italian trattoria that is both good and cheap. There's no menu; you order from the huge menu board displayed above the open kitchen. Afterwards you scramble for a table (the ones on the patio, shaded by umbrellas, are the best on warm afternoons), and a server will bring your meal. It's all hearty, home-cooked Italian. Standout dishes are the green-bean salad, tangy Caesar salad, focaccia sandwiches, and the roasted rotisserie chicken stuffed with rosemary and garlic. The freshly made pastas come with a variety of sauces; our favorite is the zesty marinara. Wine is available by the bottle, and the espresso is plenty strong. Everything on the menu board is available to go, which makes Café Citti an excellent resource for picnic supplies.

# Appendix A:
# San Francisco in Depth

## 1 San Francisco Today

Shaken but not stirred by the Loma Prieta earthquake in 1989, San Francisco has witnessed a spectacular rebound in recent years. The seaside Embarcadero, once plagued by a horrendously ugly freeway overpass, has been revitalized by a multimillion-dollar facelift, complete with palm trees, a new trolley line, and wide cobblestone walkways. SoMa, the once shady neighborhood south of Market Street, has exploded with new development, including the world-class Museum of Modern Art, the beautiful Yerba Buena Gardens, and a slew of hip new clubs and cafes. Even the city's dress code has improved: Hit the clubs wearing jeans, sneakers, and a T-shirt and you may just be asked to leave (even dress-down Fridays have changed to dress-up Fridays). In short, it's hot to be hip these days in San Francisco: Black is back, cigars are in, the blues rule, pool is cool again, and the 1950s are back with a vengeance.

And though it seems hard to believe that one man could turn a city around, ever since Willie Brown was voted into office as mayor of San Francisco, things have been looking up for the city's state of affairs. After giving just about every member of former mayor Frank Jordan's administration the boot, the legendary ex-Speaker of California's State Assembly has been administering steady doses of shock therapy to this proud but oft-troubled city. Public transportation, always a thorny issue with the people, has improved; homelessness is no longer a crime, and shelters and work programs are on the rise; the city's beleaguered 911 system is back on track; and San Franciscans in general are starting to take a renewed pride in their city since "Da Mayor" started running the show.

All that glitters is not the Golden Gate, however. At the end of World War II, San Francisco was the largest and wealthiest city on the West Coast. Since then it has been demoted to the fourth-largest city in California, home to only 750,000 people, less than 5% of the state's total. The industrial heart of the city has been knocked out and shipped off to less costly locations such as Oakland and Los Angeles, and increasingly San Francisco has had to fall back on tourism as a major source of revenue. If the process continues unabated, the city may someday become another Venice or (egad!) Las Vegas, whose only raison d'être will be fleecing its visitors like one vast Fisherman's Wharf—a frightening premonition.

Then, of course, there are the typical big-city problems. Crime is up along with drug use, homelessness and panhandling have gotten way out of hand, and a nationwide resurgence in racism hasn't left San Francisco—once a bastion of free-thinkers—untouched. (One odd predicament is the increase in drivers who run red lights, which has plagued the city and created fearful, angry pedestrians and nasty fender benders.)

But as a whole, San Francisco is doing just fine these days. Its symphony is in the black, its convention halls are fully booked, levels in city coffers are on the rise, the mayor's fired up—even AIDS is on the decline. It's hard to think of a whole city as having its ups and downs, but after nearly a decade of getting thumped by the recession and poor management (among other things), San Francisco is on a definite upswing. Though it may never relive its heady days as the king of the West Coast, San Francisco will undoubtedly retain the title as most everyone's favorite California city. As one resident put it, "Anything but LA."

## 2 A Look at the Past

Born as an out-of-the-way backwater of colonial Spain and blessed with a harbor that would have been the envy of any of the great cities of Europe, San Francisco boasts a story that's as varied as the millions of people who have passed through its Golden Gate.

**THE AGE OF DISCOVERY**  After the "discovery" of the New World by Columbus in 1492, legends of the fertile land of California were discussed in the universities and taverns of Europe, even though no one really understood where the mythical land was. (Some evidence of arrivals in California by Chinese merchants hundreds of years before Columbus's landing has been unearthed, although few scholars are willing to draw definite conclusions.) The first documented visit by a European to northern California, however, was by the Portuguese explorer Joaño Cabrillo, who traveled around the southern tip of South America to as far north as the Russian River in 1542. Nearly 40 years later, in 1579, Sir Francis Drake landed on the northern California coast, stopping for a time to repair his ships and to claim the territory for Elizabeth I of England. He was followed several years later by another Portuguese, Sebastiaño Cermenho, "discoverer" of Punta de los Reyes (Kings' Point) in the mid-1590s. Ironically, all three adventurers completely missed the narrow entrance to San Francisco Bay, either because it was enshrouded in fog or, more likely, because they simply weren't looking for it. Believe it or not, the bay's entrance is nearly impossible to see from the open ocean.

### Dateline

- **1542** Juan Cabrillo sails up the California coast.
- **1579** Sir Francis Drake lands near San Francisco, missing the entrance to the bay.
- **1769** Members of the Spanish expedition led by Gaspar de Portolá become the first Europeans to see San Francisco Bay.
- **1775** The *San Carlos* is the first European ship to sail into San Francisco Bay.
- **1776** Captain Juan Bautista de Anza establishes a presidio (military fort); San Francisco de Asís Mission opens.
- **1821** Mexico wins independence from Spain and annexes California.
- **1835** The town of Yerba Buena develops around the port; the United States tries unsuccessfully to purchase San Francisco Bay from Mexico.
- **1846** Mexican-American War.
- **1847** Americans annex Yerba Buena and rename it San Francisco.
- **1848** Gold is discovered in Coloma, near Sacramento.
- **1849** In the year of the gold rush, San Francisco's population swells from about 800 to 25,000.

*continues*

- **1851** Lawlessness becomes acute before attempts are made to curb it.
- **1869** The transcontinental railroad reaches San Francisco.
- **1873** Andrew S. Hallidie invents the cable car.
- **1906** The Great Earthquake strikes, and the resulting fire levels the city.
- **1915** The Panama Pacific International Exposition celebrates San Francisco's restoration and the completion of the Panama Canal.
- **1936** The Bay Bridge is built.
- **1937** The Golden Gate Bridge is completed.
- **1945** The United Nations Charter is drafted and adopted by the representatives of 50 countries meeting in San Francisco.
- **1950** The Beat Generation moves into the bars and cafes of North Beach.
- **1967** A free concert in Golden Gate Park attracts 20,000 people, ushering in the Summer of Love and the hippie era.
- **1974** BART's high-speed transit system opens the tunnel linking San Francisco with the East Bay.
- **1978** Harvey Milk, a city supervisor and America's first openly gay politician, is assassinated, along with Mayor George Moscone, by political rival Dan White.
- **1989** An earthquake registering 7.1 on the Richter scale hits San Francisco during a World Series baseball game, as 100 million watch on TV; the city quickly rebuilds.
- **1991** Fire rages through the Berkeley/Oakland hills, destroying 2,800 homes.
- **1993** Yerba Buena Center for the Arts opens.
- **1995** New San Francisco Museum of Modern Art opens.

*continues*

It would be another two centuries before a European actually saw the bay that would later extend Spain's influence over much of the American West. Gaspar de Portolá, a soldier sent from Spain to meddle in a rather ugly conflict between the Jesuits and the Franciscans, accidentally stumbled upon the bay in 1769, en route to somewhere else, but then stoically plodded on to his original destination, Monterey Bay, more than 100 miles to the south. Six years later, Juan Manuel de Ayala, while on a mapping expedition for the Spanish, actually sailed into San Francisco Bay, and immediately realized the enormous strategic importance of his find.

Colonization quickly followed. Juan Bautista de Anza and around 30 Spanish-speaking families marched through the deserts from Sonora, Mexico, arriving after many hardships at the northern tip of modern-day San Francisco in June 1776. They immediately claimed the peninsula for Spain. (Coincidentally, their claim of allegiance to Spain occurred only about a week before the 13 English-speaking colonies of North America's eastern seaboard, a continent away, declared their independence from Britain.) Their headquarters was an adobe fortress, the Presidio, built on the site of today's park of the same name. The settlers' church, built a mile to the south, was the first of five Spanish missions later developed around the edges of San Francisco Bay. Although the name of the church was officially Nuestra Señora de Dolores, it was dedicated to St. Francis of Assisi and nicknamed San Francisco by the Franciscan priests. Later the name was applied to the entire bay.

In 1821, Mexico broke away from Spain, secularized the Spanish missions, and abandoned all interest in the Indian natives. Freed of Spanish restrictions, California's ports were suddenly opened to trade. The region around San Francisco Bay supplied large numbers of hides and tallow for transport around Cape Horn to the tanneries and factories of New England and New York. The prospects for prosperity persuaded an English-born sailor, William Richardson, to jump ship in 1822 and settle on the site of what is now San Francisco. To impress the commandant of the Presidio, whose daughter he loved, Richardson converted to Catholicism and established the beginnings of what would soon became a thriving trading post and colony. Richard named his trading post Yerba Buena (or "good herb") because of a species of wild mint that grew there, near the site of today's Montgomery Street. (The city's original name was recalled with endless mirth 120 years later during San Francisco's hippie era.) He conducted a profitable hide-trading business and eventually became har-bormaster and the city's first merchant prince. By 1839, the place was a veritable town, with a mostly English-speaking popu-lace and a saloon of dubious virtue.

Throughout the 19th century, armed hos-tilities between English-speaking settlers from the eastern seaboard and the Spanish-speaking colonies of Spain and Mexico erupted in places as widely scattered as Texas, Puerto Rico, and along the frequently shifting U.S.-Mexico border. In 1846, a group of U.S. Marines from the warship *Portsmouth* seized the sleepy main plaza of Yerba Buena, ran the U.S. flag up a pole, and declared California an American territory. The Presidio (occupied by about a dozen unmotivated Mexican soldiers) surrendered without a fuss. The first move the new, mostly Yankee citizenry made was officially adopting the name of the bay as the name of their town.

- **1996** Former Assembly Speaker Willie Brown elected mayor of San Francisco.
- **1997** Pulitzer Prize–winning *San Francisco Chronicle* columnist Herb Caen dies of cancer.
- **1998** El Niño deluges San Francisco with its second-highest rainfall in history, causing billions in damage throughout California.
- **1999** San Francisco City Hall opens to much praise and fanfare after a multimil-lion dollar renovation.

**THE GOLD RUSH** The year 1848 was one of the most pivotal years in European history, with unrest sweeping through Europe, horrendous poverty in Ireland, and widespread disillusionment about the hopes for prosperity throughout Europe and the Eastern Coast of the United States. Stories about the golden port of San Francisco and the agrarian wealth of the American West filtered slowly east, attracting slow-moving groups of settlers. Ex-sailor Richard Henry Dana extolled the virtues of California in his best-selling novel *Two Years Before the Mast,* and helped fire the public's imagination about the territory's bounty, particularly that of the Bay Area.

The first overland party crossed the Sierra and arrived in California in 1841. San Francisco grew steadily, reaching a population of approximately 900 by April 1848, but nothing hinted at the population explosion that was to follow. The historian Barry Parr has referred to the California gold rush as the most extraordinary event to ever befall an American city in peacetime. In time, San Francisco's winning combination of raw materials, healthful climate, and freedom would have attracted thousands of settlers even without the lure of gold. But the gleam of the soft metal is said to have com-pressed 50 years of normal growth into less than 6 months. In 1848, the year gold was first discovered, the population of San Francisco jumped from under 1,000 to 26,000 in less than 6 months. As many as 100,000 more passed through San Francisco in the space of less than a year on their way to the rocky hinterlands where the gold was rumored to be.

If not for the discovery of some small particles of gold at a sawmill that he owned, Swiss-born John Augustus Sutter's legacy would have been far less flamboyant. Despite Sutter's wish to keep the discovery quiet, his employee, John Marshall, leaked word of the discovery to friends. It eventually appeared in local papers, and smart investors on the East Coast took imme-diate heed. The rush did not start, however, until Sam Brannan, a Mormon preacher and famous charlatan, ran through the streets of San Francisco shouting, "Gold! Gold in the American River!" (Brannan, incidentally, bought up all the harborfront real estate he could get, and cornered the market on shovels, pickaxes, and canned food, just before making the announcement that was heard around the world.)

A world on the brink of change responded almost frantically. The gold rush was on. Shop owners hung GONE TO THE DIGGINGS signs in their windows. Flotillas of ships set sail from ports throughout Europe, South America, Australia, and the East Coast, sometimes nearly sinking with the weight of mining equipment. Townspeople from the Midwest headed overland, tent cities sprang up, and the sociology of a nation was transformed almost overnight. Not since the Crusades of the Middle Ages had so many people been mobilized in so short a period of time. Daily business stopped; ships arrived in San Francisco and were almost immediately deserted by their crews. News of the gold strike spread like a plague through every discontented hamlet in the known world. Although other settlements were closer to the gold strike, San Francisco was the famous name, and therefore, where the gold-diggers disembarked. Tent cities sprang up, demand for virtually everything skyrocketed, and although some miners actually found gold, smart merchants quickly discovered that more enduring hopes lay in servicing the needs of the thousands of miners who arrived ill equipped and ignorant of the lay of the land. Prices soared. Miners, faced with staggeringly inflated prices for goods and services, barely scraped a profit after expenses. Most prospectors failed, many died of hardship, while others committed suicide at the alarming rate of 1,000 a year. Yet despite the tragedies, graft, and vice associated with the gold rush, within mere months San Francisco was forever transformed from a tranquil Spanish settlement into a roaring, boisterous boomtown.

**BOOMTOWN FEVER**  By 1855, most of California's surface gold had already been panned out, leaving only the richer but deeper veins of ore, which individual miners couldn't retrieve without massive capital investments. Despite that, San Francisco had evolved into a vast commercial magnet, sucking into its warehouses and banks the staggering riches that overworked newcomers had dragged, ripped, and distilled from the rocks, fields, and forests of western North America.

Investment funds were being lavished on more than mining, however. Speculation on the newly established San Francisco stock exchange could make or destroy an investor in a single day, and several noteworthy writers (including Mark Twain) were among the young men forever influenced by the boomtown spirit. The American Civil War left California firmly in the Union camp, ready, willing, and able to receive hordes of disillusioned soldiers fed up with the internecine warmongering of the eastern seaboard. In 1869, the transcontinental railway linked the eastern and western seaboards of the United States, ensuring the fortunes of the barons who controlled it. The railways, however, also shifted economic power bases as cheap manufactured goods from the East undercut the high prices hitherto charged for goods that sailed or steamed their way around the tip of South America. Ownership of the newly formed Central Pacific and Southern Pacific railroads was almost completely controlled by the "Big Four," all iron-willed capitalists—Leland Stanford, Mark Hopkins, Collis P. Huntington, and Charles Crocker—whose ruthlessness was legendary. (Much of the bone-crushing labor for their railway was executed by low-paid Chinese newcomers, most of whom arrived in overcrowded ships at San Francisco ports.) As the 19th century came to a close, civil unrest became more frequent as the monopolistic grip of the railways and robber barons became more obvious. Adding to the discontent were the uncounted thousands of Chinese immigrants, who fled starvation and unrest in Asia at rates rivaling those of the Italians, Poles, Irish, and British.

During the 1870s the flood of profits from the Comstock Lode in western Nevada diminished to a trickle, a cycle of droughts wiped out part of California's agricultural bounty, and local industry struggled to survive against the flood of manufactured goods imported via railway from the well-established factories of the East Coast and Midwest. Often, discontented workers blamed their woes on the now-unwanted hordes of Chinese workers, who by preference and for mutual protection had congregated into teeming all-Asian communities.

Despite these downward cycles, the city enjoyed other bouts of prosperity around the turn of the century thanks to the Klondike gold rush in Alaska and the Spanish-American War. Long accustomed to making a buck off gold fever, San Francisco managed to position itself as a point of embarkation for supplies bound for Alaska. Also during this time, the Bank of America emerged, which eventually evolved into the largest bank in the world. Founded in North Beach in 1904, the Bank of America was the brainchild of Italian-born A. P. Giannini, who later funded part of the construction for a bridge that many critics said was preposterous: the Golden Gate.

**THE GREAT FIRE** On the morning of April 18, 1906, San Francisco changed for all time. The city has never experienced an earthquake as destructive as the one that hit at 5:13am. (Scientists estimate its strength at 8.1 on the Richter scale.) All but a handful of the city's 400,000 inhabitants lay fast asleep when the ground beneath the city went into a series of convulsions. As one eyewitness put it, "The earth was shaking . . . it was undulating, rolling like an ocean breaker." The quake ruptured every water main in the city, and simultaneously started a chain of fires that rapidly fused into one gigantic conflagration. The fire brigades were helpless, and for 3 days San Francisco burned.

Militia troops finally stopped the flames from advancing by dynamiting entire city blocks, but not before more than 28,000 buildings lay in ruins. Minor tremors lasted another 3 days. The final damage stretched across a path of destruction 450 miles long and 50 miles wide. In all, 497 city blocks were razed, or about one-third of the city. As Jack London wrote in a heartrending newspaper dispatch, "The city of San Francisco is no more." The earthquake and subsequent fire so decisively changed the city that post-1906 San Francisco bears little resemblance to the town before the quake. Out of the ashes rose a bigger, healthier, and more beautiful town, though latter-day urbanologists regret that the rebuilding that followed the San Francisco earthquake did not follow a more enlightened plan. So eager was the city to rebuild that the old, somewhat unimaginative gridiron plan was reinstated, despite the opportunities for more daring visions that the aftermath of the quake afforded.

In 1915, in celebration of the opening of the Panama Canal and to prove to the world that San Francisco was restored to its full glory, the city hosted the Panama Pacific International Exhibition, a world's fair that exposed hundreds of thousands of visitors to the city's unique charms. The general frenzy of civic boosterism, however, reached its peak during the years just before World War I, when investments and civic pride might have reached an all-time high. Despite Prohibition, speakeasies did a thriving business in and around the city, and building sprees were as high blown and lavish as the profits on the San Francisco stock exchange.

**WORLD WAR II**    The Japanese attack on Pearl Harbor on December 7, 1941, mobilized the United States into a massive war machine, with many shipyards strategically positioned along the Pacific Coast, including San Francisco. Within less than a year, several shipyards were producing up to one new warship per day, employing hundreds of thousands of people working in 24-hour shifts (the largest, Kaiser Shipyards in Richmond, alone employed more than 100,000 workers). In search of work and the excitement of life away from their villages and cornfields, workers flooded into the city from virtually everywhere, forcing an enormous boom in housing. Hundreds found themselves separated from their small towns for the first time in their lives and reveled in their newfound freedom.

After the hostilities ended, many soldiers remembered San Francisco as the site of their finest hours and returned to live there permanently. The economic prosperity of the postwar years enabled massive enlargements of the city, including freeways, housing developments, a booming financial district, and pockets of counterculture enthusiasts such as the beatniks, gays, and hippies.

**THE 1950s: THE BEATS**    San Francisco's reputation as a rollicking place where anything goes dates from the Barbary Coast days when gang warfare, prostitution, gambling, and drinking were major city pursuits, and citizens took law and order into their own hands. Its more modern role as a catalyst for social change and the avant-garde began in the 1950s when a group of young writers, philosophers, and poets challenged the materialism and conformity of American society by embracing anarchy and Eastern philosophy, expressing their notions in poetry. They adopted a uniform of jeans, sweater, sandals, and beret; called themselves Beats; and hung out in North Beach where rents were low and cheap wine was plentiful. The *San Francisco Chronicle* columnist Herb Caen, to whom they were totally alien, dubbed them *beatniks* in his column.

Allen Ginsberg, Gregory Corso, and Jack Kerouac had begun writing at Columbia University in New York, but it wasn't until they came west and hooked up with Lawrence Ferlinghetti, Kenneth Rexroth, Gary Snyder, and others that the movement gained national attention. The bible of the Beats was Ginsberg's *Howl*, which he first read at the Six Gallery on October 13, 1955. By the time he finished reading, Ginsberg was crying, the audience was chanting, and his fellow poets were announcing the arrival of an epic bard. Ferlinghetti published *Howl*, which was deemed obscene, in 1956. A trial followed, but the court found that the book had redeeming social value, thereby reaffirming the right of free expression. The other major work, Jack Kerouac's *On the Road*, was published in 1957, instantly becoming a bestseller. The freedom and sense of possibility that this book conveyed became the bellwether for a generation.

While the Beats gave poetry readings and generated controversy, two clubs in North Beach were making waves, notably the hungry i and the Purple Onion, where everyone who was anyone or became anyone on the entertainment scene appeared—Mort Sahl, Dick Gregory, Lenny Bruce, Barbra Streisand, and Woody Allen all worked here. Maya Angelou appeared as a singer and dancer at the Purple Onion. The cafes of North Beach were the center of bohemian life in the 1950s: the Black Cat,

Vesuvio's, Caffè Trieste and Caffè Tosca, and Enrico's Sidewalk Cafe. When the tour buses started rolling in, rents went up and Broadway was turned into a sex-club strip in the early 1960s. Thus ended an era, and the Beats moved on. The alternative scene shifted to Berkeley and the Haight.

**THE 1960s: THE HAIGHT**   The torch of freedom had been passed from the Beats and North Beach to Haight-Ashbury and the hippies, but it was a radically different torch. The hippies replaced the Beats' angst, anarchy, negativism, nihilism, alcohol, and poetry with love, communalism, openness, drugs, rock music, and a back-to-nature philosophy. Although the scent of marijuana wafted everywhere—on the streets, in the cafes, in Golden Gate Park—the real drugs of choice were LSD (a tab of good acid cost $5) and other hallucinogenics. Timothy Leary experimented with its effects and exhorted youth to "Turn on, tune in, and drop out." Instead of hanging out in coffeehouses, the hippies went to concerts at the Fillmore or the Avalon Ballroom to dance. The first Family Dog Rock 'n' Roll Dance and Concert, "A Tribute to Dr. Strange," was given at the Longshoreman's Hall in fall 1965, featuring the Jefferson Airplane, the Marbles, the Great Society, and the Charlatans. At this event, the first major happening of the 1960s, Ginsberg led a snake dance through the crowd. In January 1966, the 3-day Trips Festival, organized by rock promoter Bill Graham, was also held at the Longshoreman's Hall. The climax came with Ken Kesey and the Merry Pranksters Acid Test Show, which used five movie screens, psychedelic visions, and the sounds of the Grateful Dead and Big Brother and the Holding Company. The "be-in" followed in the summer of 1966 at the polo grounds in Golden Gate Park, when an estimated 20,000 heard the Jefferson Airplane perform and Ginsberg chant, while the Hell's Angels acted as unofficial police. It was followed by the Summer of Love in 1967 as thousands of young people streamed into the city in search of drugs and sex.

The 1960s Haight scene was very different from the 1950s Beat scene. The hippies were much younger than the Beats had been, constituting the first youth movement to take over the nation. Ironically, they also became the first generation of young, independent, and moneyed consumers to be courted by corporations. Ultimately, the Haight and the hippie movement deteriorated from love and flowers into drugs and crime, drawing a fringe of crazies like Charles Manson, and leaving only a legacy of sex, drugs, violence, and consumerism. As early as October 1967, the "Diggers," who had opened a free shop and soup kitchen in the Haight, symbolically buried the dream in a clay casket in Buena Vista Park.

The end of the Vietnam War and the resignation of President Nixon took the edge off politics. The last fling of the mentality that had driven the 1960s occurred in 1974 when Patty Hearst was kidnapped from her Berkeley apartment by the Symbionese Liberation Army and taken on a bank-robbing spree before surrendering in San Francisco.

**THE 1970s: GAY RIGHTS**   The homosexual community in San Francisco developed at the end of World War II, when thousands of military personnel were discharged back to the United States via San Francisco. A substantial number of those men were homosexual and decided to stay on in San Francisco. A gay community grew up along Polk Street between Sutter and California. Later, the larger community moved into the Castro, where it remains today.

The gay political protest movement is usually dated from the 1969 Stonewall raid that occurred in Greenwich Village. Although the political

*Of all cities in the United States I have seen, San Francisco is the most beautiful.*

—Nikita S. Khrushchev

movement started in New York, California had already given birth to two major organizations for gay rights: the Mattachine Society, founded in 1951 by Henry Hay in Los Angeles; and the Daughters of Bilitis, a lesbian organization founded in 1955 in San Francisco.

After Stonewall, the Committee for Homosexual Freedom was created in spring 1969 in San Francisco; a Gay Liberation Front chapter was organized at Berkeley. In fall 1969, Robert Patterson, a columnist for the *San Francisco Examiner,* referred to homosexuals as "semi males, drag darlings," and "women who aren't exactly women." On October 31, at noon, a group began a peaceful picketing of the *Examiner.* Peace reigned until someone threw a bag of printer's ink from an *Examiner* window. Someone wrote "Fuck the Examiner" on the wall, and the police moved in to clear the crowd, clubbing them as they went. The remaining pickets retreated to Glide Methodist Church and then marched on city hall. Unfortunately, the mayor was away. Unable to air their grievances, they started a sit-in that lasted until 5pm, when they were ordered to leave. Most did, but three remained and were arrested.

Later that year, an anti-Thanksgiving rally was staged at which gays protested against several national and local businesses: Western and Delta airlines, the former for firing lesbian stewardesses, the latter for refusing to sell a ticket to a young man wearing a Gay Power button; KFOG, for its antihomosexual broadcasting; and also some local gay bars for exploitation. On May 14, 1970, a group of gay and women's liberationists invaded the convention of the American Psychiatric Association in San Francisco to protest the reading of a paper on aversion therapy for homosexuals, forcing the meeting to adjourn.

The rage against intolerance was appearing on all fronts. At the National Gay Liberation Conference held in August 1970 in the city, Charles Thorp, chairman of the San Francisco State Liberation Front, called for militancy and issued a challenge to come out with a rallying cry of "Blatant is beautiful." He also argued for the use of what he felt was the more positive, celebratory term *gay* instead of *homosexual,* and decried the fact that homosexuals were kept in their place at the three Bs: the bars, the beaches, and the baths. As the movement grew in size and power, debates on strategy and tactics occurred, most dramatically between those who wanted to withdraw into separate ghettos and those who wanted to enter mainstream society. The most extreme proposal was made in California by Don Jackson, who proposed establishing a gay territory in California's Alpine County, about 10 miles south of Lake Tahoe. It would have had a totally gay administration, civil service, university, museum—everything. The residents of Alpine County were not pleased with the proposal. But before the situation turned really ugly, Jackson's idea was abandoned because of lack of support in the gay community. In the end, the movement would concentrate on integration and civil rights, not separatism. They would elect politicians who were sympathetic to their cause and celebrate their new identity by establishing National Gay Celebration Day and Gay Pride Week, the first of which was celebrated in June 1970 when 1,000 to 2,000 marched in New York, 1,000 in Los Angeles, and a few hundred in San Francisco.

By the mid-1970s, the gay community craved a more central role in San Francisco politics. Harvey Milk, owner of a camera store in the Castro, decided to run as an openly gay man for the Board of Supervisors. He won, becoming the first openly gay man to hold a major public office in the United States. He and liberal Mayor George Moscone developed a gay-rights agenda, but in 1978 both were killed by former supervisor Dan White, who shot them after Moscone refused his request for reinstatement. White, a Catholic and former police officer, had consistently opposed Milk's and Moscone's more liberal policies. At his trial, White successfully pleaded temporary insanity caused by additives in his fast-food diet. The media dubbed it a "Twinkie defense," but the murder charges against White were reduced to manslaughter. On that day, angry and grieving, the gay community rioted, overturning and burning police cars in a night of rage. To this day, a candlelight memorial parade is held on November 27. Milk's martyrdom was both a political and a practical inspiration to gay candidates across the country.

The emphasis in the gay movement shifted abruptly in the 1980s when the AIDS epidemic struck the community. AIDS has had a dramatic impact on the Castro. While it's still a thriving and lively community, it's no longer the constant party it once was. The hedonistic lifestyle that had played out in the discos, bars, baths, and streets changed as the seriousness of the epidemic sank in and the number of deaths increased. Political efforts shifted away from enfranchisement and toward demanding money for social services and research money to deal with the AIDS crisis. The gay community developed its own organizations, such as Project Inform and Gay Men's Health Crisis, to publicize information about the disease, treatments available, and safe sex. Though new cases of AIDS within the gay community are on the decline in San Francisco, it still remains a serious problem.

**THE 1980s: THE BIG ONE, PART 2**   The 1980s may have arrived in San Francisco with a whimper (compared to previous generations), but they went out with quite a bang. At 5:04pm on Tuesday, October 17, 1989, as more than 62,000 fans filled Candlestick Park for the third game of the World Series—and the San Francisco Bay Area commute moved into its heaviest flow—an earthquake of magnitude 7.1 struck. Within the next 20 seconds, 63 lives would be lost, $10 billion in damage would occur, and the entire Bay Area community would be reminded of their humble insignificance. Centered about 60 miles south of San Francisco within the Forest of Nisene Marks, the deadly temblor was felt as far away as San Diego and Nevada.

Though scientists had predicted that an earthquake would hit on this section of the San Andreas Fault, certain structures that were built to withstand such an earthquake failed miserably. The most catastrophic event was the collapse of the elevated Cypress Street section of Interstate 880 in Oakland, where the upper level of the freeway literally pancaked the lower level, crushing everything with such force that cars were reduced to inches in height. Other structures heavily damaged included the San Francisco–Oakland Bay Bridge, shut down for months when a section of the roadbed collapsed; San Francisco's Marina District, where several multimillion-dollar homes collapsed on their weak, shifting bases of landfill and sand; and the Pacific Garden Mall in Santa Cruz, which was completely devastated.

President Bush declared a disaster area for the seven hardest-hit counties, where at least 3,700 people were reported injured and more than 12,000 were displaced. More than 18,000 homes were damaged and 963 others destroyed. Although fire raged in the city and the water-supply systems were damaged, the major fires sparked in the Marina District were brought under control within 3 hours, due mostly to the heroic efforts of San Francisco's firefighters.

After the rubble had finally settled, it was unanimously agreed that San Francisco and the Bay Area had pulled through miraculously well, particularly when compared to the more recent earthquake in Kobe, Japan, which killed thousands and displaced an entire city. After the quake, a feeling of esprit de corps swept the city as neighbors helped each other rebuild and donations poured in from all over the world. Though it has been nearly a decade since, San Francisco is still feeling the effects of the quake, most noticeably during rush hour as commuters take a variety of detours to circumvent freeways that were damaged or destroyed and are still under construction. That another "big one" will strike is inevitable: It's the price you pay for living on a fault line. But if there is ever a city that's prepared for a major shakedown, it's San Francisco.

# Appendix B:
# Useful Toll-Free Numbers & Web Sites

## AIRLINES

**Air Canada**
☎ 800/776-3000
www.aircanada.ca

**Alaska Airlines**
☎ 800/426-0333
www.alaskaair.com

**American Airlines**
☎ 800/433-7300
www.aa.com

**America West Airlines**
☎ 800/235-9292
www.americawest.com

**British Airways**
☎ 800/247-9297
☎ 0345/222-111 in Britain
www.british-airways.com

**Canadian Airlines International**
☎ 800/426-7000
www.cdnair.ca

**Continental Airlines**
☎ 800/525-0280
www.flycontinental.com

**Delta Air Lines**
☎ 800/221-1212
www.delta-air.com

**Hawaiian Airlines**
☎ 800/367-5320
www.hawaiianair.com

**Kiwi International Air Lines**
☎ 800/538-5494
www.jetkiwi.com

**Midway Airlines**
☎ 800/446-4392
www.midwayair.com

**Northwest Airlines**
☎ 800/225-2525
www.nwa.com

**Southwest Airlines**
☎ 800/435-9792
www.iflyswa.com

**Tower Air**
☎ 800/34-TOWER
   (800/348-6937) outside
   New York
☎ 718/553-8500
www.towerair.com

**Trans World Airlines (TWA)**
☎ 800/221-2000
www.twa.com

**United Airlines**
☎ 800/241-6522
www.ual.com

**US Airways**
☎ 800/428-4322
www.usair.com

**Virgin Atlantic Airways**
☎ 800/862-8621 in
   Continental U.S.
☎ 0293/747-747 in Britain
www.fly.virgin.com

## CAR-RENTAL AGENCIES

**Advantage**
☎ 800/777-5500
www.arac.com

**Alamo**
☎ 800/327-9633
www.goalamo.com

**Auto Europe**
☎ 800/223-5555
www.autoeurope.com

**Avis**
☎ 800/331-1212 in
Continental U.S.
☎ 800/TRY-AVIS in Canada
www.avis.com

**Budget**
☎ 800/527-0700
www.budgetrentacar.com

**Dollar**
☎ 800/800-4000
www.dollarcar.com

**Enterprise**
☎ 800/325-8007
www.pickenterprise.com

**Hertz**
☎ 800/654-3131
www.hertz.com

**Kemwel Holiday Auto (KHA)**
☎ 800/678-0678
www.kemwel.com

**National**
☎ 800/CAR-RENT
www.nationalcar.com

**Payless**
☎ 800/PAYLESS
www.paylesscar.com

**Rent-A-Wreck**
☎ 800/535-1391
rent-a-wreck.com

**Thrifty**
☎ 800/367-2277
www.thrifty.com

**Value**
☎ 800/327-2501
www.go-value.com

# MAJOR HOTEL & MOTEL CHAINS

**Best Western International**
☎ 800/528-1234
www.bestwestern.com

**Clarion Hotels**
☎ 800/CLARION
www.hotelchoice.com/
    cgi-bin/res/webres?clarion.html

**Comfort Inns**
☎ 800/228-5150
www.hotelchoice.com/
    cgi-bin/res/webres?comfort.html

**Courtyard by Marriott**
☎ 800/321-2211
www.courtyard.com

**Days Inn**
☎ 800/325-2525
www.daysinn.com

**Doubletree Hotels**
☎ 800/222-TREE
www.doubletreehotels.com

**Econo Lodges**
☎ 800/55-ECONO
www.hotelchoice.com/cgi-
    bin/res/webres?econo.html

**Fairfield Inn by Marriott**
☎ 800/228-2800
www.fairfieldinn.com

**Hampton Inn**
☎ 800/HAMPTON
www.hampton-inn.com

**Hilton Hotels**
☎ 800/HILTONS
www.hilton.com

**Holiday Inn**
☎ 800/HOLIDAY
www.holiday-inn.com

**Howard Johnson**
☎ 800/654-2000
www.hojo.com/hojo.html

**Hyatt Hotels & Resorts**
☎ 800/228-9000
www.hyatt.com

**ITT Sheraton**
☎ 800/325-3535
www.sheraton.com

**La Quinta Motor Inns**
☎ 800/531-5900
www.laquinta.com

**Marriott Hotels**
☎ 800/228-9290
www.marriott.com

**Motel 6**
☎ 800/4-MOTEL6 (800/
    466-8536)

**Quality Inns**
☎ 800/228-5151
www.hotelchoice.com/cgi-
  bin/res/webres?quality.html

**Radisson Hotels International**
☎ 800/333-3333
www.radisson.com

**Ramada Inns**
☎ 800/2-RAMADA
www.ramada.com

**Red Carpet Inns**
☎ 800/251-1962

**Red Lion Hotels & Inns**
☎ 800/547-8010

**Red Roof Inns**
☎ 800/843-7663
www.redroof.com

**Residence Inn by Marriott**
☎ 800/331-3131
www.residenceinn.com

**Rodeway Inns**
☎ 800/228-2000
www.hotelchoice.com/
  cgi-bin/res/webres?rodeway.html

**Super 8 Motels**
☎ 800/800-8000
www.super8motels.com

**Travelodge**
☎ 800/255-3050
www.travelodge.com

**Vagabond Inns**
☎ 800/522-1555
www.vagabondinns.com

**Wyndham Hotels and Resorts**
☎ 800/822-4200 in Continental
  U.S. and Canada
www.wyndham.com

# Index

See also separate Accommodations and Restaurant indexes, below

General Index

Restaurant Index

# FROMMER'S® COMPLETE TRAVEL GUIDES

Alaska
Amsterdam
Arizona
Atlanta
Australia
Austria
Bahamas
Barcelona, Madrid & Seville
Beijing
Belgium, Holland & Luxembourg
Bermuda
Boston
Budapest & the Best of Hungary
California
Canada
Cancún, Cozumel &
  the Yucatán
Cape Cod, Nantucket & Martha's Vineyard
Caribbean
Caribbean Cruises & Ports of Call
Caribbean Ports of Call
Carolinas & Georgia
Chicago
China
Colorado
Costa Rica
Denmark
Denver, Boulder & Colorado Springs
England
Europe
Florida
France
Germany
Greece
Greek Islands
Hawaii
Hong Kong
Honolulu, Waikiki & Oahu
Ireland
Israel
Italy
Jamaica & Barbados
Japan
Las Vegas
London
Los Angeles
Maryland & Delaware
Maui
Mexico
Miami & the Keys

Montana & Wyoming
Montréal & Québec City
Munich & the Bavarian Alps
Nashville & Memphis
Nepal
New England
New Mexico
New Orleans
New York City
Nova Scotia, New Brunswick &
  Prince Edward Island
Oregon
Paris
Philadelphia & the
  Amish Country
Portugal
Prague & the Best of the Czech Republic
Provence & the Riviera
Puerto Rico
Rome
San Antonio & Austin
San Diego
San Francisco
Santa Fe, Taos &
  Albuquerque
Scandinavia
Scotland
Seattle & Portland
Singapore & Malaysia
South Africa
Southeast Asia
South Pacific
Spain
Sweden
Switzerland
Thailand
Tokyo
Toronto
Tuscany & Umbria
USA
Utah
Vancouver & Victoria
Vermont, New Hampshire
  & Maine
Vienna & the Danube Valley
Virgin Islands
Virginia
Walt Disney World & Orlando
Washington, D.C.
Washington State

## FROMMER'S® DOLLAR-A-DAY GUIDES

Australia from $50 a Day
California from $60 a Day
Caribbean from $70 a Day
England from $70 a Day
Europe from $60 a Day
Florida from $60 a Day

Hawaii from $70 a Day
Ireland from $50 a Day
Israel from $45 a Day
Italy from $70 a Day
London from $85 a Day
New York from $80 a Day

New Zealand from $50 a Day
Paris from $85 a Day
San Francisco from $60 a Day
Washington, D.C.,
   from $60 a Day

## FROMMER'S® PORTABLE GUIDES

Acapulco, Ixtapa &
   Zihuatanejo
Alaska Cruises & Ports of Call
Bahamas
Baja & Los Cabos
Berlin
California Wine Country
Charleston & Savannah
Chicago

Dublin
Hawaii: The Big Island
Las Vegas
London
Maine Coast
Maui
New Orleans
New York City
Paris

Puerto Vallarta, Manzanillo
   & Guadalajara
San Diego
San Francisco
Sydney
Tampa & St. Petersburg
Venice
Washington, D.C.

## FROMMER'S® NATIONAL PARK GUIDES

Family Vacations in the
   National Parks
Grand Canyon

National Parks of the
   American West
Rocky Mountain

Yellowstone & Grand Teton
Yosemite & Sequoia/
   Kings Canyon
Zion & Bryce Canyon

## FROMMER'S® GREAT OUTDOOR GUIDES

New England
Northern California

Southern California & Baja
Washington & Oregon

## FROMMER'S® MEMORABLE WALKS

Chicago
London

New York
Paris

San Francisco
Washington D.C.

## FROMMER'S® IRREVERENT GUIDES

Amsterdam
Boston
Chicago
Las Vegas

London
Los Angeles
Manhattan

New Orleans
Paris
San Francisco

Seattle & Portland
Vancouver
Walt Disney World
Washington, D.C.

## FROMMER'S® BEST-LOVED DRIVING TOURS

America
Britain
California

Florida
France
Germany

Ireland
Italy
New England

Scotland
Spain
Western Europe

## THE UNOFFICIAL GUIDES®

Bed & Breakfast in
  New England
Bed & Breakfast in
  the Northwest
Beyond Disney
Branson, Missouri
California with Kids
Chicago

Cruises
Disneyland
Florida with Kids
The Great Smoky &
  Blue Ridge
  Mountains
Inside Disney
Las Vegas

London
Miami & the Keys
Mini Las Vegas
Mini-Mickey
New Orleans
New York City
Paris
San Francisco

Skiing in the West
Walt Disney World
Walt Disney World
  for Grown-ups
Walt Disney World
  for Kids
Washington, D.C.

## SPECIAL-INTEREST TITLES

Born to Shop: France
Born to Shop: Hong Kong
Born to Shop: Italy
Born to Shop: New York
Born to Shop: Paris
Frommer's Britain's Best Bike Rides
The Civil War Trust's Official Guide
  to the Civil War Discovery Trail
Frommer's Caribbean Hideaways
Frommer's Europe's Greatest Driving Tours
Frommer's Food Lover's Companion to France
Frommer's Food Lover's Companion to Italy
Frommer's Gay & Lesbian Europe
Israel Past & Present
Monks' Guide to California

Monks' Guide to New York City
The Moon
New York City with Kids
Unforgettable Weekends
Outside Magazine's Guide
  to Family Vacations
Places Rated Almanac
Retirement Places Rated
Road Atlas Britain
Road Atlas Europe
Washington, D.C., with Kids
Wonderful Weekends from Boston
Wonderful Weekends from New York City
Wonderful Weekends from San Francisco
Wonderful Weekends from Los Angeles

# WHEREVER YOU TRAVEL, *H*ELP IS NEVER FAR AWAY.

From planning your trip to providing travel assistance along the way, American Express® Travel Service Offices are always there to help you do more.

---

## *San Francisco*

---

American Express Travel Service
455 Market Street
(415) 536-2600

American Express Travel Service
560 California Street
(415) 536-2600

Ethan Allen Travel, Inc (R)
1585 Sloat Blvd.
(415) 242-0277

Travel Consultants (R)
1245 Market Street
(415) 558-9796

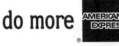

**do more** AMERICAN EXPRESS

**Travel**

www.americanexpress.com/travel

**American Express Travel Service Offices are located throughout the United States. For the office nearest you, call 1-800-AXP-3429.**